PRINCE2®

STUDY GUIDE

Third Edition—2017 Update

PRINCE2®

STUDY GUIDE

Third Edition—2017 Update

PRINCE2®

ACCREDITED BY AXELOS

DAVID HINDE

Development Editor: Kathi Duggan
Technical Editor: Duncan Wade
Copy Editor: John Sleeva
Book and Cover Designer: SelfPublishingLab
Indexer: SelfPublishingLab

Published by Orgtopia

ISBN: 978-0-9955275-2-2

For general information on our other products and services or to obtain technical support, please see www.orgtopia.com or contact (44) 208 720 7440

A catalogue record for this book is available from the British Library.

To Louise,
Thanks for all your help and support whilst I was writing this book. I couldn't have done it without you.
—*Love,* Dave

Acknowledgments

Whilst writing this book I have had the help and support of many people. Firstly, I would like to thank my partner, Louise, for putting up with me this past year. Without her advice, support, and love, I could not have written this book.

Then, I need to thank the fantastic team at Wiley who helped me put the first edition of the book together. First, there is Birgit Gruber for encouraging me to start this project in the first place. Next, Kathi Duggan, the development editor and John Sleeva the copy editor, for all your fantastic comments and advice while I was preparing the manuscript. Thank you to the project manager gurus Duncan Wade and Antony Perritt for all your invaluable advice on how to describe PRINCE2.

I would also like to thank Learning Tree, who 10 years ago sponsored me when I applied for the PRINCE2 teacher qualification and continue to support me in keeping that qualification up-to-date and providing me with PRINCE2 courses to teach. Particular thanks to Duncan Wade (again) for writing such a great course for me to teach and Graham Williams for helping me through the early stages of becoming an accredited PRINCE2 teacher.

Finally, I must thank the people at AXELOS who have developed an excellent new version of the PRINCE2 approach, the PRINCE2 2017 update.

About the Author

David Hinde has more than 25 years of experience in directing and managing projects and change programmes in the digital industry. He spent the early years of his career working for Mars Global before switching to the world of software development, broadcast, and IT. He worked in the engineering departments of MFN and RedBox, delivering projects to clients such as Deloitte and Touche, BP, and GroupTrade. He has had many years of experience in implementing best-practice approaches such as PRINCE2, PMI, Scrum, XP, Six Sigma, and MSP.

In 2002, David founded the consultancy practice Orgtopia and has since led many projects, working with clients such as Citi, Eli Lilly, and the BBC. His work focuses on pragmatic implementations of best-practice approaches in change, programme, and project management. He believes in a holistic approach that includes improving both processes and people skills. Another part of his work with Orgtopia is training and coaching. He has trained more than a thousand people in PRINCE2, coaching skills, project management, and strategic directing and governance. He is a qualified management coach with the Association for Coaching and a PRINCE2-qualified trainer and was certified as a Project Management Professional with the Project Management Institute in 2001. He also works regularly for Learning Tree International, running their project management courses.

David regularly writes about the subject of leadership and management. In addition to the first edition and this second edition of the *PRINCE2 Study Guide*, he is the author of *The Project Manager and the Pyramid* (Orgtopia, 2016), which is an ideal book to introduce people to the concepts of project management.

When he isn't working, David is a keen tennis player.

.

About the Technical Editor

Duncan Wade has a varied and rich background—4 years in sales, 11 years in software development and management, and 20 years in consultancy (www. hic.co.uk), specializing in project management and agile delivery. A passionate advocate of the value of coaching and mentoring in a business context, Duncan works with organizations to realize their potential for smart and effective management of projects, whatever their delivery preference, traditional waterfall, or agile framework. He is the author and lead trainer for Learning Tree International's offerings for PRINCE2 and PRINCE2 Agile.

Contents at a glance

Introduction

PRINCE2 is a globally recognized approach to successfully managing projects. It is widely adopted across many countries, industries, and sectors. Many projects have found that adopting the PRINCE2 approach considerably increases the likelihood of project success.

Becoming PRINCE2 accredited is an important career development objective for anyone connected with project work. Increasingly, job ads for project-related work are asking for people with the PRINCE2 accreditation.

This study guide will help you pass the PRINCE2 accreditation exams. It has been written by someone who has trained thousands of individuals from many different backgrounds to prepare for the PRINCE2 Foundation and Practitioner exams. It provides explanations of all parts of the PRINCE2 approach, many examples that show how the method is applied in practice, and a whole range of mock exam questions to test your knowledge.

Introduction to PRINCE2

PRINCE2 is a best-practice project management approach. It can be used on any type of project in any type of environment. PRINCE2 is used to deliver projects in industries as diverse as IT, banking, pharmaceuticals, telecommunications, and construction. It has been implemented widely in both the private and the public sector. In the private sector, companies such as Deloitte, Citi, KPMG, and Eli Lilly have used the method. In the public sector, the UK, Canadian, Dutch, Danish, and German governments are using PRINCE2.

Since its creation in 1996, PRINCE2 has become one of the most widely adopted project management methods in the world and is currently used in more than 50 countries. More than one million people have taken the PRINCE2 examinations. The exams are available in 16 languages, including English, French, Dutch, German, Chinese, Polish, Danish, Italian, and Spanish. More than 120 training organizations provide PRINCE2 training.

PRINCE stands for PRojects IN a Controlled Environment. PRINCE2 was derived from PRINCE, a method created in 1989 as a project management approach for the UK government's Central Computer and Telecommunications Agency (CCTA). PRINCE2 took the common-sense ideas of PRINCE and widened the method so that it could be used across all industries. It has been updated a number of times to take account of the latest ideas in project management. The last major revision was in 2017. This new version has vastly improved the method, making it far easier to apply, more concise, and a lot more flexible. The new version also has a lot more guidance on how to adapt PRINCE2 to work within a range of different environments, such as projects within programmes, projects using agile approaches, smaller projects, and projects that involve external suppliers. This study guide is based on the PRINCE2 2017 edition.

Why Should You Use PRINCE2?

Managing projects is notoriously difficult. The news is full of high-profile projects that failed to deliver. Why is this?

The main reason is that project work is much more difficult than business as usual. Business-as-usual work tends to be repetitive; what happens this month is pretty similar to what happened last month. Projects, however, often involve working with new people, sometimes in other organizations. They often involve working in new ways with new management processes. They involve creating new products and services and maybe new technologies. All this unfamiliarity leads to uncertainty. It is difficult to predict how long things will take, how things will work out, or whether people will accept new ways of doing things.

PRINCE2 provides a structured way of working through this uncertainty. It says, okay, your project involves a great deal of unpredictability, but there are many things that are the same as any other project. Whether you are building a hotel, a new IT system, or a nuclear-powered submarine, you will have to go through these similar processes. For example, any team needs to decide what the objectives of their project are at the outset and have management mechanisms to check throughout the project that things are on track, and at the end of the project, to check that the objectives have been met. Many other commonalties exist across projects, such as approaches for managing risk, quality, changes, and so on. PRINCE2 has captured these common steps and set them out in a process model. It also describes a range of management roles with responsibilities to carry out these steps and provides a range of management documents to hold and report on project information.

Following the PRINCE2 framework does not guarantee a project's success. However, it does substantially increase the likelihood of any project achieving its objectives.

PRINCE2 provides a lot of ideas, some of which might not be practical to follow. However, comparing how your project is being managed against how PRINCE2 says it should be managed provides an excellent diagnostic tool to see what might be missing in your project management approach. Some (not all) of these gaps might be beneficial to fill.

In the uncertain world of managing projects, PRINCE2 provides a solid, tested, structured approach for the project management team to decide on the way forward.

The PRINCE2 Accreditations

There are two PRINCE2 accreditations: the Foundation level and the Practitioner level. Candidates must first pass the Foundation level before attempting the Practitioner level. In order to gain the Foundation-level and Practitioner-level accreditations, candidates need to pass an exam. This study guide focuses on how to pass both the Foundation and the Practitioner exams.

I talk further about the Foundation and Practitioner exams later in this Introduction, in the section "The Accreditation Exams."

Reasons to Become PRINCE2 Certified

These days, most work environments are subject to rapid change. Most of this change will be implemented through project work. As I said at the beginning of this introduction, PRINCE2 has become a widely recognized and adopted approach for managing projects, making it a valuable career progression accreditation to hold. The following benefits are associated with PRINCE2 accreditation:

- Demonstrates proof of project management competency
- Increases career marketability
- Raises customer confidence

Demonstrates Proof of Project Management Competency

You must have a thorough understanding of the best-practice approach to managing projects in order to pass the Foundation and Practitioner levels of PRINCE2. Those holding the PRINCE2 accreditations are showing that they are capable of managing a project in a way that substantially increases the likelihood of the project's success.

Increases Career Marketability

PRINCE2 is globally recognized as a professional best-practice approach for project management. When an organization recruits project managers, a PRINCE2 accreditation is often a prerequisite. Even if this is not the case, a PRINCE2-accredited candidate will probably be looked on favorably.

Many senior managers need to be able to demonstrate that they can successfully implement change programmes within their departments and organizations. PRINCE2 is a best-practice way of implementing change, so holding the accreditation also makes senior directing–level employees more marketable.

Raises Customer Confidence

Many businesses deliver project work to their clients. The project itself can include anything from building a hotel to creating new software to building an aircraft carrier. Businesses need to be able to demonstrate to their clients not just a technical ability in their specialist area but also an ability to competently deliver projects. Potential clients will often expect to see proof that the business follows best-practice approaches when managing projects. An excellent way of doing this is to train project managers in PRINCE2 and align in-house project-delivery approaches to the PRINCE2 model.

How to Become Accredited

The first step is to thoroughly review PRINCE2 by reading this study guide. You then have one of two choices:

- Contact a PRINCE2 Strategic Accredited Training Organization (ATO). (For a full list of ATOs, refer to the AXELOS website at https://www.axelos.com/find-a-training-provider.) ATOs have been licensed by AXELOS to deliver PRINCE2 training and to provide PRINCE2 exam testing centers. AXELOS is the group that owns PRINCE2. There are ATOs in most major countries. ATOs may provide any of the following products:
  - A 2- or 3-day training course, providing last-minute preparation and a proctored Foundation exam
  - A 2- or 3-day course, providing last-minute preparation and a proctored Practitioner exam for those already holding the Foundation level
  - A 5-day course that includes a proctored Foundation and Practitioner exam (usually on different days) and last-minute preparation training for both
  - A proctored Foundation or Practitioner exam without any preparation training
- Contact PeopleCert (www.peoplecert.org). PeopleCert runs and administers the PRINCE2 exams on behalf of AXELOS. Through the PeopleCert website, you can either organize an online PRINCE2 exam or locate one of the worldwide Test Centers where you can take the exam.

Which Organizations Own and Administer PRINCE2?

A number of organizations are involved with developing and maintaining PRINCE2 and delivering and administering the exams. First, there is AXELOS, which owns PRINCE2. They also own a range of other best-practice methodologies, including ITIL®, MSP®, and RESILIA. They develop and maintain the best practices and accompanying examinations. For more information about AXELOS, go to www.axelos.com.

Then there's a whole range of training companies around the world that have been accredited by AXELOS to teach PRINCE2. They pay AXELOS a license fee and have to comply to a range of standards in order to deliver the PRINCE2 training courses. They are known as Accredited Training Organizations (ATOs). For a full list of ATOs, go to https://www.axelos.com/find-a-training-provider.

Next there is PeopleCert, a global testing and certification service provider. They administer the PRINCE2 exams on behalf of AXELOS.

Finally, there is the Stationery Office, which publishes the official PRINCE2 manual Managing Successful Projects with PRINCE2.

About This Study Guide

This study guide will help you prepare and (if you work hard enough!) pass the PRINCE2 Foundation and Practitioner accreditation exams. This section describes the objectives and content of the book and provides general advice about how best to approach your exam preparation.

Objectives of This Study Guide

The overall objective of this study guide is to provide the resources necessary for an individual to prepare for and pass the PRINCE2 Foundation- and Practitioner-level accreditations.

The Foundation level examines whether the candidate has the necessary knowledge to work within (but not lead) a project team. To demonstrate this level, a candidate must have a firm understanding of the theory of the PRINCE2 model. This study guide explains this theory by setting out the model in an informal, accessible way, explaining the terminology in simple, everyday language.

The Practitioner level examines whether the candidate can not only explain the theory of PRINCE2 but also demonstrate how the model is applied in practice. A PRINCE2 Practitioner candidate should be able to justify her application of the model. This level of understanding is required for someone leading a project team. This study guide sets out many examples of how the theory is used in practice, both throughout the main body of the text using simple examples and through the use of case studies from actual projects where PRINCE2 was employed.

The final objective of this guide is to give you plenty of practice with the types of questions you will encounter in the PRINCE2 accreditation exams. This book includes more than 200 mock Foundation questions and more than 150 mock Practitioner questions for you to test your knowledge.

Contents of This Study Guide

The study guide covers all the areas of the syllabus for the Foundation- and Practitioner-level accreditations. The information is set out in an accessible style, using plenty of examples to help you understand both the theory of the topic and how it is applied. Each chapter contains the following useful elements:

- Exam Objectives—A description of what you must achieve in order to thoroughly understand that chapter's topic.
- Case Studies—Real-life applications of that chapter's topic, to help you understand how PRINCE2 works in practice. This is an essential skill for the Practitioner level.
- Exam Spotlights—Tips and techniques to help you tackle the PRINCE2 exams.
- Summary—An overview of all the relevant PRINCE2 topics covered within that chapter.
- Exam Essentials—All the key revision points relating to that chapter's topic.
- Review Questions—A set of mock Foundation- and Practitioner-level questions. (The answers and explanations are provided in Appendix A, "Answers to Review Questions.")

There are 15 examinable syllabus areas: the seven PRINCE2 themes, the seven PRINCE2 processes, and an area covering an overview of projects and PRINCE2. These are covered in this study guide as follows:

- The overview of PRINCE2 is covered in Chapter 1, "Overview of PRINCE2."
- The seven PRINCE2 processes are covered in Chapter 2, "Starting a Project Successfully with PRINCE2"; Chapter 10, "Managing the Middle of a Project Successfully with PRINCE2"; and Chapter 11, "Managing the End of a Project Successfully with PRINCE2."
- The seven PRINCE2 themes are covered in Chapter 3, "Organization Theme"; Chapter 4, "Business Case Theme"; Chapter 5, "Plans Theme"; Chapter 6, "Quality Theme"; Chapter 7, "Risk Theme"; Chapter 8, "Change Theme"; and Chapter 9, "Progress Theme."

Chapter 12, "Passing the Accreditation Exams," provides many useful tips and techniques on how to tackle the rather unusual style of questions in a PRINCE2 exam. There are also some useful appendices that will help you prepare for the exams:

- Appendix A, "Answers to Review Questions," provides the answers and useful explanations to the mock Foundation and Practitioner questions at the end of each chapter.
- Appendix B, "Practitioner Exam Scenario," contains the exam scenario that you will need to refer to when answering the Practitioner exam questions at the end of each chapter.
- Appendix C, "Management Products in PRINCE2," summarizes all the management products used in PRINCE2, such as the records, plans, registers, and logs.
- Appendix D, "Bonus Foundation Exam," offers another sample Foundation exam that you can use for practice, in addition to answering the Foundation questions at the end of each chapter.
- Appendix E, "Bonus Practitioner Exam," offers another sample Practitioner exam that you can use for practice, in addition to answering all the Practitioner questions at the end of each chapter.

How to Use This Study Guide

The good news when it comes to revising PRINCE2 is that none of the material is particularly complex. The bad news is that there is a lot of it! Also, many parts of PRINCE2 are interrelated. So, when you're first reviewing a topic in this study guide, you may run across references to things you haven't learned about yet.

Therefore, I suggest that you first read Chapter 1, "Overview of PRINCE2," to understand the whole PRINCE2 model in a high-level way, followed by Chapter 2, "Starting a Project Successfully with PRINCE2," and Chapter 3, "Organization Theme," to understand the beginning of a PRINCE2 project. You can then tackle the other chapters and topics in any order you wish.

(Throughout this book, I have predominantly used the male pronoun. This is only to make the text easier to read, not to imply any difference between male and female project management professionals.)

Other Resources You Will Need

This study guide provides a full explanation of PRINCE2 in enough detail for you to pass the accreditation exams. However, you will also need a copy of the official PRINCE2 manual, Managing Successful Projects with PRINCE2 (Stationery Office, 2017).

The reason for this is that during the Practitioner exam, you are allowed to refer to Managing Successful Projects with PRINCE2. You are not allowed to take in any other reference material, including this study guide. This means that part of your exam preparation should include familiarizing yourself with how the topics are set out in the manual. In the Exam Spotlights throughout this book, as well as in Chapter 12, I explain how to use the manual to help you pass the exams.

The Accreditation Exams

There are two accreditation exams: the Foundation level and the Practitioner level.

Foundation Exam

The Foundation-level exam is the lower-level accreditation. You must pass it in order to take the Practitioner exam. Here are some key facts about the Foundation exam:
- It is a one-hour exam.
- The exam consists of 60 multiple-choice questions. You are given four possible answers to each question, only one of which is correct.
- You need to get 55 percent to pass the exam.
- The exam tests to see if you have the ability to act as a member of a project team running a project with PRINCE2. It requires you to understand the theory of PRINCE2.
- You are not allowed to refer to any material during the exam.

Practitioner Exam

The Practitioner exam is the higher-level accreditation. Here are some key facts about the Practitioner exam:
- The exam is two and a half hours.
- It has 68 questions, grouped into 15 syllabus sections. The 15 syllabus areas are the principles, the seven processes (starting up a project, directing a project, initiating a project, controlling a stage, managing product delivery, managing a stage boundary and closing a project) and the seven themes (business case, organization, quality, plans, risk, progress and change).

- The exam includes a project scenario that each question will refer to.
- The exam tests to see if you are capable of leading a project according to PRINCE2. To pass the exam, you not only need to understand the theory of PRINCE2 but also know how to apply it and justify its application.
- You need to get 55 percent to pass the exam.
- You are allowed to refer to Managing Successful Projects with PRINCE2. You are not allowed to use any other reference material.

How to Contact the Author

I welcome feedback from you about this book or about books you'd like to see from me in the future. You can reach me by writing to davidhinde@orgtopia.com. For more information about my work, visit my website at www.orgtopia.com.

Assessment Test

Find out how much you know about PRINCE2 before you start studying this book by answering the following questions. They are in the same format as the PRINCE2 Foundation exam questions. You will find the answers at the end of this chapter.

1. Which process occurs before the project has been commissioned?
   A. Initiating a project
   B. Managing a stage boundary
   C. Starting up a project
   D. Controlling a stage

2. During which PRINCE2 process is the project's management team designed?
   A. Starting up a project
   B. Initiating a project
   C. Controlling a stage
   D. Managing product delivery

3. Which information does NOT appear in the PRINCE2 business case?
   A. Business options
   B. Delivery options
   C. Project costs
   D. Duration over which benefits will be measured

4. During which process is the stage plan for the initiation stage created?
   A. Starting up a project
   B. Initiating a project
   C. Managing a stage boundary
   D. Directing a project

5. The fact that project work often spans multiple organizations and functional divisions relates to which characteristic of a project?
   A. Change
   B. Risk
   C. Cross-functional
   D. Uncertainty

6. Which of the following are NOT examples of situations that PRINCE2 can be tailored for?
   A. Multi-organization projects
   B. Small projects
   C. Commercial customer/supplier environment
   D. Business as usual

7. Which of the following is NOT a quality review technique activity?
   A. Review preparation
   B. Review meeting
   C. Review follow-up
   D. Review approval

8. Which PRINCE2 process is used to review and, if necessary, update the project management team?
   A. Managing a stage boundary
   B. Directing a project
   C. Controlling a stage
   D. Managing product delivery

9. During which process would a change budget for a stage be authorized?
   A. Initiating a project
   B. Managing a stage boundary
   C. Controlling a stage
   D. Directing a project

10. Which PRINCE2 risk response type cannot be applied to an opportunity?
    A. Accept
    B. Enhance
    C. Avoid
    D. Share

11. Which of the following is a task in the approach to defining and analyzing products?
    A. Prepare estimates
    B. Identify activities and dependencies
    C. Create the product breakdown structure
    D. Document the plan

12. Which role might the project manager consult during the activities of the initiating a project process to ensure that the various sections of the project initiation documentation meet the needs of the project board?
    A. Project assurance
    B. Project support
    C. Change authority
    D. Team manager

13. The [?] is responsible for managing, monitoring, and controlling all aspects of a particular risk.
    A. Risk owner
    B. Risk manager
    C. Risk actionee
    D. Project manager

14. Which is NOT one of the six aspects of project performance that needs to be managed?
    A. Quality
    B. Contracts
    C. Scope
    D. Timescales

15. Which of the following describes a PRINCE2 risk?
    A. A certain event that will affect the project in a positive or negative way
    B. A certain event that will affect the project in a negative way
    C. An uncertain event that will affect the project in a positive or negative way
    D. An uncertain event that will affect the project in a negative way

16. Which management product does the project manager use to pass responsibility for the delivery of the products to the team manager or team members?
    A. Product descriptions
    B. Team plans
    C. Work package
    D. Configuration item record

17. Which management product sets out the procedures, responsibilities, and tools and techniques necessary to ensure that the project delivers what users expect?
    A. Project product description
    B. Quality management approach
    C. Product descriptions
    D. Quality register

18. Which management product does the project manager regularly create during the controlling a stage process to report progress to the project board?
    A. Checkpoint report
    B. Highlight report
    C. End stage report
    D. Exception report

19. Which of the following management products might be used to capture an issue?
    (1) Daily log (2) Issue register (3) Issue report (4) Risk register
    A. 1, 2, 3
    B. 1, 2, 4
    C. 1, 3, 4
    D. 2, 3, 4

20. The purpose of which theme is to provide a forecast for the project's objectives and control any unacceptable deviations?
    A. Business case
    B. Plans
    C. Quality
    D. Progress

21. During which process is the quality register created?
    A. Starting up a project
    B. Initiating a project
    C. Controlling a stage
    D. Managing product delivery

22. How would the project manager escalate a situation where stage tolerances are forecast to be exceeded?
    A. Exception report
    B. Highlight report
    C. Exception plans
    D. End stage report

23. Which role is responsible for assembling the project initiation documentation?
    A. Executive
    B. Project manager
    C. Project support
    D. Senior user

24. Which level of management would make a decision regarding a breach of project tolerances?
    A. Corporate, programme management, or the customer
    B. Project board
    C. Project manager
    D. Team manager

25. Which is the only PRINCE2 role within the project management team that has post-project responsibilities?
    A. Senior user
    B. Executive
    C. Senior supplier
    D. Project manager

26. During which process are specialist products created?
    A. Initiating a project
    B. Controlling a stage
    C. Managing product delivery
    D. Managing a stage boundary

27. The three types of issue are request for change, off-specification, and [?].
    A. Potential opportunity
    B. Dis-benefit
    C. Problem or concern
    D. External product

28. What is a purpose of the quality theme?
    A. To ensure that issues affecting quality are appropriately managed
    B. To identify, assess, and control uncertainty that might affect the quality of the project's products
    C. To establish mechanisms to provide a forecast for the project's objectives
    D. To ensure that the project's products meet business expectations

29. Which is NOT one of the benefits provided by PRINCE2?
    A. It presents a generic approach that can be applied to any type of project.
    B. It improves leadership capabilities.
    C. It provides a thorough and economical set of reports.
    D. It provides explicit recognition of project responsibilities.

30. Which of the following management products may be updated during the managing a stage boundary process?
(1) Project brief (2) Change control approach (3) Business case (4) Project approach
A. 1, 2, 3
B. 1, 3, 4
C. 1, 2, 4
D. 2, 3, 4

31. Which principle does the organization theme primarily implement?
A. Continued business justification
B. Learn from experience
C. Tailor to suit the project environment
D. Defined roles and responsibilities

32. Which plan provides the business case with planned costs and timescales?
A. Project plan
B. Stage plans
C. Team plan
D. Exception plan

33. The project manager reviews the [?] to identify any organization that needs to be informed when the project is closing.
A. Communication management approach
B. Work package for closing a project
C. Change control approach
D. Notification from the project board

34. Weighing a project's benefits against ongoing operational and maintenance costs is one aspect of [?].
A. Benefits review planning
B. Investment appraisal
C. Cost planning
D. Sensitivity analysis

35. Which of the following are the three primary interests that are represented on a PRINCE2 project board?
(1) Business (2) Customer (3) User (4) Supplier
A. 1, 2, 3
B. 1, 3, 4
C. 1, 2, 4
D. 2, 3, 4

36. Which of the following statements describes the general approach to tailoring PRINCE2?
    1) Use PRINCE2 with a lightness of touch.
    2) Omit elements of PRINCE2 to suit the situation.
    3) Avoid introducing unnecessary bureaucracy.
    4) Adapt the method to external and project factors.
    A. 1, 2, 3
    B. 1, 2, 4
    C. 1, 3, 4
    D. 2, 3, 4

37. Which of the following are NOT examples of PRINCE2 reports?
    A. Risk register
    B. Product status account
    C. Highlight report
    D. Checkpoint report

38. Which one of the following is NOT a step in the PRINCE2 risk management procedure?
    A. Communicate
    B. Plan
    C. Identify
    D. Mitigate

39. What is the first plan created during the PRINCE2 process model?
    A. Project plan
    B. Stage plan for the initiation stage
    C. Stage plan for the first delivery stage
    D. Programme plan

40. Which of the following is the fundamental philosophy behind the PRINCE2 approach to plans?
    A. Just-in-time planning
    B. Product-based planning
    C. Brainstorming
    D. Use of work breakdown structures

41. Which role is responsible for producing the outputs from the closing a project process?
    A. Corporate, programme management, or the customer
    B. Project board
    C. Project manager
    D. Team manager

42. Which process describes the work of the project manager in handling the day-to-day management of each delivery stage?
    A. Starting up a project
    B. Initiating a project
    C. Controlling a stage
    D. Managing product delivery

43. During which PRINCE2 process is the outline business case created?
    A. Starting up a project
    B. Initiating a project
    C. Controlling a stage
    D. Managing a stage boundary

44. Which process is used to create the change control approach?
    A. Starting up a project
    B. Initiating a project
    C. Controlling a stage
    D. Managing a stage boundary

Answers to the Assessment Test

1. C – The starting up a project process occurs before the project has been commissioned. The process's purpose is to collate information upon which the project board can make a decision whether to commission the project during the authorizing initiation activity. See Chapter 2, "Starting a Project Successfully with PRINCE2."
2. A – The project management team is designed in the starting up a project process, during the design and appoint the project management team activity. See Chapter 2, "Starting a Project Successfully with PRINCE2."
3. B – Delivery options will appear in the project approach, not the business case. See "The Contents of the Business Case" section in Chapter 4, "Business Case Theme."
4. A – The stage plan for the initiation stage is created in the starting up a project process in order for the project board to review the work necessary for the initiation stage before authorizing it. See Chapter 5, "Plans Theme."
5. C – The cross-functional characteristic of a project means that often projects involve several groups of people who don't usually work together. The groups could come from different functional divisions or even different organizations. See Chapter 1, "Overview of PRINCE2."
6. D – PRINCE2 is not used to manage business-as-usual situations. See Chapter 1, "Overview of PRINCE2."
7. D – The quality review technique has three steps: review preparation, review meeting, and review follow-up. See Chapter 6, "Quality Theme."
8. A – At the end of each stage, the project manager reviews the project management team to see if it needs to be updated for the next stage. See Chapter 3, "Organization Theme."

9. D – A change budget, along with the stage budget and any risk budget for that stage, would be authorized by the project board in the directing a project process, during the authorize a stage activity. See Chapter 8, "Change Theme."
10. C – The avoid response is used only for threats, not opportunities. See the "Plan" section under "Risk Management Procedure" in Chapter 7, "Risk Theme."
11. C – Defining and analyzing products consists of four tasks: writing the project product description, creating the product breakdown structure, writing the product descriptions, and creating the product flow diagram. See Chapter 5, "Plans Theme."
12. A – Project assurance will check and audit the work of the project manager during the project to ensure that it will be acceptable for the people on the project board. See Chapter 2, "Starting a Project Successfully with PRINCE2."
13. A – The risk owner's role is to manage and monitor an assigned risk. See the "Implement" section under "Risk Management Procedure" in Chapter 7, "Risk Theme."
14. B – According to PRINCE2, the six aspects of project performance that need to be managed are costs, timescales, quality, scope, risk, and benefits. See Chapter 1, "Overview of PRINCE2."
15. C – In PRINCE2, a risk is something that may or may not happen—in other words, it is uncertain. You might normally think of a risk as a negative event, but in PRINCE2 it could also have a favorable impact on the project. See the "How Does PRINCE2 Use the Word Risk?" section in Chapter 7, "Risk Theme."
16. C – The work package is used by the project manager to pass on information to the teams in order for them to understand what to deliver and how to do it. It is used to pass authority to the teams for the delivery of one or more products. See the "Project Manager Controls" section in Chapter 9, "Progress Theme."
17. B – The quality management approach sets out how the project will be managed to ensure that it delivers products that meet the users' expectations. See Chapter 6, "Quality Theme."
18. B – The project manager creates the highlight report to regularly report progress to the project board during the controlling a stage process. See Chapter 10, "Managing the Middle of a Project Successfully with PRINCE2."
19. A – If the issue is informal, it might be captured in the daily log. If the issue is to be treated formally, an entry in the issue register would be created and maybe also a corresponding issue report. The risk register is used to capture risks, not issues. See Chapter 8, "Change Theme."
20. D – The purpose of the progress theme is to establish mechanisms to monitor and compare actual achievements against those planned; to provide a forecast for the project objectives and the project's continued viability; and to control any unacceptable deviations. See Chapter 9, "Progress Theme."
21. B – The quality register is created in the prepare the quality management approach activity in the initiating a project process. See Chapter 6, "Quality Theme."
22. A – The project manager uses the exception report to escalate to the project board situations where stage tolerances are forecast to be exceeded. See the "Tolerances and Exceptions" section in Chapter 9, "Progress Theme."
23. B – The project manager is responsible for assembling the project initiation documentation. This is the final activity in the initiating a project process. See Chapter 2, "Starting a Project Successfully with PRINCE2."
24. A – Corporate, programme management, or the customer makes decisions regarding a breach of project-level tolerances. See the "Tolerances and Exceptions" section in Chapter 9, "Progress Theme."

25. A – The senior user must demonstrate that the forecast benefits have been realized. In most projects, many of the benefits will not occur until after the project. See the "Business Case Responsibilities" section in Chapter 4, "Business Case Theme."
26. C – The teams create specialist products during the execute a work package activity in the managing product delivery process. See Chapter 10, "Managing the Middle of a Project Successfully with PRINCE2."
27. C – There are three types of issues in PRINCE2: request for change, off-specification, and problem or concern. See Chapter 8, "Change Theme."
28. D – Ensuring that the project's products meet business expectations is a purpose of the quality theme. See Chapter 6, "Quality Theme."
29. B – PRINCE2 does not focus on people-management or leadership skills. See Chapter 1, "Overview of PRINCE2."
30. D – All elements of the project initiation documentation may be updated during the managing a stage boundary process. The change control approach, the business case, and the project approach are all elements of the project initiation documentation. The project brief is not updated after the starting up a project process. See Chapter 10, "Managing the Middle of a Project Successfully with PRINCE2."
31. D – The organization theme ensures that everyone involved in the project's team—at the directing, managing, and delivering levels—is clear about what is expected of them. See Chapter 3, "Organization Theme."
32. A – The project plan provides the business case with planned costs and timescales. See Chapter 5, "Plans Theme."
33. A – The communication management approach details the requirements for reporting to the project's stakeholders, including the stakeholders who must be notified of the project closing. See Chapter 11, "Managing the End of a Project Successfully with PRINCE2."
34. B – One of the key sections of the business case is investment appraisal. This balances the forecast benefits against project costs and ongoing operational and maintenance costs. See "The Contents of the Business Case" section in Chapter 4, "Business Case Theme."
35. B – The three primary interests of stakeholders that are represented on the project board are business, represented by the executive; user, represented by the senior users; and supplier, represented by the senior suppliers. Refer to the "The Three Project Interests" section in Chapter 3, "Organization Theme."
36. C – Tailoring PRINCE2 consists of applying the method to the level required, not omitting elements of the method (which would weaken the approach). See Chapter 1, "Overview of PRINCE2."
37. A – A risk register is a record, not a report. See Chapter 1, "Overview of PRINCE2."
38. D – Although you may talk about mitigating a risk in everyday speech, this is not a PRINCE2 term. The steps in the PRINCE2 risk management procedure are identify, assess, plan, implement, and communicate. See the "Risk Management Procedure" section in Chapter 7, "Risk Theme."
39. B – The stage plan for the initiation stage is created in starting up a project, so it is the first one that is created. The project plan is created later, in the initiating a project process, the delivery stage plans are created later, in the managing a stage boundary process, and the programme plan is not created within the PRINCE2 model. See Chapter 5, "Plans Theme."

40. B – A fundamental philosophy behind the PRINCE2 approach to plans is that the products required are identified before the activities and resources to deliver those products are identified. This is known as product-based planning. Just-in-time planning, brainstorming, and work breakdown structures are not PRINCE2 techniques or approaches. See Chapter 5, "Plans Theme."

41. C – The project manager is responsible for producing the management products within the closing a project process. See Chapter 11, "Managing the End of a Project Successfully with PRINCE2."

42. C – The controlling a stage process contains a set of activities used by the project manager to manage each delivery stage. See Chapter 10, "Managing the Middle of a Project Successfully with PRINCE2."

43. A – During the starting up a project process, the executive will draft the outline business case. See Chapter 4, "Business Case Theme."

44. B – The change control approach is created along with the other approaches in the initiating a project process. See Chapter 8, "Change Theme."

Chapter 1

Overview of PRINCE2

PRINCE2 Foundation Exam Objectives Covered in This Chapter:

☑ **Recall:**
- The definition and characteristics of a project
- The six aspects of project performance to be managed
- The integrated elements of PRINCE2: principles, themes, processes and the project environment
- What makes a project a PRINCE2 project

☑ **Describe:**
- The features and benefits of PRINCE2
- The customer/supplier context on which PRINCE2 is based, including considerations when undertaking projects in a commercial environment

☑ **Explain the PRINCE2 principles:**
- Continued business justification
- Learn from experience
- Defined roles and responsibilities
- Manage by stages
- Manage by exception
- Focus on products
- Tailor to suit the project

☑ **Explain which aspects of a project can be tailored, who is responsible, and how tailoring decisions are documented**

PRINCE2 Practitioner Exam Objectives Covered in This Chapter:

☑ **Analyze the application of PRINCE2 principles in context:**
- Continued business justification
- Learn from experience
- Defined roles and responsibilities
- Manage by stages
- Manage by exception
- Focus on products
- Tailor to suit the project

This is a really important chapter—it sets out the overall framework of PRINCE2. You learn about the main components of the PRINCE2 model and how they all fit together. Each section of PRINCE2 often has many relationships with other parts of the methodology, so the first step in learning the approach is to understand how the structure links together. Then when I discuss a particular PRINCE2 topic, you will see how it fits into the model.

I also introduce some of the main PRINCE2 terms. You have quite a lot of terminology to learn! You might need to do some translation between the project management vocabulary you are familiar with and the PRINCE2 terms.

PRINCE2 is a management method that is used in project situations. In this chapter, you see how PRINCE2 defines a project and how it differs from "business as usual." I describe the main groups of project management activities as well as what needs to be achieved for a successful project.

The PRINCE2 model adheres to seven principles. I describe the details of these principles and show you why they contribute to successful project management.

There are many types of project situations that PRINCE2 can work within: a project might be small and simple, or large and complex; a project might involve people within only one organization or span many different commercial organizations; or a project might utilize different delivery methods, such as agile. To be successful, the project management team needs to adapt and tailor the methodology to work effectively within the environment they are faced with. In this chapter, I explain the more common situations that PRINCE2 can be adapted for and start to discuss how this tailoring is done.

Finally, I use an example project scenario to walk you through each step of a PRINCE2 project.

Project Work

In this section, you will see how PRINCE2 defines a project. This is important: only project situations are managed with PRINCE2, so the first task is to understand whether a piece of work is a project or business as usual. You will then learn how PRINCE2 defines project management. Finally, you will see what objectives can be set for a project.

What Is a Project?

PRINCE2 is *only* used to manage projects. So the first step for a *project manager* is to ensure that the situation they are faced with is indeed a project. Sometimes, this is not so easy. If an IT manager is asked to update a website, is that a project? If the update is quite small, the work might be considered a normal operational task. If it's a larger piece of work, then it might be treated as a project. At what point does the small update become too big to be business as usual?

The answer to this question relates to risk. An approach such as PRINCE2 provides a management framework that considerably increases the likelihood of project success. For small jobs, however, the framework might introduce a large and unnecessary management overhead. So deciding whether to treat a situation as a project is all about balancing the management overhead that would be introduced against such things as the decrease in the level of risk, the importance of the work, and the increase in the likelihood of success.

PRINCE2 defines a *project* as "a temporary organization that is created for the purpose of delivering one or more business products according to an agreed business case." The definition mentions a temporary organization. In PRINCE2, a group of people called the *project management team* comes together for the duration of the project. Business products are ones that will ultimately deliver some return for the organization running the project. Also note that the definition mentions a business case. PRINCE2 places a great deal of importance on the justification of the project. Anyone involved with the project should be able to justify why they are doing it.

The following characteristics of project work distinguish it from business as usual:

Change

The organization will be different after the project. For example, if the project implements a new invoice-processing system, the finance department will be working in quite a different way after the project than it did before it.

Temporary

Projects don't go on forever (although a few I've worked on have felt as if they have). They should have a start point and an end point. The end point occurs when the desired change has been implemented.

Cross-functional

Cross-functional projects often involve a collection of people drawn from many different sets of skills, different departments, and sometimes even different organizations. Often each group of people has different perspectives on the project and different motivations for getting involved. When these perspectives and motivations do not align, this can cause strain and sometimes conflict among the different groups.

Unique

To some extent, all project work is unique. On the one extreme, the project could be completely unique, such as the 1960s Apollo missions to send a man to the moon. Alternatively, the project could be just slightly different from what has been done before. For example, the installation of a new version of office software might be similar to the installation of the last version; however, this time the software is a little different and maybe new people are involved.

Uncertainty

The previous four characteristics introduce a great deal of uncertainty into project work. It is not quite clear how things will turn out. All sorts of unforeseen threats might occur. This uncertainty introduces a lot more risk compared with business as usual.

Cross-Functional Aspect of Project Work

My consultancy was involved in a project that was a good example of one with cross-functional characteristics. The project's objective was to install a new Internet system in a UK government education department. The site was to hold examination syllabus information for the various national curriculums. Within the government department, two main divisions were involved: the IT division and an information division. There were also a number of senior managers. The website was being built by a third-party software house. The teaching unions were represented because they needed to specify their informational requirements. There was a government quality assurance group who audited the project to ensure it met UK government standards. We all came from different backgrounds, saw the project with different perspectives, and had our own way of working. All these parties had to come together and work as a unified team on a temporary basis. They did, and the project was a success, although at times it was difficult. The key was to pay particular attention to how we all communicated with each other throughout the project. I talk about how PRINCE2 meets this challenge in Chapter 3, "Organization Theme."

What Is Business as Usual?

PRINCE2 is not used to manage situations that could be regarded as *business as usual*. Business as usual is any work that is part of an organization's normal operations—for example, supporting a company's IT systems, cleaning the rooms of a hotel, or running a call center. It has no predefined end. It usually involves people from the same area of the business and doesn't introduce any major change into the organization. It isn't unique—what was done last week is pretty much what will be done next week. Therefore, far less uncertainty exists regarding the work.

Project work often leads to business-as-usual work. For example, if there is a project to build a hotel, once that hotel opens, there will be a lot of business-as-usual work. This normal operational work might consist of a range of activities, including supporting the hotel's IT systems, manning the reception desk, dealing with clients' queries, running the restaurant, and so on.

What Is Project Management?

There are four main areas of *project management*: plan, delegate, monitor, and control. The four areas ensure that the specialist work of the project is co-coordinated in an effective way so as to deliver what is required within certain constraints, such as budgets and delivery dates. For example, if the project is to build a hotel, it ensures that all the hundreds of tasks, people, and resources work together to produce a hotel of the right quality. Following are some brief descriptions of each area of project management:

Figure 1.1: Project management

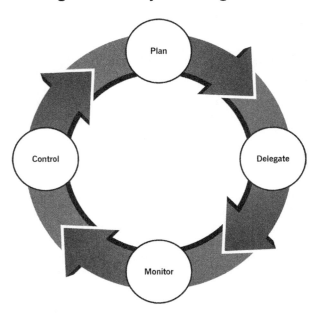

Plan

The first area is to plan what needs to be created and how this will be done. This ensures that all the work is coordinated effectively. In the hotel example, it stops situations such as the painters arriving on site before the builders have finished building the hotel walls.

Delegate

Effective delegation by the project manager ensures that the right people do the right work at the right time. When delegating, the project manager must communicate all the information that the person doing the work needs to know, such as what to create, how much time they have, what budget that have, how often to report progress, and so on. (In PRINCE2, the project manager uses work packages to delegate work—more on this in Chapter 10, "Managing the Middle of a Project Successfully with PRINCE2.")

Monitor

It would be a naïve project manager who believes that once the work has been delegated, it will all be completed to plan. The project manager needs to constantly monitor the ongoing progress of the project, spotting problems that might delay things as well as opportunities to move the project forward.

Control

Through the previous three areas, project management exerts *control* over the project. It controls all the work of all the people involved. It ensures the right activities occur at the right time to create the right products. Control is also about taking corrective action when the project looks like it will go off course.

Figure 1.1 shows the four areas of project management in a wheel, to signify that they will need to be done again and again throughout a project.

Measuring the Performance of a Project

A project's performance can be measured in six areas:
- How much money it spends; this relates to a project's costs.
- How ahead or behind schedule it is; this relates to a project's timescales.
- How well the project's products meet the required specification; this relates to a project's quality.
- How many of the required products have been delivered and whether any products have been delivered that were not asked for; this relates to a project's scope.
- How much uncertainty the project has that might lead to the project being negatively impacted; this relates to the level of project risk.
- How much value a project has delivered to the organization either during or after the project; this relates to a project's benefits. This is the most important performance objective because the ultimate point of any project—its raison d'être—is to deliver benefits.

It may be not possible to judge how well a project has performed against its benefits' targets until sometime after the initiative has finished. For example, if the project were to build a website to sell a company's products, online sales can't be measured until after the website has been launched.

Figure 1.2 shows these six different areas. PRINCE2 calls these areas the six aspects of project performance that need to be managed.

Figure 1.2: Six aspects of project performance

The Six Aspects of Performance for the London Crossrail Project

How do the six aspects of performance relate to a real project? I will use a project from London in the UK as an example. (Sharp-eyed readers might challenge me on calling Crossrail a project and tell me it would probably be classed as a programme. You are right, but let's pretend it's a project for now since it will help me explain the six aspects of project performance.) The London Crossrail project is a major initiative to upgrade the rail infrastructure of the capital. The project is building two enormous rail tunnels that will stretch across London from east to west. The new railway will link up to the existing network and provide much-needed new train capacity for the busy capital. After it has been built, travellers will be able to take a train nonstop from Heathrow (London's main airport in the west of the city) to Canary Wharf (the capital's major financial centre in the east of the city), thereby substantially cutting down commute times.

Will the project be successful? To answer that question, you need to consider the project's performance against the six aspects of project performance: cost, time, scope, quality, risk, and benefits. First, there is the cost aspect. The budget was £15 billion and, at the time of this writing, the project looks like it will deliver the system within budget. Second, the first trains are scheduled to run in 2019. Once again, at the time of writing, it looks likely that this target will be hit.

The scope of the project contains all the different products that need to be delivered, including the trains, tunnels, new stations, staff uniforms, and so on. Closely linked to the scope objective is the quality objective. In PRINCE2, a quality product is one that will be fit for its purpose. For example, a train in the Crossrail project will be fit for purpose if it can reach the right speed, have the right number of seats, be able to run without any breakdowns for the right amount of time, and so on. Before the product is created, the project management team needs to define what characteristics will make it fit for purpose. Then once it has been created, the product needs to be quality-checked to ensure it is indeed fit for purpose. At the time of writing, it looks like the Crossrail project will be able to deliver a full scope of quality products.

For any project, risk is involved. The commissioning organization will need to identify the major risks to the project, establish to what extent the risks can be mitigated, and decide whether they are comfortable with the risk situation. One key risk for the Crossrail project was that the tunnel might cause instability above ground and damage some of London's key buildings. The project management team devised an effective way to respond to this risk. Any key building above the path of the tunnel was rigged up with a laser-measuring device. The device could detect if the building has moved by the tiniest amount. If this occurred, the team could dig a shaft near the building and then inject a concrete-like substance called grout into the ground under the building that, when set, would stop any further movement.

The final aspect of project performance is benefits. The business case for the Crossrail project highlights a whole range of benefits. For example, during construction, the project has helped support 55,000 jobs, both within the project team itself and throughout the supply chain of companies that have provided products and services for the project. Once the project has finished, it will add approximately 10-percent extra capacity to London's rail network and help to increase the appeal of London as a global capital of business, culture, and tourism. Whether the project will hit all its targets for benefits remains to be seen. It has certainly delivered on the target of supporting jobs across the capital, but the post-project benefits will need to be measured over a period of time after the project has completed.

Introducing PRINCE2

The previous section looked at projects. I explained that project work involves a lot of uncertainty and risk. When a project is started, it can be difficult to see ahead, to know what to do next. Where PRINCE2 helps is that it says no matter what project you are involved with, certain steps must be carried out to ensure success. Many of these steps are just common sense. For example, at the outset of all projects, those involved should agree on its objectives. Then at the end of the project, everyone should meet again to decide whether the objectives have been met. Another set of commonsense steps is that all projects should involve those who will ultimately use the project products, so that they can define what they require and later can verify that the products that have been created are fit for their purpose. There are many other commonalities in how all projects are managed, such as general approaches to managing areas like risks, changes, quality, and communication.

The PRINCE2 model combines all these commonsense ideas about managing projects. It gives a range of processes with steps to ensure the right management activities are done, defines roles to ensure the right people take responsibility for doing the steps, and suggests a range of management documents to hold and report on useful management information. It supports everyone on the project to follow these commonsense ideas by appointing assurance roles, which checks whether the steps are being followed.

The Structure of PRINCE2

PRINCE2 is made up of four main parts, or what PRINCE2 refers to as *integrated elements*. These are the *principles*, the *themes*, the *processes*, and the *project environment*. These integrated elements are shown in Figure 1.3.

Figure 1.3: The structure of PRINCE2

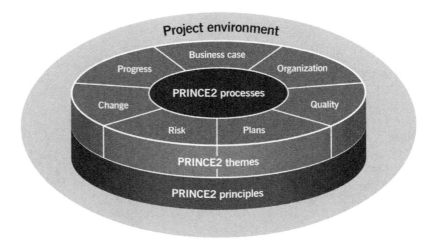

The Principles

The first integrated element of PRINCE2 is the principles. You can think of these as the core concepts that the rest of PRINCE2 adheres to. If a project management team is not practicing all of the principles, it is not a PRINCE2 project. There are seven PRINCE2 principles, which are described in detail later in this chapter. An example is "learn from experience," which means (rather obviously) that before anything is done to manage a project, it is always worth considering any prior experience that might be useful.

The Processes

The second integrated element of PRINCE2 is the seven processes, all of which provide a set of activities showing how to manage various parts of a project. The processes cover the management work from the time just before the project starts (when the question is whether the project should be done) to the end of the project. The processes show which roles should be responsible for each activity and which management documents (such as plans or reports) would be useful to create, review, or update at this time.

Each process covers a specific time during the project. For example, the starting up a project process gives six activities that should be considered for a successful start to a project. The closing a project process, as the name suggests, covers the management activities that need to take place at the end of the project.

I describe the seven PRINCE2 processes in more detail in the "An End-to-End Walk-through of PRINCE2" section later in this chapter. In the meantime, here's a brief overview of each process:

Starting Up a Project

Starting up a project covers the activities you use to investigate whether to start the project. I describe this process in detail in Chapter 2, "Starting a Project Successfully with PRINCE2."

Directing a Project

Directing a project covers the activities of the *project board*, which is the main decision-making body on a PRINCE2 project. It includes making decisions such as whether the project should start, whether to move on to the next stage of the project, and whether the project can close.

Initiating a Project

Initiating a project covers the planning activities done at the beginning of the project. I describe this process in detail in Chapter 2.

Controlling a Stage

Controlling a stage covers the project manager's day-to-day work, such as delegating work, reporting, and dealing with issues and risks. I describe this process in detail in Chapter 10, "Managing the Middle of a Project Successfully with PRINCE2."

Managing Product Delivery

Managing product delivery covers the day-to-day work of the people creating products in the project. The activities detail accepting work, creating it, reporting progress, and delivering work. I describe this process in detail in Chapter 10.

Managing a Stage Boundary

Managing a stage boundary covers the work of the project manager at the end of a major part or stage of the project. It involves activities such as reporting on the achievements in the last stage and detailed planning for the next stage. I describe this process in detail in Chapter 10.

Closing a Project

Closing a project covers the work that the project manager does to prepare for the end of the project. It involves work such as preparing the end project report, handing the products to the operational teams, and archiving project documents. I describe this process in detail in Chapter 11, "Managing the End of a Project Successfully with PRINCE2."

The Themes

The third integrated element of PRINCE2 is the themes. The themes describe how PRINCE2 recommends carrying out various aspects of project management. The risk theme, for example, describes how PRINCE2 recommends managing risk throughout a project, and the organization theme describes how PRINCE2 recommends defining the project management team's roles and responsibilities.

Each of these themes may be useful throughout all the processes. For example, the risk management approach described in the risk theme is used in all the processes. And any one process may use numerous themes. For example, in the starting up a project process, the project management team is appointed (the organization structure and the accompanying roles are described in the organization theme), risks for the project will need to identified (risk identification and estimation approaches are described in the risk theme), and the outline business case is created (the composition of the business case is described in the business case theme).

There are seven themes in PRINCE2, and this study guide has a chapter explaining each one. Here's a brief overview of each theme:

Business Case

The *business case theme* describes how to ensure the project has a solid justifiable reason to exist, not just at the outset of the project, but throughout its life. It shows how to create a business case and how to plan the tracking of the project's benefits using a benefits management approach. It sets out various activities related to justifying the project and shows which roles should be responsible for them. I describe this theme in detail in Chapter 4, "Business Case Theme."

Organization

The *organization theme* defines the project management team structure. It describes the various roles within the structure and sets out their responsibilities. I describe this theme in detail in Chapter 3, "Organization Theme."

Quality

The *quality theme* describes how to ensure that the project's products are fit for the purpose for which they will be used. I describe this theme in detail in Chapter 6, "Quality Theme."

Plans

The *plans theme* describes how to plan which products to create and which activities are needed to build those products. I describe this theme in detail in Chapter 5, "Plans Theme."

Risk

The *risk theme* describes how to manage potential threats and opportunities to the project. I describe this theme in detail in Chapter 7, "Risk Theme."

Change

The *change theme* describes how to control and manage changes to the project's products. I describe this theme in detail in Chapter 8, "Change Theme."

Progress

The *progress theme* describes how to track the progress of a project, which mechanisms to use to keep the project on track, and what to do when things go astray. I describe this theme in detail in Chapter 9, "Progress Theme."

The Project Environment

The fourth integrated element of PRINCE2 is the project environment and how to tailor PRINCE2 to that situation.

There are many types of projects and many environments in which they might run. Examples include very large, complex initiatives, involving various organizations and running over many years, as well much smaller activities, involving only a few people over a number of days. Every possible industry you could think of runs projects, each creating very different products or services. Some projects run in the private sector, others in the public sector, and still others in charities. Some projects use a variety of specialist approaches alongside PRINCE2, such as the one set out in the Project Management Institute's (PMI) *A Guide to the Project Management Body of Knowledge* (2017) or the agile approaches used in many different industries.

PRINCE2 can be applied to all of these types of situations for two reasons. First, as I discussed earlier in the chapter, no matter what type of project you are running, there will be a common set of management activities that need to be done, which are set out in PRINCE2. Second, the framework is flexible—that is, it can be tailored in many ways to suit the various situations described previously.

I look at tailoring PRINCE2 to the project environment in more detail in the section "Tailoring PRINCE2 to Different Project Types and Environments" later in this chapter.

Other Parts of PRINCE2

In addition to the four main integrated elements of PRINCE2 (processes, themes, principles, and the project environment), there are two other main parts to PRINCE2: the roles and the management products.

> ## Exam Spotlight
>
> There are four integrated elements to PRINCE2: the principles, the themes, the processes, and the project environment. The roles and the management products are also important parts of the method, but PRINCE2 does not define them as integrated elements.

Roles

I discuss the PRINCE2 management roles in more detail in Chapter 3, but it is important to understand the basic details at this point.

PRINCE2 gives a recommended project management team structure. It looks like a company organization chart, as shown in Figure 1.4.

The four levels of hierarchy in the PRINCE2 project management structure are as follows:

Corporate, Programme Management, or the Customer
This level sits outside and above the project management team.

Directing Level
The project board is responsible for this. It is the top level of the project management team.

Managing Level
The project manager is responsible for this, the middle level of the project management team.

Delivering Level
The team manager and their teams are responsible for this. It is the bottom level of the project management team.

Figure 1.4: Project management team structure

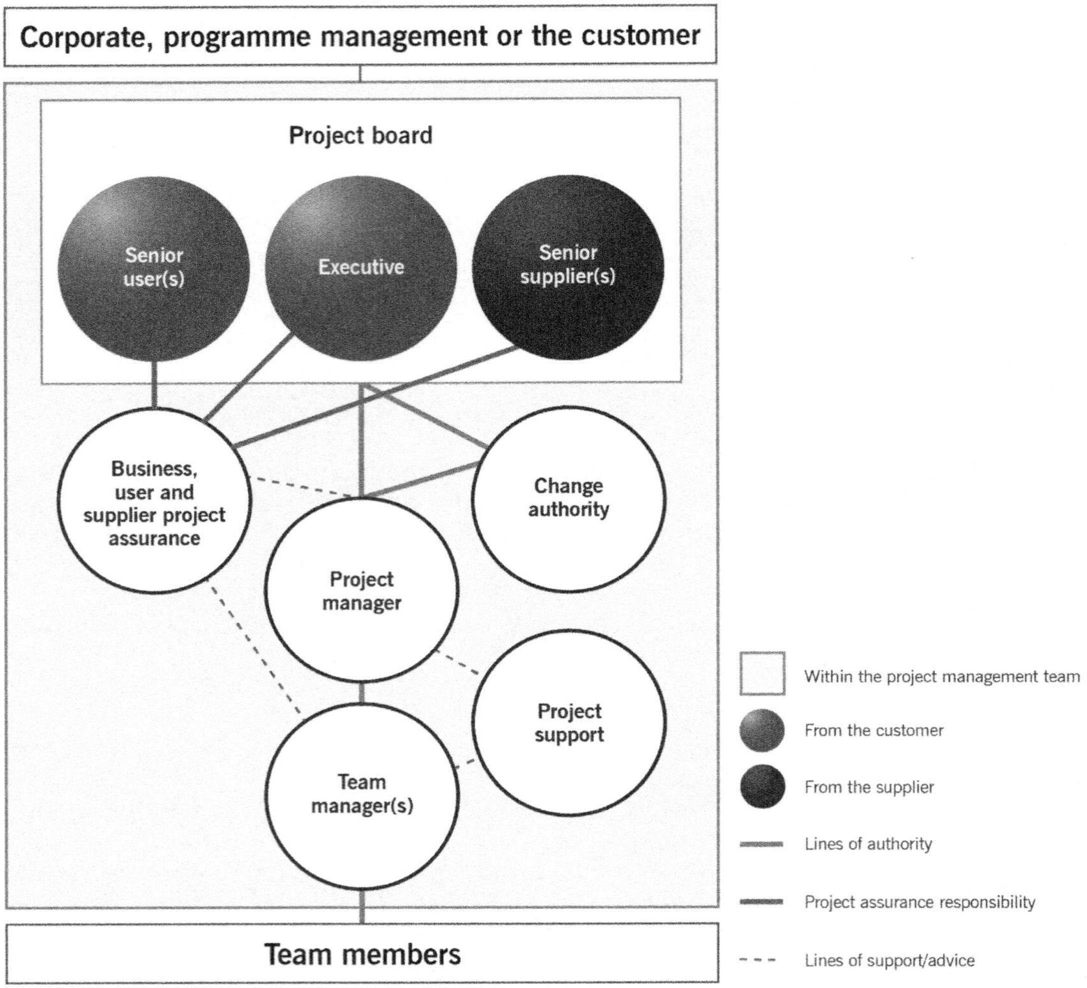

Corporate, programme management or the customer

Project board

Senior user(s)

Executive

Senior supplier(s)

Business, user and supplier project assurance

Change authority

Project manager

Project support

Team manager(s)

Team members

Within the project management team

From the customer

From the supplier

Lines of authority

Project assurance responsibility

Lines of support/advice

At the top of the project organization structure is *corporate, programme management, or the customer*. (A *programme* is a collection of related projects being run in a coordinated way.) This consists of a rather ambiguous group of people. All we know about them is that they are "high up"—that is, they have enough authority to start a project. How "high up" they are in their organizations depends on the size of the project and how much authority is needed to start it. If it is a very large project, corporate, programme management, or the customer might be the board of directors of the company; if it is a smaller project, they may be the head of a department. It is important to note that they trigger the start of the PRINCE2 process model, but corporate, programme management, or the customer is *not* part of the project management team. All the management levels below corporate, programme management, or the customer, however, *are* part of the project management team.

Below corporate, programme management, or the customer in the project management structure is the directing level. The project board is responsible for this level. The project board is given authority for the overall direction and management of the project by corporate, programme management, or the customer. They are the main decision-making body on the project. They make key project decisions, such as whether the project should start, whether it should it go on to its next major part, and finally, whether it is ready to close. They need to be high enough up in their own organization's hierarchy so as to have the authority to make these decisions.

A number of people make up the project board. Between them, they must represent three key perspectives on the project: the business perspective, the user perspective, and the supplier perspective.

The *business perspective* focuses on the returns the project will give their organization. For example, if the project were to build a hotel for a leisure company, the business perspective would be concerned with factors such as the potential sales of rooms. They also would be interested in how much investment would be needed to get those returns—in other words, what value they might get for their money. This business view is represented by the *executive* role. The executive sits on the project board. There is always *only* one executive, who is considered the leader of the project.

The *user perspective* focuses on how the project's products will be used post-project. This perspective is represented on the project board by the *senior user* role. In the hotel example, the senior user role could be carried out by representatives of those who will stay in the hotel or who understand these travelers' needs, such as a tourist board or a market research person specializing in tourism. There might be a number of people on the project board who share the senior user role.

Finally, the *supplier perspective* focuses on creating the project's products. This is represented on the project board by the *senior supplier* role. In the hotel example, the senior supplier role could be taken by operational managers from architectural or construction firms. Like the senior user role, there might be a number of people who share the senior supplier role.

Below the project board in the project management structure is the managing level. It is the responsibility of the project manager to manage the project on a day-to-day basis and within the constraints set by the project board. There is only *one* project manager in a PRINCE2 project. This individual is responsible for planning the project, delegating work, reporting on the project's progress, managing risks and issues, and creating and updating the project management documents.

At the bottom of the project management structure is the delivering level. This is the responsibility of the *teams* that create the products of the project. In the hotel project, there could be teams of architects, builders, electricians, plumbers, and so on. In some cases, such as a small project, the project manager might manage the teams directly. In other, larger projects, the project manager might delegate work to several *team managers*, who, in turn, delegate work to the teams.

As illustrated earlier in Figure 1.4, there are several other roles, such as project assurance, change authority, and project support. I explain these roles in Chapter 3.

Management Products

Management products are things that help the project management team manage the project, such as plans, registers, logs, and reports. They are a means to an end, not the end itself. Although you might think of these items as management documents, PRINCE2 calls them management products because the management information could be communicated verbally. In fact, you could run a PRINCE2 project without any documents at all.

Examples of PRINCE2 management products include the *project plan*, which is used to track and monitor the work of the project; *product descriptions*, which help specify the products to be delivered; and the *risk register*, which contains information on all the identified risks to the project. There are 26 management products in all—you can find further information on each one throughout this study guide as well as in Appendix C, "Management Products in PRINCE2."

PRINCE2 defines three types of management products: baselines, records, and reports.

Baseline management products might go through a number of versions during the life of a project. If someone needs to make an update to a baseline management product, the amendments are made to a new version of the document. Then at the end of the project, the project team can review all the versions of the document (the latest and all the old ones) and see how the information has evolved. An example of a baseline management product is a plan.

Records are the registers and the logs that the project manager uses to record information on things such as risks, issues, and lessons. An example of a record is the issue register. As with all records, there is only one issue register document; new versions are not made of the document when it needs to be updated. The updates are just added to the bottom of the register as a new line.

Reports are … well, reports. They are the progress reports that are sent during the project to update various people of the latest situation on the project. An example of a report is the highlight report that the project manager sends to the project board on a regular basis.

Specialist Products

In addition to the management products, there is another type of product called *specialist products*. These are the deliverables from the project. A project to build a hotel, for example, has numerous deliverables, such as the architectural plans, the rooms, the furniture, the swimming pool, and a hotel brochure, to name a few.

What PRINCE2 Does Not Cover

A whole range of skills and approaches are needed to manage projects successfully. PRINCE2 by no means covers them all. It does not focus on any specialist techniques that might be needed in specific industries, such as an IT project as opposed to a construction project. The framework does not provide all of the specific project management techniques that might be used, such as stakeholder analysis, critical path analysis, or risk identification techniques. An organization can use its own recommended techniques alongside PRINCE2. In some cases, PRINCE2 explains and recommends using certain techniques (for example, the risk management procedure), but an alternative approach can be used as long as it meets the requirements set out in PRINCE2. It also does not cover motivational approaches, team building, or leadership development.

Benefits of Using PRINCE2

The benefits of using PRINCE2 to manage a project include the following:
- The ideas in PRINCE2 have been developed over many years and tested successfully on many types of projects. It is highly likely that any project will benefit from these ideas, and organizations that adopt the method as a standard can improve their project management capability.

- PRINCE2 has been designed to be used on any type of project in any type of industry. It focuses on the management activities that are common to all projects rather than how to do specialist work that would be particular to one type of industry.
- PRINCE2 can be tailored and adapted to suit many different types of projects. For example, it can just as successfully be applied on a small project as to a large one, or to a project within one organization as well as to a project that spans many different commercial entities.
- PRINCE2 provides a common vocabulary of project terms. This makes it easier to communicate on projects, especially when several different organizations and people are involved.
- PRINCE2 defines specific project management responsibilities and shows how a project management team should be structured. This ensures that those involved in the management team are clear on their responsibilities. It also ensures that all the people who are needed to manage a project are included in the management team.
- PRINCE2 focuses attention on what needs to be created. This ensures there is clarity and agreement on the outputs from the project.
- PRINCE2 provides a range of reports and plans as well as other management documents to meet the needs of different levels of management.
- The PRINCE2 management-by-exception approach ensures the efficient and economic use of management time. (I describe management by exception in more detail in the next section.)
- Before, during, and after a project, PRINCE2 focuses attention on the justification for undertaking that project. This ensures that projects are run as a means to an end rather than as an end in themselves. It also ensures that organizations take on projects that provide value.
- Adopting PRINCE2 allows people within an organization to learn how to improve their management skills. It provides consistency in project work, which means that project management assets can be reused, and reduces the impact of changes in management personnel. Many PRINCE2-accredited consultants and project managers are available around the world.
- PRINCE2 provides a theoretical management framework through which actual projects can be viewed. This helps organizations identify problems and missing elements of the project's approach to management.

PRINCE2 Principles

I introduced the seven PRINCE2 principles earlier in this chapter. These are guiding concepts that the rest of the model adheres to. All the other elements and parts of PRINCE2 ensure that one or a number of these principles are implemented.

As you work through this study guide and learn about the different parts of the PRINCE2 model, ask yourself which principle each part is supporting. This will help you answer the exam questions about the linkages between the various parts of PRINCE2. For example, Chapter 4 covers the business case theme, which helps implement the principle of continued business justification.

Continued Business Justification

The principle of *continued business justification* ensures there is a documented justification for starting a project. It ensures this justification is reviewed and possibly updated throughout the life of the project. You should use the latest version of the justification to decide whether to move on to each major stage of the project. Often, this justification is written up in some form of business case.

It is important that the justification for a project aligns with the overall business strategy of the organization that is commissioning the project. If this is not the case, an organization could end up running multiple projects that are inconsistent with one another and start to work against each other.

Even projects that are driven by legislation changes or the need to be compliant with new regulation should have a business case. In this case, the business case should show that the project is delivering compliance in a value-for-money way.

PRINCE2 provides a range of activities with associated responsibilities to ensure continued business justification. These are described throughout the process model and also in the business case theme. PRINCE2 provides two important business-related management products: the business case, which documents the justification for undertaking the project, and the benefit management approach, which plans the reviews of the project's benefits.

Learn from Experience

When you're managing a project, it is a good idea to take into account the good practice and the mistakes made in past projects. It is also a good idea to collate the lessons learned during the management of the current project and pass them on to teams managing subsequent projects. During many of the management activities throughout the process model, PRINCE2 constantly highlights the need to take account of past experience and collate new knowledge. It provides two important management products to help implement the *learn from experience* principle: the *lessons log*, which is used to record both previous and current experience, and the *lessons report*, which is used to pass on experience from the current project to those who will manage subsequent projects. The progress theme (covered in Chapter 9) describes how to control the flow of experience.

Defined Roles and Responsibilities

It is important that each role in the project management team be performed by someone who understands what is expected of them and who is willing to take on that role. This is the PRINCE2 principle of *defined roles and responsibilities.* The project management team must include people from a broad range of stakeholder perspectives, especially those viewing the project from business, user, and supplier perspectives. The project management team should include appropriate roles for the various management levels of the organizations involved.

PRINCE2 provides a project management team structure. For each role within the structure, it sets out a range of responsibilities. For each activity in the process model, there is a defined role (or roles) responsible for that activity. The project management team structure and the associated roles are first set out in the project brief and then in the project initiation documentation (PID). The communication management approach (covered in Chapter 3) describes how the communication between these people will be managed.

Manage by Stages

The *manage by stages* principle ensures that PRINCE2 projects are divided into a number of time periods, called *management stages (or often just called stages).* These stages could last days, weeks, or even months (or, in some of the military projects I've been involved with, years). A collection of products is created within each stage. The project board gives the project manager the authority to manage one stage at a time. After a stage is complete, the project manager must report back to the project board members, who then review the stage's performance and other factors, such as the current state of the project's business case, and decide whether to authorize the next stage. The project management team decides *how* to divide the project into stages when preparing the project plan at the outset of the project.

A project to build a hotel, for example, could be divided into the following four stages:

- During stage one, the project is planned.
- During stage two, the hotel is designed.
- During stage three, the hotel is built.
- During stage four, the interior of the hotel is decorated and fitted with electricity, plumbing, furniture, and so on.

This approach has two benefits. First, it helps with planning. There is always a planning horizon beyond which it is difficult to forecast. For example, at the beginning of the designing work in stage two, it is impossible to plan in detail the building work of stage three, because at this point, the specification of the hotel has not been decided. With the PRINCE2 manage-by-stages approach, the detailed stage plan for each stage is not created until the end of the previous stage. The project plan, which covers the whole project and is created at the outset, is done from a high-level perspective.

The other major benefit is that the senior managers taking on roles in the project board do not need to get involved with the day-to-day management of the stages. However, they can retain control of the project by authorizing progress a stage at a time. This is an efficient way of using senior management time. Senior managers can also vary the amount of control they have by shortening or lengthening the stages.

Every PRINCE2 project always has at least two stages: a planning stage (or what PRINCE2 calls the *initiation stage*) and at least one other stage where specialist products are delivered.

Manage by Exception

In PRINCE2, each management level manages the level below using the *manage by exception* principle. As I discussed in the "Roles" section earlier in this chapter, the PRINCE2 project management structure has four levels of management. At the top is a group called corporate, programme management, or the customer, who instigate the project. Below them is project board, the main decision-making body on the project. Then comes the project manager, who manages the project on a day-to-day basis. Finally, at the bottom, are the team managers and their teams, who create the project's products. So corporate, programme management, or the customer manage the project board by exception, then the project board manages the project manager by exception, and, finally, the project manager manages the team manager by exception.

Manage by exception means that the upper level of management gives the level of management below them a piece (or all) of the project to manage on their behalf. The upper level of management also sets certain boundaries around the lower level of management's authority. The lower level of management then needs further authorization from the level of management above them in only one of two circumstances: either they have finished delivering their piece of the project and they want to move on to a new piece of work or they realize that a situation has arisen that breaches the boundaries of their delegated authority.

The upper level of management defines the authority they give to the level of management below them by setting constraints around six areas: time, cost, scope, quality, risk, and benefits. A certain amount of leeway, or what PRINCE2 calls *tolerances*, may be allowed around these constraints. If at any time it appears these constraints may be breached, the lower level of management must escalate the situation to the level of management above them. This situation is called an *exception*. Here are some examples of the six areas where constraints can be set:

Time

The upper level of management gives the level of management below them a certain amount of time to carry out their work within certain tolerances. For example, the work must be finished in six months, with a permissible early delivery of two weeks and late delivery of one week. If the lower level of management believes they cannot deliver the work within this three-week range, they must escalate the situation to the level of management above them.

Cost

The upper level of management gives the level of management below them a certain budget to spend, possibly with some permissible leeway. For example, the budget could be $10,000 with an allowable under-expenditure of $1,000 and no allowable over-expenditure. If the lower level of management forecasts that they cannot deliver their work for $9,000 to $10,000, they must escalate the situation to the level of management above them.

Scope

The upper level of management gives the level of management below them a set of products that need to be delivered with any possible variation allowed. For example, the product could be a website with pages that contain information on all the company's primary services and, if time permits, the secondary services. If the lower level of management realizes they will not be able to deliver even the primary service pages, they must escalate the situation to the level of management above them.

Quality

The upper level of management gives the level of management below them a set of specifications for all the products that should be created. These are specified in an appropriate manner to an appropriate level of detail for that management level. Any tolerance around the specifications will also be shown—for example, create an Olympic stadium 50-60 meters high. (Obviously you'd have a few more details to work with than this.) If the lower level of management cannot deliver products within these specification ranges, they must escalate the situation to the level of management above them.

Risk

The upper level of management gives the level of management below them a threshold level of aggregated risk. An example is that expected costs of the predicted threats must not exceed $20,000. (For more information on risk tolerances, see Chapter 7, "Risk Theme.") If the lower level of management realizes this threshold level of risk will be breached, they must escalate the situation to the level of management above them.

Benefits

The objectives for the project's benefits may also be given some allowable deviation by corporate, programme management, or the customer. For example, sales from the project must be in the range of $500,000 to $600,000. If this forecast looks as though it won't be possible, the situation should be escalated back to corporate, programme management, or the customer.

Management by exception provides for efficient use of the senior managers' time. They don't have to get involved in the day-to-day work of the level below. However, they can control the work of the level below by setting tolerances around these six areas.

Focus on Products

A product can be tangible like a train or intangible such as trained staff. They are always inputs or outputs from a series of activities. For example, if my project were to develop a training course and train a group of staff, the products might include the existing corporate training standards that my training course needs to comply with, the set of slides that I need to create to show during the course, and the final product, which is a group of trained staff. In PRINCE2, products are sometimes referred to as *outputs* or deliverables.

The principle of *focus on products* ensures that through every step of the project, what the project is creating is clearly defined and agreed to. In PRINCE2, these product specifications are set out in product descriptions. The product descriptions are then used as the basis of planning the activities needed to create the products, manage proposed changes to the products, and verify approval and acceptance of the products once they have been built. This seems like a rather obvious thing to do. However, many projects miss this simple approach, and as a result, disputes occur over the acceptance of the products, uncontrolled changes are introduced, or the wrong outputs are created. Also, when a project management team is not focused on the end goal of the project's activities, which is to create the agreed products, they sometimes do unnecessary work or start to create products that were not agreed.

Tailor to Suit the Project

I provided an overview of how the project management team can *tailor PRINCE2 to suit the project* environment in "The Project Environment" section earlier in this chapter, and, as mentioned, I discuss this topic in more detail in the next section of this chapter. In addition to defining this important approach as an integrated element of the model, PRINCE2 restates it as one of the seven principles.

Tailoring PRINCE2 to Different Project Types and Environments

Projects come in many different shapes and sizes. There are small projects, large projects, engineering projects, construction projects, public sector projects, and so on. The key to using PRINCE2 successfully is to tailor the method so that it suits the situation.

What Is Tailoring?

When you are managing a small project, it is important not to overburden the team with unnecessary management documents and processes. In this case, you might want to cut back how you apply PRINCE2. However, you would need to be careful—if you cut it back too much, you might not adequately cover important project management activities, such as planning, risk management, and project governance. This will probably lead to a chaotic situation in which, instead of project managing, you end up with a highly uncoordinated and incohesive initiative where all your time will be spent dealing with problems and issues. When applying PRINCE2, it is important to apply just enough of the approach that avoids the chaos of no management but does not overburden the project with unnecessary bureaucracy.

PRINCE2 is a flexible model. A project management team should always consider how to tailor PRINCE2 to best suit the particular project situation they face.

What Cannot Be Tailored?

Before I show you what parts of PRINCE2 can be tailored, the best place to start is to show you what cannot be tailored.

You learned earlier in this chapter about the seven PRINCE2 principles. Every PRINCE2 project, no matter how small, must abide by the principles. For example, even a tiny project should have a clear description of the justification for the work in order to adhere to the PRINCE2 principle of continuing business justification.

Each theme might be tailored by the project management team; however, each theme has a set of minimum requirements that must be applied. I explain each of the seven themes in Chapters 3 through 9 in this book. In the tailoring section of each of those chapters, I describe the minimum requirements for that theme. For example, when you learn about the plans theme in Chapter 5, you will see that PRINCE2 says every project must have at least two management stages.

PRINCE2 places some limits on how you might tailor what it calls techniques. There are a number of places in the PRINCE2 model where you are told to do something such as investment appraisal, estimating or reviewing a product, but you are not told exactly how to do it. This is because, although the activity must be done to be PRINCE2-compliant, the technique you might use to do it would vary widely, depending on factors such as the industry, the company, or the country your project is operating within. For example, the technique you use to appraise an investment would be very different in a small venture capital–funded company than in a large public-sector organization; or the technique you might use to quality-review an IT system would be quite different from how you would review a document. PRINCE2 often suggests a technique, but it is not mandatory that you use that technique. However, when the project management team is considering how to tailor PRINCE2, they must make sure to swap the PRINCE2-recommended technique with another, more-appropriate approach, rather than not doing the activity at all.

The "An End-to-End Walk-through of PRINCE2" section later in this chapter takes you through the process model; and in Chapters 2, 10, and 11, you learn more about these processes. Each process has a number of key purposes and objectives that you will find in the Exam Essentials sections of Chapters 2, 10, and 11. The project management team must make sure that any tailored process still achieves these purposes and objectives.

When the project management team is considering how much tailoring is required, they should balance the cost of training the project teams in the new approach against the benefits that the adapted method will bring.

Why Tailor PRINCE2?

PRINCE2 says that it is mandatory to tailor the method. There are many reasons why a project management team would want to tailor PRINCE2. You've already seen that if you are faced with a small project, you would want to cut back your application of PRINCE2. The opposite is also true: If you are faced with a very large initiative, you might want to increase your project management approach (and also use a programme management approach, as described in more detail later).

Applying PRINCE2 helps reduce the project risk, so anything that makes the project more complicated and more risky might mean you want to apply PRINCE2 in a more rigorous way. For example, projects running across multiple organizations or countries have much more scope for miscommunication, so you would want to be more careful in your project management approach.

Tailoring isn't just a matter of increasing or decreasing PRINCE2—there are many other ways of adapting the method. For example, the project might be operating in an industry that uses differing delivery methods or lifecycle models. A common approach in the IT industry is the waterfall method, where the project follows a number of prescribed phases: First, the client's requirements are established and recorded; then the IT system is designed; then it is built and tested; and finally, it is deployed. The project management team would want to adapt PRINCE2 so that there is a decision point at the end of each phase where the project board decides whether to proceed.

The project might be operating in a legal or regulatory environment. For example, I did a web project in the pharmaceutical industry where every web page had to be reviewed by the legal team to ensure it met regulatory standards. I adapted the quality management approach to ensure that all quality reviews included a legal compliance review. The project management approach might need to include certain mandatory processes or frameworks. For example, public sector projects often have to follow a mandatory procurement process.

An organization might have a range of pre-existing project management terms. For example, many companies create something similar to PRINCE2's PID at the beginning of a project. (You learn more about this important management product in the "An End-to-End Walk-through of PRINCE2" section later in this chapter.) I've seen these documents called many things: project charters, project terms of reference, project definition documents, and so on. Rather than change the document's name, the project manager could use the existing term that everyone is used to and just check that the document fulfills all the criteria of the PID.

Other factors that might influence how PRINCE2 is tailored include the capability of the project management team, the maturity of the organization, and any legal contracts that apply to the project's work.

What Can Be Tailored?

What specific parts of the model can be tailored? The simple answer is: everything, as long as you follow the rules I gave you in the preceding "What Cannot be Tailored?" section. However, you must ensure that the tailoring of PRINCE2 does not increase the risk of the project failing.

I provide you with a lot of tailoring guidance throughout this book. For example, all the themes can be tailored, and I explain how this can be done in each theme's chapter. Some themes can be tailored more than others. For example, the organization theme can be adapted in all sorts of ways to suit all sorts of situations, which you learn about in the "Tailoring the Organization Theme" section of Chapter 3. And in Chapters 2, 10, and 11, I explain how other processes can be tailored.

Generally, a tailored process shouldn't be too complicated—a simple process is more likely to be used. You will learn many different ways to tailor the processes: Sometimes processes might be combined; sometimes activities might be split; sometimes the role responsible for an activity might be amended; or, on simple projects, the processes might be followed in a more informal way.

The management products can also be tailored. As I explained earlier in this chapter, management products are things such as the project plan, the risk register, and the lessons log. Throughout this book, you will see that the management products can take many formats, such as a slide deck, an email, or something called an *information radiator*. (An information radiator is a chart with a lot of easy-to-read graphs and diagrams describing the status of the project. You learn more about information radiators in Chapter 10.)

Management products might not even be documented; they might be a simple verbal agreement. Or they might be combined, or some of the parts of the documents that are not relevant could be omitted. The opposite is also true: For more complicated projects, some of these management products might be split up to create more documents.

It is very important that everyone involved with the project clearly understands how PRINCE2 will be amended for the upcoming project. The project manager must record the approach to tailoring in the PID.

In the following sections, I describe some of the common situations for which PRINCE2 can be tailored.

Simple Projects

A simple project is one that is perceived as straightforward and low risk. PRINCE2 prefers the term *simple* rather than *small* because size is a relative term. A small project for a large corporation might be perceived as very large for a small company.

As I said earlier, if you were to apply all aspects of PRINCE2 to a simple project, you would overburden the project management team with a great deal of unnecessary project management processes, documents, and procedures. Throughout this book, I discuss how each aspect of PRINCE2 can be cut back to suit a simple project. You will see, for example, that certain processes can be combined, one person can do more than one PRINCE2 role, and some of the management products can combined or omitted.

Programme Environments

What is a programme? Simply put, it is like a big project. Earlier in this chapter, I used the example of the Crossrail initiative in London to explain the six aspects of project performance. Crossrail is a good example of a programme. It is made up of a set of interrelated projects. One project might focus on digging the tunnels under London, another on creating the trains, another on building one of the new stations, and so on.

Because of the size and complexity of a programme, a different set of skills than PRINCE2 is needed to carry out programme management. However, PRINCE2 can be used to manage any individual project within the programme. What generally happens is that in an individual project, the project board will report directly to a higher-level programme board or steering committee.

As you will see throughout the book, there are many ways that PRINCE2 can be adapted to a programme situation. For example, a number of PRINCE2 documents might be fully or partially created at the programme level, such as the business case and the differing approaches to risk, quality, change, and communication management. So the project manager might not need to re-create these documents at the project level. A more pragmatic concern is that it would be easy to confuse programme-specific documents with project-specific documents, so it would be important to create a naming convention to distinguish the two.

PRINCE2 sometimes refers to a specific programme-management approach called *Managing Successful Programmes* (MSP). This is another best-practice approach from AXELOS, the company that owns PRINCE2. You learn more about MSP in the "Tailoring the Organization Theme" section of Chapter 3 and elsewhere in this book. However, it is not a mandatory requirement to use MSP if you find yourself in a programme situation.

Commercial Customer and Supplier Environments

PRINCE2 often refers to the fact that projects operate within what it calls a customer and supplier environment. This just means there is always a customer, who specifies what is required and usually pays for the work, as well as a supplier (or a number of suppliers), who provides the skills and resources to deliver the result. The suppliers might be internal suppliers (people who work within the customer's organization) or they might be external organizations (if the customer has outsourced the work).

Obviously, projects will be more difficult to manage if a number of organizations are involved. Throughout this book, I explain how to tailor PRINCE2 to cope with this situation. For example, key PRINCE2 documents, such as the PID, and work packages might form the basis of a legal contract, so the project management team needs to decide whether the management product becomes part of the legal contract or is a separate document referred to in the contract. The latter is usually better; otherwise, changing the document might involve expensive legal work.

Throughout an initiative, the project manager needs to review and monitor a delivery team's work. This will be more difficult if the delivery team is a separate organization, especially if that organization uses certain confidential processes to create their work. The project manager needs to ensure that she has the right to review what the team is doing, at least to a certain level.

The situation might be more complicated than a customer outsourcing work to a number of suppliers. The commissioning organization might do part of the work in-house and outsource the rest to separate commercial suppliers, or the suppliers themselves might outsource some of their work or operate in partnership with one another. As you learn in this book, PRINCE2 can be tailored to suit all these situations.

There might be more than one commissioning organization. For example, this might happen in a collaborative research project or an intergovernmental project. In this case, there might be multiple reasons for doing the project, multiple business cases, and multiple organizational cultures. It will not be easy to set up a project board that can make quick decisions, because it will probably be difficult to identify one key person to perform the main decision-making role of the executive. Decisions might take a long time and require a period of consensus building. It would probably be better to use some of the programme-governance concepts to direct this sort of project.

Agile Environments

Agile is another common environment that PRINCE2 can work effectively within. Agile refers to a collection of approaches that originated in the software industry, many of which were first developed in the 1990s, such as rapid application development, the dynamic systems development method (DSDM), and Scrum. In 2001, a collection of experts in agile approaches published the Agile Manifesto, which outlined the following four principles of the agile approach:
1. Individuals and interactions are valued more than processes and tools.
2. Working products are valued more than comprehensive documentation.
3. Customer collaboration is valued more than contract negotiation.
4. Responding to change is valued more than following a plan.

Over the last decade, agile approaches have started to be used successfully in all sorts of industries, and if you haven't come across them yet, I'm sure you soon will. The purpose of this book isn't to teach you agile—many good books and other information sources are available—but it is helpful to know some of the common ideas and terms of agile in order to understand how PRINCE2 can be tailored for it.

Agile approaches tend to deliver their products over a series of iterations rather than all at the end of the project. These iterations are often referred to as *sprints* and are often quite short, maybe three or four weeks. This has a number of benefits. First, although the client will not get everything they want in the earlier releases, at least they do not have to wait too long until they get some useful products. Second, releasing in short bursts avoids the situation where, if a deadline is a long way away, the natural human tendency is to prevaricate and work more slowly. In an agile world, the deadline for release is always only a few weeks away, which motivates the team to get down to their work. And third, there is always the risk that what the teams are creating isn't really what the clients want. Clients can do their best to put across their requirements, and suppliers can do their best to understand them, but often the only time when a client can really see if the supplier understood them is when they are handed the final product. Agile approaches find out if there's been a miscommunication about requirements much quicker and so save more time and money than if everything is delivered at the end. Agile calls this *failing fast* since it's obviously better to know you're doing the wrong thing as quickly as possible. Finally, the client can give feedback to the teams when they start using products from earlier releases, which can help the team create better products in later releases.

PRINCE2 is entirely compatible with this iterative way of delivering. As you have learned, one of the PRINCE2 principles is managing the project by stages, and the project team could release products at the end of each stage if required. You can also see that this focus on delivering regularly is aligned to the PRINCE2 principle of focus on products.

Timeboxing is another agile concept. This is when a sprint of work is fixed to a certain amount of time (for example, three weeks), and if the delivery team falls behind in their work, rather than slip the deadline, they must deliver less. In order for timeboxing to work, the team must be given some flexibility on the scope of work that they need to create. In the "Tailoring the Progress Theme" section of Chapter 9, you see how you can use scope tolerances and the PRINCE2 principle of managing by exception to implement this agile idea.

A backlog is another common agile term. A backlog is a list of requirements that the customers want in the finished product. However, agile approaches steer away from the word requirements because it sounds like a mandatory feature. As I have just said, agile works best when there is some flexibility around what the customer wants. So rather than use the term requirements, agile approaches often use the term user stories because they describe a particular journey that a user would take with the product. For example, if the end product is going to be a website, a story might describe how the user wants to be able to log into the website, select a certain report, and send it to their printer. I talk more about using user stories within a PRINCE2 project in Chapter 6.

A backlog is a list of user stories that the customer wants to see in the finished product, (called a *product backlog*) or a list of user stories that the delivery team will create in a particular sprint (called a *sprint backlog*). Sometimes, if a user story is particularly big, it is referred to as an *epic*. The items in a backlog should be ordered by the value that they will provide to the client. This helps agile teams to prioritize which user stories to address in earlier releases and which to eliminate if they are running out of time. Focusing on what to deliver and prioritizing by value is very much aligned to the PRINCE2 principles of focus on products and continued business justification.

One of the principles of PRINCE2 is defined roles and responsibilities, and as you will see in Chapter 3, there are PRINCE2 roles that help to manage a successful project. Many of the agile approaches also have certain defined roles. In Chapter 3, I show you how these agile roles and PRINCE2 roles can work together. Two roles from the Scrum agile approach that are regularly used are the *scrum master* and the *product owner*. The scrum master leads a scrum delivery team, and a product owner represents the customer and collates the user stories that are required for the product.

You will learn a lot more about tailoring PRINCE2 to an agile environment throughout this book. In fact, in every chapter that describes the themes and the processes, I will explain how to adapt that area to suit an agile approach.

An End-to-End Walk-through of PRINCE2

Thus far in this chapter, you've learned about some of the major parts of PRINCE2, including its underlying principles, processes, themes, roles, and management products. Now it's time to see how these parts fit together in a project.

In this section, I use a sample project—constructing a new hotel for a leisure company—to show you how the processes are used both before and during the project. I also discuss where each role becomes involved in the model and how some of the main management products are used.

At this point, I am going to discuss the various areas at a high level. To use an analogy, I want you to see how the major pieces of the jigsaw puzzle fit together before I discuss each piece on its own. It will then be easier, when I discuss a particular part of PRINCE2 in the later chapters, to show you how that part fits into the whole model.

For this section, I will use the process overview diagram shown in Figure 1.5.

Figure 1.5: PRINCE2 process model

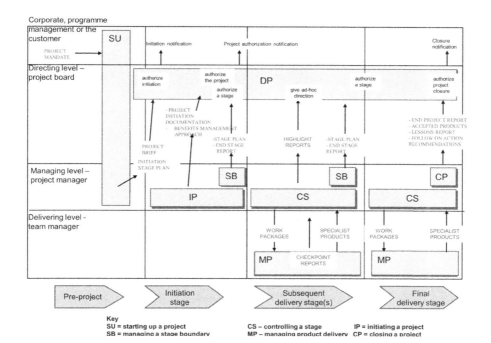

Take a look at the composition of Figure 1.5. First, there are four horizontal rows that correspond to the four levels of the project management structure.

The various rectangles and squares on the diagram represent the seven processes. The processes are positioned to show which level of management is involved with that process. For example, all the activities in the directing a project process occur at the project board level, and all the activities of the managing product delivery level occur at the team level. Some processes are carried out by a number of the management levels. For example, the starting up a project process involves corporate, programme management, or the customer; the project board; and the project manager.

The four columns in Figure 1.5 show the work that is done during four different times in the project, as follows:

- Work that happens before the project (pre-project)
- Work that happens at the beginning of the project (initiation stage)
- Work that happens in the middle of the project (subsequent delivery stages)
- Work that happens at the end of the project (final delivery stage)

Pre-Project Activities

Figure 1.6 highlights the work that takes place before a PRINCE2 project. The numbered circles on the diagram correspond to the five steps described in this section.

Figure 1.6: Activities before the project

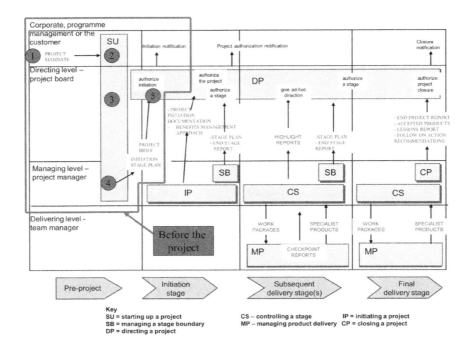

Step One: Corporate, Programme Management, or the Customer Creates a Project Mandate

In PRINCE2, before a project can start, a number of activities and authorizations must occur. First, someone (or a group of people) with an appropriate level of authority to authorize this project must create a project mandate. The project mandate will begin to answer basic questions about the project, such as the following:

- What is the project all about? What is it creating?
- Who will be involved in the project? Who will be using the project's products after the project?
- Where will the project happen? Where will the products be built?
- When will the project start and finish? When will there be any return from this project?
- How will the project be done? How will the products be built?
- Why do this project? What is the justification for it?

The project mandate will answer these basic what, why, when, who, where, and how questions. At one extreme, the information might be high-level, in which case, as you will see, the first set of activities in PRINCE2 is partly about refining and expanding these details. At the other extreme, the information in the project mandate might be in great detail, in which case the first set of activities in PRINCE2 will be more about checking that it is correct. The latter is more likely in a programme situation, where the project is part of a group of projects. In this case, the specific definitions of each project will probably be agreed to at the beginning of the programme.

For our hotel project example, let's say someone in the leisure company has an idea for a new hotel. They may have many hotels across the world, but they decide they would like to create one in Shanghai because they see China as a growing market. Someone who has the authority to start a project of this size will create a project mandate. In this example, the head of business development in the Asia Pacific region is assigned this task.

Step Two: Corporate, Programme Management, or the Customer Appoints the Executive

Once the project mandate is created, the PRINCE2 process model starts. The first process is starting up a project. (I describe the starting up a project process in much more detail in Chapter 2.)

The first step in the starting up a project process is for corporate, programme management, or the customer to appoint a senior-level person to the executive role. This person should see the initiative from a business perspective and will act as the key decision maker for the project. (The executive role is described in more detail in Chapter 3.)

Let's say in the example project, the head of business development in the Asia Pacific region is appointed as executive. She is now straddling two of the PRINCE2 management levels: She created the project mandate while sitting in the corporate, programme management, or the customer level, and now she takes on the executive role that sits in the project board level.

Step Three: The Executive Appoints the Project Manager
The next step in the starting up a project process is for the executive to appoint the project manager. The executive can then focus on directing, decision-making, and business-related activities, and the project manager can focus on the day-to-day management of the pre-project work.

Step Four: The Executive and the Project Manager Create the Project Brief and Recruit the Project Management Team

The remaining activities in the starting up a project process focus on answering the following question: Is the project idea set out in the project mandate worthwhile and viable? With regard to the hotel project example, is it worth committing major resources to start a project to build a new hotel in Shanghai? As such, a PRINCE2 project doesn't actually start during the starting up a project process. Instead, the starting up a project process is a set of activities that are performed *before* the project to decide whether or not to do that project.

To begin, the project mandate needs to be reviewed, and if necessary, the information needs to be expanded so as to provide enough details to form the basis of the decision of whether to commission the project. The output of this work goes into a new management product called the *project brief*. The project brief will answer exactly the same set of what, why, when, who, where, and how questions about the project that the project mandate did.

The "why" question is answered by creating an outline business case, which forms part of the project brief. This will start to show, at a high level at least, the justification for undertaking the project. It is the executive's responsibility to create this section of the project brief.

The rest of the project management team members are now appointed. So people are assigned to the other two project board roles of senior user and senior supplier. (These roles are described in more detail in Chapter 3.) Some of the project board members might appoint separate project assurance roles, which will monitor the project to find out if it is being run in the correct way for their perspective on the project. A project support person or people might also be appointed.

This initial project management team might get updated and added to as the initiative proceeds. At this point, however, the team needs to reflect the range of stakeholder perspectives of business, user, and supplier at the right level of authority. That way, a thorough analysis of the project idea can be done and a meaningful authorization can occur if the project idea looks to be worthwhile and viable.

For the hotel project example, let's say the leisure company's marketing director for Asia is appointed a senior user and will use the hotel to increase her sales figures. A travel market research consultant is also appointed as a senior user to represent the needs of the tourists and business travelers who might stay in the hotel. To represent the interests of the supplier side of the project, the head of procurement for Asia Pacific is appointed as senior supplier. (Later, people from the suppliers contracted to do work on the hotel might also take on the senior supplier role.)

Once the project brief has been finished, the project board will review it and decide whether to authorize things to go any further. If they decide to allow the initiative to proceed, the project will officially start with what PRINCE2 calls the initiation stage. In this stage, the project will be planned out, at least at a high level. (Remember that the manage by stages principle means that more detailed planning is done before each stage.) Before committing resources to the initiation stage, the project board will want to see a plan for the work that will be involved. So the final activity in the starting up a project process is for the project manager to create a stage plan for the initiation stage, detailing the time, effort, and costs needed to plan the project.

Step Five: The Project Board Authorizes Initiation

Now that the starting up a project process is complete, the PRINCE2 model moves on to the directing a project process. This process covers the work of the project board, which mainly involves making decisions.

The project board's first decision is called *authorize initiation*. The project board reviews the project brief to see whether the project is a worthwhile and viable initiative. If they think it is, they then review the stage plan for the initiation stage to see what would be involved in planning this project. If they decide that the resources requested for the initiation (planning) stage are reasonable, they authorize the project manager to proceed. In effect, they are giving the project manager the authority to manage just the initiation stage, after which the project manager must ask the project board, once again, for authority to continue any further.

Activities at the Beginning of the Project

Figure 1.7 shows the process diagram again, with the initiation stage highlighted and its steps numbered.

Figure 1.7: Activities at the beginning of the project

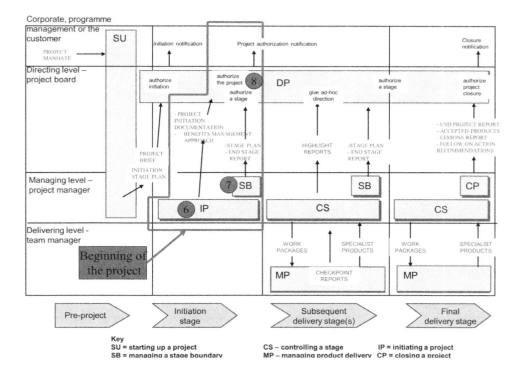

Step Six: The Project Manager Creates the Project Initiation Documentation

The initiating a project process describes a set of activities to create the project initiation documentation (PID.) The project manager does most of the work to create the PID. The information in the PID answers the same what, why, when, where, who, and how questions that the project mandate and then the project brief answered. This time, the document has greater detail because now that the project has been authorized, the project team will have more time and resources to consider these questions.

The PID is actually a collection of documents and contains the following information:

- The project plan, which describes the major products and the activities and resources required to create them, as well as how the project will be divided into stages. This plan can be high-level, because the manage by stages principle of PRINCE2 allows for more detailed planning to be left until just before a particular stage.
- A set of approach documents that set out how the project will be managed with regard to such areas as risk, change, quality, and communication.
- A detailed business case.
- Information on the project management team.
- Information on how the project will be delivered (project approach).
- A project definition, giving information on areas such as the background to the project, the project's objectives, and the project's scope.
- Information on how the project will be controlled, such as how to monitor the progress of the project and what reports are required.
- Information on how PRINCE2 will be tailored for the project.

With regard to the hotel project, the project plan section might set out the individual delivery stages as follows:

Delivery Stage One
Create architectural plans for the hotel. Obtain planning permission for construction. Create tender documents for outsourced contractors and send to potential suppliers. Select suppliers.

Delivery Stage Two
Construct hotel exteriors.

Delivery Stage Three
Decorate interior of the hotel; fit with electricity, plumbing, furniture, and so on.

In addition to creating the PID, the project manager will create the benefits management approach during the initiating a project process. The benefits management approach specifies how and when the project will be reviewed with regard to whether it's achieving the stated benefits. Many of these reviews might be planned for some time after the project. In the hotel project example, a review might be scheduled for a year after the hotel opens, to see if the hotel is meeting its targets for room sales, restaurant sales, and so on—but the planning for that review would start at this point in the project.

Step Seven: The Project Manager Creates a Plan for the First Delivery Stage

Once the project manager has almost finished the PID, she can start planning the next stage of the project. In the hotel example, she will plan in detail the work for the first delivery stage, which is when architectural plans for the hotel are created and the tender process takes place. This work is done in the managing a stage boundary process.

At this point, the project manager might have two focuses: finishing the PID (using the initiating a project process) and creating the plan for the first delivery stage (using the managing a stage boundary process). Chapter 10 describes the managing a stage boundary process in detail.

Step Eight: The Project Board Authorizes the Project and the First Delivery Stage

The project manager sends the PID and the stage plan for the first delivery stage to the project board. The project board reviews both of these management products in their directing a project process.

The project board has two directing a project activities to carry out at this point. First, they review the information in the PID and decide whether to authorize the project. Second, they review the information in the stage plan and decide whether to authorize the first delivery stage of the project.

The way that PRINCE2 has set out the directing a project activities at this point can be confusing for two reasons. First, it says the project board authorizes the project here. However, the project has already started at this point. (It has just finished the initiation stage.) What PRINCE2 means is that the project board needs to decide whether to authorize the delivery part of the project, where specialist products are created.

The second reason it can be confusing is that although the project board authorizes the delivery part of the project, the project manager cannot move ahead and manage the whole project. The project manager has authority to manage only the next delivery stage, after which she must again ask the project board for authority to continue further. In the hotel example, the project manager will have authority only to manage the work to create the architectural plans, obtain planning permission, and carry out the tender process.

Activities in the Middle of the Project

In Figure 1.8, I have highlighted the section of the process model we are now focusing on: delivering specialist products in the middle of the project. In the hotel example, this will involve creating deliverables such as tender documents, architectural plans, parts of the hotel building, computer software to run the booking system, and so on. The delivery of these specialist products will be managed on a stage-by-stage basis.

Figure 1.8: Activities in the middle of the project

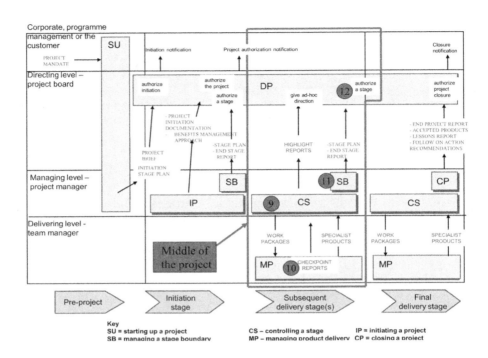

Step Nine: The Project Manager Manages a Delivery Stage

The project manager will manage each delivery stage using the activities in the controlling a stage process. This process sets out management activities such as how the project manager delegates work to various teams, reports on progress, and deals with problems and issues.

In the hotel example, the project manager will use the controlling a stage process to manage the first delivery stage (and all the other stages, too, once they've been authorized). The project manager might delegate work to an architectural firm to create the hotel designs. She might also delegate work to the leisure company's procurement department to create and issue the tenders as well as delegate work to the people who are dealing with the planning authorities in Shanghai. In PRINCE2, the project manager assigns work to teams using a work package. A work package gives team members all the information they need to know in order to do some work, such as what to create, how much time and money they have, how often to report back to the project manager, and so on. Teams are not authorized to do any work until they have received a work package.

The project manager reports progress to the project board throughout the stage by creating highlight reports. The project board decides how regularly they would like to receive these reports, but let's say, in our example, they are sent every week.

The controlling a stage process is described in a lot more detail in Chapter 10.

Step Ten: The Teams Create the Stage's Specialist Products

The team managers and their teams carry out their work in the managing product delivery process. The teams carry out three PRINCE2 activities during this process:

- Accept the work from the project manager via the work packages
- Create the specialist products as instructed in the work packages
- Deliver the specialist products back to the project manager

During the first delivery stage in the hotel project example, the architects creating the hotel's plans, the procurement team creating tenders for the construction work, and the team dealing with the Chinese planning authorities will all use the managing product delivery process.

The teams must also regularly report on the progress of their work to the project manager. They do this by creating checkpoint reports.

Step Eleven: The Project Manager Plans the Next Stage

This step is similar to step seven. Once the project manager sees that the work of the current delivery stage is nearly finished, she will start planning the next delivery stage. In the hotel example, the project manager will plan in detail the work to construct the hotel's exteriors. Just as in step seven, this work is done in the managing a stage boundary process.

Also just as in step seven, at this point, the project manager might have two focuses: finishing managing the work in the current delivery stage (using the controlling a stage process) and creating the stage plan for the next delivery stage (using the managing a stage boundary process).

The project manager also creates an end stage report for the delivery stage just ending and, if necessary, updates some of the major management products within the PID, such as the project plan and the business case.

Step Twelve: The Project Board Authorizes Another Delivery Stage

Once all the specialist products of the stage have been delivered, the project manager will send the end stage report, the next stage plan, and the updated PID to the project board. In the hotel example, this will take place when the architectural designs for the hotel are finished, contractors have been sourced for the construction work, and planning permission for the hotel has been obtained.

The project board will review the next stage plan, the updated business case, and the updated project plan in their directing a project process and decide whether to authorize the next delivery stage. In our hotel example, they will decide whether the project can move on to building the hotel's exteriors.

Steps Nine, Ten, Eleven, and Twelve Again and Again and...

Steps nine, ten, eleven, and twelve are repeated again and again, managing the delivery of each stage of the project, until the project team reaches the last stage. The final stage is handled a little differently, as you will see in the next section.

In our hotel example, which has an initiation stage and then three delivery stages, steps nine, ten, eleven, and twelve will be carried out twice: first to manage delivery stage one, and then again to manage delivery stage two.

Activities at the End of the Project

The final delivery stage is managed slightly differently. In our hotel example, this would correspond to the management of delivery stage three, when the hotel is decorated and the electricity, plumbing, furniture, IT systems, and so on are installed. Figure 1.9 highlights the section of the process model discussed in this section.

Figure 1.9: Activities at the end of the project

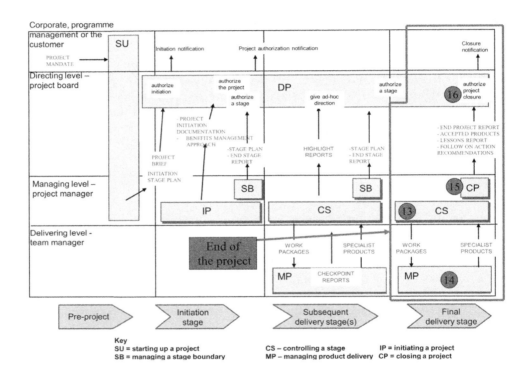

Step Thirteen: The Project Manager Manages the Final Delivery Stage

This step is exactly the same as step nine from the previous delivery stages. The project manager uses the controlling a stage process to create work packages, which delegate the final stage's delivery work to the appropriate teams. In the hotel project example, the project manager might give out work to the electrical fitters, the plumbers, the furniture moving companies, and so on. The project manager also reports to the project board using highlight reports and deals with problems and issues.

Step Fourteen: The Teams Create the Specialist Products of the Final Stage

This step is exactly the same as step ten from the previous delivery stages. The teams involved with creating this delivery stage's specialist products use the managing product delivery process to accept work via work packages, create the specialist products, and give them back to the project manager. They also report on progress to the project manager using checkpoint reports.

In the hotel example, the teams involved with creating the last delivery stage's specialist products will now be involved. These could be decorators painting the hotel, electricians wiring the lighting, IT specialists installing software, and so on.

Step Fifteen: The Project Manager Prepares for the End of the Project

The first difference between the final delivery stage and the previous delivery stages is that at the end of this last stage, instead of using the managing stage boundary process to prepare for the next stage, the project manager uses the closing a project process to prepare for the end of the project.

During the closing a project process, the project manager will do the following:

- Ensure that the project's products are signed off and accepted by the ultimate clients. In the hotel example, the ultimate clients might be the head of the Asia Pacific region that ultimately will need to accept the new hotel.
- Create an end project report. This report will review the project's performance against the original objectives that were set out in the first version of the PID.
- Update the benefits management approach to check that all the post-project benefit reviews are included.
- If any products have been delivered to the clients in earlier stages of the project, measure any benefits that have been made so far. In the hotel example, maybe the hotel's gym was built first and opened before the rest of the hotel was finished. If so, the project manager should measure the revenue gained so far from selling gym memberships. Give a list of follow-on action recommendations to the people who will operate the project's products.
- Create a lessons report that can be passed on to subsequent projects.
- Archive the project documentation.

Step Sixteen: The Project Board Authorizes the Project to Close

The second difference between the final delivery stage and the previous delivery stages is that at the end of it, the project board will authorize the closure of the project rather than another stage. Board members will review all the management products prepared by the project manager in the closing a project process, and if they are satisfied that everything is complete, they will authorize the end of the project. The project board will carry out this authorization in the directing a project process.

Summary

This chapter presented a broad summary of all the features of PRINCE2 and showed you how they fit together. I described the main sections of PRINCE2: principles, themes, processes, roles, and management products.

Projects have five key characteristics that distinguish them from business as usual: they change the organization; they are temporary, with a start and an end; they involve different functions and divisions within an organization; they involve unique work that has not been done before; and they involve a lot of uncertainty.

Given all the challenges that projects introduce, project management attempts to lower the risks and increase the likelihood of a successful outcome. As you saw, there are four main areas of project management: planning work, delegating work, monitoring the progress, and controlling the project. These four main areas of project management attempt to deliver the project to its objectives. In PRINCE2, there are six ways of describing a project objective: in terms of cost, time, scope, quality, risks, and benefits. PRINCE2 describes these as the six aspects of project performance.

After discussing what constitutes a project, I introduced a framework that you can use to manage them: PRINCE2. The PRINCE2 method consists of four integrated elements: principles, processes, themes, and the project environment. There are seven principles of PRINCE2: continued business justification, learn from experience, defined roles and responsibilities, manage by stages, manage by exception, focus on products, and tailor to suit the project environment. These are core concepts that the rest of the PRINCE2 model adheres to. Next, you learned about the PRINCE2 processes, which describe the activities to be performed by the various project roles both before and during a project. The chapter then covered the seven themes—business case, organization, quality, plans, risk, change, and progress—which explain how certain aspects of project management should be approached throughout a PRINCE2 project.

In addition to the four integrated elements of PRINCE2, you learned that there are a number of other important parts. Certain roles need to be carried out on each project, such as a project manager, who manages the project on a day-to-day basis. There are also 26 PRINCE2 management products, including plans, registers, logs, approaches (showing how the project will be managed), and a variety of reports. This chapter covered the whole range of benefits that PRINCE2 can bring to a project. These range from providing a common vocabulary for project management to providing a tested best-practice approach to managing projects.

In this chapter, you learned how PRINCE2 can be tailored to suit the type of project and the environment that the project will operate within. You saw that PRINCE2 is a very flexible approach. Common situations that PRINCE2 is tailored for include simple projects, projects operating within a programme, projects that involve outsourcing work to separate commercial suppliers, and projects that use an agile delivery method.

Finally, you saw how the major parts of PRINCE2 are used throughout the life of a project. I suggest that you review this section a number of times—it will give you a good idea how all the parts of PRINCE2 fit together.

Foundation Exam Essentials

Recall the definition and characteristics of a project.
Be able to define a project as a temporary organization created for the purpose of delivering one or more business products according to an agreed business case. Be able to name the five characteristics of a project: change, temporary, cross-functional, unique, and uncertainty. These characteristics distinguish project work from business as usual.

Recall the six aspects of project performance to be managed.
Recall that the six objectives of a project can be written in terms of cost, timescales, risk, benefits, quality, and scope.

Recall the four integrated elements of PRINCE2.

Recall that the four integrated elements of PRINCE2 are the principles, the processes, the themes, and tailoring to suit the project environment. Recall that the principles are the guiding obligations and good practices that determine whether a project is genuinely being managed using PRINCE2. Recall that the processes describe a progression from the pre-project through the stages of the project lifecycle to project closure. Recall that the themes show how to do various aspects of project management. Recall that tailoring is about amending the PRINCE2 approach to suit the project type and the environment.

Recall what makes a project a PRINCE2 project.
For a project to be following PRINCE2, it must at a minimum be applying the PRINCE2 principles, meeting the minimum requirements of each theme, meeting each process's purpose and objectives, and either using PRINCE2's recommended techniques or using alternative equivalent techniques.

Describe the features and benefits of PRINCE2.
Describe the features of PRINCE2, such as: It is a generic project management method; it separates the management of a project from the specialist work; and it focuses on describing on what needs to be done rather than prescribing how everything is done. Describe the benefits of PRINCE2, such as: it is an established, proven approach to managing projects; it can be tailored to meet the needs of the organization; and it provides a common project vocabulary that aids communication about project management matters.

Describe the customer/supplier context on which PRINCE2 is based, including considerations when undertaking projects in a commercial environment.
PRINCE2 assumes that there will be a customer who will specify the desired result and at least one supplier who will provide the resources and skills to deliver the result. Sometimes the suppliers are external organizations.

Explain the PRINCE2 principles.
Be able to explain the seven principles of PRINCE2: continued business justification, learn from experience, defined roles and responsibilities, manage by stages, manage by exception, focus on products, and tailor to suit the project environment. Explain how adhering to these principles helps increase the likelihood of project success.

Explain which aspects of a project can be tailored, who is responsible, and how tailoring decisions are documented.
Know that a range of PRINCE2 aspects can be tailored: Processes can be combined or adapted; themes can be used with techniques that are appropriate for the project; roles can be combined or split; management products may be combined or split into any number of data sources; and terminology may be changed. The project manager is responsible for identifying and documenting the levels of tailoring needed for the project in the PID. The project board will make the final decision on what tailoring to apply to the project.

Practitioner Exam Essentials

Analyze the application of PRINCE2 principles in context: continued business justification, learn from experience, defined roles and responsibilities, manage by stages, manage by exception, focus on products, and tailor to suit the project environment.

Assess and critique an approach to applying the seven PRINCE2 principles, including how the principles might be adapted to different project contexts—for example, a small project, an agile project, a project with external third-party organizations, or a project operating within a programme environment.

Review Questions

The remainder of this chapter contains mock exam questions, first for the Foundation exam and then for the Practitioner exam.

Foundation Exam Questions

1. Which two statements about tailoring are correct?
   (1) PRINCE2 projects should use the recommended PRINCE2 techniques.
   (2) Management products might be split into many data sources.
   (3) PRINCE2 projects can comprise as many management stages as are necessary.
   (4) Principles that are not relevant to the project can be excluded.
   A. 1 and 2
   B. 2 and 3
   C. 3 and 4
   D. 1 and 4

2. Which of the following describes an advantage of applying the focus on products principle?
   A. The project management method used is appropriate to the project.
   B. Projects that can longer be justified are stopped.
   C. Senior management's time is not wasted managing the project on a day-to-day basis.
   D. The project does no more work than necessary to deliver its products.

3. Which aspect of project performance that needs to be managed helps set the objectives for the expected return on the project?
   A. Costs
   B. Risks
   C. Benefits
   D. Scope

4. Which option represents a characteristic of projects?
   A. Involves work with no defined end point
   B. Involves work across multiple functional divisions
   C. Involves predictable, recurring work
   D. Involves work that brings little change to an organization

5. Which principle ensures that the range of stakeholder perspectives is represented within the project management team?
    A. Defined roles and responsibilities
    B. Continued business justification
    C. Learn from experience
    D. Tailor to suit the project environment

6. Delegating authority from one management level to the next supports which principle?
    A. Continued business justification
    B. Learn from experience
    C. Manage by stages
    D. Manage by exception

7. Which principle addresses the problem that planning beyond a certain planning horizon is difficult?
    A. Continued business justification
    B. Manage by stages
    C. Manage by exception
    D. Tailor to suit the project environment

8. How is the principle of continued business justification applied?
    A. By re-evaluating the reason for the project throughout the life of the project
    B. By seeking opportunities to implement improvements throughout the life of the project
    C. By using product description to provide clarity around user's requirements
    D. By ensuring that there are review and decision points throughout the project

9. Which of the integrated elements of PRINCE2 provides a stepwise progression through the project life cycle?
    A. Principles
    B. Themes
    C. Processes
    D. Tailoring to the project environment

10. What is one of the benefits provided by PRINCE2?
    A. Sets out how to manage projects in particular industries
    B. Provides motivational techniques
    C. Provides a common project vocabulary
    D. Shows how to manage business as usual

Practitioner Exam Questions

The following Practitioner questions are based on the Practitioner exam scenario in Appendix B.

1. The project is approaching the end of stage two and the project manager has heard that a competitor is launching a similar website. The chief executive has called a meeting to discuss the viability of carrying on with the project. Which principle is being applied, and why?
    A. Continued business justification, because the justification for the project should remain valid throughout the life of the project
    B. Learn from experience, because as the project progresses, the project should continually review and learn from outside events
    C. Defined roles and responsibilities, because the project manager is responsible for collating all the information regarding threats to the business case
    D. Manage by exception, because a threat to project tolerances should be escalated to the chief executive

2. The project is in stage two. The project manager has just met with the team creating the requirements document, which tells him their work is delayed. The project manager realizes this delay will cause a breach in stage tolerances. He is meeting with the team that is dealing with the website supplier procurement next week, who also might report a delay. To ensure he understands the full situation, he has decided to wait until after this meeting to escalate the tolerance breach to the project board. Is this an appropriate application of the manage by exception principle, and why or why not?
    A. Yes, because avoiding having to escalate two problems to the project board does not waste senior management's time.
    B. Yes, because it is the project manager's responsibility to escalate forecast breaches of stage tolerances to the project board.
    C. No, because if tolerances are forecast to be exceeded, the situation should be escalated immediately.
    D. No, because the team creating the requirements document should escalate the issue straight to the project board.

3. The project is in stage two. The requirements for the website are being collated. The marketing manager has created a long list of features he would like to see in the product. The IT manager has pointed out that in order to deliver all of these features, the project will not be completed within a reasonable time. The project manager has asked the marketing manager to categorize the features into mandatory requirements and features that are desirable but not essential. Which principle is being applied, and why?
    A. Defined roles and responsibilities, because it is the responsibility of the project manager to create product descriptions
    B. Manage by exception, because categorizing features as either mandatory or desirable will allow the project management team to define a scope tolerance
    C. Manage by stages, because categorizing features as either mandatory or desirable will allow the project manager to plan effective control and decision points
    D. Tailor to suit the project, because the project will be adapted so as not to deliver all the original requirements

Chapter
2

Starting a Project Successfully with PRINCE2

PRINCE2 Foundation Exam Objectives Covered in This Chapter:

☑ **Explain the purpose, objectives, and context of the starting up a project process, directing a project process and the initiating a project process.**

☑ **Explain the purpose of the project brief.**

☑ **Explain the purpose of the project initiation documentation.**

PRINCE2 Practitioner Exam Objectives Covered in This Chapter:

☑ **Carry out the starting up a project process activities, and recommended associated actions:**
- Appoint the executive and the project manager.
- Capture previous lessons.
- Design and appoint the project management team.
- Prepare the outline business case.
- Select the project approach and assemble the project brief.
- Plan the initiation stage.
- Demonstrating an understanding of:
  - The recommended roles and responsibilities within the process
  - How the themes may be applied

☑ **Assess whether starting up a project process activities/ actions, roles and responsibilities are effective and fit for purpose, taking into consideration: the context, the PRINCE2 principles, and the purpose and objectives of the process.**

☑ **Carry out the directing a project process activities that are used at the beginning of a project, and recommended associated actions:**
- Authorize initiation.
- Authorize the project.
- Authorize a stage.

- Demonstrating an understanding of:
  - The recommended roles and responsibilities within the process
  - How the themes may be applied

☑ **Carry out the initiating a project process activities, and Recommended associated actions:**
  - Agree the tailoring requirements.
  - Prepare the risk management approach.
  - Prepare the change control approach.
  - Prepare the quality management approach.
  - Prepare the communication management approach.
  - Set up the project controls.
  - Create the project plan.
  - Refine the business case.
  - Assemble the project initiation documentation.
- Demonstrating an understanding of:
  - The recommended roles and responsibilities within the process
  - How the themes may be applied

☑ **Assess whether initiating a project process activities/ actions, roles and responsibilities are effective and fit for purpose, taking into consideration: the context, the PRINCE2 principles, and the purpose and objectives of the process.**

In this chapter, you learn how PRINCE2 recommends that you begin a project. The two main steps are using the starting up a project process to investigate whether the project idea is a worthwhile and viable one, and then using the initiating a project process to plan the project at a high level.

You use two key management products at the beginning of a PRINCE2 project: the project brief and the project initiation documentation. In this chapter, you learn how to create them and then use them to define and gain consensus on what your project is all about.

Beginning a PRINCE2 Project

Figure 2.1 is repeated from the "An End-to-End Walk-through of PRINCE2" section in Chapter 1, "Overview of PRINCE2." If you haven't read that section yet, I recommend that you do so before reading this chapter, as it gives a high-level overview of the PRINCE2 process model. You will then be able to understand the context of the three processes discussed in this chapter: *starting up a project, directing a project and initiating a project.* In Figure 2.1, I've highlighted where the starting up a project and initiating a project processes sit within the whole model. I have highlighted only a part of the directing a project process, as this chapter describes only the part of that process that occurs during the beginning of the project. I describe the other parts of the directing a project process in Chapter 10, "Managing the Middle of the Project Successfully with PRINCE2," and Chapter 11, "Managing the End of a Project Successfully with PRINCE2." You can see that the starting up a project process happens before the project starts. It contains a set of activities that help the project board determine whether to do the project. If the board decides to proceed with the project in the directing a project process, then the activities in the initiating a project process are done. This is the official start of the project, during which you plan the project at a high level.

Figure 2.1: Pre-project and beginning of the project

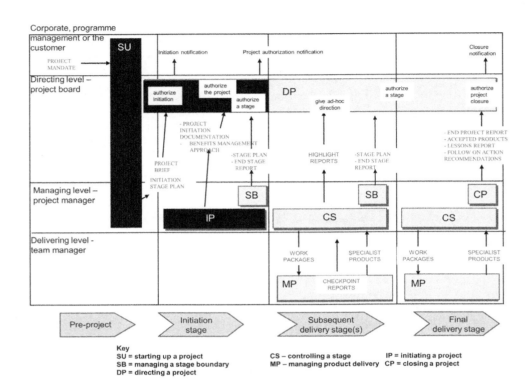

The Starting Up a Project Process

As you can see in Figure 2.1, starting up a project is the first process in the PRINCE2 model. It contains the following six activities, which are carried out before a project starts:

- *Appoint the executive and the project manager*
- *Prepare the outline business case*
- *Capture previous lessons*
- *Design and appoint the project management team*
- *Select the project approach and assemble the project brief*
- *Plan the initiation stage*

You learn about these activities in more detail in the following section. Their main purpose is to help the project management team consider the project idea and decide whether it is a viable and worthwhile proposal.

The activities in the starting up a project process shouldn't take too long relative to the potential length of the project. That way, time and money won't be wasted on initiatives that aren't taken any further. The starting up a project process is as much about stopping poorly conceived initiatives as it is about identifying good ones.

Exam Spotlight

The Foundation and Practitioner exams are based on the information in the official PRINCE2 manual: *Managing Successful Projects with PRINCE2* (Stationery Office, 2017). The manual provides a great deal of detail regarding each of the 41 activities that are found within the seven separate processes. So how much of this do you need to know before tackling the exams?

For the Foundation exam, you should memorize what happens in each individual process but not necessarily what happens in each of the processes' activities. This is the level of detail that I discussed in the "An End-to-End Walk-Through of PRINCE2" section in Chapter 1. This gives you the high-level detail for each process and shows you how they all fit together. Then for each individual process, for the Foundation exam, I suggest you read the following relevant chapters in this study guide:

- Chapter 1, "Overview of PRINCE2," which covers the directing a project process
- Chapter 2, "Starting a Project Successfully with PRINCE2," which covers the starting up a project and initiating a project processes
- Chapter 10, "Managing the Middle of a Project Successfully with PRINCE2," which covers the controlling a stage, managing product delivery, and managing a stage boundary processes
- Chapter 11, "Managing the End of a Project Successfully with PRINCE2," which covers the closing a project process

Each of these chapters provides a detailed description of what happens in each activity, which you need to understand but not necessarily memorize for the Foundation exam. Also within these chapters, I give you a key facts table for each process. I recommend that you *do* memorize these key facts for the Foundation exam.

The Practitioner exam is a different matter. It will ask you detailed questions about the activities. In this exam, however, you can refer to the PRINCE2 manual, *Managing Successful Projects with PRINCE2*. So, you don't need to memorize all the activity detail; instead, you need to know how to use the manual to find the answers during the exam.

Managing Successful Projects with PRINCE2 has a chapter on each process. Within each of those chapters is a section on each activity. These sections describe what happens in the activity and include a table of responsibilities. A flow diagram accompanies each description.

For example, the following illustration shows the flow diagram for the first activity of the starting up a project process: appoint the executive and the project manager. You can see that it shows that the project mandate is needed for this activity—it is an input to the activity. You can also see what is created by the work done in the activity—the outputs of this activity. The outputs are the executive and project manager role descriptions, an appointed executive and project manager, and finally, the daily log.

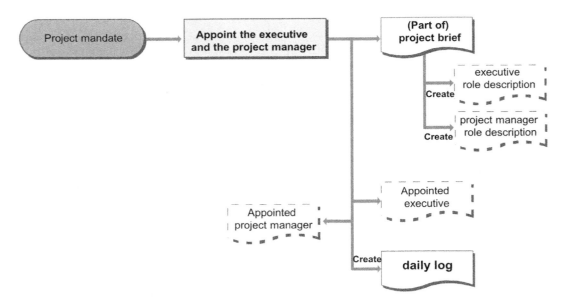

Flow diagrams are very useful. You can quickly flick through them and see which management products are involved in which activity. If you need further information, you can then refer to the activity section's text or the table of responsibilities.

When you come to the review questions for the Practitioner exam at the end of this chapter, you might want to practice using the *Managing Successful Projects with PRINCE2* process chapters as a reference.

Starting Up a Project Process Activities

Figure 2.2 shows an overview of the activities in the starting up a project process. As indicated by the arrows, dependencies exist between some of the activities. For example, the appoint the executive and the project manager activity needs to be done before the capture previous lessons activity. Apart from these dependency constraints, you can accomplish the activities in any order: sequentially, simultaneously, or iteratively.

Figure 2.2: Overview of the starting up a project process

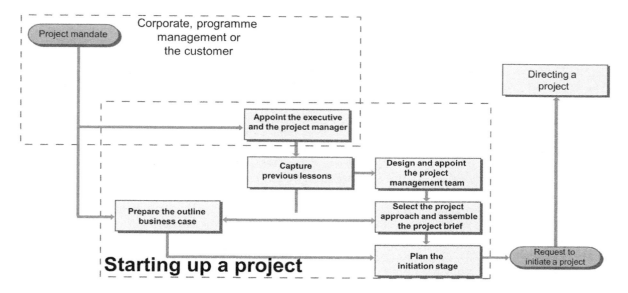

As you can see in Figure 2.2, the starting up a project process is triggered when corporate, programme management, or the customer creates the project mandate. The six activities in the starting up a project process are then carried out. When this process is completed, the project manager sends the project board a request to initiate the project. This triggers the *directing a project* process, during which the project board decides whether to proceed further with the initiative.

The following sections describe in detail each activity in the starting up a project process. You should read each section, but you don't have to memorize all the details for the Foundation exam. After these sections, you'll find a facts table for the starting up a project process that you *do* need to memorize for the Foundation exam. During the Practitioner exam, you may be asked detailed questions on the activities in the starting up a project process, but during that exam, you can use the official manual, *Managing Successful Projects with PRINCE2*, as a reference.

Appoint the Executive and the Project Manager

This is the first step of the PRINCE2 process model. It occurs after the project mandate has been created by someone in the corporate, programme management, or customer level of management.

The first step in this activity is for corporate, programme management, or the customer to appoint the executive. This is a critical role in the project management team. This person will have the necessary authority, budget, and resources to move the initiative from just an idea to a fully funded project, with the necessary resources to deliver the products. The executive will also represent the commissioning organization's business perspective to ensure that the idea represents value for money and will provide an adequate return on investment. Corporate, programme management, or the customer will create a role description for the executive based on the PRINCE2 executive role description and then recruit a suitable candidate.

The executive will probably be a senior-level manager, so it is unlikely that they will want to involve themselves in the day-to-day management of the project. Therefore, the executive will create a job description based on the PRINCE2 project manager role description and then recruit a suitable candidate.

The project manager creates a *daily log* to track personal action points and informal issues that are not tracked in the other PRINCE2 registers and logs. The daily log is sometimes referred to in PRINCE2 as the project manager's diary. During the starting up a project process, the daily log also has another use. At this point in the initiative, the risk register and the issue register have not been created. (They are created later, in the initiating a project process.) Until the registers are created, the daily log acts as a repository to record information for all project risks and issues.

Prepare the Outline Business Case

This activity has two major focuses. First, the executive is responsible for creating an outline business case and, if necessary, getting it approved by corporate, programme management, or the customer. Second, the project manager is responsible for creating the project product description.

The executive sets out the justification for the project in the outline business case. The exact composition of the business case is covered in Chapter 4, "Business Case Theme." For now, you should know that it will contain the forecast returns that the project will give the organization balanced against the time, cost, and risk that need to be taken on to get those returns. For example, if the project involves building a hotel, the business case will contain a forecast of the likely room sales compared to the cost of the hotel construction, how long the hotel will take to build, and the risks of building it. It will also consider how the project will be funded.

Remember that the time taken to carry out the activities during starting up a project process should be less compared to the rest of the processes. This is so that time isn't wasted on initiatives that shouldn't go further. As the name suggests, the business case will only be in outline form at this point, though it must have sufficient detail for the project board to decide the viability of the project. The business case will be refined if the project is given authorization to move to the initiation stage.

The other main focus in this activity is the project manager creating the *project product description*. This document will be a high-level description of the main products that the project will deliver. It should specify the product(s) that are capable of delivering the returns set out in the outline business case. For example, for the hotel project, if the forecasts in the business case include very high room rates, then the project product description would probably describe a luxury hotel. While creating the project product description, the project manager liaises with the senior users to find out their product requirements. The project manager also liaises with the senior suppliers, to see what sort of product is possible to create, and with the executive, to understand the business perspective on the project's products.

The exact composition of the project product description is covered in Chapter 6, "Quality Theme." It has a number of sections, but the two sections I'll look at now are the customer quality expectations and the acceptance criteria.

The customer presents their *customer quality expectations* to indicate what they require. In the hotel example, the client might say that their expectations are for a luxury hotel. However, the word "luxury" is ambiguous. My idea of what luxury means could be very different from yours. In order to avoid disputes at the end of the project about what should have been created, the project manager, the senior users, and the senior suppliers review the customer quality expectations and define a set of measurable specification criteria for the project's products. In PRINCE2, these are called *acceptance criteria*. These criteria are used at the end of the project to verify that the correct products have been delivered.

In the hotel example, acceptance criteria could be things such as the number of rooms the hotel will have or the size of the lobby. When the project is finished, the end customers can use these acceptance criteria to determine whether the "right" hotel has been built.

The final task for the project manager is to put together a high-level schedule to deliver the project. This schedule will include important delivery milestones and risks. Later, if the initiation stage is authorized, a more detailed version of this schedule will go into the project plan.

Capture Previous Lessons

The project manager captures useful experiences that could help the project. These lessons could come from numerous sources, such as the following:

- Lesson reports from previous projects
- Workshops or talks with people with relevant experience
- Lessons from the corporate or programme management level in the organization or from the customer
- Conversations with external organizations

During this activity, the project manager creates the *lessons log*, which acts as a repository for any lessons learned. The project manager can refer to this log throughout the PRINCE2 process model, to guide and direct how he manages the project and how to create the variety of management products. He can also use it to record lessons learned during the current project that might be useful to other projects or the organization.

As the project moves through its life and more becomes known about what lies ahead, it might be useful to repeat the exercise of capturing previous lessons.

Design and Appoint the Project Management Team

During this activity, the executive and the project manager work together to design an appropriate project management team structure and develop descriptions for all the roles in the structure (with the exception of the role descriptions for the executive and the project manager, which were written in the appoint the executive and the project manager activity). The executive then appoints people who have the level of authority necessary to move the project forward as well as the time to dedicate to the project.

Chapter 1 introduced the PRINCE2 project management team structure. It is the basis on which the project's team structure is designed. This structure ensures that the three main perspectives on the project—the business, the ultimate users of the project's products, and the suppliers of the project's products—are represented on the main decision-making unit, the project board.

All PRINCE2 project boards include senior users and senior suppliers. The senior users are senior-level people who represent those who will use the final outputs of the project. The senior suppliers are senior-level people who control the resources that will create the outputs of the project. The project manager should create job descriptions for both these roles based on the recommended PRINCE2 job descriptions. The executive then approves these job descriptions.

The project manager and the executive must next decide what other roles will be necessary to ensure that the project is effectively managed. At this point, job descriptions might be developed for project assurance (the people who monitor the project to ensure it is being run correctly), project support (those who provide a range of support services, such as administration, to help the project manager), and team managers (the people who manage the teams).

The next step is to recruit people into the roles. Not all these roles are filled at this time. For example, the project might involve using an external supplier who at this point has not been contracted. Later in the project, people from this external contractor might take on the senior supplier and team manager roles.

More than one person might fill any of the roles created in this activity. That means the project might have two or three senior users. (Remember that the executive and the project manager roles created earlier in the process are different—each project has only one executive and one project manager.)

Having multiple senior users and senior suppliers ensures that a broader range of perspectives is represented on the project board. However, it might take longer for the project board to come to a decision.

When looking for suitable candidates for the project roles, the project manager should perform a thorough analysis of all the people the project might impact. Some of these people might be suitable for the project management team. If they don't wish to take on roles in the project, they will at least probably want to be informed of its progress. This is called *stakeholder analysis*. This analysis will be done again, in more depth, if the project reaches its initiation stage during the prepare the communication management approach activity.

The people appointed to the project management team should clearly understand and accept what is expected of them. They might need some training in order to carry out their roles.

Chapter 3, "Organization Theme," covers the project management team structure in even more detail.

Select the Project Approach and Assemble the Project Brief

This activity has two focuses: create a project approach that shows how the project will be delivered, and assemble the *project brief*, which the project board will use as the basis of their decision regarding whether to proceed to the first stage of the project.

The project manager describes the *project approach*. It answers how the project's products will be delivered and how they will be brought into the operational environment, if there is one. For example, will the products be created in-house, outsourced, or bought as an off-the-shelf solution? For the hotel project, a reasonable approach might be to outsource the hotel's construction to a building firm. The project approach might also look at technical approaches used in particular industries. For example, in the construction of a hotel, the rooms might be built as individual units and then shipped to the site, rather than being built at the hotel location. The project approach specifies any supplier, organizational, or industry delivery standards. The project approach might also specify how PRINCE2 will be tailored to suit the particular project environment or the particular characteristics of the project.

PRINCE2 sometimes refers to the project approach as the *delivery solution*. This terminology can be rather confusing, because the word "solution" typically refers to the end result, not how the end result is delivered. Remember, in PRINCE2, delivery solution is synonymous with project approach.

At the end of this activity, the project manager assembles the project brief. Figure 2.3 shows the composition of this management product. Many of the sections of the project brief will have been created during the previous activities—such as the project product description, the outline business case, the project management team structure, the role descriptions, and the project approach. The only section that needs to be created at this point is the project definition, which describes the project's background, objectives, scope, and the amount of flexibility for the delivery dates and budgets.

Figure 2.3: The composition of the project brief

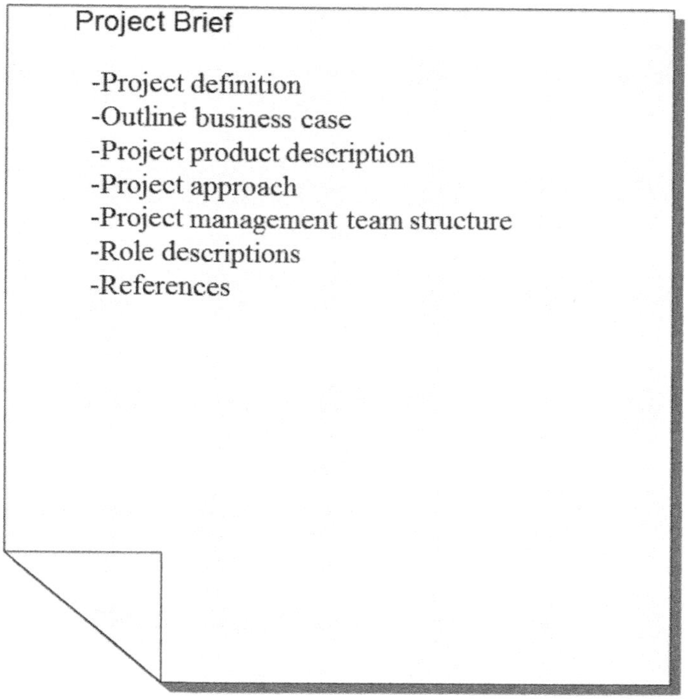

Project Brief

-Project definition
-Outline business case
-Project product description
-Project approach
-Project management team structure
-Role descriptions
-References

Plan the Initiation Stage

After the starting up a project process is completed, the project board reviews the information in the project brief and decides whether the project should start. The first stage of the project is the *initiation stage*, where the detailed planning is addressed. In addition to the project brief, the project board will want to see a plan for this first stage, to understand the time and resources needed to plan the project. In effect, they will want to see a plan for the planning. In this activity, the project manager creates the *stage plan for the initiation stage*.

Key Facts for Starting Up a Project

For the Foundation exam, you do not have to memorize all the details from the previous starting up a project process activities. You should, however, learn the important facts for this process, as specified in Table 2.1. The Practitioner exam, on the other hand, may contain detailed questions about the activities in the starting up a project process. During the exam, however, you can refer to the official PRINCE2 manual, *Managing Successful Projects with PRINCE2*, so there is no need to memorize all the details.

Table 2.1: Starting up a project process—key facts

Activity	Key Facts
Appoint the executive and the project manager	Corporate, programme management, or the customer appoints the executive. The executive appoints the project manager. The project manager creates the daily log. He uses it as a personal project diary, recording personal actions and informal issues.
Prepare the outline business case	The executive creates the outline business case. This justifies the undertaking of the project, although at this point, it may be quite high level. The project manager liaises with the executive, senior user(s), and senior supplier(s) to create the project product description. This outlines the specifications for the major products. It is used at the end of the project to verify that the right products have been created.
Capture previous lessons	The project manager creates the lessons log and populates it with past experience that will help the management of the project.
Design and appoint the project management team	The executive and the project manager design the project management team structure and create job descriptions for all the roles. They appoint as many people to the project management team as is possible at this early point in the initiative. This will include recruiting whom they can to the project board.
Select the project approach and assemble the project brief	The project manager creates the project approach. This describes the overall approach to delivering the products, such as in-house development or outsourcing the work. The project manager assembles the project brief. This defines the scope and objectives of the project. It contains some of the outputs from previous activities, such as the project management team structure, role descriptions, outline business case, project product description, and the project approach.
Plan the initiation stage	The project manager creates the stage plan for the initiation stage. This plan shows the project board what resources, money, and time would be needed to carry out the next step, the initiation stage. The initiation stage is when the project is planned to a high level. The project board reviews the stage plan for the initiation stage to decide whether to authorize the initiation stage.

Tailoring the Starting Up a Project Process

In Chapter 1, you learned that PRINCE2 can be successfully tailored to suit many different situations. For example, PRINCE2 can work effectively in a programme environment, when an agile delivery approach is used, or when there is a separate commercial organization delivering some of the project's products. This section looks at how the starting up a project process might be adapted to suit some of these situations.

In a simple, less-complicated project, the executive might decide to complete the starting up a project process in a very informal way. The project brief might be a simple statement defining the project's goals or simply an elaboration of the project mandate. In either case, it should be clear what the business rationale for the project is, what roles and responsibilities are required, and how the initiation of the project should be done. The temptation might be to skip the starting up a project process altogether, but it is an important step during which the organization commissioning the project tests to see if it is a viable, worthwhile initiative.

On a simple project, the executive might decide it is not worth recruiting a project manager for the starting up a project process. In this case, he would create the processes' management products.

At the other extreme, the project might be a very large change that's part of a programme. In this case, many of the activities in the starting up a project process might be done at a programme management level, with someone like the programme manager appointing the executive and the project manager and preparing many of the elements of the project brief. It may be that there is no separate business case for the project—just one for the overall programme—so there is no need for a project outline business case.

Another possible situation is that the project might work within an agile environment. You learned about agile in the "Tailoring PRINCE2 to Different Project Types and Environments" section of Chapter 1. At this point in the initiative, it might be too early to make any decision on whether to use an agile approach, but when the project manager is creating the project brief, he could start to assess the pluses and minuses of using it. He could start to assess factors such as whether the improved communications that a co-located agile team might bring are outweighed by the costs of providing an office space, or whether the increased engagement with the customers that frequent releases would bring might be outweighed by the overhead of more quality checks.

If an agile approach is used, the project management team needs to consider how the PRINCE2 roles relate to agile roles, such as the scrum master and the product owner.

If the project is of an investigative type, such as a research and development project, it might be very difficult to start to write measurable acceptance criteria for the final outputs in the project product description. At this early point in the initiative, it might be impossible to envision the final solution. If this is the case, the project product description should at least be clear about what business problem the final products will solve and what outcome(s) they will create.

Finally, if the project will outsource a lot of the delivery work to separate third-party organizations, the activities in the starting up a project process are likely to take place before the customer has signed a contract with the suppliers. However, some of the information that goes into the project brief will need to come from the suppliers. Typically, the customer will send out a request for information to the suppliers, who will then provide information such as early estimates of costs and timescales before they sign a contract with the customer.

The Directing a Project Process – Part I

As you learned in the "An End-to-End Walk-through of PRINCE2" section of Chapter 1, the directing a project process spans across the entire PRINCE2 process model. It starts at the completion of the starting up a project process and ends when the project board authorizes the closure of the project. I am going to cover this process across a number of chapters:

- This chapter describes how the directing a project process is used at the beginning of the project.
- Chapter 10 describes how the directing a project process is used during the middle of the project.
- Chapter 11 describes how the directing a project process is used at the end of the project.

The directing a project process is used by the project board to make key decisions about the project. The project board is accountable for the project's success. As you learned in Chapter 1, the project board is made up of three roles: the executive, who looks at the project from a business perspective, the senior user(s), who will use or maintain the project's products, and the senior supplier(s), who will provide resources to create the project's products. The ultimate decision-maker in the project board is the executive. There should only ever be one executive, but there may be a number of senior users and senior suppliers.

The project board does not manage the project on a day-to-day basis during the directing a project process; they delegate this task to the project manager. During the beginning of the project, the project manager will be managing the project on day-to-day basis, first using the starting up a project process and then, if the project board authorizes it, during the initiation stage.

The following section describes how the project board makes their first key decision: whether to authorize the initiation of the project. This decision takes place after the starting up a project process. Later in this chapter, I will come back to the directing a project process and describe how the project board makes their next key decisions, which are whether to authorize the project and the first delivery stage. This takes place after the initiating a project process.

Authorize Initiation

Once all the activities in the starting up a project process are finished, the project manager will send a request to initiate a project to the project board. The project board considers this request in the directing a project process in the authorize initiation activity (refer to Figure 2.1). They may or may not do this in a formal meeting. The basis of their decision will be all the information in the project brief. They can also use project assurance to review this material and test its validity.

Sometimes at this early point in the initiative, there may be no senior supplier representative—for example, if an outsourced supplier has not been contracted at this point. Even without the senior supplier, PRINCE2 allows the project board to authorize the initiation stage (although I think it would be a good idea to represent the outsourced supplier by a proxy—maybe using the procurement department).

If the project board decides to proceed, they will obtain the resources required by the stage plan for the initiation stage. Then the executive will give the project manager documented instructions to proceed with the delivery of just the initiation stage. At this point, they should inform all stakeholders that the project is being initiated.

The Initiating a Project Process

In Figure 2.1, you can see that once the project board has authorized initiation, the next process is initiating a project. This is where the project begins. The project manager uses this process to run the first stage of the project, the initiation stage. It contains the following nine activities:

- *Agree the tailoring requirements*
- *Prepare the risk management approach*
- *Prepare the quality management approach*
- *Prepare the change control approach*
- *Prepare the communication management approach*
- *Set-up project controls*
- *Create the project plan*
- *Prepare the benefits management approach*
- *Assemble the project initiation documentation*

The main focus of these activities is to plan the project. PRINCE2's definition of the purpose of this process is "to establish solid foundations for the project, enabling the organization to understand the work that needs to be done to deliver the project's products before committing to a significant spend."

The main output from the initiating a project process is the project initiation documentation. You learn about the exact composition of this management product in the "Assemble the Project Initiation Documentation" section later in this chapter. Many of the sections from the project brief will be transferred to the project initiation documentation, although at this point, there will be more time to refine them. Additional information needs to be added, such as the project plan, the project's approaches, and how PRINCE2 will be tailored for this particular situation.

After the initiating a project process is completed, the project initiation documentation is passed to the project board. The board uses this documentation to decide whether to authorize the project to proceed. All the activities in the initiating a project process create information that goes into the project initiation documentation. Rather than wait until the document has been finished, the project board might decide to review the information as it is created, or they may ask their project assurance representatives to do so for them.

CASE STUDY

Using PRINCE2 to Sell Projects

Many companies sell projects, such as building firms that sell their ability to deliver construction projects, software companies that deliver bespoke software, and office moving companies that deliver projects to move office furniture.

I was involved with a company of this type several years ago. They created the IT infrastructure used by large organizations for their websites. They would procure a range of types of computers and software for their clients and then install this hardware and software in secure data centers, making sure there were all sorts of fail-safes incorporated to keep the websites up in an emergency—for example, gas generators that would start if there was a blackout. They would then maintain and operate the infrastructure on behalf of their clients.

One of the challenges for the project teams was that the sales teams would often promise potential clients unrealistic delivery dates and miscommunicate the scope of the products that would be delivered. This, of course, caused a lot of problems when the project was handed over from the sales team to the delivery team.

To resolve this problem, I set up a handover process between the sales team and the project teams based on PRINCE2. Every time a salesperson felt a potential client was about to sign up for the company's services, they had to put a proposal together for that client. A representative from the project team helped them. This proposal was based on the PRINCE2 project brief. In effect, the pre-sales work was the starting up a project process. Then if the client decided to proceed with the work, it was with the understanding that there would be some time devoted to expanding on this proposal to create the project initiation documentation. At this point, if any significant new pieces of information arose, the quote might be allowed to change.

This approach allowed for a much more consistent message to be given to the clients through the pre-sales and project work. This approach led to more satisfied customers.

Initiating a Project Activities

Figure 2.4 shows an overview of the activities in the initiating a project process. As you can see, these activities are carried out in a certain sequence. First, the tailoring requirements are agreed to, then the approaches are created, and then the project plan and project controls are set up. Finally, the business case is refined and the project initiation documentation assembled.

Figure 2.4: Overview of initiating a project

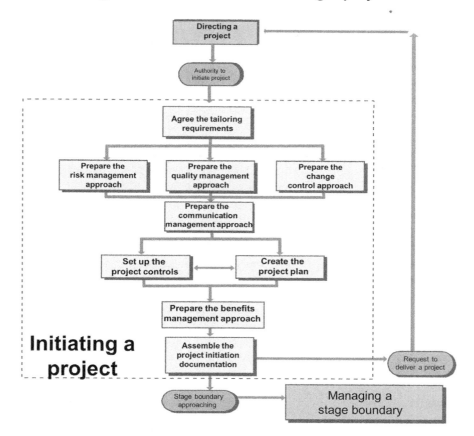

You learn about each of the nine activities over the following sections. You should read these sections and make sure you understand them, but again, you don't necessarily need to memorize the details. After these sections, you will find an "initiating a project—key process facts" table that you *do* need to memorize for the Foundation exam. As I said in the starting up a project process section, you will be asked detailed questions about the process activities in the Practitioner exam— but, of course, you can refer to the official PRINCE2 manual.

Agree the Tailoring Requirements

As you learned in Chapter 1, an important aspect of applying PRINCE2 is tailoring it so that it can work effectively given the characteristics of the project or the environment the project is operating within. For example, PRINCE2 would be used differently in a small and simple project compared to how it might be used if the project was part of a larger programme of change. In this activity, the project manager and the project board will agree to how the project management approach will need to be tailored.

Preparing the Approaches

The next four activities in initiating a project create four approaches, as follows:

- Prepare the risk management approach creates the risk management approach.
- Prepare the quality management approach creates the quality management approach.
- Prepare the change control approach creates the change control approach.
- Prepare the communication management approach creates the communication management approach.

These four management products will show how the project team will manage risks and quality, how they will assess and authorize proposed changes to the project and how they will communicate effectively with all the project's stakeholders. You will learn about the contents of each approach later in the book. (The risk management approach is covered in Chapter 7, "Risk Theme"; the quality management approach is covered in Chapter 6, "Quality Theme"; the change control approach is covered in Chapter 8, "Change Theme"; and the communication management approach is covered in Chapter 3, "Organization Theme.") However, this section will give you a brief overview of what an approach is.

An approach provides all the information needed to describe how to manage a particular area of project management. For example, if the project manager wanted to describe how quality on the project should be managed, what information would they need to provide? PRINCE2 recommends that each approach contain at least six sections: procedure, timings, roles and responsibilities, tools and techniques, reporting, and records (some of the approaches contain more sections.) The following list presents examples of the type of information that might go into these six sections for a quality management approach. Of course, you'd need a lot more information in each category to fully describe an approach to quality management, but these examples will give you an idea of how to set up an approach:

Quality Management Procedure

This is basically the set of activities that the project needs to do (maybe a number of times) to ensure it builds the right products. The project team identifies who will use the products, talks to them to find out their requirements, documents those requirements, ensures that those creating the products use the documented requirements when they are deciding what to build, and finally, gets the users back at the end of the project to agree that the products that have been built are what was initially specified. All these activities together form a basic quality procedure.

Timing of Quality Management Activities

Are there any particular dates, times, or schedules that are important to ensuring the project is building the correct products? For example, maybe at the end of each stage of the project, project assurance will carry out an audit of all the quality checks that have occurred.

Quality Management Roles and Responsibilities

Who will be involved during the project to ensure the right products are built? What responsibilities will these people have? For example, maybe one role will represent those who will use the products. That individual's responsibilities will be to fully specify what all the users require from the products, check the products as they are being built to ensure they are being created correctly, and finally, sign off on the product.

Quality Management Tools and Techniques

Will any special techniques be used in quality management? For example, if the project involves building software, a particular technical test may be available that measures whether the product is sufficiently robust to be used in operations. Will any quality standards need to be followed? For example on a construction project the building might need to adhere to certain health and safety procedures and construction regulations.

Quality Management Reporting

What quality reports need to be created, who do they need to be sent to, and what sort of format will they have? For example, maybe the project manager's regular progress report should include a section describing how the products are progressing through their quality checks.

Quality Management Records

What information does the project need to record on the quality activities carried out throughout the project? For example, many quality checks may be done during the project. It would be useful to record who was involved in those checks, what date the checks occurred, what each check revealed, and whether the quality check passed or failed.

The preceding examples deal with quality management. However, you could use the same six categories to describe how to manage risk, change control, and communication.

Prepare the Risk Management Approach

The project manager creates the *risk management approach*, which defines how to manage risk. In particular, it describes how to decrease the likelihood and/or the impact of potential threats to the project. Threats are potential problems that would detrimentally affect the project's objectives. But risks could also be opportunities—potential events that could positively affect the project's objectives. So the risk management approach also looks at how to increase the likelihood and/or impact of potential opportunities to the project. (You'll learn more about risk in Chapter 7.

The risk management approach sets out the six pieces of information common to all approaches, which were discussed in the previous section: procedure, timings, roles and responsibilities, tools and techniques, reporting, and records. Chapter 7 describes what type of information goes into each of these sections.

This approach also specifies the threshold of risk that corporate, programme management, the customer, or the project board are willing to accept—in other words, their risk tolerance levels. Risk can be measured in a variety of ways, such as adding together the expected financial impact of all the potential threats to the project. If this overall level goes over the risk tolerance levels, the project manager needs to ensure that this situation is escalated to the correct management level.

In addition, the risk management approach considers how risks will be assessed in terms of their probability, their impact on the project, what category of risk they are, and how their likelihood will vary over time. It will specify whether there will be any money set aside to fund responses to risks. Early warning indicators will be taken into account, which if monitored, might indicate an increase or decrease of the project's exposure to risk.

Finally, project support creates the *risk register*. You learn how to compose this management product in Chapter 7. For now, think of it as containing all the details of the identified threats and opportunities that might affect the project objectives. There might be a number of risks that were identified in the starting up a project process and that the project manager recorded in the daily log; in that case, these risks will now be transferred to the risk register.

Prepare the Quality Management Approach

In the next step, the project manager creates the *quality management approach*, which describes how the project management team will ensure that the end result of the project will be a product (or products) that are suitable for their intended purpose. This approach should include information in the six categories previously described in the "Preparing the Approaches" section earlier in this chapter: procedure, timings, roles and responsibilities, tools and techniques, reporting, and records.

To develop the quality management approach, the project manager should review the project product description that was created in the starting up a project process. This describes, at a high level, the specification for the main product or products that the project will need to create. The project manager will also need to take into account any organizational quality approaches of both the customers and suppliers involved with the project.

Project support creates an empty *quality register*. As the project progresses, this register will be used to record information on the quality checks that are carried out on the products that are created. You will learn more about how the quality register is used in Chapter 6.

Prepare the Change Control Approach

Creating the *change control approach* is also the job of the project manager. This approach describes how the project team will manage and control any proposed changes to the project's products as well as how to manage and control issues that arise during the project. This approach should include information in the six categories previously described in the "Preparing the Approaches" section: procedure, timings, roles and responsibilities, tools and techniques, reporting and records.

The procedure section of the approach will describe how to capture proposed issue and changes, evaluate them, and then authorize any proposed response to them at an appropriate level of authority. The change control approach also describes the format of the issue register. The *issue register* is used to record and track all proposed changes, as well as unauthorized changes that have been made to the product by mistake (which are called off-specifications) plus general problems and concerns that might arise during the project.

Project support creates the project's issue register at this point. Some issues may have already been recorded in the daily log; if so, these will be transferred to the issue register. In addition, project support may create a set of configuration item records for the project's management products, such as the project initiation documentation. Configuration item records track the status, version, and variant of a product. You will learn more about configuration item records and the PRINCE2 approach to change control in Chapter 8.

Prepare the Communication Management Approach

Next, the project manager creates the *communication management approach*, which describes how the project will manage communication between the people on the project management team as well as between the project and stakeholders outside the project team. The project manager should create this approach last, since the preceding three approaches might have identified various reports that should be included in the communication management approach.

You will learn how to create the communication management approach in more detail in Chapter 3. For now, remember that it also contains the six common types of approach information: procedures, timings, roles and responsibilities, tools and techniques, reporting, and records.

Remember that the project manager might have conducted a stakeholder analysis during the starting up a project process (during the designing and appointing the project management team activity). If this is the case, the project manager should review the results of that work and, if necessary, conduct further analysis. If no stakeholder analysis were done in the starting up a project process, the project manager will have to do it here.

Set Up the Project Controls

Anything that ensures that the project is heading toward its objectives is a *project control*. For example, the project board controls the project manager by giving them only one stage of the project to manage at a time, setting specific objectives for that stage in terms of the products that must be built and the time and money that are available for that stage. So one of the controls established in this activity is how the project plan will be divided into stages and when the end-stage assessment meetings between the project board and the project manager will occur.

Many of the ways of controlling the project will have already been defined in the four approaches. For example, the reporting system, defined in the communication management approach, allows the project to be monitored. Monitoring is an important aspect of control—it allows the monitoring body to get an early warning of problems, which they can then rectify in a timely manner.

The approaches might also set out new responsibilities for the various project management team roles. In this activity, the project manager adds these responsibilities to the role descriptions and makes sure the individuals concerned accept these amendments.

Create the Project Plan

Next, the project manager creates the *project plan*. It shows how the major products in the project will be delivered. It covers the time directly after the initiation stage to the end of the project and will probably be fairly high-level. Remember that the more detailed planning is done on a stage-by-stage basis. (Refer to the "Manage by Stages" section in Chapter 1.) However, if the project is short, the project manager might be able to plan the entire project in detail at this point.

The project plan should be based on the work that was done in the starting up a project process. The project brief will have specified important delivery dates and the project approach. The project plan needs to be consistent with both of these.

The project manager needs to decide how to format the project plan. There are many ways of presenting the information in a plan, including the popular Gantt chart format (a graphical way of showing a schedule), spreadsheets, or purely text-based. You don't need to know about these formats for the PRINCE2 exam—you just need to know that this is when the project manager decides on the plan format.

The project manager should also decide what estimating techniques will be used. For example, some projects use the Delphi method to estimate durations. (The Delphi method is a process used to come to a consensus estimate with a group of people.) Once again, estimating techniques are not covered in the PRINCE2 syllabus—you just need to know that this is the point at which the project manager decides which techniques to use.

PRINCE2 plans contain not only schedule information such as tasks, dates, and resources, but also detailed specifications of the products that will be built during that plan. In PRINCE2, these specifications are the product descriptions. Remember that the project plan is probably fairly high-level, so at this point, the project manager will only be able to identify the major deliverables. The project manager will create product descriptions for these major deliverables. These descriptions need to be consistent with the higher-level project product description created in the starting up a project process and agreed to by the senior users.

Prepare the Benefits Management Approach

The project manager will create a detailed business case, using the information in the outline business case created in the starting up a project process and the more detailed estimates of costs and timescales available from the newly created project plan. He will confer with the executive to do this.

The project manager also creates the *benefits management approach*. This management product will be covered in more detail in Chapter 4. For now, you just need to know that the project manager uses this approach to specify how achievements of the project's benefits will be measured and what management actions will be needed—probably post-project—to ensure that the benefits are achieved. Many of the activities in this approach are likely to occur after the project has finished, because many benefits from projects aren't realized until after all the products have been built.

Assemble the Project Initiation Documentation

During this activity, the project manager gathers all the information needed for the *project initiation documentation*. Figure 2.5 shows the composition of the project initiation documentation. Many of the sections come directly from the project brief, although the information within them might be more detailed at this point. The new sections are the approaches, a project plan, a detailed business case, and a description of how PRINCE2 will be tailored for this project. The project initiation documentation might be a collection of individual documents.

Figure 2.5: The composition of the project initiation documentation

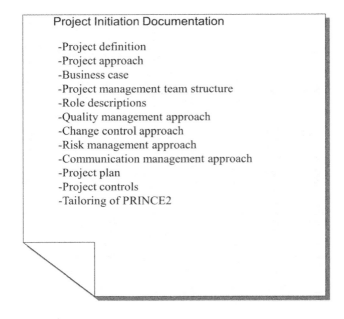

Project Initiation Documentation

-Project definition
-Project approach
-Business case
-Project management team structure
-Role descriptions
-Quality management approach
-Change control approach
-Risk management approach
-Communication management approach
-Project plan
-Project controls
-Tailoring of PRINCE2

As the project progresses, the project manager will create a new version of the project initiation documentation at the end of each stage. The project board will authorize these new versions. However, the first version of the project initiation documentation is particularly important. It describes the stakeholder's expectations of the project at the point it was authorized. PRINCE2 recommends that the project board review this first version at the end of the project, in order to evaluate how the project performed.

At the end of this activity, the project manager will use the managing a stage boundary process to prepare for the next stage. (Refer back to Figure 2.1 to see how the process model fits together at this point.) The managing a stage Boundary process is covered in more detail in Chapter 10. At this point, all that you need to know about this process is that it is used to create a detailed plan for the next stage. The project manager will show this stage plan to the project board and ask them for permission to manage that section of the project.

Finally, the project manager sends a request to deliver the project to the project board.

Key Facts for Initiating a Project

For the Foundation exam, you do not need to memorize all details contained in the previous initiating a project activity sections. Read through those sections and make sure the information makes sense. You should, however, learn the important facts for this process set out in Table 2.2. The Practitioner exam, on the other hand, might ask you detailed questions about the initiating a project activities; however, in that exam, you are allowed to refer to the official PRINCE2 manual, *Managing Successful Projects with PRINCE2*, so there is no need to memorize all the details.

Table 2.2: Initiating a project process—key facts

Activity	Key facts
Agree the tailoring requirements	The project manager will create a description of how the project management approach and PRINCE2 will be tailored for this specific project
Prepare the risk management approach	The project manager creates the risk management approach that sets out how risk will be managed during the project. Project support creates the risk register that will be used to record the project risks.
Prepare the quality management approach	The project manager creates the quality management approach that sets out how the project will ensure it creates products that are fit for the purpose for which they will eventually be used. Project support creates the quality register that will be used to record details on all the quality checks made on the project's products.
Prepare the change control approach	The project manager creates the change control approach that sets out how changes to the project's products will be controlled and how issues will be managed. Project support creates the issue register that will be used to record all project issues. The project board decides whether to delegate any authority to authorize changes and so create a change authority.

Activity	Key facts
Prepare the communication management approach	The project manager creates the communication management approach that sets out how communication between those involved with the project and other stakeholders will be managed.
Set up the project controls	The project manager documents how they and the project board will control work on the project and make sure the right things are done.
Create the project plan	The project manager creates the project plan.
Prepare the benefits management approach	The project manager creates the first version of the detailed business case and the benefits management approach.
Assemble the project initiation documentation	The project manager assembles all the information from the preceding activities to create the project initiation documentation.

Tailoring the Initiating a Project Process

Earlier in this chapter, you saw how starting up a project process can be successfully tailored to suit different situations. In this section, you will see how the initiating a project process can also be adapted.

On a small and simple project, the project initiation documentation might be a fairly simple document or maybe a set of presentation slides. Some of the components of the project initiation documentation might be combined. For example, there might be an overall management approach document rather than separate ones for risk, quality, change control, and communication. Also, rather than having separate risk and issue registers, these documents might be combined—a common way of doing this is by creating a RAID log. (RAID stands for risks, assumptions, issues and dependencies. RAID is not a PRINCE2 term and you won't be tested on this in the exams.)

In addition to the aforementioned adaptations for small projects, the management products might be adapted in a number of other ways. The area of change control is referred to by different names in different industries. For example, in an engineering project, it might be called asset management; in a software development project, it might be called configuration management; and in a project that creates documents, it might be called version control. It would be best to use these industry-specific terms when naming the change control approach. In some environments, it is common to have a change register as well as the issue register. In some projects, there are many very detailed quality checks and inspections of the products. If this is the case the quality register might be far more complex or split up into a number of interrelated documents. Particularly in larger projects, the project initiation documentation is rarely a single document, but a group of connected documents, such as reports, presentation slides, or information garnered from planning software tools.

One of the key ways that PRINCE2 projects are tailored is through using organizational or industry-specific methods of managing areas such as quality and risk. These will be described in the approaches that are created in the initiating a project process.

If the project is part of a programme, there might be programme-wide approaches to management areas such as risk, quality, change control, or communication. If this is the case, there might not be a need to create separate approaches for the project, or maybe the project approaches might simply refer to the programme approaches while highlighting some deviations that are peculiar to the project. Often in a programme situation, someone such as a business change manager is responsible for the realization of the benefits for the entire programme. If this is the case, the benefits management approach is likely to be created at the programme level by the business change manager rather than by the project manager.

The initiating a project process might be adapted in a number of ways if an agile approach is used. The product descriptions that appear in the project plan might be written in the form of user stories or epics. Also, only high-level product descriptions might be used, with an allowable flexibility on the detailed specifications. (In the "Tailoring the Quality Theme" section of Chapter 6, you will learn more about how to write product descriptions in the form of user stories and epics and how to baseline high-level product descriptions.) In fact, the project product description and the main product descriptions in the project plan might focus more on the required outcome or value that the product will bring, rather than its specifications.

When using an agile approach to plan a project, the project management team needs to take into account the level of uncertainty. If there is a great deal of uncertainty about how the product will be built, the project manager might include some agile "spikes" early on in the plan. A spike is a time-limited investigation into a technical area, so that the team can ascertain how much time and effort will be needed to build certain products and what approach works best. It might involve building a number of experimental prototypes. A similar approach might be used if the clients are unclear about their requirements. In this case, the project manager might include activities in the project plan where the delivery teams build a number of mock-ups to show to the client to get their feedback on what they like and don't like.

If the project team is delivering the work to an external client, the project initiation documentation might form the basis of a legal contract. It is best to keep the legal contract and project initiation documentation as separate documents with the legal contract referring to the project documentation as necessary. This will help minimize the need for expensive legal counsel when making any changes to the project documentation.

Finally, if the project will outsource a lot of the delivery work to separate third-party organizations, some of the activities in the initiating a project process are likely to take place before the customer has signed a contract with the suppliers. This is because the supplier needs to investigate the approaches, plans, and controls in order to assess the viability and desirability of getting involved with the project. However, initiating a project cannot be completed until a contract has been signed and the customer's project board authorizes the project.

The Directing a Project Process – Part II

As previously mentioned, I am going to cover the directing a project process in a number of steps. You last saw the directing a project process at the end of the starting up a project process, when the project board considered whether to authorize the initiation stage. Now that the initiation stage is coming to an end, it is time for the project board to consider whether to authorize the initiative to proceed any further. This decision-making is done once again in the directing a project process.

By the end of the initiation stage, the project manager will have used the initiating a project process to create the project initiation documentation. The project board will now review this using the authorize the project activity from the directing a project process. The project manager will have also used the managing a stage process to create the first delivery stage plan. The project board will now review this using the authorize a stage activity from the directing a project process. (Refer to Figure 2.1 to see how the process model works at this point.)

Authorize the Project

During this activity, the main management product that the project board (or their project assurance representatives) will review is the project initiation documentation. They look through all the information and make sure they are happy with it. They will want to see evidence that any previous experience in the lessons log was taken into account when the project manager assembled the project initiation documentation.

The project board also reviews the benefits management approach to ensure that there is adequate planning for the review of the achievements of the project's benefits and for any management actions that will be required to ensure that the benefits are realized.

The board will then need to decide whether to authorize the project. If they decide not to authorize the project, they will instruct the project manager to close the project prematurely. In this case, the project manager will start the closing a project process. You learn more about this process in Chapter 11. For now, all you need to know is that during this process, the project manager performs various activities to close the project, such as creating the end project report. After the closing a project process, the project manager goes back to the project board for a final time to request authorization to close the project.

The alternative is, of course, that the project board decides, based on the information in the project initiation documentation, that this project is a viable and worthwhile initiative. In this case, they will obtain or commit the resources needed for the project. Remember, however, that they will release these resources to the project manager only on a stage-by-stage basis.

Finally, the project board will notify corporate, programme management, or the customer and any other interested parties that the project has been authorized.

Authorize a Stage

After deciding to authorize the project, the project board will then move on to reviewing the stage plan for the first delivery stage and decide whether to authorize this work.

During the authorize a stage activity, the project board (or their project assurance representatives) will review the plan for the next stage and any new product descriptions for products that will be created in that stage. They will also want to check that any risks associated with this stage are covered by suitable countermeasures.

Then either they either approve the stage plan and set time, cost, and scope tolerances that the project manager must abide by, or they will ask the project manager to revise the plan and give guidance on what would make it acceptable.

Finally, the project board will notify corporate, programme management, or the customer and any other interested parties that a new stage is starting.

Themes to Start a Project Successfully

All seven themes are used throughout the activities at the beginning of the project. It is important for you to understand how these themes link to the activities in the starting up a project and initiating a project processes, because this will be a potential topic for exam questions.

Business Case Theme

The business case theme describes how to ensure that the project is desirable, viable, and achievable throughout the project's life. It shows how to write the project's business case, assigns a variety of business-related responsibilities to the roles within the project management team, and shows where in the process model the major business-related activities should occur. This section describes how the business case theme is implemented at the beginning of the project.

Prior to starting a PRINCE2 project, corporate, programme management, or the customer creates a project mandate. In a programme management situation, this might be a document that includes a detailed business case. For most projects, however, this is a very high-level document that includes the reasons the project is being considered and the background of the project, both of which will be transferred into the business case.

During the starting up a project process, corporate, programme management, or the customer appoints an executive for the project. The executive should represent the commissioning organization's business viewpoint. Their responsibility is to check that the project represents value for money and will yield adequate returns given the investment needed. The executive will create an outline business case, which will justify the undertaking of the project.

During the initiating a project process, the project manager refines the outline business case to create the first detailed business case. The project manager also creates the benefits management approach, which describes how the achievements of the project's benefits will be measured and what management actions might be required to ensure that the benefits will be realized.

During the directing a project process, the project board has a number of decisions to make. First, they authorize initiation, then the project, and finally, the first delivery stage. In all these decisions, they must verify that there is a solid justification for carrying on with the project based on the information in the business case.

You learn more about the business case theme in Chapter 4.

Organization Theme

The organization theme sets out a project management team structure with associated roles and responsibilities. During the starting up a project process, the project management team is designed and then appointed. Corporate, programme management, or the customer appoints the executive; the executive appoints the project manager; and then together, they design the rest of the project management team and appoint as many people to the roles as possible at this early point in the initiative.

During the initiating a project process, the project manager will carry out a full stakeholder analysis, identifying anyone who will be impacted by the project, the type of information that the project management team requires from them, and also the type of information that they require from the project management team. The output of this analysis work is put into the communication management approach.

You learn more about the organization theme in Chapter 3.

Quality Theme

The quality theme shows how a project should be managed to ensure it creates the right products. It covers how to specify which products to build, how to check the quality of the products, and who will be involved in product-focused activities. This section describes how the quality theme is implemented at the beginning of the project.

The project manager creates the project product description during the starting up a project process. This will set out the high-level specifications for the major project outputs. The project manager will work with the senior users in order to create this management product. The project product description contains the customer's quality expectations and the measurable acceptance criteria that the final products should conform to when finished.

During the initiating a project process, the project manager creates the quality management approach, which shows how the project will be managed to ensure that the correct products are created. Project support creates a blank quality register, which is used to record information on all the product quality checks that will take place throughout the project. The project manager also creates the project plan during this process. This plan includes product descriptions for the major products to be delivered.

You learn more about the quality theme in Chapter 6.

Plans Theme

The plans theme shows how to plan the work of the project using three different levels of plans: the project plan, the stage plan, and the team plan. It describes the roles involved with planning as well as the steps needed to create a plan. The plans theme also describes how to use the stages that help the project board to control and monitor a project. (See the "Manage by Stages" section in Chapter 1.) This section describes how the plans theme is implemented at the beginning of the project.

Plans are created during the following processes at the outset of a project:
- During the starting up a project process, the project manager creates the stage plan for the initiation stage; it describes the work needed to create the project initiation documentation.
- During the initiating a project process, the project manager creates the project plan, which describes at a high level the work for the entire delivery part of the project. The project manager works with the project board to decide how to split the project plan into stages.
- During the managing a stage boundary process that occurs at the end of the initiation stage, the project manager creates the first delivery stage plan.

You learn more about the plans theme in Chapter 5.

Risk Theme

The risk theme describes how to identify, assess, and control the potential threats to and opportunities for the project, and thus improves the likelihood of the project success. This section shows how the risk theme is implemented at the beginning of the project.

During the starting up a project process, the project manager logs identified threats or opportunities in the daily log. The executive then summarizes the risk situation in the outline business case.

During the initiating a project process, the project manager creates the risk management approach, which describes how risk will be managed during the project. Project support creates a risk register and transfers into it any threats or opportunities logged in the daily log. The risk register is then used to record details of identified risks throughout the project. The project manager summarizes the risk situation in the detailed business case.

You learn more about the risk theme in Chapter 7.

Change Theme

The change theme covers how to control proposed changes to the project's products and how to manage issues that might arise throughout the project. This section describes how the change theme is implemented at the beginning of the project.

During the initiating a project process, the project manager creates the change control approach, which describes how proposed changes to the project's products and project issues will be managed. Project support creates the issue register, which is used to record all issues, including requested changes to the project's products.

Also during the initiating a project process, the project board decides whether to establish a separate change authority. The individual(s) with change authority will be able to authorize some changes to the project's products.

You learn more about the change theme in Chapter 8.

Progress Theme

The progress theme shows how the work of the project will be controlled and kept on track. It covers the topic of tolerances, which are used to delegate authority with certain constraints. (See the "Manage by Exception" section in Chapter 1.) This section describes how the progress theme is implemented at the beginning of the project.

In the initiating a project process, the project manager creates the project controls section in the project initiation documentation. This sets out how the project will be controlled and monitored. It shows how the project plan will be divided into stages and specifies the various decision-making responsibilities in the project. Corporate, programme management, or the customer sets cost, time, and scope tolerances for the objectives in the project plan. The project board sets cost, time, and scope tolerances for the objectives in the stage plan for the first delivery stage.

You learn more about the progress theme in Chapter 9.

Using the PRINCE2 Principles to Start a Project Successfully

The seven PRINCE2 principles are used at the beginning of the project as follows:
- *Continued business justification* is implemented by the creation of the outline business case and then the detailed business case, the appointment of the executive to represent the business interest, and the verification that a business case exists during all the directing a project process authorization points.
- *Learn from experience* is implemented during the starting up a project process by the creation of the lessons log, which is populated with previous useful experience, and by considering lessons when carrying out any of the activities in the starting up a project and initiating a project processes.
- *Defined roles and responsibilities* is implemented by the establishment of a project management team in the starting up a project process, the appointment of people to the various roles, and the verification that they understand their project responsibilities.
- *Manage by stages* is implemented by the creation of a project plan divided into various management stages, and by the project board's authorization of the project manager's work one stage at a time—first for the initiation stage and then for the first delivery stage.

- *Manage by exception* is implemented by the project board defining certain tolerances within which the project manager must manage the initiation stage and the first delivery stage. It is also implemented by corporate, programme management, or the customer setting tolerances for the project board for the project.
- *Focus on products* is implemented first by specifying the overall output of the project in the project product description, then by specifying the major products in their product descriptions, and finally by creating the quality management approach, which defines how the project will be managed to ensure that the right products are created.
- *Tailor to suit the project environment* is implemented by including a section in the project initiation documentation that shows how PRINCE2 will be tailored for the project.

Summary

In this chapter, you learned how to start a project successfully with PRINCE2. You saw that the starting up a project, initiating a project, and directing a project processes include activities that ensure a disciplined beginning to a project.

In the starting up a project process, the executive and the project manager work together to ensure that the project's scope and objectives are defined clearly. They also design a project management team and appoint people to the roles. The executive creates an outline business case containing a justification for the project. The main outputs from the starting up a project process are a project brief, which defines the project idea, and a stage plan for the initiation stage, which specifies the resources necessary for the initiation stage.

In the directing a project process, the project board reviews the project brief and stage plan for the initiation stage. They use these documents to decide whether to authorize the initiative to continue.

The project manager then carries out the initiating a project process. This process covers the work of planning the project, at least at a high level. The project manager creates four approaches: the risk management approach, the quality management approach, the change control approach, and the communication management approach. These approaches show how the project will be managed. In addition, the project manager creates a project plan and refines the business case. All these outputs are assembled into the project initiation documentation.

After the initiating a project process, the project manager uses the managing a stage boundary process to create a stage plan for the next delivery stage. The project manager then takes this plan and the project initiation documentation to the project board. The board reviews both management products and decides whether to authorize the project manager to proceed with the project.

In this chapter, you saw how the starting up a project and initiating a project processes can be tailored to suit different project situations, such as when the project is operating within a programme or agile environment.

The final part of the chapter covered how the PRINCE2 themes and principles are implemented in these early parts of a project. You saw that all seven themes and principles are used throughout the processes covered in this chapter.

Foundation Exam Essentials

Explain the purpose, objectives, and context of the starting up a project process.
The purpose of the starting up a project process is to answer the question, "Do we have a worthwhile and viable project?" It has a number of objectives: to ensure that there is business justification for the project, to understand the scope of the project, to investigate the various ways of delivering the project, to appoint the project management team, to plan the work for the initiation stage, and to ensure that time is not wasted initiating a project that is not viable or worthwhile.

Starting up a project is a pre-project process that starts once the project mandate has been created. After the starting up a project process is completed, the project board decides whether to authorize the initiation stage of the project.

Explain the purpose, objectives, and context of the initiating a project process.
The purpose of the initiating a project process is to establish a solid foundation for the project that enables all stakeholders to understand the work that needs to be done to create the project's products. The process has a number of objectives: to ensure that there is a common understanding of the business case for the project, the scope of the project, the plan for the project, the approach to risk, quality, change control, and communication management, and how PRINCE2 will be tailored to meet the needs of the project.

The initiating a project process occurs during the initiation stage, which is the first stage of the project.

Explain the purpose, objectives, and context of the directing a project process.
The purpose of the directing a project process is to enable the project board to be accountable for the project's success by making key decisions and exercising overall control while delegating day-to-day management of the project to the project manager. The process has a number of objectives: to ensure that there is authority to initiate the project, to deliver the project's products, to authorize each stage of the project, and to authorize the closure of the project. The directing a project process also needs to ensure that the project remains viable and that there is a plan to realize the post-project benefits. The process starts at the completion of the starting up a project process and then spans the entire project, ending when the project board authorizes the closure of the project.

Describe the purpose of the project brief.
The project brief provides a full and firm foundation for the initiation of the project. It contains a number of sections: project definition, outline business case, project product description, project approach, project management team structure, and role descriptions. The executive and the project manager develop the project brief in the starting up a project process, and the project board reviews it in the directing a project process, when deciding whether to initiate the project.

Describe the purpose of the project initiation documentation.
The project initiation documentation forms the contract between the project manager and the project board regarding the definition of the project. It is used at the end of the project to see how successfully the project performed. It contains a number of sections: project definition, project approach, business case, project management team structure, role descriptions, quality management approach, risk management approach, change control approach, communication

management approach, project plan, project controls, and the tailoring of PRINCE2. The project manager develops the project initiation documentation in the initiating a project process, and the project board reviews it in the directing a project process, when deciding whether to authorize the delivery part of the project.

Practitioner Exam Essentials

Demonstrate an understanding of the six activities in the starting up a project process, and demonstrate an understanding of the recommended roles and responsibilities within the process.
There are six activities within the starting up a project process. The first activity is appoint the executive and the project manager, during which corporate, programme management, or the customer appoints the executive, who, in turn, appoints the project manager. Then, during the prepare the outline business case activity, the executive creates an outline business case, and the project manager creates the project product description. Next, during the capture previous lessons activity, the project manager creates a lessons log and records any useful experience that might help the project succeed. Then, the executive and the project manager put together the project team in the design and appoint the project management team activity. The project manager then assembles the project brief, which refines and expands on the information in the project mandate and defines what the project is all about. This is done in the select the project approach and assemble the project brief activity. Finally, during the plan the initiation stage activity, the project manager creates a stage plan for the initiation stage to plan the work to create the project initiation documentation.

Demonstrate an understanding of how the PRINCE2 themes can be applied during the starting up a project process.
All seven themes are applied during the starting up a project process. The business case theme is applied when the executive creates the outline business case. The organization theme is applied when the executive and the project manager design and appoint the project management team. The quality theme is applied when the project manager creates the project product description. The plans theme is applied when the project manager creates the stage plan for the initiation stage. The risk theme is applied when the project manager records any early project risks in the daily log and the executive records the major risks in the outline business case. The change theme is applied when the project manager creates the project product description, which shows an early baseline for the major products. Finally, the progress theme is applied when the stage plan for the initiation stage is given any tolerances around the plan's targets.

Assess and critique an approach to applying the starting up a project process.
Assess how the process might be adapted to different project contexts (for example, a small project, an agile project, a project with external third-party organizations, or a project operating within a programme environment) and whether the approach aligns with the principles of PRINCE2.

Demonstrate an understanding of the three activities in the directing a project process, and demonstrate an understanding of the recommended roles and responsibilities within the process.
Three activities within the directing a project process are used at the beginning of the project. The first activity is authorize initiation, during which the project board reviews the project brief and

decides whether to authorize the project manager to proceed with the initiation stage. Then, during the authorize the project activity, the project board reviews the project initiation documentation and decides whether to authorize the project to proceed in concept. At the same time as this activity, the project board also reviews the first delivery stage plan during the authorize the stage activity and decides whether to give the project manager the authority and budget to deliver the first delivery stage.

Demonstrate an understanding of how the PRINCE2 themes can be applied during the directing a project process.

All seven themes are applied during the directing a project process used at the beginning of the project. The business case theme is applied when the project board reviews and authorizes first the outline business case contained in the project brief and then the detailed business case contained in the project initiation documentation. The organization theme is applied when the project board reviews and authorizes the project management team structure contained in the project brief. The quality theme is applied when the project board reviews and authorizes the project product description contained in the project brief and then later when they review the quality management approach and the product descriptions of the main products contained within the project initiation documentation. The plans theme is applied when the project board reviews and authorizes the project plan and the stage plan for the first delivery stage. The risk theme is applied when the project board reviews the key project risks contained within the outline business case and then later the detailed business case. The change theme is applied when the project board reviews and authorizes the change control approach and decides whether or not to set up a separate change authority. Finally, the progress theme is applied when the project board reviews and authorizes the project controls contained in the project initiation documentation.

Demonstrate an understanding of the nine activities in the initiating a project process, and demonstrate an understanding of the recommended roles and responsibilities within the process.

There are nine activities within the initiating a project process. The first activity is agree the tailoring requirements, during which the project manager works with the project management team to decide how to tailor PRINCE2 to the project. In the next four activities—prepare the risk management approach, prepare the quality management approach, prepare the change control approach, and prepare the communication management approach—the project manager creates the approaches that will be followed to manage risk, quality, change control, and communication, respectively. Project support creates the risk register, the quality register, and the issue register. Next, the project manager creates the project plan during the create the project plan activity and show how the project will be controlled in the set up project controls activity. Then, using the outline business case created in the starting up a project process, the project manager creates a more detailed business case in the refine the business case activity. Also during this activity, the project manager creates a benefits management approach showing how to ensure that the outcomes of the project are implemented and measured. Finally, in the final activity, assemble the project initiation documentation, the project manager collates all the information created during the initiating a project process.

Demonstrate an understanding of how the PRINCE2 themes can be applied throughout the initiating a project process.

All seven themes are applied during the initiating a project process. The business case theme is applied when the project manager creates the detailed business case and the benefits management approach. The organization theme is applied when the project manager carries out a stakeholder analysis as he creates the communication management approach. The quality theme is applied when the project manager creates the quality management approach and project support creates the quality register. The plans theme is applied when the project manager creates the project plan. The risk theme is applied when the project manager creates the risk management approach and project support creates the risk register. The change theme is applied when the project manager creates the change control approach and project support creates the issue register. Finally, the progress theme is applied when the project plan is given any tolerances around the plan's targets, and the project manager records the controls that will be used throughout the project.

Assess and critique an approach to applying the initiating a project process.
This includes how the process might be adapted to different project contexts (for example, a small project, an agile project, a project with external third-party organizations, or a project operating within a programme environment) and whether the approach aligns with the principles of PRINCE2.

Review Questions

The remainder of this chapter contains mock exam questions, first for the Foundation exam and then for the Practitioner exam.

Foundation Exam Questions

1. Which product is used at the end of the project to assess how the project performed?
   A. Project brief
   B. Project initiation documentation
   C. Project product description
   D. Project mandate

2. Which of the following is a purpose of the initiating a project process?
   A. To answer the question, "Do we have a viable and worthwhile project?"
   B. To prevent poorly conceived projects from being initiated
   C. To make key decisions in and exercise overall control over the project
   D. To enable the commissioning organization to understand the work that needs to be done to deliver the project's products

3. Which of the following might be used by the commissioning organization to provide information for the project mandate?
   (1) A feasibility study (2) A request for proposal
   (3) A project brief (4) A project initiation documentation
   A. 1 and 2
   B. 2 and 3
   C. 3 and 4
   D. 1 and 4

4. Which of the following are objectives of the initiating a project process?
   (1) To ensure that there is common understanding of how the quality required will be achieved
   (2) To identify who needs information, in what format, and at what time
   (3) To ensure that all the necessary authorities exist for initiating the project
   (4) To plan the work required for project initiation
   A. 1 and 2
   B. 2 and 3
   C. 3 and 4
   D. 1 and 4

5. Which process provides information that the project board uses when deciding whether to initiate the project?
   A. Starting up a project
   B. Directing a project
   C. Initiating a project
   D. Managing a stage boundary

6. Which of the following is a purpose of the starting up a project process?
   A. To establish solid foundations for the delivery of the project
   B. To assign and monitor work packages
   C. To enable the project board to be accountable for the project's success
   D. To resource and allocate key roles and responsibilities

7. Which of the following is an objective of the starting up a project process?
   A. To plan the management activities needed to ensure that the project outcomes are achieved
   B. To describe how to tailor the commissioning organization's project management method
   C. To create a business justification for the initiation of the project
   D. To provide management direction and control throughout the project

8. Which process ensures that the project remains aligned to the commissioning organization's strategy?
   A. Starting up a project
   B. Directing a project
   C. Initiating a project
   D. Controlling a stage

9. Which process provides the base information needed to make a rational decision about commissioning a project?
   A. Directing a project
   B. Starting up a project
   C. Initiating a project
   D. Managing a stage boundary

10. Which of the following is an objective of the starting up a project process?
    A. To evaluate the various ways the project can be delivered
    B. To decide whether to appoint a change authority
    C. To ensure that there is common understanding of how the quality required will be achieved
    D. To prepare a plan to show how the achievement of the project's benefits will be measured

Practitioner Exam Questions

The following Practitioner questions are divided into two sections by question type and are based on the Practitioner exam scenario in Appendix B.

Section 1: Matching Questions

Column 1 in the following table describes five actions that take place during the starting up a project process for the Website Project, and Column 2 lists the six PRINCE2 themes. For each action (1–5), identify the theme (A–E) that it is carrying out. Choose only one theme for each action. Each theme can be used once, more than once, or not at all.

Column 1	Column 2
1. The project manager discusses the responsibilities of project support with the personal assistant to the chief executive	A. Business case
2. The project manager records in the daily log a concern from the chief executive that Quality Furniture's lack of experience in online sales may lead them to choose a poor website supplier which would lead to an impact in the quality of the final product.	B. Organization
3. The project manager is working with the project management team to understand the time required and resources needed in order to create the project initiation documentation.	C. Quality
4. The executive is working with the marketing team to forecast the likely online sales from the new website.	D. Risk
5. The executive is recording that the reason for the project is that Quality Furniture is missing a sales opportunity due to the poor design of the current website.	E. Plans
	F. Progress

Exam Spotlight

Remember that during the Practitioner exam, you are allowed to refer to the official PRINCE2 manual (*Managing Successful Projects with PRINCE2*). This is a great help. One of the key differences between passing and failing the Practitioner exam is knowing how to use the PRINCE2 manual during the exam. Some exam questions rely on your ability to find specific pieces of information quickly from the manual.

The topics in this chapter mainly revolve around the starting up a project and initiating a project processes. All the process chapters in the PRINCE2 manual are set out in the same way: The first two pages discuss the purpose, objectives, and context of the process; and then the body of each process chapter looks at the activities that take place within that particular process. Some Practitioner exam questions may test you on quite obscure facts about a process's activity. The key to getting these questions correct is to understand which activity the question is testing you on. For example, if a question asks about recruiting the project management team during the starting up a project process, you are most likely being tested on the design and appoint the project management team activity. Look carefully at the relevant pages for that activity. Do any of the bullet points help you? Does the activity's table of responsibilities give you a clue about who might be creating a management product mentioned in the question? Maybe the activity's flow diagram helps?

At the end of each process chapter in the PRINCE2 manual is a section on how to tailor the process. If you come across a question about how to tailor the process to a programme environment or a commercial supplier environment, for example, the information in that section of the manual might help.

If you are tested on a management product related to a process, the project brief, or the project initiation documentation, the best place to look for this information is Appendix A.

If you are tested on a process's roles and responsibilities, you should not only refer to each activity's table of responsibilities, but you might also find useful reference material in Appendix C.

Section 2: Classic Multiple-Choice Questions

1. The project manager is preparing the project brief. Because Quality Furniture has not done an e-commerce project before, the marketing manager has asked the project manager to arrange a workshop to capture useful experience. He has suggested inviting a range of people, including some external consultants. The project manager has scheduled the meeting but invited only Quality Furniture personnel, because he felt it was too early in the project to involve external resources. Is this appropriate, and why or why not?
    A. Yes, because the aim of the starting up a project process is to do the minimum necessary in order to decide whether to initiate the project.
    B. Yes, because running a workshop is one way to capture previous lessons.
    C. No, because if an organization has little experience in the type of project, it may be helpful to ask people external to the organization for their experience.
    D. No, because the marketing manager should schedule the workshop.

2. The project is in the initiation stage. The project manager has noticed that a number of issues recorded in the daily log during the starting up a project process should be treated formally. He has transferred these issues to the issue register. Is this appropriate, and why or why not?
    A. Yes, because formal issues recorded in the daily log during the starting up a project process should be transferred to the issue register during the initiation stage.
    B. Yes, because formal issues should be recorded in both the daily log and the issue register.
    C. No, because formal issues should be recorded in the daily log with a corresponding issue report.
    D. No, because issues that need to be treated formally should be escalated to the project board using an exception report.

3. The project is part of a programme that includes a range of marketing projects. The programme manager has prescribed a risk management approach for the website project. The project manager believes it is his responsibility to create the project's approaches and has escalated this concern to the executive. Is this appropriate, and why or why not?
    A. Yes, because the project manager is responsible for creating the project initiation documentation.
    B. Yes, because concerns about the interface between the project and the programme should be resolved by the executive.
    C. No, because if a project is part of a programme, the programme team might create some parts of the project initiation documentation.
    D. No, because if a project is part of a programme, there is no need for the project initiation documentation, as this will exist at the programme level.

Chapter

3

Organization Theme

PRINCE2 Foundation Exam Objectives Covered in This Chapter:

☑ **Explain the purpose of:**
- The organization theme
- Key management products:
  - Communication management approach

☑ **Describe what PRINCE2 requires as a minimum for applying the organization theme**

☑ **Describe the roles and responsibilities of:**
- Project board
- Executive
- Senior user
- Senior supplier
- Project assurance
- Change authority
- Project manager
- Team manager
- Project support
- Including:
  - Which roles can be combined

☑ **Explain key concepts related to organization:**
- Stakeholder
- The three project interests and how they are represented within the four levels of management

PRINCE2 Practitioner Exam Objectives Covered in This Chapter:

☑ **Apply the PRINCE2 requirements for the organization theme, demonstrating an understanding of:**
- Key management product:
  - Communication management approach
- The recommended roles and responsibilities within the theme
- The recommended project management team structure

☑ **Assess whether an approach to applying the organization theme is effective and fit for purpose, taking into consideration: the context, the PRINCE2 principles, and the purpose and requirements of the organization theme**

In this chapter, you learn who gets involved in a PRINCE2 project and which roles and responsibilities they might be given. PRINCE2 calls the information described in this chapter the organization theme. PRINCE2 recommends a project management team structure that ensures all the relevant levels of management are involved. It also ensures a broad range of stakeholder interests are represented. According to the official PRINCE2 manual (Managing Successful Projects with PRINCE2), the purpose of the organization theme is to establish the project's structure of accountability and responsibilities.

This chapter takes you through each of the PRINCE2 roles and shows what their responsibilities are throughout the project (and sometimes pre- and post-project). You learn about the management products that are important for organizing people, such as the communication management approach. As usual, this chapter describes a number of case studies to illustrate how all this works in practice and gives you plenty of example exam questions.

Common Project Organizational Challenges

What are the challenges when it comes to organizing people on projects? First, losing contact with senior stakeholders (those who have an interest in the project) is one of the prime reasons projects fail. For example, often a senior manager who funds the project gets involved only at the beginning, and then expects the project manager to be totally responsible for the project. The project manager, however, is nearly always at a fairly low or middle level of the organization; she won't have enough authority to overcome all the challenges of the project. At various times, she needs the help of senior managers.

Another reason projects need continual involvement of senior managers is that they operate in a dynamic environment, and there will be times when the original direction needs to be refocused. PRINCE2 deals with both of these challenges by describing roles for senior managers in the project team and ensuring their involvement at key points.

Another challenge is finding a way to involve the ultimate users of the project's products. Sometimes, these people are involved only at the outset of a project, when they are asked what they want, and then at the end, when they are shown the product. Of course, in the interim, their requirements might have changed. Another challenge here is that people often don't understand exactly what they want until they start to see some initial work that shows them what is possible. To mitigate both of these challenges, PRINCE2 sets out specific roles for the users of the products and gets them involved in the important decisions throughout the project.

Many projects suffer from unrealistic schedules. PRINCE2 reduces this problem by giving roles to those with authority over the resources that deliver the project's products. They must agree to the project's plans.

Even in small projects, the day-to-day coordination of all the different types of work and people involved can be complicated. PRINCE2 helps this situation by appointing one key person, the project manager, to be responsible for this task. In difficult, time-consuming projects, however, PRINCE2 provides another role, project support, to help the project manager.

The Three Project Interests

Many people may have an interest in the project's outcome. These people, called *stakeholders*, might support or oppose the project for all sorts of reasons. PRINCE2 groups some of these stakeholders into three categories. First are those who are looking at the project from a business point of view, thinking about whether the project gives good value for money or, in other words, a good return given the money invested. Next are those who will be using the project's products and services on an ongoing basis after the project has finished. Finally, there are those who will be supplying resources and people to create the project's products. PRINCE2 ensures these three perspectives on the project are represented in the project's decisional body, the project board. Figure 3.1 shows these three interests.

Figure 3.1: The three project interests

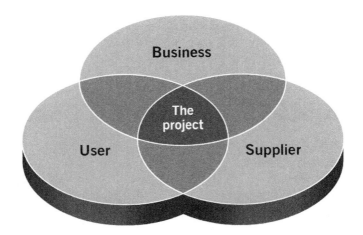

The Business Interest

The executive represents the business interest on the project and sits on the project board. Unlike the senior supplier and the senior user roles, only one person can carry out the executive role. The executive is focused on whether the project is providing good value for the money invested, whether the products of the project meet a business need that justifies the investment in the project, and whether an adequate return on the project's investment will be achieved. PRINCE2 sees this as the primary interest, outranking the needs of the users and the suppliers. As such, the executive is the ultimate level of authority within the project board. However, the executive should take into account the views of the user and supplier interests (represented on the project board by the senior user and senior supplier) when making decisions.

For example, in a project to build a new hotel, the executive should be thinking about such things as whether the cost of the hotel represents good value compared to other hotels that have been built of an equivalent standard and whether the forecast sales will pay back the initial investment in a reasonable amount of time. Rather than focusing on the quality of the hotel for its own sake, the executive should be thinking about whether the hotel will be capable of achieving the estimated returns.

The User Interest

This perspective is involved with using the products and services the project creates. The user interest is represented by the senior user role on the project board. This stakeholder category can include a number of subcategories, such as the following:

- Those who will use the products and services directly
- Those who might use the products and services as a tool to create value for themselves or their organizations
- Those who might maintain and support the products in their operational use
- Those who will be impacted by the project's products

As such, several people might carry out the senior user role.

Let me give you an example. Suppose a project's aim is to create a website for a company. The website will sell the company's products. Who has a user interest in this initiative? First, there are the company's clients, who will go onto the website and buy products. The company might have hundreds or even thousands of clients. They can't all take on senior user roles. Instead, the project might represent them using a market research company that, by doing research, understands these people's requirements.

Another type of user interest will be those who will use the website as a tool to sell products. The company's marketing director could represent this perspective. In addition, the company's IT department may support the website in operational use, so the IT director could also become as senior user. Finally, maybe the company occasionally uses a promotions agency to run marketing campaigns. The agency will be impacted by the website, as they need to consider how any future campaigns would need to be adapted to take account of it, so a senior consultant from the agency may also become a senior user.

All these various perspectives have one thing in common: Users are interested in specifying the project's products and services. They also want to get involved in validating the products and services when they are finished.

The Supplier Interest

The supplier interest is the final perspective on the project. Suppliers create the project's products and services by providing resources and the necessary skills. The senior supplier role represents this interest on the project board. A number of people might take on the senior supplier role. This is because there could be several groups of people creating different types of products and services. All these groups should be represented on the project board. The senior suppliers are senior people from these groups who can provide supplier resources to the project. The suppliers may be internal to the organization running the project or an external third party.

For example, in a project to build a new hotel for a leisure company, there might be a building firm doing the construction work. The building firm's operations manager could assume a senior supplier role. Also, if the leisure company's PR department is doing work to promote the hotel, the head of PR could also take on a senior supplier role.

The supplier perspective is focused on ensuring that the products meet the quality standards set by the project and that the project's targets—in terms of time, cost, and scope—are feasible.

Achieving Consensus Between the Project Interests

The three project interests initially will probably not agree. For example, the user's requests for product features might not represent value for money as far as the business is concerned. The business's idea of a reasonable project cost might be well below what the suppliers are quoting. It is the role of the project board to come to an agreement on these differing and sometimes inconsistent points of view when they are making decisions about the project. But remember, the executive has the ultimate authority. When conflict exists between the three interests, the business perspective has the final word.

The Four Levels of Management

In any PRINCE2 project, there are four distinct levels of management, as shown in Figure 3.2. As you go up the levels, the authority of the managers increases.

Figure 3.2: The four levels of management

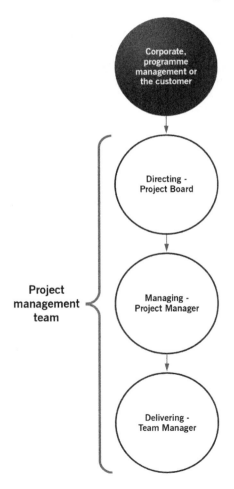

Corporate, Programme Management, or the Customer

The corporate, programme management, or the customer level, as the name suggests, could represent one of three types of people. First, they could represent the corporate level of the organization commissioning the project. For example, the board of directors of an organization might commission a website project to sell their products online. Another example would be if within a large corporation, the senior managers in a particular country commission a project to move their territory offices. With larger projects, you would expect these people to come from higher up the organization.

When a project is within a programme (a collection of projects with a coherent aim), then the corporate, programme management, or the customer level would be the programme's main decision-making body, such as a programme board.

Finally, there might be a situation whereby one company (the customer) commissions another company (the supplier) to carry out some work. For example, a company outsources a promotional campaign to a PR agency. In this case, the corporate, programme management, or the customer level would be the customer commissioning the work.

Corporate, programme management, or the customer is the top level of management in a PRINCE2 project. They instigate the project by creating the project mandate. This management product is the first document to describe the project. Its details may be very high-level, and it is up to the project board and the project manager to refine them. However, in some instances, particularly when the project is part of a programme, the project mandate may be quite detailed. This is because a programme should be clear on the definition of upcoming projects in order to coordinate them. After corporate, programme management, or the customer has created the project mandate, they appoint the executive. From that point on, the executive is responsible for taking the project forward. Corporate, programme management, or the customer set certain boundaries that the executive (and, once the executive has appointed the senior users and senior suppliers, the whole project board as well) needs to keep the project within. PRINCE2 calls these boundaries *project tolerances*. These tolerances are mainly leeway around the project's forecast budget and delivery time. If the executive or the whole project board think the project tolerances will be breached, they no longer have authority to continue with the project and must escalate the situation back up to corporate, programme management, or the customer. (You learn more about tolerances in Chapter 9, "Progress Theme.")

Once corporate, programme management, or the customer has appointed the executive, they become involved with the project only if the project tolerances are forecast to be breached. The project board will send regular notifications to corporate, programme management, or the customer about significant project events, such as the decision to move on to the next major part of the project (stage). Corporate, programme management, or the customer may also choose to receive regular progress reports from the project manager.

Figure 3.3 shows the PRINCE2 project management team structure. One important thing to note about this diagram is that the project management team includes the project board, the project manager, and the team manager levels, but not the corporate, programme management, or the customer level. Corporate, programme management, or the customer is separate from the project management team.

Figure 3.3: PRINCE2 project management structure

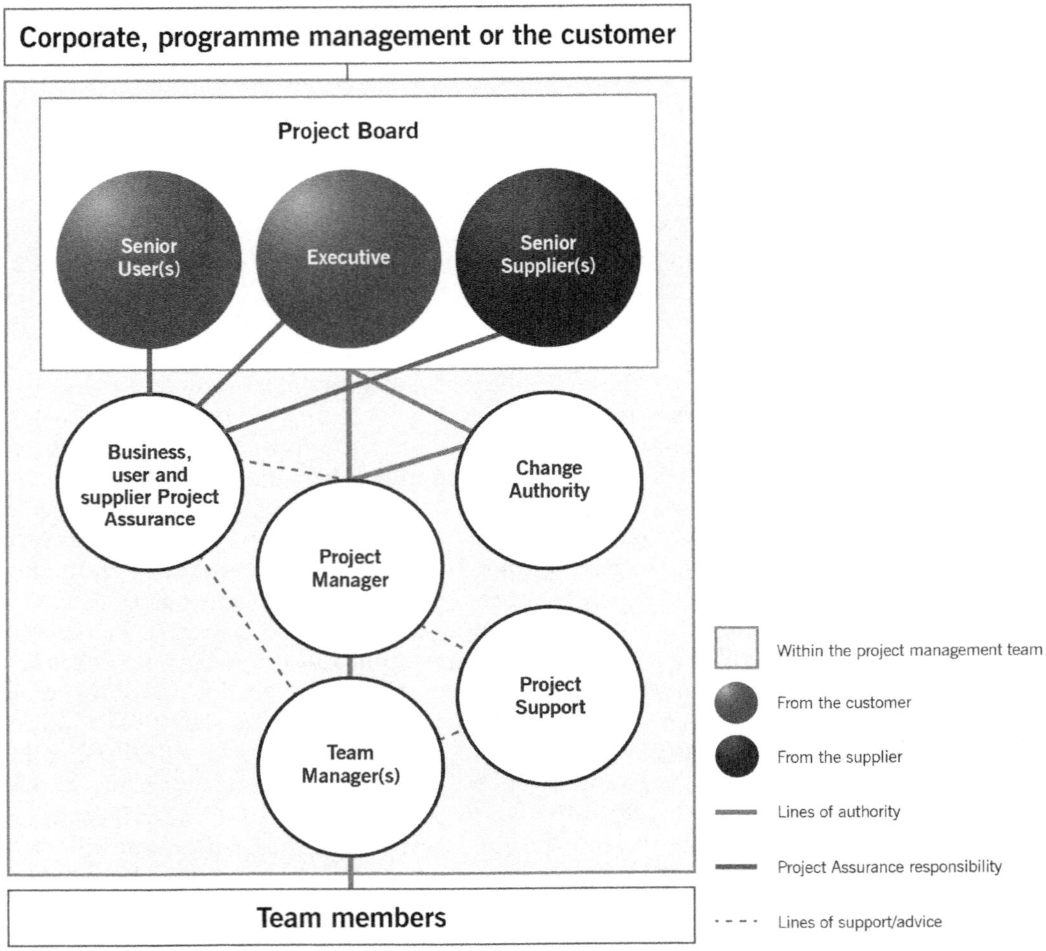

Directing

The directing level is the responsibility of the project board. They are responsible for the project within the constraints (such as project tolerances) given them by corporate, programme management, or the customer. The board makes the important project decisions, such as authorizing the beginning of the project, the beginning of each stage, and finally, the end of the project. The project board delegates the day-to-day management of the project to the project manager by authorizing the project manager to manage a stage of the project on their behalf within predefined limits or tolerances. These stage tolerances are usually defined in terms of costs or timescales. For example, the project board might say to the project manager: "You have

3 months and $100,000 to deliver the next part of the project. If you forecast that you will breach these targets by more than 10 percent, please refer to us for a decision." (For a full discussion on tolerances, see Chapter 9.)

In Figure 3.3, you can see where the project board sits in the project management team structure. You can also see that the project board is made up of three roles: the executive, the senior user, and the senior supplier.

Managing

The project manager is responsible for managing the project on a day-to-day basis within the tolerances given her by the project board. She focuses on ensuring that the project creates the required specialist products by planning, delegating work to the specialist teams, and monitoring all the separate activities that need to be done. The project manager delegates work to the teams by creating work packages. A *work package* is a management product that tells the teams what work they need to do, details such as time and cost targets, and how to report progress to the project manager. (You learn more about work packages in Chapter 9.) The project manager also regularly updates the project management team and stakeholders outside the project management team on the progress of the project.

Just as corporate, programme management, or the customer sets project tolerances for the project board and the project board sets stage tolerances for the project manager, the project manager, when delegating work to the teams, sets work package tolerances. (Again, you learn more about tolerances in Chapter 9.)

Only one project manager should be assigned to each project. If more than one project manager were assigned, there would be a risk that work on the project would lack coordination.

Delivering

In PRINCE2, the team managers are responsible for the delivering level. They manage the teams creating the project's specialist products. Remember that there are two types of products in PRINCE2: *management products* (the PRINCE2 documents, such as the risk register and the project plans) and *specialist products* (the deliverables for the project, such as websites, hotel swimming pools, or submarines). The specialist products vary depending on the type of project, whereas the management products do not. So it is mainly specialist products that are created at this bottom delivering level. (I say mainly because some management products are created at this level, such as the team's progress report, called a *checkpoint report*.)

In some circumstances, such as a small project, there may be no need for separate people to take on the team manager role. In this case, the project manager will manage the teams directly. When there are team managers, the project manager delegates work to them, who, in turn, delegate work to their teams.

The Project Management Team

The PRINCE2 project management team consists of a variety of roles to ensure that a broad perspective is represented when making key project decisions and that the right collection of skill is available to direct, manage, and deliver the project. This section describes the responsibilities of all the PRINCE2 roles.

The Project Board

The project board consists of three main roles: the executive, the senior users, and the senior suppliers. Each of these roles represents potentially conflicting perspectives on the project: the business, the users, and the suppliers, respectively. However, they need to come together and reach consensus to ensure that the project is directed effectively and that important project decisions are made in a timely, informed way. The project board as a whole is accountable for the success or failure of the project, although the key accountability rests with the executive who leads the project board.

The Executive

As stated earlier, in the "The Business Interest" section, the executive role represents the business interest in the project. The executive is focused on whether the project is delivering value for money, whether the products that are being created are capable of delivering the forecast benefits and will create an adequate return on the project's investment.

The executive is ultimately responsible for the project. Only one person should assume this role so that there will be clear accountability and responsibility for the project. The executive is also the chief decision-maker. She makes decisions supported by the other members of the project board, the senior users, and the senior suppliers, but ultimately she has the final say.

The executive is also responsible for securing the funding for the project.

The Senior Users

The senior users are responsible for representing those who will ultimately use the project's products. As discussed earlier, in the "The User Interest" section, there could be a number of different types of "users." PRINCE2 defines four types of senior users. Here is a brief description of each user type, along with examples relating to a project to build a new hotel for a leisure company:

- Users who will directly use the project's products (such as the people who might stay in the hotel)
- Users who might maintain or support the products when they go into their operational life (such as the people who might maintain the hotel's heating system or the booking software)
- Users for whom the project will achieve an objective or a benefit (such as the marketing director of the leisure company, who will use the hotel to increase her sales figures)
- People who will be impacted by the hotel (such as a local government or neighborhood group)

The senior users should be in a position to have authority over the people who will be using the products. They must ensure that these people are available to define the characteristics and requirements of the products and then to review the products once they've been built to see whether they meet these requirements.

In addition, the senior users have an important role in connection with the business case. They are responsible for forecasting the project's benefits and then demonstrating that those benefits have occurred. Many benefits might not occur until after the project has finished. For example, the hotel won't start selling rooms until after it has been built. As such, fulfilling the senior user role is likely to involve a commitment beyond the life of the project.

Why should the senior users be involved with forecasting and then demonstrating that benefits have occurred? Let me give you an example. In the hotel project, the marketing director is a senior user. She will use the hotel as a tool to create benefits for the leisure company, such as room sales. Putting the project to one side for a moment, as a marketing director, this individual is involved in projecting and tracking sales for the leisure company. Thus, she is in an ideal position to do this for the project as well.

Identifying Senior Users in a Pharmaceutical Project

My consultancy company recently worked on a project to build a pharmaceutical company's website. The site would provide medical information on a range of drugs and serve as a reference for doctors and nurses.

In this project, there were numerous types of "users" of the website. First, there were the doctors and nurses, and, of course, thousands of health-care practitioners. How did we represent them on our project board? We used a market research company, which carried out a range of focus groups with doctors to understand their requirements. A senior consultant from this company was assigned a senior user role.

The pharmaceutical company's marketing department would use the website to propagate information on the drugs, which might ultimately lead to more drugs being prescribed. The website was to roll out across Europe, and within each country, there was a separate marketing department with a separate brand manager in charge of their territory. A collection of brand managers in key countries took on another set of senior user roles. Because the website didn't launch in all the countries at the same time, the brand manager for the next territory to launch would be involved in the project board just for his part of the project.

In the pharmaceutical company was a department called Medical Information. Their responsibility was to build a database of information on all the company's drugs and distribute it to doctors and nurses. They would use the website as a tool to carry out this objective, so they were interested in the editing and storage features of the web system. A senior person from this department also took on a senior user role.

Finally, there was the pharmaceutical company's IT department. They wouldn't be building the website, because this task was outsourced to a third-party supplier, but they would be involved in maintaining the site. Their focus was on how easy the website was to maintain and operate once it had been built. The pharmaceutical company's IT director also became a senior user.

In the end, our project board had six people who represented all these perspectives on using the website.

The Senior Suppliers

The senior suppliers represent those who will be delivering the project's specialist products. In some projects, the word "delivering" might not be appropriate. The project's products might be procured, facilitated, written, or implemented, depending on the type of specialist products the project will create. As you learned in the section "The Supplier Interest," the senior suppliers have authority over the resources used to create the project's products. They are able to commit and authorize the supplier resources. They could be people from the organization that has commissioned the project or from external third-party organizations.

One of the common challenges for the project manager is that they often have to delegate work to teams over whom they have no authority. Senior suppliers are useful for overcoming this problem. For example, what does the project manager of a construction project do if the builders are working ineffectively? In a PRINCE2 project, she could escalate this situation to the head of the building company who has taken on a senior supplier role. This person is the boss of the builders, so she should be in a position to manage her workers.

There could be problems sharing confidential information if the senior suppliers are from organizations external to the commissioning organization. Would the third-party supplier want to share with the project board how much profit she is making? I doubt it! In this case, there might be two types of project meetings: meetings that are held to discuss confidential information (which take place in the separate customer and supplier organizations) and meetings that are attended by all those involved in the project. It can be quite challenging to have all external suppliers represented on the project board, but the important decisions in the project must take account of their views. They can point out unreasonable deadlines or budgets.

Project Assurance

Project assurance is a role that checks and monitors that the project is being run correctly and is capable of delivering the project's objectives in terms of time, cost, quality, scope, risks, and benefits. Each of the project board roles is responsible for a project assurance role that aligns to their area of interest. So the executive, senior users, and senior suppliers are responsible for business, user, and supplier assurance, respectively.

What does this checking and monitoring entail? A project assurance role could involve a range of activities, such as meeting with the project manager and team managers and discussing their activities, auditing project documents, or observing project meetings and quality reviews.

Who assumes the project assurance roles? If they have enough time, the project board members might choose to do so themselves. Otherwise, they might delegate the day-to-day assurance activities to other people. The project board will still be accountable for the project assurance actions aligned to their area of interest, even if they delegate them to separate individuals.

The *business assurance* role checks that the project is providing value for money and that the project's products are capable of delivering the benefits forecast in the business case. They are interested in things such as the amount of money being spent, how realistic the project's business case is, and whether risks are being managed effectively.

The *user assurance* role checks that the project is creating products that will be fit for their ultimate purpose. They are interested in whether all the user perspectives were represented when the products were specified, whether the requirements for the products have been captured in the project documentation, whether suppliers are using the correct specifications to carry out their product-creation work, and whether there is an effective user acceptance process for signing off the products when they are finished.

The *supplier assurance* role checks the project from a delivery perspective. They look at whether the supplier resources are capable of delivering the project on time and on budget. They consider the technical feasibility of the products. If the supplier is external to the organization that commissioned the project, there could actually be two perspectives on supplier assurance: the commissioning organization, which will want to check how the external organization is carrying out their work, and the external organization, which will want to check their own work.

It is important that project assurance is independent of the project manager, project support, team managers, and the teams, because project assurance will be checking these other roles during reviews of the project. If, for example, someone were given both the project assurance and the project manager roles, there would be a conflict of interest. However, as part of their role, project assurance will be expected to provide advice and guidance to the project manager, project support, team managers, and the teams.

Structuring the Project Board
There are no exact rules for how many people should be on the project board. In small projects, some of the roles might be combined. For example, if the same people are paying for and using the project's products, one person might take on the roles of executive and senior user. So, there might be as few as two people on the project board: one person shares the executive and the senior user roles, and the other person is the senior supplier. In larger projects, this number will increase, although if there are too many people, it might become more difficult to get agreement on decisions. If you have a large number of users and suppliers, it might be better to create separate *user groups* and *supplier groups*, each of which sends representatives to project board meetings.

Allocating the Right People to the Project Board
In PRINCE2, an effective project board displays four key characteristics: authority, credibility, an ability to delegate, and availability. Let's look at each of these in turn.

Without the right level of authority, the project board will be unable to drive the project forward. Having to constantly refer to people above them in their organizations in order to make decisions can cause unnecessary delay to the project. Without the right level of authority, the project board will not be able to provide resources and money to the project and sort out potential conflicts. However, if the people on the project board are too high up within their organizations, the project might not be important enough for them to get involved.

Credibility is closely linked to authority. Without credibility, the people on the project board may not be able to influence others to provide the resources and budgets necessary to achieve the project's objectives.

The ability to delegate is another important characteristic of an effective project board member. Project board members rarely have the right expertise to make management- and delivery-level decisions. Unfortunately, if the project board *does* involve themselves too heavily in the day-to-day management and delivery of the project, team members tend to follow their bad advice out of respect for their level in the organization. It is usually far better if project board members concern themselves with strategic project decisions and leave the management and delivery to those who have the relevant skills.

Finally, project board members must be available for the project. They do not need to get involved on a day-to-day basis, but only when the key decisions need to be made. If they are busy on other work, then the project will likely stall while it waits for a key authorization.

In addition to these four PRINCE2 characteristics, remember that project board members must be looking at the project from the correct perspective. The executive must keep track of whether the project is delivering value for the money invested in it; the senior user must keep track of whether the project is delivering products that are fit for their purpose; and the senior supplier must ensure that the supplier resources are capable of delivering products of the required quality.

Change Authority

From time to time, someone might ask for a change to one of the project's products. In the hotel project discussed previously, the marketing director of the leisure company might ask for an upgrade to the room design. Or the construction manager might want to change the materials used to build the hotel's foundation because she realizes the original materials won't meet safety standards. PRINCE2 calls these *requests for change*.

The project board is the usual authorization body for requests for change. However, on a project where there may be many requests for change, the project board can delegate part of this authority to a group called the *change authority*. This could also be useful when the project board does not have the necessary technical skills to fully understand the implications of a proposed request for change or the time available to fully analyze all the changes. The change authority is allowed to authorize changes within certain limits. It is up to the project board to specify these limits. Examples of such limits might be that the change authority can authorize changes up to an agreed cost or changes that don't impact the project plans by more than a certain number of days.

The project manager might also be given some authority to authorize changes. For example, a project might have a number of levels of change authority: The project board authorizes large changes; the change authority authorizes medium-sized changes; and the project manager authorizes smaller changes. Also, when faced with a large requested change to the project's products or scope, the project board might escalate the decision to implement the change to the corporate, programme management, or the customer. The people with project assurance responsibilities may also have change authority responsibilities.

The change authority and requests for change are discussed in more detail in Chapter 8, "Change Theme."

The Project Manager

The project manager manages the project on a day-to-day basis on behalf of the project board. She is given authority by the project board to run a part of the project, referred to as a *stage* in PRINCE2, at any one time. (For a full discussion of PRINCE2 stages, see Chapter 5, "Plans Theme.") After each management stage, the project manager must ask the project board for authority to move on to the next stage. As previously mentioned, to avoid problems with coordination of tasks, there should be only one project manager per project.

The project manager will carry out the following roles:

- Delegate work to the teams using *work packages*. Work Packages are a management product that tells the team what work they need to do.
- Deal with issue and change control management. This might mean escalating forecast breaches of stage tolerances to the project board. (This is covered in more detail in Chapter 9.)
- Deal with reporting. The project manager receives progress reports, called *checkpoint reports*, from the teams. The project manager also sends progress reports, called *highlight reports*, to the project board.
- Track the status of the products being created, the project costs, the schedule, and the scope of the project.

- Ensure that the project is being managed in line with the risk management approach (described in Chapter 7, "Risk Theme"), the quality management approach (described in Chapter 6, "Quality Theme"), the change management approach (described in Chapter 8, "Change Theme"), and the communication management approach (described later in this chapter).

The project manager will manage any team that does not have a team manager. If no one is available to carry out the project support role, the project manager will have to do this as well.

Project Support

The project support role is the responsibility of the project manager. The project manager can delegate the work of project support to a separate person or people. If no one is available to delegate project support activities to, the project manager will need to carry them out herself.

The project support role supports the project manager and the team manager(s) in their day-to-day management work. Their responsibilities can consist of the following:

- Providing administration services, including maintaining the project's logs and registers
- Providing guidance on the use of project management or change management tools
- Providing specialist management functions, such as planning or risk management
- Maintaining the change management procedure

In some organizations, project support will be supplied by a project office, which provides support for all the organization's projects.

Team Manager

Sometimes the project manager will manage a team directly, and sometimes a separate person will have the team manager role. For example, a team may be small enough for the project manager to manage it herself. However, for a large team, it might not be feasible for the project manager to delegate work to each individual, so the project management team might decide to assign a separate person as the team manager. Team managers might be required for a variety of reasons. If the team were in another town or even another country from the project manager, it might make sense to have a team manager at the same location as the rest of the team. Another reason is that the project manager might not fully understand the technical nature of the team's work. In such cases, it is useful to have an expert in that specialist area as a team manager.

The team manager role is responsible for the following activities:

- Accepting work on behalf of the team via a work package from the project manager. A work package is a management product that tells the team what is expected of them.
- Planning, delegating, monitoring, and controlling the team's work.
- Reporting to the project manager on a regular basis (as defined in the work package) by creating checkpoint reports. A checkpoint report is a report on the progress of the team's work.
- Escalating any forecast breach of work package tolerances to the project manager. (You learn more about tolerances in Chapter 9.)

If the team comes from a separate organization, in addition to reporting to the project manager within the project, the team might also report to their boss within their own organization. It might be a good idea for this boss to become a senior supplier, because this might help to resolve any potential conflicts of interest between the project manager and the team's manager in their own company or any undermining of the project manager's authority within the team.

Team Managers and Seniority

Although team managers are below the project manager in the PRINCE2 organizational structure, they may be more senior than the project manager. For example, a highly skilled engineer may be leading a team of specialists within the project. Alternatively, their job title within their organization might be project manager, but within the context of the project they are carrying out the team manager role.

I worked on a project in which I allocated someone a team manager role. I had discussed the responsibilities of the role with him but neglected to tell him the role was called team manager. Unbeknown to me, he had recently been promoted within the organization, so his job role within the company had been changed from team manager to project manager.

He was visibly upset later, when he came to talk to me. He told me that I had circulated the project initiation documentation and labeled him as a team manager and put him below a project manager who was his junior in the company. I had to explain to him that even though the project manager was his junior, that person was simply coordinating all the work packages of the project, whereas we needed him to play the team manager role, as his work package was particularly complex.

Other Stakeholders

A *stakeholder* is any individual, group, or organization that can affect, be affected by, or perceive itself to be affected by, a project. Stakeholders can be advocates for the project or against the project. All the people who are allocated roles on the project management team are stakeholders, but there may be many other people outside the team who are stakeholders as well. At the beginning of the project, the project manager will work with the other members of the project management team to identify all the project stakeholders and determine how they would like to be updated on the project. The project manager will also determine what information the project needs from the stakeholders. The output of this work is detailed in the communication management approach. (You learn more about the communication management approach in the following section of this chapter.)

Not all the stakeholders will agree with the project. It is still important for the project manager to identify those who might not support the initiative so that the project management team can consider how to deal with them.

Here are some examples of people who might be stakeholders in the project to build a new hotel for a leisure company:

- A local government agency where the hotel will be sited
- The trade union representative of the builders of the hotel
- The quality assurance manager for the leisure company
- The local tourism office in the city where the hotel will be built
- The leisure company's legal department

Communication Management Approach

The communication management approach describes how the project management team and the external stakeholders will communicate with each other. In any project, effective communication is vital between all the various parties involved or with an interest in the project. Sitting down at the beginning of the project and thinking about how communication will take place, and then regularly checking that this approach is followed, helps ensure that everyone has information relevant to them in a timely manner.

The project manager is responsible for creating the communication management approach in the initiating a project process. She will liaise with the project board members and external stakeholders to ensure that the approach will meet all their informational needs. The project manager should review the approach at each stage boundary. This is particularly important if new people will be involved in the next stage to make sure their informational needs will be meet. When planning the final stage of the project, the project manager should ensure that anyone who wants to be advised that the project is closing is included in the approach.

Contents

I'll now go through the different sections of the communication management approach and give you some examples of what they might contain in the project to build a new hotel for a leisure company.

Exam Spotlight

The Practitioner exam will test you on where a particular piece of information should be placed in a management product. For example, you might be given a sentence such as "Project support to file all external communication," and be asked under which heading belongs. As you learn later in this chapter, this would belong in the roles and responsibilities heading.

However, consider this sentence: "The personal assistant to the managing director will chair a daily conference call among the project team to discuss project progress." This piece of information describes how communication will be done on the project, so it should go into the communication management approach, but in which section? The sentence contains a procedure (carry out project progress updates), a schedule (daily), a technique (conference call), and a responsibility (personal assistant to chair the meetings). If we were running a real project, the answer would be it doesn't really matter. In reality, the communication management approach might not be subdivided so neatly into the different sections. The project manager must still make sure that all the types of information described by the section headings are in the document, but how the document is formatted is not so important.

The Practitioner exam will contain artificial sentences that really can belong under only one particular heading. So you shouldn't be tested on a sentence similar to the previous example. Instead, the exam might include an artificial sentence such as this: "Conference calls conducted throughout the project must use the company's standard video conferencing platform." This sentence can belong only in the tools and techniques section.

Introduction

The introduction states the purpose, objectives, and scope of the document and identifies who is responsible for the approach. For example, the introduction for the hotel project might say the following:

This document outlines how the project to build a new hotel in Shanghai will ensure that all stakeholders in the project are informed of all relevant project information. The executive of this project, the Asian business development manager, is responsible for effective communication.

Communication Procedure

This section contains any communication methods to be used during the project. The organization running the project may have their own communication standards that the project may or may not follow, so any variance to these standard approaches should be mentioned in this section. This might also be the case when the project is running within a programme or for a certain customer. The best way of thinking about this is that this section will contain "things to do" regarding communication. For example, the communication procedure section for the hotel project might say the following:

All project communication issued to external parties to be checked by the communication department. A copy of all external communication to be filed in the communication folder in the project file.

Tools and Techniques

This section contains specific techniques that might be used in the steps highlighted in the communication procedure section. For example, the project might use email or Internet collaboration tools, such as Yahoo! Groups. Agile projects might use daily Scrum meetings to aid communication within the team. Here are some examples of tools and techniques entries for the hotel project:

Daily project conference calls to take place to update all teams on the project progress and issues.

Formal press releases to be issued regarding major project milestones.

Records

This section states how the project will store information on the communication that has taken place. Here's an example of a records entry for the hotel project:

Keep a log of all communication sent to external parties. The log should state whom the communication was sent to, the format of the communication, the date issued, and a description of the contents of the communication.

Reporting

This section specifies any reports that will be created to track the implementation of the communication procedure. Here's an example of a reporting entry for the hotel project:

Send a report to the project board at the end of each stage detailing all communication that has been sent from the project management team to any external third party.

Timing of Communication Activities

This section specifies when communication activities should take place. For example, the timing of communication activities section for the hotel project might include the following entry:

The communications department to carry out a performance audit on the way communication has been managed at the end of each stage.

Roles and Responsibilities

This section describes who will be responsible for the various steps set out in the communication procedure section. For example, the roles and responsibilities section for the hotel project might include the following entry:

Project support to file all external communication.

Stakeholder Analysis

This section contains a list of all parties who have been identified as having an interest in the project. These can include people who are advocates of the project and/or those who are against it. For example, the stakeholder analysis section for the hotel project might list the following stakeholders:

- Trade union representative for the building firm
- Global business development director
- Shanghai tourist board

Information Needs for Each Interested Party

This section describes the type of information that needs to be provided to the stakeholders. Stakeholders might be interested in a variety of types of information about the project, such as up-to-date progress information, information on particular project risks or issues, or statistics on how many quality checks on the project's products are passing or failing. It will also show what information the project needs from stakeholders. For example, the hotel project might include the following entry in this section:

The human resource manager for Asia to be sent details of all risks and issues related to personnel. Please send an extract from the relevant registry entry.

The Life of the Communication Management Approach

The project manager creates the communication management approach during the initiating a project process at the beginning of the project. (The initiating a project process, described in Chapter 2, "Starting a Project Successfully with PRINCE2," contains a set of steps that the project manager and the project board carry out to plan the project.)

At the end of each stage of the project, the project manager should review the communication management approach to check that it contains all the key stakeholders for the next part of the project. When the project manager is planning the end of the project, she should also review the document to check which stakeholders must be informed of the closing of the project.

Other Management Products Used by the Organization Theme

In addition to the communication management approach, the project brief and the project initiation documentation are important organization theme management products.

The Project Brief's Use in the Organization Theme

The project manager creates the project brief in the starting up a project process. Two sections are relevant to the project organization. The project management team structure section describes the various roles of the project and how they interrelate. This may be in the form of an organization chart. The role descriptions section describes the responsibilities for each role.

The Project Initiation Documentation's Use in the Organization Theme

Once the project board has authorized the project brief described in the previous section, the project manager will then create the project initiation documentation. The project manager will copy the project management team structure and the roles and responsibilities sections from the project brief into the project initiation documentation. During the initiating a project process, the project manager might have to add more detail to these sections.

The project manager also documents in the project initiation documentation whether a change authority will be set up for the project. This information will go in the change management approach.

Organization Theme Responsibilities

Thus far in this chapter, I have outlined most of the major responsibilities of the different PRINCE2 roles. The one area I haven't discussed is who appoints whom. I covered this in Chapter 2, but for those of you not reading the book in order, I will give you a summary of that information in this section.

At the beginning of the PRINCE2 process model, in the starting up a project process, corporate, programme management, or the customer will appoint the executive. Then, in turn, the executive will appoint the project manager. Then, still in the starting up a project process, the executive and the project manager will work together to design an appropriate project management team structure for this particular project. You learn more about how the structure can be tailored for different situations in the next section of this chapter.

Once the project management team structure has been created (but still in the starting up a project process), the project manager will create role descriptions, and the executive will appoint the relevant people to the roles. However, some people may not be appointed until later in the project. For example, a senior supplier or a team manager from an external contractor might be appointed in a later stage.

Tailoring the Organization Theme

The key to using PRINCE2 successfully is adapting and tailoring the method to suit the project's environment, scale, and complexity. Of all the themes, the organization theme is the most affected by a project's scale, complexity, and environment. The following sections discuss how the organization theme can be adapted to suit certain situations, which is something the Practitioner exam might test you on.

Minimum Requirements

Organizations with a less formal project management approach or that are running smaller, less-complicated projects might choose to cut back on some of the organization theme ideas. However, some minimum requirements must be followed in order for a project team to claim they are following the PRINCE2 organization theme.

At the very minimum, the project management team must outline their organizational structure containing the project roles. These roles might not necessarily be the same as the PRINCE2 roles, but they must include all the responsibilities covered in the PRINCE2 role descriptions.

Another minimum criterion is that the project management team should define their approach for communicating and engaging with the identified stakeholders of the project.

Finally, if the project management team decides to set up a change authority, they need to document the change authority's responsibilities and describe the circumstances in which the change authority would make decisions on changes, as opposed to the project board making decisions on changes.

Scaling the Organization Theme

For smaller projects, one person on the project management team might be allocated more than one PRINCE2 role. For example, one person might take on the project manager, project support, and the team manager roles. Another common combination is if the senior user and the executive come from the same organization, these two roles might be done by one person. Or the people on the project board might choose to do their own project assurance.

Some roles, however, cannot be combined. First, the executive role and the project manager role cannot be combined. PRINCE2 says it is important to keep the key decision-maker separate from the person managing the project. Second, the people performing the project assurance role cannot also perform one of the roles they might be reviewing as part of their assurance responsibilities. This means that the people performing the project manager, project support, or the team manager roles cannot also perform a project assurance role.

PRINCE2 recommends that the project management team not combine the senior user and the senior supplier roles, because there is usually a conflict of interest between the two. However, this is not a mandatory requirement, because in some circumstances, it might be a good idea to combine the two roles. For example, in an IT project, maybe the IT department is both creating the computer system (a perspective normally represented by the senior supplier) and maintaining the system in its operational life (a perspective normally represented by the senior user).

When someone performs more than one PRINCE2 role, the obvious downside is that they have more work to do. When combining roles, the project management team must ensure that the people who will be tasked with carrying out multiple roles have the time and availability to do the work successfully. The project management team should also be careful that combining roles doesn't create any unnecessary conflicts of interests.

For larger projects, it is usually more appropriate for one person to do one PRINCE2 role or for more than one person to do one role. For example, as you saw in the earlier case study in this chapter about the pharmaceutical industry, several people might be performing the senior user role, each person representing a certain type of "use" of the product. If there are a lot of users, the project management team might consider setting up a user forum, which is separate from the project board. This user forum would then send representatives to the project board meetings who would sit on the board as senior users.

The same is true of the senior supplier role: In a project with multiple suppliers, it might be appropriate to give each one a senior supplier role on the project board. Once again, if there are a lot of suppliers, the project management team might consider setting up a supplier forum, which would send representatives to the project board meeting to sit on the board as senior suppliers.

When multiple people are performing one role, the project management team needs to ensure that the limit to each person's responsibilities is absolutely clear; otherwise, important work might not be done. For example, in the pharmaceutical project described earlier in the chapter, it should be clear what the senior user from the marketing team is responsible for compared to the responsibilities of the senior user, who is representing the doctor's interests.

Some roles cannot be allocated to more than one person. First, only one person can perform the executive role. It is more difficult to make quick, effective decisions if more than one person takes on the key decision-maker role. Also, if there are two or three executives, and the project starts to go wrong, the temptation for each executive is to blame the others for the failure. So, only one person can be the executive, and that one person is completely accountable for project's success.

Second, only one person can perform the project manager role. Many years ago, I tried to ignore this rule and shared the project manager role with a colleague. I managed the project Monday through Wednesday, and he managed it Thursday and Friday. It was a disaster! We found that people would say one thing to my colleague and another to me, or I forgot to pass on some vital piece of information to my colleague or vice versa, which caused all sorts of communication and coordination challenges.

Commercial Customer/Supplier Environment

Figure 3.4 shows a PRINCE2 project management team spanning across two organizations in a commercial customer/supplier environment. You learned about this sort of environment in Chapter 1, "Overview of PRINCE2."

Figure 3.4: Organizational structure in a commercial customer/supplier environment

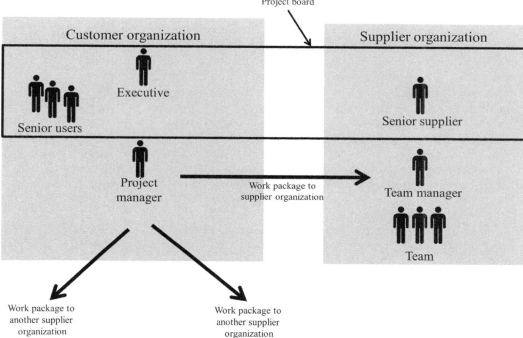

In the diagram, there is a customer organization, which might be a leisure company running a project to build a hotel. In such an example, the project's executive, the senior users, and the project manager will all work for the leisure company, and three of the project's work packages will be outsourced to other organizations. In the diagram, I have expanded the internal organizational structure of one of those suppliers to show which of their personnel will be involved in the project. This might be the organization that will provide the electricians, for example. The supplier will provide one of their personnel to be a senior supplier. This would be someone who has authority to provide electricians to the initiative, such as the operations director of that company. Below the senior supplier, the supplier organization will provide a team manager. As previously mentioned, this person's job title in their company might be project manager, but in the context of the project's organizational structure, this person is the team manager. At the bottom level of the supplier's organizational structure is the team of electricians.

In this hotel scenario, there will be two business cases for the project: the leisure company's business case (i.e., the customer's business case), which will justify the creation of the hotel based on the forecast room sales and conference sales, and the electrical company's business case (i.e., the supplier's business case), which is based on making a profit by providing electricians to the initiative. Usually when PRINCE2 talks about the business case, it is referring to the customer's business case.

In the hotel example, the electrical company might treat the leisure company's work package as a project in its own right within their company. If they are using PRINCE2, they might decide to set up their own project board to govern this project, meaning two project boards might exist. The project management team needs to be careful, when talking about a project board, that they don't muddle them up. Who might be on the supplier's project board? The executive might be the managing director of the electrical company, who is focused on the profitability of the work. The senior user might be a salesperson or account manager from the electrical company, who runs the leisure company's account and is focused on using the project to generate sales. The senior supplier would probably once again be the operations director. This means, of course, that the operations director would become a senior supplier on two project boards.

Although Figure 3.4 depicts the internal structure of only one supplier, the project manager is actually dealing with three outsourced suppliers. The executive might decide that each supplier should send a senior supplier to the project board. This sort of approach could be challenging for some projects or some organizations. The customer's project board members might not want to share sensitive information with the suppliers' personnel. If this is the case, two types of meetings could take place at the board level: one for customer staff only and one for all project board members. However, it is a good idea for the customer to be as open as possible with the suppliers, as the more information that is available to the board members, the better decisions they can make.

A number of alternative configurations exist when there are multiple third-party suppliers. For example, one supplier might be a lead contractor; they send a person onto the board to be the senior supplier, and then they deal with all the other suppliers and represent their views on the project board. Alternatively, someone from the customer organization might represent the outsourced suppliers. An ideal person for this sort of approach would be someone who is judged on selecting the right suppliers and ensuring they deliver to their contracts, such as a procurement manager. The procurement manager might also take on the senior supplier role before the suppliers have been chosen, and then be replaced by people from the outsourced suppliers later in the project.

How might the project manager's role be tailored in a commercial customer/supplier environment? First, the project manager should have a good understanding of the legal contract with another company; indeed, she might want to be involved in the creation of the contract. For example, the project manager needs to monitor the work package, so it might be reasonable to stipulate in the delivery contract that the supplier allows site visits to review progress.

In Figure 3.4 the project manager comes from the customer organization. However, in some cases the project manager might come from the supplier organization. Perhaps nearly all the work is being outsourced to one company, or maybe the work is of a highly specialized nature. In both these circumstances, it might be better for the supplier organization to provide the project manager. One of the challenges with this approach is who in the customer organization the supplier project manager would liaise with on a day-to-day basis. As mentioned previously, the project board members are not working on the project every day, so the customer organization might need to provide someone who would be available regularly to communicate with the supplier project manager. There is no PRINCE2 role name for this sort of person.

If the project manager comes from the supplier organization, the customer organization might want to increase the rigor of their project assurance. They will want to ensure that this supplier project manager is managing the project appropriately and following the standards and techniques outlined in the project approaches.

Projects within Programmes

In Chapter 1, you learned that a programme delivers a large-scale business change and is probably made up of a collection of projects, plus maybe some other smaller pieces of work. I discussed in Chapter 1 that one way of managing a programme is to use the Managing Successful Programmes (MSP) framework. You do not need to learn much about MSP for the PRINCE2 exams, but it would be useful to learn a little about some of the MSP roles. Don't worry, however. You don't need to buy a book on MSP, because this section describes all you need to know.

Figure 3.5 shows some common ways of integrating a programme environment with project environments.

Figure 3.5: Integrating a programme environment with project environments

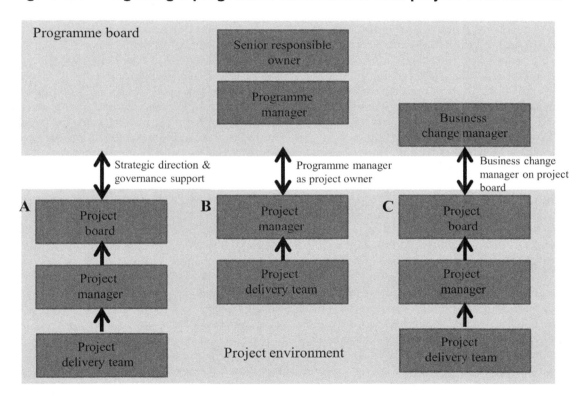

Before describing the connections between the programme and the three projects shown on the diagram, I'd like to take you through the programme board. The *programme board* is a programme's equivalent of the PRINCE2 project board. The purpose of the programme board is to drive the programme forward and deliver the programme's objectives. The programme board is led by the *senior responsible owner*, which is the programme's equivalent of the PRINCE2 executive. Like the executive, the senior responsible owner role should be done by only one person. That person is the key decision-maker for the programme and is singly accountable for the programme's success.

In Figure 3.5, you can see two other roles in the programme board. The *programme manager* is the programme equivalent of the PRINCE2 project manager. This role will be managing the programme on a day-to- day basis and is responsible for leading and managing the setting up of the programme through to the delivery of whatever new capabilities the programme needs to create. The other role in the diagram is called the *business change manager*. This is a complementary role to the programme manager and focuses on ensuring that the new capabilities are used and that they deliver benefits for the organization.

The difference between the programme manager and the business change manager can be difficult to see, so I will give you an example. Imagine that the programme is to deliver a new, corporate-wide IT system. The programme manager would focus on delivering the new system and all the accompanying products, such as training, documentation, new business processes, and so on. The business change manager would focus on ensuring that the IT system is used in the correct way and that it delivers benefits for the organization. There is a strong link between the business change manager and the PRINCE2 senior user role. As described previously, the senior user role is focused on how a project's products are used and is responsible for forecasting the benefits that will be created through the use of the products and then demonstrating that those benefits occurred.

One difference between a programme and a project is that a project tends to focus on delivering products, such as a hotel or an IT system, whereas a programme focuses on delivering products *plus* the benefits that are gained from using the products. In a PRINCE2 project, once the products have been delivered, the project often ends. The benefits that arise from using the products often happen after the project. The lifetime of the programme includes not only delivering the products but often also ensuring that the organization is using the products in the right way to deliver the right level of benefits.

Figure 3.5 shows three ways a programme could connect to a project. In approach A, the programme board appoints the executive role, who then appoints the rest of the project board—or maybe the programme board will appoint all the project board members. The programme board may want to integrate the programme's assurance approach with project assurance. For example, they might appoint the corporate quality manager to monitor some of the quality aspects of the project. Then the project would probably proceed in a normal PRINCE2 way, with the programme board acting as the corporate, programme management, or the customer level.

For a smaller project, the programme manager might decide to become the project owner (or, in PRINCE2 terms, the executive) and also carry out the roles of the senior user and the senior supplier. (shown in Figure 3.5 as approach B). In this approach, there is no project board, and the project manager reports directly to the programme manager.

As mentioned previously, there is a strong link between the senior user role and the business change manager role. In approach C, the business change manager also takes on the role of senior user on the project board.

There are variations on these three broad approaches. For example, the programme board might decide to combine a number of projects under one project board, or the business change manager might take on the executive role within one of the projects.

One of the problems with having a programme board as well as multiple project boards is that it creates more demand on senior management's time. Therefore, it is a good idea to avoid any unnecessary duplication of meeting and reports. For example, the programme board should try to align the stage boundaries of projects that have common board members so that they can meet collectively to conduct end project stage assessments.

The programme board needs to consider the process for authorizing requests for change. As described in the "Change Authority" section earlier in this chapter, a number of levels of change authority could exist. The project manager would authorize small changes; the project's change authority would authorize medium-size changes; and the project board would authorize large changes. In a programme environment, there might be an extra upper level, where very big changes need to be referred upwards to the programme board. You learn more about how to measure the size of a change in Chapter 8.

Another MSP role might be involved in the change process: the design authority. The *design authority* provides expert, specialist advice to the programme board around the areas of the organization that will be affected by the programme's work. For example, if the programme were to deliver an organization-wide IT system, the design authority might be an IT specialist. This design authority might be involved with the programme or the project's change authority. Alternatively, the design authority might take on a project assurance role.

I discussed the communication management approach earlier in the chapter. The programme board might decide to create a programme-wide approach, thereby avoiding the necessity to create one for each project.

Finally, a programme environment might include a *programme office*. This office might provide a range of support services, both to the programme as a whole and to all the individual projects within the programme. These services could range from administrative tasks to storing and tracking documentation to helping with planning software. On any individual project, the programme office might take on the role of project support.

Projects within an Organizational Environment

All organizations have their own organizational structure, and it is important to ensure that the project's organizational structure can work within it. Many organizations, for example, are structured on a functional basis. There might be a marketing department, an IT department, a finance department, and so on. One challenge for the project manager would be if she is trying to manage teams drawn from multiple functions, and each team member has to report both to the project manager and to their line manager within the function. The team members will probably give precedence to directions from their functional manager, who is probably their boss, rather than directions from the project manager. Therefore, the project manager needs to liaise closely with the functional manager to avoid any conflicts between project work and functional work. This situation might be helped if the functional managers sat on the project board as senior suppliers.

Agile Environments

At first sight, the PRINCE2 approach to project management is very different from agile project management. PRINCE2 has roles that "manage" and "control" teams, whereas agile has teams that organize themselves (i.e., there is no team manager). However, the PRINCE2 and agile approaches to managing people can work together very effectively.

Agile frameworks such as Scrum recommend a servant-leadership approach to leading delivery teams. Agile approaches do not like to use the terms "manager" or "management," because such terms imply an autocratic approach to leading teams and a lack of trust in team members. Servant leaders support their teams by using facilitating and collaborating styles of leadership. They provide a range of management services, such as removing impediments for the teams, helping the teams run progress meetings, and providing tools and techniques that enable the teams to do their job better. They even might provide a disciplinary service, if one individual is causing unnecessary friction within the team.

The key to combining an agile environment with a PRINCE2 environment is getting the balance right between the need to control and manage the project, which increases the likelihood of project success, and the need to allow the delivery teams to be self-organizing, collectively responsible for their work, and empowered, which increases the motivation and engagement of the team. The connection point between these two concepts is the link between the project manager and the teams. Getting this link right is a very important in ensuring that the PRINCE2 and agile environments work well together.

The first important thing to consider is whether you need someone called a team manager to liaise with the project manager. Given the fact the word "manager" and an autocratic style of management are anathemas to agile, using the term team manager may not be the best choice. What is important, though, is that the responsibilities of the PRINCE2 team manager are covered. As you have seen, these responsibilities include planning, monitoring, and managing progress; liaising with the project manager and other stakeholders; managing issues and risks; and final acceptance and handover of the products. In a highly agile environment, where the teams are organizing themselves effectively, the project manager might review the team manager responsibilities with the agile team and make sure they agree to cover them all collectively. When the project manager needs to liaise with such a team, talking to more than one person might be required.

In a less-agile environment, the project manager might use a similar approach but request only one point of contact. Maybe in a Scrum environment, this point of contact might be the scrum master. You learned about the scrum master role in Chapter 1. The scrum master leads a team but uses the servant leadership approach discussed previously in this chapter.

In an environment where the agile team is even less mature, the team might have a team manager who is responsible for all the PRINCE2 team manager responsibilities. However, it would be better if the team manager used a highly collaborative approach to managing her team, so as to start to embody some of the concepts of servant leadership.

Agile teams require a high degree of autonomy to work effectively. Agile teams (and any team) work best when they don't have to constantly refer upwards for a decision but are instead left to do their work without interruptions. The PRINCE2 principle of management by exception helps create autonomous teams. You learned about the principle of management by exception in Chapter 1, and I discuss it in more detail in Chapter 9. Using this principle, the project manager delegates work packages describing the targets for the cost, time, and scope for the work. Some of these objectives might have some leeway, known as a *tolerance*. In the hotel project example, the team building the spa might be required to deliver the swimming pool and the whirlpool, but if they run out of time to do so during this initial project, they could leave the sauna for next year's hotel upgrade project. This is an example of a scope tolerance. Using tolerances and the principle of management by exception allows the delivery team to have more autonomy because they don't have to refer up to the project manager about a decision on whether or not to build the sauna if they are running out of time.

Many agile approaches have quite a lot to say about the makeup of the teams. The teams need to be fairly small—approximately three to nine people. If the teams are bigger, the project manager might consider breaking up the work to create two or more smaller teams. The teams should have people with the right range of skills to complete the work and who might come from different functions within the organization.

Many agile approaches represent the user's and the customer's view in a different way from PRINCE2. For example, Scrum defines the role of the product owner. (You learned about the product owner in Chapter 1.) In Scrum, there is only one product owner, and they are singly accountable for collating the list of product requirements and features that are needed by the users and customers. This sounds similar to the PRINCE2 senior user role; however, the two roles are unlikely to map directly onto each other.

Having one person represent the customer and business views works fine when the project is focused on one product and doing regular upgrades on that product, but it is often not sufficient for larger, more complex projects. In a larger project, there is often a wide range of views and perspective about how the product will be used. For example, consider the case study earlier in the chapter about the project I worked on in the pharmaceutical industry. There were four distinct perspectives on how the website would be used, so having one product owner would not have been sufficient.

Another challenge is that some customers have a more strategic view on requirements for the products, whereas other customers have a more detailed, specialist view on the product's requirements.

Many approaches might work to overcome the preceding challenges. The senior user on the project board might be seen as a super product owner, directing the work of individual product owners operating within each delivery team. Each delivery team might have a number of customer subject-matter experts, who act as a conduit for all the views from a particular customer or user of the products. These customer subject-matter experts are similar to the product owners and might also sit on the project board as senior users. There might also be some specialists (often called *business analysts* or *requirements engineers*) who are trained in understanding business requirements, mapping out business processes, and translating this information into product designs. These people might be team members within a requirements-gathering team or spread out across a number of other teams. All these approaches can be blended together to create a workable representation of the customer or business view within a PRINCE2 agile environment.

Agile environments often allow flexibility around the scope of the project. When faced with a request for change, the change authority needs to understand what flexibility exists around the scope of work.

Learning More about Adapting PRINCE2 to an Agile Environment

I could talk a lot more about how to adapt PRINCE2 to an agile approach, but I have confined myself in this book to the key things you need to know to pass the Practitioner exams. (The Foundation exams will not test you on how to tailor PRINCE to agile environments.) If you would like to learn more about this subject, I highly recommend the book *PRINCE2 Agile* (The Stationery Office, 2015). It describes how to combine agile approaches, such as Scrum, Kanban and the Dynamic Systems Development Model, with PRINCE2 to create a really robust but flexible approach to managing projects. After you've passed the PRINCE2 exams, you could also try to obtain a PRINCE2 Agile certificate with AXELOS—but I would recommend a bit of a rest between the two!

Linking the Organization Theme with the PRINCE2 Principles

Although all seven PRINCE2 principles are implemented in part by using the ideas within the organization theme, the main principle implemented is the defined roles and responsibilities. The organization theme makes it clear which responsibilities need to be done in order to increase the likelihood of a successful project and suggests a number of roles and an organizational structure that will be accountable for these responsibilities.

Summary

This chapter described how the PRINCE2 organization theme is used to organize the people on a project. The organization theme ensures that everyone involved in the project—at the decision, management, and delivery levels—understands what is expected of them. It also ensures that all the roles necessary for a project to be successful are covered.

As you learned in this chapter, there are three main perspectives on any project: business, user, and supplier. PRINCE2 calls these the three project interests. These interests are represented on the main decision-making body in a PRINCE2 project: the project board. The executive represents the business interest; the senior user represents the user interest; and the senior supplier represents the supplier interest.

You saw in this chapter that four main management levels are represented within the PRINCE2 project management team structure. The highest level of authority is corporate, programme management, or the customer, which triggers the project at the outset. Next is the project board, which directs the project and makes key decisions. Below the project board is the project manager, who manages the project on a day-to-day basis. Under the project manager are the teams, which deliver the project's products.

You learned that the PRINCE2 project management team is made up of a variety of roles, each with its own set of responsibilities. These roles can be taken by people on the customer side or the supplier side of the project. PRINCE2 specifies that all projects take place in a customer/supplier environment.

A key management product related to the organization theme is the communication management approach. This approach defines how communication will be managed between the people inside and outside the project management team. It contains a list of people with an interest in the project (stakeholders) and defines how the project team needs to communicate with them.

You saw that the organization theme is an important part of PRINCE2. Every activity in the process model defines which role should be involved with that activity. You also saw that the organization theme implements the principle of defined roles and responsibilities.

Finally, you learned how to tailor the ideas in the organization theme to work in a range of different circumstances, such as smaller projects, projects working in a commercial customer and supplier environment, projects operating within a programme, and agile projects.

Foundation Exam Essentials

Explain the purpose of the organization theme.
The organization theme defines and establishes the project's structure of accountability and responsibilities.

Know the purpose of the communication management approach.
The communication management approach specifies how the project management team and the stakeholders of the project will communicate with each other. It also describes any analysis that has been done to determine who has a vested interest in the project and what their communication needs are. This approach is created by the project manager during the initiating a project process and then updated during the managing a stage boundary process. It is then referred to continually for reporting requirements of the project management team and other stakeholders.

Describe what PRINCE2 requires as a minimum for applying the organization theme.
As a minimum for applying the organization theme, PRINCE2 requires that a project do the following:
- Defines its organizational structure and roles. This must minimally ensure that all the responsibilities in PRINCE2's role descriptions are fulfilled.
- Document the rules for delegating change authority responsibilities, if required.
- Defines its approach to communicating and engaging with stakeholders.

Describe the responsibilities of the project board.
The project board is the main decision-making body on the project and contains three roles: the executive, the senior user, and the senior supplier. Their work takes place in the directing a project process.

Describe the responsibilities of the executive.
The executive represents the business perspective on the project board and is the ultimate decision-maker. She must secure the funding for the project and ensure that the project provides value for the money.

Describe the responsibilities of the senior users.
The senior users represent the user perspective on the project board. They must ensure that the project's products are fit for their purpose. They also provide user resources to help specify the products before they are created and then again to review them during and after their creation.

Describe the responsibilities of the senior suppliers.
The senior suppliers represent the supplier perspective on the project board. They are responsible for providing resources to the project that will create the project's products to the required level of quality.

Describe the responsibilities of project assurance.
There are three types of project assurance: business, user, and supplier assurance, which align with the project board roles of the executive, senior users, and senior suppliers, respectively. The project assurance roles monitor the project to ensure that it meets the needs of their unique perspective. The roles may provide guidance to the project manager and the team managers.

Describe the responsibilities of the project manager.
The project manager manages the project on a day-to-day basis on behalf of the project board. Her work takes place across many of the PRINCE2 processes, including starting up a project, initiating a project, managing a stage boundary, controlling a stage, and closing a project.

Describe the responsibilities of the change authority.
The change authority is given authority by the project board to authorize some changes to the project's products within certain predefined constraints.

Describe the responsibilities of the team manager.
The team manager manages the team's work in designing, creating, and delivering the project's products. Her work takes place in the managing product delivery process.

Describe the responsibilities of project support.
Project support provides a range of support activities to the project manager, team manager, and the team. Their work takes place across many of the PRINCE2 processes, including starting up a project, initiating a project, managing a stage boundary, controlling a stage, managing product delivery, and closing a project.

Describe which roles can be combined.
The PRINCE2 roles can be combined within the following constraints:
- The executive and the project manager roles cannot be combined.
- There cannot be more than one executive or project manager.
- The executive's accountability for the project's success cannot be delegated.
- The project board should not assign any project assurance roles to the project manager, team manager, or project support.

Typically on smaller, simpler projects, a number of the roles are combined. One person might carry out the responsibilities of the project manager, the team manager, and/or project support; the project board members might do their own project assurance; and the executive and senior users roles might be combined, especially if they both come from the customer environment. PRINCE2 roles can be combined but never eliminated.

Understand the term stakeholder.
The term *stakeholder* means any individual, group, or organization that can affect, be affected by, or perceive itself to be affected by an initiative (project, programme, activity, or risk).

Explain the concept of the three project interests.
The three project interests are the business, the users, and the suppliers, which are represented on the project board by the executive, senior users, and senior suppliers, respectively.

Explain the four levels of management.
The four levels of management are as follows: the corporate, programme management, or the customer level; the directing level (represented by the project board); the managing level (represented by the project manager); and the delivering level (represented by the teams and the team managers).

Practitioner Exam Objectives

Demonstrate an understanding of the communications management approach.
Demonstrate an understanding that the project manager creates the communications management approach during the initiation stage and that it shows how to manage communication throughout the project. Understand that the approach might be derived from the project brief and any corporate, programme management, or customer strategies or policies that exist, and that it could be a stand-alone document or part of the project initiation documentation. Know the composition of the communication management approach.

Assess and critique an approach to applying the organization theme.
Demonstrate an understanding of the purpose and format of the communication management approach. Describe the recommended roles and responsibilities within the organization theme and the recommended project management team structure. Show how the organization theme might be adapted to different project contexts (for example, a small project, an agile project, a project with external third-party organizations, or a project operating within a programme environment). Show why a given approach to applying the organization theme aligns with the principles of PRINCE2.

Review Questions

The remainder of this chapter contains mock exam questions, first for the Foundation exam and then for the Practitioner exam.

Foundation Exam Questions

1. Which PRINCE2 role is responsible for securing the funding for the project?
   A. Corporate, programme management, or the customer
   B. Executive
   C. Business sponsor
   D. Project manager

2. Why might a separate person be appointed as a team manager?
   (1) A team has insufficient motivation due to micromanagement.
   (2) A team is sited at a different geographic location from the project manager.
   (3) A team is building products using a specialist skill.
   (4) A team already has a project manager.
   A. 1 and 2
   B. 2 and 3
   C. 3 and 4
   D. 1 and 4

3. Which is a minimum requirement for applying the organization theme?
   A. To establish both a customer and supplier project board
   B. To appoint the design authority to the role of change authority when the project is part of a programme
   C. To appoint at least one person to carry out each of the PRINCE2 roles
   D. To ensure that all the responsibilities in the PRINCE2 role descriptions are fulfilled

4. Which level of management would authorize any deviation that exceeds stage tolerances?
   A. Corporate, programme management, or the customer
   B. Directing
   C. Managing
   D. Delivering

5. Which PRINCE2 management product helps establish a controlled flow of information between all the project stakeholders?
   A. Project brief
   B. Risk management approach
   C. Communication management approach
   D. Project approach

6. Who does the senior supplier represent when making decisions?
   A. Those who will benefit from using the products
   B. Corporate, programme management, or the customer
   C. Those who ensure the project is following a cost-conscious approach
   D. Those who are responsible for the technical integrity of the product

7. Which of the following options represents the user interest on a project?
   (1) Someone who can assess and confirm the viability of the project approach
   (2) Someone who will represent those who maintain the project's products in their operational life
   (3) Someone who can represent those who will buy the project's products once they have been developed
   (4) Someone who will be in charge of marketing the project's products once they have been developed
   A. 1 and 2
   B. 2 and 3
   C. 3 and 4
   D. 1 and 4

8. Which of the following statements is true of project assurance?
   A. Project assurance has three focuses aligned to the three interests of the project board.
   B. Project support can be assigned project assurance responsibilities.
   C. The project manager can be assigned project assurance responsibilities
   D. Project assurance creates the communication management approach.

9. Which of the following is a purpose of the organization theme?
   A. To manage uncertainty within the project
   B. To define the means of delivering the products
   C. To establish an effective approach for communication
   D. To define how the project will verify that products are fit for purpose

10. In a small project, it may be appropriate for the project manager to also carry out the responsibilities of which of the following roles?
   A. Executive
   B. Project assurance
   C. Project support
   D. Quality assurance

Practitioner Exam Questions

Exam Spotlight

When you're preparing for the Practitioner exam, it is particularly important to study the organization theme for a couple of reasons. First, one of the 15 syllabus sections in the Practitioner exam will be focused on this topic. Second, questions on any of the other syllabus areas might also ask about responsibilities relevant to that particular topic. For example, one of the quality questions might ask which of the PRINCE2 roles has quality responsibilities.

The following Practitioner questions are divided into sections by question type and are based on the Practitioner exam scenario in Appendix B.

Section 1: Matching Questions

Column 2 in the following table lists the five individuals connected to the Website Project described in the "Additional Information" section of Appendix B. Which project management role (A–F) would be most appropriate for each individual? Choose only one role for each individual. Each role can be used only once or not at all.

Column 1	Column 2
1. Operations director at Digital Design	A. Executive
2. Project manager at Digital Design	B. Senior user
3. Marketing manager at Quality Furniture	C. Senior supplier
4. The IT manager at Quality Furniture	D. Project manager
5.Chief executive of Quality Furniture	E. Project assurance
	F. Team manager

Exam Spotlight

Remember that the Practitioner exam allows you to refer to the official PRINCE2 manual (*Managing Successful Projects with PRINCE2*). This is a great help. One of the key differences between passing and failing the Practitioner exam is knowing how to use the PRINCE2 manual during the exam. Some of the questions in the exam rely on your ability to find very specific pieces of information quickly from the manual.

For organization theme questions, where might you look in the PRINCE2 manual for useful information? The first (and most obvious) place is the organization theme chapter itself. The chapter begins by discussing the purpose of the organization theme, and then moves on to talk about the three interests represented on the project management team, the four levels of management, and the minimum requirements for applying the organization theme. Next, there is a long section that describes each PRINCE2 role and the rules for combining the roles. Then there is a small section on the communication management approach. After that, there is a section that provides guidance for applying the organization theme and how to tailor the theme to different situations. The final section on creating an effective project team is not examinable, so you can ignore that in the exam. I would recommend that you look through the organization theme chapter in the PRINCE2 manual and familiarize yourself with how the information is laid out before taking the exam.

In addition to the organization theme chapter, a few other places in the PRINCE2 manual might be useful. For information on the format and sections of a communication management approach, you should look in Appendix A and find the communication management approach product description. Appendix C is also extremely useful, as there is an easy-to-read set of bullet points describing each PRINCE2 role's responsibilities.

Section 2: Classic Multiple-Choice Questions

1. Digital Design has told the project manager that they use an agile approach. The project manager has had a bad experience of agile in a previous project, so he wants to ensure strong control of the work. He has created a work package for Digital Design's work that stipulates no tolerances for the scope, time, and cost targets, and allows the project manager regular onsite visits. Is this appropriate, and why or why not?
   A. Yes, because the project manager uses the work package to control the team's work.
   B. Yes, because allowing no tolerances helps implement the management by exception principle.
   C. No, because this approach will not empower the agile delivery team and allow them to self-organize their work effectively.
   D. No, because the project manager receives checkpoint reports to monitor a team's progress.

2. The chief executive has requested that Digital Design be represented on the project board. However, he is concerned about divulging sensitive information to the supplier. He has asked the project manager to arrange a separate meeting for Quality Furniture staff before each project board meeting to discuss what can be shared with Digital Design. Is this appropriate, and why or why not?
   A. Yes, because in a commercial customer/supplier environment, there should always be a customer meeting before a project board meeting.
   B. Yes, because the executive decides how to solve the dilemma of whether to share sensitive information with external suppliers on the project board.
   C. No, because Digital Design should be represented on a separate supplier project board.
   D. No, because to enable effective decision-making, all information should be shared among project board members.

3. The project manager is planning stage three, in which an outsourced supplier will work on the design of the website. This supplier was chosen in stage two. The project manager is updating the communication management approach to include any personnel from the supplier who will now become involved in the project. Is this appropriate, and why or why not?
   A. Yes, because the project manager should review and possibly update the communication management approach at stage boundaries to ensure that it still contains all key stakeholders.
   B. Yes, because the communication management approach describes the communication between parties both internal and external to project.
   C. No, because the project manager creates the communication management approach in the initiating a project process.
   D. No, because the supplier is external to the commissioning organization and should not be included in the customer's communication management approach.

Chapter

4

Business Case Theme

The justification for a project should always be clear. A solid set of reasons should show why the project is being undertaken. These reasons should be valid, not only at the outset, when those involved with the project are putting together an argument to secure financing, but also throughout the life of the project. It is easy for the justification for a project to disappear as things progress. Perhaps costs rise, new competitive forces enter the marketplace, or technologies change. It is also important to check that projects meet the objectives set out in their business case. This often can't be evaluated until sometime after a project has finished, at which point those involved with the project probably will have moved on to other things. It is therefore easy to forget to verify that the expected return on the project's investment did actually happen. The business case theme helps overcome these challenges.

What Is the Business Case Theme?

The purpose of the *business case theme* is to set up a series of mechanisms to ensure that the project remains desirable, viable, and achievable. PRINCE2 uses these terms a lot within the business case theme, so here are some quick definitions for your reference:

- A *desirable* project is one where the positives that a project will bring to an organization, such as increased sales or decreased operating costs, outweigh the costs and risks of carrying it out.
- A *viable* project is one where, given any technical, time, and/or resource constraints, it is actually possible to deliver the project's products.
- An *achievable* project is one where the end result is that people are able to the use the products as intended and achieve the predicted benefits.

The business case theme helps evaluate whether a business justification exists for carrying out the project. It ensures that the desirability, viability, and achievability of the project are considered in all the major decisions made about the project—such as whether it should start, whether it should go on to the next major part (stage), or whether it should finish. It also ensures that when the project management team is making decisions on proposed changes or how to deal with risks, the impact on the business case will be taken into consideration.

The business case theme covers the following topics:

- The relationships between outputs, outcomes, benefits, and dis-benefits
- The purpose and contents of two management products:
  - The *business case*, which sets out the justification for the project
  - The benefits management approach, which plans how to measure the returns from the project and plans any management actions that need to take place (often post-project) to ensure the project's products are used as envisioned

- The activities involved with developing the justification for the project, using the justification to drive decision making, ensuring the project is capable of bringing about its predicted returns, and planning to measure those returns
- The PRINCE2 roles responsible for developing the justification for the project

Outputs, Outcomes, and Benefits

In Figure 4.1, you can see the causal relationship between outputs, outcomes, and benefits.

Figure 4.1: Outputs, outcomes, and benefits

Outputs are the things the project produces. Maybe your project builds a hotel, designs a new website, or writes a book. All of these are examples of outputs. Sometimes, outputs aren't tangible things you can see and touch. For example, a project might create a new financial process. As you saw in Chapter 1, "Overview of PRINCE2," outputs are also called *specialist products*. (As you also saw in Chapter 1, there is another type of product called *management products*. These are the documents that are created to help manage the project. For example, the business case and the benefits management approach, which I discuss later in this chapter, are management products.)

The ultimate aim of projects isn't just to produce outputs. You want to get some *benefit* for your organization out of these outputs. If you just produced an empty hotel that never sold any rooms, the hotel chain wouldn't be too pleased. Although this example sounds ridiculous, it is all too easy to focus on the outputs of the project and forget to measure if the organization benefited in the way you predicted. This is mainly because benefits usually happen sometime after the project has finished. For example, it may be months (or even years) before you will know whether online sales justify the investment in a website project.

Before you get to benefits, PRINCE2 introduces an interim step called outcomes. An *outcome* is the result of the change derived from using the project's outputs. If you build a new hotel, the outcome is the ability to sell rooms in the new location. If you create a new financial process, the outcome might be the ability to process invoices quicker.

A benefit is the measurable improvement that results from the outcome. In the hotel project example, a measurable benefit might be that selling rooms in the new location has increased sales by 20 percent. In the new financial process project example, a measurable benefit might be a $10,000 decrease in administrative costs resulting from processing invoices quicker.

Sometimes, a project might have negative consequences. For example, if a project were to merge together two departments in order to lower costs, the morale of the staff might decrease. Or if you fund a project to build a new website, there is not enough money to upgrade everyone's laptops. These negative consequences are called *dis-benefits*. Don't confuse dis-benefits with risks. There is uncertainty over whether a risk will occur, whereas a dis-benefit is a definite consequence of the project.

Exam Spotlight

The exams might ask you to distinguish between an output, an outcome, a benefit, and a dis-benefit. Here are some tips to help you spot which is which:

- Memorize the exact PRINCE2 definitions for the four terms. These come from *Managing Successful Projects with PRINCE2* (The Stationery Office, 2017). They are:
  - A project's *output* is any of the project's specialist products that are handed over to a user or users.
  - An *outcome* is the result of the change derived from using the project's outputs. It is something new that can be done as a result of the project's outputs.
  - A *benefit* is the measurable improvement resulting from an outcome that is perceived as an advantage by one or more stakeholder.
  - A *dis-benefit* is an outcome perceived as negative by one or more stakeholder.
- Although the definition of an output is a product, sometimes it is not a product in the conventional sense (such as a computer or a car). For example, a decision can be a product. The best way to think about outputs is that they are the result of a series of tasks or activities. For example, the project management team might discuss a number of potential approaches to a project (the discussions are activities), and the result of the discussions is a decision on which option to pursue (the decision is a product or an output).
- Don't confuse outcomes and benefits. The definition of an outcome—the result of the change derived from using the project's outputs—sounds like it could be a benefit. But benefits are measurable, whereas outcomes are not.
- Don't confuse dis-benefits with risks. Risks can be potentially bad things that result from the project, whereas dis-benefits are actual consequences that will definitely occur.

CASE STUDY

Business Case in the Pharmaceutical Industry

One of the challenges of applying the business case theme is determining whether there was a link between a benefit and a project. For example, my consultancy worked on a web project in the pharmaceutical industry. A new website was created to give doctors information on a range of drugs. One of the forecast benefits of the project was an increase in the number of those drugs prescribed by physicians. But if this occurred, was it due to the website, or was it due to other factors, such as more sales activity, an increase in the disease, or a lack of competitor activity? It is better to focus on outcomes that are directly linked to the website, such as the reduction in printing drug information leaflets. So a benefit for the project might be something like "Forecast 40 percent reduction in printing drug information leaflets."

Business Cases Where Money Isn't the Motivation

The term "business case" suggests that all PRINCE2 projects must operate in a business environment. However, this doesn't have to be the case. I have worked on PRINCE2 projects in the public sector, in charities, in the military, and in research and development departments, where the focus isn't immediate payback.

For example, I did some work for a trade union's training and development department. Their projects developed their members' job-related skills and encouraged their employers to invest in training. How do you measure whether a project like this has been successful? The answer is by focusing on various success metrics, such as the number of members attending a specific training course, and then comparing which projects would achieve this aim for the best value for money. If a website costing $100,000 gets 100 members signed up for a course, it is not as good a value as a $10,000 seminar that signs up 1,000 members.

I often work with NATO and the UK military forces. Once again, they aren't looking for a profit on their new aircraft carriers. They will focus on what level of investment can achieve certain quantifiable military capabilities.

Using the Business Case Theme

The following four main groups of business case theme–related activities are carried out before the project, during the project, and after the project:

Develop
The business case document—or more correctly, the management product—is created in the develop activity. I describe its composition later in the chapter, but for now, think of it as containing a prediction of the benefits the project will bring and details of the costs, time, and risks of the project.

Verify
At various times, the business case is reviewed to see if the project is still a worthwhile initiative. In the verify activity, the project team regularly reviews the predicted benefits to see if they still outweigh the estimated costs, time, and risks that the project needs to take on.

Maintain
As the project progresses, things will change. Costs might rise, new competitors might enter the marketplace, or work might overrun. All these changes might have an impact on the business case, so the business case needs to be regularly updated in the maintain activity.

Confirm
The purpose of the confirm activity is to determine whether the benefits predicted were achieved. For example, if the project were to build a hotel, did it reach its predicted target in room sales? Confirming benefits usually takes place post-project.

Figure 4.2 shows a summary of when these groups of activities occur before, during, and after the project.

Figure 4.2: The development path of the business case

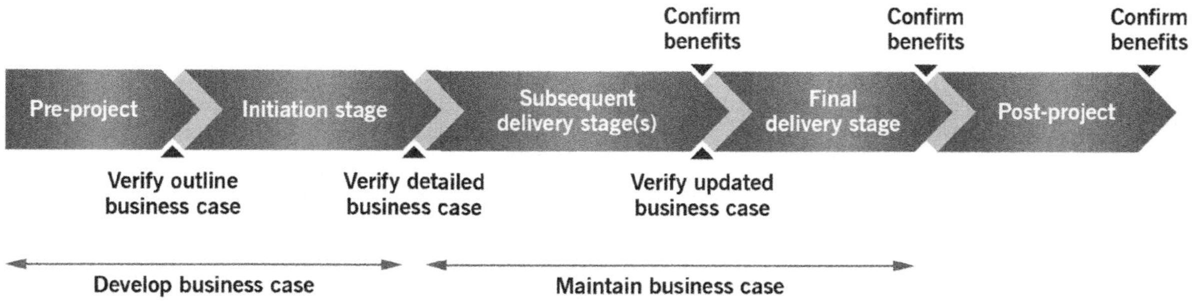

Developing the Business Case

The business case is developed both before the project starts and during the initiation stage. I talked about how the pre-project and initiation stage are managed both in Chapter 1, "Overview of PRINCE2," and in Chapter 2, "Starting a Project Successfully with PRINCE2."

Before the project starts, corporate, programme management, or the customer creates a project mandate, which contains the reasons for the project. Remember that the project mandate can be either high-level or detailed. Whatever form it takes, it should at least have some valid reasons for the project.

Once the project mandate has been created, the starting up a project process begins. This is a pre-project process with a set of activities focused on determining whether the project idea is worthwhile and viable. The executive role (the main decision maker and the representative of the business perspective on the project) is accountable for creating an outline business case based on the information in the project mandate. The executive may delegate the preparatory work to someone else, such as the project manager, but they are still accountable for ensuring this work is completed properly.

The next step occurs in the initiation stage. The initiating a project process is used to manage this stage. The project manager creates the project plan. He takes the estimates for time, cost, and potential risks from the project plan and uses this information to refine the business case. At this point, it becomes the initial business case. You can think of it as version one of the detailed business case.

As I discuss in more detail later in this chapter, the project team does not have to create a separate business case document. For small or less-formal projects, for example, they may decide to just include a few lines of text in another document or a set of slides in a presentation to explain the business justification for the project. Whichever format the business justification takes, it must clearly explain why the project is desirable, achievable, and viable.

Maintaining the Business Case

As the project progresses, it is likely that the information in the business case will become outdated. Costs will rise, new risks will be identified, and estimates for the project's benefits will change. So it is important to regularly update the business case. The project manager does this at the end of each delivery stage in the managing a stage boundary process. The managing a stage boundary process sets out how to do this in the update the business case activity. This is the maintain step of the business case development path that you saw earlier in Figure 4.2.

There is one other situation when the project manager might maintain the business case. In Chapter 5, "Plans Theme," you learn about exception plans. The project board might ask the project manager to create an exception plan to show how the project will recover after a forecast breach in stage or project tolerances. As you learn in Chapter 5, the exception plan is also created in the managing a stage boundary process, and once the plan has been created, the project manager will update the business case with any new information.

For a more detailed explanation of how the managing a stage boundary process helps the project manager manage the end of a delivery stage or an exception situation, refer to either Chapter 1, "Overview of PRINCE2," or Chapter 10, "Managing the Middle of a Project Successfully with PRINCE2."

Verifying the Business Case

At the end of each stage (both initiation and delivery), the project manager must go to the project board (the main decision-making body of the project) and ask for authorization to move to the next stage. Again, refer to Chapter 1 if you need to remember how this stage-by-stage approach works.

The business case is one of the main things that the project board considers when giving authorization to move forward. They will want to see that the business case is up-to-date and that it presents a valid business argument for continuing with the project. Throughout the project, the project manager will be regularly reviewing the issue-and-risk situation. When a new risk or issue is discovered, the project manager will review how it will affect the project objectives, including the business case. For an issue, this is referred to as carrying out an *impact analysis*. For a risk, this is called a *risk assessment*. In both cases, the business case will be reviewed to verify that there is still a valid business argument for proceeding with the project.

Confirming the Benefits

The confirming the benefits activities look to see if the benefits were achieved. As I said at the beginning of this section, most benefits will become apparent after the project has finished. If the project is to build a website to sell products, the sales won't happen until after the site is complete. However, there are circumstances when benefits happen before the end of a project. For example, consider a project to build a new block of apartments. Sometimes, building developers sell apartments before they have been built. People buy off the architectural plans. In this case, the benefits, in the form of sales, could accrue before the project ends.

The benefits management approach is used to plan the review of benefits. I describe its composition in detail later in this chapter. For now, think of it as containing a series of activities necessary to see if the project's benefits have occurred, along with who is responsible for those activities and when they will occur. Most of these activities will be planned for after the project.

The project manager creates the benefits management approach during the initiation stage. He then updates it with any relevant new information at the end of each delivery stage. Finally, he updates it at the end of the project to ensure all the post-project reviews of benefits are included. The senior user has a leading role in confirming the benefits. I talked about the senior user in Chapter 3, "Organization Theme." Remember that the senior user is a role within the project board, the main decision-making body. A number of people may be carrying out senior user roles. They all will be representing some form of use of the project's products. For example, if the project were to build a website to sell a company's products, there might be a senior user representing the customers, another representing the marketing director, who uses the website to sell products, and another representing the product information department, who load details of the company's range of products onto the site.

In PRINCE2, the senior user has two important responsibilities that are connected to the business case theme: first, to forecast the benefits from the project, and second, to be accountable that the project's products are used and that the benefits actually happen—in other words, to confirm the benefits. To see why they have these responsibilities, consider the marketing director in the previous example. He uses the website to create sales. He is thus in the ideal position to forecast how many sales (benefits) the website will bring as well as to track the sales (benefits) after the project, once the website has been built. It is in his interest to ensure that the website works correctly and is used to generate sales. Therefore, fulfilling the senior user is likely to involve a commitment beyond the project.

Finally, in relation to confirming the benefits, two other roles are important. The executive is responsible for managing benefits reviews during the project. Corporate, programme management, or the customer is responsible for managing post-project benefits reviews.

Another aspect of confirming the benefits is making sure the products from the project are used in the way that was envisioned. There are many examples of projects that create great products, but for a variety of reasons no one uses them post-project, so the benefits are never achieved. For example, I did a project several years ago where I worked with a company to create a new project management method (based on PRINCE2). The project's scope included creating a series of document templates, setting up a project assurance role, and training project staff. At the time the project closed, everyone was enthusiastic about the new approach. When I visited the company six months later, however, the project teams were using the old, pre-project method.

The preceding scenario is quite common. Organizations may underestimate how difficult it can be to change to a new way of working and not provide enough support or training to staff post-project, or not all of the organization and/or senior management is totally bought into the change (as was the case in the scenario I described).

To try to mitigate this problem, PRINCE2 recommends that the project team plan management actions in the benefits management approach to ensure the products will be used. In hindsight, what we should have done in my project was to ensure that the project personnel and some senior management's job descriptions were amended and that they were rated on their adoption of the new project approach as part of the company appraisal system. These management actions should have been included in the project's benefits management approach. Quite often these actions will take place after the project has finished, as this is often the time when a project's products are used. Corporate, programme management, or the customer is accountable for ensuring these post-project management actions take place. However, as I said earlier in this section, sometimes benefits are realized during the project, in which case, the executive would be accountable for any such management actions.

The Business Case Management Product

Rather confusingly, "business case," in addition to being the name of a theme, is also the name of a management product. The theme, as you have seen, describes the activities, roles, processes, and management products involved with ensuring that there is business justification for the project. One of the management products that the business case theme describes is the business case management product.

The Purpose

The purpose of the business case is to set out the justification for the project. It provides a compelling argument to show why the project represents value for money and will give a good return on investment. In order to do this, the business case balances the benefits that can be expected from the project against the cost of the initial project and any ongoing costs of operating the project's products. It also takes into account any risks that the project or the organization will be exposed to as a result of the project.

The business case is used to drive decision making in the project. For example, when project board members are considering whether to authorize the project to start, go on to the next stage, or close, they use the business case as an input into their decision. It is also used when the project management team is deciding whether to implement a change to the project's products. In this case, they want to check that the change doesn't have adverse effects on the business case.

The executive is accountable for the creation and timely updating of the business case, although he may delegate the preparatory and maintaining work to the project manager. If he does this, he is not absolving himself of the accountability for the document; it is just that he will not be doing the activities to create and update it. The business case is created in outline in the starting up a project process, created in detail in the initiating a project process, and then updated at the end of each stage in the managing a stage boundary process. The project board reviews the business case in the directing a project process, particularly when considering whether to authorize a new stage.

The Contents of the Business Case

In this section, I use the hotel example to help you understand the type of information that goes into each section of the business case. For this exercise, assume you are working for an international hotel chain and need to put together a PRINCE2 business case for a new site in Shanghai.

Executive Summary

Every PRINCE2 business case should start with a high-level summary of the contents of the business case. This is useful for senior stakeholders of the project, such as those at the corporate, programme management, or the customer level.

Reasons

On the PRINCE2 exam, as well as when you're working on an actual PRINCE2 project, you need to know exactly what to put in the reasons section of a business case. Although the main "reason" that you are doing the hotel project may be to make a profit, this would go in the expected benefits section of your business case. The reasons section of a PRINCE2 business case should explain the *background* of the project, such as a challenge you are facing or an opportunity that has arisen. Another way of distinguishing a reason from a benefit is that a reason relates to something that has happened, whereas a benefit is a forecast of something that will happen.

For the hotel project, you might include one of the following statements in the reasons section:

Our competitors are opening successful hotels in China's major cities, and to remain competitive, we need to do the same.

Or

Our market share of the international business market is falling due to our lack of representation in the Asian marketplace.

Business Options

The business options show different ways of responding to the challenges and opportunities set out in the reasons section. In the example, the reason you are doing this hotel project is that you are underrepresented in the Chinese market. In response to this, you might include the following options in your business case:

- Build new hotels under your brand in some of the major Chinese business centers.
- Form a partnership with an established chain of Chinese hotels.
- Buy an established chain of Chinese hotels.

Be careful not to confuse these business options (which explain *how* you will meet the business challenge) with the project approach (which explains *how* you will deliver the chosen business option). In the example, the business option you might choose is to build a new hotel. The project approach you might use to deliver this option is outsourcing the construction to a building company. This information belongs in the project brief and is created in the starting up a project process.

PRINCE2 suggests you should always consider the "do nothing," "do the minimum," and "do something" options. The do nothing option is used as a baseline to compare the other options against.

A decision on which business option to pursue needs to be made either in the project mandate or during the starting up a project process. Decisions, however, can take some time, and starting up a project is supposed to be a relatively quick step in relation to the rest of the project. So how do you deal with this?

In some cases, you might be able to decide quickly which business option to choose. Maybe the hotels are renowned for their stylized modern architecture, and it wouldn't make sense to do anything but build new hotels. However, if this is not case, you might consider doing two projects. In the first project, you would conduct a feasibility study to review the different business options and make a recommendation on which option to pursue; in the second project, you would implement that recommendation.

Expected Benefits

The expected benefits are the ultimate aim of the project. As you learned in the "Outcomes, Outputs, and Benefits" section earlier in this chapter, the project creates products, such as a hotel, and then the products produce benefits, such as room sales. Because of the causal link between outputs and benefits, ultimately what products a project creates is determined by what benefits the organization commissioning the project wants. So an expected benefit for the hotel project could be phrased as follows:

Sell $10 million worth of room sales in each of the first 3 years of opening.

Although most expected benefits happen after the project has finished, you might start to receive benefits during the project. Remember the hotel gym example—you first build the gym, open it, and start selling memberships, and then you build the hotel. You get some benefit from the gym before the project is finished. All benefits should be measurable. Statements such as "increase the competitiveness of the hotel," "increase the morale of workers," or "lower costs" do not represent benefits. In all these cases, it would be difficult to determine whether they've been achieved. Instead, they need to focus on an objective measurement. For the hotel project, the benefits section might include the following:

Increase the market share of business travelers from 20 percent to 30 percent in the Asian market.

As I said in the "Reasons" section earlier, don't confuse benefits with reasons. Benefits are forecast events, whereas reasons are things that have happened, that have led to the project.

In Chapter 9, "Progress Theme," I describe tolerances. A *tolerance* is an allowable leeway around the target that is set for the project. The business case might define a benefits tolerance for the project, as in the following example:

Sell $10 million worth of room sales; however, an absolute minimum of $8 million would be acceptable.

Expected Dis-benefits

PRINCE2 defines a dis-benefit as "an outcome that is perceived as negative by one or more project stakeholders." Be careful not to confuse this with a risk. Risks are uncertain events—they may or may not happen. Dis-benefits have happened or will happen. They are definite consequences of the project that will impact someone or something in a bad way.

Maybe for the hotel project, one of the consequences of building a hotel in Shanghai is that there are no funds left for the European Division to carry out their hotel expansion plans.

Timescales

Various timescales need to be reviewed. Over what period will the project run? When will the project's benefits occur? Over what period will the benefits from this project be tracked? With the latter, in theory, you could track the benefits over the entire operational life of the hotel, but it might be more reasonable just to track them over the next few years. This could be because this is the period over which the project will recover its costs.

For the hotel project, the timescales section could read as follows:

Construction will start in March 2020 and continue until September 2021. Bedroom sales, meeting room sales, and restaurant and bar sales will be received immediately on opening, and these will be tracked for the following 3 years.

Costs

The benefits need to be weighed against the cost of the project and the operational costs of running the products. Also, you need to set out how the project will be funded.

For the hotel project, the costs section could read as follows:

The Shanghai hotel is estimated to cost $150 million to build. The annual operational costs of the hotel in the first 3 years are estimated to be $20 million per annum. The project will be funded by the Asia-Pacific business expansion budget.

Major Risks

It is important with any investment decision to weigh the risk. For example, if I had $1,000 in savings, I could invest in the stock market and get a much higher return than investing in a government bond. I might decide that the bond is better, however, since there is very little risk with this investment.

Any project is full of uncertainty, which makes it risky. An important part of the business case is an evaluation of the risk. The risks section should contain a summary of the key risks to the project, the project team's assessment of the likelihood and impact of those risks, and a description of how the project team plans to respond to those risks to lower their likely impact on the project.

PRINCE2 suggests that this section include a summary risk profile, like the one shown in Figure 4.3. In the figure, each circle represents an individual risk. Risk number 1 is estimated to have a very high probability of happening, and if it does happen, it would have a high impact on the project. An example might be that there is a very high likelihood that a competitor will also open a Shanghai hotel, and this will have a large impact on the forecast sales figures. I discuss risks in more detail in Chapter 7, "Risk Theme."

Figure 4.3: Summary risk profile

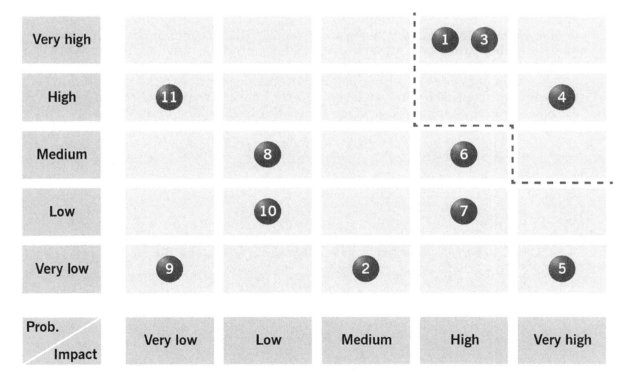

- - - - - **Risk tolerance line**

Investment Appraisal

The investment appraisal section compares the expected benefits with the project and operational costs over a period of time. There are many ways of doing this. For example, you could state how many years it would take to pay back the original investment. Maybe the hotel will generate $30 million in profit each year, so it will take 5 years to pay back the original $150 million investment. Another approach would be to work out the rate of return the hotel project will give. For the hotel, this would be $30 million profit divided by $150 million investment, which is 20 percent.

PRINCE2 does not prescribe a particular investment appraisal technique—it simply states that some appraisal of the investment should be set out in the business case. *Managing Successful Projects with PRINCE2* describes a number of investment appraisal techniques, but they are not part of the accreditation exam syllabus.

Exam Spotlight

Remember that on the Practitioner exam, you can refer to the official PRINCE2 manual, *Managing Successful Projects with PRINCE2*. This is useful if you encounter a question about the contents of a management product, such as the business case or the benefits management approach. I've studied PRINCE2 for many years, but I still have difficulty remembering exactly what goes into each section of each management product and have to refer to the manual from time to time. The best place to look is appendix A, which shows the composition of all the PRINCE2 management products.

CASE STUDY

Business Cases in the Dot-com Era

During the 1990s, I worked for two Internet startups. The business cases that justified their projects were very different from ones in more established organizations. To balance their risk exposure, they'd fund an entire portfolio of businesses, with the expectation that only a minority would actually succeed.

The Benefits Management Approach

The benefits management approach plans the activities necessary to see whether the expected benefits from the project are achieved, any management actions that will ensure that the products are used in the correct way to create the predicted benefits, and activities to see how the products have performed in their operational life.

Figure 4.4 shows the composition of the benefits management approach. This is the management product that I talked about previously in the "Confirming the Benefits" section.

Figure 4.4: The composition of the benefits management approach

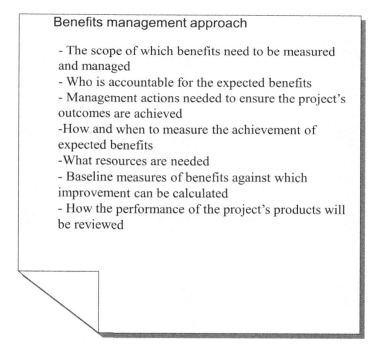

Benefits management approach

- The scope of which benefits need to be measured and managed
- Who is accountable for the expected benefits
- Management actions needed to ensure the project's outcomes are achieved
-How and when to measure the achievement of expected benefits
-What resources are needed
- Baseline measures of benefits against which improvement can be calculated
- How the performance of the project's products will be reviewed

Determining whether a benefit has occurred as a result of a project is not always straightforward. For example, it may be necessary to use accountants to calculate financial benefits such as profit and sales. Or you may need to have a human resources (HR) expert design an employee survey in order to objectively measure a subjective benefit such as increased morale. All this work needs to be scheduled in the benefits management approach.

It needs to be clear that it was the project that led to any benefits, not some other cause. Therefore, any pre-project benefits should be measured and their levels set out in the benefits management approach.

As I said in the "Confirming the Benefits" section earlier in this chapter, the benefits management approach includes any management actions that need to take place to ensure a project's products are used. These might include additional monitoring and control activities by management to ensure their staff is using the project's products to their full extent. Often these management actions occur after the project has finished.

The project manager and the executive should also plan how to review the operation of the project's products. In the hotel example, you could measure the hotel's occupancy rate or the number of times crucial systems like the heating or the accounting software broke down.

Corporate, programme management, or the customer is responsible for ensuring any post-project activities planned in the benefits management approach occur, whereas any activities planned in the benefits management approach for the time when the project is running are the responsibility of the executive.

Business Case Responsibilities

PRINCE2 assigns a number of responsibilities to the various roles within the project management structure to ensure that the desirability, viability, and achievability of the project are reviewed throughout the project.

Corporate, Programme Management, or the Customer

Using the project mandate, corporate, programme management, or the customer must instigate a project that has a viable business case. They must also appoint an executive who will be responsible for the project's business case throughout the life of the project.

After the project, corporate, programme management, or the customer takes responsibility for the benefits management approach and must ensure that the project's benefits (or lack of them) are reviewed and that any management actions planned to ensure the use of the project's products are carried out.

Executive

Throughout the life of the project, the executive is accountable for ensuring that there is a desirable, achievable, and viable business case; that the project represents value for money; and that it is aligned with the overall objectives of the organization or programme. He is also responsible for securing the funding for the project. His work includes checking that a business case is created during the starting up a project process, refined during the initiating a project process, and updated during the managing a stage boundary process. In all the decisions that the executive makes during the project, he ensures that the latest business case still justifies the continuation of the project.

Most of the project's benefits occur once the project is completed. However, some might occur during the project. For example, if you are building residential apartments, some might be sold before they are built. The executive is responsible for ensuring benefits that occur during the project are reviewed as specified in the benefits management approach.

Once the project is completed, the executive's role is finished. Any post-project benefits reviews are the responsibility of corporate, programme management, or the customer.

Senior User

In the "Confirming the Benefits" section earlier in this chapter, you learned that the senior user is responsible for forecasting the benefits from the project and ensuring that they actually occur. Refer back to that section if you need to remember why this is.

Don't confuse the executive responsibility (weighing the forecast benefits with the costs, time, and risks that need to be taken on) with the senior user's responsibility (which is focused purely on the benefits side of the business case equation).

Project Manager

Although the executive is accountable for the business case, he will probably delegate the creation and updating of the document to the project manager. The project manager must also ensure that the effects on the project's business objectives are taken into account when assessing risks and issues.

Other Roles

The senior suppliers are expected to raise any issues, such as delayed delivery dates or increased costs, which might impact the business case.

The project assurance role, which focuses on business assurance on behalf of the executive, checks that the project remains on target to deliver products that will achieve the expected business benefits and will deliver value for money.

Project support, if they exist, will be involved in the administration of creating, updating, and tracking the different versions of the business case.

Tailoring the Business Case Theme

The key to the successful use of PRINCE2 is adapting and tailoring the method based on the characteristics of the project and the environment the project is operating within. The following sections describe how the business case theme might be adapted to better suit certain situations. The Practitioner exam might test you on this.

Minimum Requirements

Organizations with a less-formal project management approach or that are running smaller, less-complicated projects might choose to cut back on some of the business case theme ideas. However, there are some minimum requirements that must be followed in order for a project team to claim they are following PRINCE2's business case theme.

Some sort of business justification must show why the project is desirable, viable, and achievable. Whatever format this takes, it needs to be updated with any new relevant information throughout the project and be a key factor in any major decision. This business justification may or may not be called a business case.

The project team should plan activities to ensure that the project's products are used to realize the forecast benefits and plan activities to measure these benefits. These activities might occur after the project has finished, but during the project, someone in corporate, programme management, or the customer must be assigned the task of ensuring these activities take place.

The project team should also document who is responsible for carrying out these minimum requirements.

Tailoring the Management Products

The business case could take many forms: It might be just a few lines of text in an organization's business plan, or it could be a set of slides in a presentation. The format of the business case might be prescribed by certain organizational standards (most likely coming from the finance department), and it might be referred to by different names (such as "a statement of work"). Regardless of its name or format, the business case must clearly show the desirability, achievability and viability of the project.

The benefits management approach might be combined with the detailed business case, either in the body of the document or as an appendix.

Regulatory Compliance

Organizations sometimes run projects to ensure they are compliant with certain industry regulations. For example, in 2016 the European Union introduced the General Data Protection Legislation (GDPR) which introduced a range of new regulatory requirements around the privacy of data. In order to be compliant with these new requirements, many companies had to launch projects to create new corporate processes and information systems. The business justification for these projects was not to create profit or decrease costs, but to avoid the possible fines that might be levied against the organizations for noncompliance.

Projects within Programmes

In PRINCE2, a *programme* is a collection of projects that are managed together. The outcomes of all the projects are connected with each other or contribute to each other in some way. For example, the activities to create the infrastructure for the Olympics could be collectively considered a programme of work. Multiple projects exist within the programme, such as one project to create the main stadium, another project to promote the event, and so on.

Each project's business case will need to align with the programme's business case. In some situations, there may be just a programme business case and no business case at the project level. In other situations, each project's business case might be very limited compared to a project run outside of a programme. For example, it might just contain a list of benefits, a budget, and a statement describing how the project is contributing to the overall aims of the programme.

At the beginning of the project, the programme may provide an outline business case in the project mandate, so there is no need for the project team to create this in the starting up a project process. After the project is completed, its benefits would probably be tracked and managed by the programme management team, and the project's benefits management approach may be part of the programme's benefits realization plan.

Commercial Customer and/or Supplier Environments

In any one project, there might be many different parties either working on the project or in some way impacted by it. Consider the hotel project. There might be a leisure company that has commissioned the building of the hotel and will own and run the hotel once it has been built. Then, there might be a construction company that builds the hotel. Each party will have a different business case, justifying their involvement in the project. The leisure company's business case will focus on the sales of hotel rooms, whereas the construction company's business case will focus on the profit they will make by building the hotel. When a project has multiple business cases, it is important to be clear about which one is being referred to in documents and discussions. For example, in PRINCE2, the leisure company's business case would be referred to as the customer's business case, and the construction company's business case would be referred to as the supplier's business case.

Agile Environments

In an agile environment, a project's scope and the associated benefits that scope will bring will probably be more fluid than in a more traditional environment. For example, an agile project might be initiated to upgrade an existing software system. At the outset of the agile project, the project team will list all the new feature ideas for the upgraded software, predict the cost and time of implementing each feature, and forecast the measurable benefit that each feature would give to the users. This list is often called a *product backlog*, particularly in Scrum agile environments, and might serve as the Scrum environment's version of the business case. The project team would then deliver these features over a series of short sprints. In Scrum environments, a *sprint* is a short period of time-boxed work, usually lasting around a month, during which a potentially releasable piece of work is created.

At the beginning of the first sprint, the project team would review the product backlog and decide which features to deliver within that sprint based on the available time and resources. Their aim would be to deliver features that would bring the highest benefits to the users first. At the end of the sprint, the new features can be released, and people can start using the new software.

Once the first sprint has finished, the second sprint can start. The first step of the next sprint is for the project team to plan which features to build in the second sprint. However, before they begin this new planning process, they might want to update the product backlog, as things might have changed since the beginning of the project, new competitors might have launched products, technology might have changed, and/or the users might have provided some important feedback about the first release. For example, some of the released features from the first sprint might not be as useful as predicted or might be delivering unforeseen benefits. Given this information, some previously planned features might be removed from the product backlog and new ones might be added.

This process of constantly re-evaluating which features to deliver at the beginning of each sprint means that the project's initial predicted scope of work and associated benefits might be different from what actually is delivered at the end of the project. To allow for this, the PRINCE2 business case should outline acceptable benefit tolerances. It might forecast the best case, expected case, and worst case for the project's benefits, given the project team's initial ideas on the overall scope of the project. The initial business case might also show the minimum amount of benefits that the project needs to deliver to make the overall initiative viable.

The business case should also take into account the positives and negatives of incrementally delivering the product through a series of sprints. On the upside, users might get beneficial products earlier, and delivering incrementally might help to fund subsequent sprints. On the downside, there might be a cost of releasing a new product every month or so, such as a disruption to the organization's ongoing operations.

Linking the Business Case Theme with the PRINCE2 Principles

In Chapter 1, I talked about the seven PRINCE2 principles. Although all seven principles contribute to implementing the business case theme in some way, the two that are most important are the principles of continuous business justification and the defined roles and responsibilities. As I said in the "Minimum Requirements" section of this chapter, it is essential that however the business case theme is implemented, there is at least a clear business justification for the project that is updated throughout the project and taken into account when making key decisions. This is essentially what the continuous business justification principle outlines. The other minimum requirement is that the project team is clear about who has which business case responsibility, which aligns with the defined roles and responsibilities principle.

Summary

This chapter described the business case theme, which sets out how PRINCE2 ensures each project has a desirable, achievable, and viable business case.

As you learned in this chapter, there is a causal link between the outputs that a project produces, the changes that these outputs make to the environment, and the benefits that might result because of these changes. For example, a project might produce a new accounting procedure. This is a PRINCE2 *output*. The result of the new procedure produces a change, which is that invoices are processed quicker. PRINCE2 calls this change an *outcome*. Finally, if you measure the result of this change, you might find that productivity has increased by 20 percent. In PRINCE2, this measurable result is called a *benefit*.

A project could have undesirable consequences, which PRINCE2 calls *dis-benefits*. PRINCE2 defines a dis-benefit as the impact of one or more outcomes that is perceived as negative by one or more stakeholder. For example, if two departments were merged together to lower costs, a negative consequence might be that employee morale decreases.

Some projects, such as military projects, are not done for financial payoff. In this case, you need to define the measurable objectives and compare different ways of achieving those objectives. Some options might to cost less, to take less time, or to involve less risk.

Throughout the project, certain steps must be taken to ensure continued business justification. At the beginning of the PRINCE2 process model, in the starting up a project process, the executive develops an outline business case. Then, in the initiating a project process, the project manager refines the business case. This more detailed version becomes "version one." At the end of each stage, in managing a stage boundary, the business case might get updated to a new version. As you learned in this chapter, the project board uses the latest version of the business case to determine whether a project should proceed to the next step.

You also learned that the most important management product in this theme is the business case. It shows the positive effects of the project and the forecast benefits, and balances those against the project's timescale, costs, and risks. The other important management product is the benefits management approach. This plan specifies when, how, and who will be involved with the reviews to see if the project's benefits have been achieved as well as any management actions that may need to take place to ensure that the project's products are used to generate benefits.

This chapter also described the PRINCE2 roles that have relevant business case responsibilities. Corporate, programme management, or the customer must instigate projects by setting out the business reasons in the project mandate. They must also appoint an executive who will be responsible for the business case throughout the life of the project. Post-project, corporate, programme management, or the customer ensures that the benefits are reviewed. Throughout the life of the project, the executive has primary responsibility of ensuring that the project is delivering value for money and that the products are capable of achieving the forecast benefits. The senior users are responsible for forecasting the likely benefits the project can expect and ensuring that these benefits have been achieved both during and after the project. The project manager manages the creation and maintenance of the business case and the benefits management approach.

Foundation Exam Essentials

Explain the purpose of the business case theme.
The purpose of the business case theme is to establish mechanisms to judge whether the project is (and remains) desirable, viable, and achievable as a means to support decision-making in its (continued) investment.

Explain the purpose of the business case management product.
The purpose of the business case is to document the business justification for undertaking the project, based on the estimated costs (both the project costs and any ongoing operations and maintenance costs) against the anticipated benefits to be gained and offset by any associated risks.

Explain the purpose of the benefits management approach.
The purpose of the benefits management approach is to show how and when management actions will take place to ensure that the projects outcomes are achieved and to show how and when measurements of the achievement of the project's benefits can be made.

Describe what PRINCE2 requires as a minimum for applying the business case theme.
As a minimum for applying the business case theme, PRINCE2 requires that the project management team create a business justification for the project (usually called a business case) and update this justification in response to any decisions or events that might impact the achievability, desirability, or viability of the project. The project management team should also plan any management actions necessary to ensure the project's outcomes will be achieved, as well as schedule reviews of the benefits of the projects to confirm they have been achieved. Finally, the project management team should define and document roles and responsibilities related to managing the business justification for the project and managing the benefits.

Define the concepts of project outputs, outcomes, benefits, and dis-benefits and understand the differences between them.
PRINCE2 projects create outputs in the form of products that result in changes within the organization or environment where these products are used. These changes, called outcomes, allow the organization to realize the benefits set out in the business justification for the project. A dis-benefit is an outcome that is perceived as negative by one or more stakeholder.

Practitioner Exam Essentials

Demonstrate an understanding of the business case.
Demonstrate an understanding that the executive creates a draft outline business case during the starting up a project process, and the project manager creates the first version of the detailed business case during the initiation stage. Understand that the project manager will update the business case at every stage boundary. Understand that the business case might be derived from the project mandate, the project brief, the forecast benefits from the senior users, or the organization's definition of value for money. Know that it could be a stand-alone document, an entry in a project management tool, a spreadsheet, presentation slides, or part of the project initiation documentation. Know the composition of the business case.

Demonstrate an understanding of the benefits management approach.
Demonstrate an understanding that the project manager creates the benefits management approach during the initiation stage and may update it at each stage boundary and at the end of the project. Know that it shows how to measure the achievement of the project's benefits and what management actions should be in place to ensure the project's products are used in the intended way and that they will deliver the forecast benefits. Understand that the approach might be derived from the business case, the project product description, and any corporate, programme management, or customer strategies or policies that outline a benefit realization approach. Know that it could be a stand-alone document, an entry in a project management tool, a spreadsheet, or a set of presentation slides. Know the composition of the benefits management approach.

Demonstrate an understanding of the recommended roles and responsibilities within the business case theme.
- Demonstrate an understanding that corporate, programme management, or the customer provides details of any corporate, programme management, or customer business case standards to follow and also provides the project mandate upon which the business case will be based.
- Demonstrate an understanding that the senior users provide forecasts of the benefits that will be derived from using the project's products and are accountable for providing actual versus forecast statements of benefits at the benefits reviews.
- Demonstrate an understanding that the project manager is responsible for preparing and maintaining the business case under the direction of the executive.

Assess and critique an approach to managing business justification.
Know which roles are responsible for which business case–related activities. Understand how and why the business case and benefits management approach should be used throughout a project and what they should contain. Show how the business case theme might be adapted to different project contexts (for example: a small project, an agile project, a project with external third-party

organizations, or a project operating within a programme environment). Show whether a given approach to managing the business case aligns with the principles of PRINCE2.

Review Questions

The remainder of this chapter contains mock exam questions, first for the Foundation exam and then for the Practitioner exam.

Foundation Exam Questions

1. Which of the following is a purpose of the business case theme?
    A. To help establish whether the project is still viable when making key decisions
    B. To understand whether the outputs from the project are fit for purpose
    C. To establish a structure of accountability for the project
    D. To assess and control uncertainty throughout the project

2. Which of the following is a purpose of the benefits management approach?
    A. To describe how and when the performance of the project's products can be measured
    B. To document the justification for the project
    C. To define the project
    D. To pass on details of unfinished work and ongoing risks

3. At what time in the project is the business case reviewed and maybe updated?
    (1) When refining the business case during the initiation stage
    (2) When creating the project mandate
    (3) At the end of each management stage
    (4) When delivering specialist products
    A. 1 and 2
    B. 1 and 3
    C. 3 and 4
    D. 1 and 4

4. Which of these options is a minimum requirement for managing business justification for the project?
    A. To split the project into at least two management stages
    B. To record all quality activities carried out during the project
    C. To define a method for baselining products
    D. To identify actions to ensure that the project's outcomes are achieved

5. Which of the following options represents an example of an output?
    A. Benefits management approach
    B. New computer software
    C. Quicker processing of invoices
    D. A 20-percent increase in productivity

6. Which two management products does the business case theme require be produced and maintained?
    (1) Risk register
    (2) Communication management approach
    (3) Business case
    (4) Benefits management approach
    A. 1 and 2
    B. 2 and 3
    C. 3 and 4
    D. 1 and 4

7. During which of the following processes is the outline business case refined into the detailed business case?
    A. Starting up a project
    B. Initiating a project
    C. Managing a stage boundary
    D. Directing a project

8. Which role is responsible for ensuring that the benefits forecast in the business case represent value for money and align with the organization's objectives?
    A. Executive
    B. Project manager
    C. Project support
    D. Senior user

9. Which of the following is an example of the business case being developed?
    A. The executive drafting the outline business case
    B. The project board reviewing the justification for the project
    C. The senior user providing a statement of the achievement of benefits during a benefit review
    D. The project manager updating the business case at the end of a stage

10. Who is responsible for specifying the benefits and subsequently realizing the benefits by using the project's product?
    A. Project manager
    B. Executive
    C. Senior supplier
    D. Senior user

Practitioner Exam Questions

Exam Spotlight

Remember that for the Practitioner exam, you are allowed to refer to the official PRINCE2 manual (*Managing Successful Projects with PRINCE2*). This is a great help. I would say one of the key differences between passing and failing the Practitioner exam is knowing how to use the PRINCE2 manual during the exam. Some of the questions in the exam rely on you finding very specific pieces of information quickly from the manual.

For business case theme questions, where might you look in the PRINCE2 manual for useful information? The first (and most obvious) place is the business case theme chapter itself. The chapter begins by discussing the purpose of the business case theme; explaining the concepts of outputs, outcomes, and benefits; and defining the terms *desirable*, *viable*, and *achievable* within a PRINCE2 context. Then the chapter looks at the minimum requirements for applying the business case theme. The next few sections look at how the business case is created and developed throughout the project. Next, a section outlines which role is responsible for the range of business case–related responsibilities. Then, a section gives guidance for effective management of business justification and shows how to tailor the theme to different situations. The last section, which focuses on investment appraisal techniques, is not examinable, so you can ignore that in the exam. I would recommend having a look through the business case theme chapter in the PRINCE2 manual before the exam and familiarizing yourself with how the information is laid out.

In addition to the business case theme chapter, a few other places in the PRINCE2 manual might be useful. As you learned in this chapter, two management products are related to the business case theme: the business case and the benefits management approach. In the PRINCE 2 manual, Appendix A is the best source of information about these two management products. You also might find Appendix C useful for business case questions about roles and responsibilities. Although there is information on the responsibilities within the business case theme chapter, you'll often find more information about business case–related responsibilities in Appendix C.

The Practitioner questions in Section 1 and Section 2 are based on the Practitioner exam scenario described in Appendix B.

Section 1: Matching Questions

The executive is drafting the outline business case for a website project during the starting up a project process. Column 1 in the following table lists the five items of information that will be included in the business case. Choose the appropriate heading (A–F) in Column 2 for each item of information. Each heading can be used once, more than once, or not at all.

Column 1	Column 2
1. Continue with the current website.	A. Reasons
2. Financing the web project mean there will be no available budget for the factory extension project.	B. Business options
3. Sales increases will be measured over three years.	C. Expected benefits
4. The current website is difficult to use and attracts very few visitors.	D. Expected dis-benefits
5. Increase sales by 20 percent per annum in the next 3 years.	E. Timescale F. Costs G. Risks

Section 2: Classic Multiple-Choice Questions

1. The operations director of Digital Design has experience in understanding the potential for online sales. He has been asked by the executive to write the business case for the project. Is this appropriate, and why or why not?
    A. Yes, because the executive is accountable for the business case but might delegate the development of the document to someone else.
    B. Yes, because Quality Furniture has not been involved in selling products on the Internet before.
    C. No, because there is a conflict of interests if the supplier writes the customer's business case.
    D. No, because the supplier confirms the viability of the project approach.

2. During the initiation stage, the executive has asked Quality Furniture's finance director to create a report of the current sales of furniture through the four shops. The executive has asked the project manager to include the current sales report in the benefits management approach. Is this appropriate, and why or why not?
    A. Yes, because the benefits management approach should include baseline measures from which improvements will be calculated.
    B. Yes, because the finance director has the financial skills required to analyze current sales.
    C. No, because the benefits management approach should focus only on benefits forecast after the project.
    D. No, because the online sales will not be produced until the project has finished, so the benefits management approach should be developed then.

Chapter

5

Plans Theme

☑ **Explain the purpose of:**
  - The plans theme
  - Types of plan:
    - Project plan
    - Stage plan
    - Exception plan
    - Team plan

☑ **Describe the PRINCE2 minimum requirements for applying the plans theme**

☑ **Recall the steps in:**
  - The recommended approach to planning, including:
  - The recommended approach to defining and analyzing the products, and explain
  - The factors to consider when structuring the project into management stages

PRINCE2 Practitioner Exam Objectives Covered in This Chapter:

☑ **Apply the PRINCE2 requirements for the plans theme, demonstrating an understanding of:**
  - Key management products:
    - Project plan
    - Stage plan
    - Exception plan
    - Team plan
  - The recommended roles and responsibilities within the theme
  - The recommended approach to planning, including the recommended approach to defining and analyzing the products, excluding detailed estimating and resource scheduling techniques

☑ **Assess whether an approach to applying the plans theme is effective and fit for purpose, taking into consideration: the context, the PRINCE2 principles, and the purpose and requirements of the plans theme (excluding detailed estimating and resource scheduling techniques)**

The plans theme describes an approach that helps you forecast the people, resources, and activities needed in order to create your project's products. It helps the project management team predict how long the project will take and how much it will cost. The plans theme describes how to document these forecasts into plans, which can then be used to track and monitor your project's progress. The plans help to communicate time, cost, and resource information to the project management team and external stakeholders.

You will see that there are different types of PRINCE2 plans containing different levels of detail. Each type of plan is useful for a different level of management. You will learn what information each of these PRINCE2 plans contains.

This chapter covers an important PRINCE2 planning approach, called *product-based planning*. Product-based planning starts with understanding the products that need to be delivered before identifying the work that has to be done.

Along with the theory, as usual there are plenty of tips to help you prepare for the exams and practice Foundation and Practitioner questions about the plans theme.

Levels of Plans

In PRINCE2, three levels of plans can be created in a project: project plans, stage plans, and team plans (as shown in Figure 5.1). Above these levels of plans, there may be a higher-level corporate, programme management, or customer's plan that the activities of the project need to align to. However, this plan will not be created within the project by the project management team, so it is not considered a PRINCE2 plan level. The corporate or programme management plan would be created either by those taking on senior positions within the organization that commissioned the project or by those running a programme that the project is part of. There might be a customer's plan if the project is delivering work to a client, and the project is only part of a wider piece of work that the customer is running.

The exception plan that you can see to the right of Figure 5.1 is a special sort of plan. It is not considered to be a PRINCE2 plan level. The exception plan shows how the project will recover after there has been a forecast breach in stage or project tolerances. Once approved by the project board, the exception plan replaces either a project plan or a stage plan. You learn more about the exception plan later in this section.

Figure 5.1: The PRINCE2 planning levels

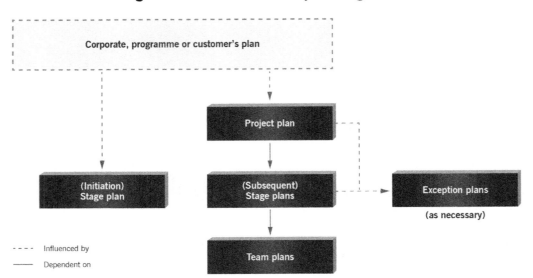

The Project Plan

The project plan is the top level of plans. The project manager creates the project plan in the initiating a project process. It shows the work that needs to be done from the point after the initiation stage to the end of the project. The project plan provides the business case with the planned costs and time. It allows the project manager to refine the business case during the initiating a project process.

The project plan shows the highest level of detail out of all the three levels of PRINCE2 plans. It describes the main products that are to be delivered in the project and shows broadly the activities and resources that are needed to deliver them. It should indicate how the project will be divided into various management stages and show any key milestone points in the project.

After the project manager creates the project plan in the initiation stage, the project board reviews its contents and decides whether to authorize the project. They do this review in their directing a project process.

Once the project is active, the project board uses the project plan (again during the directing a project process) to track and monitor the progress of the project. The project plan provides an appropriately high level of detail for the members of the project board, because, given their seniority in the project, it is unlikely they will want to get involved in the day-to-day details.

At the end of each stage during the managing a stage boundary process, the project manager updates the project plan with high-level details of what occurred in that stage as well as any new high-level details for the subsequent stages that are now known.

Figure 5.2 shows the project plan's timeline. The figure shows an example of a four-stage project. The first stage is the initiation stage, and then there are three delivery stages. You can see in this example that in order to manage the project, the project management team has created one project plan, four stage plans, and eight team plans.

Figure 5.2: Example plans for a four-stage project

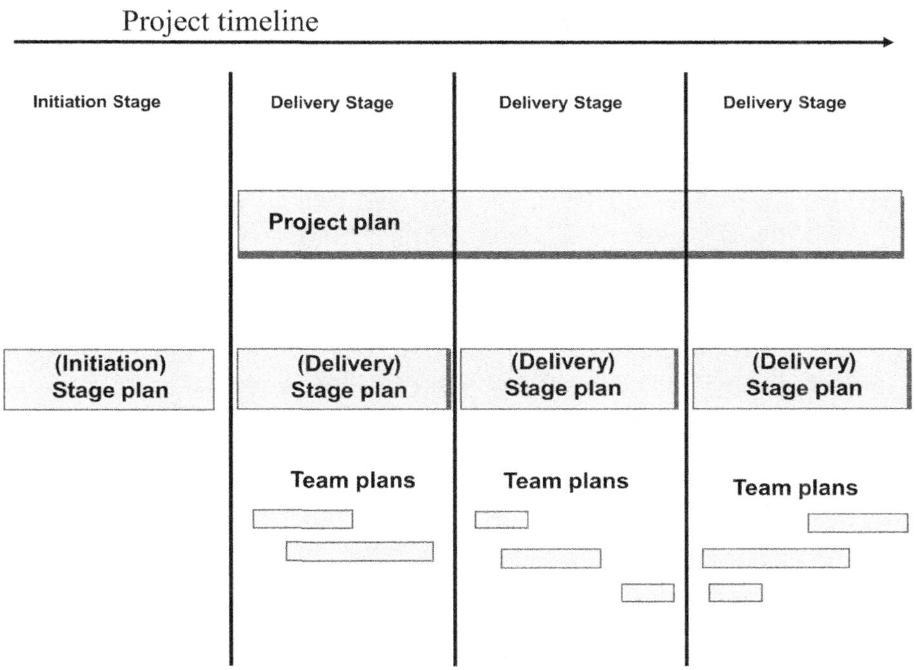

The Stage Plans

After the project plan, the next level of plans is the *stage plan*. Stage plans are created by the project manager and provide a lower level of detail than the project plan. They include enough information to allow the project manager to track and control the work done in the stages on a day-to-day basis.

Because the stage plans are more detailed than the project plan, it is usually difficult to create them until near the time the work described in the plan will be done. For example, if you were managing a project to build a hotel, it would be difficult to create the stage plan for the construction of the building until after the stage in which the architectural plans were created. This is called the *planning horizon problem*, which PRINCE2 overcomes by creating each stage's plan just before that stage starts.

There are two processes where the project manager will create stage plans. First, the stage plan for the initiation stage is created in the starting up a project process. This plan shows the work that needs to be done to create the project initiation documentation. The project manager updates the stage plan for the initiation stage with progress information during the initiating a project process, as the work of that stage proceeds.

Secondly, the project manager uses the managing a stage boundary process to create stage plans for all the stages after the initiation stage. The order of events here would be as follows:

1. Towards the end of the previous stage, the project manager uses the managing a stage boundary process to create the next stage plan.

2. Then the project board reviews it, using the directing a project process, and decides whether to authorize the project manager to proceed with the next stage.
3. If the project board authorizes the stage, the project manager updates the stage plans with progress information during the controlling a stage process, as the work of the delivery stage progresses and specialist products are delivered.

Later in the chapter, I describe product-based planning. One of the important ideas of this approach is that plans should describe not only the work to do but also which products need to be delivered as part of the scope of the plan. In PRINCE2, this is done by creating a range of product descriptions, so a stage plan will contain product descriptions for all the outputs to be delivered within that stage.

The Team Plans

Team plans are the lowest level of plans. These plans contain the necessary level of detail for individual teams to both forecast and then track and control the work that has been assigned to them by the project manager in one or more work packages. PRINCE2 says that these plans are optional, because there might be enough detail within the stage plan and the work package for the team to use. Also, because the teams might be working for different organizations that may follow other project approaches, PRINCE2 does not specify the format and composition of the team plans. The formality of a team plan could vary—it could be a simple schedule appended to a work package or a fully formed plan following the PRINCE2 composition (which you will see later in this chapter).

The team manager (or the team members, if there is no team manager) creates and updates the team plans in the managing product delivery process. The team plans may be created at the same time that the project manager creates a stage plan. However, don't get confused with the processes—if the teams are creating their team plans while the project manager is creating her stage plan at the end of the stage, the teams will still be within the managing product delivery process, and the project manager will be within the managing a stage boundary process. In fact, the stage plan may simply be an amalgamation of the team plans that cover that stage's work.

Exception Plans

Exception plans are created to show how the project or a stage will recover from a breach in project or stage tolerances. To understand how exception plans work, you must understand a little about tolerances and exceptions. Chapter 9, "Progress Theme," includes detailed descriptions of tolerances and exceptions, but for now, the following explanation will be enough.

Remember that there are four levels of management in PRINCE2: corporate, programme management, or the customer; project board; project manager; and the team manager (or the team members themselves, if there is no team manager). Each level of management sets out certain constraints within which the level below must work. These constraints are mainly defined in terms of the amount of money and/or time that a level of management must work within. (Constraints could be set around other things as well, such as quality, scope, benefit, and risk.) It might be that the constraints are set with some flexibility. For example, corporate, programme management, or the customer could tell the project board that the objective is to deliver the project within 12 months, but it would be acceptable to deliver it two months earlier or one month later. In PRINCE2, these allowable deviations are called *tolerances*.

There are different levels of these tolerances that align with the levels of management. Corporate, programme management, or the customer sets project tolerances for the project board;

the project board sets stage tolerances for the project manager; and the project manager sets work package tolerances for the team or team manager. Obviously, project tolerances are the largest, and then stage tolerances, and finally, the smallest are work package tolerances.

If any level of management realizes they are forecasting to breach the tolerances given to them by the management level above, they are in what PRINCE2 calls an *exception situation*. The exception signals that that level of management has run out of authority and must escalate the situation to the level of management above. As discussed in the following subsections, the exception situation might eventually lead to the creation of an exception plan.

Example of Using an Exception Plan to Replace a Stage Plan

In a project to build a hotel, the project has reached the stage where each of the floor's bedrooms is being built. Maybe when building one of the floors, there has been a mistake. Instead of creating 20 double rooms, 10 smaller single rooms and 15 double rooms have been built. The project manager consults with the construction manager and finds out that this situation could be handled in one of the following ways:

- Leave the rooms as they are and build five more double rooms and no single rooms in the next floor to be built.
- Rebuild the single rooms as double rooms. Doing so will take an additional eight weeks of work.

When the project board authorizes a project manager to deliver a stage, they also authorize a set of product descriptions that describe exactly what the project manager is expected to deliver within that stage. The product description for this floor of rooms says there should be 20 double rooms, which in this case, there aren't.

The project manager checks to see if she can authorize work to correct the problem without breaching the stage tolerances that the project board has given her. In this example, she has been given a two-week time tolerance for this stage. However, the work to correct the problem will take an additional eight weeks. She cannot correct the problem within the stage time tolerance, so she is in exception and must escalate this situation to the project board.

The project manager escalates the situation to the project board by first sending them a copy of an issue report describing the situation and then creating and sending them an exception report. The exception report describes the various options to deal with the problem and recommends one. In this case, the project manager would describe the two options, and maybe she would recommend rebuilding the single rooms as double rooms and taking the additional 8 weeks.

On receiving the exception report, the project board can do a number of things. In the extreme case, they could decide the problem is so serious that the project needs to be closed prematurely. But that seems unlikely in this situation. Alternatively, in the case of products that have been created incorrectly (called *off-specifications*, which you learn about in Chapter 8, "Change Theme"), the project board could approve the incorrect products (called *giving a concession*, which you also learn about in Chapter 8).

Finally, the project board could decide to investigate in more detail the project manager's recommended option. They could ask the project manager for an exception plan that showed what work was involved with rebuilding the single rooms as double rooms. In this situation, the exception plan would show the work that needed to be done from the time of the exception to the end of the current stage. Much of the work it details could be exactly the same as the original stage plan for this stage, showing the remaining work involved with building all the other floors' bedrooms. However, there would now be some additional tasks to change those incorrect single rooms into double rooms—and of course, the exception plan would run eight weeks longer than the original stage plan to allow for this additional work.

The final part to this story is that the project board will review the exception plan (in their directing a project process) and decide whether to authorize it. If they do authorize it, the exception plan becomes the new current stage plan that the project manager will then use to control and monitor the remaining work in that stage, plus the new additional corrective work. You can see this situation as Option 1 in Figure 5.3.

One final point to cover is the process the project manager uses to create the exception plan. Rather bizarrely, the exception plan is created in the managing a stage boundary. This can sometimes be confusing, because, of course, at the point that the exception occurs (represented by the dotted vertical line in Figure 5.3), the project has not reached the end of the stage. A good way of thinking about this is that because of the breach of tolerances, the project needs an emergency stage boundary. During this emergency stage boundary, the project board needs to review a new detailed plan to see how to recover from the exception. Therefore, the project manager must use the managing a stage boundary in order to prepare to meet with the project board. (By the way, "emergency stage boundary" is not a PRINCE2 term—I'm just using it to better explain the situation.)

Figure 5.3: Exception plans

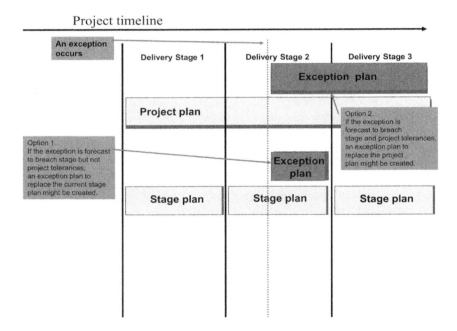

Example of Using an Exception Plan to Replace a Project Plan

In the previous example, the exception plan was created at the stage plan level. It covered the work from the point of the exception to the end of the current stage. In some situations, however, the exception plan might have to cover the work from the point of the exception to the end of the project. In such a case, the exception plan would be created at a project plan level. You can see this situation as Option 2 in Figure 5.3.

Why would the project manager create an exception plan at the project plan level? It all depends on how badly tolerances are forecast to be affected by whatever problem the project is facing. Imagine that in the last section's situation, the project manager once again recommends to the project board the option to rebuild the room, and once again this is forecast to take an additional eight weeks. However, this time the additional eight weeks will breach not only the stage time tolerances but also the project time tolerances.

In this example, corporate, programme management, or the customer has given the project board a six-week time tolerance within which they must deliver the project. When the project manager escalates the problem with the bedrooms to the project board, the board realizes that the recommended remedial action will breach their project time tolerances.

In this situation, if the project board wants to pursue the project manager's recommended option, they will ask for an exception plan that not only details the work to finish the stage but also shows what effect that work will have on subsequent stages. In this example, it looks like the only effect would be that the work in the subsequent stages is delayed, but in another situation, it could be that the work in subsequent stages might change as well.

The project manager once again creates this project-level exception plan in the managing a stage boundary. This time, however, this project-level exception plan needs to be approved at the corporate, programme management, or customer level. Once approved, the exception plan becomes the new project plan.

Breaches in Work Package Tolerances

In PRINCE2, exception plans can replace stage plans or project plans. They are not used to replace team plans. If a team manager (or team member, if there is no team manager) realizes there will be a breach of their work package tolerances, they will raise an issue. If the issue does not breach the project manager's stage tolerance, the project manager can then deal with this problem by amending the work package or issuing a new work package.

The Plan Management Product

In this section, you learn about the PRINCE2 recommended format for a plan. Stage plans, project plans, and exception plans created at the project or stage level follow this recommended format. Team plans could follow the recommended format, but it is not obligatory. It could be that the team plans are created by a third-party organization that is not following PRINCE2. In this case, they may have different planning standards. Even if this is not the case, the team plans could simply be a schedule attached to the work package.

A PRINCE2 plan should cover not just the activities to create products but also the activities to manage product creation, including activities for assurance, quality management, risk management, change control, communication, and any other project controls required. It also describes the products that are to be delivered.

Exam Spotlight

A Practitioner exam question might ask about the types of information that belong in different sections of a plan. For example, a question might ask in which section of the plan a project manager should write an amount of money that has been set aside to fund risk responses. The answer, if you didn't know it already, is the budgets section.

Remember that you can refer to the official PRINCE2 manual, *Managing Successful Projects with PRINCE2* (Stationery Office, 2017) during the Practitioner exam. When the exam asks in which section of a management product various pieces of information should go, Appendix A in the PRINCE2 manual is a good source of information. Appendix A shows the format of all the management products.

One potentially confusing situation when using the PRINCE2 manual is when the exam asks what should go where in a specific sort of plan, such as a project plan or a stage plan. If you look in Appendix A of the PRINCE2 manual, there is no project plan or stage plan section. This is because there is a generic plan section, which covers the format of the project plan, stage plans, and exception plans.

When I teach PRINCE2, I have my class write a note next to the plan section in Appendix A of the PRINCE2 manual that this covers the other types of plans as well. I recommend that you do the same.

Many plans that I have worked with contain only scheduling information, such as who is doing what on a particular date. In addition to containing a schedule, PRINCE2 plans contain a lot more information, such as details on any assumptions that have been made, prerequisites that must be in place before the plan starts, and the product descriptions for the products within the scope of the plan.

Figure 5.4 shows the composition of a PRINCE2 plan. This format is used for project plans, stage plans, and exception plans.

Figure 5.4: Composition of a plan

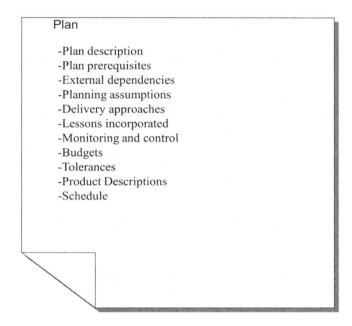

The following section describes the type of information that might go into the different sections of a stage plan, using the example of a project to build a hotel. Imagine that this plan is for a particular stage in that project in which the bedrooms will be decorated and furnished.

Plan Description

The plan description should give the reader an idea of what the work in this plan encompasses and what type of plan this is (project, stage, or exception).

In this case, the plan description might say something like the following:

This plan covers the work of the stage to decorate and furnish all the bedrooms of the hotel. The work in the plan will install each room's electricity and plumbing, decorate the rooms, and install bathroom suites and the room's furniture.

Plan Prerequisite

A plan *prerequisite* is something that must be in place before the work of the plan can begin and must remain in place for the plan to succeed. For example, a prerequisite for the building of the rooms is that the health and safety officer has signed off on the safety of the main hotel building that was built in the previous stage.

Spotting a prerequisite can be difficult in the exam, so have a good look at the related exam spotlight on this subject.

Exam Spotlight

Spotting a prerequisite can be tricky. Consider the example of the stage plan to decorate and furnish the bedrooms in the project to build a hotel. Here are three possible prerequisites for this stage plan, one of which is right, and the other two are wrong:

1. The gym building (sited on a plot next to the hotel and built in the previous stage) is completed.
2. The decorators (needed three weeks into the stage) are available to paint the rooms.
3. The engineering director of the construction company must sign off on the structural integrity of the hotel building before work can begin on fitting the interior.

Option one looks suspiciously like a prerequisite, but it is not. It is true that the gym building will probably have been completed by the time the project moves on to furnishing and decorating the rooms, but work on furnishing the rooms could begin if the construction of the gym overran. There is no dependency between the gym work and the decorating of the bedrooms in a separate building.

Option two again looks suspiciously like a prerequisite, but once again, it is not. Something is a prerequisite only if the plan cannot even start without the prerequisite happening. In this case, the plan could start without the decorators; it is just that work would be delayed if they were still not available by week three.

Option three is, of course, the correct one. In this case, no work can begin furnishing the rooms until the structural integrity of the outer building has been confirmed. The plan's work cannot even start until this sign-off has occurred.

External Dependencies

External dependencies are products that will be needed for the work described within the plan, but they will be created outside the scope of the plan. In other words, the project manager will not delegate work to anyone to create the external dependencies. Another project or group of people could be creating the external dependency products, or maybe those products already exist.

In the project to create a hotel, an example of an external dependency might be the tender responses from potential construction suppliers. These are needed for the stage during which third-party vendors are procured, but the project manager will not manage the work to create the tender responses.

External dependencies could also be activities that are being performed outside the scope of the plan but which need to be done in order to carry out some of the plan's activities.

Planning Assumptions

This section of the plan contains the planning assumptions that have been made when forecasting the work in the plan. For example, in the hotel project, the manager of the electricians might have told the project manager they will be available to do their work as long as another job they are currently doing doesn't overrun. When putting the stage plan together, the project manager would write in this section that the plan is based on the assumption that the electrician's current work finishes on schedule.

Delivery Approaches

This section of the plan shows if any main delivery approaches will be used to deliver the work. For example, if the plan's work involves using skills that the organization commissioning the project does not currently have, that organization might decide to either train their own staff to do the work or outsource the work to a specialist supplier.

Lessons Incorporated

This section of the plan shows what previous relevant experience has been considered when putting the plan together.

In the hotel project, a lesson might be the following:

A previous hotel construction project found that it was important to include penalty fees for late delivery in third-party supplier contracts to reduce the risk of delays.

Monitoring and Control

One of the main reasons for having a plan is to use it as a yardstick to continually compare actual versus planned progress so that the project manager can quickly tell if the work is behind schedule. If work starts to be delivered late, the project manager will have to take corrective action to bring things back on track.

Here are a few examples of how the stage plan could be monitored and controlled:

- Review the stage plan at the end of each day to compare forecast work against actual work.
- Request a product status account from project support to track the progress of the stage's products. (The product status account is a report generated from the project's configuration management system that gives a snapshot of the state of the project's products. You learn more about this in Chapter 8, "Change Theme.")
- Produce a highlight report every two weeks and send it to the project board and any other recipients, as detailed in the communication management approach. (A highlight report is a type of progress report sent from the project manager to the project board. You learn more about this in Chapter 10, "Managing the Middle of a Project Successfully with PRINCE2.")
- Instruct all teams in their work packages to produce a weekly checkpoint report updating the project manager on the progress of their work. (A checkpoint report is a type of progress report sent from the team manager to the project manager. You learn more about this in Chapter 10.)

Budgets

This section contains information about the following:

- The amount of money budgeted for the plan's work.
- The amount of time budgeted for the plan's work.
- The amount of money set aside to fund changes to the plan's products or scope, which is called the *change budget* (You learn about change budgets in Chapter 8, "Change Theme.")
- The amount of money set aside to fund countermeasures to deal with risks, which is called the *risk budget* (You learn about risk budgets in Chapter 7, "Risk Theme.")

Here is a sample budget entry for the stage plan to decorate and furnish the hotel:

$500,000 has been budgeted for the work to furnish and decorate the bedrooms. Four months has been budgeted to carry out the work. A risk budget of $50,000 has been set aside to fund the hiring of extra contractors, should the work overrun. A change budget of $20,000 has been set aside to fund minor changes (up to $500 each) to the specifications of any of the room fittings.

Tolerances

This section describes the plan's time, cost, risk, and scope tolerances. For example, there might be some time tolerance in the stage plan. Maybe the objective is to deliver the stage in four months, but the project board would allow it to overrun by two weeks, if needed.

Scope tolerance is the allowable flexibility on the products that will be delivered within the plan. For example, if there is time, Wi-Fi will be fitted to all the rooms, but it is not essential to do so within this stage.

Product Descriptions

As I mentioned in the introduction to this chapter, product-based planning is an important PRINCE2 concept. A product-based planning approach ensures that the project management team is very clear about which products will be created before they start to plan the necessary activities and resources. To help implement this approach, all PRINCE2 plans contain product descriptions for each product that will be delivered within the scope of the plan. The product descriptions contain detailed and measurable specifications for a product, together with a description of how these specifications will be checked and who should be responsible for signing off on the products.

This section might also contain the product descriptions for products that are external dependencies for this plan. (You will find a more detailed explanation of the purpose and composition of product descriptions in Chapter 6, "Quality Theme.")

So, in the example, the stage plan for the decoration and furnishing of the bedrooms might contain the product descriptions for the bedrooms and product descriptions for some of the individual components of the bedrooms, such as items of furniture or bathroom fittings.

Schedule

This section shows which activities are needed in order to deliver the products described in the preceding section. It also shows the sequence of those activities, which resources will be needed, which people will carry out the tasks, and which dates the different tasks are forecast to start and finish. As the work in the plan progresses, this section will be updated with what actually happened.

The schedule could be shown in a variety of formats, such as a Gantt chart (a graphical way of showing schedules), a calendar, or simply a list of tasks with dates and peoples' names next to them. One format that PRINCE2 suggests is a product checklist like the one shown in Figure 5.5. The product checklist shows a list of the products to be delivered within the scope of the plan, together with relevant key status dates for each product, such as forecast delivery date, actual delivery date, and forecast approval date.

Figure 5.5: Product checklist

Product identifier	Product title	Product description approved		Draft ready		Final quality check completed		Approved		Handed over (if applicable)	
		Plan	Actual	Plan	Actual	Plan	Actual	Plan	Actual	Plan	Actual

This section might also contain a product breakdown structure and product flow diagram. (You learn about these two diagrams in the "Defining and Analyzing the Products" section later in this chapter.)

Structuring the Project into Management Stages

You have already seen that an important principle in PRINCE2 is to manage by stages. Dividing the project into stages allows the project board to control the progress of the project. The project board gives authority to the project manager to manage only one stage at a time. At the end of each stage, the project manager must report back to the project board and ask for permission to move on to the next stage. The end of each stage acts as a review and decision point for the project board and enables them to control the project without needing to dedicate much time to the initiative.

In a simple or a short project, the project board might be happy to control the project using two stages: The first would be the initiation stage where the project plan is created, and the second would be where the work would be delivered. On more complicated projects, however, the project board likely will want more control over the project; therefore, they will want the project to be structured into more stages.

The term management stage is used in PRINCE2 interchangeably with *stages*. The definition of a management stage is the section of the project that the project manager is managing on behalf of the project board at any given time during the project. The project board commits resources and gives the project manager authority to spend for one management stage at a time. Once that management stage has finished, the project manager must return to the project board and ask for authorization to move on to the next management stage (or if that stage is the final stage, ask for authorization to close the project). So, don't get confused by the term *management stage*—it is, in effect, a stage of the project. As you have seen, the project manager plans each management stage by creating a stage plan.

The project manager creates the project plan during the initiating a project process. At this early stage in the initiative, particularly for longer projects, it might be difficult to forecast all the activities that will need to be done. Because of this, the project plan will probably be quite high-level. At this point, however, the project manager together with the project board must use this limited information to decide how to divide the project into management stages. How do they do this? PRINCE2 recommends taking the following factors into account:

How far ahead in the project is it sensible to plan in detail?

In the hotel example, it is difficult to plan in detail the construction of the building until the hotel has been designed. So it would be sensible to place the design work in one stage and the construction work in a subsequent stage.

Where are the key decision points going to be?

The project board will probably need to be involved in the key decisions, so it would be sensible to make these decisions at the end of a stage, when the board meets to decide whether to continue with the project.

How risky is the project?

If a project is riskier, the project board will probably want to have more control. The project board gains more control by having a project with more short stages rather than fewer but longer stages. This means the project manager has to report back to the project board more frequently at the end of each of the short stages.

How confident is the project management team about the project?

If the project board and the project manager are not confident about the initiative, they will probably want to have more stages and therefore more review points.

If the project is part of a programme, how might this affect the placement of stage boundaries?

It might be sensible to align project review points with programme review points.

What major delivery steps will the project progress through in order to deliver the work?

Many projects go through some major steps in order to deliver their work. For example, the key delivery steps in a software project might be to gather requirements for the product, design the software, build the software, and then test the software. These delivery steps might affect how the project will be divided into management stages.

The last factor deserves more explanation. In many organizations, typical projects will go through a well-defined set of delivery steps. For example, I recently worked with an Internet marketing agency. Many of their client projects went through the same set of steps. They called their first step "discovery," which involved researching the client's marketplace. Then they moved on to the next step, called "strategy," where they formulated a marketing plan for their client. The third step was called "execution," where they implemented the marketing plan. The fourth (and final) step was called "refine," where they collected data to see how well the marketing plan was working and made adjustments to improve its success. PRINCE2 would call each of these steps *delivery steps*. A delivery step is a group of work within a project that is characterized by using similar techniques or specialist skills or creating specialist products of a certain type. A *delivery approach* is a set of these delivery steps used by an organization to create their specialist products.

Figure 5.6 shows another example of a set of delivery steps. You can see a high-level project plan put together at the beginning of a project. All the project team knows at this stage is that the project will involve five delivery steps: specifying, designing, building, training, and commissioning. This is not so unrealistic—sometimes at the outset of a project, the project team can give only a high-level forecast of the work to be done.

Figure 5.6: High-level project plan

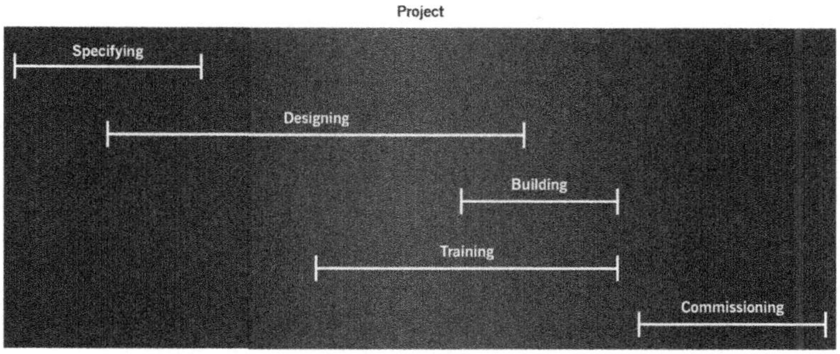

The challenge at the outset of the project is how to divide a high-level project plan into various management stages. Figure 5.7 shows how the project team has decided to divide their project into management stages. The first management stage involves doing the specifying work and the first part of the designing work; the second management stage involves doing most of the rest of the designing work and starting the training work; and so on.

Figure 5.7: High-level project plan divided into management stages

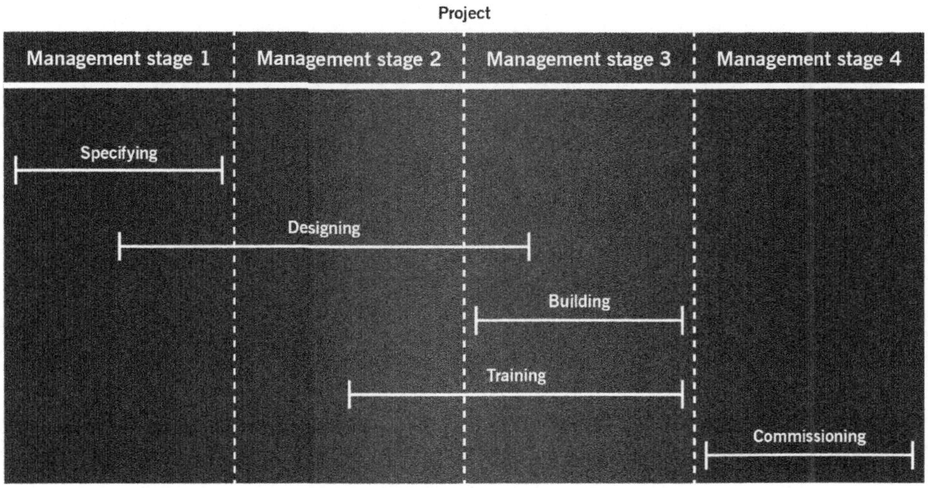

There is one problem with the project plan in Figure 5.7. A primary benefit of management stages is that they provide a review and decision point for the project board. However, at the end of management stage one, it may be difficult to review the designing work because it has only just started. Similarly, at the end of management stage two, it may be difficult to review the progress of the designing and training work, because it hasn't yet finished. The only way to review the progress of these pieces of work is to give a percentage-complete figure, which is often quite subjective. One person's 80-percent complete is another's 50-percent complete. People are overly optimistic about the work that remains, or they forget about all the little things that need to be done at the end, which, when they are added together, become one big thing!

Contrast this with reviewing the progress of the specifying work at the end of stage one. The specifying work has either finished or not finished. The project team can be completely objective when they report on the progress of this work, as they can also be with the designing, building, and training work at the end of stage three and the commissioning work at the end of stage four.

Figure 5.8 shows a solution to the problem of reviewing work that spans multiple management stages. Here, the delivery steps have been split up so that they fit into the management stages. For example, the designing delivery step is now done in three parts: The overall design is done in management stage one; the detailed design is done in management stage two; and the peripheral design is done in management stage three. Now it is easier to be more objective when the progress of the designing work is reviewed at the end of stages one, two, and three. For example, at the end of management stage one, the project manager can (hopefully) report to the project board that the overall designs have been finished.

Figure 5.8: Delivery steps divided across management stages

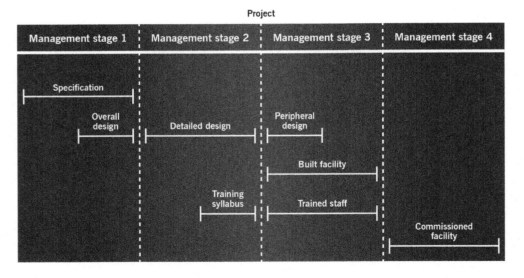

In PRINCE2 terms, the challenge in Figure 5.6, Figure 5.7, and Figure 5.8 is to work out how to divide the delivery steps into the management stages. The solution in this example is shown in Figure 5.8, where a number of the delivery steps have been subdivided so that they fit into the management stages.

Don't be confused here, though. In Figure 5.8, the overall design, detailed design, and peripheral design together form just one delivery step: the designing delivery step. This is because each of those three pieces of work involves the same set of specialist skills: designers.

Exam Spotlight

The Foundation exam often includes questions relating to delivery steps and management stages. They can be quite confusing. The best approach is to remember that delivery steps are just big pieces of work that involve people with similar skills. These big pieces of work might take place across one management stage or many management stages. Here are some questions to test how well you understand the differences between delivery steps and management stages:

1. Do delivery steps and management stages always end at the same time?
   If you look at Figure 5.7, you can see that the answer to this is no. The designing delivery step ends before management stage three.
2. Can management stages overlap?
   You can see from Figure 5.7 (and maybe you knew this already) that the answer is no.
3. Can delivery steps overlap?
   You can see from Figure 5.7 that the answer is yes. For example, at the beginning of stage three, the designing, building, and training delivery steps are all running concurrently.
4. Can you have more than one delivery step running over one management stage?
   You can see from Figure 5.7 that there are three delivery steps—designing, building, and training—running across management stage three. So the answer to this question is yes.
5. Can you have more than one management stage running over one delivery step?
   You can see from Figure 5.7 that the designing delivery step runs over three management stages. So the answer to this question is yes.

Delivery Steps in the Software Industry

Every industry's projects have different delivery steps. For example, in software engineering, the order of events in a project might be as follows: First, the software business experts gather the client's requirements for the software; next, the software experts design the software; and then the software engineers build the software, the testing team tests it, and, finally, the consultants install it. Each one of these steps is a delivery step.

If the software project is using PRINCE2, the project management team needs to decide how they are going to control the project using the management stages. One way would be to simply align the management stages with the delivery steps. So, at the end of the requirements gathering, there is a meeting with the project board, during which they review the requirements and decide whether to authorize the project to proceed to the designing stage.

However, if one of the delivery steps is very long—perhaps building the software takes a year, for example—the project board might not be comfortable committing resources for this length of time. In this case, the team could see if the software could be built in a number of modules, each of which created within its own management stage.

The software project I've just described uses what is called the *Waterfall approach*. The first set of activities defines the requirements, and then the software is designed, built, tested, and commissioned. This method is used throughout the software industry but has one big disadvantage. Clients find it difficult to specify what they want in the unfamiliar world of software engineering, even with the help of experts. Also, there are often difficulties in communication between technical people and business people. Unfortunately, with the Waterfall approach, the first time you can tell for sure whether the correct requirements have been defined is after all the work to design, build, test, and commission the product has been done and the client has finally received the product.

To reduce the risk of collecting incorrect requirements, the software team could follow another approach. The project team might decide to quickly gather an initial set of requirements from the client and then quickly build a working prototype, which they can show to the client to get some early feedback. Using this early feedback, they can quickly build another new prototype. By going through this process a number of times, the team gains a better understanding of the client's needs. After several iterations, they then design, build, and test the real product, just as they did in the first example.

How does this approach relate to the PRINCE2 management stages and delivery steps? Well, the last piece of the project—the designing, building, and testing of the real product—can be divided into management stages in the same way as the Waterfall project. What is more difficult is the prototyping work. A number of steps are involved in each iteration of the prototyping work: gathering initial requirements, designing the prototype, building the prototype, and maybe some quick testing of the prototype. Each iteration also involves multiple concurrent delivery steps. How does the project team divide this work into management stages?

One approach is to run each prototype iteration in a management stage. At the end of each iteration, the project board can then decide whether to move on to the next iteration during their end-stage assessment.

One of the main ideas related to management stages in PRINCE2 is that their placement shouldn't be dictated by the specialist work. Obviously, the specialist work will be a factor in the decision about where to place the management stages. It may be useful to finish a management stage at the end of a major delivery step so that the project board can review its output. However, the ultimate decision about the placement of management stages should be driven by an understanding of how to control the project, not by the specialist work.

The PRINCE2 Approach to Plans

Figure 5.9 shows the seven steps of the PRINCE2 approach to planning. When the project manager creates the project plans and each stage plan, she will follow the seven steps in the planning approach. With team plans, the situation is a little different. As you have seen, team plans are optional, and the teams could be working for another organization that isn't following PRINCE2 and may use a different approach to planning.

One fundamental planning concept in PRINCE2 is that the project management team should clearly define which products will be delivered before planning the activities and resources necessary to work on those products. This concept is called *product-based planning*. This means that although there might be a certain amount of iteration and repetition of the steps in the planning procedure, defining and analyzing the products should be done at least once before going on to the next steps. The next three steps—identifying activities and dependencies, preparing estimates, and preparing a schedule—are primarily focused on what PRINCE2 calls *activity-based planning*. So, in the approach to planning, there is both product-based planning, which focuses on what to create, and activity-based planning, which focuses on how to create the products.

Figure 5.9: The PRINCE2 approach to plans

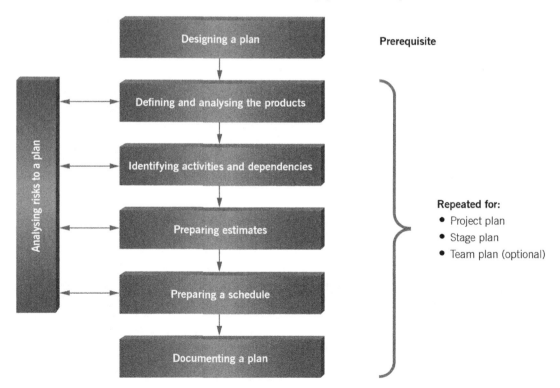

Designing a Plan

The first step is designing a plan. The first thing that the project management team must decide is how they would like to present the plans within their project. There is, of course, a variety of plan formats, from Gantt charts to a list of tasks on a spreadsheet to a far more basic set of sticky notes on a wall. In this step, the project management team chooses a suitable format for their project.

In addition to deciding on the format of plans, this step is where the project management team decides what estimating techniques to use. There are many ways to estimate how long tasks will take and how much they will cost—for example, reviewing records from similar initiatives, using statistical methods (such as three-point estimating), or consensus approaches (such as the Delphi technique). For the PRINCE2 exam, it is not necessary to understand any of these approaches to estimating. You just need to know this is when the estimating technique is chosen.

Another area the project management team needs to consider is whether to use any planning tools, such as project software.

Although the planning procedure might be carried out numerous times in any project, this particular step might be done only once. After the project management team has chosen the plans' format, estimating techniques, and planning tools, there is no need to repeat this step.

During the designing a plan step, the project management team may need to review corporate, programme management, or customer documentation to see if there are any standards for plan formats, estimating approaches, and/or planning tools that they need to follow.

When the project manager is designing the project plan, she will also need to consider how to split the plan into a number of management stages. As you have seen in the previous section of this chapter, "Structuring the Project into Management Stages," the project manager will need to consult with the project board on this decision, and there are a number of factors that will need to be considered.

Defining and Analyzing the Products

The next step is defining and analyzing the products. This is the step where the product-based planning approach is used. You learn more about this approach later in this chapter. It involves identifying all the products that will be delivered within the plan and then describing them in sufficient detail so that the teams understand what needs to be created and the project manager can track and monitor their work. In addition to identifying specialist products, this step lists the management products, such as progress reports that will be created.

The main output from this step is a collection of product descriptions describing the outputs from (and inputs to) this plan.

Identifying Activities and Dependencies

The third step is identifying activities and dependencies. Once the products within the scope of the plan have been identified, the next step is to understand what activities will deliver those products. The teams that will do this work should be involved with this step.

In addition to identifying the work to deliver the products, the plan identifies quality activities to check the products and the management activities involved with controlling and monitoring the work.

Finally, any dependencies between the activities should be described. There are two types of dependencies in PRINCE2: internal or external. An *internal dependency* is when one activity cannot start until another activity has finished. An *external dependency* is when the project management team needs something from outside of the project, such as a product or a decision, before starting some work detailed in the plan.

Preparing Estimates

During the preparing estimates step, the project management team forecasts how long the tasks will take, how much they will cost, and what effort and resources are required to carry out the activities in the plan. The estimates will inevitably change as more is discovered about the project.

Preparing a Schedule

Now that all the tasks have been identified, and the time, effort, and cost of those tasks have been estimated, the next step is preparing a schedule, which involves forecasting the dates that the tasks will start and finish. The project manager will consider resource and team availability, as well as the availability of the people involved with reviewing and approving the products.

Once the schedule is complete, it can be presented graphically so that it is easy for everyone to see what needs to be done and when. It is usual to identify key milestone dates within the schedule, showing when key outputs need to be created.

Having assigned people and resources to the various pieces of work, the project manager can create a cost budget for the plan. This should include any provision for dealing with risks (risk budget) and changes (change budget) and whether there is any proposed flexibility around the costs targets (cost tolerance). The appropriate level of management must authorize these costs: project manager for a team plan, project board for a stage plan, and corporate, programme management, or the customer for a project plan.

Analyzing Risks to a Plan

Because plans are forecast and predicting the future is difficult, all plans contain some element of uncertainty, or in PRINCE2 terms, risk. The analyzing risks to a plan step should be carried out in parallel with the other steps in the planning procedure. Any threats or opportunities that are identified are dealt with using the PRINCE2 risk management procedure. (You learn how PRINCE2 approaches risk management in Chapter 7, "Risk Theme.")

Each plan should be considered a draft until the risks inherent in that plan have been identified and assessed, and countermeasures to deal with the risks have been put into place.

Documenting a Plan

The last step is documenting a plan. Here, the outputs from preceding steps are put together in a document. This document will probably contain the overall schedule and some narrative areas describing the risks associated with the plan, external dependencies, and planning assumptions.

It might be a good idea to have a number of document formats, such as a higher-level format for senior executives and a more detailed format to use for the day-to-day management of the project.

Defining and Analyzing the Products

Defining and analyzing the products is done in the second step of the planning procedure. The approach includes four steps, as shown in Figure 5.10.

Figure 5.10: The approach to defining and analyzing the products

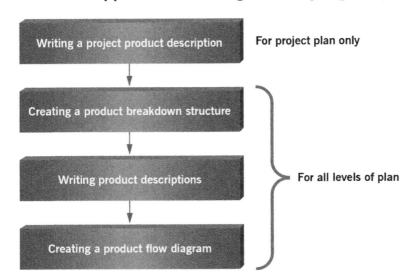

The focus of defining and analyzing the products is to identify all the individual products that need to be delivered within the scope of the plan and to understand what characteristics will make these products fit for their purpose. In order to do the latter, the project manager, in consultation with the senior users, will create a number of product descriptions. These product descriptions will describe in a measurable way what sort of products to create. They will be used by those creating the products, as well as by those checking and reviewing the products, to ensure the right products are delivered.

Writing a Project Product Description

The first step is writing a project product description. The *project product description* is a special sort of product description. It describes, at a high-level, the overall outputs of the project. For example, in the hotel project, the project product description would describe the broad (but measurable) characteristics of the hotel, including the number of bedrooms, the number of floors, and main components (such as restaurants, bars, and health centers).

The project manager, in consultation with the senior users and the executive, creates the project product description in the starting up a project process. It is used in the closing a project process to check whether the project has delivered what was expected. In any PRINCE2 project, there will ever be only one project product description (but there will be many product descriptions). You can find more information about the project product description, such as its recommended composition and how it is used throughout the project to control the quality of the final outputs, in Chapter 6, "Quality Theme."

Creating a Product Breakdown Structure

The next step is creating a product breakdown structure. A *product breakdown structure* is a graphical tool that helps the project management team identify all the products that will be delivered within a plan. It usually has a hierarchical structure rather like an organization chart, although it could be in the format of a mind map or simply an indented list. The project management team can draw the product breakdown structure together, starting by identifying the big components that need to be delivered, and then breaking each component into smaller and smaller pieces until they are down to a level where the products at the end of any particular branch of the structure can be individually installed, created, or modified.

The following "Conference Scenario" is taken from *Managing Successful Projects with PRINCE2* and will help you understand how to create a product breakdown structure. This scenario involves a project to organize a conference.

Conference Scenario*

A project is required to organize and run a conference for between 80 and 100 delegates. The date and subject matter are set, and the focus of the conference is to bring members of a particular profession up to date on recent developments in professional procedures and standards. The project team will need to identify a venue and check its availability, facilities, and price before booking it. They will also need to identify suitable speakers and book them, before producing a detailed agenda and programme. A mailing list of delegates is available, and once the venue has been booked, the project team will need to issue a press release based on the agreed programme. Part of the project will involve producing 100 delegate handouts, with a cover reflecting the selected subject matter. These handouts must contain a printed agenda covering the agreed programme, copies of the slides and notes used by the speakers, and a feedback form to capture attendee reviews. Booking arrangements for attending the conference, including details of the programme and venue, must be sent out in the mail shot (a bulk mailing to potential delegates). The team will need to regularly update the attendance list based on responses to the mail shot, and make arrangements to recruit staff to help on the day, based on the final attendance list.

Product Breakdown Structure for the Conference Project

Figure 5.11 shows the product breakdown structure for the conference scenario. It identifies all the products that need to be delivered. The word "product" can be misleading. Many people imagine a product to be a tangible "thing" that you could see and touch. However, look at some of the "products" in Figure 5.11. "Booked venue" is a product, which is not a tangible thing at all. A good way of thinking about PRINCE2 products is that they are outputs from a series of activities. A series of activities is involved in booking a venue, such as meeting with the owners of the venue, negotiating terms, and signing contracts. The output of these activities is the "booked venue."

---

* Scenario based on material from *Managing Successful Projects with PRINCE2*®. Copyright © AXELOS Limited 2017. Used under permission of AXELOS Limited. All rights reserved.

Figure 5.11: Conference product breakdown structure

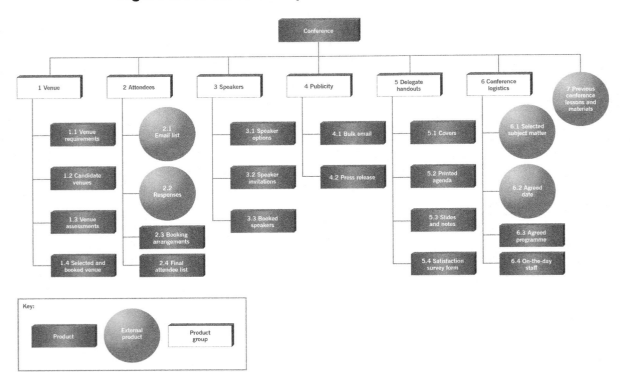

One common misconception PRINCE2 exam candidates have about the product breakdown structure is that the diagram shows the sequence in which the products will be delivered. It doesn't! It just shows the products needed for the plan. The fact that the "potential venues" is to the left of the "speaker options" does not necessarily mean that the "potential venues" product needs to be delivered before the "speaker options" product. The sequence of delivery will be shown in the product flow diagram, which you'll learn about in a minute.

You'll note that the diagram has grouped together certain products. This could mean one of two things. They could be a group of similar products, such as the four products under the "Venue" box. In this case, the "Venue" box is not actually a real product—it is a product grouping. The project team won't deliver a venue (i.e., they won't build something like a conference center within the scope of this project). The "Venue" box is there just to group together the four products underneath in a neat way. If it weren't there, you'd have to put "venue requirements," "potential venues," "venue assessments," and "booked venue" on the level above. This is fine, but it would make the diagram very wide.

The other sort of grouping shows when one product is physically composed of a collection of other products. You can see an example of this in the conference product breakdown structure. "Delegate handouts" is physically made up of "covers," "printed agenda," "slides and notes," and "satisfaction survey." Unlike in the venue example, this time the product at the top of this branch, "delegate handouts," is a real product. The project team creates "delegate handouts," and they consist of the four products below it in the product breakdown structure.

This product breakdown structure goes down to three levels. However, it could go down to many more levels. For example, the "booked speakers" could be split up into different types of speakers.

External Products in the Conference Project

On the product breakdown structure shown in Figure 5.11, you can also see that some products are shaped as ellipses. These are *external products*. External products are ones that already exist or are being created or updated outside the scope of the plan, but are required in order to create one or more of the plan's products. They are inputs into the plan's work. For example, the scenario says that the "mailing list" already exists, so this is an external product. It is not within the scope of the project team's work to create the list.

The "responses" from people wishing to attend the conference are another external product. They won't be created or updated by the teams involved with this project, but they are needed in order to deliver the conference.

One way of identifying an external product is to ask yourself whether the project manager needs to delegate the work to create the product to any of the project teams. If the answer is no, then it is an external product.

One common trap that exam candidates fall into with regard to external products is thinking that these are products created outside of the organization that commissioned the project. Take the press release product in the scenario. The scenario says, "The project team will need to issue a press release." This is a product that is created by the project team, and because it is within the scope of work of the plan, it is not external. However, imagine the scenario had said, "An external publicity company will issue a press release for the project team." Does this sentence change the "press release" to an external product?

The answer is no. The fact that a third-party supplier is now creating the press release does not make it external. The product is still within the scope of the plan, and the project manager will still have to delegate the work to the publicity company. In most modern projects, a lot of work will be delegated or outsourced to third-party suppliers, but as long as those products are within the scope of the work of the plan, they are not external.

Because people outside of the project management team create external products (unless, of course, they exist already), there is more uncertainty about whether they will be delivered on time and to the correct specification. PRINCE2 suggests that there should be a corresponding entry in the risk register for any external products and that the uncertainty should be managed using the PRINCE2 risk management procedure. It might be useful to create a product description for the external product and give this to the people involved with its creation to reduce the risk of the wrong specification being delivered.

Writing Product Descriptions

The third step is writing product descriptions. Once the product breakdown structure has been used to identify all the products that are needed for a plan, the next step is to gain an understanding of the specifications for those products. A *product description* is written for each product. This describes the measurable characteristics of the product, known as *quality criteria*, which can be used to confirm that the right product has been delivered. It also shows any techniques or approaches that will be used to ensure that a product complies with its quality criteria and who is responsible for reviewing and approving that product. (You learn more about product descriptions in Chapter 6, "Quality Theme.")

The project manager creates the product descriptions, although it is sensible to include other parties that have specialist knowledge of the products, such as the senior users, the senior suppliers, and the teams.

Product descriptions for any product should be started as soon as the need for that product has been identified. At this point, they may be in draft form; as more is known about the products, the product descriptions will become more refined. A product's product descriptions should be signed off at the same time as signing off the plan that will be used to deliver it.

In a small project, it may be only necessary to create a project product description. This might contain enough level of detail for the project management team to understand unambiguously what needs to be delivered.

Creating a Product Flow Diagram

The final step is creating a product flow diagram. The *product flow diagram* puts the products identified in the product breakdown structure into the order that they will be delivered. The product flow diagram allows the project management team to conceptualize the dependencies between the products. The diagram is also useful in the next step of the planning procedure, (identifying activities and dependencies) when the project management team considers the sequences of activities needed to create the products. The final product in the product flow diagram is the final output of that plan.

Figure 5.12 shows the product flow diagram for the conference scenario project that you saw earlier in this section. The diagram shows the order in which the products from the product breakdown structure are delivered. It also shows that some of the products are external products, by putting them into ellipses.

Figure 5.12: Conference product flow diagram

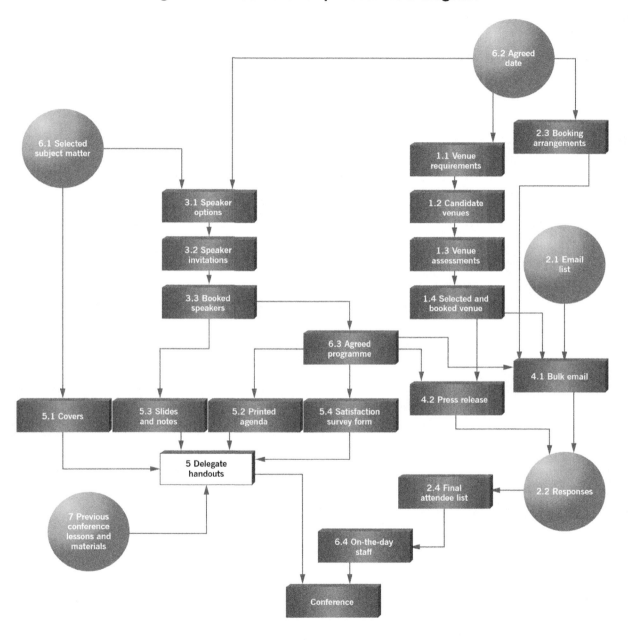

Most of the boxes and circles from the product breakdown structure have been copied across to the product flow diagram. The only exception is the product grouping products from the product breakdown structure, such as "venue" and "speakers." As you learned in the "Creating a Product Breakdown Structure" section, these are not real products. The project team will not deliver them. They were in the product breakdown structure only to make the diagram easier to follow by collating similar products in the same place.

Benefits of the Product-Based Planning Approach

The product-based planning approach brings a number of benefits to planning, including the following:
- It helps to clearly define the scope of the plan and reduces the risk of "scope creep" or the team forgetting essential products.
- It provides clarity over what needs to be delivered.
- If the users are involved with the creation of the product descriptions, it reduces the risk of acceptance disputes once the products have been delivered.
- It helps the project management team identify products that will be delivered outside of their project team so that they can take countermeasures against potential delivery problems.
- It helps provide clarity about who will review and approve products and how this will be done.

Planning Responsibilities

The roles and responsibilities for planning are fairly straightforward. The project manager creates and also updates all the plans apart from the team plans, which would be created by the team manager. The project board will review and decide whether to authorize the project plan after the initiation stage and each stage plan before each stage begins.

The project manager will use the stage plans to track and control the day-to-day activities of each stage, whereas the project board will use the higher-level project plan to track the progress of the project. If team plans exist, the team manager will use them to track and control the team's work.

Project support will provide administrative support to the project manager. For example, project support might help the project manager with the compilation of the plans, help provide support in the use of complicated planning software, help with archiving or storing the plans, or help with tracking different versions of the plan. Project assurance will review the plans to ensure they are being created and updated appropriately and that the plans will deliver the products as needed by the project's business case.

Tailoring the Plans Theme

The key to using PRINCE2 successfully is adapting and tailoring the method given the characteristics of the project and the environment the project is operating within. The following sections show how the plans theme might be adapted to better suit certain situations. This is something you might be tested on in the Practitioner exam.

Minimum Requirements

Organizations with a less-formal project management approach or that are running smaller, less-complicated projects might choose to cut back on some of the plans theme's ideas. However, some minimum requirements must be followed in order for a project team to claim they are following the PRINCE2 plans theme.

The project manager must use the product-based planning approach in order to create the project plans, exception plans, and stage plans. This means the project management team must be clear on what products will be delivered as part of each plan. In order to do this, the project manager should create a project product description, a product breakdown structure (which could be simply a list of products), and product descriptions for each product that will be delivered in each stage. As you will see in the "Agile Environments" section later in this chapter, the format of the project product description and the product descriptions could vary between environments. The product flow diagram is recommended for product-based planning, but it is not required.

The project management team must be able to show how the plans will deliver the outcomes and benefits forecast in the business case. The project must have at least two management stages (an initiation stage and at least one delivery stage), and there should be an overall project plan and a stage plan for each management stage. If the project needs to recover from an exception situation, the project manager should create an exception plan to show how this will happen.

The project management team should be clear about who will take on the various responsibilities outlined in the plans theme. Finally, when the project management team is planning, they should consider any useful experience or lessons that will help improve the accuracy of the plans.

Tailoring the Management Products

The plans could be presented in many formats, depending on the type of project and the specialist industry area. In an agile environment, for example, the project plan might be in the form of a product backlog. You learned about these in Chapter 1, "Overview of PRINCE2." Many organizations use planning software tools, so the plans might be held within these tools and might produce a range of views on the information (such as a Gantt chart). On a simple project, the plan might be a simple list of accountabilities, products, activities, and dates.

Projects within Programmes

If a project is part of a programme, the project's planning approach will be influenced by the programme's planning approach. For example, there might be certain programme planning standards that the project manager needs to adhere to when creating the project's plans. There might also be dependencies between the project and the rest of the programme. For example, the project team might need another product from another part of the programme in order to deliver their work. The project manager will need to take account of these internal programme dependencies when planning the project.

Another thing the project manager may need to consider within a programme environment is whether the project's stage ends need to be aligned with key decision points or milestones within the rest of the programme. Finally, the programme may have a team of dedicated planners that can help the project manager prepare the project's plans.

Commercial Customer/Supplier Environments

There are a number of planning challenges when an organization (the customer) outsources work to separate third-party organizations (the suppliers). In the context of a PRINCE2 project, a supplier's plan will probably become a team plan, showing part of the work (or maybe all of the work) to deliver a stage. These team plans will not necessarily follow the PRINCE2 format of a plan, and/or the supplier may not be following PRINCE2. However, the customer's project manager will need the supplier to provide sufficient details in their plans, such as activities and key milestones, so that the project manager can track the progress of the supplier's work and use that information to update the stage plan. It may be a good idea to specify in the supplier's contract what information the supplier needs to provide in their plans and what rights the customer has to inspect those plans.

The customer's and supplier's plans might contain confidential information that neither party wants to share with the other. However, this contradicts one of the key purposes of plans: to facilitate communication about how people will work together to deliver the products. To overcome this problem, each party could prepare a nonconfidential version of their plans that, while omitting commercially sensitive information, provides enough data for each party to work together to coordinate their activities.

Plans should also include procurement-related activities, such as purchase orders and deadlines for payments.

Agile Environments

As you saw in the "Different Project Types and Environments" section of Chapter 1, agile projects often create a document called a *product backlog*. The product backlog gives a list of requirements—which agile approaches call *user stories*—that the project may deliver. Each user story describes the feature in a measurable, testable way, and gives an indication of the value of the item. Like the project product description and the product breakdown structure, this product backlog identifies the main outputs of the project, so it might replace those products.

A common approach in an agile project would be for the project manager to create a high-level vision and product roadmap in the starting up a project process. This would play the same role as the project product description, giving the overall purpose of the products to be delivered and a high-level description of what will be delivered. Then, in the initiating a project process, the project manager would create the product backlog, giving more details on the individual requirements or user stories that may be delivered and an indication of the value and priority of each one.

Then there would be a series of management stages delivering a release of the product. Each management stage might contain one or more sprints of work, lasting around two to four weeks. At the end of each sprint, a working release would be handed over to the users.

Before each sprint, a sprint planning process would take place. The project management team would work together to plan which requirements from the product backlog to deliver in the upcoming sprint. They would take into account the resources available and the priorities of the requirements. The output of this work would be a sprint backlog. If PRINCE2 product descriptions were created, the initial versions of the product descriptions would likely only address the purpose and quality criteria of the products, with the rest developed during the execution of the work package.

If there were only one sprint per stage, this sprint planning would be the equivalent of stage planning in PRINCE2. If there were more than one sprint per stage, the stage planning would probably focus on an initial idea of the likely scope of the stage, including some idea of a minimum viable scope, and then this scope might be adapted as the project team plans each sprint within a stage.

Linking the Plans Theme with the PRINCE2 Principles

In Chapter 1, I talked about the seven PRINCE2 principles. The plans theme helps to implement all seven principles.

The plans should clearly show how to create the products that will be used to deliver the outcomes and benefits forecast in the business case, so the first principle that the plans theme helps to implement is the continued business justification principle. A key concept of planning is always to consider any useful experience that might improve the plans, which helps to implement the learn from experience principle. A minimum requirement of the plans theme is that the project team is clear on who will take on the various planning responsibilities, which helps to implement the defined roles and responsibilities principle. The project is broken up into a number of management stages; the project manager creates a plan for each stage; and the project board authorizes a stage at a time—all of which help to implement the principle of manage by stages.

The last three principles are also all implemented in some way by the plans theme. If the project gets into an exception situation, the project board might request that the project manager create an exception plan to show how to recover from the exception. This helps to implement the manage by exception principle. Product-based planning helps to implement the focus on products principle. Finally, the plans theme can be adapted to work in different situations—such as an agile project or a project operating within a programme—which helps to implement the tailor to suit the project principle.

Summary

In this chapter, you learned about the PRINCE2 plans theme. This theme helps define how the products of the project will be delivered. It identifies which activities will be needed and who will do them, and helps estimate the duration and cost of the project. The plans theme helps to create information that allows the different members of the project management team to communicate about the work that needs to be done.

You saw that there are a number of levels of plans. The highest level created within a project is the project plan. This plan has the broadest level of detail and is used by the project board to monitor the progress of the project. Then, for each stage, there will be a more detailed stage plan. This helps the project manager control the day-to-day activities of a stage. Finally, the lowest and most detailed plan is the team plan.

In addition to the different levels of plans, PRINCE2 provides an exception plan. This plan is used to show how the project will recover from a breach in tolerances and might replace a project plan or a stage plan.

You learned that every PRINCE2 plan (whether at the project, stage, or team level) should include a number of pieces of information, such as a schedule, planning assumptions, lessons learned from previous projects, and product descriptions for the products that are within the scope of the plan.

You also learned about the factors to consider when dividing the project into management stages, such as how far ahead to plan, how risky the project is, how confident the project management team is in proceeding, and which delivery steps will be used during the project. You learned that a delivery step is a group of work within a project that is characterized by using similar techniques or specialist skills, or by creating specialist products of a certain type.

You also learned that PRINCE2 recommends an approach to planning. This approach implements the PRINCE2 concept of product-based planning. First, the products to be delivered are identified and described, and then the activities and the resources needed to create those products are forecast.

Defining and analyzing the products is one step within the PRINCE2 planning procedure. The approach consists of four parts. In the first part, the overall outputs from the project are described using a project product description. In the second part, the individual products for a particular plan are identified using a product breakdown structure. In the third part, each product is described using product descriptions. And in the fourth part, the sequence in which the products will be delivered is shown in a product flow diagram.

Foundation Exam Essentials

Explain the purpose of the plans theme.
The purpose of the plans theme is to facilitate communication and control by defining the means of delivering the products (the where, how, and by whom, as well as estimating the when and how much).

Explain the purpose of the project plan.
The project plan provides a statement of how and when a project's time, cost, quality, and scope performance targets are to be achieved. It also shows the major products, activities, and resource requirements for the project. It provides the planned costs and timescales for the business case, identifies major control points, such as management stages and milestones, and is used by the project board as a baseline against which to monitor project progress management stage by stage.

Explain the purpose of the stage plan.
The stage plan covers the products, resources, activities, and controls specific to a management stage. The project manager uses a stage plan to control the day-to-day activities of a stage.

Explain the purpose of the team plan.
The team manager or team creates the team plan to facilitate the execution of one or more work packages.

Explain the purpose of the exception plan.
The exception plan shows the actions required to recover from either a forecast project or forecast stage tolerance deviation. Once the exception plan has been approved, it becomes the project plan or a stage plan, depending on whether the exception is forecast to breach project or stage tolerance, respectively.

Describe what PRINCE2 requires as a minimum for applying the plans theme.
As a minimum for applying the plans theme, PRINCE2 requires that the project management team do the following:
- Create a project plan for the entire project, a stage plan for each management stage, and exception plans, if required, to show how to manage exceptions
- Use lessons learned to inform planning and the product-based planning approach to create the plans
- Create plans that will enable the business case to be realized
- Ensure that each project has at least two management stages: an initiation stage and at least one other management stage
- Define the roles and responsibilities for planning

Recall the steps in the recommended approach to planning.
The PRINCE2 approach to planning involves seven steps: designing a plan, defining and analyzing the products, identifying activities and dependencies, preparing estimates, preparing a schedule, documenting a plan, and analyzing the risks to a plan.

Recall the steps in the recommended approach to defining and analyzing the products.
The recommended approach to defining and analyzing products involves four steps: writing a project product description, creating a product breakdown structure, writing product descriptions, and creating a product flow diagram.

Recall the factors to consider when structuring the project into management stages.
The project management team should consider a range of factors when structuring the project into management stages, such as how far ahead it is possible to plan, where the key decision points in the project will take place, the overall risk of the project, the delivery steps of the project, the confidence of the project board and project manager in proceeding, and the project's alignment with programme activities.

Practitioner Exam Essentials

Demonstrate an understanding of the project, stage, exception and team plans.
Demonstrate an understanding that the project manager creates the project, stage, and exception plans, and that the teams or team manager create the team plan. Understand that the project plan is created during the initiation stage and shows the major products and activities for the project; that the stage plan is created during the managing a stage boundary process and shows the work needed to deliver a stage; that an exception plan is created, if required, during the managing a stage boundary process and shows the work needed to recover from an exception situation; and that a team plan might be created during the managing product delivery process and shows the work needed to deliver one or more work packages. Understand that the plans might be derived from the project approaches, the resource availability, and the project's registers and logs. Know that plans could take a number of formats, such as a stand-alone document, an entry in a project management tool, a spreadsheet, slides or mind maps, or as part of the project initiation documentation. Know the composition of a PRINCE2 plan.

Demonstrate an understanding of the recommended roles and responsibilities within the plans theme.
Demonstrate an understanding that the project manager is responsible for preparing the project plan, stage plans, and, if required, the exception plans, and that the project manager will use stage plans to control each management stage. Also understand that the project board is responsible for approving stage plans and tracking the project's progress using the project plans, and that, if required, the team manager is responsible for preparing the teams plans.

Assess and critique an approach to applying the plans theme.
Understand the purpose and format of the project plan, stage plan, exception plan, and team plan. Understand the recommended approach to planning, including the recommended approach to defining and analyzing the products. Show how the plans theme might be adapted to different project contexts (for example, a small project, an agile project, a project with external third-party organizations, or a project operating within a programme environment). Show how an approach to planning aligns with the principles of PRINCE2.

Review Questions

The remainder of this chapter contains mock exam questions, first for the Foundation exam and then for the Practitioner exam.

Foundation Exam Questions

1. Which of these options is a minimum requirement for managing the plans of the project?
    A. To split the project into at least two management stages
    B. To record all quality activities carried out during the project
    C. To define a method for baselining products
    D. To identify actions to ensure that the project's outcomes are achieved

2. How does the plans theme help to implement the manage by exception principle?
    A. By stating that all plans should contain a lessons incorporated section
    B. By providing stage plans to help the project manager manage the day-to-day aspects of a stage
    C. By stating that all plans should contain a tolerance section
    D. By providing a product-based planning approach

3. Which of the following levels of plans might be created by organizations that are not following the PRINCE2 method?
    A. Project plan
    B. Stage plan
    C. Team plan
    D. Exception plan

4. Which of the following statements apply to an exception plan?
    (1) The project board approves an exception plan that replaces a project plan.
    (2) An exception plan may show actions required to recover from the effect of a forecast breach in project tolerance levels.
    (3) Once approved, an exception plan could become the new baselined stage plan.
    (4) An exception plan may show the actions required to recover from the effect of a forecast breach in work package tolerance levels.
    A. 1 and 2
    B. 2 and 3
    C. 3 and 4
    D. 1 and 4

5. Which of the following options is a factor to consider when structuring the project into management stages?
    A. The availability of the project board
    B. The estimating techniques used for planning
    C. The critical path of the project
    D. Alignment with programme activities

6. Which of the following are purposes of the plans theme?
   (1) To define the project's structure of accountability and responsibility
   (2) To establish whether the targets for time and cost are achievable
   (3) To provide a baseline against which progress can be measured
   (4) To establish mechanisms to judge whether the project is desirable, viable, and achievable
   A. 1 and 2
   B. 2 and 3
   C. 3 and 4
   D. 1 and 4

7. Which of the following options does PRINCE2 recommend in the designing a plan step of the approach to planning?
   A. Creating a product breakdown structure to help identify products
   B. Identifying the types of resources required for each activity
   C. Identifying uncertainties inherent in the plan
   D. Identify the number and length of management stages

8. In which of the following steps in the approach to planning does PRINCE2 recommend using the product-based planning approach?
   A. Designing the plan
   B. Defining and analyzing the products
   C. Identifying activities and dependencies
   D. Preparing estimates

9. Which is the first step in the recommended approach to defining and analyzing the products?
   A. Creating a product flow diagram
   B. Creating a product breakdown structure
   C. Writing a project product description
   D. Writing a product description

10. Which of the following is one of the benefits of product-based planning?
    A. It helps to define products that are in and out of scope of the plan.
    B. It helps to identify the shortest possible completion time of the project.
    C. It helps to identify how the performance of the project's products will be reviewed.
    D. It helps to define techniques for estimating throughout a project.

Practitioner Exam Questions

Exam Spotlight

Remember that for the Practitioner exam, you are allowed to refer to the official PRINCE2 manual (*Managing Successful Projects with PRINCE2*). This is a great help. One of the key differences between passing and failing the Practitioner exam is knowing how to use the PRINCE2 manual during the exam. Some exam questions rely on you finding very specific pieces of information quickly from the manual.

For plans theme questions, where might you look in the PRINCE2 manual for useful information? The first (and most obvious) place is the plans theme chapter itself. The chapter begins by discussing the purpose of the plans theme, explaining the concepts of using plans to enable control, how to deal with the planning horizon, and what product-based-planning is all about. Then the chapter looks at the minimum requirements for applying the plans theme. The next few sections explain the different types of plans and plans theme–related responsibilities. After the responsibilities table, the chapter describes the seven steps of the planning approach, including the four steps of defining and analyzing the products. Then there is a section that provides guidance for the effective management of plans and describes how to tailor the theme to different situations. The last section, which focuses on techniques, is not examinable, so you can ignore that in the exam. I recommend that you look through the plans theme chapter in the PRINCE2 manual before the exam and familiarize yourself with how the information is laid out.

In addition to the plans theme chapter, a few other places in the PRINCE2 manual might be useful. For information on the format and sections of a plan, you should look in Appendix A and find the plan product description. You might find Appendix C useful for plans questions that test you on roles and responsibilities. Although there is information on the responsibilities within the plans theme chapter, you'll often find more information about plans-related responsibilities in Appendix C. Appendix D gives an excellent example of how to define and analyze products.

You might also be tested on how to tailor any of the plans. There is quite a lot of information in the processes chapters about this, but the trick is to know where to look. The rule is that information on how to tailor management products is always in the chapter that describes the process in which that particular management product was created. The information is always set out as a table towards the back of the relevant process chapter, under the tailoring guidelines section. So for the information on the initiation stage plan, look in the starting up a project process chapter; for questions about tailoring the project plan, look in the initiating a project process chapter; for information about tailoring the team plan, look in the managing product delivery process chapter; and for information about tailoring the stage plan or the exception plan, look in the managing a stage boundary process chapter.

The following Practitioner questions are divided into two sections by question type and are based on the Practitioner exam scenario described in Appendix B.

Section 1: Matching Questions

The project manager is planning stage two of the project. Column 1 in the following table lists the five items of information that will be included in the stage plan. Choose only the appropriate heading (A–I) in Column 2 for each item of information. (Each heading can be used once, more than once, or not at all.)

Column 1	Column 2
1. Quality Furniture's existing standard terms of conditions will be sent to potential suppliers. The chief executive is currently revising these in another project.	A. Plan description
2. The personal assistant to the chief executive said that in her experience, suppliers can take up to a month to respond to a request to tender.	B. Plan prerequisites
3. If no suitable responses are received from the list of potential suppliers given to Quality Furniture by First Tech, $5,000 has been set aside to fund a request for tender advertisement in the technical press.	C. External dependencies
4. The project board must approve the project initiation documentation.	D. Planning assumptions
5. A weekly highlight report will be sent to the project board.	E. Lessons incorporated
	F. Monitoring and control
	G. Budgets
	H. Tolerances
	I. Schedule

Section 2: Classic Multiple-Choice Questions

Exam Spotlight

One of the Practitioner questions in Section 2 asks about the application of the defining and analyzing the products approach. To get it right, you need to understand the difference between a product and an activity in PRINCE2. You could use a number of methods to tell the difference between products and activities in the Practitioner exam. First, products will be nouns in the question's text. For example, "technical requirements" is a noun and is, in fact, a product. Be careful, though—not all the nouns are products; for example, "potential supplier" is a group of people who will be involved with the work of the project. Activities will be verbs in the question's text, so the phrase "choosing the potential suppliers" is describing an activity with the verb, to choose.

Another way to tell the difference between products and activities is to think of products as inputs to or outputs from an activity or series of activities. For example, maybe the project team is reviewing and selecting a potential web page design for the Quality Furniture website. During the review, they will need to refer to the existing branding standards. What products would be involved in this activity? First, there are the existing branding standards, which are an input into the activity of reviewing the designs. Then, the output of reviewing the designs is a selected design. The reviewing and selecting are activities.

Thinking of the words "selected design" as a product can sometimes confuse candidates of the PRINCE2 exams. Selected design could simply be an email that says, "Let's go for design number two." It isn't a product in the sense that you could box it up and give it to someone. However, it is the output to a series of activities, so it *is* a PRINCE2 product.

Remember that in the PRINCE2 approach to planning, when the project manager is conducting the defining and analyzing products step, she is purely focused on products. Therefore, the diagrams that the project manager might create in this step—such as the product breakdown structures and the product flow diagrams—contain only products. The project manager will only focus on activities in the later steps of the approach to planning, such as identifying activities and dependencies.

1. The project manager is preparing the stage plan for stage two and is creating a product flow diagram. The project manager has added review tender responses as a dependency for the short list of potential suppliers. Is this appropriate, and why or why not?
   A. Yes, because the tender responses will be reviewed before the short list of potential suppliers is created.
   B. Yes, because the review of the tender responses happens within the scope of stage two.
   C. No, because review tender responses should only be shown in the derivation heading in the product description for the short list of potential suppliers.
   D. No, because review tender responses is an activity.

2. First Tech has suggested to the chief executive that an agile approach might be beneficial for the website project. The chief executive is keen to adhere to a PRINCE2 approach but has asked the project manager to create a product backlog during the initiation stage. Is this appropriate, and why or why not?
   A. Yes, because product-based planning should be considered before activity-based planning.
   B. Yes, because product-based planning can be applied very easily to agile delivery.
   C. No, because a product backlog is not part of the project initiation documentation.
   D. No, because PRINCE2 and agile are not compatible approaches.

3. The project manager took longer than expected to create the stage plan for stage two. The personal assistant to the chief executive, who is providing project support, has suggested that the project manager use a new planning tool to create the stage plan for stage three, to make it easier to prepare the plan. She has had experience using the tool in a previous project and has offered to help create the plan. Is this appropriate, and why or why not?
   A. Yes, because project support can provide specialist expertise to help administer the project.
   B. Yes, because project support will help to baseline the stage plans.
   C. No, because the project manager should prepare the stage plan.
   D. No, because the stage plan for stage three should be created in the same way as the previous stage plans.

Chapter

6

Quality Theme

PRINCE2 Foundation Exam Objectives Covered in This Chapter:

☑ **Explain the purpose of:**
- The quality theme
- Key management products:
  - Product description
  - Project product description
  - Quality management approach
  - Quality register

☑ **Describe PRINCE2's minimum requirement for applying the quality theme.**

☑ **Explain key concepts related to quality, and the differences between them:**
- Quality planning and quality control
- Project assurance and quality assurance
- Customer quality expectations and acceptance criteria

PRINCE2 Practitioner Exam Objectives Covered in This Chapter:

☑ **Apply the PRINCE2 requirements for applying the quality theme, demonstrating an understanding of:**
- Key management products:
  - Product description
  - Project product description
  - Quality management approach
  - Quality register
- The recommended roles and responsibilities within the theme
- Key activities:
  - Quality planning
  - Quality control
  - Quality assurance

☑ **Assess whether an approach to applying the quality theme is effective and fit for purpose, taking into consideration: the context, the PRINCE2 principles, and the purpose and requirements of the theme.**

This chapter covers the PRINCE2 approach to quality. You learn how the PRINCE2 processes, roles, and management products are used to ensure the project creates products that are fit for purpose.

All projects are exposed to a number of quality risks. At the end of a project, it is all too common to have disputes about what should have been delivered as well as user dissatisfaction with the end result. The quality theme helps mitigate these risks by ensuring that project team members are clear about what they are delivering and follow procedures that ensure these products are created.

The quality theme shows how to describe an approach that ensures that quality products are created on a project. This approach is documented in the quality management approach. The approach covers how the project will carry out quality planning activities, such as working with the ultimate users of the products to capture their requirements and then ensuring that these requirements are documented. It covers how the project will approach quality control activities, in which the product will be inspected or tested to see if the product has been built correctly. It will also cover how to assign people to assurance roles to check that the project is being managed according to the approaches and any other applicable management standards.

In this chapter, you learn the PRINCE2 approach to quality planning, quality assurance, and quality control.

What Is Quality?

Normally, the word *quality* is almost synonymous with *luxury*. In my dictionary, the definition of this word is "degree or standard of excellence, especially to a high standard." If I tell my friends that I bought a quality suit, for example, they might think I have a tailor-made garment—maybe even from Saville Row, a street in London that sells very expensive suits, sometimes to royalty. (Unfortunately, unless you get all your colleagues to buy this book, that's a bit beyond my price range!)

In PRINCE2, the word *quality* is used a little differently from its everyday usage—it means fit for purpose. Taking my suit example, if I were to consider what sort of suit would be fit for my purpose, I would think about what I need my suits for. My work requires a lot of travel, so my suits need to be pretty durable. I need a suit to be able to survive being crumpled up in various suitcases and sat on during long plane journeys. I also need a suit that will look good in front of my clients.

The PRINCE2 quality theme is focused on ensuring that a project creates products that are fit for the purpose for which they will be used. It also focuses on ensuring that the project is managed in a way that is appropriate for the type of project. Therefore, processes as well as products need to be fit for purpose.

The PRINCE2 definition of the word quality is a mouthful, but for completeness, here it is:

The degree to which a set of inherent characteristics of a product, service, process, person, organization, system, or resource fulfills requirements.

I don't recommend that you spend time memorizing that long sentence. Just keep in mind that quality is all about making something fit for the purpose it is ultimately needed for.

What Is Scope?

It is important to understand that the terms *scope* and *quality* refer to different concepts. *Scope* defines the number and range of products to be delivered. For example, the scope of the hotel project identifies all the individual products of the hotel, so it might contain a set of bedrooms, a restaurant, a spa, and a lobby. Many projects suffer from *scope creep*, in which more and more things are added to the original project requirements without thought about how these additions might impact project objectives such as quality, costs, and timescales.

Once the scope of the project has been defined, the specifications for each product within that scope must be defined. The specifications that will make any individual product fit for its purpose should be clearly stated in measurable terms. You can think of these specifications as the *quality* of any individual product within the *scope* of the project.

In PRINCE2, you will see the word *scope* used to describe the number of products to be delivered within a particular plan. So PRINCE2 might refer to the scope of a project plan, a stage plan, or a team plan. In each case, this means the number and range of products to be delivered by that plan.

What Is Quality Management?

In PRINCE2, *quality management* is the coordinated activities to direct and control an organization with regard to quality. There are three main areas that help to do this:

Quality Assurance
Quality assurance provides an independent check that the project's direction and management are adequate for the nature of the project.

Quality Planning
Quality planning is about defining the specification for the project's products. It is also about understanding how the products will be checked to see if they conform to these specifications.

Quality Control
The last area of quality management, *quality control*, involves determining whether the project's products have been (or are being) built correctly. Each product is checked against the specifications in its product description. Another goal of quality control is to eliminate causes of unsatisfactory performance, which could include looking at the processes used to manage the project and seeing if they could be improved.

Quality Assurance and Project Assurance

The term *quality assurance* is used in the following two ways in PRINCE2:
- As a function or a department within an organization whose responsibility is to establish and/or maintain the quality management system

- As an activity to review a project independently to ensure it is being managed in a way that is appropriate given the objectives that have been set for it and any organizational, industry, or project standards and policies that exist

Quality assurance is done by a group of people who will be independent of the project management team. Maybe these people come from a dedicated quality assurance department whose responsibility is to check the organization's operations on an ongoing basis to ensure that things are being done properly. Now and again, this department is asked to carry out quality assurance activities on particular projects, to independently check that the project is being conducted in an appropriate manner. If no such department exists, corporate, programme management, or the customer may appoint people to carry out the quality assurance activities for a project or may decide to do the activities themselves.

Do not confuse the term *quality assurance* with *project assurance*. Project assurance is the responsibility of the project board, which checks to see if the project is being conducted properly. Each of the project board roles (executive, senior user, and senior supplier) has an accountability to carry out project assurance (business assurance, user assurance, and supplier assurance, respectively).

The activity of quality assurance is similar to the activity of carrying out the responsibilities of project assurance. Both involve reviewing the project to determine whether it is being conducted in an appropriate manner. The difference is that whoever is doing project assurance reports to the project board (or the members of the project board might do it themselves), whereas whoever is carrying out quality assurance reports to corporate, programme management, or the customer. Project assurance is independent of the project manager but is within the project management team, whereas the people doing quality assurance are independent of the project management team.

I keep saying that assurance (both project and quality) involves reviewing the project to see if it is being conducted in an appropriate manner. But what is "appropriate"? Both project assurance and quality assurance need to ensure that the project management team is managing the project in a way that aligns to the four management approaches set out in the project initiation documentation: risk management approach, quality management approach, change control approach, and communication management approach. Project assurance and quality assurance also might need to ensure that the project management team is following any relevant corporate, programme, client, or industry standards or procedures. So quality assurance and project assurance are not only reviewing quality activities, such as checking whether products meet their product descriptions, but they are also checking the whole area of project management, including risk management, managing business justification, and so on.

Sometimes, a project might be reviewed by external authorities. In the hotel project, for example, building regulators appointed by the local government might need to review the construction of the building to ensure the project management team is following local planning and construction standards. This type of review doesn't fit very well into the PRINCE2 model, because these sorts of people are not project assurance or quality assurance. They are carrying out an important assurance role, however, so they need to be incorporated into the project's quality management approach.

Figure 6.1 shows where project assurance and quality assurance sit within the project management team structure that you learned about in the section "The Four Levels of Management" in Chapter 3, "Organization Theme."

Figure 6.1: Quality assurance and project assurance

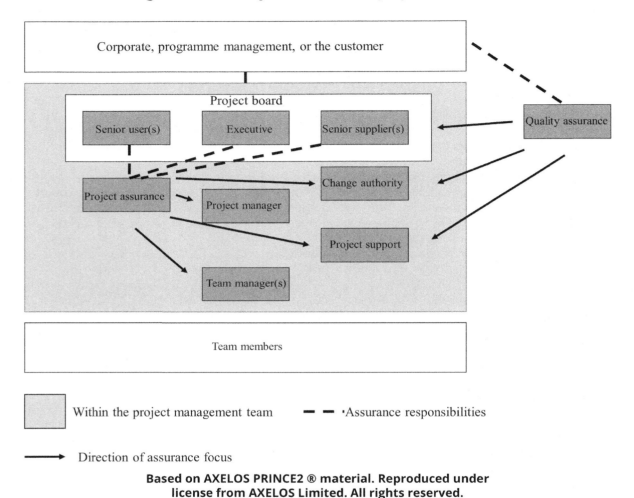

Quality Planning

Quality planning involves the following aspects:
- Defining the specification of the project's products
- Understanding how the products will be inspected and reviewed to see if they conform to their specifications and who should have responsibility for this review
- Defining who should have responsibility for final approval of the products

In PRINCE2, the project product description and the product descriptions define the specifications of the project's products. The difference between the two is that for any project, there is only one project product description that describes the overall output of the project, whereas there may be many product descriptions that describe all the individual components of the overall output.

If you are the project manager of a project to build a hotel, for example, you write one project product description that describes the hotel at a high level. This document provides the overall specifications, such as how many rooms the hotel should have of each type (penthouse, double, single, and so on), how many floors it should have, and what the hotel's main parts are (such as the lobby, a restaurant, a gym, or a swimming pool).

Then you write a product description for each component of the hotel. For example, you create a product description for the swimming pool, the lobby, the penthouses, and so on.

Both the project product description and the product descriptions describe specifications in a measurable way so that when the products have been built, there can be no argument over whether the right products have been created. For example, the product description of the swimming pool should contain the exact dimensions that the pool needs to conform to. The product description also describes how the products are to be reviewed to determine whether they meet their specifications. Finally, the product description outlines who is responsible for signing off on the products.

The next two sections describe both the project product description and the product descriptions in greater detail.

The Project Product Description

The customer's requirements from the project deliverables are described in the project product description. In this section, you learn about the purpose of the project product description: where in the PRINCE2 process model it is created, reviewed, and updated, and, finally, what it contains.

The Life of the Project Product Description

I am hoping that by now you have a fairly good grasp of the overall PRINCE2 process model. You're going to need it to follow the information in this section properly. If you feel you haven't, I recommend you reread the section "An End-to-End Walk-through of PRINCE2" in Chapter 1, "Overview of PRINCE2," before tackling this section.

The project manager liaises with the customer, senior users, senior suppliers, and the executive to create the project product description during the starting up a project process. At the end of that process, the description is put into the project brief. The starting up a project process is used to provide information to the project board in order for them to decide whether to commission the project. They make this decision by reviewing the project brief in their directing a project process.

The starting up a project process is fairly lightweight, so time isn't wasted on initiatives that aren't taken any further. At this point, the project product description needs to contain only enough detail to enable the project board to decide whether to commission the project.

If the project board does decide to commission the project, the initiation stage starts. The project manager uses the initiating a project process to refine the project product description, if necessary. This is then put into the project plan section of the project initiation documentation. (In PRINCE2, plans contain descriptions of the products that will be created within the scope of that plan, as you learned in Chapter 5, "Plans Theme.") After the initiation stage, the project board reviews the project initiation documentation with its project product description and decides whether to authorize the project to move on to delivering specialist products.

Moving on from the beginning of the project, the project product description is reviewed at the end of each stage by the project manager during the managing a stage boundary process. At this point, the project product description may be updated to reflect new information available at that point in the project. If it is updated, this new version needs to be approved by the project board while they are approving the next stage.

When products are handed over from the project team to the customers or those who will operate the products on behalf of the customers, the project product description is used to verify that the correct deliverables have been created. The handing over of the product from the project team will take place at the end of the project during the closing a project process, or if the products are handed over in a staged way throughout the project, this will also occur for the interim deliverables during the managing a stage boundary process.

The Composition of the Project Product Description

Figure 6.2 shows the composition of the project product description.

Figure 6.2: The composition of the project product description

Project Product Description

-Title
- Purpose
- Composition
-Derivation
-Development skills required
-Customer's quality expectations
-Acceptance criteria
-Project-level quality tolerances
-Acceptance method
-Acceptance responsibilities

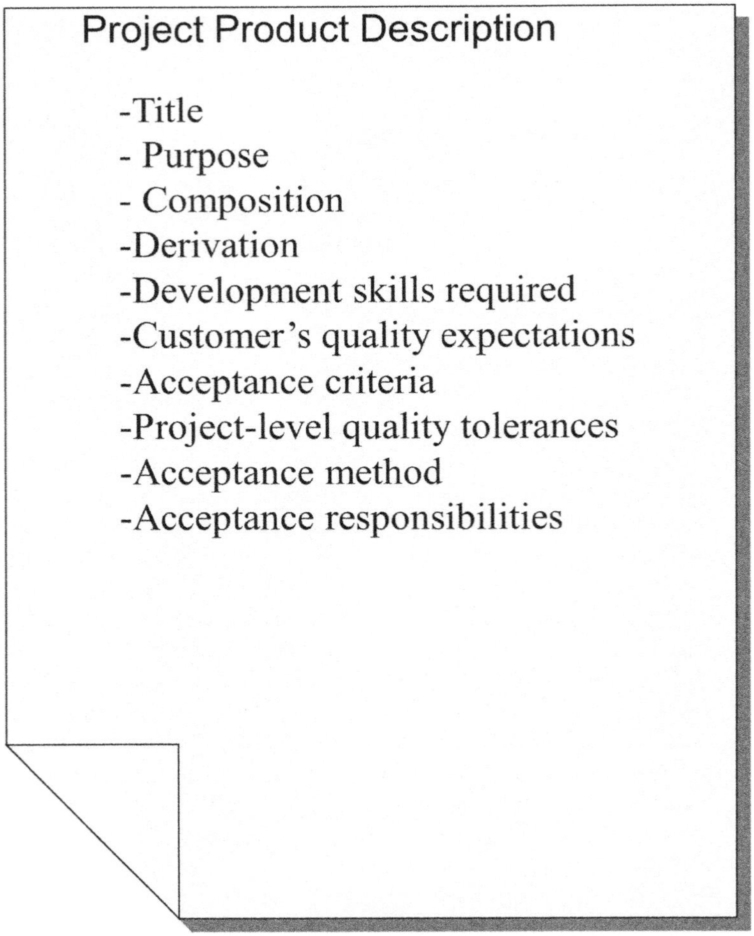

As you can see in Figure 6.2, the project product description has 10 sections. Here is a brief description of what each section contains, using the example of a project to build a new hotel in Shanghai aimed at the business traveler for a hotel chain:

Title

The title is the name of the project, which in this example is "Shanghai International Hotel."

Purpose

The purpose describes what function the overall outputs of the project will fulfill and who will use them. In the hotel project example, the purpose for the hotel chain might be to move into the Chinese market and remain competitive in the business traveler market.

Composition

Composition lists the major products and outcomes that the project will deliver. It basically defines the scope of the project. For the hotel project, this section lists all of the hotel's major parts, including the lobby, the restaurant, the gym, the swimming pool, how many of each type of rooms there will be (such as 10 penthouse suites, 30 luxury double rooms, 50 standard rooms), and so on. In addition, other products, such as an invitation to tender documents, promotional literature, or websites that are part of the scope of the project, may be listed here.

Derivation

This section shows what products are needed before the project starts. For the hotel project, this may be the project mandate or architectural plans that were drawn up before the project started.

Development Skills Required

This section presents a broad idea of the sorts of skills required to build the overall outputs of the project. For the hotel, this section may include bricklaying, plumbing, or electrical skills. The section may also indicate where these skills could be sourced, such as recruitment agencies or supplier names.

Customer's Quality Expectations

Customer's quality expectations are the expectations that the customer has about the overall outputs and outcomes of the project. These expectations are often presented in a broad, subjective form and help to get an initial understanding and common agreement about what sorts of products to create. The customer for the hotel project, for example, might ask for a luxury hotel. One person's idea of luxury could be quite different from another's, of course, so the project manager will work with the customers and the users to evolve these subjective quality expectations into more measurable acceptance criteria, which is the next section of the project product description. The customer's quality expectations could also cover any standards or processes that need to be applied during the project. For example, maybe the hotel project needs to follow some industry-defined building regulations.

Acceptance Criteria

To overcome potential delivery disputes because of subjective customer quality expectations, the project manager should work with the customer to define measurable product attributes that are derived from the quality expectations. These are called *acceptance criteria*. In the hotel project example, the use of acceptance criteria makes it much easier to prove that the right hotel has been built. The measurable attributes can cover a range of areas about the products, such as ease of use, ease of support or maintenance, appearance, major functions, development or running costs, capacity, availability, reliability, security, accuracy, and/or performance. The acceptance criteria should be set out as a prioritized list so that the project management team can decide which characteristics are the most important. This will help the project management team set quality and scope tolerances. (You learn more about tolerances in Chapter 9, "Progress Theme.") Acceptance criteria examples for the hotel can include the number of rooms, the size of the hotel, and/or how many hours per day security services will be available. Once the project management team can demonstrate that the acceptance criteria have been met, then the project can close.

Project-level Quality Tolerances
This section details any acceptable leeway that the customer will allow around the acceptance criteria. In the hotel project example, the hotel should have 200 bedrooms but 190 would be acceptable.

Acceptance Method
The acceptance method describes how the customer will accept the products once they have been built. In the hotel example, this can be as simple as counting the number of rooms that have been built. For some products, however, it could be complex. For example, if the project were to build a car, one of the acceptance criteria may relate to how many hours of continuous use the car can withstand, and the acceptance method may involve a technical stress test.

Acceptance Responsibilities
The acceptance responsibilities section defines who is responsible to sign off on the overall outputs from the project. When the hotel is accepted, it stops being the responsibility of the project team and starts to become the responsibility of the customer or the group of people who will maintain and operate the hotel. It should be clear who has signed off on the product so that there are no disputes over who should fix problems that might arise during the hotel's operation—the project team or the operational team.

The Importance of Being Clear About When Projects End

It is critical to be clear about when the products of a project have been handed over from the project team to either the client or the operations team. I worked for a company that created the computer infrastructure for organizations' websites. The computer infrastructure consisted of large, high-capacity computers. These computers were sited in datacenters that had high-capacity links to the Internet and all sorts of ways of ensuring that the computers kept running in the event of problems. For example, they had gas generators in case the local electricity supply failed. Once the company built the infrastructure, they operated and maintained it as well on behalf of the client.

When I started working for this company, what tended to happen was that one group of people built the sites and then also supported them. The problem with this arrangement is that the two types of work were very different in nature and needed to be managed in entirely different ways. The building of the infrastructure had to be planned, whereas the support work was far more ad hoc in nature. The result of having one team manage both types of work was that the planned building of infrastructure for new clients was delayed while engineers dealt with support calls from old sites. The team was not set up to manage, prioritize, and deal with the growing amount of support calls that came in every day.

The company overcame this problem by dividing the engineers into two teams: One built the products and the other supported them. This arrangement worked much better. The project teams could focus on building infrastructure for new clients and could more easily plan out their work, without the constant interruptions of support calls.

The support team set up systems that collected all the support calls that were coming in, prioritized them, and dealt with them in a timely manner. They also created a new sign-off process. They took on the responsibility of supporting a new client's infrastructure only once the other team had created support documentation and ensured the products they had created complied with standards defined by the support team.

The result of splitting the team into two was that the building work was done in a more timely manner, support calls were dealt with more effectively, and the standards that the infrastructure was built to improved.

Product Descriptions

Now that you have learned about the project product description, I will talk about the product descriptions. In this section, you learn about the purpose of product descriptions, where in the PRINCE2 process model they are created, reviewed, and updated, and, finally, what they contain.

The Purpose of Product Descriptions

Product descriptions specify each of the project's products. They set out measurable criteria that the finished product can be compared against to see if the right product has been created. Product descriptions are more than just specifications, however. They also give information on the skills required to develop, review, and approve the products; who will use the product when it is complete and for what purpose; and what method will be used to ensure that the product has been created properly.

When writing a product description, the project manager should strike a balance between creating too much detail, which would lead to an unnecessary cost in quality, and too little detail, which could lead to acceptance disputes when the product is being reviewed by the customer.

The Life of the Product Descriptions

During the life of a project, increasingly detailed descriptions of the project's outputs are needed in order to plan the work to create those products. As you saw in the previous section, the project manager creates the overall project product description in the starting up a project process. In the hotel project example, this management product describes the attributes of the hotel at a high level, such as the number of rooms it will have and its main components (the lobby, restaurant, and so on).

However, the broad descriptions in the project product description won't be detailed enough to manage the building of all the individual components of the hotel, so the project uses product descriptions to describe the project's outputs in more specific detail. During the initiating a project process, the project manager creates the project plan. The plan specifies, at a high level, how the major products of the project will be delivered. At this point, the project manager also creates product descriptions for these major products. He does this in consultation with the senior users, the senior suppliers, and perhaps the teams who will be involved in these products' creation. So at this point in the hotel project, product descriptions for things like the lobby, the swimming pool, and the types of bedrooms are created.

Now imagine that the project has moved on to a point when, during the next stage, the work to furnish the guest rooms will be done. The project manager must create a stage plan for this work. The stage plan shows which products will need to be created or procured in order to furnish the rooms—the beds, the baths, the desks in the rooms, and so on. The project manager (again with the help of the senior users, the senior supplier, and maybe the teams) creates product descriptions for these products so that the teams involved will understand the work they need to do. These more specific product descriptions are created during the managing a stage boundary process alongside the creation of the stage plan.

Finally, perhaps the teams need even more detailed product descriptions in order to do their work to furnish the bedrooms. For example, say the plumbers require a detailed description of the types of faucets that will be fitted to the bath. In this case, they can include even more detailed product descriptions for things like the faucets when they are creating their team plans. It is the responsibility of the team managers to do this during the managing product delivery process.

Each of these even more detailed product descriptions must, of course, align and be consistent with the higher-level product descriptions and also the very high-level project product description. In each case, the project manager has to liaise with the members of the project board, project assurance, and the teams in order to create the product descriptions. This is especially the case when the products are of a technical nature and the project manager does not have expertise in that area.

The product descriptions are then used both during and after the product has been created to check that the right output is or has been created. Basically, the product that has been created is compared with the measurable specification in the product's product description (in the quality criteria section) to see if they match. This is done in the managing product delivery process. The product descriptions define who is responsible for reviewing the products as well as who is responsible for final approval of the products. This is called the *appraisal* approach to quality control. The product descriptions may also be used throughout the building of the products to perform a continual check that the products being created are heading in the right direction. This is considered the *in-process* approach to quality control. These two approaches to quality control will be described in more detail later in this chapter.

The Composition of a Product Description

Figure 6.3 shows the composition of a product description.

Figure 6.3: The composition of the product description

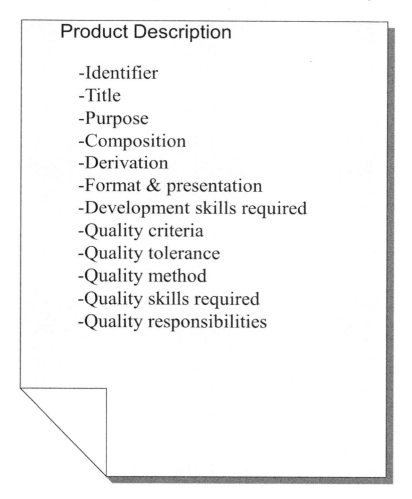

Product Description

- Identifier
- Title
- Purpose
- Composition
- Derivation
- Format & presentation
- Development skills required
- Quality criteria
- Quality tolerance
- Quality method
- Quality skills required
- Quality responsibilities

As you can see in Figure 6.3, the product description has 12 sections. Here is a brief description of what each section should include, using as an example the product description of a penthouse room in the hotel chain project:

Identifier

Every product in a PRINCE2 project is assigned a unique identifier. This identifier helps the project manager track and monitor all the project's products.

Title

The title in our example is "Penthouse Suite."

Purpose

This section defines the product's purpose and who will use it. Some products are ends in themselves, whereas others are created as a means to an end. For example, the purpose of the foundations is to hold up the rest of the hotel, whereas the purpose of the penthouse is to fulfill the needs of the high-end business traveler.

Composition

This section lists the main components that this product contains. In the penthouse example, this can include items such as the bedroom, lobby, bathroom, and furniture.

Derivation

This section lists other products that are needed in order to create this product. For the penthouse example, maybe the project team needs to create the design of the rooms before they begin building them.

Format and Presentation

If the product is a document or a report, this section shows the characteristics of how this product will be presented.

Development Skills Required

This section specifies the sorts of skills needed to create the products. It may also indicate where these skills can be sourced. It will not contain the actual names of people—those will go into the relevant stage plan or the team plan that plans the work to create this product. For the penthouse, this may include a list of relevant skills, such as carpentry, plumbing, or decorating.

Quality Criteria

The *quality criteria* describe the measurable specifications that the product must comply with. The end product can then be compared against these specifications to see if the right thing has been created. For the penthouse, these criteria may specify the dimensions of the room, the color of the walls, the type of materials that will be used, and so on. This section might also refer to any relevant standards that must be followed during product creation. For example, the electricity wiring for the penthouse might need to adhere to some building regulations.

Quality Tolerance

This section describes any leeway that the client will allow for the quality criteria. For example, a king-sized bed has been specified for the penthouse, but a queen-sized one would be acceptable.

Quality Method

The *quality method* describes how the product will be checked to see if it meets its quality criteria. Sometimes, this can be as simple as using a measuring tape to check the dimensions of the room. Other times, the quality method might be more complicated, such as using a decibel meter to check that the soundproofing in the walls is providing the necessary noise insulation. As you will see in the upcoming "Types of Quality Methods" section, there are two categories of quality methods: in-process and appraisal.

Quality Skills Required
This section describes the skills required to carry out the quality methods and indicates where the skills can be sourced. It will not contain the names of people—these are entered in the relevant stage or team plan where the quality activities are planned. For the penthouse, perhaps there is a specialist company that checks buildings for soundproofing qualities.

Quality Responsibilities
This section contains the names of the producer, the reviewers, and the approvers of the product. The approvers of the product have the ultimate sign-off for the penthouse.

Exam Spotlight

As discussed in previous chapters, you will be able to refer to the official PRINCE2 manual, *Managing Successful Projects with PRINCE2* (Stationery Office, 2017), during the Practitioner exam. This is particularly useful if you are asked a question about the contents of one of the management products, such as either the project product description or the product descriptions. Appendix A of *Managing Successful Projects with PRINCE2* shows the information that all 26 management products should contain. It would take a far better memory than mine to remember all the nuances of what goes where in each document, so when you are asked a question about the composition of a management product in the exam, make it easy on yourself and refer to Appendix A.

However, if you are asked a question about either the project product description or the product descriptions, be careful not to refer to the wrong one. When I give candidates mock questions on the project product description or product descriptions in my classes, I can confidently predict that at least half the class will refer to the wrong management product in Appendix A. The project product description and the product descriptions are similar products, but they are *not* the same. Don't confuse them in the exam.

Quality Control

Quality control is the fourth area of quality management that was introduced in the "What Is Quality Management?" section earlier in this chapter. This area involves checking that the products meet the quality criteria described in their product descriptions by carrying out the quality methods (also described in the product descriptions).

A number of levels of quality control exist in PRINCE2:
- A series of *quality checks* may be carried out on each product. For example, the penthouse described in the preceding section might require a quality check of the dimensions of the

room, a quality check of the soundproofing of the walls, a quality check testing the fire safety of the room, and so on. The quality checks will use the approaches described in the product descriptions' quality methods section. Once each check has passed, a quality record should be kept to provide evidence that the product has been reviewed. Project support will file these *quality records*. The project management team will define the format of these quality records in the quality management approach. For example, the records could consist of a form that the reviewers of a product are required to sign when they are satisfied a product has passed a quality check. The quality records should reference any relevant quality inspection documentation that has been used during the quality checks, details of any relevant defect statistics, details of any actions required to correct errors in the products, and any quality-related reports.

- Once each product has passed all its quality checks, it is ready for *approval*. This is the official signing off on the product. The product will be signed off by the person or people defined in the quality responsibilities section in the product description. An *approval record* should be kept to provide evidence of this signing off. Project support will file the approval records. Once again, PRINCE2 does not specify the format of this approval record, so it is up to the project management team to decide this. It could be a note in the minutes of a meeting, an email, a letter, a signature on a document, or a certificate.

- Once a group of products is ready to be delivered to the final customer, the client must accept them. *Acceptance* is where the final output(s) of the project, such as the hotel, are "handed over" to the customer. In many projects, this might take place only at the end. For example, once the hotel has been built, it will be "handed over" from the ownership of the project management team to the group who will operate and maintain the hotel on behalf of the hotel chain. However, many projects will hand over interim deliverables. For example, the hotel project might first build the hotel gym and deliver it to the hotel chain for them to open and operate before the rest of the hotel is finished. The project product description describes who is responsible for providing acceptances (acceptance responsibilities section), how they will do this (acceptance method section), and what measurable characteristics the products need to comply with in order for them to be acceptable (acceptance criteria). *Acceptance records* are kept to provide evidence of these acceptances. Project support will file these acceptance records. Acceptance is frequently required from a number of groups. For example, the ultimate customer should give their acceptance the products are complete, but a project might also require approval from the end users as well as those who will maintain and operate the products post-project. Sometimes there might be a known problem with the final products, so the customer might decide to give a qualified acceptance with the understanding that there will be some corrective work done later. In PRINCE2, this is known as giving a *concession*. You will learn more about concessions in Chapter 8, "Change Theme."

Using the Quality Register

Project support creates the quality register during the initiating a project process. The quality register is used to track all the quality events carried out during the project. These events could be all sorts of quality-related activities, such as workshops to plan the quality of a product, quality checks, reviews and approvals of products, inspections, or pilots. The quality register is a little like a diary of quality events. Along with the quality records that are kept for each event, the quality register provides a useful summary and audit tool of what quality events were planned in the quality management approach and the product descriptions as well as what actually took place. Each entry in the quality register should be backed up by the relevant quality records that were collated for that quality event. Basically, the quality records provide evidence that the event referred to in the register actually happened. Figure 6.4 shows the composition of the quality register.

Figure 6.4: The composition of the quality register

Quality Register

-Quality identifier
-Product identifier(s)
-Product title (s)
-Method
-Roles and responsibilities
-Dates: Planned, forecast and actual dates for:
    -The quality activity
    -Sign off that the quality activity is
     complete
- Result
-Quality records

To illustrate, the following paragraphs describe how the quality register is used to check the quality of the penthouse product for the hotel project.

First, the project manager plans the stage in which the penthouse rooms will be built and quality-checked. Working with the team managers and the senior suppliers, the project manager produces the stage plan for that stage. This stage plan includes the product descriptions for the penthouse as well as the activities that create the penthouses and quality-check them. This planning work is done in the managing a stage boundary process.

Once the stage plan is created, the project manager reviews the plan to find all the quality activities. This is also done in the managing a stage boundary process. For each quality check activity found, the project manager creates a corresponding entry in the quality register. At this point in the project, the quality register entries show only the planned details. So for a quality check to verify the dimensions of the penthouse rooms, the project manager fills out the following details:

Quality Identifier
For example, if this is the 23rd check on the project, the project manager enters **23** here.

Product Identifier(s)
The project manager takes this ID from the product's product description.

Product Title(s)
In this example, the project manager enters **Penthouse** here.

Method
This is the quality method that has been specified in the product description. This entry might be as simple as **Use a measuring tape** for the penthouse example.

Roles and Responsibilities
These are the names of the people specified in the stage plan for this quality activity. In the penthouse example, this includes the name of the person or team creating the rooms, the people responsible for reviewing the rooms, and the person responsible for signing off this quality check—all of which are found in the product description.

Planned Date of Quality Check
For this section, the project manager refers to the stage plan and writes in the date for which the quality check has been planned.

Planned Date of Sign-off of Quality Check
For this section as well, the project manager refers to the stage plan and writes in the date when the quality check is scheduled to be signed off.

Figure 6.5 shows the quality register entry for the quality check to verify the dimensions of the penthouse rooms, as it will look during the planning of the stage.

Figure 6.5: Example of a quality register entry during stage planning

Quality identifier	Product identifier(s)	Product title(s)	Method	Roles & responsibilities	Planned date of quality check	Planned date of sign-off of quality check	Actual date of quality check	Actual date of sign-off of quality check	Result	Quality records
23	121	Penthouse	Measuring	Simon - producer Jack - reviewer Jane - approver	08-Feb	10-Feb				

Once the stage plan is authorized, the project manager manages the work in that stage using the controlling a stage process. At some point, the project manager authorizes the work to build and then quality-check the penthouse rooms by giving a work package to the relevant team or team manager.

The work of building and checking the quality of the penthouse rooms takes place in the managing product delivery process and is the responsibility of the team manager or the team. Once the quality checks have been done, quality records are collated and the quality register is updated with the results. The work package describes who should update the quality register with the results. At this point, the entry in the quality register for the quality check that verifies the dimensions of the penthouse rooms would look like Figure 6.6.

Figure 6.6: Example of a quality register entry after a quality check

Quality identifier	Product identifier(s)	Product title(s)	Method	Roles & responsibilities	Planned date of quality check	Planned date of sign-off of quality check	Actual date of quality check	Actual date of sign-off of quality check	Result	Quality records
23	121	Penthouse	Measuring	Simon - producer Jack - reviewer Jane - approver	08-Feb	10-Feb	11-Feb	11-Feb	Pass	

If a product fails its quality check and has to be resubmitted for a new quality check after some remedial work has been done, a new entry in the quality register is created that refers to this resubmission quality check.

Types of Quality Methods

As I have said previously, each product that is created will go through a number of quality checks and then finally be approved. How will the products be quality checked? I am sure that every industry has hundreds of different ways of checking that products are fit for purpose. For example, a piece of software can be tested for its usability, security, and robustness, to name just three types of quality checks. In PRINCE2, you have seen that the quality method section of a product's product description describes how a product will be quality checked. PRINCE2 has the following two categories of quality methods:

In-process Methods

In-process methods are checks that are done during the creation of the product. They might involve interim checks during the building of the product. Or they might involve a special way of building a product that ensures that it conforms to its quality criteria—for example, a car manufacturing line using robots to build the parts of the car. In the hotel project, there might be a detailed process that the builders need to follow to build each bedroom. This will make it more likely that they will create bedrooms matching the quality criteria.

Appraisal Methods

Appraisal methods are checks that are done on the product after it has been finished. There are two types: *testing*, whereby an objective criterion is measured to indicate whether it meets its quality criteria, and *quality inspection*, whereby some sort of professional judgment needs to be reached. In the hotel project, for example, a building inspector from the local government office might come to conduct a thorough inspection of the hotel to check that it complies with all the necessary building and health and safety legislation. These quality inspections often follow a planned and systematic process.

CASE STUDY

Using the PRINCE2 Quality Approach

If you use the PRINCE2 quality approach, you should be pragmatic about how you implement it. Do you really need to create a lot of separate product descriptions for every product created, or can you somehow combine much of this information? The point of the product descriptions is to define the measurable criteria for each product so that the creators of the products know what they are aiming for. If there were separate product descriptions for all the products, this could create a lot of documentation. Also, some of the information in the quality register replicates information in the product descriptions, such as the responsibilities and the quality methods.

A number of PRINCE2 software tools are available that can help you create these PRINCE2 management products. The tools provide templates and replicate information between different products to avoid double entry. If you are going to use PRINCE2 in a detailed way, you'll find it useful to look at these tools.

Application of the Quality Theme in a Project

This section pulls together the quality approaches discussed in the preceding sections of this chapter. I will take you through the project to build a hotel for a hotel chain and describe how the PRINCE2 quality approach is applied.

Figure 6.7 shows what PRINCE2 calls the *quality audit trail*. As you can see, there are six major steps in the PRINCE2 quality approach to a project, and these steps produce auditable records. In the following sections, you learn what is involved in each of these six steps.

Figure 6.7: The quality audit trail

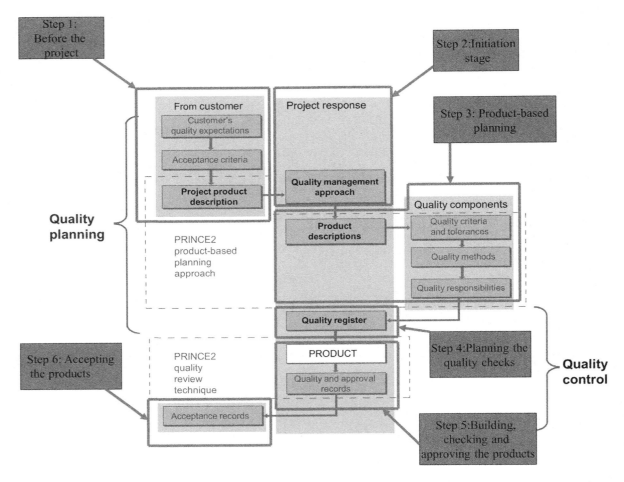

Before tackling the following sections, you should have a basic understanding of how the PRINCE2 process model fits together, at least at a high level. If you don't know this yet, go back to Chapter 1 and read the section "An End-to-End Walk-through of PRINCE2."

Step 1: Before the Project

The first step in the PRINCE2 quality approach is to understand what the customer's quality expectations are regarding the outputs of the project. These might be rather ambiguous (such as the customer asking for a luxury hotel or one aimed at the business traveler), so from these subjective customer's quality expectations, objective acceptance criteria are derived.

For example, if the customer's quality expectations of the hotel are that it will be suitable for the business traveler, some relevant acceptance criteria could be that each room will have laundry service, each television will have news channels in all main business languages, and room service will be available on a 24-hour basis.

When corporate, programme management, or the customer creates the project mandate that triggers the start of PRINCE2, it may contain an idea of their quality expectations and their acceptance criteria for the final products, although it may be left to the project management team to develop these expectations and criteria in the starting up a project process.

In the hotel example, corporate, programme management, or the customer could be the hotel chain's board of directors. They decide that they would like to open a luxury hotel aimed at the business traveler in Shanghai. They create a project mandate outlining this customer's quality expectations.

Once the project mandate has been created, the starting up a project process begins. The executive and the project manager design and appoint the project management team, including the senior users. The senior users are responsible for establishing the requirements for the project's products. There may be a number of perspectives on how the products will be used, and therefore, a number of senior users. In the hotel example, senior users may represent the marketing team of the hotel, who will use the hotel as a tool to create sales for the hotel chain. There may also be senior users who represent actual customers of the hotel, such as a market research company who are experts on the business traveler.

During the starting up a project process, the senior users are responsible for ensuring that the customer's quality expectations and the acceptance criteria correctly define products that are fit for their purpose. They work with the project manager to document the customer's quality expectations and acceptance criteria in the project product description. For example, the senior users of the hotel project might set the following acceptance criteria: The hotel must be located within 30 minutes travel time of the airport; it must have a capacity of 300 bedrooms; and it must attain a four-star Chinese hotel standard rating.

In some projects, it might be difficult to define all the acceptance criteria at the beginning of the project. For example, a research and development project team might not know exactly what will be created at the end of their work. In such cases, the acceptance criteria might evolve during the project, with new criteria being added at the end of each stage. However, the impacts of these new additions need to be evaluated and then added only once they have been reviewed through the change control process. (You learn more about change control in Chapter 8.)

After the starting up a project process, the project board reviews the project brief. The project brief contains the project product description along with other outputs from starting up a project, such as the outline business case. The project board uses the information in the project brief to decide whether to commission the project. They make this decision in the directing a project process.

Step 2: Initiation Stage

During the initiation stage, the project manager is responsible for the activities in the initiating a project process. One of these activities is to prepare the quality management approach. The quality management approach sets out how the project will be managed to ensure that the outputs meet the customer's needs. The next section of this chapter, "The Quality Management Approach," describes this management product in more detail, but for now, all you need to know is that it establishes how quality planning, quality control, and quality assurance are to be carried out during the project. It also describes the various documents (such as the quality register), roles, and reports that have to be created in order to manage the quality of the products effectively.

During the initiation stage, the project product description is reviewed and refined, if necessary.

Step 3: Product-Based Planning

As the project progresses, the specification details contained in the project product description will probably be too broad to plan the building of all the individual components that the project will create. To resolve this problem, the project manager creates product descriptions that describe all the components of the main outputs from the project. In the hotel example, the project manager might create product descriptions for the hotel's lobby, the different types of bedrooms, the restaurant, and so on.

A product's description is created at the same time as the plan that shows the activities needed to create it. For example, the project plan shows how to create the major products of the project and also contains the product descriptions for these major products. In the hotel example, these major products might be things like the hotel lobby and the different types of rooms. The project manager creates the project plan and the accompanying product descriptions for the major products in the initiating a project process.

The initiating a project process may not be the only place where product descriptions are created in the PRINCE2 process model. When the project manager develops the stage plans, he can create more detailed product descriptions or refine old ones to aid in the planning of that stage. When team managers create team plans, they might also create even more detailed product descriptions.

In the hotel example, imagine that the project manager is planning the stage during which the swimming pool will be constructed. He does this planning during the managing a stage boundary process. First, the project manager creates a product description for the swimming pool (unless it has already been created). This product description describes the measurable quality criteria for the pool, such as the dimensions, the materials that will be used to construct it, and the type of heating system that will be used. It also defines what quality methods will be used both during and after the pool's construction to ensure the product's compliance with the quality criteria. For example, perhaps safety tests will be applied to check the pool. Finally, the product description describes the quality responsibilities, such as who is responsible for producing the pool, reviewing it, and finally approving it.

Step 4: Planning the Quality Checks

When the project manager is planning the work for creating the products in any stage, he also plans the quality control activities needed to ensure that the right product is being and has been built. For each quality activity planned, the project manager creates a corresponding entry in the quality register, just as you saw in the "Using the quality register" section earlier. So for the swimming pool example, the project manager may make separate quality register entries for the dimension quality check, the safety test quality check, and a test of the swimming pool's heating system.

Step 5: Building, Checking, and Approving the Products

During the fifth step, the swimming pool is built. The project manager authorizes a team manager or a team to carry out this work by creating a work package in the controlling a stage process. The work package contains the product descriptions of all the products that the team needs to create, such as the product description for the swimming pool. The team accepts the responsibility for creating the pool in their managing product delivery process. The project manager and the teams would review the planned quality checks of the pool shown in the quality register with project assurance to see if any further reviewers are necessary. If so, they update the quality register with the names of these additional reviewers.

Then the pool is created and is quality-checked by the people indicated as reviewers in the pool's product description. This occurs during the managing product delivery process. At this time, the pool is measured, the heating system is checked, and so on. The people checking the pool could come from a variety of places, with the one caveat that obviously the project management team doesn't want the people who created the pool to review and approve their own work. The reviewers of the pool could be the senior users, the customers, and/or experts in swimming pool construction who will carry out quality inspections, or they could come from project or quality assurance. The reviewers of the pool need to create quality records to show that the reviews have taken place.

Finally, after the pool has passed all of its quality checks, it is approved. PRINCE2 reserves the word "approval" for signing off on an individual product of the project (as opposed to acceptance, which is another type of sign-off, as you'll see in a moment). The product description of the swimming pool describes who should approve the product. The approver of the pool needs to create an approval record. Once the quality records and approval record are received by project support, the relevant quality register entries can be updated with the results.

Step 6: Accepting the Products

The final step is getting acceptances for the project's products. Acceptance in PRINCE2 is different from approval. Acceptance of the project's products is the ultimate approval. It is when the products transfer from the ownership of the project team to the customer or the group that will maintain or operate the products for the customer.

In all projects, a handover takes place of the products to the final client (or their operational representatives) at the end of the project. For example, at the end of the hotel project, the hotel is handed over to the operational team, which needs to give their acceptance. It is the project manager's responsibility to obtain this acceptance during the closing a project process.

In some projects, there may also be some interim products delivered during the project. For example, in the hotel project, perhaps the gym is built and delivered before the end of the project. The gym's operational team needs to give the project management team a formal acceptance that they have taken ownership of the gym. It is the project manager's responsibility to obtain this acceptance. These interim acceptances are obtained during the managing a stage boundary process.

In both cases, PRINCE2 states that records of the acceptance should be kept. As you learned earlier in this chapter in the "Quality Control" section, these are called *acceptance records*.

The Quality Management Approach

The project manager creates the *quality management approach* in the initiating a project process and will review and possibly update the approach at the end of each management stage. This approach defines how the project will be managed to ensure that products of the right quality will be created. A project may need to follow (at least in part) an existing quality management approach, such as a corporate quality policy or a programme quality management approach. In this case, the project's quality management approach need only refer to the existing approach or refer to it and describe any differences in the project's approach. Figure 6.8 shows the composition of the quality management approach.

Figure 6.8: The composition of the quality management approach

Quality Management Strategy

-Introduction
-Quality management procedure
-Tools and techniques
-Records
-Reporting
-Timing of quality management activities
-Roles and responsibilities

As you can see in Figure 6.8, the quality management approach has seven sections. The following descriptions use the hotel project example to give you an idea of what sort of information should be included in each section.

Introduction

The introduction establishes the purpose and objectives of the quality management approach. The purpose in the hotel example is to ensure that the project creates a hotel that meets the acceptance criteria defined in the project product description and that the project complies with all relevant construction and safety standards. It also states who is responsible for the quality management approach. In the hotel example, this may be the project board.

Quality Management Procedure

This section sets out the variety of steps, activities, and templates (such as product descriptions) that will be used to ensure the correct products are built. It covers the following three quality management areas:

Quality Planning

This section addresses the steps that will be taken throughout the project to define the specifications for the overall products in the project product description and the individual products in the product descriptions. In the hotel project, this may include defining the steps that will be taken to specify the designs of the hotel, such as working with architects to create prototype models, then moving on to detailed computer-aided design drawings.

Quality Control

This section addresses the steps that will be taken throughout the project to verify that the correct products are being or have been built. It defines quality standards to be followed, such as building or construction standards. It provides templates or forms, including the quality register or quality records (such as sign-off forms). There may be a certain set of quality methods that will be used repeatedly throughout the project. In the hotel project example, a fire and safety test may be required on the entire building. Such standard types of quality methods are defined here. Finally, in some cases, certain metrics are used to help determine whether the products comply with their specifications. In the hotel example, the rooms may be checked for soundproofing using the decibel range. The quality control section specifies that decibels will be used and defines threshold levels the rooms must comply to.

Quality Assurance

Throughout the project, one area of quality assurance activities may be to carry out a number of compliance audits. For example, in the hotel project, the hotel chain wants to check that the construction company is following engineering and health and safety standards. This section shows how these compliance audits are to be carried out.

There may already be a number of procedures for quality management defined at a corporate level, in which case these procedures do not have to be repeated—the quality management approach can simply refer to them. For example, there may be a procedure that is used before the opening of a new hotel, to check that all the systems are working correctly and the hotel is ready for its first customers.

In the hotel project, the construction work will probably have been outsourced to a construction company. This construction company will follow many industry-defined standards, such as health and safety and engineering standards. This section of the quality management approach can refer to these supplier standards.

Tools and Techniques

In any project, there may be specific tools or techniques used during various parts of the quality management procedure. In the construction of the hotel, for example, a variety of tools are typically used to check the safe construction of the hotel, such as a fire safety check. Or there may be a special technique for checking the soundproofing of rooms.

Records

This chapter has covered a variety of quality records that should be kept to prove that products have been signed off correctly. There may be records to show that a product has passed a variety of quality checks, records to show that products have been approved (approval records), and records to show that products have been passed over to the clients or the operational teams (acceptance records). This section defines the format of these records, where they will be stored, and how they will be used.

This section also describes the composition and format of the quality register and how the register will be reviewed and updated.

Reporting

This section describes any quality management reports, what their purposes are, their timing, and whom they should go to.

In the hotel project example, the project board wants to see a variety of information about quality in the end stage report:

- The quality activities that took place during the stage and their results
- The products that were approved during this stage
- The off-specifications that were approved (products that did not comply with their product descriptions but were approved anyway)
- The acceptances that occurred during the stage

Timing of Quality Management Activities

This section states when formal quality management activities will take place. In the hotel project example, a health and safety compliance audit of the construction work may take place at the end of each stage.

Roles and Responsibilities

This section describes the roles and responsibilities for quality management activities. For example, the senior users are responsible for checking the product descriptions to see whether they meet their expectations, and the project manager is responsible for checking that each stage plan contains quality checks for all the products to be created and that there is an entry for these quality checks in the quality register.

The Quality Review Technique

The *quality review technique* is a way of checking the compliance of a product with its product description. It is primarily designed to assess products that take the form of a document or something similar, such as a presentation. However, it could be used for any type of appropriate product.

The quality review technique entails the following three steps:

Step 1: Preparation
First, a *chair* is appointed, who will run the quality review technique process. A *presenter* is then appointed, who will represent the producer of the product under review. The presenter

sends the product and its product description to a number of *reviewers,* who will carry out a quality inspection on the product to see whether it complies with its product description. If the reviewers spot any small grammatical or typing errors, they can write directly on the document. If the reviewers spot any larger errors, they start creating a question list for the presenter. An *administrator* is also appointed to help out with . . . guess what . . . administration.

Step 2: Review Meeting

A meeting is held, run by the chair, to review the product and is attended by all the quality review technique roles. (However, in simpler reviews or when the reviewer's feedback is easy to understand, a meeting may not be necessary.) During this meeting, the attendees discuss the questions that the reviewers have about the product. The chair determines the outcome of the meeting, which could be one of the following: The product is deemed complete and signed off; it is deemed conditionally complete, and the presenter has a number of actions to remedy a few quality problems; or the product is deemed incomplete. In the latter case, the whole quality review technique will have to be repeated at a later date, after the problems with the product have been dealt with. If the chair determines that the product has not passed the quality review, an issue should be raised to the project manager.

Step 3: Review Follow-up

If there were follow-up actions to remedy problems with the product, these are coordinated by the presenter and then signed off by the reviewers. The chair then signs off that the product is complete and reports this to the approver of the product. Of course, another possibility is that the product fails this step, in which case, the chair would raise an issue to the project manager.

If the quality review technique is used, it is done in the managing product delivery process. The quality review technique roles can more or less be carried out by anyone, as long as there is no conflict of interest, such as someone producing a product and then reviewing it. However, the administrator is likely to come from project support. The product's product descriptions specify who will carry out the various quality review technique roles for its review. In less complex or smaller reviews, only two people might be involved: one taking the chair and reviewer roles and the other taking the presenter and administrator roles.

After a document-based product has gone through the quality review technique and been signed off, no changes should be made to it. It is in a state that PRINCE2 calls *baselined*. (You'll learn more about baselines in Chapter 8.) If someone wants to make changes, they must create a new version of the product and make their changes to that version.

The quality review technique is useful for involving key interested parties, such as users, in the product and getting them to buy into the product. Sometimes at the end of a project, disputes arise about whether a product is correct. However, if the people disputing the quality of the product were involved with signing off the product, it is more difficult for them to complain.

The quality review technique has a range of benefits. It helps to involve and engage key interested parties, such as the users, and encourages buy-in for the project. It helps to build the project teams, particularly when the review team includes individuals from multiple functions and companies. It also helps to reinforce a project culture focused on quality, train the participants in quality control, and create consistent and familiar quality documentation.

Roles Involved with the Quality Theme

This chapter described the various roles that are involved with the quality theme. Here is a quick review of these roles to help you prepare for the exams:

Corporate, Programme Management, or the Customer
Provides a quality assurance function and details of any established corporate, programme management, or customer quality management approach that needs to be followed by the project management team.

Executive
Approves all the main quality management products, such as the project product description and the quality management approach, and confirms the acceptance of the main outputs of the project.

Senior user(s)
Involved with specifying the project's products in the project product description and the product descriptions, providing resources to verify that the correct products have been created and accepted, and approving the key products.

Senior Supplier(s)
Involved with reviewing the specifications for the products set out in the project product description and the product descriptions to verify that they are feasible to deliver. They approve the quality methods, tools, and techniques that are set out in the quality management approach and the product descriptions to confirm that they will create the products to a necessary level of quality.

Project Manager
Creates all the major quality management products, such as the quality management approach, project product description, product descriptions, and quality register. He liaises closely with the senior users, senior suppliers, executive, and the team manager (or the teams if there is no team manager) in order to do so. When he authorizes work to the teams, he ensures that the correct quality control work is carried out.

Team Manager
Creates the products to comply with his product descriptions, ensuring that the correct quality control is carried out and that there is evidence of the quality activities with quality records. He reviews the quality register to ensure that it is updated with the results of quality activities. If there is no team manager, then these responsibilities are taken on by the team members.

Project Assurance
Assures the project board that the quality management approach is implemented correctly. Provides advice and guidance to the project manager, team managers, or the team members if there are no team managers, and those involved with quality activities on the application of the quality management approach and the suitability of quality reviewers and approvers.

Project Support
Provides administrative support and assistance, and maintains the quality register and the quality records.

Tailoring the Quality Theme

The key to successfully using PRINCE2 is adapting and tailoring the method given the characteristics of the project and the environment the project is operating within. The following sections show you how the quality theme might be adapted to better suit certain situations. This is something you might be tested on in the exams.

Minimum Requirements

Organizations with a less-formal project management approach or that are running smaller, less-complicated projects might choose to cut back on some of the quality theme ideas. However, there are some minimum requirements that must be followed in order for a project team to claim they are following PRINCE2's quality theme.

First, the project management team must define their quality management approach. They need to describe how they will carry out quality control and project assurance and how they will report on the quality activities conducted during the project. They also need to define any important quality management roles and responsibilities.

Second, the project management team must specify what the project needs to create. This should be done at a high level by specifying customer quality expectations and prioritized acceptance criteria in the project product description, and then done again at a more detailed level by specifying each product's quality criteria in a product description.

Third, the project management team needs to keep records of any quality activities that have been carried out, such as the checking and approving of products, and summarize these activities in some sort of quality register.

Finally, the project management team should take account of prior experience and lessons when planning and doing quality activities.

Commercial Customer and Supplier Environment

In a commercial customer and supplier environment, the legal contracts should specify in an unambiguous way what products need to be delivered. They might also specify how quality assurance will be carried out throughout the project, what quality control will be done, the customer's rights of inspection of the delivery process, and the internal working of the products being built.

Aligning the Quality Approach with Organizational or Programme Approaches

So far, you have seen that the project management team creates a quality management approach for their project. However, the organization that has commissioned the project might already have an organization-wide quality approach. In this case, the project management team might adopt this organizational approach for their project. A similar situation might occur if the project is part of a programme. In this case, programme management might tell the project management team to follow the programme quality management approach.

Generally, the corporate, programme management, or the customer organizational level will tell the project board if they should follow an already established corporate or programme quality management approach. Maybe not all of the broader approach would be applicable for the project, so the project management team would adopt only certain parts of the higher-level approach and create the rest of the approach just for that initiative.

Agile Environments

In an agile environment, product descriptions might be written as user stories or epics. A user story is written in the format: "As a *<name of role>*, I want to *<description of function>*, so that *<description of benefits>*."

For example, imagine if the team for the hotel project is discussing the requirements for the hotel's website. They might create the following user stories:

"As a customer, I want to see all rooms available for a particular day so that I can decide whether to stay in the hotel."

"As a manager, I want to see all rooms booked for a particular day so that I can instruct the cleaning teams to prepare the rooms."

In addition to including the "who, what, and why" format of the user story, it is important that the product descriptions meet all the other PRINCE2 requirements. For example, a product description should also contain a list of quality criteria, which agile approaches often call acceptance criteria, in addition to indicating the skills and resources needed to implement the user story.

Most agile approaches also attach a value to each user story. This is different from the PRINCE2 approach. The nearest equivalent of the agile term *value* is the PRINCE2 term *benefit*, which, of course, is not set at a product level but only at a project level. However, there is nothing stopping a PRINCE2/agile project management team from attaching a value to each product description, which might help them understand how to prioritize and flex what is delivered.

Epics can be thought of as super-user stories, or a group of requirements that are ill defined and need to be broken down. The nearest PRINCE2 equivalent of the epic is the project product description.

In the "Application of the Quality Theme" section earlier in this chapter, I talked about how the project management team would use the product-based planning approach throughout the project to create more and more detailed product descriptions. For example, in starting up a project, the project manager creates a broad, high-level description of the main outputs of the project, which is the project product description. Then in initiating a project, he creates product descriptions of the major products, which describe the outputs at a medium level. Then in managing a stage boundary, the project manager creates more-detailed product descriptions of products to be delivered within the upcoming stage. This sort of approach is aligned to the idea in agile of evolving the requirements for the products throughout the project. However, to avoid a chaotic situation where everything could change, a pragmatic approach would be to baseline or freeze higher-level product descriptions at a reasonable point in time, while allowing lower-level product descriptions to evolve as long as their evolution does not impact on the frozen higher-level requirements.

Agile approaches deliver the products across a series of iterations. Each iteration usually lasts for a short period of time—maybe a sprint of three to four weeks. This way of working often involves a much higher frequency of quality checking than in a non-agile environment. For example, towards the end of each sprint, the team building the product will want to get feedback from the customers by demonstrating the new release. In the software industry, in order to create complicated systems within a relatively short period of time, automated tests are used that can quickly test a lot of aspects of the system. The automated testing approach might be difficult to transfer to a non-IT environment; however, regardless of which industry the project is operating within, the project management team needs to carefully plan and budget for the higher frequency of quality checking that is needed in order to deliver robust products in a short period of time.

Linking the Quality Theme with the Principles

In Chapter 1, I talked about the seven PRINCE2 principles. In some ways, all seven principles contribute to implementing the quality theme; however, the three principles that are most important are focus on products, defined roles and responsibilities, and learn from experience.

Throughout the project, the project management team is focused on products. They create a project product description and product descriptions to clearly define what will be created, and then use these management products to verify and review that the correct outputs have been created. The quality management approach will define who is doing what with regard to quality activities so that the principle of defined roles and responsibilities is implemented. This principle is also implemented by the creation of product descriptions, as they state which people will be involved with reviewing, producing, and approving the products.

Throughout the process model, PRINCE2 advocates learning from experience to ensure that the activities of quality planning, quality assurance, and quality control are carried out in the best possible way. Quality control also involves eliminating causes of unsatisfactory performance, so it could include looking at the processes used to manage the project and seeing if they could be improved.

Summary

In this chapter, you learned about the PRINCE2 quality theme. The quality theme ensures that a project creates products that are fit for their purpose.

The first thing you learned in this chapter was the PRINCE2 meaning of the word *quality*. In everyday speech, quality is often used to mean luxury or high specification. In PRINCE2, however, quality means fit for purpose. Quality management is the means by which a project ensures that products that are fit for purpose are created. There are four areas of quality management: a quality system, which defines an approach to quality; a quality assurance function, which checks that the quality system is being implemented; quality planning, where the specifications of the products are defined; and quality control, which is a set of activities to verify that the right products have been or are being built.

Two important management products are involved with quality planning: the project product description and the product descriptions. The project product description describes the overall characteristics of the major output(s) of the project, and product descriptions describe the lower-level characteristics for each of the component parts of the major outputs.

You saw that there is one important management product used for quality control: the quality register. This register is used to track all the quality checks that are carried out on the project's products. It contains information about when the check took place, who was involved, and whether the check passed or failed.

The quality management approach defines how the project will approach the four aspects of quality management. The project manager creates the quality management approach during the initiation stage of the project.

You also learned about the quality review technique. This gives a particular approach for reviewing paper-based or electronic documents and verifying whether they have been created in accordance with their product description.

Finally, you saw how the quality theme can be adapted so that it can work in a number of situations. You learned how to adapt the theme to smaller, less-complicated projects and how to use it in commercial customer and supplier environments, programme environments, and agile environments.

Foundation Exam Essentials

Explain the purpose of the quality theme.
The purpose of the quality theme is to define and implement the means by which the project will verify that products are fit for purpose. The quality theme covers the four areas of quality management: quality systems, quality assurance, quality planning, and quality control.

Explain the purpose of the project product description.
The project product description is a special form of product description. The purpose of the project product description is to describe the customer's quality expectations and the acceptance criteria, the acceptance method, and acceptance responsibilities for the project, and to gain agreement with the user on the project's scope and requirements. The project manager creates the project product description during the starting up a project process, refines it in the initiating a project process, and may update it during the managing a stage boundary process. It is used in the closing a project process to verify that the project has delivered what was expected of it and the acceptance criteria have been met.

Explain the purpose of the product description.
The purpose of the product description is to describe the nature, purpose, function, and appearance of the product. It contains the product's quality criteria and describes how the product will be tested and reviewed and who will carry out these quality checks. The project manager creates product descriptions during the initiating a project process, when formulating the project plan, and during the managing a stage boundary process, when formulating a stage or exception plan. The team manager creates product descriptions as part of putting together the team plans during the managing product delivery process.

Explain the purpose of the quality management approach.
The purpose of the quality management approach is to describe how quality will be managed on the project. It describes how quality planning, quality control, and quality assurance will be carried out. The project manager creates the quality management approach during the initiating a project process.

Explain the purpose of the quality register.
The quality register is used to summarize all the project's quality management activities and provide information for the end stage reports and end project reports. It acts as a pointer to all

the quality records that have been created for each product. The project manager creates the quality register in the initiating a project process and updates it when planning a stage during the managing a stage boundary process with the details of planned quality activities. The authority defined in the work package updates the quality register with the results of quality activities during the managing product delivery process.

Describe PRINCE2's minimum requirement for applying the quality theme.
As a minimum for applying the quality theme, PRINCE2 requires that the project management team does the following:
- Define its quality management approach, which must cover the project's approach to quality control and project assurance, how to communicate the management of quality throughout the project, and who will be responsible for the quality activities throughout the project
- Specify measurable quality criteria for each product in the product descriptions and specify the customer quality expectations and acceptance criteria for the project in the project product description
- Maintain quality records to show which quality activities are planned and which have taken place, and summarize these records in some sort of quality register
- Use lessons to inform the management of quality throughout the project

Define the concepts of quality planning and quality control.
Quality planning is about defining the project's products, with their respective quality criteria, quality methods, and the quality responsibilities of those involved. Essentially, it is about specifying what sorts of products to create and how they will be checked and reviewed. Quality control is about checking that products meet their quality criteria and identifying ways of eliminating unsatisfactory project performance by, for example, introducing process improvements in response to lessons learned.

Define the concepts of project assurance and quality assurance.
Quality assurance is the responsibility of corporate, programme management, or the customer and involves independently monitoring that the project's direction and management are adequate for the nature of the project and that it complies with relevant corporate, programme management, or customer standards and policies. Project assurance is the responsibility of the project board and involves monitoring that the project is being conducted properly. There are three types of project assurance: business assurance, which is the responsibility of the executive; user assurance, which is the responsibility of the senior user; and supplier assurance, which is the responsibility of the senior supplier.

Define the concepts of customer quality expectations and acceptance criteria.
The customer's quality expectations describe the overall level of quality expected of the project's products and the standards and processes that must be applied to achieve that quality. Acceptance criteria are a prioritized list of measurable criteria that the project's products must meet before the customer will accept them.

Practitioner Exam Essentials

Demonstrate an understanding of the quality management approach.
Demonstrate an understanding that the project manager creates the quality management approach during the initiation stage and that it shows how to manage quality throughout the project. Understand that the approach might be derived from the project brief, the project product description and any corporate, programme management, or customer strategies or policies that exist, and that it could be a stand-alone document, an entry in a project management tool, or part of the project initiation documentation. Know the composition of the quality management approach.

Demonstrate an understanding of the quality register.
Demonstrate an understanding that project support creates the quality register during the initiation stage and it is used to record details of quality activities that are carried out throughout the project. Understand that it could be a stand-alone register, a spreadsheet, a database, part of an integrated project register for all risks, actions and issues, sticky notes on walls, or an entry into a project management tool. Know the composition of the quality register.

Demonstrate an understanding of the project product description.
Demonstrate an understanding that the project manager creates the project product description during the starting up a project process. Understand that the project product description might be derived from the project mandate, discussions with the senior users, the senior suppliers and the executive or, if the project is operating within a commercial customer/supplier environment, a request for proposal. Know that the project product description could be a document, a set of presentation slides, a mind map, or an entry in a project management tool. Know the composition of the project product description.

Demonstrate an understanding of product descriptions.
Demonstrate an understanding that the project manager creates product descriptions when creating the project plan or stage plans, and the team manager or the team would create product descriptions when creating a team plan. Understand that product descriptions might be derived from a product breakdown structure, the quality management approach, the change control approach, or from discussions with the end users of the product. Know that product descriptions could be a document, a set of presentation slides, a mind map, or an entry in a project management tool. Know the composition of product descriptions.

Demonstrate an understanding of the recommended roles and responsibilities within the quality theme.
- Demonstrate an understanding that corporate, programme management, or the customer provides details of any corporate, programme, or customer quality standards to follow and also provides quality assurance.
- Demonstrate an understanding that the senior users provide customer quality expectations and acceptance criteria, help create the project product description, provide quality criteria for individual products, and help create the product descriptions.
- Demonstrate an understanding that the project board approves the project product description, the quality management approach, and the product descriptions.

- Demonstrate an understanding that the project manager prepares the project product description, the quality management approach, and the product descriptions and ensures that the teams implement the quality-control measures agreed upon in product descriptions and work packages.
- Demonstrate an understanding that the team manager creates the products according to their product descriptions, manages the quality control approaches for the products created, and assembles quality and approval records as evidence that the products have been properly reviewed and approved.
- Demonstrate an understanding that project assurance monitors and ensures that the quality management approach is correctly applied and provides advice and guidance to the project manager.
- Demonstrate an understanding that project support provides administrative support, helping to collate and store quality records and maintain the quality register.

Understand the quality planning activities that take place using the project product description and which roles are responsible for these actions.
The project manager, with the help of the senior users and the executive, creates the project product description that outlines the customer's quality expectations and the acceptance criteria. The project product description describes the acceptance methods, showing how the product will be checked for compliance with its acceptance criteria and who is responsible for accepting the products.

Understand the quality planning activities that take place using the product descriptions and which roles are responsible for these actions.
The project manager, with the help of the senior users, creates product descriptions that contain the quality criteria for each product. The product descriptions describe the quality methods to be used to verify that the products comply with their quality criteria and who is responsible for carrying out the quality methods and approving the products.

Understand the quality control actions that take place in a project and know which roles are responsible for these actions.
The person indicated in a product's product description carries out quality control actions to verify that the product matches its quality criteria and that quality and approval records should be kept as evidence that the product has been checked and approved. The person specified in the project product description carries out the ultimate approval of a product, and acceptance records should be kept as evidence of a product's ultimate approval.

Understand how to carry out quality methods.
Each product's completeness is verified by using quality methods defined in that product's product description.

Understand the objectives of the quality review technique.
The objectives of the quality review technique are to assess the conformity of a product with its quality criteria, to involve key interested parties, and to baseline a product for change control.

Understand the responsibilities of the various quality review technique roles.
The chair has overall responsibility for the quality review technique; the reviewers review the product; the presenter represents the producer of the product; and the administrator provides support.

Be familiar with the actions that take place in the quality review technique.
The three main stages of the quality review technique are review preparation, review meeting, and review follow-up.

Assess and critique an approach to applying the quality theme.
Understand the purpose and format of the project product description, product descriptions, the quality management approach, and the quality register. Show how the quality theme might be adapted to different project contexts (for example, a small project, an agile project, a project with external third-party organizations, or a project operating within a programme environment). Show how a given project approach aligns with the principles of PRINCE2.

Review Questions

The remainder of this chapter contains mock exam questions, first for the Foundation exam and then for the Practitioner exam.

Foundation Exam Questions

1. Which is a purpose of the quality register?
    A. To define the project's approach to quality control
    B. To specify a product's quality criteria
    C. To act as a pointer to quality records associated with a product
    D. To specify a product's quality methods

2. Which of the following describes how to manage quality throughout a project?
    A. Project product description
    B. Quality management approach
    C. Product description
    D. Quality register

3. Which of the following statements are true of both project assurance and quality assurance?
    1. They provide assurance that the project is being run to corporate standards.
    2. They are independent of the managing level of the project management team.
    3. The role is carried out on behalf of the business, user, and supplier perspectives of the project board.
    4. They are independent of the directing level of the project management team.
    A. 1 and 2
    B. 2 and 3
    C. 3 and 4
    D. 1 and 4

4. Which of the following statements describes a minimum requirement for applying the quality theme?
   A. To review the business justification when exceptions are raised
   B. To define how to identify ways of eliminating causes of unsatisfactory performance
   C. To ensure that the project has at least two management stages
   D. To define the project's approach to communicating and engaging with stakeholders

5. Identify the missing word(s) in the following sentence:
   [?] is achieved by implementing, monitoring, and recording the quality methods of the project.
   A. Quality planning
   B. Quality control
   C. Quality assurance
   D. Project assurance

6. Which of the following is a purpose of the project product description?
   A. To gain agreement from the user on the project's scope and requirements
   B. To define how the project will be managed in order to deliver products that are fit for their purpose
   C. To define how the project will control uncertainty
   D. To define how the project will control proposed modifications to the project's products

7. Which of the following is a quality planning activity?
   (1) Creating product descriptions to understand what is required of a product
   (2) Scheduling the development activities of a product so that it will match its product description
   (3) Carrying out a quality inspection on a completed product
   (4) Defining the quality methods that will be used to check that a product conforms to its quality criteria
   A. 1 and 2
   B. 2 and 3
   C. 3 and 4
   D. 1 and 4

8. Which of the following statement describes a minimum requirement for applying the quality theme?
   A. Using the quality review technique to inspect the project's products
   B. Using quality inspections to assess a product's fitness for purpose
   C. Using both in-process and appraisal quality methods
   D. Maintaining records of quality activities

9. Which principle is being applied when quality criteria are specified in product descriptions?
   A. Learn from experience
   B. Continued business justification
   C. Focus on products
   D. Manage by exception

10. Which of the following statements is a definition of customer quality expectations?
   A. A summary of the quality activities planned for the project
   B. A description of the measurable attributes of a product
   C. A description of the quality expected of the project's products
   D. The measurable improvement resulting from an outcome

Practitioner Exam Questions

The following Practitioner questions are divided into sections by question type and are based on the Practitioner exam scenario that you will find in Appendix B.

Section 1: Matching Questions

Column 1 in the following table describes five actions related to managing quality carried out during the Website Project, and Column 2 lists the different quality-management areas. For each action statement in Column 1, select the area of quality management (A–C in Column 2) where it is applied. Choose only one area of quality management for each action. Each quality management area can be used once, more than once, or not at all.

Column 1	Column 2
1. Using the quality review technique to inspect each web page design	A. Quality planning
2. Specifying that the website must adhere to international accessibility standards	B. Quality control
3. Reviewing the application of the risk management approach in stage one and proposing a more efficient approach for the rest of the project	C. Quality assurance
4. Ensuring that the quality management approach adheres to Quality Furniture's quality policy	
5. Deciding on the most appropriate testing plan for reviewing the final website	

Section 2: Classic Multiple-Choice Questions

Exam Spotlight

Remember that during the Practitioner exam, you are allowed to refer to the official PRINCE2 manual (*Managing Successful Projects with PRINCE2*). For quality theme questions, where might you look in the manual for useful information? The first (and most obvious) place is the quality theme chapter itself. The chapter begins by discussing the purpose of the quality theme and gives some useful definitions for a number of quality terms, such as quality management, the customer's quality expectations, acceptance criteria, and quality criteria. It then goes on to discuss the difference between quality planning and quality control, before discussing the minimum requirements for applying the quality theme. Next there is a table of quality responsibilities, and then there's some general guidance for effective quality management when you're dealing with projects in different environments (such as projects within a programme and projects that use different delivery approaches). Finally, the last section looks at the quality review technique.

In addition to the quality theme chapter, a few other places in the PRINCE2 manual might be useful. For questions about the quality theme management products, the quality management approach, the project product description, product descriptions, or the quality register, you can refer to Appendix A. For questions around the quality theme roles and responsibilities, you can refer not only to the table of responsibilities in the quality theme chapter, as I mentioned previously, but you can also find information about quality-related responsibilities in Appendix C.

1. The project is in stage three, and the project manager is working with the marketing manager and the lead consultant (who are both senior users) at First Tech to understand their requirements for the web pages. After a discussion with these two senior users, the project manager updates the quality management approach with the quality criteria for the pages. Is this appropriate, and why or why not?
   A. Yes, because the quality management approach describes how quality will be managed on the project.
   B. Yes, because the senior users provide the customer quality expectations and acceptance criteria.
   C. No, because it is the product descriptions that should contain the quality criteria for the products.
   D. No, because the quality management approach should be created in the initiation stage.

2. The marketing manager wants to ensure that more people use the new website than the old one. Visitors to the old site found it very difficult to use and so rarely returned after their initial visit. The project manager has therefore recorded as one the quality criteria that the new website must be easy to use. Is this appropriate, and why or why not?
    A. Yes, because the project management team should use lessons to inform quality planning and creating quality criteria.
    B. Yes, because quality criteria describe the quality specifications that the product must meet.
    C. No, because the senior users should provide the quality criteria for the products, and these criteria should be recorded in a product description.
    D. No, because quality criteria must provide sufficient detail and clarity to ensure that reviewers can unambiguously confirm that a product meets its requirements.

3. The project is in stage three, and the web page designs have been created. The marketing manager is chairing a quality review meeting to carry out a quality inspection of the designs. Digital Designs created the designs, and their project manager has been given the presenter role, is talking through the product, and taking questions from reviewers. Is this appropriate, and why or why not?
    A. Yes, because the presenter role represents the producer of the products.
    B. Yes, because the quality review technique should be used for reviewing a project's products.
    C. No, because external suppliers should not be involved in customer quality inspections.
    D. No, because the quality reviews should take place during the closing a project process.

Chapter

7

Risk Theme

PRINCE2 Foundation Exam Objectives Covered in This Chapter:

☑ **Explain the purpose of:**
- The risk theme, including the purpose of a risk budget
- Key management products:
  - Risk management approach
  - Risk register

☑ **Describe PRINCE2's minimum requirement for applying the risk theme**

☑ **Define key concepts related to risk, and the differences between them:**
- A risk: threat and an opportunity
- Recommended risk response types
- Risk owner and risk actionee
- Cause, event and effect
- Risk probability, risk impact and risk proximity

☑ **Describe the recommended risk management procedure**

PRINCE2 Practitioner Exam Objectives Covered in This Chapter:

☑ **Apply the PRINCE2 requirements for applying the risk theme, demonstrating an understanding of:**
- Key management products:
  - Risk management approach
  - Risk register
- The recommended roles and responsibilities within the theme
- The recommended risk management procedure (excluding risk estimation and risk evaluation techniques)

☑ **Assess whether an approach to applying the risk theme is effective and fit for purpose, taking into consideration: the context, the PRINCE2 principles, and the purpose and requirements of the theme**

Because of the unique nature of projects, you will face many potential threats and opportunities when managing them. Rather than passively waiting for threats or opportunities to materialize, you use risk management to deal with them proactively. The PRINCE2 risk theme provides a simple but effective procedure for managing risks. The approach includes steps that help you identify, assess, and control potential risks in your project, as well as effectively communicate the risk situation to the project stakeholders. The risk theme helps you increase the likelihood of delivering the benefits from a project by managing the uncertainty associated with the initiative. PRINCE2 says that the purpose of the risk theme is to identify, assess, and control uncertainty and, as a result, improve the ability of the project to succeed.

Why Are Projects So Risky?

One of the challenges that you face when managing a project is uncertainty. This varies from project to project. Imagine you were managing the Apollo missions to send a man to the moon—it would be difficult for you to predict exactly how things would turn out. At the other extreme, imagine you are working for a hotel business and your job is to manage building new sites. When you're ready to build a new hotel, even though it might be at a new location, with a different design and some new personnel, it will be far easier for you to predict things.

The amount of uncertainty therefore depends on how familiar the project situation is to those involved with the initiative, and this is a key indicator of your likely overall exposure to risk. Basically, when you are unclear as to how things might turn out, all sorts of things can go wrong!

Now let's compare this uncertainty with the amount of risk you face in non-project or business-as-usual work. Here, there is little uniqueness or uncertainty—what you do one week is probably pretty similar to what you did the week before. For example, once you've built the hotel and it is open for business, every week will be a cycle of cleaning rooms, cooking for guests, checking them in and out, and so on. You can far more easily predict potential problems, so there is far less risk.

The PRINCE2 Approach to Risk

How does PRINCE2 deal with the fact that all projects contain an amount of risk? Basically, it disciplines everyone involved with the project to regularly ask the following questions:

- What could potentially go wrong?
- What could the team do (or plan to do) that would reduce the effects of these threats on the project?
- What potential opportunities could occur?
- What could the team do to enhance the effects of these opportunities on the project?

One interesting thing to note is that PRINCE2 uses the word *risk* to cover potential opportunities as well as threats (more on this in the next section). Once the project management team has asked these questions, they must ensure that they carry out their responses to the risks.

How should a PRINCE2 project management team implement risk management? There are various parts to it, which I've set out here. Don't worry—we'll go through all of these in more depth throughout this chapter.

Risk Management Approach
At the outset (during the initiation stage), the project manager writes a risk management approach, which specifies how the project management team will manage risk.

Risk Responsibilities
Some of the PRINCE2 roles will be given risk management responsibilities.

Risk Management Procedure
The project management team will follow the PRINCE2 risk management procedure, which involves a number of general risk management steps, or "things to do." They must ensure these happen regularly throughout the project.

Risk Management Products
The project management team will create and use a number of management products (usually documents) where they can store risk-related information, such as the risk register and the risk management approach.

How Does PRINCE2 Use the Word Risk?

Normally, when you talk about facing risk, you think of it as a negative thing. My dictionary defines risk as "the possibility of incurring misfortune or loss." For example, it might rain, which would slow down the building of your hotel. However, PRINCE2 also thinks of risk as the possibility of good things occurring. For example, the price of concrete might fall and reduce your construction costs.

The definition of risk according to *Managing Successful Projects with PRINCE2* (AXELOS, The Stationery Office, 2017) is "An uncertain event or set of events that, should it occur, will have an effect on the achievement of objectives." There are two types of uncertain events:

Threats
Threats are events that, if they occur, would have a negative effect on the project.

Opportunities
Opportunities are events that, if they occur, would have a positive effect on the project.

Planning How to Manage Risk on the Project

In PRINCE2, the project management team sets out how they will manage risk in the risk management approach. In this section, I will explain why there should be such an approach and describe what it should contain.

An Example of a Risk Management Approach

How does a project manager lower the project's exposure to risk? Let me give you an example. The project manager decides on a simple approach. First, every Monday morning at 9:00 a.m., she chairs a risk management workshop with all members of the project management team. During the workshop, the project manager ensures that the following activities are covered:

- Attempt to spot any new project threats or opportunities. The project manager decides to facilitate the group using a brainstorming technique. She asks each individual to write down as many new risks as they can think of on sticky notes. Then the group puts all the sticky notes on a whiteboard and eliminates any duplicates. Seeing everyone else's risks may spur people to think of new ones.
- The group then decides how to respond to these new risks.
- Finally, the group reviews previously identified risks. Are they getting worse or better? Is the way the project management team is responding to those risks helping? Is there anything else the team can do to mitigate these risks?

After the workshop, the project manager has several other responsibilities:

- She must record all information about each risk in a central risk register.
- She must ensure that the team's decisions on risk responses are carried out.
- She must report on the current risk situation in her weekly progress reports.
- She must ensure that project assurance is aware of this approach to risk management and that they audit it on a regular basis.

This example is a repeatable approach that the project manager can use throughout the project to lower the exposure to threats and increase the exposure to opportunities. This approach should be described in the risk management approach. It may be simple, but in my experience, even this approach is a more robust way of managing risk than the one many large-scale projects use.

Using the Risk Management Approach

In Figure 7.1, you can see the composition of the risk management approach. This is the management product that the project manager in the preceding example uses to document her approach to risk during the project. The project manager would create the risk management approach early on in the initiative, in the initiation stage. It would become one of the components of the project initiation documentation. The project board will review the approach and decide whether it is appropriate for the project. The approach probably will be fairly consistent throughout the initiative; however, there might be occasions when it would be appropriate for it to be amended, so the project manager along with the project board will review the approach at each stage boundary.

Over the next few pages, I will discuss each section of the risk management approach in more detail and give you examples of each entry.

Figure 7.1: Composition of the risk management approach

Risk Management Approach

- Introduction
- Risk management procedure
- Tools and Techniques
- Records
- Reporting
- Timing of risk management activities
- Roles and responsibilities
- Scales
- Proximity
- Risk categories
- Risk response categories
- Early warning indicators
- Risk tolerance
- Risk budget

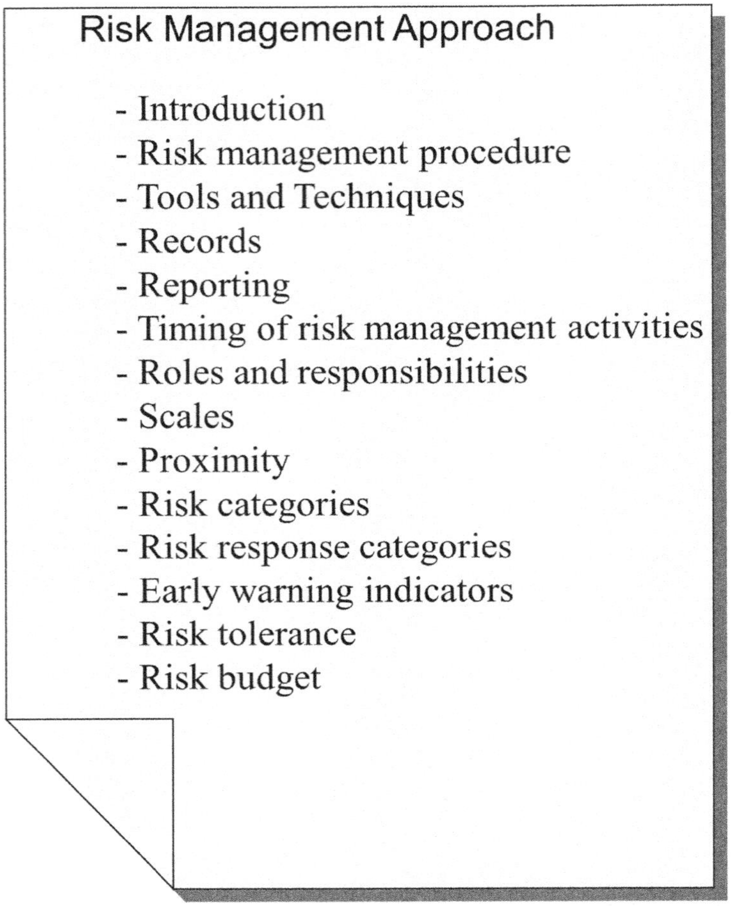

Exam Spotlight

Remember that during the Practitioner exam, you will be able to refer to *Managing Successful Projects with PRINCE2*. This is particularly useful for questions about management products such as the risk management approach. Appendix A of *Managing Successful Projects with PRINCE2* sets out the composition of the risk management approach and gives brief notes on what should be in each section. This means that you don't need to memorize all the sections of all the management products for the Practitioner exam.

Risk Management Procedure

This section contains the generic steps that the project manager regularly performs to deal with risk. PRINCE2 recommends that whatever process the project management team chooses, it should cover the following five basic areas of risk management:

- Identifying risks
- Assessing risks
- Planning your responses to risks
- Implementing your responses
- Communicating to everyone the risk situation

Looking at the steps PRINCE2 recommends, you can see that the project manager has covered all of them in the example, except assessing risks. As you will see later, PRINCE2 recommends assessing risks in terms of their likelihood, impact, and proximity (when they might occur). So the project manager in our example will add a step that includes another aim for the weekly risk workshops: assessing risks. The project manager can then write the Risk Management Procedure section as follows:

During the weekly risk management workshop, the project management team will spot any new threats or opportunities. They will assess new risks and reassess previously spotted risks in terms of their probabilities, impact, and potential timings.

During the risk management workshop, the project management team will also plan responses to any threats that will lessen their effect on the project, and plan responses to any opportunities that will increase their effect on the project.

After the meeting, the responses will be put into action and monitored and tracked to ensure they are implemented.

A weekly review of risks will be included in the weekly project progress report.

Tools and Techniques

In this section, the project manager describes any risk management tools or techniques. These can include techniques for carrying out any part of the risk management procedure, such as how to identify risks or how to estimate a risk's probability or impact. In the example, the project manager uses a brainstorming technique for identifying risks. The Tools and Techniques section describes the risk technique as follows:

During the risk management workshops, use a brainstorming technique to spot threats and opportunities. The brainstorming technique involves the following steps:
1. Each member of the project management team should individually write down at least 20 new risks on separate sticky notes.
2. The project manager puts the sticky notes on a whiteboard, removing any duplicates.
3. The team reviews the sticky notes to see if they prompt any new risk ideas and removes any that don't make sense.

Exam Spotlight

In the example, the project manager has set out a brainstorming risk identification technique. There are quite a number of other techniques that she could have used. *Managing Successful Projects with PRINCE2* lists four more in the risk theme chapter: review lessons, risk checklists, risk prompt lists, and risk breakdown structure. *Managing Successful Projects with PRINCE2* also gives a range of risk estimation and evaluation techniques, such as probability trees, expected value, Pareto analysis, and probability impact grid. However, you won't be tested on how any of these techniques work; you just need to know that these approaches would be described in the Tools and Techniques section of the risk management approach.

Records

In this section, the project manager describes how she plans to store the information on all the individual risks. Our example was a bit sketchy on this; it just stated that all the risks should be recorded in a central register. So in this section, the project manager needs to describe the format and composition of that central register.

Figure 7.2 shows the PRINCE2 recommended composition of a risk register. The project manager may decide to follow this and store the information in a spreadsheet. The Records section will then read as follows:

The project's risk register will follow the PRINCE2's recommended composition. It will be stored in the spreadsheet called `Risk_Register` under the `Project` folder.

Figure 7.2: Composition of the risk register

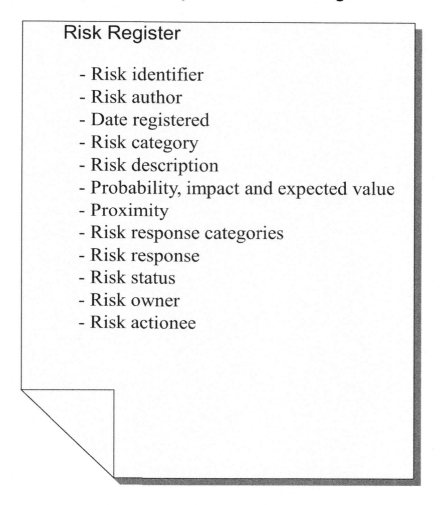

Risk Register

- Risk identifier
- Risk author
- Date registered
- Risk category
- Risk description
- Probability, impact and expected value
- Proximity
- Risk response categories
- Risk response
- Risk status
- Risk owner
- Risk actionee

Reporting

In this section, the project manager describes how the project is going to communicate the risk situation to all the project stakeholders. It shows which reports on risk will be sent out, their purpose, when they will be sent, and who will receive them. The Reporting section may read as follows:

In the weekly progress reports, include a risk situation section. This should include the top five risks to the project as well as an overall indicator of the risk exposure as Red, Amber, or Green. This weekly report will go to all the project management team members and all the project stakeholders identified in the communication management approach.

Timings

The Timings section indicates when risk management activities will occur. It can refer to a time of the week, such as Monday morning at 9:00 a.m., or to a regular time in the PRINCE2 model, such as at the end of a stage. The Timings section may read as follows:

Carry out the risk management workshop as described in the Procedure section each week on Monday morning at 9:00 a.m.

Report on the risk situation when sending out the weekly progress report on Friday afternoon.

Roles and Responsibilities

This section specifies who has risk management responsibilities. For example, the Roles and Responsibilities section might look like this:
- The project manager chairs the risk management workshop.
- All team managers attend the risk management workshop.
- The project manager must ensure that all risk responses agreed to in the workshop are implemented.
- The project board will make timely decisions on risk situations escalated to them during the project.

Scales

The Scales section describes how the project will measure the probability and impact of risks. The project management team might use broad scales such as low, medium, or high. Alternatively, they could be more specific and use percentages. When it comes to impact, the project manager might need to consider different ways of scaling, depending on which of the project objectives the risk might affect. For example, if it affects the timelines, the project manager can measure it in weeks, or if it affects the budget, she can measure it in dollars. The Scales section describes how the various aspects of risk can be measured as follows:

Categorize each risk as having high, medium, or low probability.

Review the impact of each risk in terms of its impact on time, cost, quality, scope, benefits, and the risk situation. For each one, rate the impact as high, medium, or low.

Proximity

The *proximity* of a risk gives an indication of when the risk might happen. It also shows how the risk's probability or impact might vary over time. During the project, each risk needs to be assigned a proximity category, which will indicate when it might occur. It is in this section that the project manager indicates which categories will be used. In our example, the project manager can set out the Proximity section as follows:

The timings of each risk should be categorized as: imminent, within the stage, within the project, or beyond the project.

More on Proximity

Proximity indicates when a risk might occur. It also indicates how the probability of a risk (or the impact on the project if it occurs) might vary over time. For example, if you are building a house, a risk to the project might be inclement weather. The probability of this risk will increase in the winter months and decrease in the summer months.

Risk Categories

Categorizing risks is useful for two reasons. First, it gives you some structure when you are trying to identify potential risk. Rather than start with a blank piece of paper, you can focus on a range of areas where risk can occur, which should increase the chances of spotting more potential problems. One standard set of categories is PESTLE. It stands for Political, Economic, Social (such as a managerial risk; for example, a poorly trained manager might not control her team well and thus produce poor-quality products), Technological, Legal, and Environmental (such as a risk arising because the project is within the public sector environment, such as a long and meticulous procurement process that would slow down the project).

The other reason that risk categories are useful is that they help the project management team audit how broad their risk focus is. A quick review of the risk register might reveal to the project management team that they are very good at spotting technological risks but poor at spotting legal risks. If this is the case, they might want to get legal experts involved in the risk identification workshops.

The Risk Categories section could read as follows:

Hardware, software, third-party suppliers, contractual

Risk Response Categories

It's useful to have some generic approaches on how to respond to risks; otherwise, you might employ the same techniques time and time again. Here are two common threat responses:

Avoid

In the *avoid* response, the project management team does something that either stops the risk occurring or, if it does occur, ensures it doesn't affect the project.

Reduce

In the *reduce* response, the project management team does something that lowers the probability of the risk occurring or lowers its impact on the project.

As you will see in the "Plan" section of the risk management procedure later in this chapter, PRINCE2 suggests a number of generic approaches for tackling both threats and opportunities. But for now, here's a simple example of what the Risk Response Categories section might say for the example project:

For all threats to the project that have not been accepted, first try to prevent them. If this is not possible, try to reduce their likelihood or impact on the project. As a last resort, escalate the risk to the project board and closely monitor it.

Early Warning Indicators

A number of things might indicate to the project manager that all is not well with the project. For example, the project may fall behind schedule by a certain number of days, or the customers may keep changing their minds. It is useful to set some thresholds in a number of areas that, if they are breached, indicate that the project might be at greater risk.

The Early Warning Indicators section could read as follows:

If any of the following thresholds are breached, notify all project stakeholders and allow project assurance to carry out a full risk review:
- The project schedule falls behind by more than one month.
- The number of requests for change exceeds 20.
- The number of issues recorded in the issue register as severe exceeds 10.

Risk Tolerance

Risk tolerance is the threshold level of risk that, if exceeded, needs to be escalated to the next level of management. This section sets the risk tolerance at the project and stage levels. In effect, it tells the project manager and the project board when they need to escalate the risk situation.

I will tell you more about risk tolerances in the "Identify Context" section later in this chapter. Broadly speaking, there are two ways of setting this threshold. An overall figure could be set—for example, the risk tolerance for the project is that the expected impact of all project risks is below $1 million. Alternatively, the project management team could say that if certain types of risks appear, such as risks that could result in operational failure, they need to be escalated.

The project manager in the example might set out the Risk Tolerance section as follows:

All risks that have a high probability and high impact must be escalated to the project board.

Risk Budget

The project management team may decide to set aside some of the project budget to fund various risk responses. This is called a *risk budget*. The money might be reserved for dealing with a particular set of named risks, or it might be a more general fund. I'll tell you more about the risk budget later in this chapter. In this section, the project manager states whether the project management team is going to set up a risk budget and how it will be used.

In the example, the project manager might set out the Risk Budget section as follows:

"$10,000 to be used to fund responses to any risks that have high probability and impact."

The Risk Management Procedure

Figure 7.3 shows the five steps of the PRINCE2 risk management procedure.

Figure 7.3: Risk management procedure

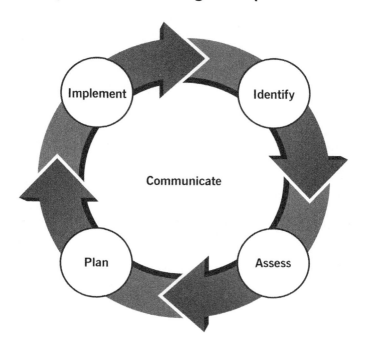

Here's a simple example of how to use this procedure. Say you are going to an important meeting tomorrow morning. You will travel by train, but there's a risk you might be late. How can you use PRINCE2's risk management procedure to help you?

1. **Identify.** A few days before your trip, you try to think of all the things that might go wrong. The alarm clock might not ring. The train might be late. The taxi to get to the train station might not arrive.

2. **Assess.** Now you measure these risks in terms of their likelihood and impact. Doing so will show you which ones you need to tackle. How likely is it that the alarm clock might not ring? It's a battered old thing, so pretty high. Without it ringing, you'll oversleep and miss the meeting. That would have a high impact. High impact, high probability—this sounds like an important risk, so you should do something about it.

3. **Plan.** In this step, you consider what to do about the high risks. You could:
   - Buy a new alarm clock.
   - Buy several alarm clocks and set them all before you go to bed.
   - Travel to the location the day before and stay in a nearby hotel.

4. **Implement.** Now you put your risk response plans into action. You buy several new alarm clocks and stay in a rather nice hotel.

5. **Communicate.** You need to ensure that everyone involved in the project is aware of the risk situation and that all new potential risks are being identified and fed back to the project manager. In the example, this doesn't make sense (unless you want to talk to yourself).

So, the PRINCE2 risk management procedure is just common sense. You probably use it every day to get around life's potential potholes.

The project manager will facilitate the implementation of these five steps again and again throughout the project. By doing so, she is helping to implement an effective risk management procedure. Now let's look at each of these steps in more detail.

Identify

The identify step has the following two focuses:

- Identify the risk context by looking at the general characteristics of the project and the environment it sits within to decide how risky it might be.
- Identify individual risks to the project.

Identify Context

In this step, the project management team will decide how risky the situation is by looking at the characteristics of the project and the environment it will operate within. Using this information, they can then formulate an approach to manage risk for the project. This approach is detailed in the risk management approach.

In certain projects, some objectives are more at risk than others. For example, if a city is hosting the Olympics, the stadium must be ready for the event. Therefore, there is probably more risk involved in delivering the project on time than delivering to the other objectives of cost, scope, quality, risks, and benefits.

Certain general characteristics make projects riskier. For example:

- Projects involving many stakeholders
- Projects involving third-party suppliers
- International projects
- Highly complex or large projects
- Projects creating highly specified or complex products

Risk management will need to be more rigorous for projects with these characteristics.

A project's risk management approach will also be determined by the commissioning organization's attitude to risk. Some organizations have a high *risk appetite*, such as a venture capital–funded company. Other organizations have a low risk appetite, such as a publicly funded government department. A project management team will probably be much bolder with risks in an environment with a high risk appetite.

The project management team will use their understanding of the organization's risk appetite to set something called a *risk tolerance*. A risk tolerance is a threshold level of risk. If this threshold is breached, the project management team might have to escalate the situation up to the corporate, programme management, or the customer level who will have to decide how to deal with the situation. You learn more about tolerances in Chapter 9, "Progress Theme."

To define a threshold level of risk, you need to measure how risky the project is at any given point in time. This is called measuring a project's risk exposure. It's rather like having an imaginary risk thermometer that you "dip" into your project from time to time to see if things have become too risky.

Unfortunately, most of us don't have a risk thermometer. There are various ways, however, of measuring the overall risk exposure of the project. One simple method would be to count how many risks appear in the risk register; the more risks there are, the greater the risk exposure. A more scientific method is the expected-value technique, as illustrated in Table 7.1. This technique shows you the expected impact of all the risks identified for the project, which in the example is $47,000. This estimate helps the project management team measure the project's overall risk exposure.

Table 7.1: Expected-value technique for risk evaluation

Risk ID	Probability (%)	Impact ($)	Expected Value ($) (probability multiplied by impact)
01	20%	$10,000	$2,000
02	50%	$30,000	$15,000
03	30%	$100,000	$30,000
Overall Expected Value:			**$47,000**

Using all this knowledge of the risk context, the project management team can then determine a relevant approach to managing risk and create an appropriate risk management approach.

CASE STUDY

Adapting the Risk Management Approach to the Risk Context

Two projects I was involved with last year looked identical at first glance. Both were to deliver an organization's public information over a website. Could I take the project management approach from one project and apply it without change to the second? When I considered the risk context, I saw that the environments were very different. One was for an insurance company in a highly competitive market, looking to take risks to get ahead; the other was for a tightly regulated pharmaceutical company, where the impact of getting information wrong could be stiff government penalties. Being clear about this difference helped me develop and follow a far more rigorous approach to risk management in the drug company project.

Identify Risks

Throughout the life of a project, the project manager must ensure that potential threats and opportunities are identified and recorded in the risk register. She may not necessarily spot all the risks herself, but she must encourage the project management team and the project stakeholders to constantly assess the risk situation and report any new risks back to her.

Remember that there are two types of risks: threats, which are uncertain events that would have a negative effect on the project objectives, and opportunities, which are uncertain events that would have a favorable effect on the project objectives. Note the emphasis on doing this activity *throughout* the project. In my experience, this step is done very well at the beginning of most projects and then is sometimes forgotten about as things progress.

PRINCE2 recommends that the project manager identify each risk's cause, the event that might follow, and the potential effect on the project. Let me give you an example. If you had a risk of being late for a meeting, what would be its risk cause, risk event, and potential effect?

Risk Cause

Risk cause is the source of the risk or the trigger point for the risk. It is sometimes called the *risk driver*. In the example, this could be the alarm clock not ringing.

Risk Event

Risk event is the uncertain event that might follow the risk cause. If the alarm doesn't ring, you might oversleep and be late for the meeting.

Risk Effect

Given the risk event, *risk effect* is how the project objectives might be affected. (Remember that the project objectives are time, cost, quality, scope, risk, and benefits.) In this case, the effect of oversleeping is that you don't sign an important client, which would affect sales figures (benefits).

Some risks might have multiple causes. You might be late for the meeting because the train broke down.

Assess

The assess step has the following two focuses:
- *Estimate* each individual risk's probability of occurring, impact, and proximity.
- *Evaluate* the overall risk exposure of the project.

Estimate

During the estimate step, the project manager needs to measure each risk. This helps her decide which are the worst threats and the best opportunities to focus on. It also helps her determine whether she has breached any risk tolerance levels, which would mean escalating to the next higher level of management.

In the beginning of this section, I discussed assessing individual risks in terms of their probability and impact. The project manager should also measure a risk's proximity, such as when it is likely to occur and whether the probability and/or impact of a risk might vary over time.

Here's another example. Say you are a project manager on a project to build a new hotel, and there is a threat that a competitor hotel might open before yours and reduce your sales as a result. You could estimate this risk as follows:

1. You measure its probability. There are several techniques you could use to estimate a risk's probability, such as a Monte Carlo analysis or even a simple guesstimate. Exactly how you do this is out of the scope of PRINCE2; however, you should try to be consistent in your approach. During the initiation stage of your project, you would specify the probability estimating

techniques you will use throughout the project. This goes in the Tools and Techniques section of your risk management approach.

In the hotel example, you might consider a number of things in order to estimate the probability of the competitor hotel opening before yours, such as the average time the competitor has taken to build other hotels and how far ahead they are with their plans. This will give you a rough idea of the likelihood of your competitor opening their hotel before yours. You then assign the risk a likelihood using the probability scales specified in the Scales section of the risk management approach. Maybe it's as simple as defining the risk as low, medium, or high likelihood.

2. You measure the impact of this risk. Any risk, if it occurs, could potentially affect any of the six project objectives: cost, time, scope, quality, risk, and benefits. In the Scales section of the risk management approach, you specify the impact scale you will use for each objective type. For example, for cost impacts, you could use scales such as "Under $1000," "$1000–$10,000," and "Above $10,000." In the example, you might decide that this risk would affect your forecast sales (benefits) and say the potential impact would be to decrease room sales by $200,000 in the first three years.

3. You measure the risk's proximity. This is the time factor of the risk, when it might materialize, and how its impact and/or probability might vary over time. Again, you should use the scales specified in the risk management approach, which this time are found in the Proximity section. Example scales might be "Imminent," "In the next month," "In the next 6 months," and so on. For your hotel risk, you might believe this threat is Imminent.

You may also want to consider how the impact or probability of the risk might change over the project's lifecycle. In addition, you might consider whether the project management team is best placed to manage the risk or whether the risk should be escalated to the corporate, programme management, or the customer level of the organization.

Exam Spotlight

PRINCE2 provides a number of risk estimation techniques, such as probability trees, expected value, Pareto analysis, and the probability impact grid. It also offers two risk evaluation techniques: using risk models or an expected monetary value technique. You will not be tested on any of these. If you want further information on the risk techniques, refer to the risk theme chapter in *Managing a Successful Project with PRINCE2*.

Evaluate

At various times, particularly at stage boundaries, the project management team will want to gauge the project's overall exposure to risk. In the "Identify Context" section, you learned that there are various methods for measuring risk exposure. In that section, I described the expected value technique; however, the project management team might decide to use another method. They should specify the project's approach to measuring overall risk exposure in the Tools and Techniques section of the risk management approach.

The project board will take into account the project's current risk exposure when deciding whether to authorize the next stage. The project management team will want to ensure that the project's risk exposure is still within the risk appetite of the commissioning organization. In order to do this, they will compare the current risk exposure to the project's risk tolerance. As I said earlier, you will learn more about tolerances in Chapter 9. If the project's risk tolerance has been breached, the project board will need to refer the situation to the corporate, programme management, or customer level.

As you have seen, one of the main concerns of the executive is ensuring that there is a business justification for the project. The executive will weigh the forecast benefits of the project against the predicted time and cost of the project to decide if there is still a business case. Another key question, however, as you saw in Chapter 4, "Business Case Theme," is whether the overall risk exposure of the project outweighs the predicted benefits of the project. The executive will review this question throughout the project, but particularly at stage boundaries.

In the next section, you will see how the project management team needs to formulate responses to each risk that they identify. These risk responses should lower the probability or impact of each risk. The project management team should measure the project's risk exposure before and after the planned risk responses.

Plan

The next step in the risk management procedure is planning one or more responses to the risks the project management team have spotted. PRINCE2 suggests a number of standard countermeasures to risks, as listed in Table 7.2. When planning responses to risks, it is important that the project management team consider past experience that might be useful. It is also important that the response to the risk is proportional to the potential impact that the risk might have. One way the team can ensure a proportionate response is to estimate the difference between the expected monetary value of the risk both before and after the response. (You learned about the expected value technique in the "Identify Context" section earlier in the chapter.) If the response costs more than the difference in the expected value, it is too expensive.

Table 7.2: Threat and opportunity responses

Threat Responses	Opportunity Responses
Avoid	Exploit
Reduce (probability and/or impact)	Enhance (probability and/or impact)
Prepare contingent plans (reduces impact only)	Prepare contingent plans (increases impact only)
Transfer (reduces the financial impact only)	Transfer
Share	Share
Accept	Accept

Planning Risk Responses to Threats

Here's an example to help you understand the standard approaches to responding to threats. During the project to build a new hotel, the project management team is concerned that if it snows, it will delay construction, potentially raise costs, and affect the quality of the building. They can respond to this threat using any of the following approaches:

Avoid

The project management team could respond in such a way that the probability of the threat occurring and/or its impact reduces to zero. In the example, they can avoid the risk by building over the summer when there is no likelihood of snow.

Reduce

The project management team could do something that reduces either the probability or the impact of the threat. In the example, they can fit snow tires to the construction vehicles, allowing them to work more easily in icy conditions. This response is often referred to as risk mitigation.

Prepare contingent plans

Preparing a *contingent plan* is a reactive response. The project management team could wait for the threat to occur and then carry out a previously planned action. In the example, if it snows, they could book the construction workers into a nearby hotel so that they won't find it difficult to get to work. Contingent plans are sometimes known as fallback plans.

Transfer

In the *transfer* response, the project management team attempts to pass on some of the potential impact of a threat to a third party. Examples of this approach are taking out insurance or specifying penalty clauses in case a third party doesn't deliver as planned. In the example, they can ask the construction company to sign a contract that makes them financially liable for late delivery.

Accept

The *accept* response involves making a conscious decision to retain the threat. The project management team should continue to monitor the risk. (If they never spotted the threat or ignored it, hoping it would go away, that's not considered an accept response.) A project team would do this when the cost of doing something about the threat is outweighed by its potential impact and/or probability. For example, if they spotted a threat that a meteorite might crash into the construction site, the probability is clearly ludicrously low, so investing in a bank of missiles to shoot down any rogue visitors from outer space probably wouldn't make sense.

Share

Share is a special response because it applies to a situation that could turn into an opportunity or a threat. There are always two parties involved. Let me give you an example. Say the hotel is going to be very luxurious and all the penthouses will have gold fittings. Normally, if the price of gold goes up, the fittings supplier would raise their prices by an equivalent amount. If the price of gold falls, however, they might not pass on the whole reduction and therefore increase their profit margins. If a project management team chooses a share response, they would write a contract with the fittings supplier to ensure that both parties equally share the costs of the threat and the benefits from the opportunity. Maybe the cost of the fittings is tied somehow to the price of gold. In these situations, both parties are sharing the risk on a pain/gain basis.

Using PRINCE2 Risk Management in the Corporate World

I consulted on a project to deliver a software system to a corporate client. Early in the project, I identified a risk that the company's procurement department could take a long time to sign off contracts with new suppliers. This could be a problem because we were planning to outsource the construction of the software to a third party. To mitigate the threat to the project timeline, we considered several approaches. We could try to reduce the risk by either engaging the procurement department earlier or allowing the company's IT department to do more of the work. In the end, we avoided the risk. Because we already had an existing contract with this client, their procurement department allowed us to quickly amend that contract to state that we would deliver the software. Then we signed a corresponding contract with a software supplier to deliver the software to us.

Planning Risk Responses to Opportunities

Here's an example to help you understand the standard approaches to responding to opportunities. In the hotel construction project, the project management team spots an opportunity. Perhaps solar panels are being installed on the roof of the hotel to generate some of the building's electricity. Maybe the project management team has learned that they could set up a special connection with the local electricity grid company, such that if the solar panels generate surplus electricity over and above what the hotel requires, it could be sold to the grid company, thus increasing the revenue of the hotel. They can respond to this opportunity using any of the following approaches:

Exploit

The *exploit* response ensures that the opportunity will happen and that it will have a favorable impact on the project. The project management team could install a very large bank of a special type of expensive solar panels that generate electricity even in low sunlight conditions and then arrange the connection with the local grid company. This will guarantee that the panels will always generate more electricity than is needed by the hotel.

Enhance

The *enhance* response increases the likelihood that the opportunity will happen and/or increases the favorable impact on the project if it does. The project management team could install more solar panels than they initially planned for, but this time, they could use less-expensive solar panels that require full sunlight to generate electricity. This will increase the likelihood of a surplus of electricity being generated, but in this option, there is no guarantee that there will be a surplus.

Transfer

With the *transfer* response to an opportunity, a third party gains a cost benefit, but the primary risk taker gains another benefit. Transferring threats is commonly used, but transferring opportunities is not. The project management team could decide to transfer some of the benefits of the potential surplus by offering to supply local businesses with electricity for a fee.

Share

This is the same response that I described earlier in the "Planning Risk Responses to Threats" section.

Accept

With the *accept* response, a deliberate decision is made to not try to enhance or exploit the opportunity. If the project management team decides to accept the opportunity, they will go ahead with the planned amount of solar panels. This may generate an electricity surplus, but there is no increased likelihood of that happening.

Prepare Contingent Plans

Similar to preparing contingent plans for a threat, you wait for the opportunity to occur and then carry out a previously planned action. In this case, the project management team would do nothing yet but plan to connect to the local grid company if a surplus of electricity is generated on a regular basis.

Exam Spotlight

Make sure that you learn the names for the various types of risk responses. Some of them are not intuitive. For example, the thought of accepting an opportunity and doing nothing to encourage it sounds strange. It is important for a candidate taking the certification exams to understand the PRINCE2 meanings for words.

Implement

In the implement step of the risk management procedure, the project manager takes all the good ideas that have been generated to respond to risks and puts them into action. For the hotel construction example, snow tires are fitted to the vehicles so that the team can continue working if it snows. For the meeting example, where you were worried you might be late, you bought several alarm clocks to ensure you wake up on time. The project manager is ultimately responsible for instigating, tracking, and monitoring the risk response plans, with the aid of the risk owners and actionees, as described in the next section.

Risk Owners and Risk Actionees

A *risk owner* might be allocated to a risk. Their role is to monitor a risk and manage any countermeasures. They should have relevant expertise. For example, a legal risk might be owned by the company lawyer. The risk owners don't necessarily have to be part of the project management team.

Risk actionees are those who actually perform the countermeasures. An example of a *risk actionee* is someone who fits snow tires to the hotel construction equipment to mitigate against bad weather.

Every entry in the risk register should identify each risk's risk owner and risk actionees. It is the responsibility of the project manager to add this information.

Risk Budget

The risk budget, if it is used, is a ring-fenced part of the project budget that would fund risk responses. In the hotel construction example, this is how the project manager might fund the purchase of all those snow tires to help in bad weather.

Table 7.3 shows how the project management team might calculate a risk budget. At the outset of the project, they spot as many potential threats and opportunities as possible. They then estimate their likely monetary impact and the potential cost of implementing countermeasures. Multiplying these two costs by the percentage likelihood gives a weighted cost for each risk, the sum of which gives a forecasted risk budget. As the project progresses, the project manager will spot other risks, so it would be prudent to set aside more than the $67,000 calculated in Table 7.3.

Table 7.3: Calculating a risk budget

Risk ID	Impact Costs	Response Costs	Total Costs	Likelihood	Weighted Cost
1	$30,000	$4,000	$34,000	30%	$10,200
2	$10,000	$1,000	$11,000	5%	$550
3	$45,000	$20,000	$65,000	50%	$32,500
4	$80,000	$15,000	$95,000	25%	$23,750
Total Weighted Cost:					**$67,000**

The project management team will describe how a risk budget will be established and calculated in the risk management approach. The value of the risk budget is described in the project's plans.

Exam Spotlight

Always spend the right budget in the right situation. For example, avoid the temptation of spending the risk budget if you need to fund a change to a product and there is no change budget left.

Inherent, Residual, and Secondary Risks

If the project management team applies a risk response to an *inherent risk* (the risk it starts off with), it might not necessarily remove the potential problem, thus leaving some *residual risk*. The countermeasure might even introduce a new *secondary risk*. Figure 7.4 shows the relationship between these three types of risk.

Figure 7.4: Types of risk

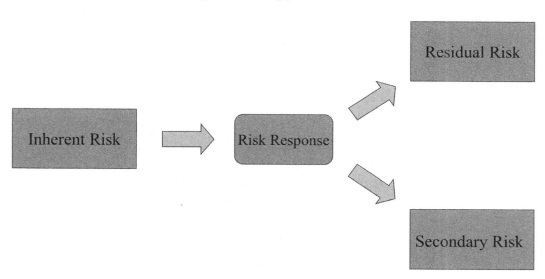

Consider this example. You are building a hotel and there is a threat of heavy rain. In response to this risk, you erect scaffolding with a tarpaulin top. There is still some residual risk left, though, because although the construction site will stay dry, the rain might affect deliveries. You have also introduced a secondary risk: The scaffolding might collapse, injuring some of the workforce.

Communicate

Good communication is vital in order for a project management team to effectively manage risk. If you refer back to Figure 7.3, you can see that PRINCE2 shows this by putting the communicate step of the risk management procedure in the center of the other steps. The project manager must ensure a broad and balanced perspective when identifying and assessing risks and then planning responses to those risks. This will mean asking the opinions of all the project management team and other stakeholders. Also, for the project manager to be effective at monitoring and controlling the work to respond to risks, she will need to closely communicate with those involved.

Exam Spotlight

In the Practitioner exam, you may be asked which of the PRINCE2 reports have a section for risk reporting. Check this by looking at the management product descriptions for highlight report, checkpoint report, end stage report, lessons report, and end project report in Appendix A of *Managing Successful Projects with PRINCE2*. The Practitioner exam might also ask if there are any other methods of communicating the risk situation, over and above the PRINCE2 reports. The PRINCE2 manual makes a number of suggestions, such as reporting risks through bulletins, notice boards, dashboards, and information radiators. An information radiator is a term from the agile approach to project management. It is sometimes also called a Big Visible Chart and is a generic name for any display of key project facts, often in easily read graphical format.

Roles Involved with the Risk Theme

Exam Spotlight

If a Practitioner exam question asks you about risk responsibilities, there is a handy table near the beginning of the risk theme chapter in *Managing Successful Projects with PRINCE2* that explains what each role does. In fact, for any question about responsibilities related to any of the seven themes, there is a similar table in each "theme" chapter in *Managing Successful Projects with PRINCE2*.

Let's now look at what the PRINCE2 project roles do when managing risk. First, consider the senior roles. Corporate, programme management, or the customer might provide an existing organizational or programme risk management approach to the project management team.

All of the project board roles consider the risk situation from their own perspective, and ensure that potential threats or opportunities affecting their interests are identified, assessed, and controlled. For example, the senior users must take into account whether there are any threats to correctly defining product requirements; the senior suppliers must ensure that there are no threats to delivering the products by the deadline date; and the executive must be looking for opportunities to increase the return-on-investment of the project.

The executive also has a broader risk management role. She is responsible for ensuring that a risk management approach exists and is being followed. PRINCE2 (and the general business world) sees the effective controlling of risk as a necessary condition to delivering value-for-money benefits.

Although the executive is responsible for ensuring the risk management approach exists, it will probably fall on the project manager to create it. The project manager also ensures that the project continually identifies, assesses, and controls risks. This doesn't mean that, for example, she has to sit in a room on her own and identify all the potential threats to the project. Rather, through activities such as risk management workshops, she facilitates the project management team to continually assess the risk situation. She must ensure that an up-to-date record of information exists on all the project's threats and opportunities in the risk register. Project support might help the project manager with risk management—for example, they might maintain the risk register.

The team managers and their teams are in the best position to spot technical, implementation, and practical risks to the project. Therefore, it is essential to include them in the process of identifying, assessing, and controlling risks.

The project assurance role will be checking that risk management is being done in line with the risk management approach. If not, they will need to escalate to the executive.

Exam Spotlight

Be careful with exam questions that ask who does what. Sometimes, there are a number of roles that do very similar things. For example, the executive is responsible for the risk management approach. (She ensures that one exists and, through her assurance role, ensures it is being followed.) However, the project manager creates and then follows the risk management approach.

Tailoring the Risk Theme

The key to successfully using PRINCE2 is adapting and tailoring the method given the characteristics of the project and the environment the project is operating within. The following sections show you how the risk theme might be adapted to better suit certain situations. This is something you might be tested on in the exams.

Minimum Requirements

Organizations with a less-formal project management approach or organizations that are running smaller, less-complicated projects might choose to cut back on some of the risk theme ideas. However, there are some minimum requirements that must be followed in order for a project team to claim they are following PRINCE2's risk theme.

First, the project management team must describe their risk management approach. This must cover all five steps that you have seen in the risk management procedure. So it should describe how risks will be identified and assessed, how responses to those risks will be planned and implemented, and how there will be effective communication about the risk situation throughout the project's lifecycle.

The project's risk management approach should also describe how the project management team will identify and assess risks that would impact the business justification for the project.

Finally, the approach should describe all the roles and responsibilities for risk management.

Once the project management team has defined the risk management approach, another minimum requirement is, rather obviously, that they follow the approach. The project management team needs to maintain some form of risk register to record all the threats and opportunities to the project. As in many parts of PRINCE2, the team should also ensure that they use prior experience and previously recorded lessons to inform the management of risks.

Scaling the Risk Theme

Project management teams faced with bigger, more-complicated projects would naturally apply the ideas in the risk theme in a more rigorous way. For example, if the project is fairly small and simple, it might be appropriate for the risk register to be a simple list on a whiteboard, whereas if the initiative is large, the risks might be recorded on a dedicated IT system. Similarly, in a small project, the project manager would probably carry out most of the risk management activities, whereas in a larger, more-complicated initiative, the project manager might delegate some of the activities to other people, such as a dedicated risk manager or risk management team.

The rigor of the risk management approach, however, is determined not only by the scale of the project. Another factor that the project management team needs to consider is the potential size of risk impacts on the rest of the organization. A quite small project might have the potential to create a very large, negative impact on the rest of the organization. For example, if a company commissioned a small project to create an online sales website, and the website was hacked and caused the customers to lose their personal data, this could have an enormous effect on the company's reputation.

Commercial Customer/Supplier Environment

When more than one organization is involved in a project, it might not be appropriate to share commercially sensitive information between those organizations. The project management team might decide to create different risk registers for each organization. However, it is generally true that the more information that can be shared between the different parties involved with the project, the more effective risk management will be.

Aligning the Risk Approach with Organizational or Programme Approaches

So far, you have seen that the project management team creates a risk management approach for their project and then ensures that they follow this approach during their initiative to control uncertainty. However, the organization that has commissioned the project might already have an organization-wide risk approach. In this case, the project management team might adopt this organizational approach for their project. A similar situation might occur if the project is part of a programme. In this case, programme management might tell the project management team to follow the programme risk management approach.

Generally, the corporate, programme management, or the customer level will tell the project board if they should follow an already established corporate or programme risk management approach. Maybe not all of the broader approach would be applicable for the project, so the project management team would adopt only certain parts of the higher-level approach and create the rest of the approach just for that initiative.

Adapting the Risk Approach to Different Delivery Approaches

In many industries, there are different approaches to delivering products. Whatever risk management approach the project management team defines, it will need to take account of whatever delivery approach they are using. Each delivery approach will have its own inherent risks and will introduce different constraints on how the project management team will manage risk.

For example, the IT industry often uses the waterfall approach, whereby the project goes through a number of defined steps. During step one, the project management team would work with customers to understand and document their requirements; during step two, they would design a solution; during step three, they would build the products; and during step four, they would test the products. There are pros and cons to the waterfall approach. Spending time considering requirements and designing a solution might lead to a really well-designed solution, which could help the project management team build a good product. On the other hand, in a dynamic environment, there is the risk that customers might change their minds or technologies might change after the requirements have been gathered and documented. The project management team might not find this out until after they have already spent a lot of time designing a solution, building and testing a product, and finally showing the products to the customer. So with a waterfall project, the project management team needs to think of a response to this risk. Maybe they could schedule regular meetings with the clients during the design, build, and test phases to ensure nothing has changed.

In Chapter 1, "Overview of PRINCE2," I discussed the agile approach. Like the waterfall approach, this also has pros and cons. The approach often requires very close collaboration with the customers throughout the project's life. The positive side of this is that the teams building the product will get a very good idea of what the clients want. The risk is that the customers might not be able to commit much time to the project. So, once again, the project management team needs to respond to this risk. Maybe they could work out a way of communicating with clients in a quick, regular way—for example, by using Internet collaboration tools.

Linking the Risk Theme with the Principles

In Chapter 1, I talked about the seven PRINCE2 principles. In some ways, all seven principles contribute to implementing the risk theme; however, the three most important principles are the continuous business justification, defined roles and responsibilities, and learn from experience.

PRINCE2 sees a strong connection between the risk theme and the continued business justification principle. Why is this? Every project is an investment for the commissioning organization. If you or I were to make an investment, one of the key things we would consider is risk. For example, we might decide to buy shares in a venture capital–funded company that is involved in a very new industry, such as driverless cars. If the driverless car industry were to take off, we would make a lot of money. However, there is a high degree of uncertainty about such a new technology, so there is a high probability we will make no money at all. Given how risky the investment is, we might decide instead to invest in a more established company that is predicting lower, but more-certain returns.

So just as when we invest in shares, when an organization invests in a project, they want to ensure that risk is managed as effectively as possible. In PRINCE2 terms, we say that effective risk management is a prerequisite to help implement the continued business justification principle.

It is more straightforward to see the link between the risk theme and the principles of defined roles and responsibilities and learn from experience. In order to do effective risk management, it needs to be clear who is doing what with regards to risk. The project management team will find using prior experience makes any risk management approach more effective. For example, when they are trying to spot new risks, rather than starting with a blank sheet of paper, they could look back at previous risk registers from similar projects.

Summary

In this chapter, you learned about the risk theme, which describes how to deal with potential threats to and opportunities for the project.

The first thing you need to understand is that the word *risk* means a slightly different thing in PRINCE2 than in everyday speech. You may be used to thinking of a risk as a potential problem, but in PRINCE2, it could also be a potential opportunity. Either way, it might affect how you deliver project objectives.

Project situations are riskier than business as usual. This is because projects are unique endeavors, and all sorts of unforeseen threats or opportunities might arise.

PRINCE2 sets out a clear procedure to deal with risk. It involves five steps: identify, assess, plan, implement, and communicate.

PRINCE2 recommends a number of standard countermeasures to a threat: avoid the threat so it will not occur; reduce the threat so that it is less likely to occur or its impact will be diminished; prepare a contingent plan to reduce the impact should the risk occur; transfer the financial effect of the risk to a third party; or make a conscious decision to accept the risk.

In this chapter, you learned that there are a number of PRINCE2 standard responses for opportunities: exploit the opportunity so it definitely occurs; enhance the opportunity so it is more likely to happen or its favorable impacts are increased; prepare a contingent plan to increase the impact of the opportunity, should it arise; and transfer an opportunity or accept the opportunity, making a conscious decision not to pursue it. In some situations, a risk can turn out to be a threat or an opportunity. In this case, PRINCE2 recommends applying a share response that allows two parties to share the costs if the situation turns into a threat and the benefits if the situation becomes an opportunity. You also learned that each risk should be assigned a risk owner who will monitor, manage, and control that risk. The risk owner might be aided by various risk actionees who carry out risk countermeasure tasks.

Finally, you learned how the risk theme might be tailored to better suit different project situations, such as small projects, projects operating within a programme environment, and projects operating with commercial customer and supplier environments.

Foundation Exam Essentials

Explain the purpose of the risk theme.
The purpose of the risk theme is to identify, assess, and control uncertainty, and as a result, improve the ability of the project to succeed.

Explain the purpose of the risk budget.
The purpose of the risk budget is to fund specific responses to the project's threats and opportunities.

Explain the purpose of the risk management approach.
The purpose of the risk management approach is to define how to manage risk throughout the project, including the procedures to follow, the risk-related roles and responsibilities, and any specific risk techniques that will be used.

Explain the purpose of the risk register.
The purpose of the risk register is to record information regarding the threats and opportunities that may impact the project.

Describe what PRINCE2 requires as a minimum for applying the risk theme.
As a minimum for applying the risk theme, PRINCE2 requires that the project management team do the following:
- Define the project's risk management approach to all five steps of the risk management procedure: identify, assess, plan, implement, and communicate
- Define the project's approach to identifying risks that might affect the business justification for the project
- Define the risk-related roles and responsibilities
- Maintain some sort of risk register to record information on the project's opportunities and threats
- Ensure that all five steps of the risk management procedure are carried out throughout the project
- Use lessons to inform risk management

Define a risk, a threat, and an opportunity.
A risk is an uncertain event or set of events that, if it were to occur, would affect any of the project's objectives. A threat is an uncertain event that would affect the project's objectives negatively. An opportunity is an uncertain event that would affect the project's objectives positively.

Explain the recommended responses to a threat.
There are a number of recommended responses to a threat, including: avoid the threat so it will not occur; reduce the threat so it is less likely to occur or its impact will be diminished; prepare a contingent plan to reduce the impact should the risk occur; transfer the financial effect of the risk to a third party; or make a conscious decision to accept the risk.

Explain the recommended responses to an opportunity.
There are a number of recommended responses to an opportunity, including: exploit the opportunity so it definitely occurs; enhance the opportunity so it is more likely to happen or its favorable impacts are increased; prepare a contingent plan to increase the impact of the opportunity should it arise; or transfer an opportunity or accept the opportunity, making a conscious decision not to pursue it. In some situations, a risk can turn out to be a threat or an opportunity. In this case, PRINCE2 recommends applying a share response that allows two parties to share the costs if the situation turns into a threat and the benefits if the situation becomes an opportunity.

Explain the concepts of a risk owner and a risk actionee.
A risk owner is someone who manages and monitors all aspects of a particular risk. A risk actionee is someone who carries out specific risk responses for a particular risk.

Explain the concepts of a risk cause, event, and effect.
Each risk can be broken down into three parts: what could cause it, the uncertain event that might follow the cause, and the effect on the project objectives if the event does occur.

Explain the concepts of risk probability, risk impact, and risk proximity.
Each risk can be assessed in three ways: the likelihood or probability that the event will occur, the impact on any one of the six aspects of project performance if it were to occur, and the likely timing or proximity of the risk.

Describe the recommended risk management procedure.
The five steps of the risk management procedure are identify, assess, plan, implement, and communicate.

Practitioner Exam Essentials

Demonstrate an understanding of the recommended roles and responsibilities within the risk theme.
Demonstrate an understanding that the project manager is responsible for preparing the risk management approach and carrying out the activities in the recommended risk management procedure. Understand that the executive needs to ensure that an appropriate risk management approach exists and is being followed throughout the project. Understand that each role on the project board is responsible for ensuring risks associated with their own interest in the project are identified and effectively controlled.

Assess and critique an approach to applying the risk theme.
Assess and critique an approach to applying the risk theme, including an understanding of the purpose and format of the risk management approach and the risk register, the recommended risk management procedure, and how the risk theme might be adapted to different project contexts (for example, a small project, an agile project, a project with external third-party organizations, or a project operating within a programme environment) and whether the approach aligns with the principles of PRINCE2.

Demonstrate an understanding of the risk management approach.
Demonstrate an understanding that the project manager creates the risk management approach during the initiation stage and that it shows how to manage risk throughout the project. Understand that the approach might be derived from the project brief, the business case, and any corporate, programme management, or customer strategies or policies that exist, and that it could be a stand-alone document or part of the project initiation documentation. Know the composition of the risk management approach.

Demonstrate an understanding of the risk register.
Demonstrate an understanding that the project manager creates the risk register during the initiation stage and uses it to record details of any risks that are identified throughout the project. Understand that it could be a stand-alone register; a spreadsheet; a database; part of an integrated project register for all risks, actions, and issues; sticky notes on walls; or an entry into a project management tool. Know the composition of the risk register.

Review Questions

The rest of this chapter contains mock exam questions, first for the Foundation exam and then for the Practitioner exam.

Foundation Exam Questions

1. Which of the following options is a step in the recommended risk management procedure?
   A. Defining and analyzing products
   B. Impact analysis
   C. Communicate
   D. Identifying activities and dependencies

2. Which of the following options is a purpose of the risk theme?
   A. To define and implement the means to verify that products are fit for purpose
   B. To establish a structure of accountability
   C. To define the means of delivering the products
   D. To identify, assess, and control uncertainty

3. Which risk response options could be applied to an opportunity?
   (1) Avoid (2) Exploit (3) Enhance (4) Reduce
   A. 1 and 2
   B. 2 and 3
   C. 3 and 4
   D. 1 and 4

4. Which step in the recommended risk management procedure formulates an appropriate risk management approach?
   A. Evaluate
   B. Identify risks
   C. Estimate
   D. Identify context

5. Which of the following options is a minimum requirement for applying the risk theme?
   A. Each risk's impact on the project's business justification must be estimated.
   B. Each identified threat must be allocated a risk owner.
   C. Probability trees must be used to estimate a risk's likelihood.
   D. Summary risk profiles must be used to summarize the set of risks.

6. You are a project manager and are buying a major input for the project from Japan. If the yen were to appreciate, it would mean a big increase in the project costs. You decide to buy some yen futures, which, if the currency did increase, would give a financial payout. What sort of PRINCE2 risk response is this?
   A. Transfer
   B. Share
   C. Fallback
   D. Avoid

7. Which two of the following options describe a purpose of the risk management approach?
   (1) To provide a record of the status for identified risks
   (2) To describe the roles and responsibilities for risk management activities
   (3) To describe the risk techniques to be applied to the project
   (4) To maintain information on opportunities relating to the project
   A. 1 and 2
   B. 2 and 3
   C. 3 and 4
   D. 1 and 4

8. What is a risk owner?
   A. An individual who is responsible for the project's risk management approach
   B. An individual who is responsible for identifying all risks within a project
   C. An individual who is responsible for monitoring all aspects of a particular risk
   D. An individual who is responsible for defining the organization's risk appetite

9. Which of the following terms is used to describe the potential trigger point of a risk?
   A. Risk impact
   B. Risk event
   C. Risk cause
   D. Risk effect

10. Which risk response type can often be achieved by implementing the cause of an opportunity?
    A. Avoid
    B. Exploit
    C. Transfer
    D. Prepare contingent plans

Practitioner Exam Questions

The following Practitioner questions are divided into sections by question type and are based on the Practitioner exam scenario that you will find in Appendix B.

Section 1: Matching Questions

The project is in stage two, and the request for tender has been sent to a number of software suppliers. The executive is concerned that because of Quality Furniture's lack of experience in IT and the Internet, there is a risk that they will choose an inappropriate or poor supplier for the work. If this happens, a number of the project's objectives, such as the timeline, costs, and the anticipated benefits, could be impacted.

Column 1 in the following table lists five responses to this risk. For each of these responses, choose the corresponding risk response type (A–F). Each risk response type can be used once, more than once, or not at all.

Column 1	Column 2
1. Add a clause in the supplier contract that makes the supplier financially liable if certain cost, quality, and time criteria are not met.	A. Avoid
2. Recruit a specialist in IT procurement and give him the role of supplier assurance on the project.	B. Reduce
3. Decide that the risk of choosing the wrong supplier is too high, cancel the project, and continue to use the old website.	C. Prepare contingent plans
4. Wait for the software development stage, and if the supplier starts to deliver poor quality, terminate the supplier's contract and use a recommended IT contractor to finish the work.	D. Transfer
5. Decide to split the tender into several parts and allocate the work to several different suppliers.	E. Accept
	F. Exploit

Section 2: Classic Multiple-Choice Questions

> # Exam Spotlight
>
> Remember that for the Practitioner exam, you are allowed to refer to the official PRINCE2 manual (*Managing Successful Projects with PRINCE2*). For risk theme questions, where might you look in the manual for useful information? The first (and most obvious) place is the risk theme chapter itself. The chapter begins by discussing the purpose of the risk theme, defining what a risk is, and giving an overview of risk management. It then looks at the minimum requirements for applying the risk theme and gives a table of the key risk-related roles and responsibilities. Then there is a section that provides guidance for effective risk management and explains how to tailor the theme to different situations. The last section goes through the five steps of the recommended risk management procedure.
>
> In addition to the risk theme chapter, a few other places in the PRINCE2 manual might be useful. For questions about the two risk theme management products—the risk management approach or the risk register—refer to the product descriptions in Appendix A. For questions about the risk theme roles and responsibilities, you can refer to the table of responsibilities within the risk theme chapter as well as to the information about risk-related responsibilities in Appendix C.

1. The project manager has been informed that a competitor plans to launch a similar website in the near future. The early release of the competitor's website might decrease the forecast sales of Quality Furniture's website. The project manager has calculated that the likely impact would be a reduction in online sales of $10,000 and has recommended that the risk response to this threat can cost anything up to this figure. Is this appropriate, and why or why not?
    A. Yes, because it is important that a risk response offers value for money.
    B. Yes, because the project manager should set the risk budget for each individual risk.
    C. No, because the project manager hasn't allowed for the probability of the risk when calculating how much to spend on the response.
    D. No, because the responses to each risk should be funded from the risk budget.

2. The project manager has heard that website supplier often uses an agile delivery approach, with deliveries happening as often as every two weeks. The chief executive has stipulated that the project must follow Quality Furniture's established risk management policy, which states that project must hold monthly risk reviews. Is the direction by the chief executive appropriate, and why or why not?

   A. Yes, because a project must align its risk management approach with any established organizational standards or approaches.

   B. Yes, because it is the executive who ensures that the risk management approach is appropriate.

   C. No, because a more traditional delivery approach should be used to control risks.

   D. No, because it is important that the approach to managing risks works with the project's chosen delivery approach.

3. The project is approaching stage three, and in the next stage, the website development company Digital Design will start to design the website. To avoid divulging any commercially sensitive information, the executive has asked the project manager to create a separate risk register for the outsourced supplier. Is this appropriate, and why or why not?

   A. Yes, because in a commercial context there may be a need for more than one risk register.

   B. Yes, because the outsourced supplier should own and manage the risks associated with their work.

   C. No, because there should only be one risk register throughout the project.

   D. No, because the risk management approach should be consistent throughout the project.

Chapter

8

Change Theme

☑ **Explain the purpose of:**
  - The change theme, including the purpose of a change budget
  - Key management products:
    - Change control approach
    - Configuration item record
    - Issue register
    - Issue report
    - Product status account

☑ **Describe PRINCE2's minimum requirements for applying the change theme.**

☑ **Describe:**
  - Types of issue
  - The recommended issue and change control procedure

PRINCE2 Practitioner Exam Objectives Covered in This Chapter:

☑ **Apply the PRINCE2 requirements for applying the change theme, demonstrating an understanding of:**
  - Key management products:
    - Change control approach
    - Configuration item record
    - Issue register
    - Issue report
    - Product status account
  - The recommended roles and responsibilities within the theme

☑ **Assess whether an approach to applying the change theme is effective and fit for purpose, taking into consideration: the context, the PRINCE2 principles, and the purpose and requirements of the theme**

The purpose of the change theme is to identify, assess, and control any potential and approved changes to the project baselines. In this chapter, you learn how PRINCE2 deals with change and what PRINCE2 means by the term "baselines." Change in a project is inevitable. There are many areas that might be subject to change: clients might change their minds about the products they require; new technology might become available, and the business environment might change; and so on.

The change theme does not prevent change; instead, it describes an approach that ensures that the decision about whether to implement changes is made at the right level of authority and only after the impact of the change has been considered.

The change theme also looks at tracking and controlling configuration items. In this chapter, you learn what a configuration item is and how being able to identify and control that item helps with change management.

Change Theme Terminology

This section defines some common terms that PRINCE2 uses with regard to the change theme.

Baselines

The PRINCE2 definition for a *baseline* is "a reference level against which an entity is monitored and controlled." What this means is that when a product is baselined, it is stored and protected from any unauthorized changes. A product might be baselined because it has just been approved. Changes to a baselined product can only be authorized using the *issue and change control procedure*. The issue and change control procedure ensures that the impact of these changes is considered and then authorized at an appropriate level of management. You learn more about the issue and change control procedure later in this chapter.

If changes are authorized for a document-based product that has been baselined, a new version will be created and the changes will be made to that new version. Some of the PRINCE2 management products will be baselined and may go through multiple versions during the life of the project. Here is a list of these baseline management products:

- Benefits management approach
- Business case
- Communication management approach
- Change control approach
- Plans (project, stage, and team)
- Product description
- Project brief
- Project initiation documentation
- Project product description

- Quality management approach
- Risk management approach
- Work package

Releases

A *release* is "a complete and consistent set of products that are managed, tested and deployed as a single entity to be handed over to the user(s)." That is, a release is a group of products that work together as a unit. Imagine, for example, that you are writing a technical book. You could think of the chapters of the book as individual products. Maybe each chapter refers to information in the other chapters (a bit like this book). When all the chapters are finished and the book is ready to be published, the set of products (or chapters) is a release.

Configuration Items

A *configuration item* is "an entity that may be a product, a component of a product or a set of products that form a release." The project management team will identify all the configuration items that the project will deliver, track the latest status of all the items throughout the project, and protect the items from any unauthorized changes once they have been baselined. Often, a configuration item will simply be a product in the project. For example, in the book project introduced in the last section, the configuration items will be the chapters of the book. If the project were to build a car, as project manager, you might want to track the progress of creating all the parts of the car, such as the engine, the wheels, the seats, and the body framework. All these car parts are examples of configuration items. You learn more about configuration items in the "Tracking and Controlling Configuration Items" section later in this chapter.

Types of Issues

There are three types of PRINCE2 issues: *request for change*, *off-specification*, and a *problem/concern*. Anyone with an interest in the project can raise an issue about anything to do with the project. If they want to do so, they should contact the project manager, who will then document the issue in the issue register (if it is a formal issue) or the daily log (if it is an informal issue). The project manager will then deal with the issue using the issue and change control procedure that you learn about later in this chapter.

Request for Change

A request for change occurs when someone asks that a change to one of the baselined products be considered.

For example, in a project to build a new hotel in Shanghai for a hotel chain, the following are examples of request for changes:

- The hotel chain's head of business development asks to change the approved architectural designs to include a gym.
- The operations director of the construction company asks to change the approved specification of the building materials to take account of changes in building standards.
- The executive asks to change the latest version of the project initiation documentation because the forecast sales for the hotel have increased.

When a request for change has been authorized, two things might need to be changed: the product itself and its product description. For example, say the hotel's gym has been built according to its product description with red walls. Then a request for change is authorized to paint the walls blue. First, the project manager will create a new version of the gym's product description that states that the walls should be blue. Next, he will authorize a work package for the painters to paint the walls blue. Obviously, if the project hasn't gotten to the point of painting the gym's walls, then only one thing needs to change: the product description.

You learn about who can authorize a request for change in the "Change Authority" section later in this chapter.

Off-Specification

PRINCE2's definition of an off-specification is "something that should be provided by the project, but currently is not (or is forecast not to be) provided. This might be a missing product or a product not meeting its specification."

An off-specification is an issue where a product or set of products either have or definitely will be delivered incorrectly. This could happen in one of the following two situations:
- Each product needs to be delivered so that it complies with its quality criteria. These quality criteria are measurable characteristics or specifications for that product. The quality criteria are contained within each product's product description. If a product has been (or will be) delivered and does not (or will not) comply with its quality criteria, then it is an off-specification.
- Each plan describes the products that need to be delivered. This is known as the *scope* of the plan. If one or more of these products is (or will be) missing, this situation is also an off-specification.

For example, in a project to build a new hotel in Shanghai for a hotel chain, the following are examples of an off-specification:
- A quality inspection on the swimming pool finds that it does not comply with the health and safety standards outlined in its product description.
- As the gym is being constructed, the building company realizes that a mistake was made when the site was surveyed: There is not enough space on the plot of land to create the building specified in the gym's product description.
- The promotional website for the new hotel has been delivered, but due to technical problems, a specified part of the site that allows online users to check room availability and book online reservations does not work.

When a product is off-specification, the project board may choose to accept the product, even though it is wrong. This is called giving a *concession*. As you learn later in this chapter, the project board might have delegated this type of decision to a change authority.

If no concession is given, then the product needs to be corrected. In this case, the project manager might be able to authorize some corrective work. Sometimes, however, the work to correct the off-specification might lead to a breach in the cost and time tolerances given to the project manager by the project board. In this case, the project manager needs to escalate this situation to the project board. (You learn more about tolerances and exceptions in Chapter 9, "Progress Theme.")

Problem/Concern

The final type of issue is a problem or a concern. PRINCE2 defines this as "any other issue that the project manager needs to resolve or escalate." Obviously, the previously described issues are problems and concerns as well, but the problem/concern category is reserved for things that cannot be categorized as either requests for change or off-specifications.

For example, in a project to build a new hotel in Shanghai for a hotel chain, the following are examples of problems or concerns:

- Notification that the Chinese authorities are taking longer than expected to grant work permits to some of the construction staff. This will delay the construction stage by over a month.
- The estimates for purchasing building materials was incorrect, they are costing 10 percent more than predicted.
- The project manager has been taken to the hospital with appendicitis and will be off work for at least a week.

Exam Spotlight

In the Practitioner exam, you might be asked to identify the type of an issue. It is sometimes unclear whether an issue is a request for change or an off-specification.

Consider, for example, the following issue:

A document is being quality-reviewed. The review team spots that the document is in color, whereas the product description specified it should be in black and white. The quality team has raised an issue asking to amend the document to black and white.

The quality team is asking for a change to the document, so it is tempting to say this is a request for change, but it is not. It is an off-specification. A request for change is primarily a request to change a product's product description. This may or may not lead to a change to the product itself. So, in this case, the quality team is not asking for a change to the document's product description. They are asking for a change to the product itself (the document) so that it matches the already written product description. The product description will stay the same.

Now consider this example:

A document is being quality-reviewed. The review team spots that the document does not match corporate branding standards. The senior user forgot to include in the product description a quality criteria specifying that corporate branding standards should be followed, and the quality team raised this as an issue.

This time, the issue is a request for change because in this scenario, not only is the team asking to change the product (the document), but they're also asking to change the document's product description.

Change Authority

It is the project board's responsibility to approve requests for change or concessions in response to an off-specification. The only caveat to this is when the project is part of a programme, but you'll learn about that in a moment.

In a project where there might be a lot of requests for change, the project board might not have time to review them all. In this case, they can delegate some authority to approve changes and off-specifications to a person or group called the *change authority*. This could also be useful when the project board does not have the necessary technical skills to fully understand the implications of a proposed request for change. The project board will place certain constraints on the authority of the change authority, such as the following:

- The authority to sign off only changes that cost less than a prearranged limit
- The authority to sign off only changes that impact the project or stage timescales by less than a prearranged limit
- The authority to sign off only changes that won't affect the broader characteristics of the final outputs of the project described in the project product description
- The authority to sign off only changes that won't affect the current operational ability of the organization

There could be a number of levels of change authority. For example, the project board authorizes large changes, a separate body of people, called the change authority, authorizes medium-sized changes, and the project manager authorizes small changes.

The project board decides how many levels of change authority there should be within the project, and what constraints will be placed on each level's authority. This is done in the initiation stage, and the decision is documented in the change control approach. A change authority might consist of people from the project management team, including project assurance. It is sensible to ensure that business, user, and supplier perspectives are all represented on the change authority.

In practice, the majority of change will be generated at work-package level. It is important that the change authority for work packages has sufficient delegated authority to ensure that change can be made without always having to escalate to the project board for approval.

If the project is part of a programme, it is up to programme management to define what level of change authority the project board will have within the project. Corporate, programme management, or the customer may also take on some responsibility for approving changes within the project, in which case, they are likely to be involved with authorizing the most severe and highest-priority changes.

Figure 8.1 shows the different levels of change authority.

Figure 8.1: Change authority levels

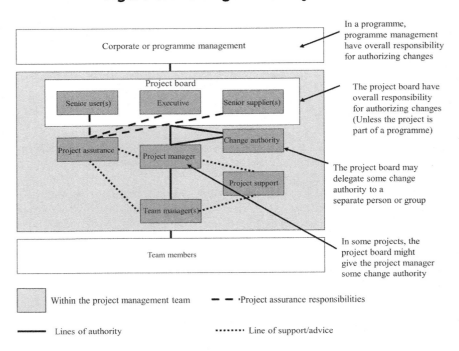

Change Budget

The *change budget* is a sum of money, agreed to by the customer and supplier, that funds the implementation of authorized requests for changes. It could also be used to pay for the initial investigation work to understand the potential impacts on the project of implementing the request for changes. The project board should decide whether there is a need for a change budget.

In the project to build a hotel, if the marketing director requests that 10 more penthouse suites be added, both investigating the impact of adding these additional rooms and then, once they are authorized, building them, would be funded from the change budget.

Change budgets are useful when there are likely to be many changes in a project. They avoid the necessity to continually refer to the next higher level of authority for every change that is requested. There are many examples of projects that might involve a lot of changes, such as in the information technology industry, where rapid technological advances take place.

The project board might authorize the use of some of the change budget to one of the lower levels of change authority, in which case, they might want to set some constraints on how the money can be spent. Typical constraints might include limiting the expenditure on any single change or limiting the overall spending within a particular stage, without reference to the project board.

A change budget might be allocated to the entire project, in which case, it would be documented in the project plan. A change budget might also be allocated to a particular stage in the project, in which case, it would be documented in the stage plan.

Exam Spotlight

It is important not to confuse when to use cost tolerances with when to use the change budget. Cost tolerances do not fund changes; the change budget funds changes. A cost tolerance is used when the costs of a stage or a project unexpectedly overrun.

Issue and Change Control Procedure

For any project, the project management team will need to decide the process that they will use to deal with the three types of issues (request for change, off-specification, and problems or concerns). In the absence of any other procedure, PRINCE2 recommends a five-step process, which you learn about in this section. As shown in Figure 8.2, this procedure is made up of the following activities: capture, examine, propose, decide, and implement. The project management team may decide to tailor the PRINCE2 issue and change control procedure for their project. The project manager will document whichever procedure will be used in the change control approach during the initiation stage. You learn more about the change control approach later in this chapter.

Figure 8.2: Issue and change control procedure

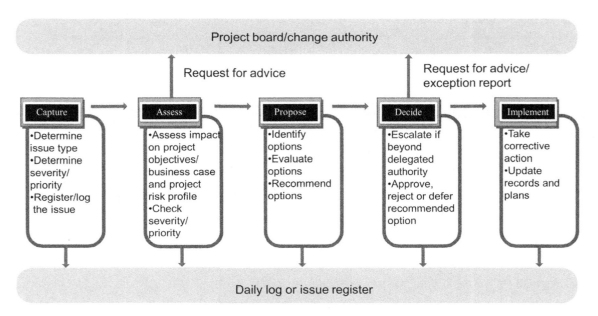

Capturing Issues

The project manager captures the issue by documenting it. Formal issues are captured in the issue register, and informal issues go into the daily log. It is the project manager who must decide whether the issue should be treated formally or informally. The change control approach will define the authority the project manager has to decide which issues he can treat as informally and also the approach to scaling the severity and priority of issues. An informal issue might be something like getting a new security pass for one of the workers or dealing with someone being out sick for the day. These sorts of things can go into the daily log that only the project manager tracks. (You learned about the daily log in Chapter 2, "Starting a Project Successfully with PRINCE2." The project manager uses the daily log as a diary or personal action list.)

For formal issues, the project manager creates an entry in the issue register. You can see sample issue register entries in Figure 8.3.

Figure 8.3: Issue register entries

Issue identifier	Issue type	Date raised	Raised by	Issue Report author	Issue description	Priority	Severity	Status	Closure date
23	RFC	08-Feb	John Smith – Head of Business Development	John Smith – Head of Business Development	Competitor is building a hotel with gym nearby –request to change architectural designs to include gym	High	High	Raised	
24	OS	11-Feb	Louise Newman	Tim Taylor	Swimming pool has not passed the health and safety review due to defects in the build	High	High	Impact analysis	
25	P/C	14- Feb	Taj Rehal	Jon Billimore	The project manager has food poisoning and will probably be sick for at least one week	High	Med	Raised	

If the entry in the issue register does not contain sufficient detail, the project manager might also create an accompanying *issue report*. Alternatively, the project manager might ask the person who raised the issue to draft the first version of the issue report. Figure 8.4 shows an example of an issue report.

Figure 8.4: Issue report

Issue Identifier: *24*	Issue Type: *Off-specification*	Issue Report Author: *Tim Taylor*
Date Raised: *11th Feb*	Raised By: *Louise Newman*	
Issue Description: *During the health and safety check, a number of defects to the swimming pool were discovered. There are no slip stones around the pool and there is no guard rail. Both of these should have been delivered according to the baselined product description for the pool.*		
Impact Analysis: *An impact analysis to correct the pool defects has been done. The work to add the missing features will take an extra 5 days and will be funded by the swimming pool construction firm.*		
Recommendation: *Proceed with the remedial work. This needs to be authorized by the project board because there is no remaining time tolerance for the stage.*		
Priority: *High*	Severity: *High*	Decision Date:
Decision:		
Approved By:		Closure Date:

The project manager captures issues in the capture and examine issues and risks activity during the controlling a stage process. You learn more about this process in Chapter 10, "Managing the Middle of a Project Successfully with PRINCE2."

Assessing Issues

The project manager is now responsible for examining the issue. This involves considering the potential impact of implementing a request for change or investigating the impact of correcting an off-specification (or the impact of authorizing a concession). Sometimes, for less severe issues, the project manager can decide it is not worth the cost and time to do a full formal impact analysis.

The *impact analysis* must consider the following:

- What impact the issue has or will have on the six aspects of project performance: cost, time, scope, quality, benefits, and risk
- Whether the issue would impact any other dependent products being created by the project or beyond

The project manager examines issues in the capture and examine issues and risks activity during the controlling a stage process. The information from the results of the impact analysis should be documented in the issue register and, if there is one, the accompanying issue report. The person who raised the issue should be updated about the results of the impact analysis.

Proposing Corrective Actions

The project manager now needs to propose how to deal with the issue. He will involve relevant people who understand the problem and weigh the benefits of implementing potential options against the time, cost, and risks that might be involved.

For example, maybe the issue under review is the off-specification you saw earlier. As the gym is being constructed, the building company realizes that a mistake was made when the site was surveyed. There is not enough space on the plot of land to create the building specified in the gym's product description.

The project manager canvasses the opinion of the building company and the architects on how a smaller gym might be created. He asks them for cost and time forecasts for this smaller gym. He asks the marketing director what effect a smaller gym would have on the forecast sales for the hotel. He also investigates the potential for buying adjacent land to create the original-sized gym. After investigation, he proposes the following two options:

- Create a smaller gym. This might have little effect on the construction costs and schedule but introduce the business risk that it might have a detrimental effect on possible gym membership sales and room sales.
- Create the original-sized gym on a plot of land that is 50 yards away from the main hotel. This would increase costs and delay construction. The marketing director may decide that whereas this wouldn't affect sales of gym memberships to nonresidents at the hotel, it might put people off staying at the hotel due to the distance the gym would be from the main building.

The project manager will describe the two options in the issue report and show the benefits of each option and the effects on the project's objectives (time, cost, quality, scope, benefits, and risks).

If either of these two options would breach the project or stage tolerances, the project manager should consider creating an exception report to send to the project board or the delegated change authority.

Deciding on Corrective Actions

The next step involves making a decision on which option to pursue to deal with the issue. Either the project manager has the authority to deal with the issue or will have to escalate the issue.

The project manager has the authority to deal with issues in the following circumstances:

- The project manager has been allocated enough cost or time tolerance to tackle the problem or concern.
- The project manager has been allocated enough cost or time tolerance to correct the off-specification.
- The project manager has the change authority to authorize a particular request for change and the change budget to fund it.

If the project manager has the authority to deal with the issue, he will pick an option from the previous propose step. This is done in the take corrective action activity during the controlling a stage process.

If the project manager does not have the authority to deal with the issue, he will escalate the situation to either the project board or the relevant change authority using an *exception report*. Before creating the exception report, the project manager would send the project board or change authority a copy of the issue report, as early warning of the issue. An exception report describes the issue, specifies the options to deal with it, and recommends one of the options. (You learn more about the exception report in Chapter 9.) This will be done in the escalate issues and risks activity during the controlling a stage process.

The project board's or change authority's response will depend on the type of issue. For example:

- If the issue is a request for change, the project board or change authority might approve it, reject it, or defer it for a later decision. They might also ask for more information.
- If the issue is an off-specification, the project board or change authority might grant a concession, instruct that the off-specification be resolved using one of the options proposed, defer the decision, or request more information.
- If the issue is a problem or concern, the project board or change authority might provide some guidance.

The project board or change authority may ask the project manager to produce an exception plan before any work is done to deal with the issue. The exception plan will plan out the work to implement the option that deals with the issue. (Exception plans are covered in more detail in Chapter 5, "Plans Theme.")

Implementing Corrective Actions

The final step in the issue and change control procedure is to implement the corrective action. If the project manager has the authority to deal with the issue, he will implement the option he has chosen; otherwise, he might create an exception plan for approval by the project board. The project manager creates the exception plan in managing a stage boundary, and the project board approves it while directing a project. (Exception plans are covered in detail in Chapter 5.)

If the actions include updating an already baselined product, the project manager needs to obtain the appropriate authorizations. If the product takes the form of a document, it is good practice to make the changes to a new version of the document and keep the old versions.

The project manager then updates the issue register and, if used, the issue report with details of the decision, and informs any interested parties. Once the issue has been closed, he updates the issue register and issue report for a final time.

Tracking and Controlling Configuration Items

Earlier in this chapter I introduced you to the term *configuration item*. If you recall, it is "an entity that may be a product, a component of a product or a set of products that form a release." This section shows you how configuration items relate to a product and how the project manager tracks and controls them.

Tracking Configuration Items

One challenge for the project manager is to keep track of the latest status of all the products being created. There might be hundreds of products being created at any one time. One way of overcoming this challenge is to keep a register that shows each product with its latest status. For this register to be useful, it needs to be kept up-to-date. That might be a lot of work. Imagine if the project were creating a car, and the project manager decided to keep track of the latest status of every nut and bolt of the vehicle. The project manager's register might contain hundreds, if not thousands, of items, and someone needs to update each of these items every time a nut or a bolt moves from one state (for example, "in design") to another state (for example, "complete").

To make the tracking approach more pragmatic, the project manager might decide to track the components of the car at a higher level. Rather than tracking at the nut-and-bolt level, he tracks at the component level, where each component can be independently modified, installed, or released. For example, there might be a steering wheel component and four wheel components. Each component contains a lot of nuts and bolts, but tracking at this level gives the project manager adequate information.

In PRINCE2, these things that the project manager is tracking the status of are called configuration items. The more granular these configuration items are, the more control the project manager has because he is able to monitor the latest product status situation in more detail. On the other hand, the more granular the configuration items are, the more work is involved in tracking them. The project management team needs to strike a happy medium between control of configuration items and the work involved in tracking them. This decision might be influenced by the importance of the project and the complexity of the relationships between its products.

It is not always easy to understand how configuration items relate to products. A configuration item might relate one-on-one with a product, but a configuration item might also track a component of a product or, maybe at the other extreme, a group of products. Obviously, there needs to be some sort of coding system so that the project management team can differentiate one configuration item from another.

Rather than create a register of information about each configuration item, PRINCE2 suggests that the project management team might create a separate configuration item record for each configuration item. A configuration item record describes the status, version, and variant of a configuration item and any details of important relationships between them. Figure 8.5 shows an example configuration item record; however, PRINCE2 does not specify the composition, format, or quality criteria for this product. The set of configuration item records for a project is often referred to as a *configuration library*.

Figure 8.5 Configuration item record

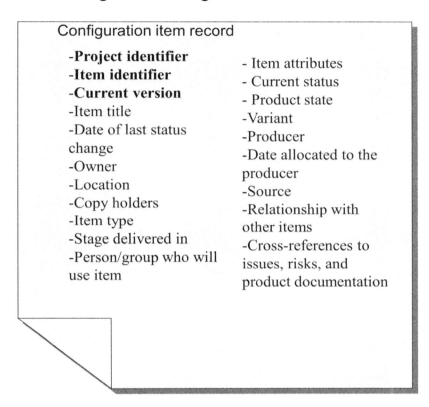

Configuration item record

-**Project identifier**
-**Item identifier**
-**Current version**
-Item title
-Date of last status change
-Owner
-Location
-Copy holders
-Item type
-Stage delivered in
-Person/group who will use item

- Item attributes
- Current status
- Product state
-Variant
-Producer
-Date allocated to the producer
-Source
-Relationship with other items
-Cross-references to issues, risks, and product documentation

Typically, project support might help the project manager maintain the information in these configuration item records. For example, imagine you are managing a project to write a book. You decide to track the status of each chapter, so each chapter needs an associated configuration item record. When the author of the first chapter completes the final draft, he or she would need to contact project support, who would then update the Chapter 1 configuration item record to show that it is finished.

From time to time, the project manager will want to know the latest status of some or all of the configuration items. For example, the project manager might be about to create a highlight report or an end stage report. He could get this information by scanning through the information in every one of the configuration item records. However, it would be a lot easier if project support could create a report that summarizes the information on either all or a specific category of the configuration item records. In PRINCE2, this report is called a *product status account*. (I don't know why PRINCE2 didn't call this a "configuration item status report," which I think would be more appropriate, but you are stuck with "product status account," so this is the name to learn!)

Figure 8.6 shows a product status account being run against a subset of the configuration item records in the project.

Figure 8.6: Product status account

A product status account provides
a snapshot of the information in either
all or a particular selected group of
configuration item records

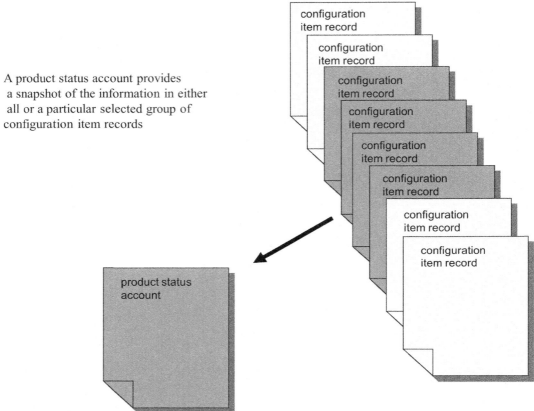

From time to time, the project management team will want to check that all the configuration item information is correct. For example, the project manager of the car project might read in the latest product status account that the left wheel is complete; however, he has just seen the parts of the wheel yet to be assembled in the engineering room, so something is wrong with that information. The project management team needs to audit the information on all the configuration item records. This would typically be done at the end of each stage and the end of the project, and project assurance might be involved.

Controlling Baselines

One of the challenges for any project is to stop anyone from making unauthorized changes to products that have been approved. Remember that once a product has been approved, PRINCE2 refers to it as being baselined. The project management team's challenge, in PRINCE2 terms, is to prevent any unauthorized changes to baselined products.

In a PRINCE2 project, changes are controlled at the configuration item level. The granularity of each configuration item will affect the level of control that the project management team has over unauthorized changes. Going back to the car project, if the team decides that each nut and bolt is a configuration item, an authorization will need to be obtained each time the engineers want to change even a minor nut or bolt on the car. It might be more sensible to control changes at a steering wheel, seat, and component of the engine level.

The project management team needs to decide who can authorize a change to a baselined configuration item. This decision is related to the issue and change control procedure that you learned about in the last section. The issue and change control procedure will define who can authorize changes to configuration items. As you have seen, this might be done by the project board or by a change authority.

Baseline control is done a little differently for document-type configuration items as it would be for physical configuration items like parts of a car. With document-based products, if an approved change is made to a configuration item, a new version of the document is created, and the old baseline is kept as a reference.

The complexity of how configuration items are tracked and controlled will vary depending on the size and complexity of the project as well as the industry sector. For example, in a simple project to write a book, the filenames for each chapter might have different suffixes depending on their state, such as "draft," "for review," and "approved." A more complicated document-based project might have a document management system that can track each document and who updated each document version, roll back to previous versions, and allow access rights to be set up for each file.

CASE STUDY

Real-World Examples of Configuration Management

One example of a configuration management tool is a document management system. This system might have a variety of features, such as safely storing multiple versions of a document, allowing the user to "roll back" to previous versions; reporting on the history of changes to the document and who made them; and allowing different levels of access, such as read/write or read-only, to certain documents.

Another example is using configuration management to help manage software development projects. On a large software project, each developer might create a small part of the product. Each part might consist of thousands of lines of code and go through many versions until it is ready for release. A software developer must ensure that their part of the product works consistently with all the other parts being developed, because mistakenly changing one line of code might cause the product to fail.

On a frequent basis, all the different parts will be combined to see if they work together. With thousands (and in some cases, millions) of ways through the different logical paths of the computer code, it takes a lot of hard work and discipline to create the many individual parts that work together properly.

What all this means is that it is essential to keep track of the status of each part of the product, who is working on it, and what its latest version is. It is also essential to be able to go back to older versions, in case a new version breaks the code base. Finally, it is critical to protect the parts of the code that have been approved, in case anyone mistakenly makes unauthorized changes to the software that prevent it from working correctly. All these activities are configuration management. In the world of computer programming, many software tools are available that carry out these tasks—identifying, tracking, and protecting all the parts of the code.

In an engineering project, where there are a lot of physical items to keep track of, some sort of asset management or parts management system might be used.

Change Control Approach

The project manager creates the change control approach during the initiation stage. It identifies how the project's products will be controlled and protected. It answers the question "how will the project management team manage issue and change control?"

The change control approach includes the following sections:

Issue Management and Change Control Process
This section describes the steps that will be repeated throughout the project to control issues and changes and authorize them at a relevant level of authority. This procedure should cover the core activities of change and issue control described earlier in the chapter (capturing, assessing, proposing, deciding, and implementing).

Tools and Techniques
This section describes tools and/or techniques that will be used to manage and control issues and change.

Records
This section describes the composition and format of the issue register, as well as the configuration item records, if they are being used.

Reporting
This section describes the various reports that will be created in issue and change management, such as the product status accounts and the issue reports, if they are being used.

Timing of Issue Management, Change Control, and Issue Activities
This section includes the timings of activities, such as auditing the configuration item records.

Roles and Responsibilities
This section describes who will be responsible for the various activities involved with issue or change management, including whether a change authority and change budget will be set up.

Scales for Priority and Severity
This section describes the scales that will be used to grade the priority and severity of issues—for example, low, medium, or high, or one to five.

Roles Involved with the Change Theme

This chapter has described the change-related responsibilities for the various PRINCE2 roles. Here is a quick review of these responsibilities to help you prepare for the exams:

Corporate, Programme Management, or the Customer
This might be the highest level of change authority in a project and will provide any corporate, programme, or customer approaches for issue resolution and change control.

Project Board
During the initiation of the project, the project board authorizes the change control approach that has been prepared by the project manager. In particular, they will need to decide whether to use a change authority and, if so, agree on the level of authority to be delegated. They will also set the scales for issue severity and priority and determine the change budget.

During the project, they will advise the project manager on issues, approve all changes (unless delegated to a change authority) and make decisions on escalated issues. Finally, they will approve exception plans when stage-level tolerances are forecast to be exceeded.

The senior users, executive, and senior suppliers should make their decisions on issues by taking into account their perspective on the project. As part of their decision-making process, the executive will take into account the effect the issues would have on the project's business justification, the senior users will consider the effect on the benefits of using the products, and the senior suppliers will review the issues' effects on the delivery and integrity of the products.

Project Manager
During the initiation of the project, the project manager prepares the change control approach and creates the issue register.

During the project, the project manager creates issue reports and exception reports, if required, and maintains the issue register. He manages the issue and change control procedure and ensures that the project management team follows the approach outlined in the change control approach. He also manages the implementation of any authorized corrective actions to respond to issues raised.

Team Manager
The team manager must escalate any issues associated with his work package to the project manager and help in the preparation of any necessary exception plans. He also needs to manage any issues as directed by the project manager and assist the project manager in examining the impact of an issue and options to deal with it.

Project Assurance
Project assurance must review issues and changes by assessing their impact on the business, user, or supplier perspective on the project. Project assurance should monitor the project management

team's adherence to the project's approach to issue and change control that is described in the change control approach. Project assurance should also be involved in configuration audits.

Project Support
Project support should help administer the change control and issue procedure by, for example, helping the project manager maintain the issue register. Project support can also help maintain configuration item records and product status accounts, if they are used.

Tailoring the Change Theme

The key to successfully using PRINCE2 is adapting and tailoring the method given the characteristics of the project and the environment the project is operating within. The following sections show you how the change theme might be adapted to better suit certain situations. This is something you might be tested on in the exams.

Minimum Requirements

Organizations with a less-formal project management approach or that are running smaller, less-complicated projects might choose to cut back on some of the change theme ideas. Some minimum requirements, however, must be followed in order for a project team to claim they are following PRINCE2's change theme.

First, the project management team must define their change control approach. They need to delineate how issues are identified, examined (particularly in terms of whether they will impact the business justification for the project), and managed throughout the project. They also need to define the roles and responsibilities for managing change, including whether there will be a defined change authority.

The next thing the project management team must do (at a minimum) is define how product baselines are created, maintained, and controlled. Then during the project, they should maintain some form of issue register to record relevant information about each issue. They should also consider any useful experience that would help in managing issues.

Aligning the Change Approach with Organizational or Programme Approaches

So far, you have seen that the project management team creates a change control approach for their project. However, the organization, customer, or programme that has commissioned the project might already have an issue and change approach or certain change- or issue-related policies and processes. In this case, the project management team needs to include those in the project's change control approach.

Agile Environments

The first time you're introduced to PRINCE2 and agile environments, you may get the impression that they approach change in very different ways. A general philosophy of agile approaches is to respond to and embrace change, whereas PRINCE2 talks about controlling change. The agile approach to change, however, can work effectively in a PRINCE2 project. It is important that the project management team avoid over exactness when creating product descriptions. Sometimes quality criteria do need to be specified precisely—for example, it might be essential that each component of a rocket project adheres to a very exact specification, whereas in the project to build the hotel, it is not necessary to specify the exact shade of blue that should be used to paint the hotel foyer's walls.

Specifying quality criteria precisely only when it is really necessary decreases the number of requests for change that need to be treated formally through the issue and change control procedure. This also allows a more flexible approach to requested changes.

The project management team should try to baseline only quality criteria that encapsulate the purpose of the product. For example, when Apple developed the computer mouse, Steve Jobs specified that the product must cost Apple less than 15 dollars to make, it shouldn't fail within two years, and it should be usable on his blue jeans. I don't know if the Apple team were using PRINCE2, but if they were, they could have baselined these high-level requirements. Then they could have changed their mind repeatedly about what materials to use, the dimensions of the device, or how many buttons it had—without having to refer those requests for changes to Steve Jobs.

Agile approaches tend to deliver over short periods of time called *sprints*. Typically, these sprints last between two to four weeks. It is important that any requests for changes raised during a sprint are dealt with speedily so as not to slow down the development of the products. A change control procedure that takes four weeks, for example, would be inappropriate for a project that delivers in three-week sprints.

Linking the Change Theme with the Principles

In Chapter 1, "Overview of PRINCE2," I talked about the seven PRINCE2 principles. In some ways, all of the seven principles contribute to implementing the change theme; however, the four principles that are most important to this particular theme are continued business justification, defined roles and responsibilities, learn from experience, and focus on products.

As you have learned in this chapter, the project manager must carry out an impact analysis on each issue that arises. The most important impact to consider is how the issue might affect the business rationale for the project. Therefore, the change theme helps continually review the business justification of the project.

The change control approach must describe, at a minimum, the roles and responsibilities that are associated with managing issues and changes, such as who must capture an issue, who must be involved in assessing issues, and who can authorize different levels of issues. In this way, the change theme helps to implement the defined roles and responsibilities principle.

The project management team must also consider any useful experience that would help them identify and/or manage issues. This helps to implement the principle of learning from experience.

Finally, the change theme is fundamentally about controlling and managing change to the project's products, which helps to implement the principle of focusing on products.

Summary

In this chapter, you learned about the change theme. The change theme describes how to control and manage changes to the project's products and how to manage issues. It ensures that the right level of authority authorizes changes and responses to issues. The change theme also covers how to track configuration items and control changes to baselined products. First, the chapter defined some change theme terminology: baselines, releases, and configuration items. A baseline is a product that is frozen at a point in time for a particular reason. It may be frozen for all sorts of reasons, such as because it is ready for review or because it has been approved. A release is a set of products that works together as a group in a consistent and coherent manner. A release might describe a group of products that will be handed over to the client. Finally, a configuration item could be a group of products, a single product, or even a part of a product. It is the status of these configuration items that the project manager will track during the project.

You then learned that there are three types of issues in PRINCE2. The first is a request for change. The second is called an off-specification. This is when a product is (or will be) missing or a product doesn't (or won't) match its specification. The final type of issue is a problem or concern. The problem or concern could be about all sorts of things, such as spending too much money, a key member of the staff being ill, or a supplier going bankrupt.

The chapter also described the change authority. This is a person or a group of people who have been given authority to approve changes to the project's products. The change authority might have a change budget that would be used to fund the changes.

You then saw how all issues and changes in a PRINCE2 project are handled by the issue and change control procedure. There are five core activities to this procedure: (1) capturing or documenting the issue; (2) assessing the issue and thinking about what sort of impact it will have on the project; (3) proposing a set of options to deal with the issue; (4) making a decision on what option to pursue; and (5) implementing the decision.

In addition to describing the issue and change control procedure, the change theme describes how to track configuration item records. In this chapter, you learned that PRINCE2 suggests using configuration item records to record information on each configuration item, such as its variant and latest status. You also saw that the change theme discusses the importance of controlling baselines to configuration items so as to prevent unauthorized changes to products.

This chapter also covered the change control approach. This management product documents how issue and change control will be done on the project. The project manager creates the change control approach near the beginning of the project, during the initiation stage.

Finally, this chapter looked at how to adapt the change theme when PRINCE2 is used in a range of different situations, such as a small project, a project operating in a programme environment, and a project operating in an agile environment.

Foundation Exam Essentials

Explain the purpose of the change theme.
The purpose of the change theme is to identify, assess, and control any potential and approved changes to the project baselines.

Explain the purpose of the change budget.
The change budget is used to fund the work to implement requests for change and possibly the analysis work looking at the impact of the change.

Explain the purpose of the change control approach.
The purpose of the change control approach is to document how issue and change control will be carried out during the project. The approach is created by the project manager during initiating a

project, and it is used and reviewed by the project manager and project assurance throughout the project to ensure that the project is following the correct approach to change and issue management.

Explain the purpose of a configuration item record.
The purpose of a configuration item record is to track information relevant to a particular configuration item. It is created as soon as the need for that configuration item is identified and then updated throughout the life of the configuration item. Project support is responsible for maintaining the configuration item records.

Explain the purpose of an issue register.
The purpose of the issue register is to track information regarding all the issues in the project. The project manager creates the issue register during the initiating a project process, and it will then be updated with new issue information throughout the project.

Explain the purpose of an issue report.
The purpose of the issue report is to track information regarding a particular issue in the project. The project manager is responsible for the creation of the issue report during the controlling a stage process, as well as updating this report throughout the life of that issue. The use of an issue report is optional if the issue register contains adequate information about a particular issue.

Explain the purpose of a product status account.
The purpose of the product status account is to provide information to the project manager regarding the status of all or a subset of the configuration items. The project manager might ask project support to create a product status account at various times throughout the project, such as when preparing a highlight report or reviewing stage status during the controlling a stage process, when preparing the end stage report during the managing a stage boundary process, or when preparing to close the project during the closing a project process.

Describe PRINCE2's minimum requirements for applying the change theme.
As a minimum for applying the change theme, PRINCE2 requires that the project management team do the following:
- Define the project's change control approach, which must cover how issues are to be identified, examined (particularly in terms of their impact on the project's business justification), and managed throughout the project. The project management team also needs to describe the change and issue management related roles and responsibilities and whether a change authority will be established for the project.
- Define how product baselines are created, maintained, and controlled.
- Maintain an issue register to record relevant information on issues throughout the project.
- Consider any useful experience that would help in managing issues.

Describe the different issue types.
The three types of issues in PRINCE2 are request for change, off-specification, and problem or concern. A request for change is a request to change a product's specifications documented in its baselined product description. An off-specification is something that should be provided by the project but currently is not and is not forecast to be provided in the future. This might involve a missing product or a product not meeting its specifications. A problem or concern is any other issue that the project manager needs to resolve or escalate.

Describe the issue and change control procedure.
The five core activities that take place in the issue and change control procedure are capture, assess, propose, decide, and implement. This procedure is used to manage and control issues and changes. It involves recording the issue in the issue register, assessing the impact that the issue will have on the project, proposing a solution to the issue, making a decision on the issue at the relevant level of management, and implementing the resolution.

Define a baseline.
A baseline is a snapshot of a release, product, and any component products, frozen at a point in time for a particular purpose.

Define a release.
A release is a complete and consistent set of products that are managed, tested, and deployed as a single entity to be handed over to the user(s).

Define a configuration item.
A configuration item is an entity that is subject to configuration management. The entity may be a component of a product, a product, or a set of products that form a release.

Understand the responsibilities of the change authority.
The change authority is a person or group given authorization by the project board to approve changes. The project board decides whether to use a change authority and what constraints to place on their authority during the initiating a project process when the change control approach is prepared.

Demonstrate an understanding of the change control approach.
Demonstrate an understanding that the project manager creates the change control approach during the initiation stage and that it shows how to manage changes and issues throughout the project. Understand that the approach might be derived from the project product description or any corporate, programme management, customer, or supplier quality strategies or systems that exist, and that it could be a stand-alone document or part of the project-initiation documentation. Know the composition of the change control approach.

Demonstrate an understanding of the issue register.
Demonstrate an understanding that the project manager creates the issue register during the initiation stage and uses it to record details of any problems or concerns, requests for change, or off-specifications that are identified throughout the project. Understand that it could be a stand-alone register; a spreadsheet; a database; part of an integrated project register for all risks, actions, and issues; sticky notes on walls; or an entry into a project management tool. Know the composition of the issue register.

Demonstrate an understanding of the configuration item record.
Demonstrate an understanding that configuration item records are created only if required by the project's change control approach. Understand that if they are used, they would provide a record of information such as the history, status, version and variant of each configuration item. Know that the set of configuration item records is often referred to as a configuration library. Understand that the records might be derived from the change control approach, the product breakdown structure, the stage plan, or the registers. Know that PRINCE2 does not define the composition, format, or presentation of this product.

Demonstrate an understanding of the issue report.
Demonstrate an understanding that when the project manager is capturing an issue by recording it in the issue register, he may also create an accompanying issue report, and that the project manager will update the issue report throughout the life of the issue. Know that the issue report might be derived from other reports or from information from the users or suppliers on the project. Know that the issue report could be a document, a spreadsheet, a database, or an entry into a project management tool. Know the composition of the issue report.

Demonstrate an understanding of the product status account.
Demonstrate an understanding that product status accounts are created only if required by the project's change control approach. Understand that if they are used, they provide a report on information such as the history, status, version, and variant of a subset of configuration items. Understand that a product status account might be derived from configuration item records or a stage plan. Know that PRINCE2 does not define the composition, format, or presentation of this product.

Review Questions

The remainder of this chapter contains mock exam questions, first for the Foundation exam and then for the Practitioner exam.

Foundation Exam Questions

1. Which of the following is an off-specification?
   (1) A missing product
   (2) A product delivered over budget
   (3) A product delivered late
   (4) A product that is forecast not to be provided
   A. 1 and 2
   B. 2 and 3
   C. 3 and 4
   D. 1 and 4

2. Which of the following describes a minimum requirement for applying the change theme?
   A. Define how product baselines are created, maintained, and controlled
   B. Define how to identify ways of eliminating causes of unsatisfactory performance
   C. Ensure that the project has at least two management stages
   D. Define the project's approach to communicating and engaging with stakeholders

3. Which of the following options might be funded by a change budget?
   A. Assessing threats to the project
   B. Analyzing the impact of a request for change
   C. Reducing the probability of a threat
   D. Implementing actions following a quality review

4. Which of the following is a purpose of the change control approach?
    (1) Describes the procedures to be used for achieving effective issue management
    (2) Describes how changes to the products will be controlled
    (3) Describes how to identify any opportunities that would have a positive effect on objectives
    (4) Describes how to achieve each product's required level of quality
    A. 1 and 2
    B. 2 and 3
    C. 3 and 4
    D. 1 and 4

5. Which of the following should be used to record issues that will be managed informally?
    A. Issue register
    B. Issue report
    C. Daily log
    D. Change control approach

6. During which step of the issue and change control procedure might the project manager need to create an exception plan?
    A. Assess
    B. Propose
    C. Decide
    D. Implement

7. Which management product is used to track all products that do not meet their specifications?
    A. Configuration control approach
    B. Issue report
    C. Issue register
    D. Configuration item record

8. If the project board decides to accept an off-specification, what is this called?
    A. Concession
    B. Threat
    C. Issue
    D. Quality issue

9. Which of the following might be created to record the latest status, version, and variant of a product?
    A. Issue report
    B. Configuration item record
    C. Product description
    D. Stage plan

10. Which of the following describes a minimum requirement for applying the change theme?
    A. Create product status accounts
    B. Create a configuration item record to track the state of each product
    C. Escalate requests for changes to the project board for a decision
    D. Maintain some form of issue register

Practitioner Exam Questions

The following Practitioner questions are divided into two sections by question type and are based on the Practitioner exam scenario that you will find in Appendix B.

Section 1: Matching Questions

The project is in stage four, and the website for Quality Furniture is being built. The chief executive recently saw a competitor's website that had a facility to view the furniture from many different angles (3D View). He would like this facility in the new website. Currently, this is not specified in the baselined designs for the site.

Column 1 in the following table describes five actions related to handling this request for change from the chief executive. For each of these actions, choose the correct step in PRINCE2's recommended issue and change control procedure (A–E in Column 2) where this action would be carried out. Each option from Column 2 can be only used once.

Column 1	Column 2
1. The project manager decides he does not have the necessary authority to implement 3D View and escalates the idea to the project board.	A. Capturing issues
2. The project manager chairs a meeting with the project team to look at the possible benefits of 3D View, the costs of creating it, and the time it will take.	B. Assessing issues
3. The project board considers the argument for implementing 3D View and how the idea might be funded.	C. Proposing corrective actions
4. The project manager records the request from the chief executive in the issue register and gives it a unique identifier.	D. Deciding on corrective actions
5. The project manager creates a plan to show how the 3D View feature will be implemented.	E. Implementing corrective actions

Section 2: Classic Multiple-Choice Questions

> ## Exam Spotlight
>
> Remember that during the Practitioner exam, you are allowed to refer to the official PRINCE2 manual (*Managing Successful Projects with PRINCE2*). For change theme questions, where might you look in the manual for useful information? The first (and most obvious) place is the change theme chapter itself. The chapter begins by discussing the purpose of the change theme and provides some useful definitions for a number of change terms, such as request for change, off-specification, baseline, configuration item record, and product status account. It then goes on to discuss the minimum requirements for applying the change theme, followed by a table of change control responsibilities. Next, there is a section that provides general guidance for effective change management, including how to carry out change control in projects of different sizes and with different delivery approaches. It also describes how to manage product baselines and establish a change authority and change budgets. Finally, the last section looks at the recommended issue and change control procedure.
>
> In addition to the change theme chapter, a few other places in the PRINCE2 manual might be useful. For questions about the change theme management products (the change control approach, the configuration item record, the issue register, the issue report, and the product status account), refer to Appendix A. For questions about the change theme roles and responsibilities, you can not only refer to the table of responsibilities within the change theme chapter that I mentioned previously, but you'll also find information about change-related responsibilities in Appendix C.

1. The project is in stage three, and Quality Furniture's marketing manager has requested that Digital Design create a Quality Furniture Facebook page as well as the new website. The project manager has recorded this as a request for change and has been discussing the impact on the project with the marketing manager and the finance director. He has decided not to discuss the impact of the change with Digital Design. Is this appropriate, and why or why not?
   A. Yes, because an impact analysis on a request for change will include discussing confidential information about Quality Furniture's business case.
   B. Yes, because including external suppliers in the impact analysis discussions could slow down the decision-making process.
   C. No, because for a project to be successful in a commercial environment, all information must be shared between the customer and suppliers.
   D. No, because the impact analysis needs to take account of the supplier's cost and effort required to implement the change.

2. The project is in stage three, and the website is being designed. There are more than 20 different components in the new system to design, and in many cases, the design of one component is linked to the design of another component. The project manager is concerned that if a request for change is raised for any of these designs, the impact analysis may not take into account the impact that changing one component may have on another component. The project manager has identified 10 components that are linked to other components and, for each case, has raised a concern in the issue register. Is this appropriate, and why or why not?

   A. Yes, because the issue register is used to record all problems or concerns raised during the project.

   B. Yes, because the project manager is responsible for maintaining the issue register throughout the project.

   C. No, because it would be better practice to create a configuration item record for each design that includes information about important relationships between them.

   D. No, because not taking into account the relationships between designs is a risk and should be recorded in the risk register.

3. The project is in stage three. Digital Design is proposing to use an agile delivery approach to create the website. Quality Furniture's chief executive is keen to use this approach. The project manager has raised the concern that if an agile approach is used, a new version of the change control approach will be needed, as it was not originally written to work within an agile development environment. Is this appropriate, and why or why not?

   A. Yes, because it is important that the change control approach works with and supports the project's chosen delivery approach.

   B. Yes, because now there needs to be two change control approaches: one for Digital Design's work and one for the rest of the project.

   C. No, because the change control approach is created in the initiation stage.

   D. No, because in an agile environment, changes are not controlled, so a change control approach will not be needed.

Chapter

9

Progress Theme

PRINCE2 Foundation Exam Objectives Covered in This Chapter:

☑ **Explain the purpose of:**
- The progress theme
- Key management products
  - Daily log
  - Lessons log
  - Lessons report
  - Work package Exception report
- Describe PRINCE2's minimum requirement for applying the progress theme
- Explain key concepts related to progress:
  - Event-driven and time-driven controls
  - Tolerances and exceptions, including how tolerances are set and exceptions are reported

PRINCE2 Practitioner Exam Objectives Covered in This Chapter:

☑ **Apply the PRINCE2 requirements for controlling progress, demonstrating an understanding of:**
- Key management products:
  - Daily log
  - Work package
  - Exception report
  - Lessons report
  - Lessons log
- The recommended roles and responsibilities within the theme
- Tolerances and raising exceptions

☑ **Assess whether an approach to applying the progress theme is effective and fit for purpose, taking into consideration: the context, the PRINCE2 principles, and the purpose and requirements of the progress theme**

The scope of the progress theme can be difficult to understand. The project management area covered by the other themes is far more obvious. For example, it's easy to understand that the organization theme describes the people who are involved in a project and what they should do, and the risk theme describes how to deal with potential problems. But it isn't obvious what the progress theme covers.

In a previous version of PRINCE2, the progress theme was called the *control component*. (In that previous version, a component was pretty much the same thing as a theme.) I think control was a better name, because the progress theme is all about *controlling* all the activities and the people in the project so that the objectives that have been set are achieved. A lot of parts of PRINCE2 help *control* what is happening on a project, many of which you have already read about in other chapters. For example, the product descriptions that you learned about in the quality theme help define what is to be delivered, and so help control the creation of the products. So in addition to introducing a few new topics, the progress theme also reviews the whole of PRINCE2 to see how the parts of the model help *control* what is happening.

To learn more about how the progress theme controls a project, read on.

Purpose of the Progress Theme

As mentioned in the introduction to this chapter, the progress theme is focused on controlling the project so that it achieves its objectives. A number of general things need to be done in order to control a project. First, the project management team must decide what they want the project to accomplish. They do so by setting objectives in terms of time, cost, scope, quality, risk, and benefits. These objectives are described in various management products, including the project's plans and various parts of the project initiation documentation, such as the business case, the approaches, and the project product description. All these management products help control the project because the project management team can use them to compare what is actually happening on the project with what they would like to happen. These products act as a measuring stick to see how well the project is progressing.

The second part of controlling a project is to work out how the project management team will constantly review what is happening in the project against what they would like to happen. Various parts of PRINCE2 help you do this. For instance, progress reports—such as highlight reports, checkpoint reports, end stage reports, and end project reports—show the project management team how the project is progressing against its objectives. There are also the various logs and registers, which help the project manager track things such as issues, risks, lessons, and personal actions. Finally, there are the stages. At the end of each stage, the project management team comes together and reviews the performance of the previous stage.

The last part of controlling the project is making timely decisions at the right level of management, either about whether some piece of work should proceed or how to handle problems in the project. PRINCE2 enables the project board to decide, one stage at a time, whether to proceed with the project, and enables the project manager to decide when to authorize the team to do the work. Both of these decisions help control the progress of the project by releasing resources a bit at a time. Another decision to make from time to time during the project is whether to escalate problems and issues. As you will learn in this chapter, the concepts of tolerance and exceptions help each level of management decide whether they could handle a problem themselves or whether they should escalate it to the level of management above.

The final decision to make is whether the project should be closed. You learn more about closing a project in Chapter 11, "Managing the End of a Project Successfully with PRINCE2," including how, in some circumstances, the project might be closed prematurely. As usual, the PRINCE2 manual has its own, rather unusual way of stating the purpose of this theme. The manual talks about the progress theme establishing "mechanisms" to monitor and compare actual achievements against those planned. Don't be put off by the word "mechanisms"—a mechanism is the way that the project management team decides to compare the project's progress against its targets. For example, they might decide to review a cost report at a weekly meeting to assess the project's progress against its budget targets.

As you can see, the progress theme is quite a collection of different aspects of PRINCE2, some of which have already been covered in other chapters of this book. But in this theme, PRINCE2 reviews these areas and asks the question, "How does this part of PRINCE2 control where the project is going?" The progress theme also introduces the concepts of tolerances and exceptions. (These concepts have been mentioned in other chapters, but they're described in more detail in this chapter.)

Tolerances and Exceptions

The definition of tolerances in *Managing Successful Projects with PRINCE2* (Stationery Office, 2017) is as follows:

> Tolerances are the permissible deviation above and below a plan's target for time and cost without escalating the deviation to the next level of management. There may also be tolerance levels for quality, scope, benefit and risk.

In other words, tolerances enable one management level to specify certain constraints on the authority of the management level below them. For example, when the project board delegates the management of each stage to the project manager, they define how much time the project manager is allowed to use. This time target might have some allowable flexibility. The project board might say to the project manager, "Deliver this stage in the next six months, although in certain circumstances, we will allow a two-week late delivery." These additional two weeks are an example of a time tolerance.

The project board might also set cost tolerances for the project manager to deliver the stage. For example, they might say to the project manager, "We will give you $50,000 for the next stage, with an allowable over-expenditure of up to $5,000 and an allowable under-expenditure spend of up to $10,000."

In addition to cost and time tolerances, there could also be scope, quality, benefit, and risk tolerances. You will learn about these later in this chapter.

The definition of an exception in *Managing Successful Projects with PRINCE2* is as follows:

An exception is a situation where it can be forecast that there will be a deviation beyond the agreed tolerance levels.

In the previous example, an exception would occur if the project manager forecasts that the stage will be delivered later than the two-week tolerance set by the project board. When an exception occurs, it must immediately be reported to the management level above; in this case, the project manager must escalate the situation to the project board. In effect, the project manager does not have authority to handle the situation and must refer to the project board for them to decide how to deal with the delay.

One question that students often ask is, "What is the point of a negative tolerance?" In the previous example, the project board has asked the project manager to escalate any situation where there might be an underspend of more than $10,000. But isn't spending less than $40,000 a good thing that does not need to be escalated?

There are two main reasons the project board might want the project manager to report forecast underspends. First, they might be concerned about the quality of the products, and second, they might be able to reallocate the money to another project or another part of the organization.

One other important point regarding exceptions is that they must be escalated when it can be *forecast* that a tolerance level will be breached, not when the level is actually breached. In the previous example, the project manager is in exception when she forecasts that the stage will spend over $55,000, not when the stage actually does spend over $55,000.

Levels of Tolerance

Figure 9.1 shows cost tolerances being set at three different levels: project, stage, and work package. On the left side of the figure, you can see which level of management sets which level of tolerance. Corporate, programme management, or the customer sets the overall project budget and any tolerances around this budget. These project tolerances are given to the project board and define their level of authority. In this case, the project board is given a project budget of $300,000 and must escalate to corporate, programme management, or the customer if they believe they will overspend on that budget by more than $100,000 or underspend on it by more than $200,000. (Project tolerances therefore are plus $100,000 and minus $200,000.) Similarly, for each stage, the project board sets a stage budget with tolerances for the project manager to work within. Figure 9.1 shows that for one stage in this project, the project manager was given a stage budget of $100,000, with tolerances of plus $50,000 and minus $70,000. Finally, for each work package, the project manager will allocate a work package budget with tolerances that the team manager or team need to work within. Figure 9.1 shows that for one work package in this project, the teams were given a budget of $50,000, with tolerances of plus $20,000 and minus $30,000.

Figure 9.1: Levels of cost tolerance

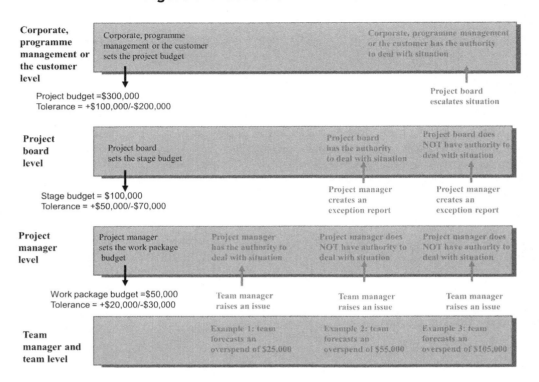

The example in Figure 9.1 shows the setting of three different levels of cost tolerances. Time, scope, and risk tolerances can also be set the same way at a project, stage, and work package level. However, the other two types of tolerances—benefit and quality—are not set at these three different levels. Benefit tolerance is set only at the project level. Quality is set at an overall project level and then at an individual product level. (You'll learn more about benefit and quality tolerances later in this chapter.)

On the right side of the diagram are three examples that show what happens when there is a forecast deviation beyond the work package tolerance, then the stage tolerance, and finally, the project tolerance.

Example 1: Overspend of $25,000

In Example 1, the team manager realizes she will spend $25,000 more than the $50,000 she has been allocated by the project manager. In this case, the project manager has set work package tolerances to be plus $20,000 and minus $30,000, so the forecast overspend will breach the work package tolerances. An exception has occurred, which the team manager must escalate immediately to the project manager.

In the PRINCE2 model, the team manager escalates forecast breaches in work package tolerances to the project manager by raising an issue in the way that has been agreed to in the work package. This might involve simply phoning the project manager or perhaps filling out an issue report form and emailing it to the project manager.

When the project manager receives the issue, she first checks that she has the authority to handle this situation. She can handle overspends as long as they do not breach the stage tolerances. In this case, there will be an overspend of $25,000, but the project manager has been given a stage tolerance of $50,000. Therefore, the project manager can handle this situation herself, without escalating it to the project board.

All of this is based on the assumption that no other work packages have overspent their budgets. If they have, this might mean that the cumulative effects of all the overspends would breach the project manager's stage tolerances.

Example 2: Overspend of $55,000

In Example 2, the team manager forecasts that she will spend $55,000 more than the $50,000 she has been allocated. As in Example 1, she will need to escalate this situation by raising an issue to the project manager. This time, however, the project manager does not have enough authority to deal with the situation, because there will be an overspend of $55,000 and the project manager has been given a stage tolerance of $50,000. This means that the project manager will have to escalate this situation to the project board.

In the PRINCE2 model, the project manager escalates forecast breaches in stage tolerances by sending the project board an *exception report*. Figure 9.2 shows an example exception report.

Figure 9.2: Example exception report

Exception Title:
Increase in the price of haulage.

Cause of the Exception:
Since estimating the costs of haulage of the materials for the hotel to the construction site, the price of oil has doubled. This has caused a substantial increase in the price of transport. The work package of the haulage company was forecast to cost $50,000. The haulage company is now predicting there will be an overspend of $55,000 taking the total cost of haulage up to $105,000.

Consequences of the Deviation:
The consequence of the deviation is that there is not enough money in the stage budget to pay the haulage company. If the materials are not transported to the site, the construction on the hotel cannot start.

Options
Increase the budget for the haulage company or procure the services of a less expensive haulage company.

Recommendation:
It seems that all haulage companies have increased their costs, so we recommend to simply increase the current haulage company's budget.

Lessons
A fixed price contract with the haulage company would have limited our exposure to the risk of the oil price increasing.

The project board will then review the predicted overspend and compare it against the project tolerances they have been given by corporate, programme management, or the customer to see if they have the authority to deal with this situation. In this case, the overspend is $55,000 and the project board has a project cost tolerance of $100,000, so they can handle this situation without referring to corporate, programme management, or the customer.

Example 3: Overspend of $105,000

In Example 3, there is a much more serious overspend. The team manager forecasts that she will spend $105,000 more than she has been allocated. As you can see in the figure, first the team manager escalates this to the project manager by raising the issue. Then the project manager escalates it to the project board by sending them an exception report. Finally, the project board realizes that they don't have enough project cost tolerance to deal with this situation, so they refer it to corporate, programme management, or the customer. With this situation, only corporate, programme management, or the customer has the authority to make a decision on how to handle the overspend.

Further Notes on Levels of Tolerance

You need to remember a few things about levels of tolerance. As you saw in the examples, when there is a breach in the level of tolerance, it is escalated first to the next level of management. If the team manager realizes that the breach of tolerance is so severe that it actually breaches the project level of tolerance (as in Example 3), she doesn't escalate this directly to corporate, programme management, or the customer—she only escalates it to the project manager. (As you have just seen in the previous subsection, the project manager will then escalate the breach of tolerance to the project board, which in turn escalates it to corporate, programme management, or the customer.)

Also remember who sets the various levels of tolerance. Corporate, programme management, or the customer sets the project level of tolerance. They do this at the beginning of the project, when they write the project mandate, but they may adjust the tolerance levels throughout the project, especially when the project brief or project initiation documentation is authorized.

The project board sets the stage level of tolerances during the directing a project process, when they authorize the project manager to deliver a management stage.

Finally, the project manager sets the work package level of tolerance when she authorizes a team to work on a work package during the controlling a stage process.

The last thing to remember from this section is that each level of management escalates an exception in a different way: The team manager would raise an issue to the project manager; the project manager would send an exception report to the project board; and the project board would send a notification to the corporate, programme management, or the customer level.

Types of Tolerance

The six types of tolerance are time and cost (which are known as the standard types of tolerance), scope, risk, quality, and benefit.

Time Tolerance

An example of a time tolerance is "Deliver this project within six months, although an early delivery of one month or late delivery of two weeks would be allowed." Time tolerances can be set at the project, stage, or work package level and are described in the project plan, stage plan, or work package, respectively.

Cost Tolerance

An example of a cost tolerance is "The budget for this work package is $1,000, plus or minus 10 percent." Cost tolerances can be set at the project, stage, or work package level and are described in the project plan, stage plan, or work package, respectively.

Scope Tolerance

Scope tolerance describes any flexibility around the number or range of products that will be delivered. For example, the client for a website project might prioritize the list of features that they want on the website. Some features will be mandatory and must be delivered; others might be "good to have" and should be delivered; others aren't essential to the project and are just "nice to have," so they could be delivered; and finally, some features are so low priority that, given the budgetary and time constraints, won't be delivered. This approach is sometimes called the MoSCoW prioritization technique, where *M* stands for must haves, *S* for should haves, *C* for should haves, and *W* for won't haves. MoSCoW isn't a PRINCE2 technique, but it is a PRINCE2-compatible approach to help the project management team define scope tolerances.

Another non-MoSCoW, simpler example from the hotel project would be: "The spa must contain a swimming pool and whirlpool, but the steam room could be left to the hotel upgrade project next year if there is not time to construct it in this project." This sentence describes an allowable flexibility around what should be delivered in the hotel's spa, so it's a scope tolerance.

Scope tolerances can be set at the project, stage, or work package level and are described in the project plan, stage plan, or work package, respectively. As you saw in Chapter 5, "Plans Theme," one step in the approach to planning is identifying what products to deliver within the plan. This is essentially the scope of the plan and is shown pictorially in the product breakdown structure for that plan. (I discussed product breakdown structures in Chapter 5.) PRINCE2 recommends that the scope tolerance for a plan be shown clearly by referencing this diagram or indicating on the diagram which of the products are part of the scope tolerance.

Risk Tolerance

Risk tolerance defines a threshold level of risk that, if exceeded, needs to be escalated to the next level of management. To be able to set a risk tolerance, the project management team must decide how to measure the level of risk on the project at any one time. One way of doing this is to simply count how many risks are currently listed in the risk register. A more sophisticated method is to use the expected value risk evaluation approach you learned about in Chapter 7. Table 9.1 is a duplicate of the table used to explain this method in Chapter 7.

Table 9.1: Expected-value technique for risk evaluation

Risk ID	Probability (%)	Impact ($)	Expected Value ($) (Probability Multiplied by Impact)
01	20%	$10,000	$2,000
02	50%	$30,000	$15,000
03	30%	$100,000	$30,000
Expected Overall Value:			**$47,000**

Each risk is given a percentage that shows its likelihood and a predicted cost impact. By multiplying the probability of each risk by its forecast cost impact, an expected value for that risk is calculated. Then, an overall value is calculated by adding together all the expected values.

This expected overall figure is the likely amount of money that risks will cost the project. It indicates the level of risk on the project and can be used to set a risk tolerance level. For example, the project board might say to the project manager, "Escalate the risk situation to us if the overall expected impact of risks rises above $50,000."

There are many other ways of defining an overall risk tolerance for the project. One method worth mentioning is using the risk profile diagram that you first saw in the section "The Contents of the Business Case" in Chapter 4, "Business Case Theme." Figure 9.3 shows that risk profile diagram again, with the addition of a risk tolerance line. If any risk is identified that is above this line, in effect a risk with a high impact and probability, then this situation should be escalated to the relevant level of authority.

Figure 9.3: Risk profile diagram showing a risk tolerance line

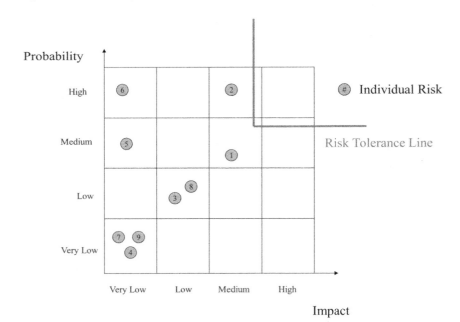

Another way of setting risk tolerances is to define certain types of risks that, if spotted, must be escalated. For example, the project board might want to be immediately informed about risks that might threaten the organization's business-as-usual operations.

Risk tolerances can be set at the project, stage, or work package level and are written into the risk management approach, stage plan, or work package, respectively.

Quality Tolerance
Quality tolerances are allowable flexibility around the specifications of products. They can be set at both a high level in the project product description and at a lower level in the product descriptions.

In Chapter 6, "Quality Theme," you learned that the main project outputs are described in the project product description at the beginning of the project. The project product description contains acceptance criteria, which are measurable specifications for the products. For example, in the project to build a hotel, an acceptance criterion might be that the hotel should be able to service 400 guests at one time. If some flexibility in the hotel's capacity were specified, that would be an example of a quality tolerance.

You also learned in Chapter 6 that as the project progresses, the project management team needs to create more detailed specifications for the products described in the product descriptions. For example, in the hotel project, product descriptions might be written for the swimming pool, the bedrooms, and/or the lobby. These product descriptions should contain quality criteria for each product, which are the measurable attributes of that product. For example, a product description for a bedroom might say that the room needs to be 20 square meters. If the specification included some flexibility, such as that the room could be anywhere between 18 to 20 square meters, this would be another example of a quality tolerance.

In summary, quality tolerances at a broad level are described in the project product description, and quality tolerances at an individual product level are described in the product descriptions. Remember that the project manager creates the project product description and product descriptions with any associated tolerances with the help of the senior users, the senior suppliers, and the teams. The project board will sign off on both management products.

Benefit Tolerance

Benefit tolerances are allowable deviations related to the forecast benefits of the project. In the hotel project, here's an example of a benefit tolerance: "Sales for the hotel are forecast to be $20 million, although a figure of $18 million would be acceptable to the board."

Benefit tolerances are set only at the project level and are described in the business case. The project board authorizes them.

Summary of Tolerance Types

Figure 9.4 summarizes the tolerance types and where they are documented.

Figure 9.4: Tolerance types

Tolerance Area	Project Level	Stage Level	Work Package Level	Product Level
Time	Project plan	Stage plan	Work package	Not applicable
Cost	Project plan	Stage plan	Work package	Not applicable
Scope	Project plan	Stage plan	Work package	Not applicable
Risk	Risk management approach	Stage plan	Work package	Not applicable
Quality	Project product description	Not applicable	Not applicable	Product description
Benefits	Business case	Not applicable	Not applicable	Not applicable

PRINCE2 Controls

As mentioned earlier, many parts of PRINCE2 help control the progress of a project. You have already learned about many of these parts in previous chapters, but this section specifically describes what role they play in controlling the progress of the project.

Project Board Controls

PRINCE2 enables the project board to control the project without the need to attend regular progress and decision-making meetings. This helps reduce the amount of management time the project board members need to dedicate to the project. The control mechanisms provided for the project board are described in this section.

Figure 9.5, a simplified version of the diagram that you saw in Chapter 1, provides an overview of the process model. Using the diagram and the explanation that follows, you will see that the project board has three main ways to control the progress of the project: by using authorizations, by monitoring progress, and by putting in place mechanisms to deal effectively with problems and changes.

Figure 9.5: Project board controls

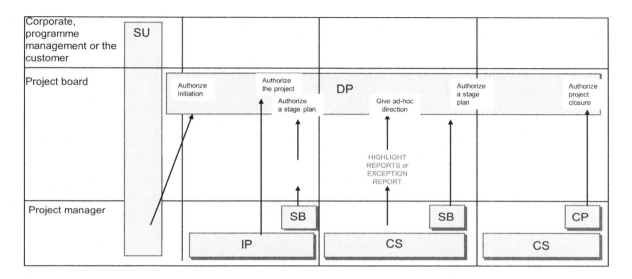

Controlling the Project Using Authorizations

First, the project board can use the directing a project authorizations to control the progress of the project. These authorizations act as gates, which the project has to go through in order to proceed. The project board controls access to these gates and thus controls the progress of the project. These authorizations are used at various times in the project, as described here:

- After the project manager has finished the work of the starting up a project process and created the project brief and the stage plan for the initiation stage, the project cannot proceed any further until the project board authorizes initiation.
- After the project manager has finished the work of the initiating a project process and created the project initiation documentation, the project cannot proceed any further until the project board authorizes the project.
- After the project manager has created the next stage plan, the project cannot proceed any further until the project board authorizes the next stage. This authorization could also be used to authorize an exception plan.
- Finally, the project cannot finish until the project board has authorized closure.

Controlling the Project by Monitoring Progress

An important part of controlling a project is keeping up-to-date on the progress of the project. Without progress updates, it is impossible to know when to do tasks such as decision making or releasing resources.

The project board monitors the progress of the project using highlight reports. During each stage, the project manager regularly creates a highlight report and sends it to the project board. You learn more about the highlight reports in Chapter 10, "Managing the Middle of a Project Successfully with PRINCE2." For now, just think of highlight reports as regular progress reports, showing what has happened in the previous period and what is planned to happen in the next period. The project board will decide on the frequency of highlight reports. For example, they might ask the project manager to send one every week. During the stage, the project board might also use project assurance to monitor progress.

At the end of each stage, the project manager will prepare an end stage report. This will show what has been achieved (or not achieved) in the stage. The project board will review the end stage report at the end stage assessment, when they are deciding whether to authorize the next stage. Once again, you learn more about the end stage report in Chapter 10.

At the end of the project, the project manager will prepare an end project report. This will show what has been achieved (or not achieved) in the entire project. The project board will review the end project report at the end project assessment, when they are deciding whether to authorize the closure of the project. You learn more about the end project report in Chapter 11.

Controlling the Project in Exception and Change Situations

Even in a well-managed project, it's inevitable that things will not go according to plan and that people will change their minds about what they require. With PRINCE2, the project board can be reassured that major problems and changes will be escalated to them, whereas smaller ones can be dealt with at a lower level of management. The project board can use the tolerances they set for the project manager to define the size of problems and changes they wish to be involved with. If the project manager realizes the tolerances she has been given will be breached, she must escalate this situation to the project board using an exception report. The project board can then decide what action to take.

As you learned in Chapter 8, "Change Theme," the project board can also delegate an amount of change authority either to a separate body (called the *change authority*) or to the project manager. The project board can set certain constraints on the ability to authorize change; for example, the project manager might be allowed to authorize changes only up to a certain amount of money. In the same way that the tolerances are used by the project board to define the size of the problems they wish to be involved with, the constraints on the change authority help the project board define the size of the changes they wish to make decisions about.

Project Manager Controls

The project manager uses various parts of PRINCE2 to ensure that each stage she has been given to manage by the project board is kept on track and delivers what is expected. There are three main ways that the project manager controls each stage: by using work packages to delegate work to the teams, by monitoring the progress of the stage, and by putting in place mechanisms to deal effectively with problems and changes.

Controlling the Stage Using Work Packages

The teams are not allowed to start their work until the project manager has authorized a work package. The work package is agreed upon by the team (or the team manager acting on the team's behalf) and the project manager. It details all the relevant information about the team's work, such as what products they need to deliver, how much time and money they have to do the work, and so on.

A Sample Work Package

To understand how a work package is used, consider once again the scenario where a hotel chain has commissioned a project to build a new hotel. Imagine that the project manager needs to delegate some work to the procurement team, because they are responsible for creating a request for tender document that will be sent to building construction companies. The work package that the project manager creates for the procurement team might contain the following information:

Date

This section contains the date that the work package was agreed upon between the project manager and the team manager (or the team members, if there is no team manager).

Team Manager or Person Authorized

This section contains the name of the person authorized to do the work. In this case, it is the name of the person leading the procurement team who will compile the request for tender document.

Work Package Description

This section describes the work to be done. In this case, it describes the type of information that should be included in the request for tender document and what is involved in putting this document together.

Techniques, Processes, and Procedures

This section describes any special approaches that should be used to deliver the specialist products. In this case, it may refer to any company procurement standards.

Development Interfaces

This section specifies the people with whom the delivery team will need to liaise during the delivery of the work package, which PRINCE2 refers to as *development interfaces*. In this case, the procurement team needs to get the hotel designs from the architects.

Operations and Maintenance Interfaces

This section describes any operations and maintenance interfaces, which are other products that the products delivered by the work package will have to work with or connect to in their operational life. The request for tender document won't go into operational life, so this section is not relevant in this example. However, imagine if the work were to create a website where clients could book hotel rooms online. The online booking website would need to connect with the hotel's sales system, so that sales system would be included in this section as an operations interface.

Change Control Requirements

This section might cover a number of change control aspects related to the work, such as how to store and place security around different versions of the products being created, how to obtain copies of other products, how to submit the products to change control, and who to advise of any status changes to the products. On the last point, project support might be tracking the status changes of each product so that they can create product status accounts for the project manager. (There is a lot more information about change control and product status accounts in Chapter 8.) Maybe in this case, the hotel chain's document management system will be used to store all the different versions of the request for tender document.

Joint Agreements

This section specifies the cost, time, and effort that the project manager and the team have agreed will be required to complete the work. It may also specify any key milestone dates when certain interim deliverables will be finished. Maybe in this case, the procurement manager and the project manager have agreed the work will take two weeks and the procurement team will charge the project $500.

Tolerances

This section specifies the time-, cost-, scope-, and risk-level tolerances that the project manager has given the team for the work. Maybe in this case, the project manager will allow a three-day tolerance if the procurement department is delayed due to other work.

Constraints

Some work will have to follow certain general constraints, such as health and safety rules or security constraints. In this request for tender document example, there might be a constraint that no company documents can be taken off site and that all documents must be regularly scanned for computer viruses.

Reporting Arrangements

In this section, the project manager defines how often the teams report to her as well as the type of information that she expects to see in a progress report. This is effectively defining the frequency and composition of the checkpoint reports. The checkpoint reports are progress reports sent from the team to the project manager on a regular basis. (You learn more about the checkpoint reports in Chapter 10.). In this case, maybe the project manager asks for a status update at the end of the first week of the work.

Problem Handling and Escalation

This section describes how the team must escalate problems and issues. In this example, the procurement team may be required to call the project manager immediately if a problem occurs and then send a written report regarding the matter within 24 hours.

Extracts or References

This section specifies other important documents that the team might need. For example, the stage plan is a useful reference because it shows the team how their work fits in with the rest of the activities in the stage. Another important set of documents is the product descriptions for the products to be delivered within the work package. In this example, a necessary reference is the product description for the request for tender document.

Approval Method

This section describes the approval method to be used for this work package, which includes the person or group who will sign off on the work from the work package and how the project manager should be advised of this. In the example, this section might specify that the head of procurement is responsible for signing off on the request for tender document.

PRINCE2 recommends that there should be a space on the work package to record both its initial authorization and then its acceptance and return when the work is completed. In this example, there might be two spaces at the bottom where the project manager and the team manager sign (or digitally sign) when the work is authorized and when the work is completed.

Exam Questions about Work Packages

The Practitioner exam might ask you detailed questions about what each section of the work package should contain. It is difficult to remember all the information about what should go where in a PRINCE2 management product. However, don't forget that in the Practitioner exam, you can refer to *Managing Successful Projects with PRINCE2.* This is especially useful for questions about management products like the work package, because Appendix A shows you exactly what each of the management products should contain.

Controlling the Stage by Monitoring Progress

Just as it's important for the project board to monitor the progress of the project using highlight reports and end stage reports, it is important for the project manager to monitor the progress of a stage using checkpoint reports. Checkpoint reports are created by the team managers (or team members, if there isn't a team manager) and sent to the project manager on a regular basis. They update the project manager on the progress of the team's work. As you saw in the previous section, the project manager defines the composition and the frequency of the checkpoint reports in the work package.

In addition to tracking the progress of work completed against the stage plan, the project manager should also look out for early warning signs of potential problems. For example, maybe the work is being completed on time, but an increasing number of issues are being raised that are not being resolved. In my experience, I have found that if the customer is raising a lot of requests for change, it could be an indication that they are not happy with the official signed-off specification of the product. The frequency of the checkpoint reports might vary in different situations. For example, with a new team, the project manager might ask for weekly reports at first, until she is satisfied that the team has gained some experience in their work. Once the project manager has more confidence in the team, she might request that reports be submitted every two weeks.

Controlling the Stage in Exception and Change Situations

The last way that the project manager controls the stage is by using the PRINCE2 logs and registers to review progress and identify any issues or risks that need to be resolved. Anyone can raise an issue or a risk in PRINCE2. When they do so, they should inform the project manager so that it can be logged in the appropriate log or register. (Informal issues are put in the daily log; formal issues, problems or concerns, requests for change, and off-specifications go in the issue register; and risks are put in the risk register.) The project manager then uses these logs and registers to review the progress of the stage and checks to see whether there are any pressing issues, risks, or actions that might throw the stage off track. For more information about the risk register, see Chapter 7; for more on the issue register, see Chapter 8.

The project manager creates the daily log in the starting up a project process. It is basically the project manager's notebook and/or personal action list, which is sometimes referred to as the project manager's diary. This diary is a useful tool that allows the project manager to track the progress of a variety of things that would not be covered in the more formal management product, such as the issue register or the stage plan. It allows the project manager to control her day-to-day activities and serves as a useful repository for the project manager to record observations about the project. One of these observations on its own might seem insignificant, but when put together with other similar observations, might alert the project manager of new issues or risks. In addition, the daily log is sometimes used to record issues and risks during the starting up a project process if the other registers have not yet been set up. (The issue, quality, and risk registers are officially set up later in the process model, in the initiating a project process.)

When the project manager delegates work, she sets tolerances for the teams. If the teams believe they will breach these work package tolerances, they must escalate the situation to the project manager. Their work package will show them how to escalate situations to the project manager. This allows the project manager to define the sorts of problems she wishes to be involved with and which ones she would prefer the teams to sort out on their own.

Event-Driven vs. Time-Driven Controls

In the last few sections, you have seen how many different areas of PRINCE2 help control the project. For example, the work package helps the project manager control the team, and the authorizations help the project board control the progress of the project. All these different areas are known as *controls*. PRINCE2 splits up controls into two types: event-driven or time-driven.

> *Event-driven controls* occur after some sort of event, such as the end of the stage or the end of the project. For example, the end stage report is an event-driven control and is driven by the end of the stage occurring. Another example is the exception report, which is driven by a forecast breach of stage tolerances.

> *Time-driven controls* on the other hand, are not driven by anything happening—they just occur at regular intervals. For example, it is Monday morning and it is time to write the weekly highlight report. Another example of a time-driven control is the team writing a regular checkpoint report.

Controlling the Capturing and Reporting of Lessons

Students always find the fact that the lessons log and the *lessons report* are covered in a theme about tracking and controlling progress rather unusual. It does seem a rather awkward admission to this area of PRINCE2, but I will attempt to explain why it is here.

As you have seen already, one of the key principles of PRINCE2 is to "learn from experience." In the starting up a project process, the project manager creates the lessons log. The lessons log is used for two purposes. First, it is used as a repository of experience from previous initiatives that might be useful in the management of this project. Second, it is used to record lessons that are being learned on the current project that might be useful for others. The lessons log is therefore a way of controlling the flow of lessons and experience in the project. You can see the composition of the lessons log in Figure 9.6.

Figure 9.6: Composition of the lessons log

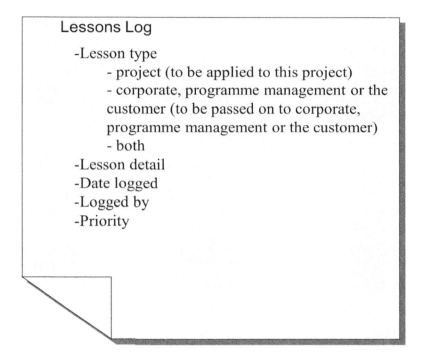

Lessons Log

-Lesson type
   - project (to be applied to this project)
   - corporate, programme management or the customer (to be passed on to corporate, programme management or the customer)
   - both
-Lesson detail
-Date logged
-Logged by
-Priority

When the project management team is reviewing the progress of the project, lessons often become apparent. For example, the team might realize they are behind schedule and that more care should have been taken over the estimating of the tasks. The lessons captured by the project manager could apply to both the management of the project and the specialist activities used to create the specialist products.

Lessons are passed on to other parts of the organization using a lessons report. A lessons report could be created at any time in the project, but typically it is created at the end of a stage or the project and is included in the end stage report or the end project report, respectively. The recipient(s) of the lessons report should be in a position to use the experience to improve the programme or the organization. Those in charge of the organization's quality management system would be one typical recipient. Another reason a lessons report might be created is when more information needs to be recorded for a particular entry in the lessons log.

Roles Involved with the Progress Theme

This chapter described the progress-related responsibilities for the various PRINCE2 roles. Here is a quick review of these responsibilities to help you prepare for the exams:

Corporate, Programme Management, or the Customer
Corporate, programme management, or the customer sets project tolerances and documents them in the project mandate. They will also make decisions regarding forecast breaches in project-level tolerances.

Project Board
The project board sets stage-level tolerances for the project manager. They will make decisions regarding forecast breaches in stage-level tolerances. The project board controls progress by authorizing the project on a stage-by-stage basis.

Project Manager
The project manager will control the progress of a stage by authorizing teams to deliver specialist products using work packages. The project manager sets work package-level tolerances for the team manager and the teams. He will make decisions regarding forecast breaches in work package-level tolerances. The project manager will use the stage plan to monitor the progress of the stage, manage the production of progress reports, such as the highlight reports and the end stage reports, and control issues and risks using the issue register and the risk register. The project manager will produce exception reports when stage-level or project-level tolerances are forecast to be exceeded and, when requested by the project board, will create exception plans.

Team Manager
The teams (and the team manager, if there is one) agree on the work packages with the project manager. They must escalate any forecast breach in work package tolerances to the project manager and regularly report progress using checkpoint reports.

Project Assurance
Project assurance monitors the project to ensure that forecast progress will not exceed project-, stage-, or work package-level tolerances. Business assurance will have a particular focus on verifying that there are no new risks to the business case for the project.

Project Support
Project support assists the project manager with the creation of progress reports and the maintenance of the project's issues and logs.

Tailoring the Progress Theme

The key to successfully using PRINCE2 is adapting and tailoring the method given the characteristics of the project and the environment the project is operating within. The following sections show you how the progress theme might be adapted to better suit certain situations. This is something you might be tested on in the Practitioner exam.

Minimum Requirements

Organizations with a less-formal project management approach or that are running smaller, less-complicated projects might choose to cut back on some of the progress theme ideas. Some minimum requirements, however, must be followed in order for a project team to claim they are following PRINCE2's progress theme.

The first minimum requirement of the progress theme is that the project should be managed by stages. That is, the project should be broken into stages, and the project board should authorize the project manager to manage one stage at a time. Although this is a progress theme requirement, rather confusingly PRINCE2 explains how to manage a project by stages in the plans theme. (If you've forgotten how to structure a project into stages, refer to Chapter 5 in this book.)

The second minimum requirement is that each level of management sets tolerance targets for the level below it, and then proceeds to manage that level using the manage by exception principle. This helps each management level clearly delegate authority to its subordinate level.

If an exception occurs, the project management team might analyze the impact of that exception on the project objectives, but at a minimum, they must review the impact on the business justification for the project.

The project management team must also describe the approach to controlling progress in the project initiation documentation. This would be put into the project controls section and summarize the project-level controls. These controls include the management stage boundaries, agreed tolerances, how the project will be monitored, and which progress reports will be created.

Finally, as with many of the minimum requirements of the themes, PRINCE2 states that the project management team must consider any lessons when implementing the ideas of the progress theme.

Tailoring the Management Products

The lessons log might be quite a formal document on some projects, whereas on other projects it might be just an informal notebook. Remember that sometimes a lessons report might be created if you want to describe a particular entry in the lessons log in more detail. The lessons reports that are created at the end of a stage or end of the project might simply be combined with the end stage report and the end project report, respectively.

The work packages might take many forms. A PRINCE2 project might be run in a whole range of different environments and be working with a whole range of different specialist teams. A work package that might be right for an architect would be completely wrong for a team of software engineers. The important thing, though, is no matter the format or what tools were used to put together the work package, the project manager must use the PRINCE2 product description of the work package as a checklist and make sure all the relevant information has been included. This product description is found in Appendix A of the *Managing Successful Projects with PRINCE2* manual.

Another factor that might change the format of the work package is whether the team is an internal or external team. An internal team's work package might be more informal, whereas an external team's work package might be a formal statement of work or part of a legal contract.

The exception reports are created by the project manager and sent to the project board to alert them of a forecast breach of stage tolerances. The key thing here is that the report contains all the useful information that the board members would need in such a situation and is in a format that is easily understood. It would not be good if the project manager, faced with a major breach of tolerances, sends a complicated, arcane report to the project board, which has no idea what it means. Therefore, the key to tailoring an exception report is to ensure that the project board approves of its format, and that they understand the importance of reading and responding to such reports as quickly as possible.

I worked on a project where the project manager was constantly sending exception reports to the project board and moaning that he never got any replies. When I looked at the reports he was sending, I could understand why. Many of them were very lengthy documents containing a lot of technical terminology that was very difficult to understand.

Exam Spotlight

As I have said, the progress theme is a slightly different one because it looks at how the whole of PRINCE2 controls the project environment. When it comes to tailoring management products, if you were applying PRINCE2, you would want to consider how to tailor all 26 of them. However, a progress theme Practitioner exam question might test you on how to tailor nine of the management products: daily log, checkpoint report, end project report, end stage report, exception report, highlight report, lessons log, lessons report, and work package. To improve the flow of this chapter, I have focused on the daily log, the exception report, the lessons log, the lessons report, and the work package. I cover the checkpoint report, the highlight report, and the end stage report in Chapter 10, "Managing the Middle of the Project Successfully with PRINCE2"; and I cover the end project report in Chapter 11, "Managing the End of the Project Successfully with PRINCE2." Don't be surprised, however, if the Practitioner exam includes a progress theme question on one of the management products I cover in the later chapters.

If you get a question on how to tailor the management products in a Practitioner exam question about a theme, it is not obvious where to find useful information in the *Managing Successful Projects with PRINCE2* manual. That is because the information on tailoring management products is in the process chapters, not in the theme where it is tested! The trick is knowing which process chapter to look in. (Remember, you can take the PRINCE2 manual into the exam, and it is an extremely useful reference when you're trying to work out the right answers.) The information on how to tailor a management product is always towards the end of the process chapter where that management product is created. For example, in the progress theme, you might be tested on how to tailor the exception report. The project manager creates the exception report in the controlling a stage process, so the information on how to tailor the exception report is towards the end of the controlling a stage chapter in the *Managing Successful Projects with PRINCE2* manual.

Remember that in Practitioner exam questions on the progress theme, you might be tested on some management products that I explain more fully in other chapters of this study guide. If you get stuck on a question about how to tailor the highlight report, for example, just remember at what point during a project's lifecycle that report is created. Since the highlight report is created in the controlling a stage

process, you would look in that chapter in the PRINCE2 manual for useful information on how to answer the exam question.

Projects within Programmes

For projects within programmes, there will probably be a programme-wide approach to controlling the progress of the project. This might include certain formats and timings of progress reports, such as for the highlight reports or end stage reports. The project management team will need to take account of these programme-wide standards when managing the project.

Agile Environments

One of the features of many agile approaches is delivering the products in a number of time-bound iterative approaches. In Chapter 1, for example, you saw that the agile approach called Scrum recommends delivering products in a number of sprints that typically last a month or less. According to the rules of Scrum, once a sprint begins, it cannot be shortened or lengthened. As I will explain later, this leads to a situation where setting scope tolerances is important.

All project managers, whether operating in an agile environment or not, are faced with the so-called iron triangle or triple constraints of project management. There is a relationship between the scope of the project, the time to deliver the products, and the cost of delivering the products. For example, if the project is running out of time, perhaps due to poor estimating, the project management team has no option but to use one of the other two constraints. They might choose to try to catch up by adding more resources and thus increasing the costs of the project, or alternatively, they might decrease the scope of products to be delivered.

In a non-agile, more traditional approach to project management, the scope of what to deliver is often seen as inflexible. (In PRINCE2 terms, this means there would be no scope tolerance.) With no flexibility over what to deliver, if the project management team gets into trouble and realizes they have underestimated how long the work will take, the project end date often starts to shift and gets later and later. This is one of the key reasons that PRINCE2 recommends setting time tolerances. No time estimate can be 100-percent accurate, so allowing some flexibility over when to deliver something gives each level of management some leeway before they have to escalate the situation.

As I said previously, however, the project manager in an agile environment might not be able to move the deadline, because she has to deliver within a time-bound delivery iteration or sprint. If the project starts to run into trouble, and with no option to shift the deadline back in time, rather than increase the cost, agile projects will often decrease what will be delivered. As you have seen, a scope tolerance is an allowable leeway on what to deliver. By allowing the project to be flexible regarding what to deliver, the likelihood that the delivery iterations or sprints will always hit their deadline dates is greatly increased. This means that in an agile environment, there is often more focus on setting scope tolerances than time tolerances.

Project managers in an agile environment will be focused more on how much scope has been delivered rather than time or cost overruns. (Scope might be measured in a number of ways, from completed products, features, user stories, or requirements.) As stated earlier, this is because once the short delivery iterations or sprints have been started, they are fixed in terms of time. As a result, there shouldn't be a time overrun, and if the only cost to the product is people who are being used on a time basis, there shouldn't be a cost overrun either. So the key part of the triple constraints that the agile project manager needs to focus on when measuring progress is the scope.

Figure 9.7: The triple constraints of project management

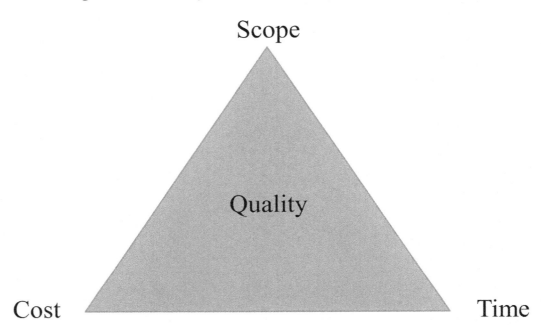

Linking the Progress Theme with the PRINCE2 Principles

In Chapter 1, I talked about the seven PRINCE2 principles. In some ways, all seven principles contribute to implementing the progress theme; however, the three that are most important are manage by exception, manage by stage, and learn from experience.

As you saw in the "Minimum Requirements" section earlier in this chapter, to be following the progress theme, the project management team must, at a minimum, set tolerances for each level of management that clearly define that level of management's authority. Then, if any level of management is forecasting to breach their tolerances, they must escalate to the level above them. This approach follows the principle of manage by exception.

Another minimum requirement is that the project be broken up into stages and that the project board authorizes a stage at a time for the project manager to deliver. This is implementing the principle of manage by stages.

Finally, at a minimum, the project management team must consider useful experience when determining how to control the progress of the project. This is the principle of learn from experience. (Incidentally, in PRINCE2, it's pretty much a given that before you do anything, you should find out if there is any useful experience that might help.)

Summary

In this chapter, you learned about the progress theme. The progress theme covers the various ways that PRINCE2 controls the activities, resources, and people on a project to ensure that the project's objectives are achieved.

The first topic you learned about was tolerances. A tolerance is an allowable deviation of the cost and time targets that have been given to one level of management by the management level above. You saw that tolerances can also be set for the specifications of a product (quality tolerances), the number of products to be delivered (scope tolerances), the level of acceptable uncertainty (risk tolerances), and the benefits that the project's products will bring to the organization (benefit tolerances).

You saw that the time, cost, scope, and risk tolerances might be set at three different levels. Corporate, programme management, or the customer sets project tolerances for the project board; the project board sets stage tolerances for the project manager; and the project manager sets work package tolerances for the team. Quality tolerances are established either at a project level or at a product level, and benefit tolerances are set only at a project level.

You learned that the tolerances help one management level manage the one below by exception. If one management level realizes that the tolerances they have been set are forecast to be breached, they are in a situation called an exception. They must then immediately escalate the situation to the management level above for a decision on how to proceed.

This chapter also showed you how the project board uses various parts of PRINCE2 to control the project's progress. First, they use the authorization activities in the directing a project process to authorize one stage of the project at a time. Second, they need to keep up-to-date on the latest progress of the project in order to control it and so receive progress reports in the form of the highlight reports and the end stage reports. Finally, the project board controls change and issue situations by defining what sorts of situations they want to be involved in and what sort of situations can be resolved by lower levels of management. This is done by setting tolerances and constraints on change authority for lower levels of management.

In addition, you saw how the project manager controls the progress of a stage. The project manager uses the work package to delegate work to the teams, checkpoint reports to monitor the teams' work, and the various logs and registers to control the actions, threats, opportunities, and issues of the project.

You learned that all the parts of PRINCE2 used to control the project are called controls. There are two types of controls: event-driven and time-driven. Event-driven controls occur after a particular thing has happened. For example, after an exception, the project manager creates an exception report. Time-driven controls occur on a regular basis, such as the regular sending of highlight reports or checkpoint reports.

Finally, you learned about how the progress theme can be adapted to better suit certain situations, such as smaller, less complex projects, projects that are within larger programmes, and projects that use agile delivery methods.

Foundation Exam Essentials

Explain the purpose of the progress theme.
The purpose of the progress theme is to establish mechanisms to monitor and compare the actual achievements against those planned, to provide a forecast for the project objectives and the project's continued viability, and to control any unacceptable deviations.

Understand the concept of tolerances and exceptions.
A tolerance is a permissible deviation above and below a plan's target for time and cost without escalating the deviation to the next level of management. There may also be tolerances for quality, scope, benefit, and risk. An exception is a situation where it can be forecast that there will be a deviation beyond the agreed tolerance levels.

Know when and how tolerances are set.
Corporate, programme management, or the customer sets project tolerances at the beginning of the project; the project board sets stage tolerances at the beginning of each stage; and the project manager sets work package tolerances when a work package is delegated to the team.

Know in which management products tolerances are documented.
Cost, time, and scope tolerances are documented at a project, stage, and work package level in the project plan, stage plan, and work package, respectively. Risk tolerances are documented at a project level in the risk management approach, at a stage level in the stage plan, and at a work package level in the work package. Quality tolerances are documented in the project product description or the product descriptions, and benefit tolerances are documented in the business case.

Know how exceptions are reported.
The team manager reports work package-level exceptions by raising an issue to the project manager; the project manager reports stage-level exceptions by escalating an issue report or an exception report to the project board; and the project board reports project-level exceptions by notifying corporate, programme management, or the customer.

Understand the different levels of tolerance and how they relate to the application of management by exception by the different levels of management.
Time, cost, risk, and scope tolerances can be set at three different levels—project, stage, and work package—and these levels are set by corporate, programme management, or the customer, the project board, and the project manager, respectively. When a management level forecasts a breach in the tolerances that have been set by the management level above, they need to escalate the situation to that higher management level.

Understand the purpose of the daily log.
The daily log is used to record informal issues, required actions, or significant events not caught by the other PRINCE2 registers and logs. It acts as the project diary for the project manager. It can also be used as a repository for issues and risks during the starting up a project process, if the other registers have not been set up.

Understand the purpose of the lessons log.
The project manager creates the lessons log in the starting up a project process and updates it throughout the project. The project manager uses it to collate lessons learned from previous initiatives that would be useful for the current project and also to collate experience from the current project that might be useful for future initiatives.

Understand the purpose of the lessons report.
The project manager creates the lessons report to pass on lessons from the project to those who might usefully employ them. The lessons report can be created at any time in the project, but it is typically created during the managing a stage boundary process as part of the end stage report, or during the closing a project process as part of the end project report. The project manager might also create a lessons report if more information needs to be recorded about a particular entry in the lessons log.

Understand the purpose of the work package.
The project manager creates the work package in the controlling a stage process in order to define the information that the team manager or team needs to deliver one or more products. Once the team manager or team member has accepted the work package in the managing product delivery process, she is responsible for delivering the products that it described.

Understand the purpose of the exception report.
The project manager creates the exception report during the controlling a stage process if she is forecasting her stage tolerance will be breached. It provides information about the exception to the project board, including options that have been considered to deal with the exception, and allows the project board to make a decision on the situation in the directing a project process.

Describe PRINCE2's minimum requirements for applying the progress theme.
As a minimum for controlling progress, PRINCE2 requires that a project management team does the following:
- Define its approach to controlling progress in the project initiation documentation
- Be managed by stages
- Set tolerances and be managed by exceptions against these tolerances
- Review the business justification when exceptions are raised
- Consider lessons that would provide useful experience when controlling progress

Understand the concepts of event-driven and time-driven controls.
Event-driven controls are used to control a particular event that has occurred, such as the end of a stage or an exception. Time-driven controls do not respond to an event but occur at a regular frequency, such as the creation of highlight reports or checkpoint reports.

Practitioner Exam Essentials

Demonstrate an understanding of the daily log.
Demonstrate an understanding that the project manager creates the daily log during the starting up a project process and that she will use the log to record informal issues, personal action points,

or other significant events not captured by the other PRINCE2 logs or registers. Understand that there may be more than one daily log because team managers may also create one. Know that PRINCE2 does not define the composition or format for this management product.

Demonstrate an understanding of the work package.

Demonstrate an understanding that the project manager creates work packages in order to delegate work to teams and to inform those teams what is required of them. Know that the project manager creates work packages during the controlling a stage process and that teams accept work packages in the managing product delivery process. Understand that work packages might be derived from an existing commercial agreement between the customer and supplier, a quality management approach, a change control approach, or a stage plan. Know that a work package could be a document, a conversation between the project manager and a team manager, or an entry in a project management tool. Know the composition of the work package.

Demonstrate an understanding of the exception report.

Demonstrate an understanding that the project manager creates an exception report in order to escalate a forecast breach of stage tolerances or a request for change to the project board. Know that the project manager creates exception reports during the controlling a stage process. Understand that exception reports might be derived from plans, a PRINCE2 register or report, or from project board advice. Know that an exception report could be a document, an issue recorded in the minutes of a progress review, or an entry in a project management tool. Know the composition of the exception report.

Demonstrate an understanding of the lessons log.

Demonstrate an understanding that the project manager creates the lessons log during the starting up a project process and uses it to record both experience from previous projects that would help the current project and experience from the current project that would help future projects. Understand that the lessons log might be derived from any of the PRINCE2 management products from both the current and previous projects. Know that a lessons log could be a document, stand-alone log, an entry in a project management tool, or part of an integrated project register for all risks, actions, and issues. Know the composition of the lessons log.

Demonstrate an understanding of the lessons report.

Demonstrate an understanding that the project manager creates a lessons report in order to pass on useful experience that could be applied on other projects. Know that the project manager could create a lessons report at any time during the project but typically would include one within highlight, end stage, or end project reports. Understand that a lessons report might be derived from the lessons log. Know that PRINCE2 does not define the composition or format for this management product.

Demonstrate an understanding of the recommended roles and responsibilities within the progress theme.

Demonstrate an understanding that corporate, programme management, or the customer sets project tolerances that the project board must direct the project within, that the project board sets stage tolerances that the project manager must manage the stage within, and that the project manager sets work package tolerances that the team must deliver work packages within.

Assess and critique an approach to applying the progress theme.
This must include the ability to understand the purpose and format of the work package, exception report, lessons log, lessons report, and daily log. It should include an understanding of how to set tolerances, raise exceptions, and manage by exception. It should also include the ability to adapt the approach to controlling progress to different project contexts (for example, a small project, an agile project, a project with external third-party organizations, or a project operating within a programme environment). Finally, it should include an ability to show how a given approach to managing progress aligns with the principles of PRINCE2.

Review Questions

The remainder of this chapter contains mock exam questions, first for the Foundation exam and then for the Practitioner exam.

Foundation Exam Questions

1. When does the project manager allocate tolerances to the team manager or team?
    A. When planning the stage
    B. When authorizing the stage
    C. When authorizing a work package
    D. When approving a product description

2. Which of the following information is recorded in the daily log?
    (1) A risk identified in starting up a project
    (2) An informal issue
    (3) A request for change
    (4) An off-specification
    A. 1 and 2
    B. 2 and 3
    C. 3 and 4
    D. 1 and 4

3. Which management product is used to collate experience that may be useful for input into the project's strategies and plans?
    A. Lessons log
    B. Exception report
    C. Issue register
    D. Project initiation documentation

4. When an exception is raised, what must be done as a minimum requirement for applying the progress theme?
    A. Send out a notification to all interested stakeholders
    B. Create an exception report
    C. Review the business justification for the project
    D. Record details of the exception in the next highlight report

5. Which management products would be used to document any flexibility on what will be delivered?
    (1) Quality register
    (2) Project plan
    (3) Stage plan
    (4) Product description
    A. 1 and 2
    B. 2 and 3
    C. 3 and 4
    D. 1 and 4

6. Which of the following management products are event-driven controls?
    (1) Highlight report
    (2) End stage report
    (3) Exception report
    (4) Checkpoint report
    A. 1 and 2
    B. 2 and 3
    C. 3 and 4
    D. 1 and 4

7. Which management product forms an agreement between the project manager and a team manager about which products the team should deliver?
    A. Stage plan
    B. Work package
    C. Product description
    D. Project product description

8. What management product should the project manager create in order to notify the project board of a forecast breach of stage tolerances?
    A. Checkpoint report
    B. Highlight report
    C. End stage report
    D. Exception report

9. Which of the following is a purpose of the progress theme?
    A. To provide a forecast for the project's continued viability
    B. To identify and control uncertainty
    C. To define how the project will verify that products are fit for purpose
    D. To establish the project's structure of accountability

10. What is a purpose of an exception report?
    A. To record options to respond to an exception
    B. To replace a stage plan following a stage-level exception
    C. To replace a project plan following a project-level exception
    D. To notify the project manager of a work-package-level exception

Practitioner Exam Questions

The following Practitioner questions are divided into two sections by question type and are based on the Practitioner exam scenario in Appendix B.

Section 1: Matching Questions

Column 1 in the following table contains five statements related to tolerances for the Website Project, and Column 2 lists the different tolerance areas. For each statement in Column 1, select the tolerance area (A–F in Column 2) that it represents. Choose only one tolerance area for each item statement. Each tolerance area can be used once, more than once, or not at all.

Column 1	Column 2
1. A customer review feature for each piece of furniture is not a mandatory requirement for the initial launch of the website, but it would be nice to have.	A. Time
2. Forecast online furniture sales should be between $1.5 million to $2 million per annum.	B. Cost
3. Users of the new website should find it easy to use and should be able to locate any piece of information from the home page within two to four mouse-clicks.	C. Scope
4. The aggregated expected monetary value of all threats to the project must remain within 15 percent of the project's budget.	D. Quality
5. The overall project budget can be exceeded by up to $20,000.	E. Benefits
	F. Risk

Section 2: Classic Multiple-Choice Questions

Exam Spotlight

Remember that for the Practitioner exam, you are allowed to refer to the official PRINCE2 manual (*Managing Successful Projects with PRINCE2*). This is a great help. I would say one of the key differences between passing and failing the Practitioner exam is knowing how to use the PRINCE2 manual during the exam. Some of the questions in the exam rely on you finding very specific pieces of information quickly from the manual.

For progress theme questions, where might you look in the PRINCE2 manual for useful information? The first (and most obvious) place is the progress theme chapter itself. The chapter begins by discussing the purpose of the progress theme, and then looks at the minimum requirements for applying the progress theme. Next, there is a section on tolerances, including a useful table that gives examples of each tolerance area and shows in which management product they would be recorded. In the middle of the chapter, there is a section on raising each level of exception. Then there is a brief section that provides guidance for effective progress management and explains how to tailor the theme to different situations. (The last section, which focuses on techniques that are relevant to controlling progress, is not examinable, so you won't need to refer to it during the exam.) I recommend that you review the progress theme chapter in the PRINCE2 manual before the exam and familiarize yourself with how the information is laid out.

In addition to the progress theme chapter, a few other places in the PRINCE2 manual might be useful. You might be tested on how to tailor any one of the management products related to controlling progress. As I said in a previous Exam Spotlight earlier in this chapter, the information on how to tailor management products is always in the chapter about the process in which that particular management product was created. The information is always set out as a table towards the back of the relevant process chapter, under the tailoring guidelines section. So, for progress theme questions about tailoring the lessons log, look in the starting up a project process chapter; for questions about tailoring the exception report, the highlight report, or the work package, look in the controlling a stage process chapter; for information about tailoring the checkpoint report, look in the managing product delivery chapter; for information about tailoring the end stage report plus the lessons log, look in the managing a stage boundary process; and for information about how to tailor the end project report plus the lessons log, look in the closing a project process.

No matter which topic you are being tested on, two rules always hold true when it comes to using the PRINCE2 manual during the exam. If you are being tested on management products, a really good reference in the PRINCE2 manual (in addition to the sections I already mentioned above for tailoring management products) is Appendix A. This appendix shows you all 26 management products and gives you a lot of useful information about each one. Many questions on the exam ask you under which heading within a management product certain types of information might go. For these types of questions, the composition section under each management product in Appendix A is very useful.

The other general rule is that when you are being tested on roles and responsibilities, Appendix C is often useful. As I said previously, there is a table of responsibilities within the progress theme chapter; however, you'll often find more information about progress-related responsibilities in Appendix C.

1. During the initiation stage, the chief executive of Quality Furniture has said that any threat identified during the project that might impact the current sales from the mail order catalogs or the existing shops must be immediately escalated to him. The project manager has updated the risk management approach with this information. Is this appropriate, and why or why not?
   A. Yes, because the project manager should record project-level tolerances in each of the approaches contained within the project initiation documentation.
   B. Yes, because the project manager should record project-level risk tolerances in the risk management approach.
   C. No, risk tolerances can be defined only in terms of an overall expected value of all the risks on the project.
   D. No, because the executive should ensure that risks associated with the business case are identified, assessed, and controlled.

2. The project is in stage two, and the First Tech consultant is in the process of collating the requirements for the website. She has reported to the project manager that some of the staff she needs to talk to have not returned her calls or have not turned up to meetings. The project manager has recorded these problems in the daily log and now realizes there is a pattern to these events. He has decided to manage this as a formal issue and is preparing an issue report. Is this appropriate, and why or why not?
   A. Yes, because when a number of items in the daily log are collated, they might indicate a new issue.
   B. Yes, because the project manager should create an issue report for each observation recorded in the daily log.
   C. No, because the daily log is for informal issues that do not require an issue report.
   D. No, because having spotted the issue the First Tech consultation should prepare the issue report.

3. The project is in stage two and the project manager is preparing the work package for a Quality Furniture team who will prepare the request for tender document. To save time, he has decided to use exactly the same format as the work package he created for the First Tech consultant who is collating the requirements. Is this appropriate, and why or why not?

    A. Yes, because the project manager is responsible for preparing the work packages.
    B. Yes, because the work package should always follow the same format.
    C. No, because work packages for internal teams and those for external suppliers are likely to differ.
    D. No, because the work package for the Quality Furniture team should have been created in the initiation stage.

Chapter

10

Managing the Middle of a Project Successfully with PRINCE2

PRINCE2 Foundation Exam Objectives Covered in This Chapter:

☑ Explain the purpose, objectives, and context of the controlling a stage process.

☑ Explain the purpose, objectives, and context of the managing product delivery process.

☑ Explain the purpose, objectives, and context of the managing a stage boundary process.

☑ Explain the purpose of the checkpoint report, the highlight report, and the end stage report.

PRINCE2 Practitioner Exam Objectives Covered in This Chapter:

☑ Carry out the controlling a stage process activities, and Recommended associated actions:
  - Work packages:
    - Authorize a work package
    - Review work package status
    - Receive completed work packages
  - Monitoring and reporting:
    - Review the management stage status
    - Report highlights
  - Issues:
    - Capture and examine issues and risks
    - Escalate issues and risks
    - Take corrective action

☑ Demonstrating an understanding of:
  - The recommended roles and responsibilities within the process
  - How the themes may be applied

☑ **Assess whether controlling a stage process activities/ actions, roles and responsibilities are effective and fit for purpose, taking into consideration: the context, the PRINCE2 principles, and the purpose and objectives of the process.**

☑ **Carry out the managing product delivery process activities, and**
  - Recommended associated actions:
    - Accept a work package
    - Execute a work package
    - Deliver a work package
  - Demonstrating an understanding of:
    - The recommended roles and responsibilities within the process
    - How the themes may be applied

☑ **Assess whether managing product delivery stage process activities/actions, roles and responsibilities are effective and fit for purpose, taking into consideration: the context, the PRINCE2 principles, and the purpose and objectives of the process.**

☑ **Carry out the managing a stage boundary process activities, and**
  - Recommended associated actions:
    - Plan the next management stage
    - Update the project plan
    - Update the business case
    - Report management stage end
    - Produce an exception plan

☑ **Demonstrating an understanding of:**
  - The recommended roles and responsibilities within the process
  - How the themes may be applied

☑ **Assess whether managing a stage boundary process activities/actions, roles and responsibilities are effective and fit for purpose, taking into consideration: the context, the PRINCE2 principles, and the purpose and objectives of the process.**

☑ **Carry out the directing a project process activities that are used in the middle of a project, and recommended associated actions:**
  - Give ad hoc direction

- Authorize a stage or an exception plan.

☑ **Demonstrating an understanding of:**
- The recommended roles and responsibilities within the process
- How the themes may be applied

☑ **Demonstrate an understanding of the following management products, and which roles are responsible for each:**
- Highlight report
- Checkpoint report
- End stage report

In this chapter, you learn how PRINCE2 is used to manage the middle of a project. In PRINCE2, the middle of the project begins at the completion of the initiation stage and ends when the project manager starts to prepare for the end of the project in the closing a project process.

The main focus of the middle of the project is to deliver specialist products (although some management products, such as the end stage report, are also delivered). For example, if the project team were building a new hotel, in the middle of the project, they would deliver specialist products such as the swimming pool, the restaurant, the furniture, and the sales systems. Before and after the middle of the project, only management products such as the project initiation documentation and the end project report are delivered.

The middle of the project could last for a few days, weeks, months, or sometimes even years. The project manager manages the middle of the project on behalf of the project board, one delivery stage at a time. At the end of each delivery stage (apart from the final one), the project manager asks the project board for authorization to move to the next delivery stage.

In this chapter, you learn how the project manager uses the controlling a stage process to manage each delivery stage. The controlling a stage process covers how the project manager delegates work to the teams, deals with reporting, and handles problems and issues.

This chapter also covers how the teams and team managers use the managing product delivery process to control the delivery of their work. This includes negotiating for resources and time with the project manager, ensuring that the delivery of their work follows quality standards, and reporting to the project manager.

Finally, this chapter covers how the end of each stage (apart from the final stage) is handled using the managing a stage boundary process. At this point, the project manager needs to plan the work for the succeeding stage and ask the project board for permission to proceed to that stage.

Overview of the Middle of a PRINCE2 Project

The "An End-to-End Walk-through of PRINCE2" section of Chapter 1, "Overview of PRINCE2," provides an overview of the process model. I recommend that you review that section again, in particular the "Activities in the Middle of the Project" subsection, before continuing with this chapter. This will help you understand how the three processes discussed in this chapter (controlling a stage, managing product delivery, and managing a stage boundary) fit into the overall method.

Figure 10.1 is taken from the section "An End-to-End Walk-through of PRINCE2" in Chapter 1. I have highlighted the part of the model you will learn about in this chapter.

Figure 10.1: Middle of the project

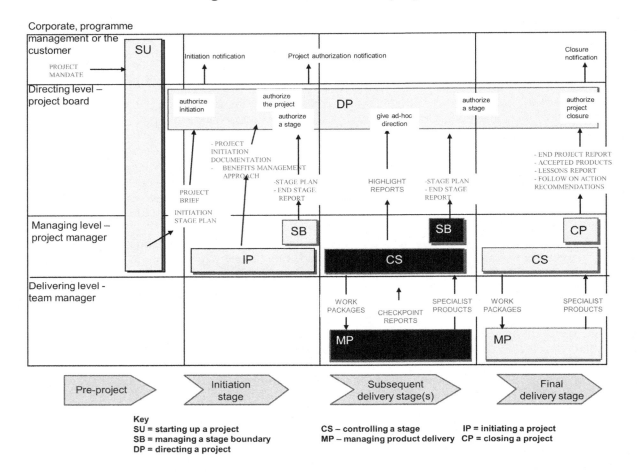

The Controlling a Stage and Managing Product Delivery Processes

The project manager uses the eight activities in the controlling a stage process to manage each delivery stage (see Figure 10.2). During each delivery stage, the teams will be working on creating the specialist products. The teams use the activities in the managing product delivery process. As you can see in the figure, the managing product delivery process involves three activities.

Figure 10.2: Controlling a stage and managing product delivery

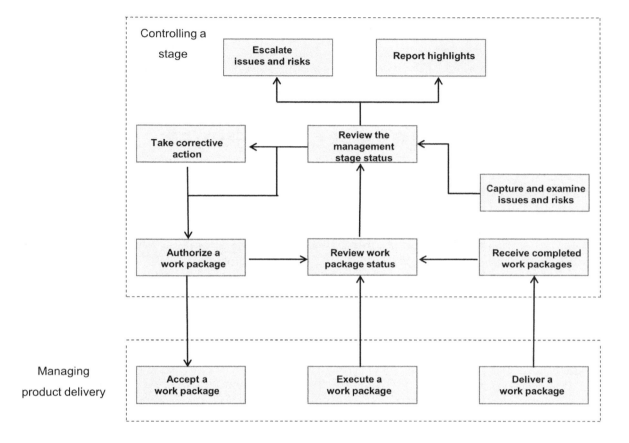

The activities in the controlling a stage process and the managing product delivery process cover the following four main areas of work:

Controlling the Delivery of the Specialist Work
The project manager uses the activities in the controlling a stage process to delegate the work to the teams, review their progress, and accept the work once it is finished. The teams use the activities in the managing product delivery process to formally accept work from the project manager, to deliver the products to relevant quality standards, to ensure quality control activities are carried out, and finally, to understand how to notify the project manager when the work is finished.

Reporting on the Progress of the Stage
The project manager uses the activities in the controlling a stage process to regularly report on the progress of the stage to the project board and any other relevant stakeholders. The teams use the activities in the managing product delivery process to report regularly to the project manager.

Dealing with Issues and Risks during a Stage

The project manager uses the activities in the controlling a stage process to capture and examine issues and risks and ensure that appropriate decisions and actions are made regarding them.

Deciding What to Do Next in a Stage

The project manager uses the activities in the controlling a stage process to decide what to do next out of options such as authorize new work, write a report, finish the stage, or finish the project.

Each of these four areas of work is covered in more detail in the following sections.

Controlling the Delivery of the Specialist Work

Figure 10.3 shows the activities in the controlling a stage and managing product delivery processes that are involved with controlling the delivery of the specialist work. All three activities in the managing product delivery process are involved, whereas only three of the eight activities in the controlling a stage process are concerned with this area.

Figure 10.3: Controlling the delivery of specialist work

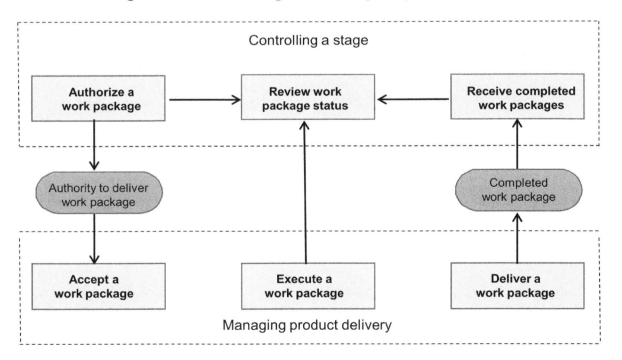

Authorize a Work Package

The authorize a work package activity in the controlling a stage process is where the project manager hands over the responsibility to deliver one or more specialist products to a team. This is done by creating and agreeing to a work package with that team. You learned about the work package in Chapter 9, "Progress Theme." Remember that it contains information such as what products need to be created, how much time and money the team is being given to deliver the products, how often to report back to the project manager, and who should approve the products once they have been created. Figure 10.4 shows the composition of the work package.

Figure 10.4: Composition of the work package

Work Package

- Date
- Person authorized
- Work package description
- Techniques, processes, and procedures
- Development interfaces
- Operations and maintenance interfaces
- Change control requirements
- Joint agreements
- Tolerances
- Constraints
- Reporting arrangements
- Problem handling and escalation
- Extracts or references
- Approval method

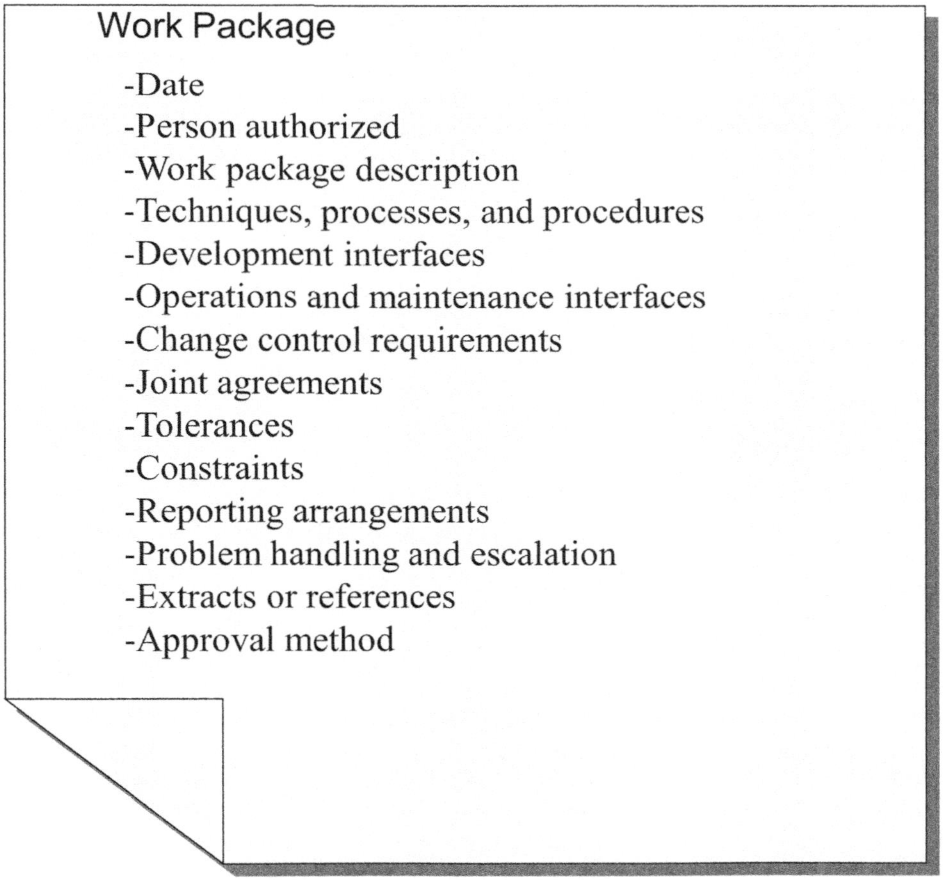

In a project to build a new hotel, the project manager would need to authorize many work packages with many teams. For example, the project manager would authorize one work package for the electrical contractor to wire the rooms, another work package for the plumbing contractor to fit the water pipes, another work package for the decorator to paint the rooms, and so on.

No team is allowed to start their work until a work package has been authorized by the project manager. This prevents teams from starting work at the wrong time or doing work that is unnecessary for the project. One work package might cover the creation of a number of products.

The project manager decides when it is time to authorize a new work package by monitoring the progress of the stage using the stage plan. Sometimes, the project manager might need to authorize a previously unplanned work package in response to an issue or a risk. This is possible as long as the work doesn't cause a forecast breach in the stage tolerances. If it will cause a forecast breach in stage tolerances, the project manager will have to refer to the project board for a decision.

Before authorizing a new work package, the project manager should review the following management products in order to understand what information the work package should contain:

Stage Plan
This tells the project manager what products need to be produced; the time, cost, and effort to be used; and the available tolerances.

Project Controls Section of the Project Initiation Documentation
This shows the project manager whether there are any project standards for controlling the team's work. For example, a standard progress report might be required from the teams.

Quality Management Approach
This shows the quality standards the team should follow.

Change Control Approach
This shows the team if there are any standard configuration management approaches they should use to store products, obtain copies of documents, place security around products, and so on. Once the team has accepted the work package, the project manager might have to update the following management products:

Stage Plan
The project manager updates the stage plan to reflect any changes to the schedule that the team is proposing in order to deliver their work. If these changes would take the stage beyond its forecast tolerances, the project manager would have to escalate the situation to the project board.

Configuration Item Records
If configuration item records are used, the project manager updates them to amend the status of the products to be delivered to "Work in progress."

Quality Register
The project manager updates this register to show any changes to planned quality checks. These quality checks will have been initially planned when the project manager created the stage plan; however, at this point, some amendments, such as extra reviewers, might be needed.

Issue Register and the Risk Register
The project manager updates these registers to show information on any new issues or risks that the work package will introduce. The project manager should discuss the issues and risks that might affect the work package with the teams.

Accept a Work Package

The accept a work package activity belongs to the managing product delivery process (refer to Figure 10.3). The team and the team manager (if there is one) carry out this activity.

The accept a work package activity is simply the reverse side of the authorize a work package activity in the controlling a stage process. It is where the team or team manager takes responsibility for delivering the work package's products. The team might not accept the initial information in the work package; they may need to negotiate with the project manager more time or resources to carry out the work.

The teams will agree with the project manager to deliver the work package within certain tolerances. As you learned in Chapter 9, a tolerance is the allowable flexibility for factors like the time and cost. For example, the project manager might agree that the team has three weeks to deliver the work package but in certain circumstances will allow the delivery to be two days late. This means that the team has authority to proceed with the work as long as they are not forecasting that they will go over their schedule by more than two days. If they are, then they must immediately escalate the situation to the project manager by raising an issue. The procedure for raising an issue is described in the work package.

The work package contains the product descriptions for the products to be delivered. In Chapter 6, "Quality Theme," you learned about product descriptions. As you recall, they contain the product specification and explain how to check and approve the product. The teams use this information in order to understand what to deliver and which quality activities to plan. It might be appropriate for the teams to check with project assurance to ensure that the quality activities are still suitable and that no extra reviewers are needed.

The team or the team manager may create a team plan to show how the work package will be delivered within the agreed-to constraints. They should consult with the supplier-side project assurance to ensure that the team plan follows any relevant supplier standards. The project manager might want to review this team plan to reassure himself on the viability of the work package, although this might not be appropriate in a commercial customer/supplier environment. If the latter is the case, the project manager might still ask to review a set of key milestones showing when interim products for the work package will be delivered.

One point to note is that the teams might have already created the team plan when the project manager was creating the stage plan. If you think about it, in order to create a plan for the stage, the project manager should ask the teams for their team plans and use that information to create the stage plan. The project manager creates stage plans in the plan the next management stage activity in the managing a stage boundary process. If the teams are creating team plans in order to help the project manager create the stage plan, they would be using the accept a work package activity in the managing product delivery process—even though at this point, the teams are not accepting the work package. I know this is a bit confusing, but just think of it as a PRINCE2 glitch.

Execute a Work Package

The execute a work package activity belongs to the managing product delivery process (refer to Figure 10.3). The team and the team manager (if there is one) carry out this activity. This is where the specialist products are developed. In the project to build a new hotel, for example, this is the activity where all sorts of specialist work will be done, such as designing architectural plans, creating tender documents, creating the building, fitting the bedrooms, and so on. You can think of this activity as where the "real work" is done rather than the management stuff, such as creating plans and the project initiation documentation.

Of course, the first focus for the teams in this activity is the production of the specialist products, but as you will see in this section, they also need to ensure that quality management, change control, and reporting are carried out as well.

The teams will develop the specialist products so that they match the specifications described in the products' product descriptions. They may have agreed with the project manager to use certain techniques, processes, or procedures when they create the products. For example, if the project manager delegated some work to create a tender document, the team may have agreed to follow the organizational standards. Any standards to be followed are described in the work package.

During the creation of the products, the teams might need to liaise with other people. For example, if the electrical contractors are wiring the bedrooms, they will want to coordinate with the plumbers to ensure their work doesn't conflict with each other. The development interfaces section of the work package will describe anyone the teams might need to liaise with.

The specialist products might have to connect with other products during their operational life. For example, the telephone system might need to connect to the booking system. The operations and maintenance interface section of the work package will describe any specialist products that the products being delivered will need to interface with in their operational life.

The teams (and also project assurance) need to ensure that quality control activities to check the products are carried out by the relevant people. As you learned in Chapter 6, quality control is all about checking that products are fit for purpose. The product descriptions specify the quality methods that must be used to check the products and who should be involved with the review and approval of the products. The teams should ensure that quality and approval records are kept to show proof that the quality activities have been done and the products are approved. The teams should ensure that the quality register is updated with the results of quality checks.

The teams will need to adhere to any configuration management approaches, if there are any, described in the work package. These could cover areas such as where the products need to be stored, how different versions of the product should be identified, or who needs to be updated if a product is completed (because this person will update the product's configuration item record with a new status).

Finally, the teams should regularly update the project manager on their progress by sending a checkpoint report. The work package will describe the format and frequency of the checkpoint report. Figure 10.5 shows the PRINCE2-recommended composition of the checkpoint report.

Figure 10.5: Composition of the checkpoint report

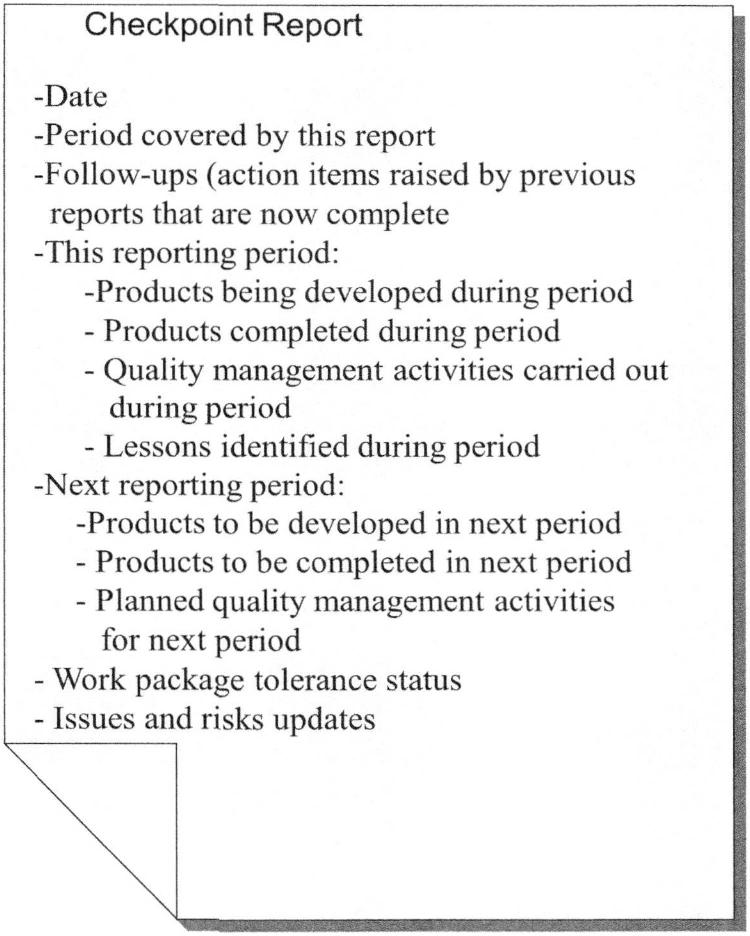

Checkpoint Report

-Date
-Period covered by this report
-Follow-ups (action items raised by previous
  reports that are now complete
-This reporting period:
    -Products being developed during period
    - Products completed during period
    - Quality management activities carried out
        during period
    - Lessons identified during period
-Next reporting period:
    -Products to be developed in next period
    - Products to be completed in next period
    - Planned quality management activities
        for next period
- Work package tolerance status
- Issues and risks updates

Review Work Package Status

The review work package status activity belongs to the controlling a stage process (refer to Figure 10.3). The project manager carries out this activity.

On a regular basis, while managing a stage, the project manager reviews the progress of each individual work package being delivered. If they aren't too far away, the project manager could just go and see the teams and review the work they are delivering. However, there are a number of PRINCE2 ways to review the specialist work:

- By reviewing the checkpoint reports that the teams send to the project manager
- By reviewing the quality register to see how quality checks are progressing
- By reviewing the configuration item records (if any have been produced) to see the current status of the products within the work package

The project manager will want to assess the overall progress of the work package and reassure himself that the work will finish in the time and cost agreed. The project manager will use this information to update the stage plan with the actual progress. The project manager constantly updates the stage plan with progress information throughout a stage. Figure 10.6 and Figure 10.7 show examples of this. Figure 10.6 shows a simple stage plan with three tasks. At this point, none of the tasks has been started, so the information in Figure 10.6 shows the planned or forecast times the project manager thinks the tasks will start and end. As you can see, the three tasks are dependent on one another. For example, Task 1 must be completed before Task 2 is started. This is the state the plan would be in at the beginning of the stage.

Figure 10.6: Stage plan with forecast details only

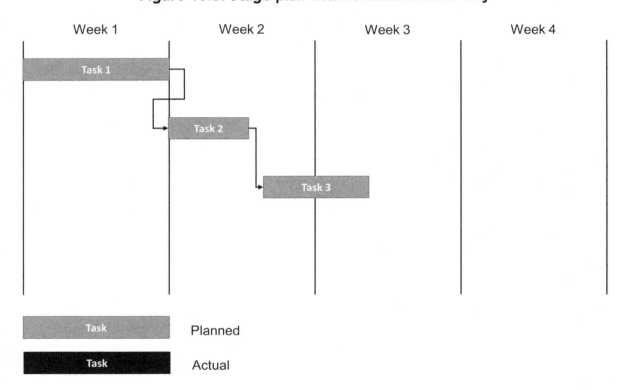

Figure 10.7 shows the situation a couple of weeks into the stage. As you can see, Task 1 has overrun—it should have taken one week, but in fact, it has taken two weeks. The project manager has updated the plan with the actual information for the duration of Task 1 and has updated the forecast start and end dates for Task 2 and Task 3. In any stage, the project manager will be constantly updating the stage plan in this manner. This updating of the stage plan is done in the review work package status activity.

Figure 10.7: Updated stage plan with to-date actuals, forecasts, and adjustments

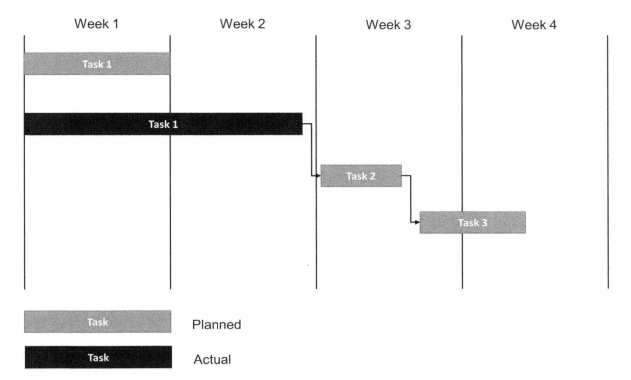

Deliver a Work Package

The deliver a work package activity belongs to the managing product delivery process (refer to Figure 10.3). The team and the team manager (if there is one) carry out this activity.

At this point, the products that the team has been working on should be complete. The team should ensure that they have approval records to prove the relevant people have signed off on the products. (The relevant people are described in the product descriptions as approvers.) The team will also check the quality register to see if all the necessary quality checks have been done.

The team should follow the procedure described in the work package to deliver the completed products. Finally, the team or the team manager must notify the project manager that the work in the work package is complete.

Receive Completed Work Packages

The receive completed work packages activity belongs to the controlling a stage process (refer to Figure 10.3). The project manager carries out this activity.

The receive completed work packages activity is simply the reverse side of the deliver a work package activity in the managing product delivery process that was described in the previous subsection. To ensure that the work has been carried out correctly, during this activity, the project manager checks approval records, the quality register, and, if used, the relevant configuration item records.

Reporting on the Progress of a Stage

One important part of controlling a stage is the project manager regularly updating the project board and any other relevant stakeholders on the progress of the work by sending them highlight reports.

The report highlights activity is part of the controlling a stage process (refer to Figure 10.2) and so is carried out by the project manager. In this activity, the project manager creates a highlight report and sends it to the project board and any other stakeholders who want to be regularly apprised of progress. The communication management approach (which was created back in the initiation stage and shows how the project team will communicate during the project) describes the format, frequency, and recipients of the highlight report.

Figure 10.8 shows the PRINCE2-recommended format for the highlight report. The project manager uses many sources of information to create the highlight report—for example, information in the registers, the logs, checkpoint reports, the configuration management system, and so on.

Figure 10.8: Composition of the highlight report

Highlight Report

- Date
- Period covered by this report
- Overview of the stage's current status
- This reporting period:
    - Status of work packages
    - Products completed during period
    - Products still to be completed
    - Corrective actions taken in period
- Next reporting period:
    - Work packages to be worked on next period
    - Products to be completed in next period
    - Corrective actions planned for next period
- Project & management stage tolerance status
- Request for change – raised, approved/rejected, and pending
- Key issues and risks updates
- Lessons

Dealing with Issues and Risks during a Stage

Throughout the stage, the project manager will probably be faced with many ad hoc problems and issues. For example, people might ask for a change to a product's specification, a product might be delivered incorrectly, or someone might spot a new threat to the project. The project manager uses the following three activities in the controlling a stage process to handle these sorts of situations:

- Capture and examine issues and risks
- Take corrective action
- Escalate issues and risks

Capture and Examine Issues and Risks

Any stakeholder can raise an issue or a risk. The project manager should be notified immediately of new issues and risks. He then ensures that they are properly recorded in the relevant log or register. He also ensures that the risk or issue's impact on the project is analyzed.

As you learned in Chapter 8, "Change Theme," there are three types of issues:

Request for Change
Someone wants to change a product or a product's product description.

Off-specification
A product(s) has or will be delivered incorrectly.

Problem or Concern
A problem or concern is any other issue which does not fit into the category of a request for change or an off-specification.

You also saw in Chapter 8 how, in the absence of any other defined approach, issues and changes can be handled using the PRINCE2 issue and change control procedure. The procedure has five steps: capture, assess, propose, decide, and implement. The project manager performs the first two steps—capture and examine—in the capture and examine issues and risks activity in the controlling a stage process.

You learned in Chapter 8 that formal issues are recorded in the issue register, and, if a lot of information needs to be recorded regarding that issue, an accompanying issue report might also be created. Informal issues are recorded in the daily log.

After the issue has been *captured*, it is *assessed*. As you learned in Chapter 8, during the assess step, the project manager works with the rest of the project management team to consider the impact the issue will have on factors (such as the cost and time of the project), the wider environment outside of the project, and the interests of the main stakeholder groups (such as the suppliers, users, and the business).

The project manager should check the communication management approach to see if any stakeholders need to be informed of this new issue.

In addition to dealing with issues in this activity, the project manager captures and examines risks. You learned about risks in Chapter 7, "Risk Theme." A risk is an uncertain event that might affect the project for good or bad. Good risks are called *opportunities*—for example, an opportunity to recruit an experienced contractor to work on the new hotel. Bad risks are called *threats*—for instance, a threat that bad weather could delay the hotel's construction.

As you learned in Chapter 7, in the absence of any other defined approach, the PRINCE2 risk management procedure is used to manage risks. The procedure consists of five steps: identify, assess, plan, implement, and communicate. A number of the risk management procedure steps might be carried out during the capture and examine issues and risks activity in the controlling a stage process. A project stakeholder might tell the project manager about a new risk. The project manager would record it in the risk register (the identify step). The project manager would then ensure that the risk is assessed in terms of its probability, impact, and proximity, and that countermeasures are planned (the assess and plan steps). The project manager should communicate information about the risk to anyone identified in the communication management approach (the communicate step).

If, because of the issue or risk, the project manager will take corrective action or escalate the situation to the project board, the project manager should first use the review the management stage status activity to see the full picture of the situation.

Take Corrective Action
In this activity, the project manager takes some action to resolve deviations from the stage plan caused by an issue. The project manager is able to take corrective action only if it does not cause a forecast breach in the stage's tolerances.

One example is authorizing the teams to correct an off-specification. Another example is authorizing more resources to work on a product that is behind schedule. The project manager should work with the teams to consider the best action to take. Once the option has been chosen, the project manager should update any relevant management products—such as the issue register, issue report, risk register, configuration item record, or stage plan—with the option's details. Finally, the project manager completes the authorize a work package activity to instruct the teams to carry out the corrective action.

Escalate Issues and Risks
Sometimes an issue or a risk (or the aggregation of a number of issues and risks) cannot be resolved without causing a forecast breach of a stage's tolerances. In this case, the project manager must escalate the situation to the project board.

The project manager uses an exception report to escalate issues and risks. As you learned in Chapter 9, the exception report describes the problem, analyzes a number of possible options to resolve the issue or risk, and recommends one of the options.

Because it could take some time to put together an exception report, PRINCE2 recommends that the project manager alert the project board of the issue before collating the necessary information for the exception report.

The project board might make a number of responses to the exception report, depending on the type of issue:

- They might request more information or time to consider the problem.
- They might approve, defer, or reject a request for change.
- For an off-specification, they might grant a concession, or reject one or defer one.
- They might increase the tolerances of the stage.
- They might instruct the project manager to create an exception plan showing the project board more details of how the recommended option from the exception report will be carried out.
- They might even instruct the project manager to close the project prematurely.

Once the project manager has received the project board's response, he should execute their decision.

Deciding What to Do Next in a Stage

You have now learned about seven of the eight activities in the controlling a stage process. As you've seen, they involve delegating work to teams, reviewing progress, dealing with issues, and writing highlight reports. In a typical week, the project manager will be juggling his time between all of these seven activities.

The final activity, review the management stage status, is a bit different from the other seven activities in the controlling a stage process. It is the activity in which the project manager pauses, reviews the whole situation of the stage, and then decides what to do next.

The project manager might use a number of sources of information to review the stage's status. For example, he might refer to checkpoint reports, the stage plan, configuration item records, or any of the logs or registers.

After reviewing the status, the project manager decides which activity is appropriate to do next. The project manager might move to another activity in the controlling a stage process, such as report highlights or escalate issues and risks. Or the project manager might realize that the stage is ending and start to do the activities in the managing a stage boundary process. Or, if this is the last stage of the project, the project manager might do the activities in the closing a project process.

Another focus for the project manager in this activity is to review the benefits management approach to check whether any benefit reviews are due. Remember that the benefits management approach is created in the initiation stage and plans how the benefits from the project will be reviewed and what management actions will be required to ensure that the project's outcomes are achieved. Most benefits from a project usually occur after the project has finished. However, in some projects, benefits might arise during the project itself. For example, if the project is to build a block of apartments, some of the apartments might be sold "off plan" before they have been completed. The project manager should ensure that these benefit reviews are executed.

At this point, some of the project's products might be handed over to the client or to the operations or maintenance teams as part of a phased handover. If this is the case, the project manager needs to ensure that these products have been approved and that the client and the operations or maintenance teams are ready to take responsibility for the products.

Key Facts for Controlling a Stage and Managing Product Delivery

For the Foundation exam, you do not have to memorize all the details from the previous controlling a stage and managing product delivery activity sections. However, you should learn the important facts for these processes as specified in Table 10.1 and Table 10.2. The Practitioner exam, on the other hand, may contain detailed questions about process activities, but you will be allowed to refer to the official PRINCE2 manual, *Managing Successful Projects with PRINCE2*, during the exam, so there is no need to memorize all the details.

> *You might want to reread the Exam Spotlight in Chapter 2, "Starting a Project Successfully with PRINCE2," that discusses how to approach the PRINCE2 processes when preparing for the exam and how to use Managing Successful Projects with PRINCE2 to answer process questions in the Practitioner exam.*

Table 10.1: Controlling a stage process—key facts

Activity	Key Facts
Authorize a work package	The project manager creates a work package that provides the team and/or the team manager with all the information they will need in order to deliver a set of specialist products.
Review work package status	The project manager reviews the status of individual work packages currently being worked on. The project manager uses checkpoint reports, configuration items records, product status accounts, and the quality register to review the team's progress. The project manager updates the stage plan with information on the progress of the work packages.
Receive completed work packages	The project manager receives notification from the team that a work package has been completed. The project manager checks the work and ensures that all the products have been approved. The project manager updates the stage plan to show the work package as completed.
Report highlights	The project manager creates a highlight report and sends it to the project board and to any other stakeholders who wish to be kept up-to-date on the project as identified in the communication management approach. The highlight report describes the stage's progress.
Capture and examine issues and risks	The project manager records new formal issues in the issue register and might also create an accompanying issue report. The project manager records informal issues in the daily log and risks in the risk register. The project manager ensures that an impact analysis is carried out on issues and that a risk assessment is carried out on risks. New risk countermeasures are planned.
Take corrective action	The project manager deals with risks and issues that can be resolved without a forecast breach in stage tolerances.

Activity	Key Facts
Escalate issues and risks	The project manager escalates risks and issues that cannot be resolved without a forecast breach in stage tolerances. The project manager escalates the situation to the project board by sending them an exception report. The project manager carries out the decision made by the project board.
Review the management stage status	The project manager reviews the stage and decides what to do next. The next action could be any of the controlling a stage activities, or the managing a stage boundary process if the stage is nearing completion, or the closing a project process if the whole project is nearing completion.

Table 10.2: Managing product delivery process—key facts

Activity	Key Facts
Accept a work package	The team or the team manager receives a work package from the project manager and agrees to carry out the work. The team might create a team plan for the work. The team checks with project assurance that the quality register describes appropriate reviewers for the products that will be created in the work package.
Execute a work package	The team creates and delivers the specialist products. The team ensures that quality activities defined in the products' product descriptions and the quality register are carried out and that products are approved. The team collects quality and approval records as evidence that the quality activities have occurred. The team regularly updates the project manager about the work package's progress by sending him checkpoint reports.
Deliver a work package	The team notifies the project manager that the products from a work package have been delivered. The team ensures that all the relevant quality activities have been carried out and that the relevant reviewers have approved the products.

Tailoring the Controlling a Stage and Managing Product Delivery Processes

As you learned in Chapter 1, PRINCE2 can be tailored to suit many different situations. For example, PRINCE2 can work effectively in a programme environment, when an agile delivery approach is used, or when an external commercial organization delivers some of the project's products. This section looks at how the controlling a stage and the managing product delivery processes might be adapted to suit some of these situations.

On large, complicated projects, particularly when you're dealing with external commercial suppliers, the work package might be a formal set of instructions. On a simple project or when you're dealing with internal teams, the work package might be more informal. Also, different industries have different ways of specifying work to be done, so work packages might look quite different depending on which industry the project is running within. Whichever form the work package takes, however, the project manager should use the work package's product description as a checklist to ensure that all relevant information is present.

On a simple project, the highlight and checkpoint reports might be more informal and could simply be verbal updates. On agile projects, the project manager or the team manager might facilitate regular standup meetings. These are short meetings where the teams can report progress and examine project issues. Also, rather than using reports, agile projects often communicate project information using an *information radiator*. Information radiators are easy-to-read wall charts that show (usually in a visual and pictorial way) information about the project's progress, issues, risks, and goals. Common components of an information radiator are a Kanban board and a burn down chart. The Kanban board tracks the work that has been assigned to each person and the current status of each task. Figure 10.9 shows an example of a Kanban board. A burn down chart tracks how much work remains against time. Figure 10.10 shows an example of a burn down chart.

Figure 10.9: A Kanban board

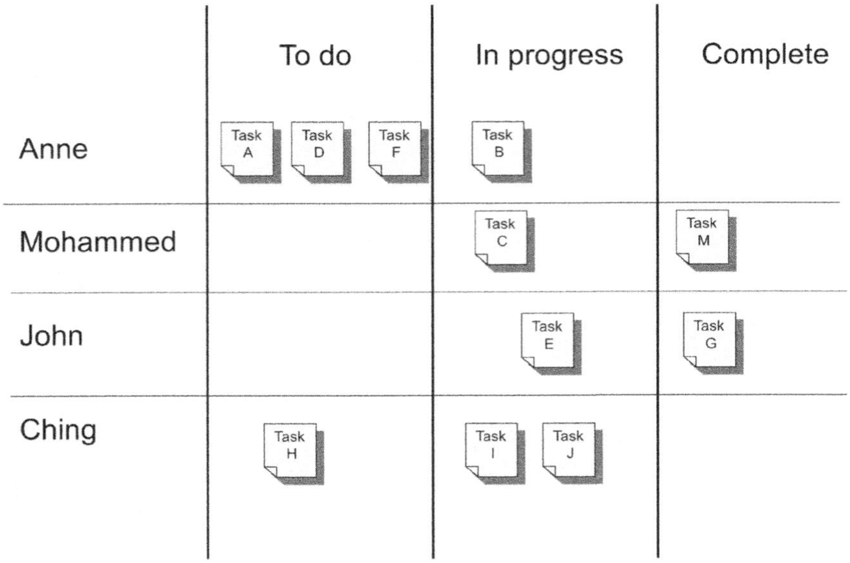

Figure 10.10: A burn down chart

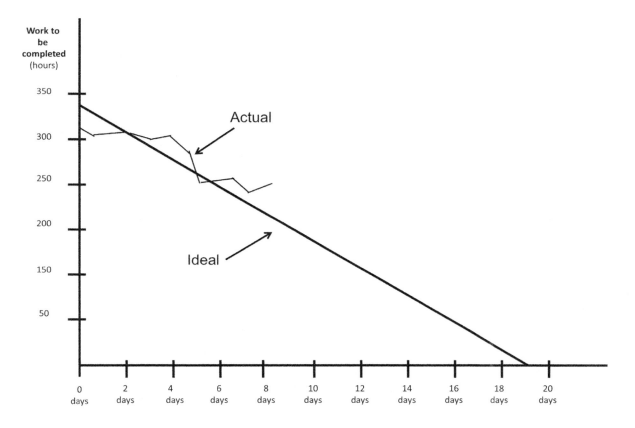

In an agile project, each work package might contain a number of sprints. A *sprint* is a time-boxed period of work that delivers a number of releasable products. The sign-off of the products might be done by giving reviews and demonstrations to the customer at the end of each sprint. At the end of each sprint, the project manager or the team manager might run a sprint retrospective. Similar to lessons learned meetings, these retrospectives can help the team learn useful experience for future work.

The frequency of the highlight reports and the checkpoint reports may change to suit the risk profile and the products being created. This would be documented in the communication management approach. Also, the reports might contain additional information, such as progress against certain key performance indicators.

If the project manager is delegating work to an external supplier, the work package might take the form of a legally binding contract. To enable to the project manager to control the work, the contract should stipulate that the supplier provide sufficient progress information to the project manager.

If a work package is very large, a team manager skilled in project management might break it down into a hierarchy of smaller work packages, each delegated to individual team members or teams. Using this approach might necessitate a hierarchy of team managers.

If the project is part of a programme, the project management team should consider the circumstances in which issues or risks would need to be escalated to the programme team. The team should also consider whether the risks and issues should be recorded in separate project registers or in an overall risk or issue register system for the entire project.

The Managing a Stage Boundary Process

The managing a stage boundary process is done in one of two situations: either at the end of a stage (except the final stage, when the closing a project process is used instead) or when the project board has requested an exception plan. In either case, the project manager does most of the work in the activities in the managing a stage boundary process.

If the managing a stage boundary process is being used at the end of a stage, the activities help the project manager to do the following three things:

- Review the work of the stage and create an end stage report.
- Look ahead to the work of the next stage and create a stage plan for it.
- Review the overall project situation and update the project plan, the business case, and the overall risk situation.

As you learned in Chapter 5, "Plans Theme," the managing a stage boundary process is also used to create an exception plan. Although the project manager is using the activities in the managing a stage boundary process to create the exception plan, the project might not be at the end of the stage. In this situation, there will have been a forecast breach of stage or project tolerances, which the project manager will have escalated to the project board. In response, the project board will have asked the project manager to create an exception plan showing how the project will respond to the forecast breach in tolerances. This request for an exception plan could occur at any time in a stage, depending on when the exception has occurred. As mentioned in Chapter 5, one way of thinking about this is that the project needs an emergency stage boundary to deal with the breach in tolerances.

Figure 10.11 shows the activities in the managing a stage boundary process. There are two routes into the process. The route to the managing a stage boundary process could be because the end of the stage is approaching, in which case the project manager uses the plan the next management stage activity to create the next stage plan. Alternatively, the route to the managing a stage boundary process might be in response to the project board's request for an exception plan, in which case, the project manager uses the produce an exception plan activity to create an exception plan. Then, the project manager does the other three activities: update the project plan, update the business case, and report management stage end.

Figure 10.11: Activities in the managing a stage boundary process

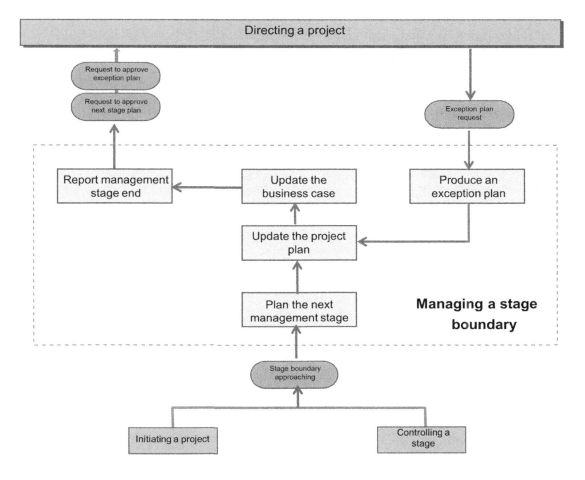

Plan the Next Management Stage

In this activity, the project manager creates the stage plan for the next management stage. As you learned in Chapter 5, the project manager creates a broad project plan at the beginning of the project, and then just before starting a new stage, the project manager creates a more detailed stage plan for the upcoming stage. This is in line with the PRINCE2 manage by stage principle.

The project manager will want to involve as many relevant people as possible to ensure that an accurate stage plan is created. He may consult with the teams that will deliver the specialist work, the senior suppliers, as well as project assurance.

The project manager will need to ensure that the stage plan takes account of the project's risk, quality, change control, and communication approaches. He will also want to ensure that the stage plan is aligned with the project plan created at the beginning of the project.

During the stage-planning process, the project manager may need to create new product descriptions. As you learned in Chapter 6, the project manager (with the help of the senior users) will first create broad product descriptions when producing the project plan. Then, during stage planning, the project manager might need to create more detailed product descriptions for the products to be delivered in the next stage. For example, in the project to build a new hotel, imagine that the next stage will furnish the hotel rooms. The project plan created at the beginning of the project might have contained overall product descriptions for each type of room. When planning the stage, more detailed product descriptions will be created for components of the rooms, such as the furniture, the bath fixtures, and the electrical equipment.

When new product descriptions are created, an associated configuration item record might also be created to track the status of that product.

If the stage plan is for the final stage of the project, the plan also needs to cover the management activities that will take place during the closing a project process. For example, if you refer to Figure 10.1, you'll see that the project manager will plan the closure activities during the second visit to the managing a stage boundary process for that particular project. If the stage plan is *not* for the final stage of the project, the plan will also need to cover the management activities that will take place during the managing stage boundary process that will take place at the end of that stage.

If new people will be involved in the next stage, the project manager will need to update the project management team structure and the roles and responsibilities section in the project initiation documentation.

Finally, the project manager may need to update the quality register with details of the quality checks planned for the stage, the issue register with new issues spotted for the stage, and the risk register to describe new threats and/or opportunities associated with the stage.

Produce an Exception Plan

In this activity, the project manager creates an exception plan. The work done in this activity is very similar to the work done in the plan the next management stage activity that you just learned about. The project manager will create a new plan and perhaps some new product descriptions and configuration item records. The project manager will also need to update a range of associated management products, such as the registers, project management team structure, and roles and responsibilities. However, in this case, the plan created shows the project board how the project can recover from a forecast breach in tolerances. For example, if the forecast breach were at the stage level, the exception plan would be at the stage plan level; if the forecast breach were at the project level, the exception plan would be at the project plan level. (See Chapter 5 for more information on exception plans.)

Another point to note is that the exception plan might contain many of the original activities from the stage plan or the project plan that it will replace (after authorization from the project board). The difference is that it also contains a variety of other activities to deal with the forecast breach in tolerance.

Update the Project Plan

The project manager should update the project plan as follows:
- Update the section of the project plan that refers to the current stage with the high-level details of what has actually occurred.
- Update the section of the project plan that refers to the next stage with any changes to the forecast work made while creating the next stage plan.

The project manager should also review the project product description to make sure it still reflects the overall outputs that will be created, given the fact that more detailed product descriptions have been created in the stage-planning process. Any changes to the project product description would need to be referred to the project board for a decision.

Exam Spotlight

In the modern world of project management, many project managers use software tools to create and update project plans. Usually, these tools provide multiple views of a plan, such as a detailed view that project managers can use to track and control work (the equivalent of a PRINCE2 stage plan) and a broader "milestone" view that project managers can show to senior stakeholders (the equivalent of a PRINCE2 project plan). This means that as project managers update the plan with the progress of the work, both views are updated simultaneously.

The scenario described in the previous paragraph does not translate to the PRINCE2 process model. As you have learned, in the controlling a stage process, the project manager updates the stage plan with the progress of the work, and then later, in the managing a stage boundary process, he updates the project plan with a broader, higher-level view of the progress of the work.

Remember this for the exam: PRINCE2 considers the stage plan and the project plan as two separate (but aligned) plans that are updated at different times.

Update the Business Case

As you saw in Chapter 1, one of the principles of PRINCE2 is continued business justification. As the project progresses, a common project management pitfall is not reviewing and updating the original business case that justified the start of the initiative. Many things might change during the project that would invalidate the project's justification: Costs might rise; schedules might be delayed; new competitors might arrive; technology might change; and so on. Because of these potential changes, PRINCE2 states that at the end of each stage, the business case needs to be updated. The project board will review the updated business case when deciding whether to authorize the project to continue to the next stage.

In this activity, the project manager and the executive review all the sections of the business case and update them, as necessary. They will use the information created from the previous activities in the managing a stage boundary process, such as the new stage plan or exception plan and updated logs and registers. The executive should also consider how changes in the outside environment, such as new technologies or new competitors, might change the forecast benefits.

The project manager should consult with the executive to consider whether any of the organizations involved with the project have changed their outlook on risk appetite. As you learned in Chapter 7, *risk appetite* is the amount of risk that an individual or an organization is willing to take. Sometimes, for example, an organization might start a risky project, but as time progresses, the outside economic environment deteriorates and the organization finds it is no longer in a position to make riskier investments. If an organization lowers its risk appetite, it may want to either close a project or change the project's objectives so that there is less risk involved, or maybe change the risk management approach to allow for a more rigorous risk management system.

The project manager should consult with the executive to reevaluate the overall risk situation to ensure that it remains within the project risk tolerances and to ensure that the main risks to the project are being managed correctly.

The project manager and executive should review the benefits management approach to check that it has been updated with the results of any benefit reviews that took place in the previous stage and compare these results with the expected results. They should also ensure that any new planned benefit reviews are in the stage and project plans.

Report Stage End

In this activity, the project manager creates an *end stage report* that the project board will review, along with the other outputs of managing a stage boundary, to decide whether to move to the next stage of the project. Figure 10.12 shows the composition of the end stage report.

Figure 10.12: The End Stage Report

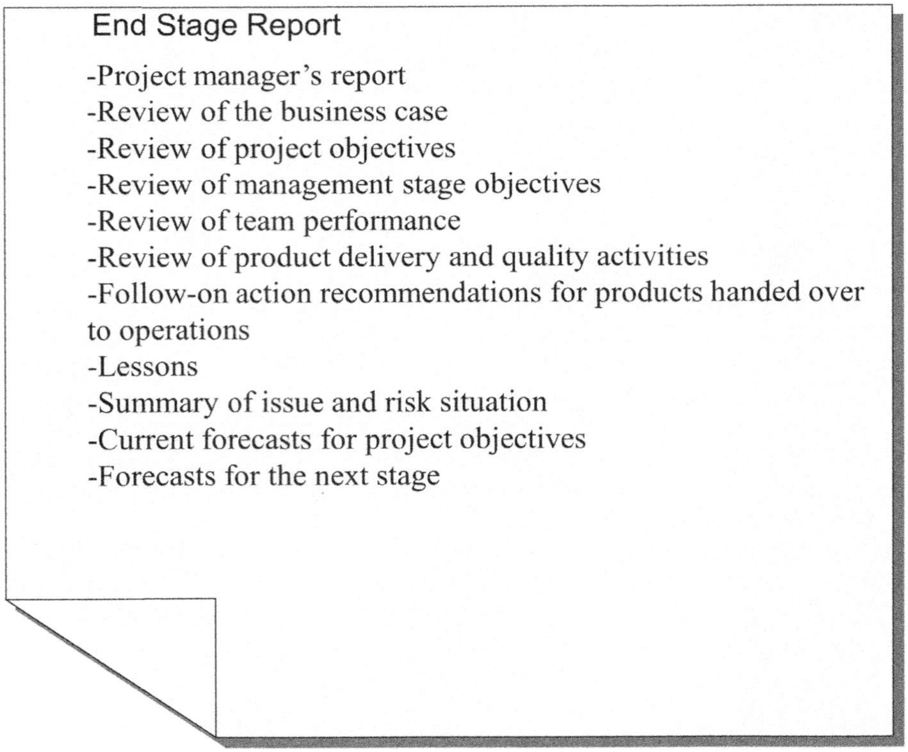

End Stage Report

- Project manager's report
- Review of the business case
- Review of project objectives
- Review of management stage objectives
- Review of team performance
- Review of product delivery and quality activities
- Follow-on action recommendations for products handed over to operations
- Lessons
- Summary of issue and risk situation
- Current forecasts for project objectives
- Forecasts for the next stage

The one caveat to this is when the project manager is using the managing a stage boundary process to create an exception plan. The previous stage boundary may have only just occurred, so there is little new information to report. In this situation, the project manager should ask the project board if an end stage report is necessary.

Some projects might hand over interim deliverables to the client or an operational team at the end of some of the stages. The project manager needs to ensure that the relevant people (such as the senior users or members of the operational team) sign off on the products by giving their acceptances. The project manager should also ensure that any relevant follow-on action recommendations associated with those products (such as requests for unauthorized changes or off-specifications that were given concessions) are handed over to the client or operational team.

At this point, the project manager might create a lessons report. On shorter projects, a lessons report might be created only at the end of the project; on longer projects, however, it might be useful to pass on experience to relevant people at the end of each stage.

The main recipient of the end stage report is the project board; however, the project manager should consult the communication management approach to see if he should include any other stakeholders.

The final part of the report end stage activity is to seek approval from the project board to move to the next stage of the project.

After Managing a Stage Boundary

Once the managing a stage boundary process activities are complete, the project board (supported by project assurance, if they exist as separate individuals to the project board members) will review whether to authorize the project manager to manage the next stage or the exception plan. The project board carries out this review in their directing a project process. The project board will use all the outputs of the managing a stage boundary process to make this decision. If the managing a stage boundary process were used to create an exception plan due to a forecast breach in project tolerances, then corporate, programme management, or the customer would also need to be involved with this decision.

One particular focus for the project board is to ensure that the updated business case still forecasts a worthwhile and viable project. This should be one of the main drivers in their decision whether to continue with the project.

After considering all the previously described factors, the project board will do one of the following:

- Approve the stage plan or exception plan and the associated product descriptions. If this is the case, the project board will set the tolerances for the new plan and obtain or commit the resources needed for the plan. In addition, the project board should approve the updated benefits management approach, business case, and project plan, as well as any other amended sections of the project initiation documentation.
- Ask the project manager to revise the plan and give guidance on what changes are needed.
- Instruct the project manager to initiate the premature closure of the project.

Finally, the project board should communicate the status of the project to any interested parties (as defined in the communication management approach), especially corporate, programme management, or the customer.

Key Facts for Managing a Stage Boundary

As with the other processes, I recommend that you familiarize yourself with the information in the preceding sections on the activities in the managing a stage boundary process. However, you need to memorize the key facts in Table 10.3 only when preparing for the Foundation exam. If any more detailed questions arise in the Practitioner exam, you can refer to *Managing Successful Project with PRINCE2* to find the information.

Table 10.3: Managing a stage boundary process—key facts

Activity	Key Facts
Plan the next management stage	The project manager creates the next stage plan and any associated product descriptions and configuration item records. If new people will take on new roles and responsibilities for the next stage, the project manager updates the project management team.
Produce an exception plan	The project manager creates an exception plan and any associated product descriptions and configuration item records. If new people will take on new roles and responsibilities for the exception plan, the project manager updates the project management team.
Update the project plan	The project manager updates the project plan with the progress from the previous stage and any new forecast information for the next stage.
Update the business case	The project manager consults with the executive and updates the business case with any new information, and then reviews the overall risk profile and major risks to the project. The benefits management approach is updated with results from benefits reviews from the previous stage and new reviews planned for subsequent stages and post-project.
Report stage end	The project manager creates the end stage report. The project manager ensures that acceptances are obtained for any interim deliverables that are being handed over to the client or the operational team. The project manager creates a list of follow-on action recommendations for products being handed over to the operational teams as well as a lessons report, if necessary.

Tailoring the Managing a Stage Boundary Process

In Chapter 1, you learned that PRINCE2 can be tailored to suit many different situations. For example, PRINCE2 can work effectively in a small project or in a programme environment, or when an agile delivery approach is used. This section looks at how the managing a stage boundary process might be adapted to suit some of these situations.

A small project might have only one delivery stage after the initiation stage. This means there would be no need to create a stage plan for the delivery stage, because it would be the same as the project plan. There also would be no need for an end stage report, only an end project report. Furthermore, the lessons report could be combined with the end project report. In fact, the managing a stage boundary process would only be needed if an exception plan were required.

If the project were delivering highly specialized products and the project manager did not have the requisite skills, he might not create the product descriptions. Instead, the project manager could delegate the product descriptions to someone with the right skill set, but he would want to verify the descriptions were created in enough detail to act as a basis for planning the stage.

If the project were operating in an agile environment, it would be important that the stage boundaries not interrupt the work of a sprint. It would be best practice to align the stage boundaries with the end of either one sprint or a group of sprints. During the managing a stage boundary process, the project management team would reevaluate the product backlog to ensure that the next stage delivered the highest value product features. (You learned about sprints and backlogs in Chapter 1.)

The Directing a Project Process

I cover the directing a project process in a number of chapters, as follows:
- Chapter 2 describes how the directing a project process is used at the beginning of the project.
- This chapter describes how the directing a project process is used during the middle of the project.
- Chapter 11 describes how the directing a project process is used at the end of the project.

During the middle of the project, the project board will use the directing a project process at the end of each delivery stage (apart from the final stage) to consider whether to authorize the next delivery stage. Although you have already learned about the authorize a stage activity in Chapter 2, I am going to describe the activity again. This time, however, I'll discuss how it is used in the middle of the project. I will also show you how this activity could be used to authorize an exception plan.

This section also discusses another directing a project activity, give ad hoc direction. This activity can be used at the beginning, middle, or the end of the project, so I could have covered it in Chapters 2 and 11 as well. For convenience, however, I am going to cover it only once, in this chapter.

Authorize a Stage or Exception Plan

This activity could be used in one of two situations. The first situation would be if the project were at the end of a management stage (but not the final stage of the project.) In this case, the project manager would use the managing a stage boundary process to prepare a next stage plan, update the project initiation documentation (particularly the business case and the project plan), and create an end stage report. Then the project manager would send the project board a request to approve the next stage plan. Finally, the project board would use the directing a project process activity called authorize a stage to consider whether to authorize the project manager to proceed to the next stage.

The second situation where the authorize a stage or exception plan activity might be used is when there has been an exception and the project board has requested that the project manager create an exception plan. (You learned about this situation in the "Exception Plan" section of Chapter 5.) In this case, the project manager first would use the managing a stage boundary process to create an exception plan, and then he would send a request to approve the exception plan to the project board. Finally, the project board would use the authorize a stage or an exception plan activity to consider whether to authorize the project manager to proceed with the work in the new exception plan. As you learned in chapter 5, the exception plan might be at the project level or the stage plan level.

The project board will review the following three types of information during the authorize a stage or exception plan activity whether they are in the situation where the project manager has just created a stage plan or in the situation where the project manager has just created an exception plan:

- The stage or exception plan itself. The project board will want to review the stage or exception plan to check that it is feasible and achievable, and they will want to review the product descriptions for the products to be delivered within the stage or exception plan to see if they deliver fit for purpose products.
- The latest updated version of the project initiation documentation. The project board will want to review any updates to the project initiation documentation but particularly whether the latest version of the business case continues to demonstrate a viable project. The project board will also want to review the benefits management approach to check that any benefits planned to be achieved within the next management stage will be measured and reviewed.
- The end stage report. The project board will want to review the performance of the previous stage. In the case of authorizing an exception plan, it may be that the current management stage has only just started. In this case, it is up to the project board whether to ask the project manager to create an end stage report.

Give Ad Hoc Direction

The give ad hoc direction activity is where the project board members can give informal guidance to the project manager. This activity could be used at any time during the project, but it is more likely to occur either during the initiation stage or when approaching management stage boundaries. The advice might be given by the whole project board or from an individual member of the project board. This activity might be triggered by a whole range of situations. For example, the project manager might simply request some advice, or an external event—such as a change in programme, customer, or corporate priorities—might prompt the project board to give new guidance to the project manager.

Themes Used to Manage the Middle of the Project

All seven PRINCE2 themes are used throughout the activities in the middle of the project. It is important to understand how the themes link to the activities in the controlling a stage, managing product delivery, and managing a stage boundary processes, because this is a common question topic in the PRINCE2 exams.

Business Case Theme

As you learned in Chapter 4, "Business Case Theme," the business case theme describes how to ensure that the project is desirable, viable, and achievable throughout the project's life. It shows how to write the project's business case, assigns a variety of business-related responsibilities to the roles within the project management team, and shows where in the process model the major business-related activities should occur.

When the project manager is reviewing the stage status during the controlling a stage process, he will review the benefits management approach to check whether any benefit reviews are due. Also, during the controlling a stage process, the project manager will ensure that the impact of new issues and risks on the business case is considered.

The project manager and the executive will update the business case during the managing a stage boundary process. The project board will then use the updated business case as a key driver in deciding whether to authorize the next stage of the project during the directing a project process.

Organization Theme

As you learned in Chapter 3, "Organization Theme," the organization theme describes the project management team structure, the project roles, and the project responsibilities. During the controlling a stage process, the project manager is responsible for managing the stage on behalf of the project board. The project manager delegates work packages to the team (or the team manager) that will be responsible for delivering the work using the managing product delivery process.

During the managing a stage boundary process, when the project manager is planning the next stage or the exception plan, he may discover that the project management team needs to be updated as new people become involved with the project or old ones are disengaging from the work. In this case, the project manager would update the project management team structure and/or roles and responsibilities sections of the project initiation documentation. The project board would review these updates when deciding whether to authorize the next stage.

Quality Theme

As discussed in Chapter 6, the quality theme shows how a project should be managed to ensure that it creates the right products. The theme covers how to conduct quality planning (which creates the product's specifications), how to do quality control (which confirms the products meet their specifications), and how to do quality assurance (which independently monitors quality management aspects of the project).

In the managing a stage boundary process, the project manager creates the next stage plan or the exception plan. This might involve creating new product descriptions for the specialist products to be delivered or using product descriptions created previously when preparing the project plan.

Stage plans or exception plans created during the managing a stage boundary process include activities that check the quality of the products. The project manager refers to the quality management approach to see if these quality checks should follow any standards. The project manager also refers to the product descriptions to see who should review and approve each product. The project manager updates the quality register with the planned details of these quality checks.

During the controlling a stage process, the project manager delegates work to the teams by assigning work packages. These work packages contain product descriptions that show the teams the quality expectations for the products to be delivered and how they should be checked. Later, when the project manager receives the completed work packages, he will want to see evidence that the products have been checked and approved by the relevant people described in that product's product description.

In the managing product delivery process, the teams deliver the specialist products according to the specifications described in the product descriptions. The teams also ensure that the relevant people carry out quality checks on the products, that the quality register is updated with the results of the quality checks, and that quality records are kept as evidence that the checks took place.

Plans Theme

As you learned in Chapter 5, the plans theme shows how to use various levels of plans (project plan, stage plan, and team plan) to plan the work of the project, what roles are involved with each plan, and what steps are needed to create a plan.

In the managing a stage boundary process, the project manager creates a stage plan and updates the overall project plan with details from the previous stage and new forecasts for the upcoming stage. The project manager uses the stage plan during the controlling a stage process to track and monitor the work of the teams.

The team or team manager may create a team plan during the managing product delivery process, which they can then use to track and monitor their work. The team plan is optional, however, as the stage plan alone may provide enough detail for the team.

If there has been a forecast breach in stage or project tolerances, the project board may ask the project manager to create an exception plan. The exception plan shows how the project will recover from the deviation caused by the exception. The project manager creates the exception plan in the managing a stage boundary process. After the project board approves it, the exception plan replaces either the stage plan or the project plan.

Risk Theme

Chapter 7 showed you that the risk theme identifies, assesses, and controls the potential threats and opportunities of the project, and thus improves the likelihood of the project's success.

During the capture and examine issues and risks activity of the controlling a stage process, the project manager records identified risks in the risk register. The project manager works with the project management team to assess the impact and probability of the risks and plan countermeasures to them. The project manager checks the communication management approach to see if he needs to inform anyone of the risk. The project manager also tracks planned risk management activities to see if they are being successful in tackling risks.

In the controlling a stage process, the project manager produces regular highlight reports for the project board and other relevant stakeholders. The highlight reports should update the recipients on the current status of risks within the project. Similarly, the teams or team manager create regular checkpoint reports for the project manager that should also include a section on the current risks to the work package that the team is delivering.

Finally, when the project manager creates the stage plan or the exception plan, he should ensure that he understands the risks associated with the plan and that there are adequate countermeasures planned for each one.

Change Theme

As you learned in Chapter 8, the change theme covers how to control issues and changes to the project's products.

During the controlling a stage process, the project manager captures and examines issues. Issues could be requests for changes, off-specifications, or problems or concerns. The project manager can deal with issues if they do not cause a forecast breach in stage tolerances or if the request for change is within the constraints of any change authority he has. If this is the case, he takes corrective action. Otherwise, the project manager will need to escalate the issues using an exception report.

The project board might ask the project manager to create an exception plan in response to an issue. The project manager would create the exception plan during the managing a stage boundary process, and the project board would approve it during the directing a project process.

The teams or the team manager need to ensure that any issues that would cause a forecast breach to work package tolerances are raised to the project manager.

Progress Theme

As you learned in Chapter 9, the progress theme describes how PRINCE2 controls the work of the project using tolerances to delegate authority, a variety of reports to monitor the progress of the project, and a number of other controls, such as work packages and product descriptions, to constrain the work that is carried out.

The managing a stage boundary process plans each stage and provides the project board with enough information to decide what tolerances to set for each stage and whether to authorize the work. The controlling a stage process describes the activities necessary for the project manager to manage and control the work of each stage. The controlling a stage process allows the project manager to delegate work using work packages to the teams and to set work package tolerances.

All the management products used throughout the middle of the project help to monitor or control the work being delivered.

Using the PRINCE2 Principles to Successfully Manage the Middle of a Project

The seven PRINCE2 principles used during the middle of the project are as follows:

Continued Business Justification
The project manager updates the business case at the end of each stage. The project board uses the updated business case to drive their decision about whether to authorize the next stage of the project. The project manager considers the impact on the business case of new issues or risks.

Learn from Experience
Previous experience is always considered when carrying out any of the activities in the controlling a stage, managing a stage boundary, and managing product delivery processes. If appropriate, the project manager includes a lessons report with highlight reports and end stage reports.

Defined Roles and Responsibilities

The project manager ensures that the roles and responsibilities for the project management team are up-to-date for each stage in the managing a stage boundary process.

Manage by Stage

The project board authorizes the project manager to manage the project one stage at a time. The project manager uses the managing a stage boundary process to prepare information for the project board to decide whether to authorize the next stage, and then uses the controlling a stage process to manage each authorized stage.

Manage by Exception

The project board defines stage tolerances within which the project manager must manage each delivery stage. The project manager has authority to manage each stage unless he forecasts that these stage tolerances will be breached, in which case he must escalate the situation to the project board. In a similar way, the project manager sets the work package tolerances that the teams must work within.

Focus on Products

The project manager creates stage plans and exception plans using a product-based planning approach to ensure that product descriptions are available for each product to be delivered in the stage. The project manager gives the teams the product descriptions to ensure that they deliver products to the correct specifications.

Tailor to Suit the Project Environment

The project manager plans how to apply the project's approach to tailoring PRINCE2 when planning each stage during the managing a stage boundary process.

Summary

In this chapter, you learned how the activities in the PRINCE2 controlling a stage, managing product delivery, managing a stage boundary, and directing a project processes work together to manage the middle part of the project.

More specifically, you learned how the project manager uses the controlling a stage process to manage the day-to-day activities of a stage on behalf of the project board. During this process, the project manager delegates work to the delivery teams, continually monitors the activities of the stage, regularly reports progress to the project board, and deals with issues and risks.

You also learned about the managing product delivery process, which the delivery teams use to create the specialist products of the project.

This chapter also looked at the managing a stage boundary process. This process includes a set of activities that the project manager will use at the end of a stage in order to prepare to meet with the project board for an end-stage assessment. You also saw that the managing a stage boundary process is used when there is a forecast breach in stage or project tolerances and the project board has asked for an exception plan.

You saw how the directing a project process is used in the middle of the project. The project board uses the authorize the stage activity at the end of each management stage to decide whether to authorize the next stage. As an input to this decision, they use the work that the project manager has prepared in the managing a stage boundary process, such as the next stage plan and the end stage report. The project board can also give the project manager informal advice using the give ad hoc direction activity and keep track of the stage's progress by reading the project manager's highlight reports and exception reports.

You saw how the processes that are used to manage the middle of the project can be tailored to suit a number of situations, such as a particularly complex project, a project within a programme, or a project using an agile delivery method. Finally, you saw how the PRINCE2 themes and the principles are used throughout the middle of the project.

Foundation Exam Essentials

Explain the purpose of the controlling a stage process.
The purpose of the controlling a stage process is for the project manager to assign work to be done, to monitor such work, to deal with issues, to report progress to the project board, and to take corrective actions to ensure that the stage remains within tolerance.

Explain the objectives of the controlling a stage process.
The objectives of the controlling a stage process are to focus attention on the delivery of the stage's products in order to avoid scope creep and to deliver the correct level of quality in the agreed-to time and cost tolerances, keep issues and risks under control, and keep the business case under review.

Explain the context of the controlling a stage process.
The controlling a stage process is used to manage each delivery stage of the project, but it may also be used to manage the initiation stage of a particularly long and complex project.

Explain the purpose of the managing product delivery process.
The purpose of the managing product delivery process is to control the link between the project manager and the team manager(s) by agreeing on the requirements for the acceptance, execution, and delivery of project work. The role of the team manager(s) is to coordinate an area of work to deliver one or more of the project's products.

Explain the objectives of the managing product delivery process.
The objectives of the managing product delivery process are to ensure that the team's work is authorized and agreed to; that the teams understand what is to be produced and the expected effort, cost, and timescales; that products are delivered to expectations and within tolerances; and that accurate progress information is provided to the project manager.

Explain the context of the managing product delivery process.
The teams and/or team manager(s) use the managing product delivery process to deliver work packages during a delivery stage. The process is initiated by the project manager during the authorize a work package activity in the controlling a stage process.

Explain the purpose of the managing a stage boundary process.
The purpose of the managing a stage boundary process is to enable the project manager to provide a stage plan, an updated project plan, an updated business case, and an end stage report to the project board so that they can decide whether to authorize the project to move to its next stage. A

secondary purpose of the managing a stage boundary process is to enable the project manager to provide an exception plan to show the project board how the project can recover from a stage- or project-level exception.

Explain the objectives of the managing a stage boundary process.
The objectives of the managing a stage boundary process are to assure the project board that all of a stage's products have been approved; to prepare the stage plan for the next stage; to review and, if necessary, update the project initiation documentation (in particular, the business case, the project plan, the project management team, and the overall risk situation); and to request authorization to start the next stage. In an exception situation, the objective of the managing a stage boundary process is to prepare an exception plan and seek approval to replace either the project plan or the stage plan with the exception plan.

Explain the context of the managing a stage boundary process.
The managing a stage boundary process is used at the end of each stage (apart from the final stage) in order to prepare for the work of subsequent stages. It is also used after an exception situation when the project board has requested an exception plan.

Explain the purpose of the highlight report
The project board (and possibly other stakeholders) uses the highlight report to monitor the progress of a management stage. The project manager creates the highlight report on a regular basis throughout a management stage. The project board defines the frequency of the highlight report.

Explain the purpose of the checkpoint report.
The project manager uses the checkpoint report to monitor the progress of a work package. The team manager or a member of a team creates the checkpoint report on a regular basis throughout the delivery of a work package. The project manager defines the frequency of the checkpoint report.

Explain the purpose of the end stage report.
The project board uses the end stage report to review the progress of a stage while deciding whether to authorize the next stage. The project manager creates the end stage report.

Practitioner Exam Essentials

Carry out the eight activities in the controlling a stage process and demonstrate an understanding of the recommended roles and responsibilities within the process.
The project manager is responsible for all eight activities in the controlling a stage process. There are four categories of activities: managing the work of the teams using the authorize a work package, review work package status, and receive completed work packages activities; managing risks and issues using the capture and examine issues and risks, take corrective action, and escalate issues and risks activities; reporting progress using the report highlights activity; and reviewing the stage and deciding what to do next using the review the management stage status activity.

Demonstrate an understanding of how the PRINCE2 themes can be applied throughout the controlling a stage process.
All seven PRINCE2 themes are applied during the controlling a stage process. The business case theme is applied when the project manager assesses the impact of issues and risks against the business case and reviews the benefits management approach to ensure any benefit reviews are carried out. The organization theme is applied when the project manager carries out his responsibilities to manage a stage on behalf of the project board. The quality theme is applied when the project manager delegates work packages to the teams by giving them product descriptions showing what products need to be created. The plans theme is applied when the project manager tracks the progress of the stage using the stage plan. The risk theme is applied when the project manager regularly identifies and assesses risks throughout the stage and records them in the risk register. The change theme is applied when the project manager carries out the issue and change control process by capturing and assessing issues and ensuring decisions on the issues are made at the appropriate level of management. Finally, the progress theme is applied when the project manager manages the teams by exception and also when he escalates any forecast deviation from stage tolerances to the project board.

Assess and critique an approach to applying the controlling a stage process.
Explain how the process might be adapted to different project contexts (for example, a small project, an agile project, a project with external third-party organizations, or a project operating within a programme environment) and whether the approach aligns with the PRINCE2 principles.

Carry out the three activities in the managing product delivery process and demonstrate an understanding of the recommended roles and responsibilities within the process.
The team manager and/or the teams are responsible for all three activities in the managing product delivery process. The work is accepted from the project manager in the accept a work package activity, created and delivered in the execute a work package activity, and handed back to the project manager in the deliver a work package activity.

Demonstrate an understanding of how the PRINCE2 themes can be applied throughout the managing product delivery process.
All the PRINCE2 themes except the business case theme are applied during the managing product delivery process. The organization theme is applied when the team manager carries out his responsibilities to manage a work package on behalf of the project manager. The quality theme is applied when the team creates products according to their product descriptions and quality control activities are carried out to ensure that the products are fit for purpose. The plans theme is applied if the team manager creates a team plan to track the progress of the work package or when the team is helping the project manager create stage plans. The risk theme is applied when the team manager escalates risks to the project manager. The change theme is applied when the team manager escalates issues to the project manager. Finally, the progress theme is applied when the team manager accepts the controls for the work as described in the work package.

Assess and critique an approach to applying the managing product delivery process.
Explain how the process might be adapted to different project contexts (for example, a small project, an agile project, a project with external third party organizations, or a project operating within a programme environment) and whether the approach aligns with the PRINCE2 principles.

Carry out the five activities in the managing a stage boundary process and demonstrate an understanding of the recommended roles and responsibilities within the process.
The project manager is responsible for the five activities in the managing a stage boundary process. The project manager will either create the next stage plan using the plan the next management stage activity or create an exception plan using the produce an exception plan activity, and will then update the project initiation documentation in the update the project plan and update the business case activities. Finally, he will create an end stage report in the report stage end activity.

Demonstrate an understanding of how the PRINCE2 themes can be applied throughout the managing stage boundary process.
All the PRINCE2 themes are applied during the managing stage boundary process. The business case theme is applied when the project manager updates the business case. The organization theme is applied when the project manager updates the project management team ready for the next stage. The quality theme is applied when the project manager works with senior users to create product descriptions for products to be delivered in the next stage and plans quality control activities for the next stage. The plans theme is applied when the project manager creates either a stage plan for the next management stage or an exception plan to show how to recover from a forecast breach of tolerances. The risk theme is applied when the project manager identifies any risks for the upcoming stage. The change theme is applied when the team manager identifies any issues for the next management stage. Finally, the progress theme is applied when the project manager proposes stage tolerances for the next management stage to the project board.

Assess and critique an approach to applying the managing stage boundary process.
Explain how the process might be adapted to different project contexts (for example, a small project, an agile project, a project with external third-party organizations, or a project operating within a programme environment) and whether the approach aligns with the PRINCE2 principles.

Demonstrate an understanding of the two activities in the directing a project process that are used in the middle of a project and demonstrate an understanding of the recommended roles and responsibilities within the process.
Two activities within the directing a project process are used in the middle of the project. The first activity is authorize a stage or an exception plan, during which the project board reviews the stage or exception plan, the updated project initiation documentation, and the end stage report, and decides whether to authorize the project manager to proceed with the work in the next stage or exception plan. The second activity, give ad hoc direction, is where the project board can give informal advice or guidance to the project manager.

Demonstrate an understanding of how the PRINCE2 themes can be applied during the directing a project process activities used in the middle of the project.
All seven themes are applied during the directing a project process used in the middle of the project. The business case theme is applied when the project board reviews the updated business case at the end of each management stage to decide if the project is still viable. The organization theme is used when the project board reviews any changes to the project management team at the end of each management stage. The quality theme is applied when the project board reviews and authorizes the product descriptions for products that will be delivered in the next management stage. The plans theme is applied when the project board reviews and authorizes the stage plan or exception plan. The risk theme is applied when the project board reviews the overall project

risk situation when deciding whether to authorize a stage or exception plan. The change theme is applied when the project board reviews and authorizes any requests for changes that have been made during the middle of the project. Finally, the progress theme is applied when the project board reviews and authorizes the project a stage at a time throughout the middle of the project.

Demonstrate an understanding of the highlight report.
Demonstrate an understanding that the project manager creates highlight reports at regular intervals throughout a management stage, and the project board uses the highlight reports to monitor the progress of a management stage. Know that the project manager creates highlight reports during the controlling a stage process. Understand that highlight reports might be derived from checkpoint reports, the issue, quality, or risk registers, stage plans, and the communication management approach. Know that a highlight report could be a presentation to the project board, a document or email, a wall chart or a Kanban board, or an entry in a project management tool. Know the composition of the highlight report.

Demonstrate an understanding of the checkpoint report.
Demonstrate an understanding that the team manager or a team member creates checkpoint reports at regular intervals throughout the delivery of a work package, and the project manager uses the checkpoint reports to monitor the progress of a work package. Know that the team manager or a team member creates checkpoint reports during the managing product delivery process. Understand that checkpoint reports might be derived from previous checkpoint reports, the work package, or the team plan. Know that a checkpoint report could be a presentation to the project manager, a document or email, a wall chart or a Kanban board, or an entry in a project management tool. Know the composition of the checkpoint report.

Demonstrate an understanding of the end stage report.
Demonstrate an understanding that the project manager creates the end stage report at the end of a management stage, and the project board uses the end stage report to review the progress of the previous management stage while deciding whether to authorize the subsequent management stage. Know that the project manager creates end stage reports during the managing a stage boundary process. Understand that end stage reports might be derived from the issue, quality, or risk registers, stage plans, the project plan, the benefits management approach, any exception reports raised in the previous stage, the lessons log, the updated business case, and completed work packages. Know that an end stage report could be a presentation to the project board, a document or email, a wall chart or a Kanban board, or an entry in a project management tool. Know the composition of the end stage report.

Review Questions

The remainder of this chapter contains mock exam questions, first for the Foundation exam and then for the Practitioner exam.

Foundation Exam Questions

1. A purpose of the managing a stage boundary process is to provide the project board with sufficient information so that it can:
    (1) Review whether the objectives set out in the original project initiation documentation have been achieved
    (2) Assess whether to commission the project
    (3) Confirm continued business justification of the project
    (4) Confirm acceptability of the project's risks
    A. 1 and 2
    B. 2 and 3
    C. 3 and 4
    D. 1 and 4

2. Which of the following is an objective of the controlling a stage process?
    A. To produce an end stage report
    B. To ensure that the host site can support the products when the project is disbanded
    C. To provide management direction and control throughout the project
    D. To keep the business case under review

3. Which activity can take place within the managing a stage boundary process?
    A. Review and, if necessary, update the project initiation documentation
    B. Produce highlight reports
    C. Accept work packages
    D. Sign off on completed work packages

4. In which process are work packages triggered?
    A. Starting up a project
    B. Directing a project
    C. Controlling a stage
    D. Managing product delivery

5. Which of the following is a purpose of the managing product delivery process?
    A. To create a fixed point at which acceptance of the project's products is confirmed
    B. To place formal requirements on accepting, executing, and delivering the project work
    C. To take corrective action to ensure the stage remains within tolerance
    D. To ensure that the prerequisites for initiating the project are in place

6. Which of the following is a purpose of the controlling a stage process?
    A. To hand over the responsibility for delivering work packages to the teams
    B. To enable the organization to understand what work needs to be done before committing to a significant expenditure.
    C. To enable the project board to be accountable for the project's success
    D. To provide information that enables the project board to decide whether to authorize the next stage

7. Which of the following is an objective of the managing product delivery process?
    A. To ensure that the team manager and the teams understand the expected effort, time, and cost needed to deliver the products
    B. To ensure that the various ways to deliver the project are evaluated
    C. To define how quality management will be carried out during the project
    D. To request authorization to start the next stage of the project

8. In which process are approvals obtained for completed products?
    A. Initiating a project
    B. Directing a project
    C. Controlling a stage
    D. Managing product delivery

9. Which of the following is an objective of the managing a stage boundary process?
    A. To ensure that there is business justification for initiating the project
    B. To approve all the products from the current stage
    C. To assure the project board that all products in the current stage have been approved
    D. To communicate breaches in project tolerance to corporate, programme management, or the customer

10. In which process are specialist products created?
    A. Initiating a project
    B. Controlling a stage
    C. Managing product delivery
    D. Managing a stage boundary

Practitioner Questions

The following Practitioner exam questions are divided into two sections by question type and are based on the Practitioner exam scenario in Appendix B.

Section 1: Matching Questions

Column 1 in the following table describes five actions taken by the project manager as part of the controlling a stage process during stage four of the Website Project, and Column 2 lists the seven PRINCE2 themes. For each action (1–5), identify the theme (A–G) that it relates to. Choose only one theme for each action. Each theme can be used once, more than once, or not at all.

Column 1	Column 2
1. The website development contractor, Digital Design, needs official instructions from the project manager to start their work.	A. Business Case
2. The marketing manager has asked whether the website could be available several weeks earlier so that the website launch could be combined with another planned corporate promotion.	B. Organization
3. The website development contractor, Digital Design, has spotted a new technology that may save the project some time. The project manager needs to assess this possibility.	C. Quality
4. The project manager is collating information regarding the work that has been done so far and what work remains.	D. Plans
5. The executive is concerned that because Quality Furniture has not worked with Digital Design before, the contractor may not understand Quality Furniture's IT standards and policies, which may lead to them delivering a system with operational difficulties.	E. Risk
	F. Change
	G. Progress

Section 2: Classic Multiple-Choice Questions

Exam Spotlight

Remember that during the Practitioner exam, you are allowed to refer to the official PRINCE2 manual (*Managing Successful Projects with PRINCE2*). This is a great help. I would say one of the key differences between passing and failing the Practitioner exam is knowing how to use the PRINCE2 manual during the exam. Some of the questions in the exam rely on you finding very specific pieces of information quickly from the manual.

This chapter covers three processes: controlling a stage, managing product delivery, and managing a stage boundary. In the manual, all the process chapters are set out in the same way. The first two pages discuss the purpose, objectives, and context of the process. Then the body of each process chapter looks at the activities that take place within that particular process. Some practitioner questions may test you on quite obscure facts about a process's activity. The key to getting these questions correct is to first understand which activity the question is testing you on. For example, if a question asks about delegating work to a team during the controlling a stage process, you are probably being asked about the authorize a work package activity. Look carefully in the manual at the relevant pages for that particular activity. Do any of the bullet points help? Does the activity's table of responsibilities provide a clue about who might be creating a management product mentioned in the question? Maybe the activity's flow diagram helps?

A process question might ask you about how to tailor the process to different situations, such as a programme or agile environment. To help with these sorts of questions, you'll find a section at the end of each process chapter about tailoring.

Process questions might ask you about a management product that is created in that process. For example, a controlling a stage process question could test you on the work package or the highlight report. The best place to look for information about management products is in the manual's Appendix A.

If you are tested on a process's roles and responsibilities, there are two good places to look in the manual: each activity's table of responsibilities and Appendix C.

1. During the managing a stage boundary process at the end of stage three, the project manager worked with Digital Design to create a stage plan for stage four. The project manager then created work packages for Digital Design and authorized them do their work. Finally, the project manager requested authorization for the stage plan from the project board. Is this appropriate, and why or why not?
   A. Yes, because the project manager is responsible for authorizing all work packages.
   B. Yes, because the project manager needs to confirm that the work packages for a stage can be delivered before requesting authorization for the stage plan that contains those work packages.
   C. No, because the project board should authorize the stage plan before the project manager authorizes work packages for the delivery of work within that stage.
   D. No, because the project board makes all authorizations within the project, so they should authorize the work packages.

2. The First Tech Consultant is carrying out a project assurance role on the project. The Digital Design team manager consulted with the First Tech Consultant when accepting the work package. The First Tech Consultant recommended that some additional reviewers be added to some of the work package's quality checks. Is this appropriate, and why or why not?
    A. Yes, because when accepting a work package, the team manager should consult with project assurance to find out if any extra reviewers are required.
    B. Yes, because project assurance is responsible for approving the products within each stage, they must ensure that appropriate reviewers are allocated to each quality check.
    C. No, because all reviewers should be allocated to a stage's quality checks when the stage plan is created during the managing a stage boundary process.
    D. No, because the managing product delivery process is focused on the work of the teams, so project assurance should not be involved during the accepting a work package activity.

3. During stage four, the marketing manager has asked for a change to the baselined home page design. It would be a small change to the tones of blue that are used to more closely match Quality Furniture's brand colors. Because this is a minor change and the marketing manager is responsible for all outward communication for the company, the project manager amends the home page work package and instructs the teams to implement the change. Is this appropriate, and why or why not?
    A. Yes, because the project manager can authorize small changes to the project's products.
    B. Yes, because the marketing manager is responsible for communication at Quality Furniture, she has the authority to instigate this change.
    C. No, because once a product has been baselined, it cannot be changed.
    D. No, because requests to change baselined products should be recorded in the issue register and be subject to an impact analysis before being authorized by the appropriate change authority.

Chapter

11

Managing the End of a Project Successfully with PRINCE2

PRINCE2 Foundation Exam Objectives Covered in This Chapter:

☑ Explain the purpose, objectives, and context of the closing a project process.

☑ Explain the purpose of the end project report.

PRINCE2 Practitioner Exam Objectives Covered in This Chapter:

☑ Carry out the closing a project process activities, and
  • Recommended associated actions:
    ▪ Prepare planned closure
    ▪ Prepare premature closure
    ▪ Hand over products
    ▪ Evaluate the project
    ▪ Recommend project closure
  • Demonstrating an understanding of:
    ▪ Recommended roles and responsibilities within the process
    ▪ How the themes may be applied

☑ Assess whether closing a project process activities/ actions, roles and responsibilities are effective and fit for purpose, taking into consideration: the context, the PRINCE2 principles, and the purpose and objectives of the process.

☑ Carry out the directing a project process activities that are used at the end of a project, and
  • Recommended associated actions:
    ▪ Authorize project closure
  • Demonstrate an understanding of:
    ▪ The recommended roles and responsibilities within the process
    ▪ How the themes may be applied

☑ Assess whether directing a project process activities/ actions, roles and responsibilities are effective and fit for purpose, taking into consideration: the context, the PRINCE2 principles, and the purpose and objectives of the process.

☑ Demonstrate an understanding of the end project report, and which roles are responsible in its use.

In this chapter, you learn how to use PRINCE2 to manage the end of a project. The close of a project can bring various challenges. For example, some projects suffer because they have no clear end. This can create a number of problems. The project's products have not been officially passed to the group who will maintain them in their operational life, but the project team believes they have finished working on them. If there are problems with the products, it is not clear whether the project or the operations team should fix them.

Another problem when there is no clear end is that the project has not been officially reviewed against its original objectives. This can cause longer-term problems for the organization: Unbeknown to them, they may be continually running projects that do not meet their business aims.

In this chapter, you learn how PRINCE2 aims to reduce the risks of these problems occurring. The closing a project process ensures that there is a point in time where all of the project's products need to be accepted by the customers and the operations teams. The closing a project process also ensures that the project is reviewed against its original objectives.

Overview of the End of a PRINCE2 Project

Figure 11.1 is taken from the "An End-to-End Walk-through of PRINCE2" section in Chapter 1, "Overview of PRINCE2." If you haven't read that section, I recommend that you do so before reading this chapter, as it gives a high-level overview of the PRINCE2 process model. You will then be able to understand the context of the closing a project process discussed in this chapter.

In Figure 11.1, I have highlighted the final delivery stage of the project. The first thing to understand is that in *most* ways, the final delivery stage is managed in a similar way to the other delivery stages. You learned how the project manager managed the other delivery stages in Chapter 10, "Managing the Middle of a Project Successfully with PRINCE2," but here's a brief summary. The project manager plans the delivery stage in the previous managing a stage boundary process, and the project board authorizes the work in the directing a project process. When the stage starts, the project manager uses the controlling a stage process to manage the work, and the teams use the managing product delivery process to deliver the specialist products.

The difference between the final delivery stage and the other delivery stages is that at the end of the final stage, instead of using the managing a stage boundary process to prepare for an end-stage assessment, the project manager uses the closing a project process to prepare for the end of the project.

Figure 11.1: End of the project

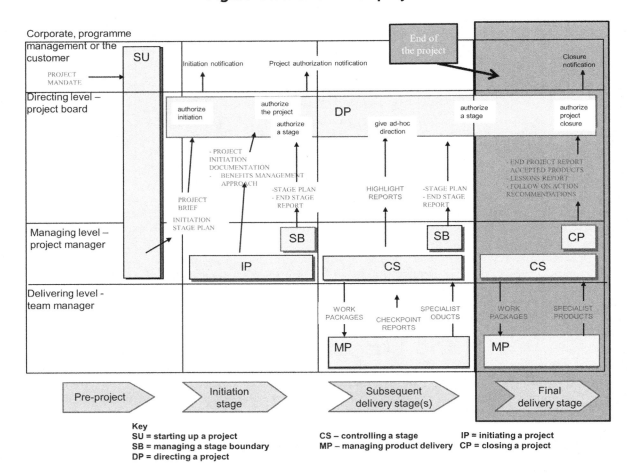

The project manager uses the activities in the closing a project process to prepare to meet the project board and ask permission to shut down the project. These activities include ensuring that the customer accepts the project's products as complete, evaluating the project against its objectives, and assigning responsibility for the post-project benefit reviews.

After the closing a project process, the project board uses the directing a project process's authorize project closure activity to make the final decision whether the project can now close.

CASE STUDY

Common Misunderstandings about the Closing a Project Process

Students have three common misunderstandings about the end of a PRINCE2 project. First, candidates think the project is closed when the closing a project process is complete—a reasonable assumption, given the name of the process. Unfortunately, however, PRINCE2 hasn't named the process very well; it should be called "preparing for the closing of a project." The project board closes the project using the directing a project process's authorize project closure activity—*after* the closing a project process.

Second, candidates mistakenly think that the project board carries out the activities of the closing a project process. This is incorrect; the project manager is responsible for this process.

Third, some candidates mistakenly think that closing a project is a stage in itself. This isn't the case. The activities in the closing a project process are only part of the final delivery stage. In that final delivery stage, there will also be work to deliver various specialist products.

The Closing a Project Process

The closing a project process provides a fixed point in time at which acceptance of the main outputs of the project can be confirmed. If the project were to build a hotel, the hotel would be officially "signed off" during the closing a project process. In PRINCE2 terms, the final sign off on the project's products is called *obtaining acceptance*. This is where ownership of the products is transferred from the project team to the clients or operations teams.

The project product description describes who can authorize acceptance. You learned about the project product description in Chapter 6, "Quality Theme." It describes the overall products and outlines measurable acceptance criteria that the products must meet, how the product should be checked against these criteria, and who should do the checking.

Many types of people could have acceptance responsibilities, including the ultimate clients, who might be internal or external to the organization running the project. In the hotel example, the customers might be senior directors of the hotel chain. The teams that will operate or maintain the products could also have acceptance responsibilities. In the hotel example, this could be the team that will run the hotel.

In Chapter 10, you learned that closing a project isn't the only place where products might be handed over to the clients or the operations teams. In some projects, there might be interim deliverables that are accepted by the clients or the operations teams in the managing a stage boundary process at the end of a particular stage.

The closing a project process is also when the project is reviewed against its original objectives to see how successful it has been. For example, how long did the project take compared to the original estimates, and how much did it cost compared to the original budget? During the project, these original objectives might have been subject to some approved changes. If this is the case, these changes obviously need to be taken into account when reviewing the project.

Figure 11.2 shows the main activities of the closing a project process:
- Prepare planned closure
- Prepare premature closure
- Hand over products
- Evaluate the project
- Recommend project closure

Figure 11.2: Overview of closing a project

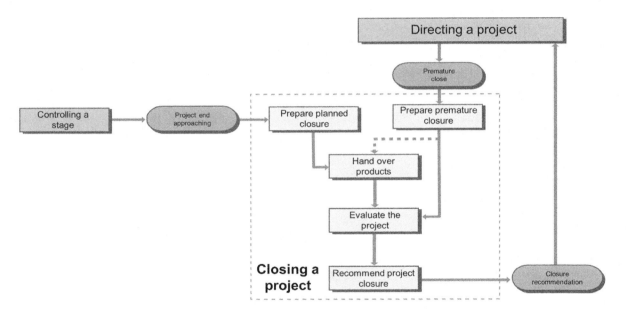

The first activity that the project manager will do in the closing a project process depends on whether this is a planned or a premature closure. If the project is closing when it was originally planned to close, the project manager will perform the prepare planned closure activity. If the project is closing earlier than originally planned (known as a *premature closure*), the project manager will carry out the prepare premature closure activity. After either one of these activities, the project manager will then do the final three closing a project activities: hand over products, evaluate the project, and recommend project closure.

You learn about each of these activities in this section. Make sure you understand the general idea of closing a project, but you don't necessarily have to remember all the details. At the end of this section is a key facts table that shows you what would be useful to memorize for the exams.

Prepare Planned Closure

Before arriving at this activity, the project manager would have been using the controlling a stage process to manage the final delivery stage. When she realizes that the final delivery stage is nearing completion, she will want to start preparing for the end of the project by using the closing a project process. In this situation, the first closing a project activity the project manager will do is prepare planned closure.

The project manager updates the project plan with the progress updates from the final stage. If the project has used a configuration management system, the project manager might request a product status account to ensure that all the products from the final stage have been approved by the relevant people outlined in their product descriptions. (You learned about product status accounts in the "Tracking and Controlling Configuration Items" section of Chapter 8, "Change Theme.") The project manager will confirm that the project has delivered what was defined in the project product description and that all the acceptance criteria have been met.

Finally, the project manager notifies the project board that the resources used in the final stage are about to be released from the project.

Prepare Premature Closure

This will be the first activity in the closing a project process if the project board has instructed the project manager to close the project prematurely. If the project has used a configuration management system, the project manager might request a product status account and review the current state of the products. In particular, she will look for products that could be useful to other projects or parts of the organization (even if the project hasn't finished them yet) and/or products that need to be secured or put into storage.

Suppose, for example, that the project is to create some new apartments for a construction firm. The construction firm may decide that because of poor economic conditions, they will prematurely close the project and restart it when conditions improve. In this case, additional work will be needed to secure the unfinished site and weatherproof the buildings.

The project manager will then create additional estimates for the work needed to finish potentially useful products or to put products into storage. The project manager will need to present these additional work estimates (maybe in the form of an exception plan) to the project board for authorization.

The project manager will also update the issue register to record the premature closure request and update the project plan with the progress updates from the final stage.

Finally, she will notify the project board that the resources used in the final stage are about to be released from the project.

Hand Over Products

In this activity, the project manager hands over the project's products to the operations and maintenance teams. The project manager reviews the change control approach to understand any special procedure for this handover. The project manager should collect acceptance records from the operations and maintenance teams as proof that they have taken on responsibility for the products. After the products have been handed over, the project manager ensures that any relevant configuration item records are updated with the change of status. (You learned about configuration item records in the "Tracking and Controlling Configuration Items" section of Chapter 8.)

Some products, such as IT systems, need a lot of support and maintenance in their operational life after the project. In this case, the project manager ensures that there is a suitable service agreement or contract between the operations team and the end users. This service agreement should have been a specialist product that was delivered as part of the project.

The project manager passes on any follow-on action recommendations for the products to the operations team. These can be things such as known product errors, requests for changes that were considered but never implemented, and/or known issues or risks for the products.

The project manager (and, in some cases, the senior users) reviews the benefits management approach to ensure that post-project benefit reviews have been planned. In addition to reviewing the benefits derived from the products, these reviews focus on how the products performed in their operational life. The project manager (and, once again, the senior users might be involved here) will also check that the approach plans all post-project management actions that are required to ensure that the project's outcomes are achieved. In Chapter 10, you learned that some projects might hand over interim releases at the end of some of the stages. If this were the case, the remainder of the products would be handed over at this point.

Evaluate the Project

In this activity, the project manager creates the *end project report*. This report compares the project's actual achievements against the objectives set in the original version of the project initiation documentation created in the initiation stage. One caveat to this is that if the original objectives have been subject to an approved change, the amended objectives will be used.

The end project report focuses on how the project performed against its planned targets for time, cost, quality, scope, benefits, and risk. Of course, at this point, not all the benefits might have been achieved, since many benefits don't occur until after the project. So all that can be done at this point is to review any benefits that occurred during the project and to ensure post-project benefit reviews are planned in the benefits management approach.

Figure 11.3 shows the composition of the end project report.

Figure 11.3: Composition of the end project report

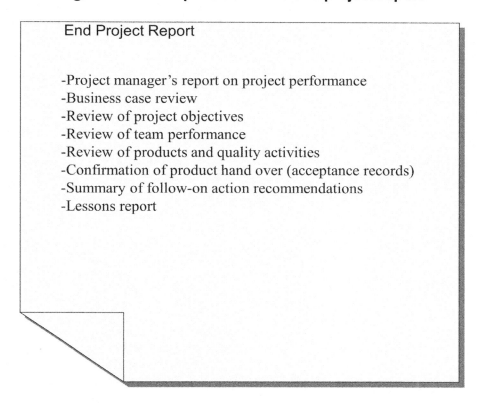

End Project Report

-Project manager's report on project performance
-Business case review
-Review of project objectives
-Review of team performance
-Review of products and quality activities
-Confirmation of product hand over (acceptance records)
-Summary of follow-on action recommendations
-Lessons report

One aim of the evaluate the project activity is to provide useful feedback to corporate, programme management, or the customer that will help to manage future projects. For example, by comparing estimates versus actual results, the organization might see ways to improve its estimating techniques. The end project report contains a lessons report for the project, which can show corporate, programme management, or the customer what worked well and/or what worked badly in managing this project. For example, the lessons report could look at how PRINCE2 was implemented and suggest improvements in its use for future projects. (You learned about the lessons report in Chapter 10.)

Recommend Project Closure

In this activity, the project manager confirms to the project board that the project is ready to be closed. The project manager creates a draft project closure notification for the project board to review.

The project manager then reviews the communication management approach to see who needs to be informed that the project is about to close.

Finally, the project manager ensures that all the project's issues and logs are closed and that all the project documentation is archived in accordance with the procedure described in the change control approach.

Key Facts for Closing a Project

For the Foundation exam, you do not have to memorize all the details from the previous activities sections. However, you should learn the important facts for each activity, as specified in Table 11.1. The Practitioner exam, on the other hand, may contain detailed questions about process activities, but you will be allowed to refer to the official PRINCE2 manual, *Managing Successful Projects with PRINCE2*, so there is no need to memorize all the details.

Table 11.1 Closing a project process—key facts

Activity	Key Facts
Prepare planned closure	The project manager requests a product status account to check that the project's products meet all their quality criteria and have been approved by the appropriate authorities. The project manager updates the project plan with actual progress from the last delivery stage.
Prepare premature closure	The project manager updates the project plan with actual progress from the last delivery stage. The project manager requests a product status account to understand which products have been completed. The project manager prepares additional work estimates for unfinished products that could be useful for other projects or for products that need to be stored or secured.
Hand over products	The project manager ensures that all products are handed over to the operations and maintenance teams and acceptance records are obtained as proof. The project manager checks the benefits management approach to ensure that it includes all post-project activities to confirm benefits that cannot be measured until sometime after the project.
Evaluate the project	The project manager creates the end project report, which evaluates how the project performed against the planned objectives outlined in the initial project initiation documentation. The project manager creates a lessons report to show useful experience learned during the project.
Recommend project closure	The project manager sends a draft project closure notification to the project board. The project manager ensures that the project documentation is archived according to the approach outlined in the change control approach.

Tailoring the Closing a Project Process

In Chapter 1, you learned that PRINCE2 can be successfully tailored to suit many different situations. For example, PRINCE2 can work effectively in a programme environment, when an agile delivery approach is used, or when a separate commercial organization delivers some of the project's products. This section looks at how the closing a project process might be adapted to suit some of these situations.

In a simple project, the closing a project process's activities might be done rapidly and informally. For example, the main activities of accepting the final products, evaluating the overall project, and approving the closure of the project might take place in a single meeting. There may be no need to prepare an end project report. Instead, circulating the meeting minutes from the closure meeting might suffice. Even when closing a simple project, however, the project manager needs to ensure that all stakeholders are informed that the project is ending and that they are all aware of any follow-on actions.

Sometimes the project team will retain responsibility for operating the products for a trial or warranty period before passing them over to a client's operations team. If this is the case, there might be a number of acceptances of the final products. First, the client might review the finished products and sign off on them, but the project team is still responsible for supporting the products. This might occur at the end of one of the later stages of the project, during managing a stage boundary. Then the products will go through their warranty period, which might be covered by a number of the last stages of the project. Finally, the products will be handed over from the project team to the client's operations team during the closing a project process.

If the project has used an agile delivery approach, many of the activities prescribed in the closing a project process might have already occurred by the time the project reaches its end. An agile approach would deliver the products into their operational environment over a number of iterations. This means that many of the products will have been accepted throughout the project and that the products will already have started to deliver benefits to the commissioning organization, so planning post-project benefit reviews might not be necessary. In addition, because agile teams often carry out retrospectives (meetings where lessons are reviewed) at the end of each release, there might be no need to write a lessons report. However, it is still good practice to hold some sort of formal project closure event.

If the project is part of a programme, someone from the programme board will take responsibility for the benefits management approach after the project. Sometimes this person is called a *business change manager* and is responsible for ensuring that all the programme's products are used in the correct way to deliver the benefits from the programme.

The main management product created in the closing a project process is the end project report. This can be adapted to suit any readership. The project manager would need to consider whether any of the elements of the report are confidential. For example, the business case review or the review of team performance might be separated from the main report and sent to a restricted audience.

The Directing a Project Process

As mentioned in Chapter 2, "Starting a Project Successfully with PRINCE2," this book covers the directing a project process in several chapters, as follows:

- Chapter 2 describes how the directing a project process is used at the beginning of the project.
- Chapter 10 describes how the directing a project process is used during the middle of the project.
- This chapter describes how the directing a project process is used at the end of the project.

At the end of the project, the project board uses the directing a project process to decide whether to authorize the closure of the project.

Authorize Project Closure

The final activity in the PRINCE2 process model is the directing a project process's authorize project closure activity. This is where the project board reviews the outputs from the closing a project process and decides whether the project can finally close.

This is the project board's last activity before the body is disbanded. The decision may need further authorization from corporate, programme management, or the customer. The project board may also use project assurance to review the end project report and validate its accuracy.

During the authorize project closure activity, the project board reviews the project against its original objectives (or, as stated previously, any approved amendments to these original objectives). They ensure that any post-project benefit reviews are planned and pass on the responsibility for these reviews to corporate, programme management, or the customer. They also ensure that useful experience highlighted in the lessons report is passed on to the relevant authorities.

Finally, the project board issues the project closure notification in accordance with the procedure described in the communication management approach.

Key Facts for Directing a Project

For the Foundation exam, you do not have to memorize all the details of the directing a project activities. However, you should learn the important facts for each activity, as specified in Table 11.2. The Practitioner exam, on the other hand, may contain detailed questions about process activities, but you will be allowed to refer to the official PRINCE2 manual, *Managing Successful Projects with PRINCE2*, so there is no need to memorize all the details.

Table 11.2: Directing a project process—key facts

Activity	Key Facts
Authorize initiation (covered in detail in Chapter 2)	The project board reviews the project brief and the initiation stage plan and decides whether to authorize the project manager to proceed with the initiation stage.
Authorize the project (covered in detail in Chapter 2)	The project board reviews the project initiation documentation and decides whether to authorize the commencement of the delivery part of the project.
Authorize a stage or exception plan (covered in detail in Chapters 2 and 10)	The project board reviews either the next stage plan or an exception plan, together with the updated project initiation documentation and an end stage report, and decides whether to authorize the project manager to proceed with the work of the stage or exception plan.

Activity	Key Facts
Give ad-hoc direction (covered in detail in Chapter 10)	The project board gives the project manager informal advice or guidance.
Authorize project closure (covered in detail in this chapter.)	The project board reviews the performance of the project by reviewing the end project report and decides whether to authorize the closure of the project.

Tailoring the Directing a Project Process

As mentioned at the beginning of this section, you have been learning about the directing a project process across three chapters of this book: Chapters 2, 10, and this chapter. What hasn't been covered so far is how to tailor the process throughout the entire project. I am going to do that here, so don't get confused—even though the rest of this chapter is about the end of the project, this particular section shows you how to tailor the directing a project process, at the beginning, middle, and the end of the initiative.

On simple projects, the project board might take a less formal approach to directing a project. Project board decisions might be communicated by email or at informal meetings. To avoid any confusion, however, it is important that there is some record showing what the decisions were. A simple project might have only two stages: an initiation stage and one delivery stage. In this case, the project board will only need to use the authorize a stage or exception plan activity to authorize exception plans.

The project board roles can be adapted; however, it is important that only one person is accountable for the project board's decisions and the success of the project. In some organizations, this person is referred to as a project sponsor rather than an executive. Sometimes the decision to release funds is made above the project board—for example, at a corporate, programme, or portfolio level.

In agile projects, where the teams are often delivering to tight, inflexible deadlines, the project board needs to make quick decisions. This is particularly important when the project manager raises exceptions to the project board. The project board must also be prepared for a more informal style of reporting. For example, they might not receive formal progress reports but instead be asked to attend sprint reviews or product demonstrations.

In the "Tailoring the Organization Theme" section of Chapter 3, "Organization Theme," you learned that a commercial customer/supplier environment could have two project boards: one set up by the customer and one set up by the supplier. In this case, the customer's executive looks after the interests of the customer, and the supplier's executive looks after the interests of the supplier. Whether there is a separate supplier project board or not, the customer's project board should have senior suppliers who represent the interests of any external suppliers. Early on in the project, when the external suppliers may not yet have been engaged, someone from the customer organization might temporarily become a senior supplier. This might be someone from the customer's procurement department.

You also learned in the "Tailoring the Organization Theme" section of Chapter 3 that if the project is part of a programme, people from the programme board might take on roles on a project board. For example, the programme manager might become a project executive, or the programme's business change manager might become a project's senior user.

Using the PRINCE2 Themes to Close the Project

This section looks at how the PRINCE2 themes are used at the end of the project. It is important for you to understand this, as this is a potential topic for exam questions.

Business Case Theme

During the closing a project process, the project manager updates the benefits management approach with any further planned post-project benefit reviews and reviews any benefits that have occurred during the project.

During the directing a project process, the project board ensures that corporate, programme management, or the customer assumes responsibility for the post-project benefits reviews and reviews the achievement of any benefits during the project. The project board also reviews the final updated business case to confirm that the final cost and time forecasts have been achieved and that the benefits forecasts have been achieved or are likely to be achieved post-project.

Organization Theme

The project manager uses the communication management approach to determine who needs to be notified that the project is ending. After the directing a project process's authorize project closure activity is complete, the project management team is disbanded. The responsibility for post-project benefit reviews is given to corporate, programme management, or the customer. The responsibility for the project's products is handed over to the operations and maintenance team.

Quality Theme

During the closing a project process, the project manager ensures that all the products from the final stage have been approved by the appropriate authorities highlighted in their product descriptions. The project manager ensures that the authorities defined in the project product description review the final outputs from the project against the acceptance criteria and give acceptances for those products. The project manager should obtain acceptance records as proof that this has happened.

Plans Theme

The project manager updates the project plan with details of what happened in the final stage during the closing a project process. If the project has closed prematurely, the project manager may need to create an exception plan to ask for authorization for any additional work, such as finishing products that might be useful for the organization or for storing products.

Risk Theme

The project manager passes on details of any relevant operational risks to the group that will maintain the products in their operational life. These risks are passed on as follow-on action recommendations during the closing a project process.

The project manager closes and archives the risk register in the closing a project process.

Change Theme

During the closing a project process, the project manager reports any off-specifications, concessions, and approved requests for change in the end project report, and archives the issue register and any issue reports.

The project manager passes on any relevant issues to the operations team as follow-on action recommendations.

Progress Theme

The end project report acts as a major project control, helping the project board monitor the results of the project. The lessons report is another project control, helping the project management team capture and disseminate useful experiences from the project.

Using the PRINCE2 Principles to Close the Project

All seven PRINCE2 principles are used to some extent at the end of the project, but the three main ones are as follows:

Focus on Products
The project manager ensures that acceptance is obtained for the final outputs of the project and that the products are reviewed against their acceptance criteria described in the project product description.

Learn from Experience
The project manager creates a final lessons report and passes it to the project board, which, in turn, passes it to the group that is focused on organizational improvement.

Continued Business Justification
The project manager ensures that the forecast benefits are reviewed and that post-project benefit reviews are planned.

Summary

In this chapter, you saw how PRINCE2 can be used to manage the end of a project. Two main processes are involved: closing a project and directing a project.

The closing a project process ensures that there is a fixed point in time to review the outputs from the project and to review the achievement (or lack of it) of the project's objectives. The project manager is responsible for closing a project, the main output of which is the end project report.

After the closing a project process, the project board uses the directing a project process's authorize project closure activity to review the end project report and decide whether the project can close. The project board ensures that corporate, programme management, or the customer accepts responsibility for any post-project benefit reviews.

You saw how the closing a project process can be adapted to suit different situations, such as when the project management team is faced with a simple project, an agile project, or a project that's within a programme environment. Finally, you saw that all the PRINCE2 themes and principles are used at the end of the project.

Foundation Exam Essentials

Explain the purpose of the closing a project process.
The purpose of the closing a project process is to provide a fixed point at which acceptance of the project's products is confirmed and to review whether the project's objectives have been achieved (or approved changes to the objectives have been achieved) or that the project has nothing more to contribute.

Explain the objectives of the closing a project process.
The objectives of the closing a project process are to gain user and operational acceptance for the products, to review the project against its baseline, to assess any benefits that have already been realized, to ensure post-project benefit reviews are planned, and to ensure that provision has been made to address all open issues and risks with follow-on action recommendations.

Explain the context of the closing a project process.
The closing a project process occurs at the end of the process model. The project manager uses the activities to prepare to meet with the project board for the final time to ask for authorization to close the project.

Explain the purpose of the end project report.
The purpose of the end project report is to review the performance of the project against the objectives set in the version of the project initiation documentation that was used to authorize it.

Practitioner Exam Essentials

Carry out the five activities of the closing a project process and demonstrate an understanding of the recommended roles and responsibilities within the process.
The project manager is responsible for all five activities in the closing a project process. If the project is closing prematurely, the project manager prepares for premature closure by updating the project plan for a final time and estimating any additional work that needs to be done to finish off potentially useful products or to make any of the unfinished products safe. If the project is closing at the appropriate time, the project manager prepares the planned closure by updating the project plan for the final time. The project manager then hands over products to the client, users, and/or the operations team, who will take responsibility for the products post-project. Next, the project manager evaluates the project by creating an end project report. Finally, the project manager recommends the project's closure.

Demonstrate an understanding of how the PRINCE2 themes can be applied throughout the closing a project process.
All seven PRINCE2 themes are applied during the closing a project process. The business case theme is applied when the project manager reviews the achievement of any benefits during the project and plans any further post-project benefit reviews. The organization theme is applied when the project manager carries out her responsibilities to close the project on behalf of the project board. The quality theme is applied when the client, users, and/or the operations team evaluate the final outputs of the

project against the project product description. The plans theme is applied when the project manager updates the project plan for the final time and, in the case of a premature close, may create an exception plan to describe any final work needed to make products safe or to finish potentially useful products. The risk theme is applied when the project manager passes on any risks that could impact the operation of the products post-project as follow-on-action recommendations to the client, users, or operations team. The change theme is applied when the project manager passes on any changes or issues that could impact the operation of the products post-project as follow-on-action recommendations to the client, users, or operations team. Finally, the progress theme is applied when the project manager reviews the achievements of the project and writes the end project report.

Assess and critique an approach to applying the closing a project process.
Explain how the process might be adapted to different project contexts (for example, a small project, an agile project, a project with external third-party organizations or a project operating within a programme environment) and whether the approach aligns with the principles of PRINCE2.

Understand the directing a project process's authorize project closure activity and demonstrate an understanding of the recommended roles and responsibilities within this activity.
In the authorize project closure activity, the project board reviews the project's performance and decides whether to authorize the closure of the project.

Demonstrate an understanding of how the PRINCE2 themes can be applied during the directing a project process's activities used at the end of the project.
All seven PRINCE2 themes are applied during the directing a project process used at the end of the project. The business case theme is applied when the project board reviews the updated benefits management approach to check that all post-project benefit reviews are planned. In addition, the project board will check that any post-project management actions to ensure the outcomes from using the project's products are achieved are also planned. The organization theme is used when the project board reviews the performance of the project management team. The quality theme is applied when the project board ensures that the final outputs of the project have been accepted. The plans theme is applied when the project board reviews the final version of the project plan containing all actuals from the project. The risk theme is applied when the project board reviews the performance of the project's risk management approach. The change theme is applied when the project board reviews the performance of the project's change control approach. Finally, the progress theme is applied when the project board reviews the performance of the project controls.

Assess and critique an approach to applying the directing a project process.
Explain how the process might be adapted to different project contexts (for example, a small project, an agile project, a project with external third-party organizations, or a project operating within a programme environment) and whether the approach aligns with the principles of PRINCE2.

Demonstrate an understanding of the end project report.
Demonstrate an understanding that the project manager creates the end project report at the end of the project and that the project board uses the end project report to review the performance of the project while deciding whether to authorize the project's closure. Know that the project manager creates the end project report during the closing a project process. Understand that the end project report might be derived from the issue, quality or risk registers, the project plan, end stage reports, the benefits management approach, the business case, any exception reports raised during the project, and the

lessons log. Know that an end project report could be a presentation to the project board, a document or email, or an entry in a project management tool. Know the composition of the end project report.

Review Questions

The remainder of this chapter contains mock exam questions, first for the Foundation exam and then for the Practitioner exam.

Foundation Exam Questions

1. What is a purpose of the closing a project process?
   A. To enable the project manager to review whether the project has anything further to contribute
   B. To enable the project board to decide whether to close the project
   C. To enable the project manager to manage the final delivery stage
   D. To enable the delivery team to create the specialist products of the final stage

2. When might the closing a project process be used in a project?
   (1) Directly following a request from the project board to prepare to close the project earlier than expected
   (2) While the project manager is planning the activities for the closure of the project
   (3) While the project board is deciding to authorize the closure of the project
   (4) Directly preceding the decision by the project board whether to close the project
   A. 1 and 2
   B. 2 and 3
   C. 3 and 4
   D. 1 and 4

3. Which of the following are purposes of the end project report?
   (1) To show the activities required to gain acceptance of the products and evaluate the project's performance
   (2) To pass on details of ongoing risks
   (3) To document lessons that could be applied to other projects
   (4) To show how and when the achievement of the post-project benefits can be made
   A. 1 and 2
   B. 2 and 3
   C. 3 and 4
   D. 1 and 4

4. Which of the following is a purpose of the lessons report?
   A. To recommend post-project actions specific to the project's products
   B. To plan how and when the project's benefits will be reviewed
   C. To collate lessons that could be usefully applied to the current project
   D. To provoke action to embed positive experience into the organization's way of working

5. Which of the following is an objective of the closing a project process?
   A. To prepare a stage plan for the early phases of operational support for the project's products
   B. To request authorization to start the final stage of the project
   C. To provide authority to close the project
   D. To ensure that any continuing threats to the project's products are highlighted in the follow-on action recommendations

6. Which of the following processes enables the project board to be accountable for the project's success?
   A. Closing a project
   B. Controlling a stage
   C. Directing a project
   D. Managing product delivery

7. Which of the following is an objective of the directing a project process?
   A. To obtain acceptance records to verify user acceptance of the project's products
   B. To create an end project report to review the performance of the project against its baselines
   C. To ensure that there is authority to close the project
   D. To prepare the stage plan for the last management stage

8. Which process allows the two-way flow of information about the closure of the project between the project board and corporate, programme management, or the customer?
   A. Controlling a stage
   B. Managing product delivery
   C. Closing a project
   D. Directing a project

9. Which process helps to ensure that the project has a clear end rather than slowly drifting into the operational usage of the project's products?
   A. Starting up a project
   B. Initiating a project
   C. Controlling a stage
   D. Closing a project

10. Which management product defines the management actions that will be put into place to ensure that the project outcomes are achieved?
    A. Project initiation documentation
    B. Benefits management approach
    C. End project report
    D. Lessons report

Practitioner Exam Questions

The following Practitioner exam questions are divided into two sections by question type and are based on the Practitioner exam scenario in Appendix B.

Section 1: Matching Questions

Column 1 in the following table describes five actions taken by the project manager as part of the closing a project process during the Website Project, and Column 2 lists the seven PRINCE2 themes. For each action (1–5), identify the theme (A–G) that it relates to. Choose only one theme for each action. Each theme can be used once, more than once, or not at all.

Column 1	Column 2
1. 1. The project manager refers to the communication management approach to identify who needs to know the project is closing.	A. Business case
2. 2. The project manager reviews the benefits management approach to check that there is a planned review of online sales in six months' time.	B. Organization
3. 3. First Tech highlights an ongoing security threat to the website. The project manager passes this on as a follow-on action recommendation to the IT personnel who will operate and maintain the site.	C. Quality
4. 4. The project manager discusses with the marketing director whether she agrees that the website has met all its acceptance criteria.	D. Plans
5. 5. The project manager gathers information about the performance of the project against its initial objectives and records it in the end project report.	E. Risk
	F. Change
	G. Progress

Section 2: Classic Multiple-Choice Questions

Exam Spotlight

Remember that during the Practitioner exam, you are allowed to refer to the official PRINCE2 manual (*Managing Successful Projects with PRINCE2*). This is a great help. One of the key differences between passing and failing the Practitioner exam is knowing how to use the PRINCE2 manual during the exam. Some of the questions in the exam rely on your ability to find specific pieces of information quickly from the manual.

This chapter covers how to use the closing a project process and the directing a project process at the end of the project. In the manual, all the process chapters are set out in the same way. The first two pages discuss the purpose, objectives, and context of the process. Then the body of each process chapter looks at the activities that take place within that particular process. Some Practitioner exam questions can test you on quite obscure facts about a process's activity. The key to getting these questions correct is to first understand which activity the question is testing you on. For example, if a question asks about obtaining acceptances for the final products during the closing a project process, you are probably being asked about the hand over products activity. Look carefully in the manual at the relevant pages for that particular activity. Do any of the bullet points help you? Does the activity's table of responsibilities give a clue about who might be creating a management product mentioned in the question? Does the activity's flow diagram help?

A process question might ask you about how to tailor the process to different situations, such as a programme or agile environment. To help with these sorts of questions, you'll find a section at the end of each process chapter about tailoring.

Process questions might ask you about a management product that is created in that process. For example, a closing a project process question could test you on the end project report or the lessons report. The best place to look for information about management products is in the manual's Appendix A.

If you are tested on a process's roles and responsibilities, there are two good places to look in the manual: each activity's table of responsibilities and Appendix C.

1. At the end of stage five, the project board asked the project manager to plan for a review of the monthly number of website visitors in six months' time. The project manager added this information to the benefits management approach. Is this appropriate, and why or why not?
    A. Yes, because during the closing a project process, the project manager might update the benefits management approach with any new benefit reviews.
    B. Yes, because the project manager needs to delegate a work package to the team that reviews the website's visitors.
    C. No, because the project manager creates the benefits management approach in the initiation stage.
    D. No, because reviewing the number of visitors to the website is outside the scope of the project.

2. During stage five, the IT manager has suggested that Digital Design be engaged to support and maintain the website after the project. The project board has approved this idea and has asked the IT manager to create a service agreement between Quality Furniture and Digital Design for this post-project operational support. Is this appropriate, and why or why not?
    A. Yes, because all projects should create support and maintenance agreements for their products.
    B. Yes, because when a product requires a lot of potentially expensive support, it is good practice to ensure a suitable service agreement has been created before the end of the project.
    C. No, because the support and maintenance of the website is outside the scope of the project.
    D. No, because the support and maintenance of the website will be planned in the benefits management approach.

3. During stage three, the chief executive has decided that the budget for the website would be better spent upgrading Quality Furniture's four shops and has asked that the website project be closed immediately. The marketing manager has suggested that it would still be a good idea, before closing the project, to increase the current website's ranking in major search engines. The project manager has created an exception plan that shows the cost and time for the search engine work while removing all further work to create the new website and sent it to the project board. Is this appropriate, and why or why not?
    A. Yes, because in the case of a premature closure, the project management team should try to salvage anything of value before abandoning the initiative.
    B. Yes, because it is the project manager who should decide what work needs to be completed before a project closes.
    C. No, because the project should now close and the search engine work should take place in a new project.
    D. No, because the marketing manager should create the exception plan.

Chapter

12

Passing the
Accreditation Exams

Two things will greatly increase your chances of becoming PRINCE2-accredited: First, you need to learn the PRINCE2 method, and second, you must understand the style and format of the two exams.

Studying a method with as much detail as PRINCE2 provides can be quite a challenge. The good news is that you don't need to remember everything. The basic Foundation exam does not test you about the detailed aspects of the method, and the more difficult Practitioner exam allows you to use the PRINCE2 manual *Managing Successful Projects with PRINCE2* (Stationery Office, 2017).

This chapter discusses what to remember for the Foundation examination and how to use the PRINCE2 manual for the Practitioner exam. You should also know how to tackle the exam formats. The Practitioner exam has a unique style. If the first time you see this style is on the exam day, a good knowledge of PRINCE2 might not be enough to ensure that you pass. This chapter offers a range of tips and tactics to improve your chances of successfully negotiating the Foundation and Practitioner exam formats.

Preparing for the Exams

As with any exam, the better you prepare, the more likely you are to pass. In this section, you learn where to focus your study time.

Preparing for the Foundation Exam

The Foundation exam is the easier of the two exams. It tests to see if you can remember the PRINCE2 methodology rather than the more difficult skill of whether you can apply the methodology. However, you do need to be fully prepared in order to pass. As mentioned in the introduction, you don't have to remember everything for this exam. In this section, I will show you what you should memorize in order to pass the Foundation exam.

It is also very important to practice taking as many Foundation mock questions as you can before taking the real exam. There are plenty of practice questions for you to try in this book. In this section, I will also discuss the best way to use these practice questions.

Syllabus Topics Tested During the Foundation Exam

There are 16 separate syllabus areas in the Foundation exam. On average, there will be about four questions on each of these topics. The syllabus area topics are as follows:

Projects and PRINCE2
This topic includes the characteristics of a project, the six aspects of project performance that need to be managed, the four integrated elements of PRINCE2, and the benefits of PRINCE2. Chapter 1, "Overview of PRINCE2," covers this topic.

The Principles
This topic includes questions on the seven PRINCE2 principles. Chapter 1 covers this topic.

The Seven Themes
The seven PRINCE2 themes are covered in Chapters 3 through 9, respectively.

The Seven Processes
Chapter 1, "Overview of PRINCE2," covers the directing a project process. Chapter 2, "Starting a Project Successfully with PRINCE2," covers the starting up a project and initiating a project processes. Chapter 10, "Managing the Middle of a Project Successfully with PRINCE2," covers the controlling a stage, managing product delivery, and managing a stage boundary processes. Chapter 11, "Managing the End of a Project Successfully with PRINCE2," covers the closing a project process.

You should learn the 16 syllabus topics to a medium level of detail for the Foundation exam. The next few sections describe what "medium level of detail" means in practice.

Learning About Projects and PRINCE2 for the Foundation Exam
Chapter 1 covers this syllabus topic. You need to be able to identify the following:
- The characteristics that distinguish a project from business as usual: change, temporary, cross-functional, unique, and uncertainty
- The four elements of PRINCE2: principles, themes, processes, and the project environment
- The benefits of PRINCE2 — see the list in Chapter 1
- The six aspects of project performance that need to be managed: cost, timescales, scope, quality, risk, and benefits
- What makes a project a PRINCE2 project and which aspects of PRINCE2 can be tailored

This information is usually the first thing people learn about PRINCE2, but by the time they take the exam, they've forgotten it. Make sure you don't fall into that trap.

Learning About the Principles for the Foundation Exam
This syllabus topic, discussed in Chapter 1, covers all seven PRINCE2 principles: continued business justification, learn from experience, defined roles and responsibilities, manage by stages, manage by exception, focus on products, and tailor to suit the project environment.

You might need to explain how the PRINCE2 principles are supported and implemented by the rest of the methodology. For example: Which theme primarily supports the manage by exception principle? The answer is the progress theme (see Chapter 9, "Progress Theme"), because it explains the use of tolerances that implement management by exception. Another example would be: Which theme primarily supports the focus on products principle? The answer is the quality theme (see Chapter 6, "Quality Theme"), because it explains how to use product descriptions to specify a product.

Learning About the Process Model for the Foundation Exam
The PRINCE2 model contains seven processes, within which are approximately 40 separate activities. Within each activity, various roles do various actions, carried out using the management approaches set out in the themes and using the various PRINCE2 management products. This is obviously a lot of detail to remember.

You can answer the vast majority of questions on the Foundation exam by knowing the model down to the process level, not to the activity level. For example, rather than trying to remember that the project manager creates the daily log during the appoint the executive and the project manager activity, it is enough to remember that this occurs in the starting up a project process. So, for each of the seven processes, memorize which management products are created, reviewed, or updated, which themes are used, and which roles are involved.

You should also understand the sequence in which the processes are used throughout the life of a project. The "An End-to-End Walk-through of PRINCE2" section in Chapter 1 is an excellent source of information for this.

The process key facts tables provided in this book are also useful for preparing for the Foundation exam. You can find these tables in the following chapters:
- Chapter 2, "Starting a Project Successfully with PRINCE2," contains a key facts tables for the starting up a project and initiating a project processes.
- Chapter 10, "Managing the Middle of a Project Successfully with PRINCE2," contains key facts tables for the controlling a stage, managing product delivery, and managing a stage boundary processes.
- Chapter 11, "Managing the End of a Project Successfully with PRINCE2," contains a key facts table for the closing a project process.

Learning About the Roles for the Foundation Exam

It is very important to understand the PRINCE2 roles and responsibilities. These are covered in detail in Chapter 3, "Organization Theme," but here's a quick rundown of what you need to know about them for the exam:
- Understand that there are three main stakeholder interests represented in the PRINCE2 project management team: the user, the supplier, and the business.
- Know the four levels of the PRINCE2 project management structure: the corporate, programme management, or the customer level; the directing level (represented by the project board); the managing level (represented by the project manager); and the delivering level (represented by the team manager and the teams). Understand how these levels interact with each other throughout a project.
- Understand the project management team organization chart. Figure 3.3, in Chapter 3, "Organization Theme," shows how the various PRINCE2 roles report to and work with each other.
- Understand the responsibilities of each PRINCE2 role.

The organization theme topic spans the entire PRINCE2 method. In every single process, theme, or activity, various roles do various things. With every management product, various roles are involved with creating, reviewing, and updating the product. This makes the organization theme one of the most important topics to learn.

Learning About the Themes for the Foundation Exam

Ironically, I have the least amount to say about how to learn the themes for the Foundation exam. It's ironic because most of your preparation time should be focused on understanding the seven themes, but there are no shortcuts with this topic. Make sure you read through the relevant chapters in this study guide to fully understand how each theme describes how to manage the project using its particular area of project management and how the theme relates to the rest of the PRINCE2 model.

The Foundation exam tests you on each theme's minimum requirements. The tailoring section of each theme-related chapter in this study guide discusses these minimum requirements. Be sure to read these sections carefully.

Learning About the Management Products for the Foundation Exam

There are 26 PRINCE2 management products, each with approximately 10 different sections of information. That is a lot of information to remember. For the Foundation exam, for most of these management products, I wouldn't recommend memorizing all the sections of all the products. You need to know each product's purpose, an overview of the information it contains, and the processes within which it is created and updated. Appendix B, "Management Products in PRINCE2," contains a reference list for all 26 management products that tells you where they are described in this study guide. With some management products, it is more important to remember exactly what they contain. I recommend memorizing the composition of the following management products:

- Business case
- Product description
- Project product description
- Project brief
- Project initiation documentation
- Work package

Learning About the PRINCE2 Terminology

It is very important to understand the PRINCE2 terminology. One of the benefits of PRINCE2 is that it provides a common project management language. For this to be useful, however, you need to be able to speak that language. This can be challenging for the following reasons:

- Before studying PRINCE2, candidates may have managed projects using a different approach, either one created specifically for their workplace or one of the other available project management best practice approaches, such as the Project Management Institute's *A Guide to the Project Management Body of Knowledge, 4th Edition (PMBOK® Guide)*. Candidates then confuse the terminology between PRINCE2 and the other approach.
- A number of PRINCE2 terms are used in a different way in everyday speech. For example, "risks" in PRINCE2 are not just potential bad things that might happen but also potential opportunities (see Chapter 7, "Risk Theme"). The "reason" for doing the project is always what has happened before the project started to trigger the initiative, not the predicted value that the project might bring (see Chapter 4, "Business Case Theme"). And "quality" doesn't mean luxurious; it means a product that is fit for the purpose it will be used for (see Chapter 6, "Quality Theme").

The meaning of a Foundation question can change if the candidate misunderstands the definition of just one word. It is important to learn all the PRINCE2 terminology by using the Glossary, which can be found on this book's companion website (www.sybex.com/go/prince2studyguide).

Testing Your Knowledge

In addition to performing all the exam preparation discussed previously, you should take as many practice Foundation questions as you can. You can find practice Foundation questions in the Assessment Test at the beginning of this book and in the Review Questions sections at the end of each chapter. There is also a complete Foundation examination, in Appendix D, "Sample Foundation Examinations."

I would recommend that you answer all of these questions.

Use the practice Foundation exam questions to focus your exam preparation. Review the questions you get wrong and make sure you understand your mistakes. Look to see if there is any pattern to your mistakes—for example, maybe you are having trouble with a particular topic. If so, you obviously need to do further work in that area.

When you answer the practice Foundation questions, try to take them in the same amount of time that you will have for the real exam. You get only one hour to answer 60 questions—an average of one minute per question. Also, try to answer the practice questions without referring to this study guide, any of your revision material, or *Managing Successful Projects with PRINCE2*.

Preparing for the Practitioner Exam

The Practitioner exam is the harder of the two PRINCE2 accreditation levels. It tests not only whether you understand the methodology but also whether you know how to apply it. Obviously, the best way to understand how to apply PRINCE2 is to actually use it in practice. However, quite a number of candidates who take the Practitioner exam have never used the method, and, for those who have, very few workplaces implement every aspect of PRINCE2. So how do you show how to apply the method if you have never or only partially used it? I suggest the following approaches:

- Answer plenty of Practitioner exam practice questions. The Practitioner exam gives you a project case study and then asks questions about how to apply PRINCE2 to it. The more of these sorts of questions you answer, the better your understanding will be on how to apply the method. This book has mock Practitioner questions at the end of most chapters, and there is a complete Practitioner Exam in Appendix E. I suggest you answer all of these questions.
- Read the case studies set out throughout this book. They show how PRINCE2 has been used in real projects.
- Read widely on the application of project approaches such as PRINCE2. If you search on the Web for PRINCE2 blogs, articles, and discussion forums, you will find plenty of resources to expand your knowledge. There are some particularly good ones on LinkedIn.®
- Implement some of the aspects of PRINCE2 in your workplace.

The Practitioner exam doesn't require you to memorize any more of the theory than you did for the Foundation exam. Remember that you can answer the more detailed questions on the Practitioner exam by referring to *Managing Successful Projects with PRINCE2*, which you are allowed to take into the exam.

Using the Managing Successful Projects with PRINCE2 Manual

You should know how to use the official PRINCE2 manual, *Managing Successful Projects with PRINCE2*, during the exam to help you answer the more detailed questions. The manual is useful for detailed questions such as what happens in a particular activity or what type of information goes into which particular section of one of the management products. I discuss how to use the manual during the exam in the "Taking the Practitioner Exam" section later in this chapter. There are a number of things you can do before the exam that will make the manual easier to use *during* the exam:

- There isn't much time in the Practitioner exam, so you have to find the information in the manual quickly. Buy some sticky tabs and place them at the beginning of the chapters. You could tab the beginning of the processes and themes chapters and the beginning of the appendices. This will make it far easier to quickly find what you are looking for.
- The Practitioner exam rules state that you are not allowed to take any reference material other than the PRINCE2 manual into the exam. This includes not being allowed to insert sheets or anything larger than a section tab into the manual. However, one loophole in this rule is that you are allowed to write notes in the manual and highlight words. I recommend

that you do this for any summary material that you have found useful in this study guide or from any other source that you feel will help you during the exam.

- When you answer the mock Practitioner exam questions in this study guide, practice using the PRINCE2 manual.

Taking the Exams

Sooner or later, the dreaded exam day will arrive. If you have followed all the advice in this study guide, you will have an excellent chance of passing both levels of accreditation. Remember that before you sit for the Practitioner exam, you must first take and pass the Foundation exam.

Obviously, having a good knowledge of PRINCE2 is a prerequisite to passing the accreditation; however, approaching the exam in the right way will increase your chances of success. This section provides some of the tips and tactics for dealing with the two exams that I have learned over the many years I have taught PRINCE2.

General Tips for Taking the Exams

This section discusses a number of general tips that will be useful for both the Foundation and the Practitioner exams.

Read the Question

When I teach PRINCE2 courses, "read the question" are three words that I repeat again and again. It sounds so obvious—and rather patronizing. However, it is very easy, especially when you are under pressure, to skim the questions, misreading or missing essential words in a question, or changing the question into something you would rather have answered.

The PRINCE2 examinations are specifically worded. They use the PRINCE2 terminology in an exacting way. This makes it even more important than normal to carefully read the questions. It might help you during the exam to use a pen to underline or highlight key words in a question.

To illustrate how easy it is to misread the exam, consider the following question about the change theme:

Which product would confirm the version numbers of all products being developed within a given stage?
A. Configuration item record
B. Product status account
C. Stage plan
D. Work package

Answer: B
The product status account provides a summary of the status information about a group of products. This status information is sourced from all those products' configuration item records. Option A is incorrect—each product has a corresponding configuration item record that holds status information on that product, such as its latest version number; however, the question asks for the product that holds the version numbers of *all* the products in a stage, not just for one product. Option C is incorrect—the stage plan shows how the products will

be created, not their version numbers. Option D is incorrect—the work package is the official instruction to the teams to build the products.

Did you get it right? If you went for product status account, well done. If you went for configuration item record, you just proved my point about reading the question. If you went for stage plan or work package, you probably need to reread Chapter 8, "Change Theme."

The key word in this question is *all*. It is easy to miss such a small word and read the question as "Which product would confirm the version numbers of *a* product being developed within a given stage?" If the question had asked this, the answer would have been the configuration item record.

Other common misread terms are confusing an exception plan with an exception report, product descriptions with the project product description, and issue reports with issue registers.

Time Management

One of the major reasons that people fail the PRINCE2 exams is that they run out of time.

The Foundation exam has 60 questions, which you need to answer in one hour. That is one question per minute. Practice answering the mock questions until you can do them at this sort of pace.

The Practitioner exam has 68 questions, for which you have two and a half hours to answer. Once again, you need to do the questions at a quick pace, although you get slightly more time per question: two minutes. When answering the mock questions, practice doing them at this speed. Candidates generally find it harder to complete the Practitioner exam than the Foundation exam in the time available.

In either exam, if you get stuck on a particular question, you must move on. Leave the question for any time you have left at the end. Keep moving through the exam at the right sort of pace so that you have the best chance of answering as many questions as possible.

Special Allowances for International and Disabled Candidates

I discussed earlier how challenging it can be to understand the PRINCE2 terminology. This is difficult enough for a native English speaker; it is obviously even harder for someone who isn't. I regularly teach PRINCE2 courses across Europe for international bodies such as NATO and the United Nations. Although the exam is available in 16 different languages, my courses are always in English and the exams are worded in English. During these courses, I spend extra time making sure that the candidates understand the language of PRINCE2.

As of this writing, AXELOS allows extra time for candidates taking the exam in English who are nonnative speakers of English, providing that they fulfill the following two criteria:

- They are nonnative speakers of English.
- They work in an environment where English is not the business language.

If the candidates meet both of these criteria, they can get an extra 15 minutes for the Foundation exam and an extra 40 minutes for the Practitioner exam. If you meet these criteria, *take* this extra time—every advantage helps. AXELOS regularly updates these rules, so check them with the organization that is providing your exam center. They will have an up-to-date copy of the AXELOS proctor or invigilator rules.

The exams have also been translated into 16 languages. You could check to see if the exam is available in your language. Once again, the organization that is providing your exam center will have all the latest details on this.

If you believe you have a disability that will affect your performance in the exam, contact your exam center to discuss it. AXELOS makes all reasonable allowances for disabilities so that everyone can have a fair chance at taking the exams. AXELOS may require you to produce a doctor's certificate.

Raising Issues During or After the Exam

If there are any issues either before or during the exam that you feel would reasonably affect your performance, you should raise them with your exam invigilator or proctor. He will write them down and submit them, along with the exam papers.

Taking the Foundation Exam

Although the Foundation exam is considered the easier of the two levels, it can still represent a challenge for candidates. If you follow all of the preceding preparation tips, however, you will arrive at the exam well prepared.

The Foundation exam has 60 multiple-choice questions. Each question gives four possible options, one of which is correct. The invigilator or proctor rules do not allow you to refer to any books or study notes during the exam. The exam tests to see if you know the methodology but not necessarily that you know how to apply it. (That comes later, in the Practitioner exam.) You must score 55 percent or better to pass.

Foundation Exam Question Formats

There are four types of Foundation exam questions: standard, negative, missing word, and list. Let's look at each in turn and talk about how you should tackle them.

Standard Questions

The standard type is the easiest. Here is an example:

Which is one of the six aspects of project performance that needs to be managed?
A. Customers
B. People
C. Benefits
D. Processes

Answer: C
Six aspects of project performance need to be managed: time, cost, benefits, risk, quality, and scope. (See Chapter 1, "Overview of PRINCE2.")

Unless the question itself is difficult, you should be able to quickly answer questions in this format.

Negative Questions

Under exam conditions, you may easily miss the word "not" in these types of questions, which, of course, will lead you to the wrong answer. However, the exam should highlight "not" by capitalizing and putting it in bold. Here is an example:

Which is **NOT** a recommended response type to respond to a threat?
A. Avoid
B. Exploit
C. Share
D. Transfer

Answer: B
This is a question about risk responses, which were covered in Chapter 7, "Risk Theme."

Missing Word(s) Questions
Here is an example of this type of question:

Identify the missing word(s) in the following sentence:

Quality planning provides the definition of the required products with their [?] as a foundation for project board agreement.
A. Customer's quality expectations
B. Quality test results
C. Quality criteria
D. Owners

Answer: C
The quality criteria of each product define the measurable specification for that product, which can then be agreed to by the project board (see Chapter 6, "Quality Theme").

This type of question is fairly straightforward. Just be careful to remember that sometimes there is a missing word and sometimes there is a missing partial sentence.

List Questions
The list type of question takes more time than the other types, because there is more to read. Here is an example of this type of question:

Which two statements about tailoring are correct?
(1) PRINCE2 projects should use the recommended PRINCE2 techniques.
(2) Management products could be split into many data sources.
(3) PRINCE2 projects can comprise as many management stages as necessary.
(4) Principles that are not relevant to the project can be excluded.
A. 1 and 2
B. 2 and 3
C. 3 and 4
D. 1 and 4

Answer: B
Option 1 is incorrect—for a project to be a PRINCE2 project, either the recommended PRINCE2 techniques should be used or an equivalent alternative. Option 4 is incorrect—a minimum requirement of PRINCE2 is that a project adheres to the seven principles.

To answer these questions quickly, read the four options and find which ones are wrong.

Taking the Practitioner Exam

The Practitioner exam is the harder of the two PRINCE2 accreditation levels. It tests not only whether you know the theory but also whether you understand how to apply it. A prerequisite for taking the Practitioner exam is that you must have passed the Foundation exam.

There are 68 questions, which are split into 15 sections, each focusing on a different syllabus topic. The 15 syllabus topics are the principles, the seven themes, and the seven processes.

You need to get 55 percent to pass.

The Practitioner exam consists of the following three booklets:

- A scenario booklet with additional information for some of the questions
- A question paper
- An answer sheet

The Scenario and Additional Information

When you take the Practitioner exam, you will get a separate booklet containing a scenario of about a page in length and some additional information, which is also about a page in length. The additional information usually describes a number of people who will be involved in the scenario's project. It will always say clearly at the top of any question whether you need to refer to a section of the additional information in order to answer that question. One common mistake Practitioner exam candidates make is trying to answer a question without referring to any necessary additional information.

As you can imagine, with only two and a half hours to finish the whole exam, you don't have a great deal of time to read this additional information. I recommend that as soon as you start the exam, you should quickly read the scenario. The exam will refer to the scenario throughout all the 68 questions, whereas the additional information is generally needed for only four or five questions, so you need a fairly good grasp of the scenario right away. Highlight any significant points and aim to understand broadly what is happening, but on this first read-through, don't concern yourself with all the scenario details. As you move through the exam, you can fill in the gaps in your knowledge. Also, at this point, you don't know what is important about the scenario until you see the questions.

Once you have read quickly through the scenario, move on to the questions. Don't read any of the additional information until you come to a question that refers to it. Even then, you should first read the question and then read the relevant section of the additional information. Using this approach, you can frame how you read the information, focusing only on what you need to answer the question.

Practitioner Exam Question Formats

There are two possible Practitioner exam question formats:

Standard Classic Multiple Choice

These are similar to the Foundation questions. You are given a question with four possible answers, and you need to pick the correct option.

Matching

You are given two lists, and you have to match one set of list items with the other set of list items.

The next few sections discuss how to tackle each of these question types. The questions come from the Review Questions sections at the end of the chapters. If you haven't reviewed all of these questions yet, don't worry—you don't need to in order to understand this section. The Practitioner exam scenario for these questions concerns a furniture manufacturing company called Quality Furniture that has started a project to create a new website. The website will sell their products.

Matching Questions

In the matching type of question, you are given two lists. For each option in the first list, you have to choose an option from the second list. The following is an example taken from Chapter 3, "Organization Theme":

> Use the "Additional Information" that you will find in Appendix B. In the following table, Column 1 lists the five individuals connected to the Website Project. Which project management role (A–F in Column 2) would be most appropriate for each individual? Choose only one role for each individual. Each role can be used once or not at all.

Column 1	Column 2
1. Operations director at Digital Design	A. Executive
2. Project manager at Digital Design	B. Senior user
3. Marketing manager at Quality Furniture	C. Senior supplier
4. IT manager at Quality Furniture	D. Project manager
5. Chief executive of Quality Furniture	E. Project assurance
	F. Team manager

Here are the answers and explanations:
1. C
    The operation director at Digital Design would be able to represent the supplier interest of the outsourced supplier and therefore could become a senior supplier.
2. F
    Although referred to as a project manager within Digital Design, this person manages only one of the work streams of the project and would therefore likely to be the team manager within the project.
3. B
    The marketing manager, along with the marketing team, would use the website to realize benefits (future sales of furniture) and therefore could become a senior user.
4. D
    The IT manager would be an ideal candidate for the project manager role. She has previously managed a similar project and is PRINCE2-qualified, so she is likely to have the relevant competencies for the role, such as planning, time management, and people management.
5. A
    The chief executive would be able to represent the business interest in the project and therefore could become the project's executive.

How did you do? One potential pitfall that exam candidates sometimes fall into is believing that all the options in Column 2 have to be used. As you can see from this example, that is not always the case. At the top of these sorts of questions, a statement such as "Each selection in Column 2 can be used once, more than once, or not at all" will appear that explains this.

Classic Standard Multiple-Choice Questions

The classic standard multiple-choice question comes in two main types. The first is the easier type, which is very similar to the Foundation exam questions. Here is an example taken from Chapter 1:

> The project is approaching the end of stage two, and the project manager has heard that a competitor is launching a similar website. The chief executive has called a meeting to discuss the viability of carrying on with the project. Which principle is being applied, and why?
> A. Continued business justification, because the justification for the project should remain valid throughout the life of the project
> B. Learn from experience, because as the project progresses, the project should continually review and learn from outside events
> C. Defined roles and responsibilities, because the project manager is responsible for collating all information regarding threats to the business case
> D. Manage by exception, because a threat to project tolerances should be escalated to the chief executive

> Answer: A
> The principle of continued business justification requires that the justification for the project remain valid throughout the project's life. The meeting that the chief executive has called is to review the justification for the web project (option A). Option B is incorrect— although it is true that the project management team should continually learn from outside events, this situation is specifically about reviewing the justification for the project, so it is more about applying the principle of continued business justification than learn from experience. Option C is incorrect—although it is true that the project manager is responsible for maintaining the risk register, the principle being applied by calling the meeting is continued business justification. Option D is incorrect—it is not clear yet whether there is any threat to project tolerances.

These types of questions should be the quickest to answer. Save time on these questions—time that you can then use for the harder formats.

The other type of standard multiple-choice question is harder. In these types of questions, you not only have to work out whether an approach to managing the project is correct, you also have to justify with PRINCE2 theory why it is correct. Here is an example of this type of question taken from Chapter 3, "Organization Theme":

> The chief executive has requested that Digital Design be represented on the project board. However, he is concerned about divulging sensitive information to the supplier. He has asked the project manager to arrange a separate meeting for Quality Furniture staff before each

project board meeting to discuss what can be shared with Digital Design. Is this appropriate, and why or why not?

A. Yes, because in a commercial customer/supplier environment, there should always be a customer meeting before a project board meeting.

B. Yes, because the executive decides how to solve the dilemma of whether to share sensitive information with external suppliers on the project board.

C. No, because Digital Design should be represented on a separate supplier project board.

D. No, because in order to enable effective decision making, all information should be shared among project board members.

Answer: B

The question makes an assertion about how the project should be managed. In this case, the assertion is that when dealing with external suppliers, it might be appropriate to have a customer pre-meeting before each project board meeting. You then have to decide whether that assertion is correct or incorrect. But then you have to think a little bit more, because you have to work out which part of the PRINCE2 method justifies your answer.

There are two approaches to questions like this. First, ask yourself whether the assertion sounds reasonable, In this case, I think it does, so the answer is probably option A or B, which at the very worst is a one-in-two guess rather than a one-in-four guess. The other approach is to forget about the question for a moment and look at the PRINCE2 theory outlined in each of the options. Are any of these options incorrect according to PRINCE2? For example, option C in the example says there should be a separate supplier project board. PRINCE2 clearly says there is only one project board per project, so option C must be incorrect.

Using *Managing Successful Projects with PRINCE2* during the Exam

Some questions are quite detailed, such as asking what type of information appears in a particular section of a particular management product. Unless you have a photographic memory and have memorized this entire study guide and/or memorized the entire official PRINCE2 manual (*Managing Successful Projects with PRINCE2*), you will not be able to answer these very detailed questions without referring to the PRINCE2 manual.

Here are a few tips about using the using the PRINCE2 manual during the exam:

- For questions about management products, refer to Appendix A in the PRINCE2 manual. Appendix A shows you exactly what type of information goes into which section of each management product.
- For questions about roles and responsibilities, refer to Appendix C in the PRINCE2 manual. This appendix contains an easy-to-read list of responsibilities for each role. There also is a table in each theme-related chapter that gives you a similar list, focusing on that theme's responsibilities.
- For questions about particular activities, use the relevant process chapter. The input/output diagrams and the responsibilities tables for each activity in the process chapters are particularly easy to read and show what management product is created, reviewed, or updated in which activity, as well as which role is responsible.
- For questions about the organization theme, you'll find useful the diagram in the organization theme chapter that shows the project management team structure. It illustrates who reports to whom and how each role fits into the project management team.

- For questions about the quality theme, you'll find useful the diagram in the quality theme chapter that shows the quality audit trail. It pulls together all the aspects of quality management. You can annotate this diagram using what you learned in Chapter 6, "Quality Theme," in this study guide.
- For questions about the plans theme, you'll find useful the diagram in the plans theme chapter that shows the PRINCE2 levels of plans. It illustrates how the plans relate to each other. You can annotate this diagram using what you learned in Chapter 5, "Plans Theme," in this study guide.
- For questions about the risk theme, you'll find useful the table in the risk theme chapter that shows the threat and opportunity responses. It demonstrates how to respond to a risk. You can annotate this table using what you learned in Chapter 7, "Risk Theme," in this study guide.
- For questions about the change theme, you'll find useful the diagram in the change theme chapter that shows the issue and change control procedure. It shows how to respond to a change. You can annotate this diagram using what you learned in Chapter 8, "Change Theme," in this study guide.

Good luck!

Appendix A

Answers to Review Questions

Chapter 1: Overview of PRINCE2

Foundation Exam Answers

1. B. Option 1 is incorrect—for a project to be a PRINCE2 project, either the recommended PRINCE2 techniques should be used or an equivalent alternative. Option 4 is incorrect—a minimum requirement of PRINCE2 is that a project adheres to the seven principles.
2. D. The focus on products principle ensures that the project management team does work only that directly contributes to producing the project outputs (option D). Option A is a benefit of the tailor to the project environment principle. Option B is a benefit of the continued business justification principle. Option C is a benefit of the manage by exception principle.
3. C. The expected returns from the project are the forecast benefits that occur as a result of the outcomes of the project.
4. B. Projects often involve work that spans a number of functional divisions and possibly spans across a number of organizations.
5. A. The defined roles and responsibilities principle ensures that all necessary perspectives and people are involved with the management of the project.
6. D. Management by exception is the approach whereby one management level delegates work to the management level below by defining constraints around the lower level's authority. The standard way of defining this authority is by setting out what costs and timescales the lower level must work within, including any permissible leeway or tolerance. If the lower level realizes they cannot meet their constraints, they must escalate the situation to the management level above.
7. B. The manage by stages principle breaks up the project into time sections. The project is planned at a high level from beginning to end. Detailed planning is done for only the next stage, just before that stage starts.
8. A. The continued business justification principle states there should be a clear reason to undertake the project and that this rationale should be re-evaluated throughout the project (option A). Option B is one of the ways the learn from experience principle should be applied. Option C is one of the ways the focus on products principle should be applied. Option D is one of the ways the manage by stages principle should be applied.
9. C. The processes provide a set of activities to be done by defined project roles throughout the life of the project.
10. C. PRINCE2 provides a common vocabulary. This makes it easier to communicate on projects, especially when several different organizations are involved.

Practitioner Exam Answers

1. A. The principle of continued business justification requires that for all projects, the justification for the project remains valid throughout its life. The meeting that the chief executive has called is to review the justification for the website project (option A). Option B is incorrect—although it is true that the project management team should continually learn from outside events, this situation is particularly about reviewing the justification for the project, so it is more about applying the continued business justification principle than applying the learn from experience principle. Option C is incorrect—although it is true that the project manager is responsible for maintaining the risk register, the principle being applied by calling the meeting is continued business justification. Option D is incorrect—it is not clear yet whether there is any threat to project tolerances.

2. C. If a tolerance is forecast to be exceeded, it should be escalated immediately to the next management level for a decision on how to proceed (option C). Option A is incorrect—although it is true that the principle of manage by exception helps avoid wasting senior management's time, it is important to escalate exceptions as quickly as possible. Option B is incorrect—although it is true that the project manager is responsible for escalating forecast breaches of tolerances, the problem with the project manager's approach is that he is not escalating the issue immediately. Option D is incorrect—the team should escalate the situation to the project manager, who will then escalate the problem to the project board.

3. B. The manage by exception principle involves establishing accountability for each level of management by setting tolerances. One area that may have a tolerance is the scope of work in terms of which products might be delivered. Categorizing features in terms of desirable and mandatory features will help establish an allowable variation on what will be delivered (option B). Option A is incorrect—although it is true that the project manager is responsible for creating product descriptions, product description have not yet been created for the features. Option C is incorrect—categorizing the features will not allow the planning of effective control and decision points. Planning effective control and decision points will take into account factors such as how far ahead it is feasible to plan and the amount of project risk. Option D is incorrect—categorizing the features does not involve tailoring the application of PRINCE2.

Chapter 2: Starting a Project Successfully with PRINCE2

Foundation Exam Answers

1. B. The project manager uses the first version of the project initiation documentation (option B) during the closing a project process to assess how the project performed against its initial objectives. This assessment is described in the end project report.

2. D. The project manager creates the project plan in the initiating a project process, which shows what work needs to be done to deliver the project's products (option D). Options A and B are purposes of the starting up a project process, and option C is a purpose of the directing a project process.

3. A. The project mandate could be based on information taken from a feasibility study (option 1) or, in a supplier environment, a request for proposal (option 2). Option 3 is incorrect—the project manager creates the project brief in the starting up a project process, which is triggered by the project mandate. Option 4 is incorrect—the project manager creates the project initiation documentation during the initiating a project process, which takes place after the commissioning organization has created the project mandate.

4. A. Option 1 is correct—the project manager creates the quality management approach, which describes how to ensure that the quality required from the products is achieved, during the initiating a project process. Option 2 is also correct—the project manager creates the communication management approach, which describes the communication needs of the project management team and stakeholders who are external to the team, during the initiating a project process. Option 3 is incorrect—defining all the necessary authorities for initiating the project is an objective of the starting up a project process. Authorizing the initiation of the project occurs immediately prior to the initiating a project process, Option 4 is also incorrect—the project manager creates the initiation stage plan in the starting up a project process.

5. A. The project manager creates the project brief, which the project board reviews when deciding whether to authorize the initiation of the project, during the starting up a project process.

6. D. The executive and the project manager design and appoint the project management team during the starting up a project process (option D). Option A is incorrect—establishing solid foundations for the delivery of the project is an objective of the initiating a project process. In order to do this, the project manager creates the project initiation documentation, which contains the project plan, during the initiating a project process. Option B is incorrect—assigning and monitoring work packages is an objective of the controlling a stage process. Option C is incorrect—enabling the project board to be accountable for the project's success is an objective of the directing a project process.

7. C. The executive creates the outline business case, which should justify the project management team carrying out the initiation stage of the project, during the starting up a project process (option C). Option A is incorrect—the project manager creates the benefits management approach, which plans the management activities to ensure the project outcomes are achieved, during the initiating a project process. Option B is incorrect—the project manager records how the project management method will be tailored for the upcoming project in the project initiation documentation during the initiating a project process. Option D is incorrect—providing management direction and control is an objective of the directing a project process.

8. B. When the project board is carrying out their activities, as described in the directing a project process (option B), one of their key responsibilities is to ensure that the project remains aligned to the overall strategy of the commissioning organization (corporate, programme management, or the customer).

9. B. The project manager creates the project brief during the starting up a project process. This provides the base information about the project, which the project board uses to decide whether to commission the first stage of the project.

10. A. The project manager creates the project approach, which evaluates how the project's products can be delivered and recommends an approach, during the starting up a project process (option A). Option B is incorrect—determining how changes will be identified, assessed, and controlled is an objective of the initiating a project process. Option C is incorrect—this is an objective of the initiating a project process. During the initiating a project process, the project manager creates the quality management approach, which describes how quality management will be conducted. Option D is incorrect—this is an objective of the initiating a project process. During the initiating a project process, the project manager creates the benefits management approach, which defines how to measure the achievement of the project's benefits.

Practitioner Exam Answers

Answers to Section 1: Matching Questions

1. B. The organization theme describes the roles and responsibilities that will be required throughout the project.
2. D. The concern is a risk to the project. During the starting up a project process, the project manager will record risks in the daily log because the risk register will not have been created yet. Recording uncertain events and their impact on the project is part of the application of the risk theme.
3. E. This statement describes the project manager creating the initiation stage plan.
4. A. The online sales will be recorded as benefits in the outline business case.
5. A. The reasons for the project will be recorded in the outline business case.

Answers to Section 2: Classic Multiple-Choice Questions

1. C. When the project manager is capturing previous lessons, it might be appropriate to ask people outside of the organization to share any related experiences (option C). Option A is incorrect—although it is true that one of the aims of the starting up a project process is to ensure it is done as quickly as possible, it would not be unreasonable to talk to people outside of the organization who have relevant experience, especially given that the Quality Furniture staff does not have any experience. Option B is incorrect—although it is true that running a workshop is one way of capturing useful experience, this is not the reason why the project manager should not invite external personnel to the workshop. Option D is incorrect—the project manager should be responsible for maintaining the lessons log and facilitating the capturing of useful lessons.
2. A. During the starting up a project process, the project manager records issus in the daily log. When the project moves into the initiation stage, the project manager transfers any issues that need to be treated formally to the issue register (option A). Option B is incorrect—the project manager needs to record formal issues only in the issue register. Option C is incorrect—the project manager should record formal issues in the issue register and, if necessary, create an accompanying issue report. Option D is incorrect—the project manager would escalate a formal issue to the project board only if a stage tolerance is forecast to be exceeded and the project manager is in exception; however, there is no indication that this is the case.
3. C. If a project is part of a programme, some parts of the project initiation documentation, such as the approaches and the business case, might be created at a programme level (option C). Option A is incorrect—although the project manager is responsible for ensuring that appropriate project initiation documentation is created, some parts of the project initiation documentation might be created by other people, such as programme management. Option B is incorrect—although the executive might work to resolve some communication difficulties with the programme team, this is not the reason why the programme team might be correct in prescribing the risk management approach. Option D is incorrect—there is always the need for the project initiation documentation, whether the project is part of a programme or not; however, when the project is part of a programme, some parts of the project initiation documentation might have been created by the programme team.

Chapter 3: Organization Theme

Foundation Exam Answers

1. B. The executive represents the business interest on the project. It is his responsibility to secure the funding for the project.
2. B. PRINCE2 states that, rather than the project manager managing the team, a separate person might be appointed to the team manager role because the project is large, a team is sited in another geographic area, and/or a team is using specialist skills.
3. D. A minimum requirement of the organization theme is to ensure that all the responsibilities in the PRINCE2 role descriptions are fulfilled (option D). Option A is incorrect—in some circumstances, where work is outsourced to an external company, that company might decide to set up their own project board, but this is not an organization theme minimum requirement. Option B is incorrect—when the project is part of a programme, the programme's design authority might take on the role of change authority, but this is not an organization theme minimum requirement. Option C is incorrect—the project must ensure that all the responsibilities described in the PRINCE2 role descriptions are fulfilled, but sometimes one person might take on more than one role.
4. B. The project board represents the directing level of management. They allocate stages with associated tolerances to the project manager. If the project manager realizes that a stage will breach those stage tolerances, he must escalate this situation to the project board, which has the authority to authorize any deviation that exceeds stage tolerances (as long as the situation does not also exceed project tolerances, in which case corporate, programme management, or the customer would need to authorize the deviation.)
5. C. The communication management approach facilitates engagement with stakeholders through the establishment of a controlled and bidirectional flow of information.
6. D. The senior supplier is responsible for ensuring that the project's products have the technical integrity to meet the users' needs (option D.) Option A is incorrect— the senior user represents those who will benefit from using the products. Option B is incorrect—corporate, programme management, or the customer is responsible for commissioning the project. Option C is incorrect—the executive is responsible for ensuring that the project is following a cost-conscious approach.
7. B. A number of different types of people could represent the user interest on the project. They might be someone who will buy the products for their own use, as they will be impacted by the outputs of the project (option 3). They might be someone who will maintain or operate the products after the project (option 2). Option 1, someone who can assess and confirm the viability of the project approach, would represent the supplier interest, and option 4, someone who wants to ensure that the business need justifies the investment in the project, would represent the business interest.
8. A. Each role on the project board—the executive, the senior user, and the senior supplier—has a project assurance responsibility aligned to its area of interest (option A). Options B and C are incorrect—project assurance is responsible for auditing the project manager and project support, so neither of these roles can also do project assurance, as this would create a conflict of interest. Option D is incorrect—the project manager is responsible for creating the communication management approach.

9. C. One purpose of the organization theme is to define the project's approach to communicating and engaging with the stakeholders. This is documented in the communication management approach (option C). Option A is a purpose of the risk theme (see Chapter 7, "Risk Theme"). Option B is a purpose of the plans theme (see Chapter 5, "Plans Theme"). Option D is a purpose of the quality theme (see Chapter 6, "Quality Theme").

10. C. In a small project, the project support and the project manager roles can be combined.

Practitioner Exam Answers

Answers to Section 1: Matching Questions

1. C. The operation director at Digital Design will be able to represent the supplier interest of the outsourced supplier, so he could become a senior supplier.

2. F. Although referred to as a project manager within Digital Design, this person is managing only one of the work streams of the project, so he is likely to be the team manager within the project.

3. B. The marketing manager and the marketing team will use the website to realize benefits (future sales of furniture), so the marketing manager could become a senior user.

4. D. The IT manager would be an ideal candidate for the project manager role. She has previously managed a similar project and is PRINCE2-qualified, so she is likely to have the relevant competencies for the role, such as planning, time management, and people management.

5. A. The chief executive will be able to represent the business interest in the project, so he could become the project's executive.

Answers to Section 2: Classic Multiple-Choice Questions

1. C. An important concept in agile environments is allowing the delivery team to self-organize and have autonomy within certain constraints. The best way to achieve this is by the project manager using the principle of management by exception to manage the agile team. This would mean setting appropriate tolerances around the work package, particularly around the scope objective, and describing in the work package how the team manager could work, without needing to constantly liaise with the project manager, unless there is a forecast breach of work package tolerances (option C). Option A is incorrect—although it is true that the project manager uses a work package to control the teams, the approach described in the question is not the best method for an agile environment. Option B is also incorrect—setting no tolerances is not an effective way of implementing management by exception. There would be no leeway around any of the work package objectives, so the team would have to liaise with the project manager on a greater basis for decisions. Option D is also incorrect—although it is true that the project manager receives checkpoint reports to monitor a team's progress, this is not the reason why the described approach would not be effective in an agile environment.

2. B. The executive should decide how to balance the risk of divulging sensitive information to third-party organizations against the benefit of having external suppliers on the project board, which might provide useful information around specialist issues and supplier resources. A reasonable response to this challenge would be to have a Quality Furniture meeting before each project board meeting to decide which information can be discussed with the supplier (option B). Option A is incorrect—it is not mandated in PRINCE2 that in a commercial customer/supplier environment every project board meeting be preceded by a customer meeting. Option C is also incorrect—sometimes a supplier might set up a supplier project board, but this isn't

a mandatory requirement in a commercial customer/supplier environment, and even if one did exist, Digital Design might still represent the supplier interest on the Quality Furniture's project board. Option D is also incorrect—although it is true that the more information that is shared among project board members, the more likely good decisions will be made, in a commercial customer/supplier environment, it might not be appropriate to share sensitive commercial information between the customer and external suppliers.

3. A. The project manager should review the communication management approach at each stage boundary to ensure that all the relevant stakeholders are included in the document ready for the upcoming stage (option A). Option B is incorrect—although it is true that the communication management approach describes the communication between parties both internal and external to the project, this is not the reason why the project manager should update the communication management approach while planning for stage three. Option C is also incorrect—although it is true that the project manager creates the communication management approach in the initiating a project process, he could still update the document at each stage boundary. Option D is also incorrect—the communication management approach should cover the means of communication for all stakeholders in the project, regardless of whether they are internal or external to the commissioning organization.

Chapter 4: Business Case Theme

Foundation Exam Answers

1. A. One of the purposes of the business case theme is establish and review the viability of the project throughout the initiative (option A). Option B is a purpose of the quality theme, option C is a purpose of the organization theme, and option D is a purpose of the risk theme.

2. A. The benefits management approach describes both how and when the benefits will be reviewed and also how the performance of the project's products will be reviewed.

3. B. Option 1 is correct—the outline business case is reviewed during the initiation stage and updated to create the detailed business case. Option 2 is incorrect—although the project mandate might contain a description of the justification for the project, the business case is not created until after the project mandate is created. Option 3 is correct—the business case is updated and reviewed at the end of each management stage. The project manager updates the business case in the managing a stage boundary process, and then the project board reviews the business case in the directing a project process, when deciding whether to authorize the next stage. Option 4 is incorrect—specialist products are delivered by the teams during the managing product delivery process, and the business case is not reviewed at this point.

4. D. The project manager records management actions that need to be put into place to ensure that the project's outcomes are achieved in the benefits management approach (option D). Option A is a minimum requirement of the plans theme, option B is a minimum requirement of the quality theme, and option C is a minimum requirement of the change theme.

5. B. An output from a project is the specialist product the project produces. Option B, new computer software, might be an output from a project. Option A, benefits management approach, is an example of a management product, not a specialist product. Option C is the result of the change of using some products, so it's an outcome. Option D is the measurable positive consequence of a project, so it's a benefit.

6. C. The business case theme requires that a business case and a benefits management approach be produced and maintained.
7. B. The detailed business case is created in the initiating a project process.
8. A. The executive ensures that the benefits forecast in the business case represent value for money and align with the organization's objectives.
9. A. The executive creates the outline business case in the starting up a project process (option A). This is part of developing the business case. Option B is incorrect—this is an example of a verify activity. Option C is incorrect—this is an example of a confirm activity. Option D is incorrect—this is an example of a maintain step.
10. D. The senior user is responsible for both forecasting the benefits from the project and then realizing the benefits by using the project's products.

Practitioner Exam Answers

Answers to Section 1: Matching Questions
1. B. The business options section shows the alternatives considered to meet the business challenges that the organization faces. The "do nothing" option should always be considered, and continuing with the current website is effectively doing nothing.
2. D. A dis-benefit is an outcome from the project that would be perceived as negative by one or more stakeholder. If the website project goes ahead, the factory-extension project will not be able to start.
3. E. The timescales section should show the period over which the benefits from the website will be realized.
4. A. The reasons section explains why the project is being undertaken.
5. C. The increase in sales by 20 percent is a measurable benefit from the project.

Answers to Section 2: Classic Multiple-Choice Questions
1. C. If a supplier were to write a customer's business case, there would be a conflict of interest (option C). Option A is incorrect—the executive is accountable for the business case, but there would be a conflict of interest if a supplier were to develop the customer's business case. Option B is also incorrect—although it is true that Quality Furniture has not been involved in online sales before, this wouldn't justify creating a conflict of interests by asking the supplier to create their business case. Option D is also incorrect—if the supplier takes on the role of senior supplier, they would confirm the viability of the project approach, but this isn't the reason why the supplier should not develop the customer's business case.
2. A. The benefits management approach will be used post-project to compare the sales of the company after the new website has been launched against the sales as they were before the website was launched (option A). Answer B is incorrect—although it is true that the finance director has financial skills, this is not the reason the baseline measures of the company's sales should be written into the benefits management approach. Answer C is also incorrect—the benefits management approach will focus on the improvement in sales due to the project, so it will need to compare Quality Furniture's sales after the project to what they were before the project. Answer D is also incorrect—the benefits management approach should be developed during the initiation stage of the project.

Chapter 5: Plans Theme

Foundation Exam Answers

1. A. A minimum requirement of the plans theme is that a project must have at least two management stages (option A). Option B is a minimum requirement of the quality theme. Option C is a minimum requirement of the change theme. Option D is a minimum requirement of the business case theme.

2. C. The manage by exception principle is implemented by specifying that each PRINCE2 plan includes time, cost, and scope tolerances. Option A describes how the plans theme implements the learn by experience principle. Option B describes how the plans theme implements the manage by stages principle. Finally, option D describes how the plans theme implements the focus on products principle.

3. C. The team plan may be created by teams that are working for separate organizations following different project management method.

4. B. Options 2 and 3 are correct. Option 1 is incorrect—corporate, programme management, or the customer approves an exception plan that would replace a project plan. Option 4 is incorrect—exception plans are not produced following breaches in work package tolerance levels. Instead, the project manager takes corrective actions by updating the work package or issuing a new work package.

5. D. It may be a requirement to align the end of a management stage with a programme milestone review. This will allow the project to contribute fully to the assessment of the ongoing viability of the programme.

6. B. Options 2 and 3 are correct. Option 1 is incorrect—establishing the project's structure of accountability and responsibility is a purpose of the organization theme. Option 4 is incorrect—the business case theme establishes mechanisms to judge whether the project is desirable, viable, and achievable.

7. D. Option A would take place in the defining and analyzing the products step. Option B would take place in the preparing estimates step. Option C would take place in the analyzing risks to a plan step.

8. B. The product-based planning approach is recommended to help define and analyze products.

9. C. Creating a project product description is the first step in the recommended approach to defining and analyzing the products.

10. A. Product-based planning helps to identify the products that are in and out of the scope of the plan by creating tools such as the product breakdown structure.

Practitioner Exam Answers

Answers to Section 1: Matching Questions

1. C. The standard terms of conditions are being revised outside the scope of this stage's plan because they are being changed in another project. Products that are needed for a plan but that the project manager is not accountable for delivering are external dependencies.

2. E. The personal assistant's experience is a lesson that can be usefully applied when scheduling this stage's activities.

3. G. The $5,000 to fund an advertisement is an amount of money used to fund a fallback response to the risk that no suitable tender responses will be received. Any money set aside to fund specific management responses to threats to the success of the plan should be itemized under the "budgets" heading as the risk budget.

4. B. The approval of the project initiation documentation must occur before the activities of stage two can commence. Plan prerequisites are any fundamental aspects that must be in place for the plan to begin.

5. F. The highlight reports are one method that the project board can use to monitor the progress of the stage.

Answers to Section 2: Classic Multiple-Choice Questions

1. D. Only products are shown in the product flow diagram (and the product breakdown structure), not activities. Options A and B are incorrect because review tender responses is an activity and therefore should not be shown in the product flow diagram. Option C is incorrect because the derivation heading should show only products that are needed in order to create the short list of potential suppliers.

2. B. Agile approaches can be used within a PRINCE2 product-based planning approach, and one common approach would be to produce a product backlog during the initiating a project process. Option A is incorrect—although it is true that product-based planning should be considered before activity-based planning, this isn't the reason that a product backlog should be created. Option C is incorrect—although it is true that a product backlog is not part of the standards project initiation documentation, the document can be tailored to suit an agile environment. Option D is incorrect—PRINCE2 can be tailored to an agile environment.

3. A. Project support can assist with the compilation of stage plans and contribute specialist expertise, such as knowledge of planning tools. Option B is incorrect—although it is true that project support will help to baseline the stage plans, this is not the reason why project support might provide help with a planning tool to prepare the plans. Option C is incorrect—although it is true that the project manager is responsible to prepare the stage plans, project support may still provide assistance to the project manager to help them create these plans. Option D is incorrect—it is not true that each stage plan must be created using the same met

Chapter 6: Quality Theme

Foundation Exam Answers

1. C. The quality register summarizes information on the quality activities that are planned or have taken place. One such quality activity might be the quality checking of a product. Every time a product is checked, a quality record should be collected as evidence. The quality register should point to where these quality records are stored (option C). Option A is incorrect—the quality management approach defines the project's approach to quality control. Option B is incorrect—a product description describes a product's quality criteria. Option D is incorrect—a product description specifies the quality methods that will be used to check if a product matches its quality criteria.

2. B. The quality management approach describes how to manage quality throughout the project.

3. A. Option 1 is correct—both types of assurance monitor whether the project adheres to a range of standards, including corporate standards. Option 2 is also correct—both types of assurance are independent of the project manager, who is the managing level of the project management team. Option 3 is incorrect—project assurance not quality assurance is split into business, user, and supplier assurance. Option 4 is incorrect—only quality assurance is independent of the project board, which is the directing level of the project management team.

4. B. At a minimum, the project management team should create a quality management approach that defines the project's approach to quality control. Quality control is focused on both checking that the project's products have been created correctly as well as continually reviewing the performance of the project to see if things can be improved by, for example, improving the management processes (option B). Option A is incorrect—reviewing the business justification of the project after an exception has been raised is a minimum requirement of the progress theme. Option C is incorrect—planning a project with a minimum of two stages is a minimum requirement of the plans theme. Option D is incorrect—defining the project's approach to communicating and engaging with stakeholders is a minimum requirement of the organization theme.

5. B. Quality control is about checking that the project's products have been created correctly. This is done by using quality methods, which are different ways of comparing a product to its quality criteria and keeping evidence that the quality checks have taken place in the form of quality records and entries in the quality register.

6. A. The project product description defines what the project will need to deliver in order for it to be acceptable to the users (option A). Option B is incorrect—the quality management approach describes the management approach, which helps the project deliver products that will be fit for their purpose. Option C is incorrect—the risk management approach defines how the project will control uncertainty (see Chapter 7, "Risk Theme"). Option D is incorrect—the change management approach defines how the project will control proposed modifications to the project's products (see Chapter 8, "Change Theme").

7. D. Option 1 is correct—quality planning is partly about specifying what will be created using product descriptions. Option 4 is also correct—quality planning is partly about specifying how products will be checked to ensure their fitness for purpose. Option 2 is incorrect—scheduling development activities to create the products is an example of applying the plans theme, not quality planning (see Chapter 5, "Plans Theme"). Option 3 is incorrect—carrying out a quality inspection on a product is an example of quality control, not quality planning.

8. D. One of the minimum requirements for applying the quality theme is collecting quality records after each quality test has been carried out on a product. These quality records could be in any format—for example, a form signed by the reviewer—but should always provide evidence that the quality activity occurred. The other options—using the quality review technique, quality inspections, and in-process and appraisal methods—are possible ways of carrying out quality control but are not mandatory requirements of the quality theme.

9. C. Quality criteria specify the measurable attributes that will make a product fit for its purpose. Therefore, specifying quality criteria helps the project management team apply the focus on products principle.

10. C. Customer quality expectations give a high-level description of the overall outputs of the project and the quality expected of those outputs (option C). Option A is incorrect—the quality register would show a summary of the quality activities planned for the project. Option B is incorrect—a product description's quality criteria would describe the measurable attributes of a product. Option D is incorrect—the measurable improvement resulting from an outcome is a benefit. (See Chapter 4, "Business Case Theme.")

Practitioner Exam Answers

Answers to Section 1: Matching Questions

1. B. Quality control is partly focused on checking and reviewing that products meet their product descriptions. The quality review technique can be used to inspect products that are documents in order to verify that they meet their product descriptions.
2. A. Quality planning is partly focused on specifying the attributes of a product. The accessibility standards are a specified attribute that the website must conform to.
3. B. Quality control is partly focused on eliminating causes of unsatisfactory performance. Reviewing the risk management approach and proposing a more efficient process helps improve the performance of the project.
4. C. Quality assurance is about continually reviewing the project to ensure that it adheres to any relevant standards or procedures. Ensuring that the quality management approach adheres to the corporate quality policy is therefore a quality assurance responsibility.
5. A. Planning how to test and review the products is a quality planning activity. This will be done either by describing quality methods in each product's product description or by describing acceptance methods in the project product description.

Answers to Section 2: Classic Multiple-Choice Questions

1. C. The web pages should be described along with their quality criteria in product descriptions, not the quality management approach. The quality management approach describes how to manage quality but does not describe what level of quality or what type of products the project should create (option C). Option A is incorrect—although it is true that the quality management approach describes how quality will be managed, the descriptions for the web pages are not a statement of how to manage quality throughout the project; instead, they are a description of the quality criteria for the products. Option B is incorrect—it is true that senior users provide customer quality expectations and acceptance criteria, but both of these would be recorded in the project product description, not the quality management approach. Option D is incorrect—although it is true that the quality management approach is created in the initiation stage, the approach might be updated throughout the project, and the characteristics of the web pages should be recorded in product descriptions, not the quality management approach.
2. D. Quality criteria should be specific and measurable, but the phrase, "easy to use" is neither of these (option D). Option A is incorrect—although it is true that lessons should be used to inform quality planning, "easy to use" is not specific or measurable and is therefore not an appropriate quality criteria. Option B is incorrect—although it is true that quality criteria describe the quality specification that the product must meet, "easy to use" is not specific or measurable and is therefore not an appropriate quality criteria. Option C is incorrect—although it is true that the senior users should provide the quality criteria and these should be recorded in product descriptions, "easy to use" is not specific or measurable and is therefore not an appropriate quality criteria.
3. A. The presenter role introduces the product for review and represents the producer of the product (option A). Option B is incorrect—the quality review technique is not necessarily used to check all of the project's products. Option C is incorrect—external suppliers can be involved in a quality inspection when they have created the products. Option D is incorrect—quality reviews will take place throughout delivery stages and will be carried out in the managing product delivery process.

Chapter 7: Risk Theme

Foundation Exam Answers

1. C. The recommended risk management procedure consists of five steps: identify, assess, plan, implement, and communicate, so option C is correct. Defining and analyzing products (option A) and identifying activities and dependencies (option D) are steps in the recommended approach to product-based planning. Option B, impact analysis, is part of the issue and change control procedure.

2. D. The purpose of the risk theme is to identify, assess, and control uncertainty and thus improve the ability of the project to succeed (option D). Option A is a purpose of the quality theme. Option B is a purpose of the organization theme. Option C is a purpose of the plans theme.

3. B. Exploit and enhance are risk response options for opportunities. Avoid and reduce are risk response options for threats.

4. D. When the project management team identifies context (during the identify step in the risk management procedure), they consider general characteristics about the project and the environment that might make it riskier than others. For example, a project with a large number of stakeholders will probably be riskier. This is a major determinant of how the project management team will manage risk, which is specified in the risk management approach.

5. A. In order to be following the PRINCE2 risk theme, the project management team must, at a minimum, estimate each risk's potential impact on the business justification for the project.

6. A. Buying the futures will help you reduce the financial impact on the project if the yen appreciates. It is a form of insurance, giving a payout if the worst happens. It is therefore a transfer response.

7. B. Two purposes of the risk management approach are to describe the roles and responsibilities related to risk management (option 2) and to describe any risk management techniques that will be used throughout the project (option 3). It is the risk register that will provide a record of the status for identified risks (option 1) and maintain information on opportunities relating to the project (option 4).

8. C. A risk owner is a named individual who is responsible for the management, monitoring, and control of all aspects of a particular risk (option C). Option A is a responsibility of the executive. Option B is a responsibility of the project manager. Option D is a responsibility of corporate, programme management, or the customer.

9. C. A risk cause is the source or trigger point of a risk (option C). Option A, the risk impact, is the potential impact the risk would have on the project's objectives. Option B, the risk event, is the uncertain event that may follow from the risk cause. Option D, the risk effect, describes the impact that the risk would have on the project's objectives.

10. B. The exploit response to an opportunity ensures that the opportunity will happen. This can often be achieved by implementing the cause of an opportunity.

Practitioner Exam Answers

Answers to Section 1: Matching Questions

1. D. By adding the clause in the contract with the software supplier, the project management team is transferring some of the financial risk to that supplier.
2. B. By bringing in an expert in the area of IT procurement, the project management team is reducing the likelihood of choosing an inappropriate supplier.
3. A. This seems rather strange, but the fact is that if the project is canceled, the risk is eradicated. The impact of a poor supplier is avoided by not having a project that necessitates selecting one.
4. C. Preparing a contingent plan is a reactive response to a potential risk. The project management team waits until the risk occurs and then, if it does, starts to follow a pre-prepared plan.
5. B. By splitting up the tender into several parts, the project management team is spreading the risk of a poor supplier. They may still pick a poor supplier, but it is less likely that they will do so for all the work. So this action reduces the impact and the likelihood of the risk.

Answers to Section 2: Classic Multiple-Choice Questions

1. C. It is important that the money used to respond to risks is proportionate given the likely probability and impact of the risk. One way of achieving this is to calculate the difference between the expected value of the risk both before and after the risk response and ensuring that the risk response costs no more than this figure. Option A is incorrect—although it is true that a risk response offers value for money, the project manager has not allowed for the likely probability of the risk in his calculations. If the probability is very low, $10,000 might be far too much to spend responding to this threat. Option B is incorrect—a risk budget is not set for each individual risk but can be set for the entire project, a stage or for a work package. Option D is incorrect—although it is true that risk responses should be funded from the risk budget, this is not the reason why the project manager's approach to determining what to spend on this particular risk is incorrect.
2. D. It is important that the project's risk management approach works with the project's chosen delivery approach. If deliveries might happen every two weeks, it is unlikely that reviewing risks every month would be appropriate (option D). Option A is incorrect—a project may need to align its risk management approach with an already established organizational approach, but in this case, that would not be appropriate. Option B is incorrect—although it is true that the executive should ensure that the risk management approach is appropriate, it is not clear if the chief executive is carrying out the executive role, and even if he were, he is recommending a risk approach that would not be consistent with the delivery approach that will be used on the project. The agile approach in option C is appropriate, but the project management team needs to be aware of the risks inherent with this approach and take steps to respond to them.
3. A. In a commercial customer and supplier environment, there may be the need for more than one risk register to avoid the issue of sharing commercially sensitive information between the various commercial parties (option A). Option B is incorrect—when work is outsourced, the customer still owns the risks associated with the work. Option C is incorrect—there may be more than one risk register in a commercial customer and supplier situation. Option D is incorrect—although the risk management approach is likely to be fairly static during the project, it could be adapted as the project progresses, and it is not clear if this situation requires an adaption to the approach. The risk management approach created at the beginning of the project might have stated that in commercial situations, two risk registers are required, and the executive might simply be reminding the project manager of this fact.

Chapter 8: Change Theme

Foundation Exam Answers

1. D. Options 1 and 4 are correct. An off-specification is a product that should be delivered by the project but has not been provided and is not forecast to be provided in the future. This could be a missing product or one that doesn't meet its specification. Option 2 refers to a product that, even though it will be delivered over budget, will be delivered—so it is not off-specification. Option 3 refers to a product that, even though it will be late, will be delivered—so it is not an off-specification.

2. A. As a minimum, the project management team must define how product baselines are created, maintained, and controlled (option A). Option B is incorrect—defining the project's approach to quality control in order to eliminate causes of unsatisfactory performance is a minimum requirement of the quality theme. Option C is incorrect—planning a project with at least two stages is a minimum requirement of the plans theme. Option D is incorrect—defining the project's approach to communicating and engaging with stakeholders is a minimum requirement of the organization theme.

3. B. The change budget can be used to fund the analysis of the potential impact of a request for change (option B). Option A is incorrect—threats to the project are risks, and assessing risks is funded from the project budget. Option C is incorrect—reducing the probability of a threat would be done by carrying out a risk response that would be funded using the risk budget. Option D is incorrect—actions following a quality review would be funded from the project budget.

4. A. The change control approach describes how to manage issues and changes within a project (options 1 and 2). Option 3 would be described in the risk management approach. Option 4 would be described in the quality management approach.

5. C. The project manager records informal issues in the daily log. The issue register and issue report are used to record formal issues (options A and B), and the change control approach describes how to carry out effective issue management throughout the project (option D).

6. D. The project manager may need to create an exception plan during the implementing corrective actions step of the issue and change control procedure if he does not have the authority to take corrective action himself.

7. C. A product that does not meet its specification is called an off-specification. Information on all the off-specifications in the project can be found in the issue register. Option B is incorrect, because an issue report would potentially hold information on just one particular off-specification, not all of them.

8. A. A concession occurs when the project board authorizes a product that does not comply with the specification described in that product's product description.

9. B. A configuration item record might be created to record the latest status, version, and variant of a product or a configuration item (option B). Option A is incorrect—an issue report records the latest information on an issue. Option C is incorrect—the product description describes the measurable aspects of a product, how the product will be tested, and who will approve the product (see Chapter 6, "Quality Theme"). Option D is incorrect—a stage plan describes the work to be done in a particular stage (see Chapter 5, "Plans Theme").

10. D. One of the minimum requirements for applying the change theme is maintaining some form of issue register to record issues (option D). Options A, B, and C—creating product status accounts and configuration item records or escalating all requests for changes to the project board—are possible ways of managing change but are not mandatory requirements of the change theme.

Practitioner Exam Answers

Answers to Section 1: Matching Questions

1. C. The third step in the issue and change control procedure is proposing corrective actions. At this time, if the project manager does not have the authority to deal with the issue, he should seek advice from the project board or the delegated change authority.
2. B. The second step in the issue and change control procedure is assessing issues. At this time, an impact analysis will be carried out, looking at how the issue will affect the project objectives, such as time, cost, benefits, risks, scope, and quality. The project manager might do this by chairing a meeting with the project management team.
3. D. The fourth step in the issue and change control procedure is to decide on corrective actions. The project board or its delegated change authority needs to decide whether to approve the request for change.
4. 4   A. The first step in the issue and change control procedure is capturing issues. In this case, it is a request for change, so it is a formal issue, and the project manager should create an entry in the issue register.
5. E. The final step of the issue and change control procedure is implementing corrective actions to resolve the issue. Either the project manager can do this himself or, if he does not have the authority, he will need to create an exception plan, which needs to be authorized by the project board.

Answers to Section 2: Classic Multiple-Choice Questions

1. D. Examining the impact of a request for change must include looking at the impact of the change from both the customer's perspective and the supplier's perspective (option D). Option A is incorrect—although having the supplier participate in the discussions on the impact of the change may include sharing some confidential information, it is important to review the impact from both a customer's and supplier's perspective. Option B is incorrect—although including the suppliers in the review of the impact of the request for change may slow the decision, it is important to review the impact from both a customer's and a supplier's perspective. Option C is incorrect—not all information needs to be shared between a customer and supplier for the project to be successful.
2. C. When there are many relationships between the project's products, it is good practice for the project team to consider creating configuration item records that include information on each product, such as status, version, and important relationships between the products. The latter would help when assessing the impact that a request for change on one product might have on another product (option C). Option A is incorrect—although the issue register records problems or concerns raised during the project, it would be better practice to record information about the relationships between products in a set of configuration item records. Option B is incorrect—although the project manager is responsible for maintaining the issue register, the relationships between products should not be recorded in the issue register. Option D is incorrect—although there is a potential threat to the project if the product relationships are not taken into account, it would be better practice to record information about the relationships between products in a set of configuration item records.
3. A. A change control approach needs to take into account the project's delivery approach, so it is appropriate to create a new version for the agile environment (option A). Option B is incorrect—there should be only one change control approach covering the project. Option C is incorrect—although the change control approach is created in the initiation stage, the approach can be changed anytime throughout the project as long as the change control procedure is used. Option D is incorrect—although one of the principles of agile is to embrace change, change will still be controlled to some degree within an agile environment.

Chapter 9: Progress Theme

Foundation Exam Answers

1. C. The project manager allocates the work package tolerances for the team when authorizing a work package.
2. A. The daily log is used to capture actions and significant events not caught by the other PRINCE2 registers or logs. Option 1 is correct because risks and issues identified in the starting up a project process are put temporarily into the daily log and then later transferred into the relevant register in the initiating a project process. Option 2 is also correct because informal issues are recorded in the daily log. Option 3 is incorrect because requests for changes are recorded in the issue register, and option 4 is incorrect because off-specifications are recorded in the issue register.
3. A. The lessons log is used to collate experience and lessons that could be useful for the current project (option A). Option B is incorrect—the project manager uses an exception report to escalate forecast breaches in stage or project tolerances to the project board. Option C is incorrect—the issue register captures requests for change, off-specifications, or problems or concerns. Option D is incorrect—the project initiation documentation is used as the main terms of reference for the project.
4. C. As a minimum requirement, when exceptions are raised, the business justification for the project should be reviewed (option C). Option A is incorrect—there is no requirement to send out notification to interested stakeholders when an exception is raised. Option B is incorrect—although PRINCE2 recommends that the project manager raises an exception report if stage tolerances are forecast to be exceeded, it is not a minimum requirement for applying the progress theme. Option D is incorrect—although PRINCE2 recommends that the project manager sends regular highlight reports to the project board to enable them to track progress, it is not a minimum requirement of the progress theme.
5. B. Scope tolerances define any flexibility in what will be delivered. Scope tolerance can be defined at three different levels—project level, stage level, and work package level—and is documented in the project plan, stage plan, and work package, respectively. Therefore, options 2 and 3 are correct, and options 1 and 4 are incorrect.
6. B. Option 1 and option 4 are time-driven reports—they are created at regular intervals rather than being driven by an event. Option 2 is an event-driven control—the end stage report is driven by the end of a stage event. Option 3 is an event-driven control—the exception report is driven by an exception event.
7. B. The work package forms an agreement between the project manager and the team manager about what the team will deliver (option B). Option A is incorrect—the stage plan shows what products need to be delivered across a whole stage, which might be delivered by a number of teams. Option C is incorrect—although a product description does define the specification for a particular product, it does not form an agreement between the project manager and a team manager about what to deliver. However, a work package might refer to a number of product descriptions to show what types of products need to be delivered within the work package. Option D is incorrect—the project product description shows what the project needs to deliver in order to gain acceptance. It is used to gain agreement on the project's scope and requirements with the users and the customers of the project.

8. D. The project manager creates an exception report to notify the project board of forecast breaches of stage tolerances. Option A is incorrect—the team manager creates checkpoint reports to report progress to the project manager. Option B is incorrect—the project manager creates highlight reports to report regular progress to the project board. Option C is incorrect—the project manager creates the end stage report to allow the project board to evaluate the performance of a stage.

9. A. The purpose of the progress theme is to establish mechanisms to monitor and compare actual achievements against those planned, to provide a forecast for project objectives and the project's continued viability, and to control any unacceptable deviations. Option B is a purpose of the risk theme; option C is a purpose of the quality theme; and option D is a purpose of the organization theme.

10. A. Option A is correct—the project manager will create an exception report to notify the project board of a stage-level or a project-level exception and to outline recommended options to respond to the situation. Option B and option C are incorrect—an exception plan would replace either a stage plan following a stage-level exception or a project plan following s project-level exception. Option D is incorrect—the team manager would raise an issue to notify the project manager of a work-package-level exception.

Practitioner Exam Answers

Answers to Section 1: Matching Questions

1. C. The statement is a scope tolerance. A scope tolerance is an allowable flexibility around what the project (or stage or work package) must deliver in terms of the set of products or range of features or requirements. The statement indicates that one particular feature, the customer review function, would be nice to have. Although the project team should try to deliver the customer review feature, it is not a necessary part of the project's scope. As such, if it is not delivered, there is no need for the project manager to escalate this situation.

2. E. The statement is a benefits statement. In the Website Project, the main benefit is the online sales that the website will generate. The statement indicates that, in order for the project to be a success, there is an allowable flexibility in the benefits that must be achieved.

3. D. The statement is a quality tolerance. A quality tolerance is an allowable flexibility around the attributes and characteristics of the products that must be delivered. In this case, the flexibility is around the ease of use attributes. Quality tolerances could also be set around other product attribute categories, such as ease of support, ease of maintenance, appearance, major functions, development costs, running costs, capacity, availability, reliability, security, accuracy, or performance.

4. F. The statement is a risk tolerance. A risk tolerance is a threshold level of risk exposure that, if exceeded, must be escalated to the appropriate level of management. The statement sets a threshold in terms of the aggregated expected monetary value of all risks to the project. This is a project-level risk tolerance—if the threshold is exceeded, the project management team will need to escalate the situation to corporate, programme management, or the customer. Risk tolerances could also focus on a particular type of risk. For example, any risk that could affect the security of the organization must be escalated.

5. B. The statement is a cost tolerance. A cost tolerance is an allowable flexibility around the budget for the overall project, stage, or work package.

Answers to Section 2: Classic Multiple-Choice Questions

1. B. The chief executive is defining a project-level risk tolerance. These are recorded in the risk management approach, which is created by the project manager in the initiation stage (option B). Option A is incorrect—only the risk management approach contains project-level tolerances, which in the case of the risk management approach, would be the risk project-level tolerances. The quality management approach, the change control approach, and the communication management approach do not contain project-level tolerances. Option C is incorrect—risk tolerances can be defined in a number of ways. They could be defined as a threshold level in the overall value of the risk situation. The project management team can use numerous techniques to define the overall value of risk in the project—for example, the expected value technique. The other way to set risk tolerances is to stipulate that certain types of risks—for example, those that might impact the on-going operations of the organization—need to be escalated to an appropriate level of management. Option D is incorrect—although it is true that the executive should ensure that risks associated with the business case are identified, assessed, and controlled, this is not the reason why the project manager would record the project-level risk tolerance in the risk management approach.

2. A. The daily log is a useful place to record individual observations about the project that, on their own, do not require formal issue management. However, when some of these observations are collated, they may alert the project manager of a new issue or a risk that needs to be managed formally. The project manager should prepare an issue report for all issues that are to be managed formally (option A). Option B is incorrect—the daily log will contain many observations that are informal issues. These will never need to be documented in an issue report. Option C is incorrect—although it is true that one of the purposes of the daily log is to record informal issues, the project manager might realize that, when aggregated, some of these informal issues contribute to creating a new formal issue. Option D is incorrect—the project manager is responsible for preparing issue reports, not the person who has raised the issue.

3. C. Although work packages must contain all the relevant content, those that are created for work that is done internally are likely to be in a different format from those created for work that is contracted out to a supplier (option C). Option A is incorrect—although it is true that the project manager is responsible for preparing work packages, this is not a reason why the format of work packages should not differ between internal and external teams. Option B is incorrect—even though it is important that work packages contain all the relevant content, the document can take many forms. Option D is incorrect—work packages are not created all at once in the initiation stage; work packages are created as they are needed in each delivery stage.

Chapter 10: Managing the Middle of a Project Successfully with PRINCE2

Foundation Exam Answers

1. C. Option 1 is incorrect—the closing a project process provides the project board with sufficient information to establish whether the objectives set in the original project initiation documentation have been achieved. Option 2 is incorrect—the starting up a project process provides the project board with sufficient information to assess whether the project is worthwhile and viable and should be commissioned.

2. D. During the controlling a stage process, the project manager ensures that the business case is taken into account when decisions are made on actions such as how to deal with issues, risks, or exceptions (option D.) Option A is incorrect—the project manager produces the end stage report in the managing a stage boundary process. Option B is incorrect—the project manager ensures that those who take control of the project's products post-project can support those products during the closing a project process. Option C is incorrect—the project board provides management direction and control by making key decisions in the directing a project process.

3. A. During the managing a stage boundary process, the project manager reviews and, if necessary, updates the project initiation documentation. He particularly reviews the business case section of the project initiation documentation to check there is still justification for the project to continue. Option B is incorrect—the project manager creates highlight reports during the controlling a stage process. Option C is incorrect—the team manager (or the team) accepts work packages during the managing product delivery process. Option D is incorrect—the project manager signs off on completed work packages during the controlling a stage process.

4. C. The project manager triggers work packages during the controlling a stage process.

5. B. The team manager and the team create specialist products within the constraints set by the work package, which defines how the products will be created and checked (option B.) Option A is incorrect—a purpose of the closing a project process is to provide a point in time when the client, users, and/or the operations team can establish whether they are happy that the correct products have been created. Option C is incorrect—taking corrective action to ensure the stage remains within tolerance is a purpose of the controlling a stage process. Option D is incorrect—one of the purposes of the starting up a project process is to ensure that the project management team is ready for initiating the project.

6. A. During the controlling a stage process, the project manager delegates work to the teams by handing over work packages (option A). Option B is incorrect—the project manager creates the project plan during the initiating a project process to enable the commissioning organization to understand what work needs to be done during the project. Option C is incorrect—a purpose of the directing a project process is to enable the project board to be accountable for the project's success. Option D is incorrect—the project manager uses managing a stage boundary to provide the information to the project board so that they can whether to authorize the next stage.

7. A. The accept a work package activity of the managing product delivery process ensures that the teams understand the expected effort, time, and cost to deliver the work package's products (option A). Option B is an objective of the starting up a project process. (The project approach evaluates how the project will be delivered). Option C is an objective of the initiating a project process. (The quality management approach describes how quality management will be carried out). Option D is an objective of the managing a stage boundary process.

8. D. During the managing product delivery process, the specialist products are not only created, but they are also approved by the authorities specified in the product's product description.

9. C. The project manager should review the quality activities and ensure that all products in the current stage have been approved (option C). Option A is incorrect—the starting up a project process is used to ensure that there is business justification for initiating the project. Option B is incorrect—the products for any stage are approved in the managing product delivery process. Option D is incorrect—the project board uses the directing a project process to communicate to corporate, programme management, or the customer.

10. C. The teams create specialist products during the managing product delivery process.

Practitioner Exam Answers

Answers to Section 1: Matching Questions

1. G. The progress theme describes how the project manager uses a work package as a way of controlling the work of the teams. The work package gives official authorization for the teams to start creating the specialist products and ensures that they start work at the correct time.

2. F. The marketing manager's request is an issue that would need to be captured in the issue register. The change theme covers the issue and change control procedure.

3. E. Digital Design has spotted what PRINCE2 calls an *opportunity*. Opportunities are types of risks that may affect the project in a favorable way. Risks are assessed using the risk theme.

4. G. The progress theme describes how the project manager will regularly review the progress of work using sources such as checkpoint reports.

5. E. The executive's concern is a risk that the project manager will need to assess using the risk management procedure. This is covered by the risk theme.

Answers to Section 2: Classic Multiple-Choice Questions

1. C. The order of events should be as follows: The project manager creates the stage plan for a stage during the managing a stage boundary process; then the project board authorizes the stage plan during the directing a project process; finally, the project manager manages the stage during the controlling a stage process, part of which will be authorizing work packages for the teams.

2. A. The project manager will initially plan quality reviews and checks on the stage's products while creating the stage plan during the managing a stage boundary process. However, the team manager and the teams should review these quality checks with project assurance when they are accepting a work package during the managing product delivery process. At this point, project assurance may recommend adding some extra reviewers to certain quality checks.

3. D. All requests for change of baselined products, no matter how small, must follow the issue and change control procedure: capture the issue in the issue register, carry out an impact analysis, and then authorize the change at the right level of change authority.

Chapter 11: Managing the End of a Project Successfully with PRINCE2

Foundation Exam Answers

1. A. The closing a project process is used to review a project's achievements against its objectives and see if it has anything further to contribute (option A). Option B is incorrect—the project board's decision to close the project is made in the directing a project process. Option C is incorrect—the project manager uses the controlling a stage process to manage the final delivery stage (as well as all the other delivery stages). Option D is incorrect—the delivery teams use the managing product delivery process to create the specialist products of the final stage (as well as the specialist products for all the other stages).

2. D. Option 2 is incorrect—the project manager plans the closure activities while planning the final stage of the project during the managing a stage boundary process. Option 3 is incorrect—the project board authorizes the closure of the project during the directing a project process.

3. B. Option 1 is incorrect—the stage plan for the final stage would show which activities are required to close the project, such as gaining acceptance for the project's products and evaluating the project's performance. Option 4 is incorrect—the benefits management approach shows how and when the achievement of the post-project benefits can be made. The benefits management approach is passed, along with the end project report, to the project board to review when authorizing the closure of the project.

4. D. The lessons report passes on useful experience to those who have responsibility for quality improvement within an organization (option D). Option A is incorrect—post-project actions specific to the project's products are described in the follow-on action recommendations. Option B is incorrect—the benefits management approach plans how and when the project's benefits will be reviewed. Option C is incorrect—the lessons log is used to collate lessons that could be applied to the current project.

5. D. In the closing a project process, the project manager creates the follow-on action recommendations, which include continuing threats to the project's products in their operational life (option D). Option A is incorrect—PRINCE2 does not manage the operational phase for the project's products. Option B is incorrect—the managing a stage boundary process is used to request authorization to start the final stage. Option C is incorrect—the directing a project process enables the project board to provide authority to close the project.

6. C. The directing a project process enables the project board to be accountable for the project's success (option C).

7. C. Option C is correct—the project board has the authority to close the project during the directing a project process. Option A is incorrect—the project manager obtains acceptance records during the closing a project process. Option B is incorrect—the project manager creates the end project report during the closing a project process. Option D is incorrect—the project manager prepares the stage plan for the last management stage during the managing a stage boundary process.

8. D. The directing a project process ensures that there is a two-way flow of information between the project board and corporate, programme management, or the customer.

9. D. The closing a project process ensures that project has a clear end.

10. B. The benefits management approach defines the benefits management actions and benefit reviews that will be put into place to ensure that the project's outcomes are achieved and to confirm that the project's benefits are realized.

Practitioner Exam Answers

Answers to Section 1: Matching Questions

1. B. The organization theme describes how to record details of all the project's stakeholders and their information needs in the communication management approach. This includes identifying who needs to be informed when the project is finishing.
2. A. The business case theme describes how the benefits management approach is used to plan how and when reviews of the project's benefits will take place.
3. E. The risk theme describes how to manage threats to the project's products.
4. C. The quality theme describes how to use the acceptance criteria detailed in the project product description to confirm that the project has produced products that are fit for their purpose.
5. G. The progress theme describes how to report on the progress of the project by writing a series of reports over the life of the project. The last report that evaluates the progress of the project is the end project report.

Answers to Section 2: Classic Multiple-Choice Questions

1. A. The project manager should check that the benefits management approach contains all post-project benefit reviews during the hand over products activity of the closing a project process (option A). Option B is incorrect—the review of the visitors to the website is outside the scope of the project, so the project manager will not need to create a work package for this activity. Option C is incorrect—although the project manager creates the benefits management approach in the initiation stage, the project manager might also update it at the end of the project. Option D is incorrect—although the visitor review will occur after the project, the benefits management approach will still plan the work of the post-project benefit reviews.
2. B. When a project is creating products that might require a lot of expensive support and maintenance, it is good practice to ensure that, as part of the project's scope, a maintenance agreement is drawn up between the support organization and the end users (option B). Option A is incorrect—not every project will create products that will need to be supported after the project. Option C is incorrect—although the support and maintenance of the website is outside the scope of the project, it is still good practice to create an agreement for the support during the project. Option D is incorrect—the benefits management approach will plan the benefit reviews and management actions needed to ensure that the project outcomes are achieved, not the support and maintenance of the project's products.
3. A. When a project is closed prematurely, the project manager might propose some additional work estimates to salvage some value out of partially created products or to make products safe. If this is the case, the project manager might create an exception plan for the project board to review (option A.) Option B is incorrect—it is the project board, not the project manager, who should decide what work needs to be completed before a project closes. Option C is incorrect—the search engine work does not necessarily have to take place in a new project. Option D is incorrect—the project manager creates exception plans.

Appendix

B

Practitioner Exam Scenario

This appendix contains an example Practitioner exam scenario. All the Practitioner questions at the end of each chapter use this scenario, so you will need to refer back to it while answering the review questions.

Scenario—Website Project

The companies and people described in this scenario are fictional.

Quality Furniture produces handcrafted wooden furniture from locally sourced timber. They sell their products through their four shops and via a mail-order catalog. Their sales figures are good, but the chief executive feels that they are missing a major business opportunity by not selling products online. Their website has a number of problems: Very few people visit the site; it is difficult to use; and it doesn't allow visitors to make purchases.

The chief executive employed First Tech, a digital marketing consultancy, to review the Quality Furniture website and make recommendations. They created a feasibility study that suggested the following:

- Redesign the website so that customers can easily browse information about furniture and the Quality Furniture marketing team can quickly upload new product information.
- Link the website to the Quality Furniture sales system and add a shopping facility so that customers can order online.
- Increase the website's rankings in the major search engines.

They also recommended that the project be managed using PRINCE2 and consist of the following stages:

- Stage 1: Initiation.
- Stage 2: Develop the requirements document for the website. Send a request for tender document to suitable web design companies for the design and development of the new website. Receive and evaluate proposals. Select a supplier.
- Stage 3: Design the website, including page designs and informational content.
- Stage 4: Build the website.
- Stage 5: Launch the website and increase its ranking in major search engines.

The project has just finished the starting up a project process, and the chief executive has recruited a PRINCE2-accredited project manager. Initial estimates are that the project will cost $150,000 and take 6 months to complete. There is a project cost tolerance of +$20,000, a time tolerance of +2 weeks/–3 weeks, a change budget of $10,000, and a risk budget of $20,000. The project is forecast to increase the sales of furniture by 20 percent over the next three years.

Additional Information

The chief executive founded Quality Furniture 20 years ago. He is always looking for ways to improve the company and has an interest in new technologies.

The finance director of Quality Furniture oversees the financial management of the company.

The personal assistant to the chief executive created and administered Quality Furniture's documentation management system, which stores and tracks all corporate documents. She provides administrative support to both the chief executive and any significant initiative at Quality Furniture.

The marketing manager at Quality Furniture oversees all sales and marketing activity of Quality Furniture's products.

The IT manager at Quality Furniture managed the delivery of the new sales system and is PRINCE2-qualified.

The operations director of Digital Design (the outsourced supplier that Quality Furniture will use to create the website) will provide the people who will build Quality Furniture's website.

The project manager at Digital Design (the outsourced supplier that Quality Furniture will use to create the website) manages a team of website developers.

The lead consultant at First Tech is an e-commerce expert. She will work as a business analyst during the project, collating requirements for the website.

Appendix C

Management Products in PRINCE2

In this appendix, you will find information on all 26 of the PRINCE2 management products. You were introduced to management products in Chapter 1, "Overview of PRINCE2." Each management product contains information that helps the project management team deliver the project. In many projects, the management products will be documents. In some circumstances, however, such as a small informal project, the information could be agreed to verbally.

Management products might be used for the following:

- To report information to various people both inside and outside the project management team
- To record information on items such as risks, issues, lessons learned, and actions
- To plan the work that needs to be done
- To define how the project should be managed
- To document the business justification for the project
- To outline the specifications for products
- To track the status of the products
- To document and agree to the project definition and scope of work

Throughout this study guide, you have learned about each of the 26 management products. In particular, you have learned about the purpose and composition of each management product. You also saw which roles create, update, and review each management product and in which of the processes this work is done.

Following is a brief outline of each management product and a reference to which chapter discusses it in detail.

Benefits Management Approach

The benefits management approach outlines the management actions that need to take place to ensure that the intended outcome of the project is achieved. It also shows how and when the benefits from the project will be reviewed and how and when the operational performance of the project's products will be reviewed. The project manager creates the benefits management approach in the initiation stage and updates it at each stage boundary. The management actions and reviews that the benefits management approach plans may occur both during and after the project.

You can learn more about the benefits management approach in Chapter 4, "Business Case Theme."

Business Case

The business case documents the business justification for the project. The executive creates an outline business case in the starting up a project process. The project manager adds more information in the initiation stage to create the first detailed business case. The business case is updated at each stage boundary and is a key input into the project board's decisions about whether to authorize initiation, the project, and each delivery stage. The project brief contains the outline business case created in the starting up a project process. The project initiation documentation contains the detailed business case, which is created in the initiation stage and updated throughout the project.

You can learn more about the business case in Chapter 4, "Business Case Theme."

Change Control Approach

The change control approach outlines how a number of areas of the project will be managed: how to manage proposed changes to the project's products, how to manage products that do not meet their specifications, and how to manage issues. The project manager creates the change control approach in the initiation stage, and it forms part of the project initiation documentation. The change control approach might be updated at a stage boundary.

You can learn more about the change control approach in Chapter 8, "Change Theme."

Checkpoint Report

The team manager (or the team members, if there is no team manager) sends a regular checkpoint report to the project manager. Checkpoint reports update the project manager on the progress of the work package that the team is delivering. The work package outlines how often the project manager wishes to receive checkpoint reports. The team manager creates checkpoint reports in the managing product delivery process, and the project manager reads them in the controlling a stage process.

You can learn more about checkpoint reports in Chapter 10, "Managing the Middle of a Project Successfully with PRINCE2."

Communication Management Approach

The communication management approach outlines how the project will approach communication among the members of the project management team. It also contains a stakeholder analysis showing all those outside the project management team who wish to be updated on the progress of the project and how they wish to receive those updates. The project manager creates the communication management approach in the initiation stage, and it forms part of the project initiation documentation. It may be updated at each stage boundary with information about new stakeholders or project management team members.

You can learn more about the communication management approach in Chapter 3, "Organization Theme."

Configuration Item Record

A configuration item record contains information on the latest status of a particular configuration item, such as the history, the status, and the latest version. Configuration item records are created only if required by the project's change control approach. A configuration item could be a product (both specialist and management), a component of a product, or a group of products.

You can learn more about configuration item records in Chapter 8, "Change Theme."

Daily Log

The project manager creates the daily log in the starting up a project process and uses it to record personal actions and informal issues. It also acts as a temporary repository of issues and risks in the starting up a project process, until the risk register and the issue register are created in the initiation stage. The daily log is sometimes known as the project manager's project diary.

You can learn more about the daily log in Chapter 9, "Progress Theme."

End Project Report

The project manager creates the end project report in the closing a project process. It reviews the project's performance against its objectives that were outlined in the original project initiation documentation (or against any approved changes to the original objectives). The end project report might also contain any lessons that have been learned during the project and any action points that need to be passed on to the operational team that will look after the products post-project. The project board reviews the end project report when considering whether to authorize the closure of the project in the directing a project process.

You can learn more about the end project report in Chapter 11, "Managing the End of a Project Successfully with PRINCE2."

End Stage Report

The project manager creates an end stage report in the managing a stage boundary process. The report reviews the performance of a stage. The project board reviews the end stage report during the directing a project process, when considering whether to authorize the next stage.

You can learn more about end stage reports in Chapter 10, "Managing the Middle of a Project Successfully with PRINCE2."

Exception Report

The project manager sends the project board an exception report if he is forecasting a breach in stage or project tolerances. The report details the problem that has caused the exception, gives a number of options to resolve the situation, and recommends one or more of the options. The project manager creates exception reports when necessary in the controlling a stage process. The project board reviews exception reports in the directing a project process and then must decide what to do next.

You can learn more about exception reports in Chapter 9, "Progress Theme."

Highlight Report

The project manager sends regular highlight reports to the project board and any other stakeholders identified as recipients in the communication management approach. Highlight reports update the project board and stakeholders of a stage's progress. The communication management approach defines the frequency of highlight reports. The project manager creates highlight reports in the controlling a stage process, and the project board reads the reports in the directing a project process.

You can learn more about highlight reports in Chapter 10, "Managing the Middle of a Project Successfully with PRINCE2."

Issue Register

The issue register records issues throughout the project. The project manager is responsible for regularly monitoring and updating the issue register. Three types of issues are recorded in the issue register: requests for changes, off-specifications, and problems or concerns. The project manager creates the issue register in the initiation stage.

You can learn more about the issue register in Chapter 8, "Change Theme."

Issue Report

If the issue register does not contain sufficient detail for a particular issue, an issue report might be created. The issue report is an optional management product for documenting details of the issue, such as a description, an impact analysis, and options and recommendations to deal with the issue. If required, the project manager creates issue reports during the controlling a stage process, when capturing and examining issues. Issue reports are updated throughout the life of the issue.

You can learn more about issue reports in Chapter 8, "Change Theme."

Lessons Log

The lessons log is used to record experience learned on previous projects that might be useful for the current project. It also acts as a repository for experience gained on the current project that might be useful for other projects. The project manager creates the lessons log in the starting up a project process and updates it throughout the project.

You can learn more about the lessons log in Chapter 9, "Progress Theme."

Lessons Report

The lessons report is used to pass on useful experience from the current project to those in the organization who are focused on quality improvement. The project manager might create a lessons report at the end of each stage as well as at the end of the project.

You can learn more about lessons reports in Chapter 9, "Progress Theme."

Plan

A plan defines which products will be delivered within the plan's scope and the activities and resources needed to deliver the products. There are three levels of plans in PRINCE2: project plan, stage plan, and team plan. Each plan level follows the same composition.

The project plan shows the major products to be delivered for the entire project and the major activities and resources needed to deliver those products. The plan will probably be at a fairly high level. The project manager creates the project plan in the initiation stage and updates it with progress information at the end of each stage. The project board uses the project plan to monitor the progress of the project during the directing a project process.

Stage plans shows the products to be delivered for a particular management stage and the activities and resources needed to deliver those products. Stage plans will probably be more detailed than the project plan. The project manager creates stage plans during the managing a stage boundary process. The project board reviews the stage plan when considering whether to authorize the next stage. The project manager uses the stage plan to monitor the progress of a stage during the controlling a stage process.

Team plans show the products to be delivered for one or more work packages and the activities and resources needed to deliver those products. The team manager (or team member, if there is no team manager) creates team plans and uses them to monitor the team's work in the managing product delivery process.

After an exception situation, the project board might request that the project manager create an exception plan. This will show how the project manager proposes that the project recover from a project- or stage-level forecast breach of tolerance. If the project board approves it, the exception plan will replace the project plan or stage plan, respectively.

You can learn more about plans in Chapter 5, "Plans Theme."

Product Description

A product description defines the specification for a particular product. The product could be a specialist or a management product. A product description shows the measurable quality criteria that the product needs to conform to, which quality methods to use to check the product, and who is responsible for reviewing and approving the product. The project manager creates product descriptions when creating a project plan, exception plan, or stage plan. The team manager might also create product descriptions when creating a team plan. When creating product descriptions, the project manager (or team manager) will probably need to liaise with the users of the products and those with specialist knowledge of the products.

You can learn more about product descriptions in Chapter 6, "Quality Theme."

Product Status Account

A product status account is an optional product and will be created if required by the project's change control approach. It shows the current status information on all, or a subset of, the project's products. This status information is sourced from the configuration item records. The project manager might create (or ask project support to create) a product status account at various times in the project, such as when creating a highlight report or an end stage report or when preparing to close the project.

You can learn more about product status accounts in Chapter 8, "Change Theme."

Project Brief

The project manager creates the project brief in the starting up a project process. The project brief defines and scopes the project at a high level. It answers basic questions, such as why the project is being done, what the project is to deliver, who will be involved with the project, when the project will start and finish, and which approach will be used to deliver the products. The outline business case and the project product description are both within the project brief.

The project board reviews the project brief during the directing a project process, when considering whether to authorize the initiation stage of the project.

You can learn more about the project brief in Chapter 2, "Starting a Project Successfully with PRINCE2."

Project Initiation Documentation

The project initiation documentation defines the project and sets out the project's overall objectives. The project initiation documentation forms a contract between the members of the project board and the project manager about what the project must achieve. The project manager creates the project initiation documentation during the initiation stage. The project initiation documentation builds on the information in the project brief to further define and scope the project. The project initiation documentation also contains a set of approaches showing how the project will be managed as well as the project plan and the project controls.

The project manager updates the project initiation documentation at the end of each stage. The project board reviews the latest version of the project initiation documentation when considering whether to authorize the project or the next stage.

You can learn more about the project initiation documentation in Chapter 2, "Starting a Project Successfully with PRINCE2."

Project Product Description

The project manager—with the help of the senior users, senior suppliers, and the executive—creates the project product description in the starting up a project process. It describes the main outputs of the project. It contains the customer quality expectations and measurable acceptance criteria for the products. It also shows how the products will be checked to see whether they conform to the acceptance criteria and who is responsible for officially accepting the products.

The project product description is used when deliverables are handed over to the client or the operations team to confirm that the products have been created correctly. The handing over of deliverables might happen at the end of a stage or at the end of the project.

You can learn more about the project product description in Chapter 6, "Quality Theme."

Quality Management Approach

The quality management approach outlines how the project management team will approach quality planning, quality control, and quality assurance throughout the project. It shows how the project will be managed to ensure that the products are fit for their purpose. The project manager creates the quality management approach in the initiation stage, and it forms part of the project initiation documentation. The quality management approach might be updated at a stage boundary.

You can learn more about the quality management approach in Chapter 6, "Quality Theme."

Quality Register

The quality register records information on the quality activities that take place during the project. Each quality check and quality inspection of a product should have a corresponding entry in the quality register. These entries provide information such as when the check took place, who was involved in the check, whether the check passed or failed, and references to any quality records that may have been collated as evidence of the check. The project manager creates the quality register in the initiation stage and updates it with planned quality activities when planning a stage. The quality register is updated with the results of the quality activities in the managing product delivery process. The work package defines who should update the quality register with the results of the quality activities.

You can learn more about the quality register in Chapter 6, "Quality Theme."

Risk Management Approach

The risk management approach outlines how the project management team will approach managing threats and opportunities throughout the project. It shows how the project will be managed in a way that decreases the likelihood and/or impact of threats and increases the likelihood and/or impact of opportunities. The project manager creates the risk management approach in the initiation stage, and it forms part of the project initiation documentation. The risk management approach might be updated at a stage boundary.

You can learn more about the risk management approach in Chapter 7, "Risk Theme."

Risk Register

The risk register records information on the threats and opportunities that the project faces. Each entry will record information such as a description of the risk, the risk's likelihood and impact, and countermeasures to address the risk. The project manager creates the risk register in the initiation stage and updates it regularly throughout the project.

You can learn more about the risk register in Chapter 7, "Risk Theme."

Work Package

The work package is an agreement between the project manager and the team manager (or the team members, if there is no team manager) that the team will deliver a set of specialist products. The work package describes the time and cost that the products must be delivered within and whether there are any tolerances around these objectives. The work package is created between two activities in the process model: when the project manager authorizes a work package in the controlling a stage process and when the team manager accepts a work package in the managing product delivery process.

You can learn more about work packages in Chapter 9, "Progress Theme."

Appendix D

Bonus PRINCE2 Foundation Exam

This is a sample PRINCE2 Foundation exam. Here are some tips to help you get the most from this mock exam:

- Try to complete the sample exam in an hour, which is the amount of time you will have for the real exam.
- Try to complete the exam without referring to this study guide or any other PRINCE2 reference material. You cannot use any reference material when taking the actual exam.
- After completing the exam, check your answers to see which ones you got right. Try to determine why you got any answers wrong. If you didn't understand a particular PRINCE2 topic, review that topic's chapter in this study guide. If you didn't understand the format of the question, review Chapter 12, "Passing the Accreditation Exams." If you ran out of time, keep practicing by taking the sample exam until you can complete it in the time allocated.

Good luck!

Foundation Questions

1. Which management product is used to document project-level risk tolerances?
   A. Project plan
   B. Risk management approach
   C. Risk register
   D. Project controls

2. Which of the following is a purpose of the controlling a stage process?
   A. To make key decisions on the project but delegate day-to-day management to the project manager
   B. To determine whether the project is viable and worthwhile
   C. To monitor the work to be done and deal with issues
   D. To produce an exception plan to show how the project can recover from a forecast breach in tolerance

3. Which of the following is a purpose of the managing product delivery process?
   A. To coordinate an area of work that will deliver one or more of the project's products
   B. To report to the project board on the progress of the stage
   C. To prepare sufficient information to allow the project board to authorize the next stage
   D. To provide a point in time when the acceptance of the project's products is confirmed

4. If the project or stage requires re-planning due to an exception situation, which process may be invoked?
   A. Initiating a project
   B. Controlling a stage
   C. Managing a stage boundary
   D. Closing a project

5. Tailoring PRINCE2 can involve which of the following?
   (1) Adapting the themes to work with relevant corporate policies
   (2) Substituting organizational project terms to replace PRINCE2 terminology
   (3) Adapting the principles to suit the environment
   (4) Not creating a business case when launching a project to comply with mandatory regulations
   A. 1 and 2
   B. 2 and 3
   C. 3 and 4
   D. 1 and 4

6. Which of the following is a purpose of the closing a project process?
   (1) To provide a fixed point in time to hand over responsibility for the project's products to the operational team
   (2) To enable the project manager to prepare for a premature close
   (3) To manage the products in the early phases of their operational life
   (4) To review all the post-project benefits from the project
   A. 1 and 2
   B. 2 and 3
   C. 3 and 4
   D. 1 and 4

7. Which of the following PRINCE2 principles does the business case theme primarily help to implement?
   A. Defined roles and responsibilities
   B. Manage by stage
   C. Focus on products
   D. Continued business justification

8. An uncertain event that could have a favorable impact on the project is known as [?].
   A. An issue
   B. An opportunity
   C. A threat
   D. A concession

9. Which of the following is a reason that PRINCE2 provides three levels of plans?
   A. To overcome the planning horizon problem
   B. To create detailed plans at the beginning of the project
   C. To enable the use of Gantt charts
   D. To provide the three roles on the project board with a plan that aligns with each of their interests

10. Which of the following are purposes of the quality theme?
    (1) To ensure that the project's products meet business expectations
    (2) To define the means of delivering the project's products
    (3) To define how to assess changes to the project baselines
    (4) To define the means by which the project will implement continuous improvement
    A. 1 and 2
    B. 2 and 3
    C. 3 and 4
    D. 1 and 4

11. Which theme ensures that there is an effective strategy to manage communication flows to and from stakeholders?
    A. Business case theme
    B. Organization theme
    C. Plans theme
    D. Quality theme

12. Which PRINCE2 process prevents poorly conceived projects from being initiated?
    A. Starting up a project
    B. Initiating a project
    C. Directing a project
    D. Controlling a stage

13. The purpose of the [?] process is to gain an understanding of the work to deliver the project's products before committing a significant sum of money.
    A. Starting up a project
    B. Initiating a project
    C. Controlling a stage
    D. Managing product delivery

14. Which of the following is a purpose of the directing a project process?
    A. To provide information to answer whether the project is a viable and worthwhile
    B. To enable the organization to understand the work needed to deliver the project's products
    C. To enable the project board to be accountable for the project by making key decisions
    D. To provide a fixed point at which the acceptance of the project's products is confirmed

15. Which of the following is **NOT** a purpose of the organization theme?
    A. To define the responsibilities for directing the project
    B. To ensure that there is business, user, and supplier stakeholder representation on the project management team
    C. To facilitate communication by defining the means of delivering the products
    D. To ensure that clearly defined accountability exists at each level of management

16. Which response to a risk would be implemented only if the threat occurs?
    A. Avoid
    B. Reduce
    C. Prepare contingent plans
    D. Transfer

17. Which of the following statements represents a time in the project when the business case would be reviewed?
    (1) During an impact assessment of a risk
    (2) During the appointment of the executive
    (3) During the creation of the project mandate
    (4) During an end stage assessment
    A. 1 and 2
    B. 2 and 3
    C. 3 and 4
    D. 1 and 4

18. Which of the following are objectives of the closing a project process?
    (1) To assess all the benefits from the project
    (2) To review the forecast post-project benefits and update if necessary
    (3) To review the planned details for post-project benefit reviews
    (4) To create a plan to show how and when to measure the project's benefits
    A. 1 and 2
    B. 2 and 3
    C. 3 and 4
    D. 1 and 4

19. Which of the following statements describes a risk actionee?
    A. An individual assigned to carry out a risk response action
    B. An individual responsible for managing and monitoring a particular risk
    C. An individual responsible for the project's risk management approach
    D. An individual responsible for regularly identifying, assessing, and controlling project risks

20. Which is an objective of the managing a stage boundary process?
    A. To record experience learned in the current stage that might help manage later stages or projects
    B. To evaluate the various ways the project can be delivered
    C. To delegate work packages to the teams for the next stage
    D. To deliver the next stage's products to expectations and within tolerances

21. Which is an objective of the managing product delivery process?
    A. To ensure that the business case for the project is kept under review
    B. To assure the project board that all products in the current stage have been approved
    C. To provide accurate information regarding the project to corporate or programme management
    D. To provide accurate progress information to the project manager at an agreed frequency

22. Which process captures issues and analyzes their impact on the project?
    A. Directing a project
    B. Controlling a stage
    C. Managing a stage boundary
    D. Managing product delivery

23. Which of the following are purposes of the risk theme?
    (1) To define the project's structure of accountability
    (2) To identify, assess, and control uncertainty
    (3) To provide a systematic approach to managing opportunities
    (4) To identify, assess, and control potential changes
    A. 1 and 2
    B. 2 and 3
    C. 3 and 4
    D. 1 and 4

24. Which of the following roles represents the business interest on the project?
    A. Executive
    B. Senior user
    C. Senior supplier
    D. Project manager

25. When conducting an impact analysis on an issue, which of the following factors should the project manager consider?
(1) The impact of the issue on the wider programme or corporate environment
(2) The supplier's perspective on the issue
(3) The probability that the issue will occur
(4) The position of the person who raised the issue
A. 1 and 2
B. 2 and 3
C. 3 and 4
D. 1 and 4

26. Which product is sometimes known as the project manager's diary?
A. Project initiation documentation
B. Daily log
C. Issue register
D. Risk register

27. Which process is invoked from the controlling a stage process toward the end of the final stage?
A. Starting up a project
B. Initiating a project
C. Managing a stage boundary
D. Closing a project

28. Which role applies the activities of the managing product delivery process?
A. Project manager
B. Team manager
C. Executive
D. Senior user

29. In a three-stage project, when should the managing a stage boundary **NOT** be undertaken?
A. At or close to the end of the initiation stage
B. At or close to the end of the final delivery stage
C. At or close to the end of the first delivery stage
D. After a request from the project board for an exception plan

30. Which of the following is **NOT** an example of a follow-on action recommendation that might be made during the closing a project process?
A. A recommendation related to unfinished work
B. A recommendation related to known risks associated with the project's products
C. A recommendation to close the project
D. A recommendation related to activities to take the products to the next phase of their operational lives

31. Which of the following statements about project outputs, outcomes, and benefits is correct?
    (1) Outcomes lead to outputs.
    (2) Benefits are the measurable improvement from an outcome.
    (3) A benefit should be perceived as an advantage by one or more stakeholders.
    (4) The project initiation documentation is an output.
    A. 1 and 2
    B. 2 and 3
    C. 3 and 4
    D. 1 and 4

32. Which of the following statements does **NOT** describe an activity in the assess step of the risk management procedure?
    A. Assess the net effect of all the identified threats and opportunities on a project
    B. Estimate the likelihood of a particular risk
    C. Understand how the impact of a risk might vary over time
    D. Review the corporate risk management procedures for possible inclusion in the risk management approach

33. Which plan might be created at the same time that the project manager is creating a stage plan?
    A. Programme plan
    B. Quality plan
    C. Exception plan
    D. Team plan

34. Which of the quality review technique roles coordinates and tracks work to correct a product following a review?
    A. Chair
    B. Presenter
    C. Reviewer
    D. Administrator

35. Which of the following is **NOT** true of project support?
    A. The project manager may take on the role of project support.
    B. Project support may provide administrative services during a project.
    C. Project support will monitor the management of the project to check that it is appropriate.
    D. Project support may be provided by a corporate project office.

36. Which of the following is an objective of the starting up a project process?
    A. To provide management direction and control throughout the project
    B. To provide a common understanding of how risks will be identified, assessed, and controlled
    C. To focus attention on the delivery of the project's specialist products
    D. To ensure that the work for project initiation is planned

37. Which of the following are objectives of the initiating a project process?
    (1) To ensure that time is not wasted initiating a project based on unsound assumptions
    (2) To ensure that the work required for project initiation is planned
    (3) To describe how baselines will be established and controlled
    (4) To ensure that there is a common understanding of how the corporate project management method will be tailored to suit the project
    A. 1 and 2
    B. 2 and 3
    C. 3 and 4
    D. 1 and 4

38. Which of the following PRINCE2 processes provides authority to close the project?
    A. Starting up a project
    B. Initiating a project
    C. Closing a project
    D. Directing a project

39. Which of the following budgets should be used to fund the identification and analysis of individual risks?
    A. Risk budget
    B. Project budget
    C. Change budget
    D. Cost tolerance

40. Which of the following roles represents the interests of those designing, developing, or procuring the project's products?
    A. Executive
    B. Senior supplier
    C. Senior user
    D. Corporate, programme management, or the customer

41. Which management product defines the quality standards to be applied throughout the project?
    A. Change control approach
    B. Product descriptions
    C. Quality register
    D. Quality management approach

42. What is the first task in the recommended approach to defining and analyzing products?
    A. Writing product descriptions
    B. Writing a project product description
    C. Creating the product breakdown structure
    D. Creating the product flow diagram

43. Which of the following does **NOT** describe a PRINCE2 approach for measuring the impact of a risk?
    A. Understand the potential effect of a risk on the project's schedule
    B. Understand the time factor of the risk
    C. Understand how the project's budgets might be affected by the risk
    D. Understand both the pre-response and post-response levels of the impact of a risk

44. What should drive decision-making in a PRINCE2 project?
    A. The corporate budget
    B. The business case
    C. The time available
    D. The preferences of the senior stakeholders

45. How might the PRINCE2 processes be tailored to suit the project environment?
    A. By omitting the starting up a project process on a project that is short of time
    B. By substituting an industry-specific lifecycle model for PRINCE2 during technical projects
    C. By using only a programme management process when the project is part of a programme
    D. By changing the responsibilities for performing the activities

46. Which management product is used to capture and maintain information on all the threats identified during a project?
    A. Risk management approach
    B. Issue register
    C. Issue report
    D. Risk register

47. How does the managing a stage boundary process help to implement the principle of management by exception?
    A. By proposing tolerances for the upcoming management stage
    B. By creating a lessons report detailing experience that might help other projects
    C. By providing the project board with sufficient information on the continued business justification of the project
    D. By creating any new product descriptions necessary for the next management stage

48. Which process shows external suppliers who are not using PRINCE2 how they can interface with the PRINCE2 method?
    A. Starting up a project
    B. Controlling a stage
    C. Managing a stage boundary
    D. Managing product delivery

49. Which management product does the project manager use to define the frequency and format of progress reports from the team?
    A. Work package
    B. Communication management approach
    C. Stage plan
    D. Team plan

50. Which of the following would **NOT** be potentially considered when defining the management stages of a project?
    A. Programme activities
    B. The availability of senior stakeholders
    C. The amount of risk in the project
    D. The planning horizon during the project

51. Which of the following aspects are used to describe a risk?
    (1) Risk mitigation
    (2) Risk cause
    (3) Risk event
    (4) Risk effect
    A. 1, 2, 3
    B. 1, 2, 4
    C. 1, 3, 4
    D. 2, 3, 4

52. Which of the following would **NOT** trigger an event-driven control?
    A. The end of a stage has arrived.
    B. The scheduled day of the month to create the regular progress report has arrived.
    C. An exception occurs, and an exception report has been written.
    D. The project manager has completed the project initiation documentation.

53. Which role is primarily responsible for the activities in the controlling a stage process?
    A. Executive
    B. Senior user
    C. Project manager
    D. Team manager

54. Which management product would the team manager review to understand with whom he might need to liaise during the delivery of specialist products?
    A. Project initiation documentation
    B. Highlight report
    C. Work package
    D. Checkpoint report

55. Which plans may be created or updated during the managing a stage boundary process?
    (1) Programme plan
    (2) Stage plan
    (3) Exception plan
    (4) Team plan
    A. 1 and 2
    B. 2 and 3
    C. 3 and 4
    D. 1 and 4

56. Which of the PRINCE2 principles is implemented by the closing a project process and provides a fixed point at which acceptance for the project's outputs are confirmed?
    A. Continued business justification
    B. Focus on products
    C. Manage by exception
    D. Manage by stage

57. Which of the following is **NOT** a characteristic of a benefit?
    A. Measurable
    B. Assigned
    C. Aligned to corporate objectives and strategy
    D. Perceived as negative by stakeholders

58. Which of the following management products describes how uncertainty will be managed on the project?
    A. Risk register
    B. Change control approach
    C. Risk management approach
    D. Issue report

59. Which of the tasks of the approach to defining and analyzing products creates an overall description of the main outputs of the project?
    A. Writing product descriptions
    B. Writing a project product description
    C. Creating a product breakdown structure
    D. Creating a product flow diagram

60. Which of the following describes the relationship between customer quality expectations and acceptance criteria?
    A. Customer quality expectations are defined in the product descriptions, whereas acceptance criteria are defined in the project product description.
    B. Customer quality expectations describe the quality expected of the project's product, whereas acceptance criteria are a prioritized list of measurable criteria needed before a customer will accept the project's product.
    C. Customer quality expectations come from the customer, whereas acceptance criteria come from the operations and maintenance teams.
    D. Customer quality expectations are agreed to at the beginning of the project, whereas acceptance criteria are agreed to at the end of the project.

Answers to Bonus Foundation Exam

1. B. The risk management approach is used to document the project-level risk tolerance. Stage-level and work package–level risk tolerances could be documented in stage plans and work packages, respectively. (See Chapter 9, "Progress Theme.")
2. C. During the controlling a stage process, the project manager monitors the progress of the work of the teams and deals with any issues. Option A is a purpose of the directing a project process. Option B is a purpose of the starting up a project process. Option D is a purpose of the managing a stage boundary process. (See Chapter 10, "Managing the Middle of a Project Successfully with PRINCE2.")
3. A. Option A is correct—during the managing product delivery process, the team manager coordinates an area of work to deliver one or more of the project's products. Option B is a purpose of the controlling a stage process. Option C is a purpose of the managing a stage boundary process. Option D is a purpose of the closing a project process. (See Chapter 10, "Managing the Middle of a Project Successfully with PRINCE2.")
4. C. If the project manager forecasts that stage or project tolerances will be breached, the project board might request that the current stage or the entire project be re-planned. As a result of this request, the project manager will use the managing a stage boundary process to create an exception plan. (See Chapter 5, "Plans Theme.")
5. A. Option 3 is incorrect—PRINCE2 principles are never amended; they are the core concepts to which all PRINCE2 projects must adhere. Option 4 is incorrect—the minimum requirements of each theme must be applied. (See Chapter 1, "Overview of PRINCE2")
6. A. Option 3 is incorrect—PRINCE2 is not used to manage products in their operational life. The closing a project process is used to hand over responsibility for the products to the operational and maintenance teams who *will* manage the products in their operational life. Option 4 is incorrect—many of the post-project benefits are often reviewed after the project has finished. (See Chapter 11, "Managing the End of a Project Successfully with PRINCE2.")
7. D. The business case theme describes how to document the justification for the project in the business case. Before each major decision on the project, the business case is updated. This updated business case is then used to check whether there is still justification for the project before making each project decision. (See Chapter 4, "Business Case Theme.")

8. B. An opportunity is a type of risk, which is an uncertain event that could have a favorable impact on the project. (See Chapter 7, "Risk Theme.")

9. A. All aspects of planning become more difficult the further into the future the plan extends. This is known as the *planning horizon problem*. PRINCE2 provides three levels of plans at different levels of detail and scope to help overcome this problem. (See Chapter 5, "Plans Theme.")

10. D. Option 2 is incorrect—defining the means of delivering the project's products is a purpose of the plans theme. Option 3 is incorrect—defining how to assess changes to the project's baselines is a purpose of the change theme. (See Chapter 5, "Plans Theme," Chapter 8, "Change Theme," and Chapter 6, "Quality Theme.")

11. B. The organization theme describes the communication management approach that defines how the project will manage communication. (See Chapter 3, "Organization Theme.")

12. A. During the starting up a project process, the project management team reviews the project idea and decides whether it is viable and worthwhile. If the idea is not a good one, the output from the starting up a project process should be a recommendation to not move ahead with the project. (See Chapter 2, "Starting a Project Successfully with PRINCE2.")

13. B. During the initiating a project process, the project plan is created; this plan describes the work and resources needed to deliver the project's products. The project board can then use this information before deciding whether to authorize the project. (See Chapter 2, "Starting a Project Successfully with PRINCE2.")

14. C. Most of the directing a project activities are focused on making key project decisions, such as whether the project should start, move to the next stage, or finish. (See Chapter 1, "Overview of PRINCE2.")

15. C. Facilitating communication by defining the means of delivering the products is a purpose of the plans theme. (See Chapter 3, "Organization Theme," and Chapter 5, "Plans Theme.")

16. C. The prepare contingent plans response creates a plan to do something *if and only if* the risk actually occurs. (See Chapter 7, "Risk Theme," in *PRINCE2 Study Guide*.)

17. D. The business case is not reviewed during the appointment of the executive or during the creation of the project mandate, because at these points the business case has not been created. (See Chapter 4, "Business Case Theme.")

18. B. Option 1 is incorrect—it is unlikely that all the benefits will have been achieved by the time the project reaches closing a project; many of the benefits may occur post-project. Option 4 is incorrect—the benefit management approach, which shows how and when to measure the project's benefits, is created in the initiating a project process. It may, however, be updated during the life of the project, particularly at the stage boundaries and the end of the project. (See Chapter 11, "Managing the End of a Project Successfully with PRINCE2.")

19. A. Each risk might be assigned to one or more risk actionees to carry out a particular risk response action. Option B is incorrect—this statement refers to a risk owner. Option C is incorrect—the executive is responsible for the project's risk management approach. Option D is incorrect—the project manager is responsible for identifying, assessing and controlling project risks. (See Chapter 7, "Risk Theme.")

20. A. The project manager creates a lessons report in the managing a stage boundary process. Option B is incorrect—the project approach, which describes the evaluation of various ways to deliver the project, is created during the starting up a project process. Option C is incorrect—the controlling a stage process is used to delegate work packages to the teams. Option D is incorrect—the managing product delivery process is used to deliver each stage's products. (See Chapter 10, "Managing the Middle of a Project Successfully with PRINCE2.")

21. D. The managing product delivery process describes how the team should report progress regularly to the project manager using checkpoint reports. Option A is an objective of the controlling a stage process. Option B is an objective of the managing a stage boundary process. Option C is an objective of the directing a project process. (See Chapter 10, "Managing the Middle of a Project Successfully with PRINCE2.")

22. B. The project manager captures and examines issues in the controlling a stage process. (See Chapter 10, "Managing the Middle of a Project Successfully with PRINCE2.")

23. B. Option 1 is incorrect—the organization theme establishes the project's structure of accountability. Option 4 is incorrect—the Change theme identifies, assesses, and controls potential changes to the project and its products. (See Chapter 3, "Organization Theme," Chapter 7, "Risk Theme," and Chapter 8, "Change Theme.")

24. A. The executive represents the business interests on the project, making sure that the project is capable of delivering its forecast benefits and is delivering value for money. (See Chapter 3, "Organization Theme.")

25. A. Option 3 is incorrect—the project manager would assess the probability of a risk, not an issue. Option 4 is incorrect—the position of the person who raised the issue is not reviewed during an issue's impact analysis. (See Chapter 8, "Change Theme.")

26. B. The daily log is sometimes referred to as the project manager's diary. The project manager uses the daily log to record informal issues, events, and personal actions that are not captured by the other PRINCE2 registers and logs. (See Chapter 9, "Progress Theme.")

27. D. The project manager uses the closing a project process toward the end of the last stage to prepare information that the project board will review when deciding whether to authorize closure of the project. (See Chapter 11, "Managing the End of a Project Successfully with PRINCE2.")

28. B. The team manager uses the activities of the managing product delivery process to manage the delivery of the specialist products. (See Chapter 10, "Managing the Middle of a Project Successfully with PRINCE2.")

29. B. The managing a stage boundary process is not used at the end of the final stage. (See Chapter 10, "Managing the Middle of a Project Successfully with PRINCE2.")

30. C. Follow-on action recommendations relate to activities that will take place after the close of the project, so Option C is incorrect. (See Chapter 11, "Managing the End of a Project Successfully with PRINCE2.")

31. B. Option 1 is incorrect—outputs might lead to outcomes, not the other way around. Option 4 is incorrect—outputs are the specialist products from a project. The project initiation documentation is a management product. (See Chapter 4, "Business Case Theme.")

32. D. The assess step of the risk management procedure includes two activities. The first activity is estimating the probability, likelihood, and proximity of individual risks—options B and C fit into this category. The second activity is evaluating the overall exposure of the project to risk—option A fits into this category. Option D is incorrect—reviewing the corporate risk management procedures to determine whether any should be included in the project's risk management approach would be done in the identify context step of the risk management procedure. (See Chapter 7, "Risk Theme.")

33. D. When the project manager is creating a stage plan, he may ask the teams involved with that stage to create team plans for their work. He can then use the information in the team plans for the stage plan. (See Chapter 5, "Plans Theme.") Note: There is no such thing as a quality plan in PRINCE2.

34. B. The presenter is responsible for ensuring that any remedial work necessary to correct a product following a quality review meeting is carried out. (See Chapter 6, "Quality Theme.")

35. C. Project assurance, not project support, is responsible for monitoring the management of the project. (See Chapter 3, "Organization Theme.")

36. D. During the starting up a project process, the stage plan for the initiation stage is created. (See Chapter 2, "Starting a Project Successfully with PRINCE2.")

37. C. Option 1 is incorrect—ensuring that time is not wasted initiating a project based on unsound assumptions is an objective of the starting up a project process. Option 2 is incorrect—planning the initiation stage is an objective of the starting up a project process. (See Chapter 2, "Starting a Project Successfully with PRINCE2.")

38. D. Although the project manager prepares the end project report and ensures that the project's products have been accepted in the closing a project process, the project is authorized to close during the directing a project process. (See Chapter 11, "Managing the End of a Project Successfully with PRINCE2.")

39. B. The project budget is used to fund the identification and analysis of risks. The risk budget is only used to fund specific management responses to risks. (See Chapter 7, "Risk Theme.")

40. B. The senior supplier represents those who will deliver the project's products. Delivery might involve designing, developing, or procuring the products. (See Chapter 3, "Organization Theme.")

41. D. The quality management approach defines the quality standards and techniques to be applied throughout the project. It defines how quality management will be conducted during the project. (See Chapter 6, "Quality Theme.")

42. B. Writing a project product description is the first task of the approach to defining and analyzing products. (See Chapter 5, "Plans Theme.")

43. B. Option B is an example of understanding the proximity of a risk, not its impact. Options A and C are correct ways of understanding a risk's impact on costs and schedules. Option D is also correct—PRINCE2 recommends forecasting the impact of a risk both before and after a risk response has been applied. (See Chapter 7, "Risk Theme.")

44. B. The business case must drive decision-making in a PRINCE2 project. The rationale behind the project, which is documented in the business case, drives decision-making in a PRINCE2 project. (See Chapter 4, "Business Case Theme.")

45. D. All the PRINCE2 processes and activities are always performed, but what might be adapted is who is responsible for performing the activities. (See Chapter 1, "Overview of PRINCE2.")

46. D. The risk register is used to capture information on all risks identified during the project. Risks can be either threats or opportunities. (See Chapter 7, "Risk Theme.")

47. A. Stage tolerances define the authority of the project manager and allow the project board to manage the project manager by exception. The project manager proposes suitable tolerances to the project board in the stage plan created in managing a stage boundary. (See Chapter 10, "Managing the Middle of a Project Successfully with PRINCE2.")

48. D. External suppliers who are not using PRINCE2 can use the managing product delivery process to determine how to interface with the rest of a PRINCE2 project. (See Chapter 10, "Managing the Middle of a Project Successfully with PRINCE2.")

49. A. The work package describes the frequency and format of the checkpoint reports that are sent from the teams to the project manager. (See Chapter 10, "Managing the Middle of a Project Successfully with PRINCE2.")

50. B. The length and placement of the management stages should not be driven by when people are available. (See Chapter 5, "Plans Theme.")

51. D. PRINCE2 recommends describing the source of the risk (risk cause), the area of uncertainty that might follow the source (risk event), and the impact on the project if the area of uncertainty occurs (risk effect). (See Chapter 7, "Risk Theme.")

52. B. Progress reporting is done on a regular frequency rather than being driven by any particular event. Progress reporting is known as a *time-driven control*. (See Chapter 9, "Progress Theme.")

53. C. The project manager is primarily responsible for the activities in the controlling a stage process, although project assurance and project support are also involved. (See Chapter 10, "Managing the Middle of a Project Successfully with PRINCE2.")

54. C. The work package describes people with whom the team manager might need to liaise during the delivery of the specialist products. These people would be listed under the development interfaces section. (See Chapter 9, "Progress Theme.")

55. B. Programme plans are not created within the PRINCE2 approach, and the team plan is created and updated in the managing product delivery process. (See Chapter 5, "Plans Theme.")

56. B. Option B is correct—accepting the project's products helps the project management team to focus on products. (See Chapter 6, "Quality Theme," and Chapter 11, "Managing the End of a Project Successfully with PRINCE2.")

57. D. Stakeholders perceive a dis-benefit, not a benefit, as negative. (See Chapter 4, "Business Case Theme.")

58. C. The risk management approach describes how the project management team will manage uncertainty. (See Chapter 7, "Risk Theme.")

59. B. The project product description describes the overall outputs from the project. (See Chapter 5, "Plans Theme.")

60. B. Customer quality expectations describe the quality expected of the project's products as well as the standards and processes that need to be applied in order to create that quality. They could be more ambiguous than the measurable set of acceptance criteria. (See Chapter 6, "Quality Theme.")

Appendix
E

Bonus PRINCE2 Practitioner Exam

472

This is a sample PRINCE2 Practitioner exam. The following list explains the exam format and rules and how to use this sample exam to prepare for the real Practitioner exam:

- This sample exam is formatted in the same way as an actual Practitioner exam. For the exam, you will be given two booklets: a scenario and additional information booklet and a question booklet. The scenario and additional information booklet contains a project case study that all the exam's questions are based on. It also contains additional information that you will need to answer some of the questions.
- The question booklet contains 68 questions. The questions are divided into 15 sections, each of which tests you on a particular syllabus topic. The 15 syllabus topics are the principles, the seven themes, and the seven processes.
- Some questions might require you to refer to the additional information. If so, it will be clearly stated at the top of the question.
- Each question is worth one mark, with a maximum of 68 marks. You need to get 38 marks, or 55 percent, to pass.
- You will have two and a half hours to complete the real exam, so I suggest that you limit yourself to that same amount of time for this sample exam. If you take two minutes to answer each question, you will have about 15 minutes to read the scenario and any additional information a particular question might include.
- During the real exam, you are allowed to refer to the official PRINCE2 manual (*Managing Successful Projects with PRINCE2*, The Stationery Office, 2017). When you are working on these questions, practice referring to the PRINCE2 manual to help you answer them. See Chapter 12, "Passing the Accreditation Exams," in this study guide for some tips.
- After completing this sample exam, mark your answers to see which ones you got right. You will find the answers at the end of this appendix. Try to determine why you got any answers wrong. If you didn't understand a particular PRINCE2 topic, review that topic's chapter in this study guide. If you didn't understand the format of the question, refer to Chapter 12. If you ran out of time, keep practicing by taking the sample exam until you can complete it in the time allocated.

Good luck!

Project Scenario and Additional Information

This section contains the project scenario on which the exam is based. This section also contains additional information that will be needed to answer some of the questions. If a question requires you to refer to additional information, that will be clearly stated in the question.

Project Scenario

Quality Furniture produces handcrafted wooden furniture from locally sourced timber. They sell their products through their four shops and via a mail-order catalog. Their production process is labor-intensive and involves skilled craftspeople, which means their products are quite expensive.

Research conducted by the marketing manager has shown that there is a big market for a range of less-expensive furniture sold under the Quality Furniture brand. The marketing manager has recommended launching a new range of furniture called QualityEconomy. To lower the costs and thus reduce the price, this new furniture range will be produced using an automated manufacturing process. The operations director believes this process will have the added benefit of improving the overall productivity figures for the manufacture and creation of the entire Quality Furniture range.

The board of directors has created a project mandate to produce a limited range of QualityEconomy products and launch them onto the market. The project mandate recommends that the project will consist of the following stages:

Stage 1: Initiation.
Stage 2: Market research. Research the market to help identify a number of products for the QualityEconomy range. Create designs for the new products.
Stage 3: Create prototypes for the new QualityEconomy products and define the requirements for the new production machinery needed to manufacture the QualityEconomy products.
Stage 4: Purchase and install the new production machinery. Train the operators of the production machinery. Market the QualityEconomy range, including sending an updated Quality Furniture catalog to existing and potential clients, updating the website, and creating and sending out press releases.

Initial estimates are that the project will take six months and cost $400,000. The project has a cost tolerance of plus or minus 10 percent and a time tolerance of plus or minus two weeks.

Additional Information

Here are some brief descriptions of some of the key roles in this project:
- The *chief executive* set up Quality Furniture 20 years ago. He is always looking for ways to improve the company and has an interest in new technologies.
- The *finance director* of Quality Furniture oversees the financial management of the company.
- The *company accountant* of Quality Furniture keeps the company accounts and prepares all the financial statements.
- The *personal assistant* to the chief executive created and administered Quality Furniture's documentation management system, which stores and tracks all corporate documents. She provides administrative support to both the chief executive and any significant initiative at Quality Furniture.

- The *marketing manager* at Quality Furniture oversees all sales and marketing activity of Quality Furniture's products.
- The *IT manager* at Quality Furniture managed the delivery of Quality Furniture's new sales system and is PRINCE2-qualified.
- The *retail manager* is in charge of the Quality Furniture retail outlets.
- The *operations director* at Quality Furniture oversees the production of all the furniture ranges.
- The *head of product development* leads a team that will design the new QualityEconomy furniture range.
- The *product designer*, who works for the head of product development, has designed many successful Quality Furniture products. He will be working on the new designs for the QualityEconomy range.
- The *account manager* at the production machinery supplier will arrange the installation of the new production line at Quality Furniture.

Questions

Here are the Practitioner exam questions. Answer all 68 questions.

Principles

1. The project is approaching the end of stage three. The team defining the production machinery requirements has discovered that the machines are much more expensive than previously thought. The executive has called a project board meeting to discuss whether the project should continue. Is this an appropriate application of the continued business justification principle, and why or why not?
   A. Yes, because each project should be aligned with corporate strategy.
   B. Yes, because stopping the initiative could allow resources to be reinvested in a more worthwhile project.
   C. No, because the project manager should update the business case at the end of each stage.
   D. No, because the business case should be created in the initiation stage.

2. The project is in stage four. The account manager for the production machinery supplier has been recruited to the project board as a senior supplier. Is this an appropriate application of the defined roles and responsibilities principle, and why or why not?
   A. Yes, because the account manager will be able to provide resources and expertise to install the production machines.
   B. Yes, because only external suppliers should take on the role of senior supplier.
   C. No, because the project board should not include people from another organization.
   D. No, because the project board was set up during the starting up a project process.

3. The project manager is preparing the project plan. The marketing manager has suggested that the press release be prepared during stage three rather than stage four because, in her experience, there is a lag of several weeks from submitting a release to it appearing in the media. Which principle is being applied, and why?
   A. Focus on products, because the marketing manager is identifying specialist products for the project plan.
   B. Focus on products, because the marketing manager is agreeing to create the products before understanding the work that will be required to do so.
   C. Learn from experience, because this lesson will help future projects be more successful.
   D. Learn from experience, because previous projects should be reviewed for relevant lessons to improve the QualityEconomy project.

4. The project is in stage four. The chief executive has just announced a new Quality Furniture branding plan and wants to ensure that the launch of the QualityEconomy range is aligned to the new branding guidelines. The project manager is treating this as a request for change and is reviewing the product descriptions for the new catalog, the updated website, and the press release to see how they might be affected. Which principle is being applied, and why?
   A. Continued business justification, because the impact of a change on the business justification of the project must be reviewed.
   B. Continued business justification, because this will avoid the QualityEconomy project having mutually inconsistent objectives with another project.
   C. Focus on products, because the impact of a change on the project's products must be reviewed.
   D. Focus on products, because this will ensure that the project only carries out work that is needed to deliver the marketing products.

5. The project is in the initiation stage, and the project manager is preparing the project controls section of the project initiation documentation. The executive has asked that the project manager escalate all forecast breaches of work package tolerances to the project board during the initiative. Is this an appropriate application of the manage by exception principle, and why or why not?
   A. Yes, because this allows the project manager to efficiently manage the project on a day-to-day basis.
   B. Yes, because this clearly defines accountability at the delivery level.
   C. No, because forecast breaches of work package tolerances should be escalated to the corporate level.
   D. No, because this is likely to waste senior management's time.

6. The project is approaching the end of stage two. The executive has asked the project manager to prepare the stage plans for stages three and four, and the project board will review and authorize both plans in the upcoming end stage assessment. Is this an appropriate application of the manage by stage principle, and why or why not?

    A. Yes, because this reduces the senior managers' time burden.
    B. Yes, because the project manager should create a stage plan for each management stage of the project.
    C. No, because the viability of the project should be reviewed at the end of stage three, before stage four is authorized.
    D. No, because the project plan should have been created during the initiation stage.

7. The project is approaching the end of stage two. The marketing manager, who is the senior user, is abroad at a meeting with international clients and cannot attend the end stage assessment meeting. Rather than delay the meeting, the project manager has sent the end stage report and next stage plan to the marketing manager by email and asked whether she will give her approval for the next stage. Is this an appropriate application of the tailor to suit the project principle, and why or why not?

    A. Yes, because effective project management requires decisions, not necessarily meetings.
    B. Yes, because the senior user is responsible for forecasting the benefits of the project.
    C. No, because the end stage assessment meeting must be attended by all the members of the project board.
    D. No, because the end stage report is a confidential document and should not be emailed.

8. The project is in stage three, and the project manager is preparing a work package for the team creating the prototypes. He agrees with the team manager that the prototyping work must be complete within three weeks, although in certain circumstances, an additional week is available if required. Which principle is being applied and why?

    A. Manage by stage, because the project manager is managing the stage on behalf of the project board.
    B. Manage by stage, because the work package will need to be authorized by the project board.
    C. Manage by exception, because the project manager is defining the team manager's authority using tolerances.
    D. Manage by exception, because the tolerances define the project manager's level of authority.

Business Case

In the following table, Column 1 contains three statements relating to the QualityEconomy project. Decide whether each statement describes an output, outcome, benefit, dis-benefit, or something different (options A–E in Column 2). Choose only one option for each statement. Each option in Column 2 can be used once, more than once, or not at all.

Column 1	Column 2
9. Because of the QualityEconomy project, there is no budget for the retail manager to upgrade the main store.	A. Output
10. The project initiation documentation for QualityEconomy project.	B. Outcome
11. Quality Furniture expands its range of products and reaches new markets.	C. Benefit
	D. Dis-benefit
	E. None of the above

12. The QualityEconomy project is part of a programme to deliver a range of strategic improvements to the business. The chief executive does not want to share this information with each project manager. He has asked each project manager to create a separate, stand-alone business case for each project that does not refer to the overall programme. Is this appropriate, and why or why not?
    A. Yes, because each project must be able to justify itself without reference to the overall programme.
    B. Yes, because the project manager is responsible for the development of the business case
    C. No, because a project's business case should be aligned with the programme's business case.
    D. No, because there is no need for a project business case if a project is part of a programme.

13. The project is approaching the end of stage two. The marketing manager, who is a senior user, is concerned that the market research results show less demand for the QualityEconomy range of products than expected. She has asked the project manager to prematurely close the project. Is this appropriate, and why or why not?
    A. Yes, because the project manager is responsible for the development of the business case.
    B. Yes, because the project must remain desirable throughout the initiative.
    C. No, because the project board should decide whether the project is still desirable.
    D. No, because the closing a project process should be used at the end of the final stage.

Organization

Use the additional information to answer this question. The project is in the initiation stage, and the project manager is preparing the communication management approach. In the following table, Column 1 lists three items of information that will be included in the communication management approach. Using the additional information provided for this project, identify the heading from Column 2 (A–F) that each item should be recorded under. Choose only one heading for each item of information. Each heading can be used once, more than once, or not at all.

Column 1	Column 2
14. The company accountant will be impacted by this project because he will need to update the sales systems.	A. Communication procedure
15. A log of all external communication regarding the QualityEconomy range—including the date the communication was sent, the recipients, and the content of the communication—should be maintained.	B. Tools and techniques
16. All press releases must conform to the Quality Furniture branding standards.	C. Records
	D. Reporting
	E. Roles and responsibilities
	F. Stakeholder analysis

17. Use the additional information to answer this question. The retail manager oversees the Quality Furniture retail outlets. He needs to understand how the shops will stock and display the new QualityEconomy range after the project. The project manager has recommended that he take on the role of senior supplier. Is this appropriate, and why or why not?
    A. Yes, because the retail outlets will be supplying the QualityEconomy range to the company's customers.
    B. Yes, because the retail manager will be able to review the viability of the plan to install the new production machinery.
    C. No, because the retail manager will be delivering the benefits of the project and should be a senior user.
    D. No, because the senior supplier role should be carried out by the account manager from the production machinery supplier.

18. Use the additional information to answer this question. The personal assistant to the chief executive will procure the services of the production machinery supplier. The executive has recruited her as a senior supplier. Is this appropriate, and why or why not?
    A. Yes, because she reports directly to the chief executive of Quality Furniture.
    B. Yes, because the senior supplier represents the people who are facilitating, procuring, and implementing the project's products.
    C. No, because someone from the production machinery supplier should become senior supplier.
    D. No, because the personal assistant should take on the role of project support, as she has skills in administration and organization.

Quality

In the following table, Column 1 lists three items of information included in the product description for the standard design document that will be used to specify the QualityEconomy furniture. For each item in Column 1, identify the heading (A–F in Column 2) that it should be recorded under. Choose only one heading for each item of information. Each heading can be used once, more than once, or not at all.

Column 1	Column 2
19. The head of product development will be the producer.	A. Quality criteria
20. Experience with the Quality Furniture production standards and health and safety standards for furniture.	B. Quality tolerances
21. PRINCE2 quality review technique.	C. Derivation
	D. Quality method
	E. Quality skills required
	F. Quality responsibilities

22. The head of product development has created the QualityEconomy bed design document, which now needs to be reviewed using the PRINCE2 quality review technique. During the review preparation, one of the reviewers spots an error in the design and raises an off-specification to the project manager. Is this appropriate, and why or why not?
    A. Yes, because an off-specification is a type of issue where a product does not meet its specifications.
    B. Yes, because the reviewer role should review the product.
    C. No, because the reviewer should have raised a request for change.
    D. No, because the reviewer should submit a question to the chair ahead of the review meeting.

23. The operations director is reviewing the QualityEconomy bed design ahead of the review meeting. She spots a number of spelling and grammatical mistakes, so she annotates the product copy. Is this appropriate, and why or why not?
    A. Yes, because any errors with the product should recorded by annotating the product copy.
    B. Yes, because it is appropriate to highlight small errors by annotating the product copy.
    C. No, because these errors should have been raised as an issue.
    D. No, because these errors should have been added to the question list to ask the presenter in the review meeting.

Plans

The project is approaching the end of stage three. In the following table, Column 1 lists three statements that the project manager considers while preparing the plan for stage four. Identify the step in PRINCE2's recommended approach to defining and analyzing the products (A–D in Column 2) that each step applies to. Choose one step for each statement. Each step can be used once, more than once, or not at all.

Column 1	Column 2
24. The training materials must be reviewed by the operations director.	A. Writing a project product description
25. The press release will consist of set of photographs of the QualityEconomy range, a market report, and a history of Quality Furniture.	B. Creating a product breakdown structure
26. Installed machinery needs to be set-up before the project creates trained operators.	C. Writing product descriptions
	D. Creating a product flow diagram

27. The project is in the initiation stage. The project manager has said that the work to purchase the production machinery and the work to install the machinery should be split into two management stages. Is this appropriate, and why or why not?
    A. Yes, because a delivery step should always equate to a management stage.
    B. Yes, because there are often benefits if the end of a management stage aligns with the end of a delivery step.
    C. No, because this approach will create an unnecessary stage boundary, which will waste the project board's time.
    D. No, because during the initiation stage it is too early to create stage plans for the later management stages.

28. The personal assistant to the chief executive is selecting the production machinery supplier. The project manager wants the supplier to be contractually bound to provide a plan showing how they will install the machines. Is this appropriate, and why or why not?
    A. Yes, because the supplier should create the stage plan for the installation of the machines.
    B. Yes, because this will allow the project manager to monitor and control his own stage plan.
    C. No, because the project manager should create the plan to track the work of installing the machines.
    D. No, because during the supplier's processes and techniques are likely to be confidential.

Risk

In the following table, Column 1 lists three items of information that will be included in the risk management approach for the QualityEconomy project. For each item, identify the heading (A–F in Column 2) that it should be recorded under. Choose only one heading for each item of information. Each heading can be used once, more than once, or not at all.

Column 1	Column 2
29. The risk register should conform to the PRINCE2-recommended composition.	A. Risk management procedure
30. Imminent risks are risks that may occur within one week.	B. Tools and techniques
31. Project assurance will monitor the project for compliance with the risk management approach.	C. Records
	D. Roles and responsibilities
	E. Scales
	F. Proximity

32. Quality Furniture has gained a reputation over the years for creating excellent handcrafted furniture. The chief executive is concerned that the QualityEconomy range may damage the company's reputation for excellence and lead to an overall reduction in sales. The chief executive has asked the project manager to assess this threat. The project manager has recommended closing the project. Is this appropriate, and why or why not?
A. Yes, because closing the project might be a valid response to a project risk.
B. Yes, because projects should always be closed if they affect the on-going operations of the organization.
C. No, because closing the project is not a valid risk response.
D. No, because the risk response should reduce the risk to the organization.

33. The risk that the new QualityEconomy range might damage the company's reputation for excellence was assessed, and it was decided to respond by upgrading the specification of the materials to be used to create the QualityEconomy range. The executive has authorized this response to be funded from the project tolerances. Is this appropriate, and why or why not?
A. Yes, because the cost tolerance is used to fund any necessary expenditure over and above original budget.
B. Yes, because tolerances are used to fund estimating errors.
C. No, because the risk budget should be used to fund responses to project threats.
D. No, because the project should be closed and a new project budget secured.

Change

In the following table, Column 1 lists three actions that are carried out to manage issues and changes throughout the project. For each action, identify the role (A–F in Column 2) that should be responsible for carrying it out. Choose only one role for each action. Each role can be used once, more than once, or not at all.

Column 1	Column 2
34. Assist in the maintenance of any records made regarding off-specifications and requests for change.	A. Corporate, programme management, or the customer
35. Set aside $40,000 to fund any suggestions raised during the initiative for improvements to the new production line.	B. Executive
36. Review the impact of issues on the integrity of the production machinery.	C. Senior supplier
	D. Senior user
	E. Project manager
	F. Project support

37. The project is in stage four, and the production machinery has been installed. When the operations director reviews the new machinery, she realizes one of the machines is the wrong model, so she raises an issue to the project manager. The project manager records this issue as a request for change. Is this appropriate, and why or why not?
    A. Yes, because if a product does not meet its specification, it will need to be changed so that it does.
    B. Yes, because the project manager is responsible for ensuring that issues are recorded.
    C. No, because project support should record this issue in the issue register.
    D. No, because this should be recorded as an off-specification.

38. The project is in stage four, and one of the installed production machines has been found to be the incorrect model. After reviewing the impact of this issue, the operations director realizes that the incorrect machine will be able to produce the QualityEconomy furniture to the right specification. The project manager escalates the issue to the project board and suggests they authorize keeping the incorrect model. Is this appropriate, and why or why not?
    A. Yes, because the project manager should escalate all decisions regarding requests for change to the project board.
    B. Yes, because when faced with an off-specification, the project board might decide to authorize a concession.
    C. No, because the machine is incorrect and should be changed.
    D. No, because this is a decision for the operations director and should not be escalated to the project board.

Progress

In the following table, Column 1 lists three statements related to tolerances for the QualityEconomy project. For each statement, select the tolerance area (A–F in Column 2) that it represents. Choose only one tolerance area for each statement. Each tolerance area can be used once, more than once, or not at all.

Column 1	Column 2
39. The project should increase Quality Furniture's productivity by $170 to $200 per item of furniture created.	A. Time
40. If any threat to the ongoing operations is identified, this must be escalated immediately to the Quality Furniture board of directors.	B. Cost
41. The QualityEconomy furniture range should include a bed, bedside cabinet, wardrobe, dining table, chairs, and bookshelf. If this is not possible within time constraints and budgets, the bedside cabinet and bookshelf can be designed in the follow-on project.	C. Scope
	D. Quality
	E. Benefits
	F. Risk

42. The project is in stage four, and the personal assistant has procured the production machinery. She found it difficult to find a suitable supplier until she joined a local business group that was able to supply a number of vetted recommendations. She described this experience in her final checkpoint report to the project manager. Is this appropriate, and why or why not?
    A. Yes, because any lessons identified by the team manager should be included in the checkpoint report.
    B. Yes, because the project manager should be kept informed of progress on a regular basis.
    C. No, because this experience should have been raised as an issue.
    D. No, because the team manager should have recorded this experience in the lessons log.

43. The project is in stage four. After surveying Quality Furniture's premises, the account manager for the production machinery supplier realizes it will take an extra two weeks to install the machinery. The work package for the installation of the machinery has a one-week tolerance. The account manager sends the project manager an exception report. Is this appropriate, and why or why not?
   A. Yes, because the work package is now in exception.
   B. Yes, because the project manager should be kept informed of progress on a regular basis.
   C. No, because the account manager should send an exception report to the project board.
   D. No, because the account manager should raise an issue to the project manager.

Starting Up a Project

In the following table, Column 1 describes three actions that take place during the starting up a project process. For each action, identify the theme (A–F in Column 2) that is being applied. Choose only one theme for each action. Each theme can be used once, more than once, or not at all.

Column 1	Column 2
44. The project manager records in the daily log that Quality Furniture has never used an automated process to create furniture, which may lead to poor quality products being created.	A. Business case
45. The chief executive designs the project management team structure for the project.	B. Organization
46. The chief executive, the marketing manager, and the operations director work together to forecast the likely sales for the QualityEconomy range of furniture and the likely production costs.	C. Risk
	D. Progress
	E. Plans
	F. Quality

47. The marketing manager has recommended that the new furniture be environmentally friendly, to meet market demand. The project manager has recorded this statement in the project product description. Is this appropriate, and why or why not?
   A. Yes, because the project product description describes the customer quality expectations for the project's products.
   B. Yes, because the project product description describes the acceptance criteria for the project's products.
   C. No, because project manager creates the product descriptions for the main products while preparing the project plan in the initiation stage.
   D. No, because the senior users are responsible for preparing the project product description.

Directing a Project

In the following table, Column 1 describes three actions that are carried out as part of the directing a project process. For each action, identify which role (A–E in Column 2) should carry it out. Choose only one role for each action. Each role can be used once, more than once, or not at all.

Column 1	Column 2
48. Make the final decision on whether to authorize the project, after reviewing the project initiation documentation.	A. Executive
49. Chair the end stage assessment to review stage three of the project.	B. Senior user
50. Review whether it is viable to install the production machinery according to the activities set out in the plan for stage four.	C. Senior supplier
	D. Project manager
	E. Team manager

51. The project is in the initiation stage, and the project manager is preparing the project initiation documentation. The project manager has asked to meet regularly with the executive during the stage, as he requires guidance regarding the creation of the detailed business case and the project approaches. Is this appropriate, and why or why not?
    A. Yes, because the need for consultation between the project manager and the project board is likely to be particularly frequent during the initiation stage.
    B. Yes, because project board is responsible for preparing the project initiation documentation.
    C. No, because the project manager will meet with the project board at the end of the initiation stage so that they can authorize the project.
    D. No, because the project board is responsible for directing the project.

Initiating a Project

Column 1 in the following table lists three statements that are included in the project initiation documentation for the QualityEconomy project. Identify which heading (A–G in Column 2) each statement should be recorded under. Choose only one heading for each statement. Each heading can be used once, more than once, or not at all.

Column 1	Column 2
52. The QualityEconomy furniture designs and prototypes should adhere to the Quality Furniture production standards.	A. Quality management approach
53. All threats to the project that might affect the continuing operation of the business must be escalated to the Quality Furniture board of directors.	B. Risk management approach
54. Following the initiation stage, the project board will assess whether to continue the project at the end of both stage two and stage three.	C. Change management approach
	D. Communication management approach
	E. Project plan
	F. Project controls
	G. Tailoring of PRINCE2

55. While preparing the risk management approach, the project manager reviewed all the threats and opportunities identified and listed them in the approach document. Is this appropriate, and why or why not?
    A. Yes, because the project manager is responsible for ensuring that the risks for a project are identified.
    B. Yes, because all the threats and opportunities for the project should be identified during the initiation stage.
    C. No, because the threats and opportunities should be recorded in the risk register.
    D. No, because project support should prepare information on threats and opportunities.

56. During the initiation stage, the project board decided to delegate the approval of any changes raised during the project that cost less than $500 to the project manager. Is this appropriate, and why or why not?
    A. Yes, because the project board should decide during the initiation stage whether they want to delegate any change authority.
    B. Yes, because the project board should set up a change authority for each stage.
    C. No, because the project board is responsible for authorizing all changes and cannot delegate this responsibility.
    D. No, because the project manager cannot assume any responsibility for authorizing changes.

Controlling a Stage

57. The operations director has told the project manager that the production machinery supplier has delayed the installation date by a week. What is the first management product that should be updated or created as a result?
   A. Risk register
   B. Lessons log
   C. Quality register
   D. Issue register

58. The project manager has recorded in the daily log that the selected supplier of the factory machines requires formal instructions to start the training of the operators. What is the first management product that should be updated or created as a result?
   A. Work package
   B. Team plan
   C. Stage plan
   D. Highlight report

59. The marketing manager has told the project manager that she believes the budget allocated to promote the QualityEconomy furniture may not be sufficient to achieve the project's sales figures. What is the first management product that should be updated or created as a result?
   A. Stage plan
   B. Lessons log
   C. Risk register
   D. Issue register

Managing Product Delivery

Stage four has started. The personal assistant to the chief executive has been given the work package to procure the supplier of the new factory machines. Column 1 in the following table describes three actions that the personal assistant will carry out while procuring the new machines. Identify the managing product delivery activity (A–C in Column 2) during which each action should be carried out. Choose only one activity for each action. Each activity can be used once, more than once, or not at all.

Column 1	Column 2
60. Send the project manager a progress report on a regular basis.	A. Accept a work package
61. Develop a request for information document to send to potential suppliers.	B. Execute a work package
62. Produce a plan showing what will be involved in selecting and then procuring a supplier for the new machines.	C. Deliver a work package

63. The project is in stage two, and the product designer is producing the designs for the new furniture. The project manager has requested a regular checkpoint report from the designer. However, the designer uses an agile approach and asks the project manager if he can provide the progress information using an information radiator. Is this appropriate, and why or why not?
   A. Yes, because checkpoint reports can be tailored to suit the delivery approach used by the team.
   B. Yes, because information radiators should be used by teams to report progress information to the project manager.
   C. No, because the team manager should send a regular checkpoint report to update the project manager on the work package's progress.
   D. No, because agile teams are self-organizing, so there is no need to update the project manager regarding the progress of the work package.

Managing a Stage Boundary

64. The project is approaching the end of stage two, the market research has been completed, and the head of the product development team has created the designs for the new furniture. Which activity should take place during the report management stage end activity?
   A. Create a set of product descriptions for the prototypes of the QualityEconomy range.
   B. Create a product flow diagram showing the order in which the requirements and prototypes will be delivered.
   C. Record that the product designers were very helpful and worked unpaid overtime to ensure that all the designs were finished.
   D. Update the forecast for the sales of the QualityEconomy range based on a new piece of market research.

65. The project is approaching the end of stage three, and the project manager is reviewing the products to be delivered in stage four with the teams. He has created a flow diagram to show the order in which the products need to be delivered. During which managing a stage boundary activity should this work occur?
   A. Plan the next management stage
   B. Update the project plan
   C. Update the business case
   D. Report management stage end

66. The production machinery company's account manager has told the project manager that Quality Furniture's electrical system does not have enough capacity to power the new machines. This means installing new circuits, which will delay the installation work by five weeks. Stage four has a three-week tolerance. The project manager adds the new work to the stage plan and sends this to the project board as an exception plan. Is this appropriate, and why or why not?
   A. Yes, because the project board should approve the new work by reviewing an exception plan.
   B. Yes, because an exception plan shows the actions required to recover from a forecast deviation from agreed tolerances.
   C. No, because the work to install the new electrical circuits is out of scope of the project.
   D. No, because the project manager should first set out the options to respond to this issue in an exception report.

Closing a Project

67. The QualityEconomy project is coming to a close. With the help of project support, the project manager is collating all the project documentation into a secure folder and backing it up. During which activity of the closing a project process should this work occur?
    A. Prepare planned closure
    B. Hand over products
    C. Evaluate the project
    D. Recommend project closure

68. The project is coming to a close, and the project manager is arranging to hand over the production machinery to the operations director. However, the operations director is refusing to sign off the machines, as no support agreement has been arranged with the production machinery supplier. Is this appropriate, and why or why not?
    A. Yes, because all completed products need a service agreement.
    B. Yes, because the production machinery is likely to need potentially expensive support and maintenance.
    C. No, because the service agreement should be an output in a follow-on project.
    D. No, because the executive is responsible for authorizing the closure of the project.

Answers to Practitioner Exam Questions

Answers to Principles

1. B. The principle of continued business justification requires that the project management team review the justification for the project throughout the initiative. If the justification is no longer valid, the project should be stopped, which might allow the project's funds to be better invested elsewhere (option B). Option A is incorrect—although it is true that each project should be aligned with any wider corporate strategy that exists, the question is about revalidated the justification for the project, not aligning that business case with a wider organizational strategy. Option C is incorrect—although the project manager is responsible for updating the business case at the end of each stage, that does not mean that reevaluating the business case is not a good example of applying the principle of continued business justification. Option D is incorrect—although the detailed business case should be created in the initiation stage, that does not mean reevaluating the business case is not a good example of applying the principle of continued business justification.

2. A. The senior supplier should be able to provide the resources and expertise required by the project (option A). Option B is incorrect—someone from Quality Furniture, such as a procurement manager, could become the senior supplier. Option C is incorrect—the senior supplier role might be done by someone external to Quality Furniture. Option D is incorrect—although the project board was initially set up in the starting up a project process, the project management team structure might be updated throughout the initiative.

3. D. This is an example of a lesson from a previous project being applied to the current project, so it is applying the principle of learn from experience (option D). Option A is incorrect—the press release has already been identified. Option B is incorrect— the question is focused on when an activity should occur, not what products should be created. Option C is incorrect—although this lesson might help future projects, the question is about the lesson helping the current project.

4. C. The focus on products principle helps manage uncontrolled change by reviewing how a change might impact the project's products (option C). Option A is incorrect—although the impact of a change on the business justification of the project should be reviewed, in this case, the project manager is reviewing the impact of the change on the project's products. Option B is incorrect—although the project's objectives should not be inconsistent with another project's objectives, in this case, the project manager is reviewing the impact of the change on the project's products, not the objectives of the two projects. Option D is incorrect—although the focus on products principle helps to ensure that only work is needed to deliver products is performed, in this case, the project manager is not reviewing what work is needed to deliver the marketing products but is reviewing the impact of the change on the product descriptions instead.

5. D. This approach means the project board will be notified of every breach of work package tolerance no matter how small. A better approach would be to give the project manager some stage tolerance so that he will escalate work packages exceptions only if they are particularly large and breach the overall stage tolerances (option D). Option A is incorrect—this will not allow the project manager to efficiently manage the project, as he will have to refer to the project board each time there is a breach of work package tolerances no matter how small. Option B is incorrect—although this helps to define the level of accountability at the delivery level, it does not define the level of accountability at the management level. Option C is incorrect—forecast breaches at the work package–level are escalated to the project manager.

6. C. The project board must review if there is still business justification for the project to continue, before authorizing a stage of the project. At the end of stage three, the business case might have changed and there may no longer be justification to continue the project. So the project board should not authorize stage four until the end of stage three (option C). Option A is incorrect—the project board must authorize only one stage at a time. Option B is incorrect—although the project manager should create a stage plan for each management stage, the project manager will create each stage plan only just before that stage starts. Option D is incorrect—although the project manager creates the project plan during the initiation stage, the project manager also creates more detailed stage plans before each stage begins throughout the project.

7. A. The end stage assessments do not necessarily have to be attended in person. What is important is that all the members of the project board review the necessary information and make a decision based on their perspective of the project (option A). Option B is incorrect—although the senior user is responsible for forecasting the likely benefits of the project, this is not the reason why using email is an appropriate application of the tailoring principle. It is describing applying the defined roles and responsibilities principle. Option C is incorrect—members of the project board are not required to attend an end stage assessment meeting; they just to be involved in the decision regarding whether to authorize the next stage. Option D is incorrect—as long as necessary security precautions are taken, there is no reason why any PRINCE2 documents should not be emailed.

8. C. By setting a tolerance around the time target for the work package, the project manager is defining the limits of the team manager's delegated authority. This will allow the project manager to manage the work package by exception, getting involved only if the team manager is forecasting a breach of this tolerance (option C). Option A is incorrect—although the project manager is managing the stage on behalf of the project board, delegating authority from one management level to another is an example of applying the manage by exception principle. Option B is incorrect—the project manager, not the project board, authorizes the work package. Option D is incorrect—the work package tolerance defines the team manager's level of authority, not the project manager's. The project manager's level authority is defined by stage tolerances set by the project board.

Answers to Business Case

9. D. A dis-benefit is a consequence of the project that is perceived as negative by one or more stakeholders. In this case, a consequence of the QualityEconomy project is that there is no money for the retail manager to upgrade the new store.

10. E. The project initiation documentation is a management product from the QualityEconomy project; therefore, it is not an output, outcome, benefit, or dis-benefit. (It is not an output because the project initiation documentation is a management product, and outputs are always specialist products.)

11. B. This statement describes a change in the real-world circumstances and behavior of Quality Furniture resulting from the project, so it is an outcome.

12. C. If a project is part of a programme, each project's business case needs to be aligned with the overall programme's business case. Typically, each project's business case will be reduced in content and may contain just an outline of the project's benefits, costs, and timescales and refer to the programme's business case for any other information (option C). Option A is incorrect—a project within a programme might not have a rationale when it is seen as a standalone project; it might have a rationale only when it is joined up with the overall programme. Option B is incorrect—although the project manager is responsible for the development of the business case, if the project is part of a programme, the project manager will need to align the project's business case with the programme's business case. This won't be possible if the chief executive is not willing to share the overall programme's goals. Option D is incorrect—it is appropriate for each project within a programme to have a business case; however, the business case might be reduced in content in this situation.

13. C. The decision to prematurely close the project should be made by the project board, not just by the senior user (option C). Option A is incorrect—it is true that the project manager is responsible for the development of the business case, but the question is asking whether it would be appropriate for the senior user to decide on her own whether to prematurely close the project. Option B is incorrect—although the project should remain desirable throughout its life, it is not up to the senior user to decide whether this is the case, without consulting the other project board members. Option D is incorrect—if the project board decides to prematurely close the project, the closing a project process can be used at any time throughout the project.

Answers to Organization

14. F. A stakeholder is anyone who can impact or be impacted by a project. Therefore, the company accountant should be recorded under the stakeholder analysis section.
15. C. The records section of the communication management approach defines which communication records are required.
16. A. The procedure section describes any corporate standards that should be followed.
17. C. The retail manager will help to deliver the benefits of the project by selling the new QualityEconomy range through the shops. The senior user role could represent those who will use the products to deliver the benefits of the project (option C). Option A is incorrect—although the retail outlets will be supplying the furniture to the customers after the project, the retail manager is not supplying any resources or products to deliver the project's products, so he should not be a senior supplier. Option B is incorrect—the retail manager is unlikely to have expertise in the installation of the new production machinery, so he is a poor choice to review the plan. Option D is incorrect—although the account manager from the production machinery supplier could be a senior supplier, there could be more than one senior supplier, so this is not the reason the retail manager should not take on that role.
18. B. The senior supplier could be someone who is procuring products and services for the project, so the personal assistant could be a senior supplier (option B). Option A is incorrect—the fact that she reports directly to the chief executive is not a reason to become senior supplier. Option C is incorrect—although someone from the production machinery supplier might take on the role of senior supplier, there can be more than one senior supplier, so this is not a reason why the personal assistant could not take on the role. Option D is incorrect—although the personal assistant has skills in administration and organization, which would mean she could take on the role of project support, this does not mean she could not take on the role of senior supplier.

Answers to Quality

19. F. The quality responsibilities section of a product description will define the producer for the product.
20. E. The quality skills required section of a product description will give an indication of the skills required to carry out a review of the product.
21. D. The quality review technique is a method that could be used to check the quality of the standard design document.
22. D. During the preparing for the review step of the quality review technique, the reviewers review the product in line with the quality criteria of the associated product description. If they spot an error, they add it to a question list that will be submitted to the chair ahead of the review meeting (option D). Option A is incorrect—although an off-specification is a type of issue where a product does not meet its specification, it is too early to raise this type of issue. The review meeting needs to be held to review any problems that the reviewers have found, and then the presenter needs to try to correct any problems during the review follow-up. If the problem were not corrected, an off-specification would be raised. Option B is incorrect—although the reviewer role should review the product, it is incorrect that the reviewer should raise an off-specification at this point in the quality review process. Option C is incorrect—although the design document might need to be changed, it is not a request for change, as the change needed would be to correct the product so that it matches its product description. A request for change is a request to change the product description (and maybe the product, too, if it had been created).

23. B. During the preparing for the review step of the quality review technique, if the reviewers spot any small errors with the product, such as spelling mistakes or grammatical errors, it is appropriate to annotate the product copy (option B.) Option A is incorrect—most errors will be recorded by compiling a question list to ask the presenter during the review meeting. Option C is incorrect—it is too early to raise an issue. First, the review meeting needs to be held to review any problems that the reviewers have found, and then the presenter needs to try to correct any problems during the review follow-up. If the problems were still not corrected after these steps, then an issue would be raised. Option D is incorrect—although most product errors that are spotted while preparing for the review should be recorded as a question for the presenter, small errors, such as spelling or grammatical mistakes, can be recorded by annotating the product copy.

Answers to Plans

24. C. The fact that the training materials must be reviewed by the operations director should be recorded in the quality responsibilities section of the training material's product description.
25. B. The fact that the press release will consist of three products should be recorded in the product breakdown structure.
26. D. The sequence in which products need to be delivered should be recorded in the product flow diagram.
27. B. The work to purchase the machinery is a different delivery step from the work to install the machinery. A delivery step is a group of work distinguished by a particular set of specialist skills or techniques. There are often benefits to splitting delivery steps into their own management stages; for example, it will be easy to assess progress at the end of a delivery step because there is often a well-defined output. However, this is only one factor to take into account when splitting the project into management stages, so it will not always be appropriate to decide to put each delivery step into its own management stage (option B). Option A is incorrect—the boundaries of management stages and delivery steps might coincide, but this is not always the case. Option C is incorrect—although this will create a stage boundary, it is not necessarily the case that this will be a waste of time. Option D is incorrect—the project manager is not proposing to create the stage plans for the later stages; he is proposing to split the project plan into management stages. The stage plans will be created later in the project, just before the stages start.
28. B. When the plans theme is being tailored for a customer/supplier situation, the contract should be clear about what rights of inspection and audit the customer has. A supplier's plan should have sufficient activities and milestones for the customer's project manager to maintain their own plans (option B). Option A is incorrect—the project manager should create the stage plan, although part of it might be based on the supplier's team plan. Option C is incorrect—although the project manager will create a stage plan to track the work of installing the machines, this stage plan will be partially based on the supplier's plan; therefore, the project manager will need to understand the work involved to install the machines by asking the supplier for a plan. Option D is incorrect—although the supplier's processes and techniques might be confidential, it is appropriate to at least understand the key milestone steps in the supplier's work.

Answers to Risk

29. C. The format and composition of the risk register should be recorded under the records section of the risk management approach.
30. F. How to scale the likely timing of a risk should be recorded under the proximity section of the risk management approach.
31. D. The roles and responsibilities for risk management activities should be recorded under the roles and responsibilities section of the risk management approach.
32. A. Closing the project is an example of an avoid response to the threat and is a valid response (option A). Option B is incorrect—closing a project is not always the only response to a threat to the ongoing operations of the organization; there's a range of other response types, such as trying to reduce the risk or transferring the risk. Option C is incorrect—closing the project is a valid risk response that avoids the risk. Option D is incorrect—the reduce risk response is not the only way to deal with a risk; there's a range of other response types, such as avoiding the risk.
33. C. Upgrading the specification of the materials is an example of a risk response to the threat that Quality Furniture's reputation will be damaged. The risk budget is used to fund responses to project threats (option C). Option A is incorrect—cost tolerances are used to fund unexpected rises in costs or estimating errors, not responses to risks. Option B is incorrect—although tolerances are used to fund estimating errors, this is a situation where money is needed to fund a response to a risk, which should be funded from the risk budget. Option D is incorrect—the project does not need to be closed; the project management team simply needs to fund the response to the risk.

Answers to Change

34. F. Project support should assist the project manager in maintaining the issue register throughout the project. The issue register is used to record information regarding off-specifications and requests for changes.
35. B. Suggestions raised to improve the new production line should be classed as requests for change. Requests for change are funded from the change budget. The change budget would be secured by the executive.
36. C. The senior supplier should review issues, with a particular focus on safeguarding the integrity of the complete solution and the specialist products.
37. D. A product that does not meet its specification is an off-specification, not a request for change (option D). Option A is incorrect—although the product might need to be changed, a request for change is a request to change the product description (and maybe the product, too, if it had been created.) In this case, the operations director wants to change the machine so that it matches its product description, which is an off-specification. Option B is incorrect—although the project manager is responsible to ensure that issues are recorded, in this case, the project manager is recording the wrong type of issue. Option C is incorrect—although project support might assist the project manager with maintaining the issue register, the problem with the action is that the wrong type of issue is being recorded.

38. B. One valid response from the project board is to accept the off-specification without immediate corrective action. This is called a *concession* (option B). Option A is incorrect—first, this is an off-specification, not a request for change; and second, the project manager might have some authority to authorize some requests for change. Option C is incorrect—although the machine isn't the one that Quality Furniture initially specified, they might decide that the best option is to keep the machine. Option D is incorrect—it is unlikely that the operations director on her own would be able to make this decision, as she only represents the user perspective. It is more likely that the project board, which represents not just the user perspective but also the business and supplier perspectives, would need to make this decision.

Answers to Progress

39. E. The improvement of productivity is a benefit from the project, so any allowable leeway in the forecast productivity improvement is a benefit tolerance.
40. F. Threats are types of risks. A threshold level of risk exposure that, if breached, must be escalated is a risk tolerance.
41. C. This statement describes an allowable deviation on the set of products that should be delivered. The set of products describes the scope of the project.
42. A. If the team manager learns any useful experience while delivering a work package, they should pass it on to the project manager in the checkpoint report (option A). Option B is incorrect—although the project manager should be kept informed of progress on a regular basis, this information relates to a lesson rather than progress in creating the specialist products. Option C is incorrect—lessons are not raised as issues. Option D is incorrect—team managers should pass on experience through the checkpoint report, and then the project manager should record the lessons in the lessons log.
43. D. If a work package is forecast to exceed its tolerances, the team manager should inform the project manager by raising an issue (option D). Option A is incorrect—although the work package is an exception, it is not appropriate to send the project manager an exception report. Option B is incorrect—although the project manager should be kept informed of progress on a regular basis, the team manager does this by sending the project manager regular checkpoint reports, not by sending an exception report. Option C is incorrect—team managers raises work package–level exceptions by raising issues to the project manager. A project manager would use an exception report to escalate a stage-level exception to the project board.

Answers to Starting Up a Project

44. C. The project manager has identified a risk to the project. During the starting up a project process, risks are recorded in the daily log because the risk register is not created until the initiating a project process.
45. B. Designing the project management team structure, thereby understanding which PRINCE2 roles need to be appointed, is helping to apply the organization theme.
46. A. The chief executive, the marketing manager, and the operations director are creating the business case for the project. This action is applying the business case theme.

47. A. "Environmentally friendly" is an example of a customer quality expectation, which can be a subjective statement describing what is required from the project's products (option A). Option B is incorrect—acceptance criteria are measurable, and in its current form, the statement "environmentally friendly" is not measurable. It would need to be changed into a measurable statement; for example, "The wood is sourced only from trees that can be regrown within 10 years." Option C is incorrect—although the project manager creates the main product descriptions while preparing the project plan during the initiation stage, the project manager creates the project product description during the starting up a project process. Option D is incorrect—the senior users will be involved in creating the project product description, but the project manager prepares the document.

Answers to Directing a Project

48. A. The executive is the ultimate decision-maker on the project board.
49. A. The executive is responsible for organizing and chairing reviews by the project board.
50. C. The senior supplier is responsible for ensuring that the proposals for developing the products are realistic.
51. A. The project manager could consult with the project board at any time throughout the project using the give ad-hoc direction activity of the directing a project process. This is likely to happen more often either during the initiation stage or when approaching management stage boundaries (option A). Option B is incorrect—the project manager, not the project board, is responsible for preparing the project initiation documentation. Option C is incorrect—although the project manager meets with the project board at the end of the initiation stage, he may also meet with the board during the stage. Option D is incorrect—although the project board is responsible for directing the project, they still might provide guidance to the project manager throughout the project.

Answers to Initiating a Project

52. A. The quality standards to be followed during the project are described in the quality management procedure section of the quality management approach.
53. B. Threats are types of risks. The threshold levels of risk exposure that, if breached, must be escalated to corporate or programme management are described in the risk tolerance section of the risk management approach. In this situation, the Quality Furniture board of directors represents the corporate or programme level of management.
54. F. This statement describes how the project board will control the project on a stage-by-stage basis. It belongs in the project controls section and should describe the management stages for the project.
55. C. Threats and opportunities are recorded in the risk register, not the risk management approach. The risk management approach describes how to manage risk; it does not contain information on individual risks (option C). Option A is incorrect—although the project manager is responsible for ensuring that risks are identified, he will record them in the risk register, not the risk management approach. Option B is incorrect—risks should be identified throughout the project, not just in the initiation stage. Option D is incorrect—although project support might prepare information regarding risks, all risks should be recorded in the risk register.

56. A. During the initiation stage, the project board should decide whether to delegate any change authority. They should identify who will be given change authority, any constraints around the limits to this authority, and whether there will be any change budget (option A). Option B is incorrect—the project board does not need to set up a change authority for each particular stage. It is more likely they will set up a change authority for the entire project. Option C is incorrect—the project board can delegate some of their authority for authorizing changes. Option D is incorrect—the project manager can assume some responsibility for authorizing changes.

Answers to Controlling a Stage

57. D. The operations director is raising a problem or concern type of issue. Issues are recorded in the issue register.
58. A. The project manager should create a work package to authorize the supplier to start work.
59. C. The fact that the budget may not be sufficient is a risk. Risks are uncertain events that might affect the project's objectives. In this case, the uncertain event might affect the benefit objective. Risks are recorded in the risk register.

Answers to Managing Product Delivery

60. B. The team manager updates the project manager about the progress of the work package using a checkpoint report. This is created during the execute a work package activity.
61. B. The request for information document is a specialist product within the project. The team develops the specialist products during the execute a work package activity.
62. A. The team manager may create a team plan to understand the work needed to deliver the work package during the accept a work package activity.
63. A. Checkpoint reports can be tailored to suit the environment. In an agile environment, teams sometime communicate progress via an information radiator, which is an easy-to-read chart showing the progress of their work (option A). Option B is incorrect—not all teams will use information radiators; many might send a regular checkpoint report document to the project manager. Option C is incorrect—although the team manager should send a regular checkpoint report to the project manager, this report might take many forms, including an information radiator. Option D is incorrect—although agile teams might be self-organizing, this does not mean they should not update the project manager on the progress of their work.

Answers to Managing a Stage Boundary

64. C. In the report management stage end activity, the project manager will review the team performance during the management stage just ending (option C). Option A is incorrect—product descriptions for the products to be created in the next stage would be created in the plan the next management stage activity. Option B is incorrect—a product flow diagram for the products to be created in the next stage would be created in the plan the next management stage activity. Option D is incorrect—the new sales forecast should be added to the business case during the update the business case activity.
65. A. During the plan the next management stage activity, the project manager might create a product flow diagram showing the order in which the next stage's products will be delivered (option A).

66. D. The project manager should first escalate this issue in an exception report that sets out the options to respond to the problem. The project board may then ask the project manager to prepare an exception plan (option D). Option A is incorrect—the project manager should send the project board an exception report. The project board may then respond to this report by asking the project manager to create an exception plan, but it is too early to create that plan. Option B is incorrect—although an exception plan shows the actions required to recover from a forecast deviation from agreed tolerances, it is too early for the project manager to create the exception plan. Option C is incorrect—the work to install the electrical circuitry was initially out of scope of the project, but the project board might decide to approve this.

Answers to Closing a Project

67. D. During the recommend project closure activity, the project manager is responsible for ensuring that all the project information is secured and archived (option D).
68. B. Because the production machinery is likely to require potentially expensive support and maintenance, a service agreement should be created. This should have been part of the scope of the project (option B). Option A is incorrect—not all products require a service agreement. Option C is incorrect—the service agreement should be a product within the scope of the QualityEconomy project. Option D is incorrect—although the executive is ultimately responsible for authorizing the closure of the project, this is not a reason not to have a service agreement.

Printed in Great Britain
by Amazon

76851970R00303